A History
of African Archaeology

Edited by Peter Robertshaw

Assistant Professor, Department of Anthropology,
California State University

James Currey LONDON

Heinemann PORTSMOUTH (N.H.)

James Currey Ltd
54b Thornhill Square, Islington, London N1 1BE

Heinemann Educational Books Inc
70 Court Street, Portsmouth
New Hampshire 03801

© James Currey Ltd 1990
First published 1990

British Library Cataloguing in Publication Data

A History of African archaeology.
   1. Africa. Antiquities. Archaeological investigation
   I. Robertshaw, Peter
960

   ISBN 0–85255–020–0
      0–85255–065–0 (pbk)

Library of Congress Cataloging-in-Publication Data

A history of African archaeology / Peter Robertshaw.
     p.   cm.
   Includes bibliographical references.
   ISBN 0–435–08040–7 (Heinemann : alk. paper). — ISBN
0–435–08041–5 (Heinemann : pbk. : alk. paper)
   1. Archaeology—Africa—History. 2. Africa—Antiquities.
I. Robertshaw, Peter.
CC101.A35H57   1990   89–26733
960′.1—dc20   CIP

Typeset in 11pt Bembo by Colset Private Limited, Singapore
Printed and bound in Great Britain by Villiers Publications, London N6

Contents

Acknowledgements

The editor would like to thank all those whom he prevailed upon to write contributions to this volume. Their hard work, enthusiasm and patience are gratefully acknowledged. Several people were kind enough to review manuscripts, while others sought out photographs.

Desmond Clark and Peter Shinnie in particular generously put a large number of photographs at the editor's disposal.

Laura Tindimubona redrew maps so that they conformed to the required style.

Lucy Shimechero translated Pierre de Maret's draft manuscript from the French.

The staff of the British Institute in Eastern Africa provided valuable support throughout the whole endeavour, as did Denyse Robertshaw.

The acknowledgments for illustrations are as follows:

1:3, 1:6, 11:2, 11:3, 11:5, 11:6 courtesy of J.D. Clark; 1:4, 5:1, 5:2 National Museums of Kenya (copyright); 1:5 J. Nenquin, by courtesy of J.D. Clark; 2:1 Leakey Family Collection; 2:2 G. Souville; 2:3 National Geographic Society (copyright); 2:4, 2:5, 2:6 J.A.J. Gowlett; 3:1 J. Deacon, from an oil painting in the Albany Museum, Grahamstown; 3:2 University of Cape Town Libraries; J.D. Clark; 3:3, 3:4, 3:5 University of Cape Town Libraries; 3:6, 3:7, 3:8, 3:9 J. Deacon; 4:1, 4:2 M. Hall; 4:3, 4:4, 7:6, 11:1 R. Tredgold, by courtesy of J.D. Clark; 4:5 Tim Maggs; 4:6, 8:2 Natal Museum; 4:7 N.J. van der Merwe; 5:3, 6:1 British Institute in Eastern Africa; 7:3, 7:4, 7:5, 7:7 Musée Royal de l'Afrique Centrale, Tervuren (copyright); 8:5 F.J. Kense; 9:1 La Société Française d'Histoire d'Outre-Mer (copyright); 9:2, 15:4, 15:5 by courtesy of M. Posnansky; 9:3 Editions recherches sur les Civilisations, A.D.P.F. (copyright) and the authors of the Tegdaoust volume; 9:4 Rod and Susan McIntosh; 10:2 Alonzo Pond collection Ref. 27-13-2-423; 10:3 Alonzo Pond collection Ref. 27-17-4-458; 10:4 Alonzo Pond collection Ref. 27-24-442; 10:5 From the archives of E-G. Gobert, by courtesy of J. Tixier; 14:1 University Museum, University of Pennsylvania (copyright); 14:2 Museum of Fine Arts, Boston (copyright); 11:4 Academic Press (copyright); 12:1, 12:2, 12:3 by courtesy of Thurstan Shaw; 8:3, 8:4, 13:1, 13:2, 13:3, 13:4, 13:5, 15:3 by courtesy of P.L. Shinnie.

Notes on Contributors

Peter Robertshaw received his PhD from Cambridge, where he had studied under Charles McBurney as an undergraduate. His thesis on the later prehistory of the Western Cape, South Africa, was mostly supervised by John Parkington. After a short spell at the Albany Museum, Grahamstown, Robertshaw was Assistant Director of the British Institute in Eastern Africa from 1979 to 1988, when he took a visiting position at the University of Georgia, Athens. He now teaches in the Department of Anthropology, California State University, San Bernardino. The greater part of his recent field research, conducted throughout Eastern Africa, has involved studies of the origins and development of pastoral societies. He has previously edited volumes on *Culture History in the Southern Sudan* (with John Mack) and *Early Pastoralists of South-western Kenya*.

J.A.J. Gowlett is also a Cambridge graduate and a former student of Charles McBurney. His introduction to studies of human origins in the field was on excavations directed by Glynn Isaac at East Turkana. While completing a thesis on the Acheulean sites in East Africa, he was appointed to a lectureship in archaeology at the University of Khartoum. Following participation in the Chesowanja Research Expedition he then served as Senior Archaeologist in the AMS Radiocarbon Dating Laboratory for seven years. In 1987 he was appointed Deputy Director of the Institute of Prehistoric Sciences and Archaeology at the University of Liverpool. He is the author of *Ascent to Civilization*. He is particularly interested in the mental abilities of early humans.

Janette Deacon was taught archaeology by John Goodwin and Ray Inskeep at the University of Cape Town, where she was later appointed as a junior lecturer. She married H.J. Deacon and they moved to the Albany Museum in Grahamstown where she analysed the stone artefacts from the Wilton name site for her MA thesis in 1969. From 1972 to 1975 Janette Deacon taught at the University of Cape Town. While a research assistant at the University of Stellenbosch, where Hilary Deacon started the Archaeology Department, she obtained a PhD in 1982 on the analysis of the Later Stone Age sequences at several sites in the Southern Cape. She is currently the archaeologist at the National Monuments Council and an honorary researcher at the University of Stellenbosch studying the archaeology of the late nineteenth-century /Xam San. She has edited the *South African Archaeological Bulletin* since 1976.

Martin Hall received his doctorate from Cambridge University for research on the Iron Age of Zululand, which he undertook while he was employed at the Natal Museum, Pietermaritzburg. From Natal he moved to Cape Town to become Head of Archaeology at the South African Museum. He is now Chief Research Officer in the Department of Archaeology, and Director of the Centre for African Studies, University of Cape Town. Martin Hall has recently published a general synthesis and interpretation of early farming communities in Southern Africa. He is currently investigating the archaeology of early colonial domination at the Cape.

Steven A. Brandt   is Assistant Professor of Anthropology at the University of Florida, Gainesville. He was educated at the University of California, Berkeley (PhD, 1982) and from 1982 to 1988 he taught at the University of Georgia. His research interests are African archaeology, hunter-gatherer palaeoecology and the evolution of food-producing systems. He is currently engaged in several long-term archaeological projects in Somalia.

Rodolfo Fattovich   is Associate Professor of Ethiopian Archaeology at the Seminario di Studi Africani of the Istituto Universitario Orientale at Naples. His major research interests lie in the protohistory of north-eastern Africa.

Pierre de Maret   is Professor of Archaeology and Anthropology at the University of Brussels and an associate of the Royal Museum of Central Africa in Tervuren, where he worked for many years. Since 1970 he has been conducting archaeological research in Central Africa. His main interests are in later prehistory and the Iron Age. He recently published the final reports on his excavations of Iron Age cemeteries in south-eastern Zaire.

François J. Kense   has worked mostly in the Gonja region in northern Ghana. His doctoral thesis (1981), supervised by Peter Shinnie at Calgary, focussed on the archaeological visibility of Gbanye rule over an indigenous population at the town of Daboya. In 1987 he initiated a two-year project in the Mamprussi region of north-eastern Ghana to investigate changing adaptations to the environment of the Gambaga Escarpment. François Kense has taught archaeology at the Universities of Calgary and Alberta. He now lives in Victoria, Canada, with his wife, who is an Arctic archaeologist, and their two sons.

Philip de Barros   is a Research Associate with the UCLA Institute of Archaeology, where he teaches ceramic analysis, and Director of Cultural Resources for a private environmental firm. His theoretical and methodological interests include technology and culture change, settlement system dynamics, ethnoarchaeology, and ceramic typology and seriation. His substantive interests include the Later Stone Age and Iron Age in both West and Central Africa. His dissertation, supervised by Merrick Posnansky, dealt with the societal repercussions of the rise of large-scale traditional iron production in Bassar (Togo).

Peter J. Sheppard   formerly a research associate at the University of Waterloo (Canada), now holds a fellowship in the Department of Anthropology, University of Auckland (New Zealand). He has participated in fieldwork in Algeria on the Capsian and made a detailed study of Capsian lithics for his doctoral dissertation, under the supervision of David Lubell. Sheppard's interests include the archaeology of hunter-gatherers and the problems of studying stylistic variation in stone tools. He is currently conducting fieldwork in Portugal and Jordan.

Desmond Clark,   after long and distinguished careers in African archaeology, now live in
Thurstan Shaw   Berkeley, Cambridge and Calgary respectively, from where they continue
and **Peter Shinnie**   their research and publishing.

David O'Connor (BA, Sydney) holds a postgraduate diploma in Egyptology from University College, London, and a doctorate from Cambridge (1969). He is currently Associate Curator of the Egyptian Section of the University Museum and Associate Professor of Egyptology in the Oriental Studies Department of the University of Pennsylvania. His chief interests are ancient Egyptian history and society, the role of archaeology in their reconstruction, and the relations between Egypt and the rest of Africa in antiquity. O'Connor has directed excavations at a pharaonic royal palace site at Malkata, western Thebes; and for several years has co-directed (with W.K. Simpson) excavations at Abydos in southern Egypt. He is a co-author of *Ancient Egypt: A Social History* (1983) and author of numerous articles.

Peter R. Schmidt was trained initially in history at Stanford. He took his MA in African history at UCLA, spending a year at Makerere University, where he studied with Merrick Posnansky. He obtained his doctorate at Northwestern, where he was supervised by Stuart Struever, Ivor Wilks and John Rowe. From 1971 to 1988 he was Associate Professor (Research) of Anthropology at Brown University. He has also served as Head of the new Archaeology Unit at the University of Dar es Salaam (1985–7). He is now Director of the Centre of African Studies at the University of Florida. Schmidt has conducted research into the Iron Age of western Tanzania, as well as the oral traditions and ethnotechnology of that region. More recently he has been involved in Iron Age research in other parts of Tanzania and in south-eastern Gabon.

Whitney Davis received his PhD in art history from Harvard University, where he was also a Junior Fellow in the Society of Fellows (1983–6). After a period as Getty Fellow in the History of Art and the Humanities at the University of California, Berkeley, he is now Assistant Professor in the Department of Art History at Northwestern University. His principal interests are the art and archaeology of north-eastern Africa and Egypt, art historical theory, and the 'archaeology of mind' and symbolism. He has published several articels on Palaeolithic, prehistoric and ancient art, and on rock art in the Nile valley, and a book on dynastic Egyptian image-making, *The Canonical Tradition in Ancient Egyptian Art*.

Augustin Holl born in Cameroon in 1954, received his MA in history at the bilingual University of Yaounde in Cameroon. He presented his doctoral thesis, on the Neolithic economy of the Dhar Tichitt region in Mauritania, to the University of Paris I, Pantheon-Sorbonne, in 1983. He is currently lecturer in prehistory at the University of Paris X, Nanterre. He has conducted fieldwork in the Sahara and is presently engaged in an archaeological project in the Cameroonian part of the Chadian plain.

Bruce G. Trigger received his PhD from Yale University in 1964. He began teaching at McGill University in Montreal, Canada, in that year and he has been Professor of Anthropology since 1969. He has divided his research between the study of ancient civilizations, North American ethnohistory, and the history of archaeology. He has carried out archaeological excavations in Egypt, the Sudan and Ontario. He has written numerous books and has recently published *A History of Archaeological Thought*. He was elected a Fellow of the Royal Society of Canada in 1976 and is the recipient of several awards, most recently the degree of DSc (*honoris causa*) from the University of New Brunswick.

1:1 *Africa under colonial rule 1924*

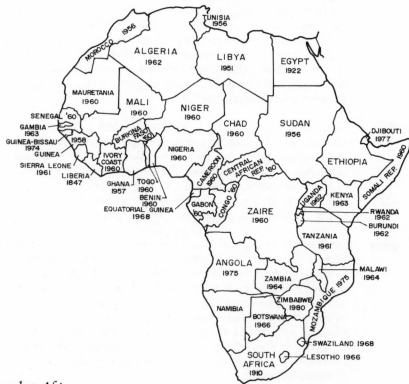

1:2 *Independent Africa*

1 *A History of African Archaeology: An Introduction*

PETER ROBERTSHAW

For many years Glyn Daniel was almost alone in his serious interest in the history of archaeology (e.g. Daniel 1950, 1962, 1967, 1968, 1975). The history of the subject was of little account to the scientific discipline of the New Archaeology of the 1960s and early 1970s. For, if the establishment of covering laws of human behaviour was the goal of archaeology, then the history of archaeology could be deemed of minor importance to what many regarded as an emergent science. Now, with the maturity of the last decade, has come an understanding that what archaeologists do and what they consider to be 'good' archaeology are products of the way in which the subject has developed, which can be linked in turn to broader social, cultural, political and economic concerns. Daniel's writings have found a new relevance and have been joined by several recent monographs and edited volumes. Almost all these works have focussed on the history of archaeology in either Europe or North America (e.g. Fitting 1973; Willey and Sabloff 1974; Klindt-Jensen 1975; Trigger and Glover 1981–2). By contrast parts of the world beyond these 'metropolitan' regions have been poorly served by historians of archaeology (see, however, Daniel 1981a). Africa is no exception to this generalization. The history of African archaeology is briefly recounted in a handful of papers (Goodwin 1935; Clark 1965a, 1965b; Shaw 1976; Fagan 1981, Posnansky 1982; Gabel 1985). The great majority of these are of a descriptive nature, particularly the most recent (Gabel 1985), and make little, if any, attempt to examine the development of African archaeology within a wider context. The present volume tries both to redress the neglect of the history of African archaeology and to analyse this history within perspectives that encompass the changing trends within archaeology as a discipline as well as the various milieux within which African archaeology has been pursued.

Several major themes thread their way through this volume. However, since none of the papers is specifically or solely directed at any of these themes, it may be worthwhile to use this introductory essay to alert the reader to some of them. The commentary chapter by Bruce Trigger which concludes the book takes up these issues in more detail.

The metropolitan parts of the world referred to above are, in a sense, the 'core' regions where most archaeological fieldwork has been undertaken, where the major centres of archaeological teaching and research are located and where issues of theory have often been prominently debated. It is there that the major works that have comprised the foundations of archaeology as a discipline were written and published, for example the works of Darwin, Morgan, Marx, Engels and Boas, and of the archaeologists Childe, Grahame Clark, Taylor, Willey and Phillips, Binford, David Clarke and Renfrew. Archaeologists from these 'core' regions travelled – and continue to travel – to the 'peripheral' regions of the world – I use the term 'peripheral' in a non-derogatory sense – to put theory into practice. Thus, they tried to impose their training and conceptions of the discipline on areas

3

which were often archaeological *terra incognita*, had no written history and were in many cases inhabited by peoples with non-industrial technologies living in a manner that western imperialism might well deem 'primitive', if not downright 'prehistoric'. Clearly the culture shock with which the archaeologist newly arrived in Africa was afflicted subtly (or not so subtly) redirected methods and goals. The results of this research were eventually carried back to the metropolis, where their dissemination served to stimulate or revise archaeological theory as well as more general views about the Third World. Therefore, the complex interplay between theory at the 'core' and practice at the 'periphery' is a theme which has considerable impact upon the development of archaeology, particularly, but by no means exclusively, in Africa. This interplay is nicely encapsulated by the phrase 'Cambridge in the Bush' that has been coined in the context of Australian archaeology (Murray and White 1981) but is equally applicable to large parts of Africa.

A simple example of the impact of African society upon metropolitan archaeological thought and of how this has changed through time is the encounter between western academics and African hunter-gatherers. Around the turn of the century this encounter enabled the academics to apply their social evolutionary schemes to living peoples and hence to flesh them out with accounts of 'survivors from the Palaeolithic era'. Yet, as some of the chapters that follow (particularly De Maret, Kense) demonstrate, the African encounter also posed challenges to some cherished evolutionary models. In Central Africa the complexity of the iron-smelting technology came to be regarded as a strong case for its antiquity and hence a denial of the notion of an unchanging African past. Similarly, the splendour of West African sculpture was not to be gainsaid. Later, in the 1960s, Richard Lee's work with Kalahari hunter-gatherers prompted a radical revision of notions of the diet and lifestyle of early humans. However, continued work in this region has exposed the fallacies of various assumptions upon which the relevance of some of Lee's work for prehistory was founded (Schrire 1980); Kalahari hunter-gatherers possess a long and dynamic history of changing patterns of subsistence within a regional economic system involving herdsmen and farmers as well as hunter-gatherers (Denbow 1984a; Denbow and Wilmsen 1986). The implications of this new understanding are now beginning to permeate archaeological theory.

Another theme, within which the concepts of theory at the 'core' and practice at the 'periphery' are embedded, is that of the socio-political context in which African archaeology developed. This theme is pervasive throughout this book as it is addressed more or less directly by all authors. No one could possibly deny the tremendous impact of colonialism and nationalism upon African archaeology (figs. 1:1, 1:2). Early colonial settlers and administrators, among whom are to be found many of the pioneers of African archaeology, sought to deny their conquered subjects a past. The logical consequence of this view – that there could be no African archaeology – was neatly sidestepped to colonialist advantage by affirming two positions. The first was that there was indeed a rich African past to be explored but that this was confined to the Stone Age, while the recent past was characterized as one of cultural isolation, stagnation and general degeneracy. The second acknowledged that there were exceptions to the first position – Great Zimbabwe being the classic example – but insisted that these were the achievements of pale-skinned outsiders (Phoenicians, Hamites, etc.) for whom Africans had served as little more than a pool of labour. Thus, colonialism – the white man's burden or *mission civilisatrice* –

was not only justified but also invested with historical precedents. The rise of nationalism and the eventual achievement of independence throughout Africa, outside of South Africa and Namibia, was reflected in shifts in the emphasis of research from the Stone Age to the more recent past and the favourable reception accorded to explanations invoking models of autochthonous development rather than diffusion or migrations.

The preceding remarks are obviously an oversimplification of a complex set of relationships between colonialism and nationalism on the one hand and changes in archaeological theory and practice on the other. There was and is no straightforward cause-and-effect relationship; for example, the enthusiasm for later prehistory must be seen against the acceptance of African history as a valid component of the discipline of history, while the embracing of models of autochthonous development was in accord with tenets applauded by adherents of the 'New Archaeology'. The complexities in the relationships between archaeology, colonialism and nationalism are particularly well illustrated in the papers by Augustin Holl and Martin Hall. However, there is another aspect to these relationships, which is mentioned in De Maret's paper and is alluded to in many others in such a way that it can be seen as another theme which runs throughout the volume and as one worthy of further examination. This is the variation between the different colonial powers – the United Kingdom, France, Belgium, Germany, Portugal and Spain – in their attitudes towards and promotion of achaeology within their colonies, as well as in the types of bureaucratic structures within which archaeology operated and, of course, in the sorts of archaeology that were undertaken and the methods of dissemination of the results. The papers by Kense and De Barros demonstrate how the centralization of archaeology in francophone West Africa under the umbrella of L'Institut Français d'Afrique Noire (IFAN), which also published a journal out of Dakar that carried archaeological reports from 1939 onwards, allowed the pursuit of research projects across national boundaries. By contrast, archaeology in English-speaking West Africa was fragmented by numerous state boundaries, as Thurstan Shaw explains in his contribution to this book. Thus, unlike the *Bulletin de l'IFAN*, the *West African Journal of Archaeology* was founded only in 1971.

The first professional archaeologists to work in Africa were trained in the universities of their respective European countries and tended to pursue their careers in the colonies of the countries from which they came. Indeed, even after independence many indigenous archaeologists found their way for training to the universities of their former colonial masters, although this pattern has begun to break down as American influence has grown and the number of training opportunities available within Africa has risen. Thus, it should come as no surprise that approaches to archaeology within particular African countries have in many ways mirrored the concerns of the archaeologists working within the colonial power; for example, Sheppard illustrates how archaeology in the Maghreb was pervaded by the debate over the origins of the French Aurignacian. These circumstances also serve to explain how it was that certain institutions came to wield a great deal of influence in African archaeology – 'Cambridge in the Bush' is again an apt phrase. Within these institutions certain individuals were of course responsible for much of the training of the Africanists and continued to act as the mentors of their protégés for many years. Two individuals would appear to have played particularly central roles in this respect – Miles Burkitt at Cambridge and the Abbé Henri Breuil (fig. 1:3) (see Gowlett's chapter). Both travelled extensively in Southern Africa and were instrumental in raising international interest in African prehistory,

1:3 *Abbé Henri Breuil at Olorgesailie 1947*

Burkitt's *South Africa's Past in Stone and Paint* (1928) being particularly influential. Other figures played less prominent but perhaps equally important roles, for example A.C. Haddon, also at Cambridge, Raymond Vaufrey and Jacques Tixier in France. In time the Africanists themselves rose to prominence – a whole generation of African archaeologists found their way to Berkeley to study under Desmond Clark and Glynn Isaac, while Ray Inskeep at Cape Town instructed numerous students who were to fill the expanding job market in South African archaeology in the 1970s, as Janette Deacon documents in her contribution.

Desmond Clark, in the introduction to his 'personal memoir' for this volume, subdivides the history of African archaeology into three periods – pioneer, formative and the modern behavioural and actualistic period. This is a scheme with which few would quibble and which is followed more or less closely by several of the other contributors (Gowlett, Deacon, Robertshaw, De Maret, Kense). Apart from Sparrman's excavations of 1779 (Robertshaw 1979) and some sporadic recording of rock paintings during the eighteenth and early nineteenth centuries (Gabel 1985), African archaeology began in the latter part of the nineteenth century at the hands mostly of amateurs, some of whom were no doubt inspired by the general acceptance of the antiquity of Boucher de Perthes's discoveries in France. Indeed, it was usually stone tools that were collected. Descriptions of these artefacts formed the core of the early regional syntheses of African prehistory: Dunn (1879–80) for Southern Africa, Stainier (1899) for the Congo and André (1882) for the whole continent. Later, as Africa became the home of numerous colonial administrators, soldiers, farmers, traders and miners, so the doctrines of social evolution which averred that African

1:4 *Louis Leakey skinning a duiker with a backed blade he has just made from Brandon flint. Examining other artefacts made by Leakey are 'Peter' Van Riet Lowe (left), Director of the South African Archaeological Survey, and Miles Burkitt, who started the teaching of archaeology at Cambridge University in 1919. The occasion was the third Pan-African Congress, Livingstone 1955*

societies were a relic of the eras of 'savagery' or 'barbarism' gained widespread credence. Thus were the policies of colonialism legitimized. Archaeology was of course not the sole means for this legitimization. Yet, in certain instances it took centre stage – most famously at Great Zimbabwe, a site that proponents of various ideologies have attempted to appropriate for the best part of a century. Martin Hall in recounting the history of the interpretations of Great Zimbabwe forces us to recognize that the ideological wrangles were founded upon political economic realities. However, Great Zimbabwe is by no means the only example of the results (real or imaginary) of archaeological research being used for ideological ends, for other papers in this volume cite similar, if less well publicized, cases.

The 'formative' years of African archaeology really began with the advent of the first professional archaeologists to take up posts in Africa. Prominent among these are John Goodwin, who arrived in Cape Town in 1923, and two of the contributors to this volume, Desmond Clark and Thurstan Shaw, who assumed their posts in 1937. One should also not forget the geologist E.J. Wayland who settled in Uganda in 1919, and, more important, Louis Leakey (fig. 1:4), who began his research expeditions to East Africa in 1926, though a number of years were to pass before he finally settled in Nairobi. In West Africa IFAN was founded at Dakar under Theodore Monod in 1939. However, it was Louis Leakey who had the great flair for publicity and who attempted to promote the idea of Africa as the cradle of mankind in the wake of Raymond Dart's discovery of the first Australopithecine fossil at Taung.

While Leakey and others strove to reach an international audience, the founding of publications for the dissemination of archaeological results within Africa was a gradual affair. Although archaeological papers appeared in the *South African Journal of Science* from the beginning of this century and in the *Bulletin de l'IFAN* from 1939, the first journal catering specifically for the subject – the *South African Archaeological Bulletin* – was founded only in 1945, with *Kush* and *Libyca* following in 1953, *Azania* (for Eastern Africa) in 1966 and the *West African Journal of Archaeology* in 1971. The *African Archaeological Review* began life only in 1983.

The first professionals were mostly interested in the Stone Age and their primary goal was the establishment of dated sequences of stone artefact industries, which they could compare with those of Europe. It seems that by such relative dating they hoped to establish patterns of migrations and the diffusion of technological innovations across the Old World. Such grand aims were often not explicitly stated, but it is clear, for example, that Goodwin thought of South Africa as a backwater of Europe from which ideas trickled down through the Sahara (see Deacon's paper), while Leakey took a more positive view of Africa's role (Robertshaw) as did many archaeologists active in the Maghreb (Sheppard). The pursuit of dated sequences led in two major directions: first was the issue of dating and second that of typology and the nomenclature to be used for the stone tool industries. Dating was achieved by studying the geomorphological contexts of archaeological occurrences and inferring past climates, which were then placed in a sequence of 'pluvials' and 'interpluvials' thought to be homologous with the European glacial sequence. Although the 'Pluvial Theory' was later discredited and rendered obsolete by new techniques of absolute dating, part of its significance for the development of African archaeology lies in the impetus it gave to multi-disciplinary research. From the time of Louis Leakey's earliest expedition it became normal practice for a Stone Age archaeologist to be accompanied in the field by at least one geologist and a palaeontologist.

Discussions of typology and nomenclature often generated a great deal of heat but very little light in African archaeology, as De Maret's chapter on Central Africa makes abundantly clear. Some, like Louis Leakey, preferred to hang on to European terms, albeit perhaps modified to suit the context, while others were in favour of developing an independent African nomenclature. The latter approach was pioneered by Goodwin and Van Riet Lowe in their epochal *Stone Age Cultures of South Africa* (1929). The problems of nomenclature were so persistent that they were a moving force behind the convening of a Wenner-Gren symposium on African prehistory held at Burg-Wartenstein in 1965 (Bishop and Clark 1967). The recommendations of that meeting concerning terminology are still widely debated and were variously applied or ignored in the 1980s.

Problems of terminology and the comparisons of regional sequences from different parts of the continent were a major theme of, and presumably part of the inspiration behind, the first Pan-African Congress of Prehistory and Quaternary Studies organized by Louis and Mary Leakey in Nairobi in 1947. This first Pan-African Congress was by all accounts a great success, bringing together for the first time very many of the archaeologists working in Africa (figs. 1:5, 1:6). Not surprisingly the exercise was repeated at more or less regular intervals thence forward, the largest of these gatherings attracting over 200 participants to Nairobi in 1977. In line with the general focus of research on the Stone Age, papers on earlier, rather than on later, prehistory, predominated at all the early congresses. Thus while they were a source of great inspiration and fellowship for the

1:5 *The first Pan-African Congress of Prehistory, Nairobi, January 1947.* Front row left to right: C. Van Riet Lowe, Raymond Dart, Alex du Toit, Henri Breuil, Robert Broom. Second row: *Sydney Haughton, E.J. Wayland, Erik Nilsson, Camille Arambourg, F. Corin, Francis Cabu, S.A. Huzayyin, Mustafa Amer Bey, Mary Leakey, Louis Leakey.* Third row: *A. Huddlestone, H.B.S. Cooke, P. Deraniyagala, Armand Ruhlmann, M. Degerbol, Bettencourt Diaz (behind Arambourg), L. Barradas, F. Mouta, A. Do Vale, A.J.H. Goodwin, B.D. Malan, Alex Galloway, E.G.P. Sherwood.* Back row: *Sir Wilfrid LeGros Clark, A.J.D. Meiring, L.H. Wells, Frederick Zeuner, M.R. Drennan, Kenneth Oakley, Wendell Phillips, Geoffrey Bond, Neville Jones, Theodore Monod, D.G. MacInnes, J. Janmart, John Waechter, E. Ganz, J.C. Pauvert, Raymond Mauny, Brigadier J.R. Jamieson, J. Desmond Clark, Rosemary Moss, Mrs Burney, G. Andrew, A.J. Arkell, D.R. Grantham, Bernard Fagg, Lester King*

1:6 *Participants at the fourth Pan-African Congress of Prehistory, Léopoldville 1959.* Left to right: *Oliver Davies, Georges Mortelmans, Camille Arambourg, Desmond Clark, Louis Leakey.* Behind: *Gunter Smolla and Merrick Posnansky.*

prehistorians, they tended to be by-passed by those interested in historical archaeology, as Peter Shinnie remarks in his paper.

The 1950s and 1960s saw rapid developments in African archaeology, only some of which can be touched upon in the space of this introduction. Radiocarbon and other absolute dating methods not only established the chronology of Africa's past but also permitted archaeologists both to excavate single-component sites where dating would have been previously impossible and to examine their data from new perspectives that need not be enslaved to the problem of chronology. Prominent among these perspectives was the study of man's adaptations to his environment. The ecological approach became and still is the dominant paradigm in African archaeology. Some of the inspiration for its adoption lies with the influence of the writings of Grahame Clark and others at Cambridge, but it is no doubt in large part due to the fact that African archaeologists could readily observe people interacting with their environment at a subsistence level using relatively simple technology. The study of past human behaviour was further enhanced by the potential of excavating 'living-floors', to which Desmond Clark draws attention and to which he and others were introduced at Olorgesailie in Kenya during an excursion of the first Pan-African Congress (see Gowlett). This type of research received a boost also from the international interest aroused by the excavations of early hominid 'living-floors' at Olduvai, and later at Koobi Fora, and their implications for the understanding of the beginnings of human culture, as is documented in Gowlett's contribution to this volume.

Radiocarbon dating is a particularly useful tool in the study of later prehistory, particularly the African Iron Age, for many of the sites are single-component open-air occurrences that could not otherwise be dated. However, the surge of interest in later prehistory in the 1960s was not simply a product of the radiocarbon revolution; its roots are more complex. In part of course it was a reaction to the existing imbalance of research effort towards the Stone Age. Yet it was also a response to the questions and challenges posed by the study of African history, a study then enjoying a phenomenal period of expansion. The nature of the interdisciplinary relationship between African history and archaeology is the subject of the paper in this volume by Peter Schmidt.

The growth of African history and, by association, the archaeological study of later prehistory are to be understood in the context of the rise of African nationalism and the pursuit of an indigenous past with which to banish the colonialist myth of 'Savage Africa', as well as other propaganda such as that of the simultaneous arrival of the Dutch colonists and Bantu-speaking farmers at the borders of South Africa. Historians and archaeologists have indeed succeeded in revealing the riches of Africa's heritage but not without risking the creation of new myths, for example 'Merrie Africa' and some of Anta Diop's interpretations of Egyptology. African nationalism provided much of the impetus too for the establishment of training opportunities in archaeology for Africans. The teaching of archaeology began remarkably early in West Africa, the department at Legon in Ghana being founded in 1951. However, another eleven years were to elapse before a Chair of Archaeology was established, at Ibadan. By contrast training opportunities were much slower to develop in East Africa. In South Africa too it was only with Ray Inskeep's appointment at Cape Town in 1959 that the numbers of locally trained archaeologists, all of them white, began to grow. In more recent years many students have studied outside Africa, particularly in North America. Indeed, there has been a steady growth in American involvement in African archaeology in the decades following the end of the Second World War. However, despite the training opportunities available over the last twenty years or so, African archaeology outside South Africa remains predominantly an expatriate pursuit. This is reflected in the authorship of the papers in this volume, among whom are numbered only two Africans.

This brief introduction has touched upon several aspects of the development of African archaeology and has attempted to outline some of the recurring themes to be found in this book. The papers that follow delve far more deeply into the history of African archaeology. In my role as editor I have urged the authors to place this history within the broader contexts of archaeology as a whole and of the changing social and political climates in which archaeology was practised. Within these broad guidelines individual authors have chosen their own courses with the result that a number of varying perspectives are presented, which I believe adds to rather than detracts from the interest of the book as a whole. The selection of topics for inclusion has been a difficult task and some readers may be irked by the omission of papers dealing with specific subjects or geographical regions. I have tried to chart a course somewhere between comprehensive geographical coverage of the continent and discussion of issues that cross-cut regional boundaries, yet keeping the volume within an acceptable length. In some cases I have not been able to find suitable authors to cover particular topics.

The first and longest section of the volume examines the development of African archaeology on a regional basis. However, the first chapter in this section, by Gowlett dealing with the study of the earlier time-ranges of prehistory, is more wide-ranging. The reason for this is that while most archaeology of the later prehistoric periods has taken place within specific regional contexts and in some cases perhaps within regional 'schools' of archaeology, the study of earlier prehistory has generally addressed goals which have transcended political or geographical boundaries. Two of the regional papers which follow are devoted to Southern Africa (Deacon, Hall). This reflects both the great amount of research that has been carried out in Southern Africa, most of it by archaeologists domiciled there, and the surpassing interest of the political, economic and ideological contexts in which archaeologists have operated. The rest of the continent receives less detailed treatment in this volume and some areas, including the Sahara and the Sudan, are almost entirely neglected. While these omissions are regrettable, the papers do provide a reasonably comprehensive but not exhaustive survey of the sorts of archaeology which Africa has witnessed.

A number of archaeologists have had fruitful and productive careers in Africa. As one might expect, their names crop up frequently as one turns the pages of this book. Some of these famous figures have passed on – Breuil, Burkitt, Goodwin, Isaac, Davies, Louis Leakey and Vaufrey and many others; happily others are still active and three – Desmond Clark, Thurstan Shaw and Peter Shinnie – kindly agreed to contribute retrospects of their careers. These are valuable contributions – not simply because they breathe life into the more analytical studies of the first section of the book, but also because their discussions of their aims and achievements significantly enhance our understanding of the development of African archaeology. While Shaw's and Shinnie's papers are very much 'personal memoirs', Desmond Clark prefaces his reflections with his own views on the history of African archaeology. In part this reflects his great interest in the subject, but also it is because an autobiographical 'retrospect' of his career was recently published in *Antiquity* (Clark 1986); thus, many of the details of the sort that Shaw and Shinnie present here have in Clark's case already been published. I regret that the memoirs of some of the other senior figures in African archaeology are not also included in this book. Some of course have published their autobiographies elsewhere (e.g. Mary Leakey 1984); others whom I solicited declined my invitations for a variety of sound reasons. Nevertheless, I am particulary conscious that there is no French representation in this part of the book.

African archaeology has not developed in academic isolation from other subjects. The nature of the changing relationships between archaeology and its sister disciplines in Africa forms the theme of the third section of the volume. The section begins with David O'Connor's paper on Egyptology and African archaeology, two disciplines which have long been remarkably divorced from each other, as is evident, for example, from the policy of various African archaeological journals of excluding Pharaonic Egypt from their terms of reference. O'Connor shows why this split has occurred but demonstrates too that the Egyptian past is intimately connected with that of much of north-eastern Africa. The relationship between archaeology and African history is the subject of Peter Schmidt's paper. Much work in this field has been concerned with attempts at verifying oral traditions through archaeological excavation. Schmidt reveals the pitfalls and potentials of this approach while arguing that much closer links need to be forged between the disciplines and between them and anthropology in any programme of research if results of real value to all these disciplines are to be accomplished. African history's involvement with archaeology is a much more recent phenomenon than the study of African rock art. Whitney Davis documents the sometimes sporadic efforts that archaeologists have made to incorporate rock art into their reconstructions of the past. In retrospect such attempts often ended in failure. However, it is also clear that substantive progress has been achieved lately in rock art studies, which has successfully brought archaeologists and art historians into real communication. The final paper in this section is by Augustin Holl and is a more personal view of the history of West African archaeology than the contributions of Kense and De Barros. Holl holds what I suspect may be a unique position – that of a black African occupying a lectureship in a European university, a reversal of usual practice. He is thus eminently well placed to comment upon the influences of colonialism and nationalism on African archaeology.

In order to draw together some of the themes in the development of African archaeology the volume concludes with a commentary chapter by Bruce Trigger. Here the history of African archaeology is examined in a more global context and the discussion builds on some of Trigger's earlier papers that have addressed the social, political and intellectual parameters within which archaeology has operated. The final chapter – indeed the volume as a whole – asserts not only the fascination of studying the history of archaeology in Africa but also the tremendous achievements of that archaeology. With such a history behind it, African archaeology can look forward to an exciting future.

2 *Archaeological Studies of Human Origins & Early Prehistory in Africa*

J.A.J. GOWLETT

Africa is the continent paramount in studies of human evolution. For the last thirty years it has reigned supreme in both human palaeontology and the archaeology of human origins. It is easy to forget that this pre-eminence is no more long-established than that. Even now the picture may change. Discoveries in other continents could alter the balance of our perspective, but it is unlikely that Africa could ever again rank behind other areas.

The aim of this chapter is to examine the main factors which have led to the prominence of African studies; and to trace the main developments of fieldwork and theory within Africa, noting at least in passing how they fit in with those on a worldwide scale in studies of human evolution. Such an account cannot be presented accurately as a history of personalities, or controversies. It has to be a consideration of major trends in the subjects, and as such concerned primarily with published evidence rather than private dealings. Nothing, of course, can alter the fact that a very few individuals have had an outstanding role in shaping the field of study.

Archaeological studies of human origins differ from other areas of African archaeology, in that in principle, and perhaps for some researchers, the prime importance lies in the subject – human evolution – rather than the place. Thus we should be wary of projecting backwards a false idealization of the concept of 'Africa'. There is a theoretical contrast with any other field of African prehistory, since scholars of later periods always have plenty of choice as to where to work, and those who choose to work in Africa have done so primarily because of their own interest in Africa. To many researchers in human evolution the continent has been important in its own right, but for others it has been merely the backdrop to a science which was the main interest. That is the theoretical position, perhaps, but in practice the emphasis on human origin studies in Africa has been moulded by people who cared deeply about Africa, and had a conviction, often against the odds, that it was the best place to look. They have been sustained by knowing that they are investigating one of the truly major issues of science.

The historical benchmark must be the phase of evolutionary anthropology which began around 1860. Before this any finds which might have been made in Africa would have found little scientific framework for their assessment – just as the Gibraltar skull was set aside for more than twenty years in Europe. Chance has it, however, that the continent most important in the study of human origins was itself little known to science until precisely the era when the appropriate sciences began to develop.

From the 1830s onwards Charles Lyell argued the evidence for the Antiquity of Man, first stating his case at length in 1863 (Lyell 1863). By then Boucher de Perthes had made his famous discoveries in the Somme valley. The implications were followed up both in England and France. Lubbock (1865) and de Mortillet (1881) in effect became champions of the cause, much as Huxley (1863) did for Darwin.

These early foundations scarely touched on Africa, since for European science most of Africa was still beyond secure surveillance, the territory of explorers apart from its fringes. Moreover, studies of human evolution did not yet rest on a collection of hominid fossils. When Darwin wrote *The Descent of Man* he was writing, in a sense, a comparative study of mankind, with as he admitted 'hardly any original facts in regard to man', but nevertheless demonstrating flashes of remarkable intuition (1871; 1874: 240):

> It is therefore probable that Africa was formerly inhabited by extinct apes closely allied to the gorilla and chimpanzee; and as these two species are now man's nearest allies, it is somewhat more probable that our early progenitors lived on the African continent than elsewhere. But it is useless to speculate on this subject.

T.H. Huxley took much the same view as a result of his work on the African apes (Huxley 1863). His anatomical comparisons showed that human beings are far more closely related to the African great apes than to the orang utan and gibbon, conclusions that have been supported by genetic studies of recent years. Huxley's selected accounts of travellers' observations also show implicitly behavioural resemblances which have received far more scrutiny in recent years. Caution was of course in order for Darwin and Huxley who both well understood that past geographic distributions of fossil species may have little to do with the present. These foundations might nevertheless have led to a great deal more, except for chances of history which diverted attention elsewhere. Primary among these were the spate of discoveries of Neandertal remains in Europe (especially from 1886 onwards), and Dubois's discoveries in Java between 1890 and 1892 (Von Koenigswald 1956).

The pioneering phases of studies of human origins cannot of course be understood in terms of the preoccupations of today. One might like to perceive gradual steady progress towards modern views in a 'field of study'. Plainly, however, a great deal depended upon a few individuals and their activities. They can only be understood as individuals. Nevertheless, they existed in the climate of ideas of their day. On the one hand, they had to be idiosyncratic and unusual, or they would not have got this subject moving; but on the other, they were in large measure products of the ideas which they encountered, both inside archaeology and circulating within other disciplines.

A few general observations about this can be made. There is a background of intertwined linguistic traditions of archaeology. English and French were not just the main languages, but for many years were the vehicles for two major archaeological schools of influence, those of Britain and France. The predominance of these two languages has remained, but now many more national traditions of archaeology have a stake in their use.

Within France, the pioneers of the mid-nineteenth century were followed by de Mortillet, a founding father of classification, and then among others the young Boule (1861–1942) and Breuil (1877–1961). Boule's editorship of the wide-ranging journal *l'Anthropologie* (founded 1891), and Breuil's broad geographic interests, were to be major influences in the shaping of the discipline on the scale of the Old World, Africa included. In the period after the First World War, British Palaeolithic archaeology was much influenced by the French tradition, particularly through the friendship of Miles Burkitt and the Abbé Breuil ('the Abbé Henri Breuil . . . my kind instructor and friend': Burkitt 1921: vi).

Throughout this formative period there is another dichotomy apart from the linguistic – the uneasy *pas-de-deux* between hominid studies and Stone

Age archaeology. Many hundreds of stone tools are found for every hominid fossil, and for every site where the two are found together, there are at least several where one is found without the other. Two aspects of human evolution which should shadow one another closely sometimes take quite separate paths. The paucity of earlier hominid finds, and the rarity of associations with artefacts, thus encouraged archaeologists and physical anthropologists to drift apart, especially in the English-speaking world. For example, in his 'Prehistory' Burkitt (1921) specifically excludes consideration of the hominid remains, building his story of earliest man around the French Somme sequence, whereas Duckworth (1912) in a textbook of physical anthropology naturally built the earlier part of his story around Eugene Dubois's discoveries of *Pithecanthropus erectus* in Java. In Africa the hominids and archaeology have stayed more closely linked, and so it is necessary to pay attention to both. But it is undeniable that over the years the hominid remains have generated the hotter controversies. This is perhaps partly a function of classification. The general stages of Stone Age development have been broadly agreed since the time of de Mortillet, and there is much scope for provisional labelling. Linnaean classification, on the other hand, has a precision which often fits ill with the uncertainties of the material, and seems ready-made for controversy. The archaeology gains the main attention here. Debates about the status of hominid fossils are extensively covered elsewhere (e.g. Johanson and Edey 1981; Lewin 1987; Reader 1988).

For most of the earlier writers of general texts geography was an incidental. The main aim was to construct an account that ran continuously through time, illustrating all the main 'stages' of human cultural development. Reliance on the home continent (nearly always Europe) was not explicit, simply natural. Equally important finds from Africa or elsewhere were often mentioned in passing, but only treated specifically when crucial data absolutely demanded it (cf. Burkitt 1921, whose subtitle limits his remit to Europe, and MacCurdy 1924 whose *Human Origins* concentrates almost entirely on Europe).

Early field collectors fell from a different mould. Their interest was naturally centred on all archaeological aspects of the places where they were. Consequently the principal experts were not, as today, specialists by period, but were professionally interested in almost every period (few, other than J. Desmond Clark, have maintained such a record up to the present day). Lower Palaeolithic finds were often peripheral. The discovery of, say, two Chellean bifaces in 1895, cannot therefore be slotted straight into a history of Lower Palaeolithic archaeology. Such finds were often merely collected and noted as evidence that the major early traditions recognized in Europe also existed elsewhere.

At this point, it is convenient to divide the history of studies of human origins in Africa into several phases, recognizing that this is a crude approximation. Some countries were strongly represented from the start, others have played little part at any time. Careers of individual researchers also run across these phases, which nevertheless through certain major events and discoveries have a rough validity.

1 *c*. 1860–1920   Early exploration; apart from expeditions, collection increasingly (1900–20) by resident amateurs and museum-based investigators.

2 *c*. 1920–40   Systematic explorations in various areas by trained archaeologists and geologists.

3 *c*. 1940–45   Second World War (melting pot).

| 4 | *c.* 1945–60 | Postwar conference phase, first large area excavations. |
| 5 | *c.* 1960– | Phase of multidisciplinary investigations by teams employing scientific techniques, e.g. radiometric dating methods. Rise of indigenous archaeology. |

It will seem, no doubt, artificial to single out a war as a phase – though we hear of Collins who 'like Major Feilden in the Zulu War . . . seized the opportunity presented by the digging of trenches to obtain implements straight from the gravel' (Collins and Smith 1915). Similar chances were taken a number of times, but even so wars up to and including the First World War scarcely merit separate treatment. There is no doubt, all the same, that these unsettled periods had remarkable effects in catching up people of intellect and flinging them hither and thither, for their hands and eyes to seize on the available opportunities. In the Second World War this happened to a sufficient degree that those years need to be considered as more than an interruption.

Early exploration (1860–1920)

For the most part, the first archaeological activity concerned with the earlier part of the Stone Age took place in established states, rather than being the result of explorers' journeys into the unknown. One exception was Richard Thornton, the geologist in David Livingstone's Zambezi expedition, who found implements in Natal around 1858–60 (Clark 1959a: 26). States and protectorates created in larger measure the stability and infrastructure which allow regular collecting. These conditions were present in the north in Algeria and Tunisia, and in the south in South Africa. Algeria had been taken by force by France in the 1830s, Tunisia became a protectorate in 1881. The Cape of South Africa had been in British hands since 1806, Natal from 1845. Egypt of course was accessible, and by 1920, following the general seizure of lands by colonial powers, archaeological work – and Palaeolithic implements – are appearing in many other places.

In Algeria, numerous archaeological expeditions took place from the 1870s onwards. The first bifaces were found near Temassinine around 1880. The first formal reference to a Lower Palaeolithic was by Rivière (1896) at Boul Baba, but there only one 'Chellean biface' was found. Other sites were discovered by Flamand and Laquière (1906), at Gassi Touil. Chantre recognized the site of Chetma in 1908 (Chantre 1908). Pallary (1911) reports bifaces at Ghardaia, mentioned again by Roffo (1934). Pallary was active in several parts of the Maghreb, publishing material from 1905 until the early 1920s (e.g. Pallary 1918–19).

In truth, though, the main importance of the early work in North Africa was in establishing foundations. As Biberson (1961a) remarks, when the Abbé Breuil came to write the first synthesis in French of African prehistory, he could find but several lines to write about the Lower Palaeolithic of Morocco (Breuil 1930). These scattered discoveries served mainly to stimulate the efforts of later workers.

Not surprisingly, Egypt also figures in the early records. The French prehistorian E. Cartailhac surveyed the discoveries in 1892 (Cartailhac 1892). Sir John Lubbock had reported bifaces from Luxor as early as 1874. Later, starting his work in 1914 in the area of the Valley of the Kings, Seligman (1921) concentrated specifically on 'the older Palaeolithic age'. In these high deserts of Egypt he found implements 'which in Europe would be classified as Chellean, Acheulean or Mousterian'. Seligman provided a concise and valuable synopsis of the difficulties of establishing the age of implements. Evidence could be sought in three directions, viz: (i) association with extinct fauna or human remains; (ii) discovery of implements *in situ* in strata of determinable Pleistocene age; (iii) the implements themselves may present a type of working which in Europe is only found in artefacts of a particular Palaeolithic age. As (i) was not available, and (iii) not proof, he rightly hoped to establish (ii), and did so in an approach subsequently followed by many others.

In South Africa collections were made in the early 1880s by Rickard, Gooch and others (Goodwin 1946). Implements had already been discovered in the search for diamonds and gold in various parts of the country. The best known early systematic collector was Dr Louis Péringuey, originally a botanist, who became the first director of the South African Museum at the Cape, and made numerous discoveries including the first early artefacts from Stellenbosch. In 1911 he published 'The Stone Ages of South Africa' (Péringuey 1911).

Other considerable early activity was reviewed by Collins and Smith (1915), who provide a summary of finds, chiefly those made by Collins during the Boer War in 1900–2. Smith compiled it mainly from his 'methodical notes taken on the spot; but being a prisoner of war in Germany, he is unfortunately prevented from making a final revision'. Finds are described from Natal, Haagensted saltpan 30 miles north-west of Bloemfontein, and Windsorton 30 miles north of Kimberley. Other early work is described by Lee Doux (1914). The geologist Johnson (1907b) notes an implement from the tin-bearing gravels of the Embabaan valley; extensive finds were made in the Zambesi gravels by Messrs Balfour, Lamplugh and others. Otto and Obermaier (1909) carefully record the stratigraphy and situation of an *in situ* hand-axe (Faustkeil) from Mariannhill in Natal.

The missionary Neville Jones also worked north of Kimberley, at sites near the railway line which leads northwards to Mafeking. In precise terms he documented artefacts found in deposits at Taungs and Tigerkloof, providing drawn valley sections, maps, photographs and drawings (Jones 1920). The implements of various ages, made from quartzite and diorite, were presented in a table of four successive periods. Jones thought that he might 'perhaps be considered greatly daring' in adding a column suggesting probable European equivalents. He intended, however, no more than 'tentative suggestion'. He stands out as a pioneer who set high standards. Neville Jones remained a missionary until he joined the Rhodesian Museum staff at the age of 55. As Professor G. Barbour wrote in his obituary (Barbour 1956) his publications are a model of clarity.

Soon Jones was to transfer his attention to the Rhodesias, and others were to handle the terminology of Southern Africa rather differently. East Africa first comes into the picture a little later than the north and south of the continent, primarily through the work of trained geologists. J.W. Gregory, author of *The Great Rift Valley* (1896) and *The Rift Valleys and Geology of East Africa* (1921), was apparently first to find stone tools and describe them. His main archaeological achievement was the discovery of Olorgesailie, but unfortunately (or perhaps fortunately) the site was lost for a further forty years. He was followed by Hobley, who wrote about the diatomite exposures of Kariandusi in 1910 (Hobley 1910), and by E.J. Wayland who began to work in Uganda from 1919 (see below).

These geologists followed archaeology mainly as a hobby, but with considerable dedication, and in Wayland's case professional achievement.

Louis Leakey reviewed the pioneering efforts in his book of 1931, and one can detect the mild exasperation of the young professional with the limitations of his predecessors. Yet Leakey thought Gregory's chapter about stone tools was important enough to reprint it in its entirety (Leakey 1931: 278–80).

A consequence of the First World War was to bring into the English-speaking arena the former German colony of Tanganyika, where Professor Reck had already found remarkable mammalian fossil assemblages at Olduvai Gorge. A human skeleton found in the gorge drew attention there (Reck 1914, 1926). It was later proven to be intrusive, but it was to play an important part in attracting Louis Leakey's attention to the potential of the gorge. For the moment, studies of early prehistory in Africa were not having a great deal of impact in the outside world. It would be exaggeration to say that all attention was focussed on the recent discoveries at Piltdown, but in his excellent survey of 1924 MacCurdy – having needed just two pages for listing hand-axe occurrences in Africa – could turn to nowhere but Java, Heidelburg and Piltdown for detailing early fossils. He accepted the stratigraphic context of Oldoway man, but from its character aligned it with the Aurignacian; about Boskop in South Africa he was far more sceptical (MacCurdy 1924: I, 422–5). Broken Hill man, discovered in 1921, could be reasonably regarded as 'a variant of the Neanderthal type' (I, 369–72).

Systematic explorations (1920–40)

After the First World War various systematic investigations began both north and south of the Sahara. So far no convincing early human remains had been found – little more than Boskop man in 1913, and Reck's controversial Olduvai man at about the same time (Haughton 1918; Reck 1914). Living-floors were virtually unknown, and dating a near impossibility. The workers of the day therefore set considerable emphasis on building regional stratigraphic sequences where possible, fitting in with these elaborate schemes of typological development, as favoured by Breuil.

In the north, M. Antoine provided much impetus, becoming secretary-general in 1926 of the newly founded Society of Prehistory in Morocco (Biberson 1961a: 13). For the next thirty years this area proved more rewarding in terms of early sites than Algeria or Tunisia. Early in 1927, Antoine accompanied J. Bourcart and Messrs Boule and Vaufrey to the Carrière Martin at Casablanca, thus marking the beginning of interest in an area of rich sites (Antoine 1935).

In Egypt, where Father Bovier-Lapierre (1925) had described industries from the fringes of Cairo, Sandford and Arkell worked along the Nile, producing a series of monographs from the late 1920s (Sandford and Arkell 1929, 1933, 1939; Sandford 1934a and b); further west, Gertrude Caton Thompson and E.W. Gardner worked in the Fayum and at Kharga Oasis (Caton Thompson and Gardner 1934, 1952; Caton Thompson 1946). This work established a succession of Lower Palaeolithic industries along the Nile in a series of terraces ranging from 30 m above the river downwards. The assemblages were labelled as Abbevillean, Acheulean, Acheuleo-Levalloisian and Levalloisian, and would mainly fall within the Acheulean as now recognized. Around the oases similar industries were found in high-level sediments, allowing the recognition of wetter phases.

In South Africa, a transfusion of energy came through the arrival of A.J.H. Goodwin, a former student of Miles Burkitt, who soon formed a working partnership with 'Peter' van Riet Lowe. Unlike Neville Jones, they felt a need to shape a new terminology specific to Africa (Goodwin 1926; Goodwin and van Riet Lowe 1929). As J.D. Clark wrote (1959a):

> In the twenties of the present century it became apparent that the old, European, classification of archaeological material would have to be revised and a new, essentially African, terminology evolved before South African prehistory could be placed on a really firm and systematic basis.

Thus came into play the Early, Middle and Later Stone Ages, which stood in place of – and naturally cannot be fully correlated with – the Eurasian Lower, Middle and Upper Palaeolithic. Those on the ground in southern Africa were almost overwhelmed with the richness of local traditions, and also produced numerous names for local 'cultures' – such as the Stellenbosch and Fauresmith – which we would now term industries or industrial traditions.

Even now it is difficult to pass judgment on the efforts of Goodwin and Van Riet Lowe in terminology. They were dealing with material somewhat different from any known elsewhere, and at the least would have needed to modify existing terminology. In fact they reworked it radically from top to bottom. The framework of classification based on this initiative was to find favour in most of sub-Saharan Africa. Its influence spread northwards, as that of the traditional Lower/Middle/Upper Palaeolithic spread southwards in the hands of both French- and English-speaking scholars. (The two systems eventually came into contact in the Nile valley in the 1960s, and paradoxically room was found for both, when both Nubian Middle Palaeolithic and Middle Stone Age were named: papers in Wendorf (1968)).

Goodwin struck off in decidedly local terms, yet he represented a major link with the external world. He stimulated lasting contacts with the great names of the World Palaeolithic. Miles Burkitt came to visit in 1927, and was sufficiently impressed to follow up the trip with several publications (Burkitt 1927a, 1927b, 1928). Burkitt encouraged the Abbé Breuil to come likewise. In 1929 Breuil made a visit of eleven weeks. On his tour Breuil inspected numbers of sites, including Kanteen Kopje near Kimberley, which he visited with Goodwin, Van Riet Lowe and Kelley. There is no doubt that he was deeply impressed both by these and later sites, including of course the rock art. His report to a conference at the Institut de Paléontologie Humaine is reproduced in its beautifully colloquial French in *L'Anthropologie* (Breuil 1930b). After paying tribute to Péringuey and other scholars, he mentions the civilizations 'similar to our Chellean, Clactonian, Acheulean, Micoquian, Levalloisian and Mousterian'. Searching for key sequences, he draws attention to a site on the end of the Cape peninsula; to Bambata Cave (Jones and Armstrong); then 'the remarkable discoveries' of the Vaal, Orange and Transvaal gravels; finally the sequence of the Gwelo gravels in Rhodesia. Only then does he drop into the South African terminology, having broken his audience in gently with familiar labels. He noted the Stellenbosch with its cleavers and Victoria West technique; the Fauresmith with its 'très jolis types bifaces' recalling La Micoque.

For all this, Breuil, like Burkitt, felt able to fit South Africa into the 'major lines' of evolution of the Stone Age in Europe, North Africa, the Middle East and India. As he says, 'Always one has the impression that one has not left this world in which Europe is the north-west corner and India the south-east corner'. No wonder that Breuil and Burkitt had a lasting respect for Africa and all that it had to offer.

For the moment, it appeared not to offer very early human remains.

Boskop (Haughton 1918) and the Rhodesian skull (found in 1921; Clark *et al.* 1947) were of great interest, but not of sufficient antiquity or primitive aspect to figure prominently in scenarios of human evolution. The discovery of the 'Taung child' in 1924 was something exceptional, hardly connected with archaeology, and too perplexing to be understood by many anthropologists. Baboon skulls were found in the limestone quarries as early as 1920. Then in 1924 the remarkable child skull of a hominid was uncovered and brought to Professor Raymond Dart, who rapidly published an account in Nature, naming *Australopithecus africanus* as a 'man-ape' (Dart 1925a; Broom 1950; Le Gros Clark 1967). His accurate interpretation drew rapid and mixed reaction (e.g. Duckworth 1925; Elliot Smith 1925; Keith 1925; Smith Woodward 1925). Influential British and American anthropologists were cautious, having in their hands neither the specimen nor any material for comparisons. The response became increasingly unenthusiastic as debate was taken up, and in some respects Dart's opinions seemed to go beyond the evidence (Le Gros Clark 1967, 16–17). The doubters were wrong, of course, to regard the find as no more than an ape, but it is important now to remember that they were judging from a short published note on a single find, a mere child's skull, without association with artefacts, and as always difficult to date.

In 1929 Dart prised apart the jaws so that the teeth could be studied. But the disappointment of the controversy was real – Robert Broom (1950) felt that the setback lost years of work. Broom was to the fore in Dart's defence, and, when the chance came, started his own work on limestone caves, 350 km to the north-east at Sterkfontein near Krugersdorp, 40 km from Johannesburg. Within months Broom had a skull, an adult *Australopithecus*. In just one month it was published in *Nature* (Broom, Sept. 1936). In 1937 Broom toured lecturing to appreciative audiences in America. He returned to discover further remains at Kromdraai, two miles from Sterkfontein, this time to be recovered from the pocket of the schoolboy Gert Terblanche (Broom 1937, 1938, 1950). These were the first remains of an adult robust australopithecine.

In 1939 the price of lime fell, and the quarry working stopped. Then the war enforced a long interruption. Astounding as the finds were, and although much headway had been made towards their international acceptance, there was still a long way to go. There was as yet no association of tools and hominids, so that it was easy to write off the 'man-apes' as primitive non-cultural sideshoots in human evolution. Similar problems of acceptance were to occur also in East Africa.

In East Africa, E.J. Wayland was appointed as the first Director of Geological Survey in Uganda in 1919. He worked at first more or less in archaeological isolation, but rapidly produced results (Wayland 1923, 1924). Wayland had limited time because of his geological work, as Louis Leakey (1934) later noted, but on the basis of former high lake shores he began to work out a pluvial-interpluvial succession, and he also found the opportunity to work out a local archaeological sequence comprised of Kafuan, Sangoan and Magosian 'cultures'. All of these subsequently gave rise to problems of definition. The Kafuan is the original 'pebble culture' (Wayland 1926). Before the First World War Wayland had seen artefacts on pebbles in Ceylon, and now he began to find them in the valleys of the Kagera, Muzizi and Kafu. As Biberson remarks (1961b), the finds did not meet the reception which might have been expected. In 1934 the Abbé Breuil wrote, 'Récemment E.J. Wayland a parlé d'une industrie très rudimentaire de galets cassés dans des graviers fort anciens, mais il est vraiment difficile, d'après sa publication et ses figures, d'être convaincu de la réalité du travail de ces objets'. Wayland, however, was not discouraged, publishing four phases of the Kafuan in his paper of 1934, and he was to convince many before the Kafuan finally found its demise in 1959 (Wayland 1934a; Bishop 1959).

The astonishing career of Louis Leakey now began to transform the scene of East African prehistory. His varied and exciting life has been recorded perceptively in both long and short biographies (Cole 1975; Tobias 1976; Clark 1976), and two autobiographies (Leakey 1937, 1974). Here there is room for little more than the essential facts.

Born in Kenya in 1903, Louis Leakey was saved from a classic English boarding school education by the First World War; already interested in prehistory, he had to wait until going to university in Cambridge for a formal training. There, like Grahame Clark and Desmond Clark after him, he was a student of Miles Burkitt. In 1926 Leakey returned to Kenya, and began a series of expeditions over eight years that set foundations of substance for East African prehistory. The expeditions ranged widely in space and time; up the Rift Valley, where he worked at Kariandusi, Gamble's Cave, and later sites; down to Olduvai where he established an outline of the cultural sequence; then to Lake Victoria, and the subsequently notorious finds of Kanam and Kanjera.

The results of the first two expeditions were rapidly published in a volume which includes excellent photographs of the bifaces from Kariandusi (Leakey 1931). Following the first expedition (1926) Leakey was awarded a Fellowship at St John's College, Cambridge, which he held for several years. The nature of the successful work in the Naivasha and Nakuru basins influenced Leakey's views. He was thereafter the foremost proponent of pluvial/interpluvial sequences as the basis of chronologies. These held sway for over a quarter of a century, although doubts were expressed by some scholars (e.g. O'Brien 1939, who found grave problems with the whole concept). During one of his visits to Europe in 1928, Louis Leakey went to Germany to meet Professor Reck and to see the remains of Oldoway man, together with the fauna collected from Olduvai in the early expeditions. Mary Leakey (1978) records that he observed artefacts among the geological samples in the German collections. Reck had failed to notice any artefacts at Olduvai, apparently expecting them to have been made of flint. Leakey soon won a bet with him by discovering lava artefacts at Olduvai within twenty-four hours of arriving there on the expedition organized with Reck in 1931.

At any rate, the decision to go to Olduvai was made (fig. 2:1). In the early days work at Olduvai Gorge was difficult. Vehicles were unreliable, roads bad, and there was little support. Water supply was a particular problem. The early work, from 1931 onwards until 1951, consisted of 'establishing a sequence of evolutionary stages of culture within the geological horizons exposed in the gorge'; locating as many different sites as possible; and 'obtaining an overall picture of the geological history . . . and its possible link with the climatic fluctuations of the Pleistocene period' (Leakey 1965: xi). Already by 1932 Louis Leakey was able to give a report of the stratigraphy and industries of Olduvai Gorge to the first congress of the International Union of Prehistoric and Protohistoric Sciences, held in London (Leakey 1934b). The sequence then ranged from 'pre-Chellean' at the base to 'Aurignacian' at the top, but in outline Leakey's early scheme has proved surprisingly durable. For various reasons the full implications of this work were not widely recognized for another 25 years.

In describing his material Leakey had to take into account the views of Wayland:

2:1 *Olduvai Gorge 1935: Louis Leakey* (centre) *with giant fossil elephant bones.* On the left *the geologist Peter Kent,* right *Mary Nicol, the future Mrs Leakey*

> Following upon the Kafuan culture came a culture step which Mr Wayland calls pre-Chellean and to which I have given the name of the Oldowan culture. I should have preferred to call it 'Developed Kafuan', but Mr Wayland holds that it is quite distinct from even the most developed Kafuan (Leakey 1936b: 39)

Louis Leakey felt nevertheless that eventually the name 'Oldowan' would 'probably be dropped'; but in the event it was the other way round.

There now came the subsequently notorious expedition to Kanam and Kanjera near Lake Victoria, where apparently early human remains were discovered. Controversy has such strong appeal that the episode of Kanam and Kanjera has made a stock story: the brash young colonial, rushing around finding new sites, until he suddenly overreaches himself, misdescribes or misinterprets his finds and their location, and is deflated resoundingly by the British establishment, in the form of the geologist Boswell.

The truth is more complex. Indeed, there was resentment in some circles in England that young men should go forth to far corners of the globe, and almost instantly return claiming major finds. First there had been Dubois, then Dart – whose find came to him – and now Leakey. British physical anthropologists seem to have been in an uneasy frame of mind, partly owing to Piltdown man. These remains were a major claim to fame, but not universally accepted, especially on the continent of Europe. Whatever opinions were voiced, competition from Africa must have been an irritating pinprick. Yet, essentially, Leakey was not on his own. He had an excellent archaeological training, enthusiastic support from his mentors which many of us might now welcome, and even in those early days often worked closely with professional geologists and palaeontologists. In this case, however, he was in isolation, seen to be arguing with an eminent geologist on the latter's own professional ground. Boswell was able to doubt the context of the finds (Boswell 1935). Neither the records, nor anything remaining on the ground, were sufficient to support Leakey's cause.

Was this episode, or was it not, a major setback for Louis Leakey's career, for his resolve, and for the development of studies of human origins? It seems not, or if so, at least that many other factors were involved. Leakey had a restless intellect, and many interests. After nine years of expeditions (he went back to Olduvai in 1935 after Kanam), he had other things to do.

Indeed there is a natural cycle in this work, completed by two more books *Adam's Ancestors* (1934) and *Stone Age Africa* (1936), the latter based on the Munro lectures given by invitation in 1936. Louis Leakey's turn to the anthropology of the Kikuyu was characteristic of several such switches of attention in his life.

In the background also were the wretched forged Piltdown remains, and the views of a school of British physical anthropologists who felt that archaeological evidence, particularly from far continents, was almost irrelevant in building up a picture of early human evolution. Otherwise, Olduvai would have counted for far more, and the pity is that no genuine associations of early hominids and artefacts were retrieved in the early days. By comparison Kanam and Kanjera were far less suitable sites for conducting arguments.

There is no doubt that Louis Leakey was deeply hurt by the aspersions apparently cast on his competence in the field. His reply to Boswell (1935) also in *Nature* makes this plain (Leakey 1936b). Leakey quotes Boswell's sentence ending, 'and the deposits (said to be clays) are in fact of entirely different rock (volcanic agglomerate)', complaining that this had been widely interpreted around the world as meaning 'Boswell says Leakey does not know the difference between a clay and a volcanic agglomerate'. He explained that this was merely the consequence of a mix-up over a photograph. This kind of detailed riposte is characteristic of the early *Nature* papers, and it may have served to compound whatever damage there was.

Particularly unfortunate was the scepticism of French prehistorians, such as Boule and de Pradenne. De Pradenne (1940) reviews African prehistory quite thoroughly without even mentioning Olduvai, but citing Boswell over Kanam to the effect that 'the observations had not been made with the method that was desirable' (p. 174). Boule and Vallois (1956) express similar doubts. Nevertheless, Leakey retained the support of allies, such as Broom (who is scathing of the critics [1950: 12–13]), and remained determined not to give up over Kanam, writing in 1953:

> Doubt has been cast on this specimen by Professor Boswell, and there are some who, with him, still prefer to regard this as a 'doubtful' specimen. An ever-increasing number, however, agree with me that it is a genuine example of Lower Pleistocene man. (Leakey 1953: 202)

This view has not prevailed.

In summarizing the period, one must note the rarity and small scale of excavation. The first Acheulean – and pre-Acheulean – sites to be discovered in sub-Saharan Africa were found, as we have seen, long before the Second World War. Even in 1921 Burkitt mentioned finds of *coups-de-poing* (hand-axes) from countries as far apart as South Africa and Somalia. But apart from the notable work in Uganda by Wayland, and later by O'Brien, at Nsongezi (Wayland 1934a and b; O'Brien 1939) and by Neville Jones in Southern Rhodesia (Jones 1949) little major excavation was carried out until after the Second World War.

The first conference of the International Union of Prehistoric and Protohistoric Sciences, held in London in 1932 (published by Oxford University Press in 1934), offered an opportunity for a round-up of knowledge in Africa as well as Europe. Egypt was well represented, with papers by K.S. Sandford on recent work in the Nile Valley and by Gertrude Caton-Thompson on recent discoveries at Kharga Oasis (Sandford 1934; Caton-Thompson 1934). R. Vaufrey was at work in the region of Gafsa, Tunisia, reporting 'Acheuleo-Mousterian' sites from the alluvial deposits

(Vaufrey 1934). Louis Leakey (1934b) presented his paper on Olduvai. This is a further reminder that workers in the pre-war period were thin on the ground. In total, however, their work added up to a very substantial contribution.

The Second World War

War generally leads to a retrenchment of cultural activities. An interruption of irresistible force, it is an eventful manipulator of men, including those archaeologists who are caught up by it. For Louis Leakey the Second World War meant a period in the Special Branch of the CID in Nairobi, but in one way or another time was still found for archaeology (cf. Clark 1976: 530). During the war the Leakeys rediscovered the enormously rich Acheulean site of Olorgesailie in the Rift Valley of Kenya, first noted by Gregory (1921) but then lost. In the years up to 1946, aided by Italian prisoners of war, they were able to carry out fieldwork at various localities.

Far to the north, the Lower Omo Valley was occupied by allied forces from Kenya. Some fossils collected were sent to the Coryndon Museum, where they attracted Louis Leakey's attention (Howell 1978). Early in 1942 he despatched his foreman, Heselon Mukiri, who spent three weeks collecting items of fossil fauna, which are now in the museum. Leakey had appreciated the potential of the area since the time of C. Arambourg's expedition (Leakey 1936b: 130, quoted by Merrick 1976). It was F. Clark Howell who eventually took up the challenge of research in the area long after the war in July–August 1959, subsequently forming the International Omo Research Expedition in 1966 (Howell 1968, 1978).

In Katanga, Brother Lauwers, and then F. Cabu, separately discovered the site of La Kamoa in gravels disturbed by road-making. In May and June 1940, Cabu published in *Katanga Illustré*, discerning three stages of 'Chellean' (Cahen 1975). Later in the war, Cabu went to South Africa. There, Cahen notes, he met several prehistorians, showing them a selection of his specimens. At Cape Town the material was examined by Goodwin, who pronounced affinities with Stellenbosch III and IV, and with Victoria West technique I and II. The collections were then examined in detail at Johannesburg by Breuil – himself there on wartime business – and van Riet Lowe, who published two articles on the subject (Breuil 1944; van Riet Lowe 1944).

Breuil was able to visit the site himself after the war with Cabu and de Faveaux, and made some soundings. He diagnosed an evolved Acheulean, and a transition to a more recent industry characterized by 'ciseaux' (Breuil 1948). This important site remains less than widely known, but further work was undertaken in the postwar period (Mortelmans 1956, 1957b; Cahen 1975; see below).

The war uprooted J. Desmond Clark from his work at the Livingstone Museum (in the present Zambia), and after passing through Nairobi, where he visited sites with the Leakeys, he spent most of 1942 and 1943 in Somalia. There he added vastly to earlier work by Seton-Kerr, de Morgan and Teilhard de Chardin (1930) emerging with sufficient material and notes to complete a doctoral thesis at Cambridge (later published: Clark 1954; the other part of his thesis was concerned with Rhodesian archaeology). Other archaeologists gained a taste for new areas during the war, including Charles McBurney, who subsequently returned to Cyrenaica in the postwar period, to tackle its archaeology in slightly more relaxed circumstances (McBurney and Hey 1955; McBurney 1967).

Integration and progress: the postwar conference phase and the time of the Acheulean

As a result of correspondence with leading prehistorians all over Africa during 1943 and 1944, it became increasingly clear that there was an urgent need for workers in the fields of Prehistory, Quaternary Geology and Palaeontology in this continent to get together and discuss mutual problems at the earliest possible opportunity.

Louis Leakey managed to achieve this by organizing the First Pan-African Congress in Nairobi in 1947 (Leakey and Cole, 1952: iii). Finding suitable accommodation was difficult, but the event was successful. The 61 delegates included many leading prehistorians, among them Breuil, Wayland, Zeuner, Oakley, Dart, Broom, Monod, Ruhlmann, Van Riet Lowe and J. Desmond Clark (see fig. 1:5). There were conference excursions to the major East African sites, including Olorgesailie and Kariandusi, where new excavations had been made for the occasion. Paper shortages hindered publication, so that the final product was drastically sub-edited to reduce length (Leakey and Cole 1952). Naturally in the circumstances the contributions appear patchy. Arkell's Palaeolithic paper was expanded and published separately, and remains the chief source on the Acheulean site of Khor Abu Anga in Sudan (Arkell 1949). The perception that studies of early prehistory must of necessity have Africa as their focus was most effectively summarized by van Riet Lowe (1952c):

> While it is now widely held that the essential home of the Hand-Axe Culture is to be sought in Africa, we find, when we set out in search of its roots that as soon as we leave this continent we flounder in mists of uncertainty. If, on the other hand, we remain here, we find that here – and here only – we have a long series of earlier well-stratified cultures which lead us naturally and directly to the establishment of the Hand-Axe Culture. When we add to this the remarkable discoveries of Dart and Broom in South Africa, of Leakey in East Africa, of Wayland in Central Africa and of Neuville (1941) and Ruhlmann (1941) and others in North Africa, we find that the only reasonable working hypothesis we can adopt at this stage is to regard this continent as the most likely centre of the origin of tool-making man.

The other papers provide support to this theme: Leakey's brief notes on Olorgesailie and Kariandusi; Desmond Clark's 200 sites from the Somalilands; Breuil's survey of raised beaches around Africa; but especially, perhaps, Le Gros Clark's interpretation of the fossil hominid evidence (Leakey 1952c; Clark 1952; Breuil 1952; Le Gros Clark 1952).

Sir Wilfrid Le Gros Clark was among the most influential of the delegates. He came to Nairobi from a visit to South Africa, where he had inspected the australopithecine remains. Convinced now of their hominid status, he gave papers on that theme at Nairobi and later in London, thus helping greatly to establish their acceptance in the scientific world (Le Gros Clark 1952, 1967).

In its methodology, however, the most striking piece is H.B.S. Cooke's cool survey of 'Quaternary events in South Africa', which lays foundations for faunal comparisons, and addresses itself critically to the issue of climatic correlations (Cooke 1952). The limited data, he felt, did not justify attempts at correlating climatic oscillations of southern Africa with other areas; and certainly not with Europe. It was more than a decade before

R. Foster Flint destroyed the idea of pluvial correlations in its entirety (Flint 1959a).

Pan-African congresses followed at five-yearly intervals. The second was at Algiers, the third at Livingstone. Gradually they began to address thorny issues of approach, terminology and typology. These congresses allowed useful meetings and debate, but in the 1950s the most significant progress in early prehistoric studies came on the ground.

An appreciation was now dawning that it was important to obtain not merely collections of artefacts, but also information about actual occupation surfaces. Not all the earlier examples of such work belong to the Palaeolithic. One may note, for example, the work of Bersu upon Iron Age farmsteads, with its meticulous recording (Bersu 1940), but even earlier Rust (1937) had excavated late glacial sites to very high standards, reached again, for example, in the methods of A. Leroi-Gourhan (1950b). In each case what was notable was the detailed plotting of minor features and finds across horizontal surfaces. Although the importance of careful stratigraphic study had long been appreciated, similarly comprehensive recording of artefact distributions was only just beginning.

Louis Leakey grasped from Olorgesailie – where the surfaces were preserved intact for visitors to see – the great value of studying relatively undisturbed occupation floors, but other workers played a larger part in subsequent developments. The first volume on Olduvai Gorge (Leakey 1951) concentrated rather on the old theme of outlining the evolution of the Oldowan and Acheulean 'cultures'. Louis Leakey was more concerned with linking stratigraphic progression and typological evolution, as were other workers at the time (cf. Van Riet Lowe 1952c, in the case of the Vaal sequence). Large-scale excavations had not yet been carried out at Olduvai, and when they did come in 1960–3, it was Mary Leakey who made a major contribution towards the study of living-floors with her exacting recording, analysis and illustration (Leakey 1967, 1971).

In the meantime, however, J.D. Clark had started excavations at Kalambo Falls in 1953, and had done at least as much to establish seriously the archaeology of the Acheulean in sub-Saharan Africa. The Kalambo sites lie in a small river basin just above the falls on the border between Zambia and Tanzania. Although the Acheulean is known from many sites in Europe, there limitations of context usually have to be recognized: even now the great majority of finds come either from cave sites, often excavated long ago by primitive techniques, or in derived condition from gravel pits, and of uncertain age. Without doubt this field of archaeology would have made more rapid progress in Europe if sealed and relatively undisturbed living-floors had been easier to find. As it happened such sites were found either too early for their 'own archaeological good' (cf. Roe 1981, speaking of Stoke Newington), or chiefly in recent years.

Kalambo Falls did provide exceptional conditions of preservation. In addition to forging an important 'strategic link' in spatial terms between the known sites in southern Africa and those in East Africa, the Kalambo Falls sites contributed a wealth of valuable archaeological data, and (as was believed) a calibrated time sequence extending through most of the Upper Pleistocene. Early radiocarbon dates of around 60,000 years now look much too young, and a racemization estimate of around 200,000 years must certainly be nearer the mark. Clark (1969) states explicitly the two main lines of approach which were undoubtedly fostered consciously at the time of excavation. First there was the traditional idea of tracing the 'technical development of prehistoric culture', then the much newer idea of recovering detailed information about living-floors:

We developed . . . a technique for excavating these 'floors', and the later disturbed surfaces, first cleaning off the overlying sterile sands and clays and exposing the floor, or section of floor, so that the relationship of everything on it could be clearly seen and plotted. In this way we were able to obtain details of the relationship of the tools, factory waste, natural stones and wood and so of the relationships between classes of shaped tools, thus supplementing the information to be obtained from a study of the artefacts themselves.

Two volumes of the Kalambo series have appeared (Clark 1969, 1974), and the analysis of the artefacts continues. Isimila, another large and rich Acheulean site, was discovered in the early 1950s near Iringa in Tanzania's Southern Highlands. Isimila is a site complex rather than a site, in the sense that occurrences have been found widely separated in the same beds. The main objectives of the work were those most encouraged by the nature of the site. Its value was summarized by the excavators (Howell *et al.* 1962):

The importance of the Isimila site is severalfold and includes its strategic location, its abundance of artefacts in archaeological context, the relative completeness of its lithic assemblages, its multiple horizons of former human occupation, and its preservation (however fragmentary) of a Pleistocene mammalian fauna assemblage.

But perhaps the main importance of Isimila was that facts from the ground added a new dimension to artefact studies, stimulating much rethinking. The authors drew attention to 'the extraordinary lateral variation, evident both on quantitative and qualitative grounds, between assemblages within a single stratigraphic horizon', observing that this lateral variation at Isimila was as well marked as differences between stratigraphically separated occurrences at Olorgesailie, the best site for comparison.

The evidence upon the ground at Isimila thus formed a direct challenge to the established assumption of progressive typological and morphological development through time, accompanied by increased refinement – the model inherited from Breuil and Van Riet Lowe. It is unlikely that anyone could have predicted the Isimila evidence on theoretical grounds. New evidence collected in the light of a traditional model clashed with that model, and made theoretical reappraisal a necessity. Similar evidence suggesting varied Acheulean activities, for example at Broken Hill, led J.D. Clark to talk of 'special purposes' camps (Clark 1959a). The first major examination of this issue in African prehistory was made by Maxine Kleindienst in her doctoral thesis of 1961. This was based mainly upon comparisons of the assemblages from Kalambo and Isimila (she had worked on both sites), together with information from Olorgesailie and other sites (Kleindienst 1961, 1962). Her work helped to lead to a more general concern with 'precision and definition' in terminology, a theme much in evidence during the next few years (e.g. Clark *et al.* 1966).

In northern Africa the 1950s were also a time of developments, with a different emphasis, more concerned with chronological and typological refinement. Until 1949 no 'pebble tools' had been found in North Africa. All was changed by C. Arambourg's discovery at Ain Hanech in Algeria of 'facetted spheroids' in association with a Villafranchian fauna in spring deposits. These were followed by Hugot's discoveries at Aoulef in the Sahara (Hugot 1955), but most important of all was the coastal sequence around Casablanca with its impressive stratigraphy.

During the war this had been monitored by Neuville and Ruhlmann (e.g. 1941), though their work had attracted criticism from Bourcart and

Antoine (Bourcart 1943; Antoine 1948). In 1948 Armand Ruhlmann was killed in an accident digging the cave of El Aïoun, and by then R. Neuville had already moved to Jerusalem as French Consul General. M. Antoine, the new inspector of prehistoric antiquities, prevailed on P. Biberson to take geological responsibility for the Casablanca sequence (fig. 2:2). Over the next few years he laboured to build up a full stratigraphic and archaeological record, culminating in twin publications which prove that the prehistory as much as the geology had captured his enthusiasm (Biberson 1961a, 1961b). Biberson elaborated four phases of 'pebble culture', followed by eight of Acheulean. His model of typological progression was clearly taken from Breuil, Wayland and Leakey, as his dutiful comparisons make clear. This was, however, one of the first works to simplify 'la civilisation du biface' to the single name of 'Acheulean', and it remains a beautiful example of classic stratigraphic research.

Early Acheulean was also investigated at Ternifine (Palikao) in Algeria, where Arambourg excavated in the 1950s (Arambourg 1955; Balout et al. 1967), and where hominid remains were also found. Ternifine was judged by Biberson to be as primitive as the early Acheulean of the S.T.I.C. quarry at Casablanca (Stage III of his scheme), and by Arambourg to belong to the beginning of the Middle Pleistocene on the basis of the fauna. The 'Atlanthropus' of Sidi Abderrahman and the finds of mandibles from Ternifine are the North African finds now generally ascribed to Homo erectus. The other main thrusts of work were in chronology and typology of bifacial tools, respectively by Balout (1955) and Tixier (1956; cf. also Balout et al. 1967).

In South Africa the postwar period opened with important discoveries by Dr Robert Broom of the Transvaal Museum at Kromdraai and Sterkfontein (Broom 1950). A general publication of the prewar discoveries also played a part in convincing the outside world of the hominid status of the australopithecines (Broom and Schepers 1946). Le Gros Clark is critical of this in detail, and especially of the contribution of Schepers, but was convinced of the essential correctness of Broom's interpretations (Le Gros Clark 1967). It was largely through his efforts that the elderly Broom received due recognition, though he remained bitter towards those British scientists who had belittled his earlier work and that of Dart and Leakey (Broom 1950). After his death in 1951 the work was continued by his assistant J.T. Robinson. In the meantime Raymond Dart had undertaken research at Makapansgat, eventually arguing for australopithecine use of tools in the form of the 'osteodontokeratic' culture, which aroused further controversy (Dart 1957).

In May 1956 there came a crucial find when Dr C.K. Brain discovered stone artefacts in the upper part of the breccias at Sterkfontein. These 'indubitable pebble-tools of Oldowan type' were 'possibly the most important discovery in the field of palaeoanthropology since the finding of implements with Peking man' (Oakley 1957). The excavations of Robinson and Mason (1957) confirmed that the artefacts were to be found in situ in a layer of breccia yielding australopithecine teeth.

Until this time the general feeling had been that a hominid more advanced than the australopithecines was responsible for the earliest stone tools found here and there in Africa: Man the toolmaker was, presumably, Homo. The direct association at Sterkfontein was sufficient to produce a near-revolution in Oakley's concepts. To him Brain's discoveries now suggested that 'pebble-tools may have been made by Australopithecus, while Professor Arambourg's finds at Ternifine ("Atlanthropus") indicate that by the time culture in Africa has reached the beginning of the Acheulean stage

2:2 *Exposures of marine sediments near Casablanca, at the base of the buried 'Anfatian' cliff on Cap Chatelier. P. Biberson* (right) *indicates remains of* Purpura haemastoma *to L. Balout and J. Tixier* (centre)

the tool-makers had attained the grade of *Pithecanthropus'*. Here, tentatively expressed, was a simple and straightforward framework which we might be living with today. The transition could have happened rapidly because of the great selection pressures putatively linked with early tool-use. Oakley was the champion of the concept of 'Man the toolmaker'; yet here in effect, he was willing to admit Australopithecus as Man, though not as *Homo*. Events in East Africa would soon sweep away this simple schema.

Three fine works published by Pelican books make a lasting monument to the efforts of the 1950s: the prehistories of East, South and North Africa by Sonia Cole, Desmond Clark and Charles McBurney (Cole 1954, 1963; Clark 1959a; McBurney 1960).

Modernisation, multidisciplinary work

The last thirty years have seen the introduction of absolute dating methods, an expansion of Lower Palaeolithic research around Africa and the Old World, an internationalization of work, large interdisciplinary projects, major changes of political environment, and developments of archaeological practice and theory. If there is one moment at which we can label a new phase, it must be the discovery of hominid remains and artefacts together in Bed I of Olduvai Gorge. Serious work at Olduvai in the postwar period started in 1951 with site BK II (found in 1935; Leakey 1959a). In the period 1951–8 SHK II had also been dug, but the truly momentous discoveries began in 1959.

The recovery of early hominid remains on site FLK in association with stone artefacts, and then the realization that there were two separate hominid species in the same beds, came as a quite rapid sequence of events. The cranium of 'Zinjanthropus' was found by Mary Leakey on 17 July 1959 at site FLK, close to the end of the digging season. One trench was dug, leading to the discovery of a tibia, and fragments of OH6 in surface soil. When work resumed in 1960 more fragments were found, and additionally the remains of OH7 and OH8 at nearby site FLK NN (Leakey 1959, 1960, 1961a and b, 1965; Leakey, M.D., 1978). The controversies over the naming of these specimens have been related elsewhere (Le Gros Clark 1967; Reader 1988; Lewin 1988). After the first discovery Louis

2:3 *Louis Leakey was a devoted practitioner of experimental archaeology. Here he uses three Oldowan spheroids in a bolas 1965*

Leakey (fig. 2:3) wrote and published a major paper for the Darwin Centennial volume (Leakey 1960), declaring that 'a new genus has been set up to accommodate this newly found, early stone-tool making man'. Following the later discoveries of a 'more advanced' hominid, the Leakeys changed their interpretation promptly: 'Zinjanthropus' could now be regarded as belonging with the robust australopithecines, and the new hominid, as the probable tool-maker, became a candidate to enter the genus of *Homo*. This entailed recognizing as *Homo* specimens with cranial capacity closer to that of australopithecines and apes than to that of modern man; and with various primitive characteristics. Philip Tobias was able to endorse this classification (Leakey, Tobias and Napier 1964), but others including Le Gros Clark and Oakley could not (Le Gros Clark 1967; in Oakley 1969 (p. 299) the specimens are listed as *'Homo' habilis*, under australopithecines). They saw no difficulty in *Australopithecus* making tools, but felt that the anatomical grounds were insufficient for recognizing a species of *Homo*. As Oakley phrased it in his colleague's obituary, 'Le Gros Clark was never convinced that this so-called Homo habilis fell outside the range of *Australopithecinae*. Was he right again?' (Oakley 1976). In the longer run, Leakey and Tobias have prevailed, but it is interesting to see that there was later something close to a re-run of this debate, when Alan Walker was reluctant to regard the 1470 specimen from East Turkana as *Homo*, for similar reasons.

Fascinating though these controversies may be, they are not central to the archaeological progress which the discoveries heralded. Palaeoanthropology was virtually transformed by the new associations, and by the new dates achieved by potassium-argon, which showed that Olduvai Bed I was approximately three times older than early glacial deposits of Europe (Leakey, Evernden and Curtis 1961; see p. 91 of Leakey 1965). The committee of the National Geographic Society was convinced of the need for support, and provided an infusion of funds which entirely changed the scale of survey and excavation. A simple verbal account does not easily make plain just how fundamentally the operations were altered. Consider, however, the size of the excavations and the numbers of finds. The excavations of FLK NN were 18 by 15 metres (270 sq m); at FLK 22 by 15 metres (330 sq m). The *Zinjanthropus* floor alone yielded over 2,000 artefacts. Mary Leakey records that Louis made over to her the direction of excavations at the gorge, and even that he accepted without demur her re-evaluation of the cultural material. Her excavations, and the published record of them with its unsurpassed drawings, are classics in this field (Leakey 1971).

This was now to become the age of the Oldowan, with the Acheulean relegated to a lesser position. Special mention must however be given to the developments at Olorgesailie in the early 1960s, since many of the intellectual or theoretical advances of the last thirty years rest on Glynn Isaac's work on that site. After the original investigations of the 1940s the Leakeys had been able to arrange the appointment of site wardens to continue the archaeological work. Merrick Posnansky (1959) conducted new excavations, locating a light-duty (Hope Fountain) facies of Acheulean. In 1961 Glynn Isaac took over, beginning a new series of excavations for museum display.

A full published account with considerable historical background is given in the Olorgesailie monograph of 1977. The simplest way to describe Isaac's approach in this, his early work, is as comprehensive. The excavations consolidated the approaches used at Kalambo, Isimila and Olduvai. Kleindienst's typology was overhauled and simplified, and complemented by a metrical approach to artefact analysis. For Isaac the measuring schemes – which were developed in parallel or earlier by others including Derek Roe – were subordinate to the goals of understanding the assemblages as series of events in ancient landscapes. The ideas are skilfully handled in his essays of the early 1970s (e.g. 1972a and b). Many see Isaac's prime contribution as being in his fieldwork and social models, but in the long term, his greatest contribution may well have been in developing robust theoretical approaches to archaeological problems in the face of uncertainties in time relationships. Also he was one of the first to take a landscape archaeology approach to early sites, and to consider site formation processes. No less careful or thoughtful was the renewed work at La Kamoa by Daniel Cahen, who dug there in 1969–70 (Cahen 1975).

As the Oldowan grew older, the Acheulean moved back into the gap. In the early 1960s the Leakeys stimulated research on the west side of Lake Natron, where the jaw of a robust australopithecine had been found. The project was carried out mainly by Glynn Isaac and Richard Leakey in a field season from July to September 1964 which yielded very early Acheulean sites dated to about 1.4 million years (Isaac 1967). Acheulean from the site of EF-HR at Olduvai, excavated by Mary Leakey in September-October 1963, proved to have a comparable age (Leakey 1971, 1975). In 1960 Louis Leakey had found the calvaria of Olduvai Hominid 9 ('Chellean man') at a considerably higher level, where Developed Oldowan was later found. Although Louis Leakey had long thought of the Acheulean as emerging directly from the Oldowan (e.g. Leakey 1936b), Mary Leakey regarded it as an intrusive phenomenon. Problems of this nature were not easily resolved: they have much to do with perceptions of resolution in the data, and with attitudes towards definitions.

In spite of its new eminence the Oldowan was not found at many more sites. Whereas the Acheulean can be counted in hundreds, if not thousands of localities, well attested Oldowan sites have probably not risen above twenty. Until this stage in East Africa (now minus the Kafuan) Olduvai Gorge stood almost alone. In North Africa, Sidi Abderrahman and Ain

Hanech were supplemented by less certainly dated sites. Since the early 1960s the list has been considerably augmented, mainly by investigations in the more northerly stretches of the Rift Valley.

The sites at Melka Kontouré in the Awash (Aouache) valley 50 km from Addis Ababa were discovered by J. Dekker in 1963, and investigated first by G. Bailloud in 1965. From the next year J. Chavaillon and colleagues worked there for several seasons, revealing an impressive sequence of Oldowan and Acheulean occurrences (Chavaillon, J. 1973, 1976b, 1980; Chavaillon, N. 1976; Chavaillon et al. 1978; Piperno 1980).

In 1966 F. Clark Howell began to organize the international Omo research expedition in the area of southern Ethiopia adjoining Lake Rudolf (now Turkana), with the support of Emperor Haile Selassie. Following an initial survey by F.H. Brown (1969), in 1967 American, Kenyan and French teams took part. The French were led by Professor Camille Arambourg, who had first worked in the area in 1932–3 (Arambourg 1952). After one season the Kenyan team transferred its attention to the eastern shores of Lake Rudolf, but the others continued with their work of building up a local sequence. This produced one of the best dated series of Plio-Pleistocene deposits anywhere in the world, with accompanying rich series of fossils, and eventually archaeological sites. The hominid remains were unfortunately highly fragmentary for the most part, but fortunately numerous. Howell and Coppens (1976) report remains from two localities in the Usno Formation, and no less than 92 in the Shungura Formation. Against four incomplete crania, there were over 200 isolated teeth. In 1969 artefacts were found at Omo for the first time in the Shungura Formation. Little more was found in 1970, but in 1971–2 both French and American teams excavated successfully on several sites (Chavaillon 1970, 1971, 1976a and b; Merrick et al. 1973; Merrick 1976). The Oldowan-like industry made from very small cobbles was dated to about 2.0–2.1 million years.

From 1968 Richard Leakey worked at East Rudolf (East Turkana) where he had noticed extensive exposures from the air. Artefact sites were rapidly discovered in and around the KBS tuff (Behrensmeyer 1970; Leakey, M.D. 1970; Leakey, R.E.F. 1970). Initially they were examined by Mary Leakey, but in view of the extent of her commitments at Olduvai, the responsibilities of description and investigation were soon passed to Glynn Isaac. This was plainly an appropriate choice: Richard Leakey and Glynn Isaac had previously collaborated at Peninj in the early 1960s (Isaac 1967), and Isaac's work at Olorgesailie had given him extensive experience of Lower Palaeolithic problems.

Richard Leakey and Glynn Isaac were to maintain a fruitful collaboration over many seasons. In the course of this research numerous archaeological and palaeontological sites were discovered (Leakey and Leakey 1978). The contributions of Leakey and Isaac to the project remained clearly separate, largely as artefacts and hominids tended to be found in different areas. Initial investigations were particularly exciting because of the very early date suggested by the first argon–argon dates (Fitch and Miller 1970). Accordingly the KBS sites were regarded as adding three-quarters of a million years to the history of tool-making (fig. 2:4), and this new vista encouraged Isaac to re-examine the earliest stages of tool-making from a theoretical perspective, considering various possible models of early hominid adaptations (e.g. Isaac 1972a and b).

Here then was the background to Glynn Isaac's formulation, and championing, of the 'food-sharing model' and the central concept of 'home bases' (e.g. Isaac 1978). The interpretative picture is summarized by Isaac et al. (1973: 548):

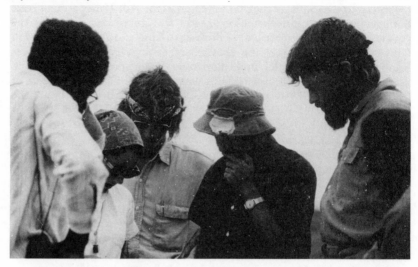

2:4 *Conference of researchers with Glynn Isaac on the KBS site at East Rudolf (E. Turkana). Flanking Isaac, left to right, are J.C. Onyango-Abuje, D. Stiles, A.K. Behrensmeyer, J.W.K. Harris and Bob Campbell*

by the time of the KBS Tuff, some hominids were already involved in behaviour patterns that were of fundamental importance for the evolutionary differentiation of our species from other living primates, namely: tool manufacture and use; meat eating (and presumably hunting); and operation out of a home base. It seems highly likely that food sharing and some cooperative division of labour would also have been involved.

The 1470 cranium found in 1972 injected into this picture precociously early *Homo* (Leakey 1973). By the following year, however, doubts were emerging about the East Turkana dates, which had been established by the argon-argon technique. The prime pointer came from comparisons with the Omo sequence, which was also very fully dated by potassium-argon. The fauna found in apparently contemporary levels of the two areas seemed incompatible: there was a kind of evolutionary offset. The issues were fully discussed at a conference held in Nairobi in 1973 (published as Coppens *et al.* 1976). Basil Cooke wrote, on the basis of data from *Mesochoerus*, that

> it would be inferred that the KBS Tuff should be fairly close in age to the top of Member F at Omo, which is apparently 2.0 my, whereas the radiometric date for the KBS Tuff is 2.6 my. The discrepancy is considerable and cannot be ignored. (Cooke 1976: 261)

Some researchers felt that differences in ecology between the two areas could partly explain the faunal offset, but it fairly soon became apparent that the Omo chronology was correct. The controversy, however, ran on until 1979, and was only finally resolved in print in 1980 (Gleadow 1980; McDougall *et al.* 1980).

Much earlier than this, two sets of archaeological sites had been distinguished at East Turkana, the early 'KBS Industry' ascribed to the Oldowan Industrial Complex, and the somewhat later Karari Industry, which could be regarded as a form of Developed Oldowan (Isaac 1976; Isaac *et al.* 1976; Harris and Herbich 1978; Isaac and Harris 1978). As a consequence of the redating the two industries are far less separated in time than had been supposed, having ages of *c.* 1.8–1.9 ma and 1.5–1.6 ma respectively. The great bulk of the material belongs to the later Karari phase. FxJj 50, on the Karari escarpment, was singled out for particularly intensive treatment (Bunn *et al.* 1980).

Further to the south, in the central region of the Rift Valley around Lake Baringo, another multi-disciplinary study was going on. This was the geological mapping project led by Professors King and Bishop of London University. In this project the Quaternary geology of a huge area was mapped at a large scale, and numerous fossiliferous localities were discovered. Australopithecine remains were found in Chesowanja, east of Lake Baringo, in 1969 (Carney *et al.* 1971), while W.B. Jones found the archaeological site of Kilombe (fig. 2:5). During the 1973 field season at Kilombe Bill Bishop revisited Chesowanja, noting for the first time numbers of artefact localities which had previously been overlooked. Following a geological reinterpretation investigations at Chesowanja were started up wth some difficulty (Bishop *et al.* 1978). Although Bill Bishop's sudden death in 1976 was a great blow, the projected archaeological work was still able to get under way (Harris and Gowlett 1980; Gowlett *et al.* 1981; Harris *et al.* 1981), but the loss of Bishop's enthusiastic support had an unsettling effect.

In the mid-1970s further investigations flourished in various parts of the Ethiopian Rift. International teams found more than 25 artefact localities in the area of Gadeb, 250 km south of Addis Ababa (Clark 1980b, Clark and Kurashina 1979). They included both Developed Oldowan and Acheulean sites, and in one instance stones appeared to have been altered by fire (Barbetti *et al.* 1980).

The more northerly part of the Rift, the Afar depression, is famous for the discoveries of early hominids made at Hadar from 1974 onwards (Johanson and Taieb 1976; Taieb *et al.* 1976; Johanson and Edey 1981). Two groups of Lower Palaeolithic sites were also found in the area. At Hadar itself Corvinus and Roche prospected in 1973, 1974 and 1975 as part of the international research expedition led by M. Taieb (Corvinus and Roche 1976, 1980). Apart from Acheulean industries in upper levels hints of *in situ* occurrences were found at Kada Gona in the upper part of the Hadar Formation, in the region of the BKT2 tuff aged about 2.6 ma. These were mainly in conglomerates, but Roche added to the finds (Roche 1980), and in later work with Don Johanson, J.W.K. Harris found artefacts *in situ* in fine-grained deposits (Harris 1983).

Remains of *Homo erectus* were found elsewhere in the Hadar area, and numerous other Acheulean sites (Kalb *et al.* 1982; Clark *et al.* 1984). The Nile Basin possesses no truly early sites, but work on the Acheulean has continued at intervals, in rescue excavations associated with construction of the Aswan High Dam (the site of Arkin 8 (Chmielewski 1968; Wendorf 1968); in middle Egypt (Vermeersch *et al.* 1980) and in the western desert (Wendorf and Schild 1977).

In South Africa the discovery of hominid remains continued, the total rising from about 1022 to 1077 specimens during the 1970s through further finds at Sterkfontein and Swartkrans (Brain 1970, 1978; Tobias 1972, 1978). R.J. Clarke reassembled hominid fragments from Swartkrans, including those assigned to 'Telanthropus capensis' in 1949 (Broom and Robinson 1949), so as to make up a partial cranium of 'Homo sp.' (Clark, Howell and Brain 1970). Early Acheulean artefacts from Sterkfontein were studied by Stiles (1979a and b), who made comparisons with Bed II Acheulean and Developed Oldowan of Olduvai. Perhaps unfairly, the South African discoveries of the 1970s did not make the same impact in the world as those from Kenya and Ethiopia. The absence of volcanic rocks which could allow potassium-argon-dating was part of the problem. The geomorphological reasoning of Partridge (1973) was accepted with reservation, and faunal comparisons, though providing

2:5 *J.W.K. Harris, Bill Bishop and Glynn Isaac examine exposures near Kilombe in the central Rift Valley 1973*

excellent estimates, did not carry the force of radiometric determinations. Not surprisingly, the archaeology of the Acheulean has received less attention again, but the work of Deacon at Amanzi Springs, Keller at Montagu Cave and of Mason at the Cave of Hearths and Doornlaagte, has a place in the history of the subject (Deacon 1970, 1975; Keller 1973; Mason 1962, 1966).

Recent years

How do we get under the skin of the subject, beyond raw details? What has really been going on in the archaeology of human origins in recent years? Inexorably, the paths of hominid palaeontology and archaeology tend to drift apart again, as soon as exciting finds come up in one which have no counterpart in the other. 1470 and the early industries of KBS can be assimilated side by side; but the three-million-year-old hominids of Hadar, or the even older Laetoli footprints (Leakey and Hay 1979) have no archaeological match. The central problem for early archaeology appears to lie in assessing how rapidly human abilities and behaviour emerged; and in determining to what extent the 'package' present in ourselves first appears as a complex, rather than accumulating trait by trait. The work of the last ten years has frequently been concerned with these problems, but also frequently has set them aside, losing them amid detail. The controversies of recent years are too close to be treated objectively. As a history, then, this account should draw to an end around 1980, since later events cannot be treated with the necessary detachment. For that reason detailed referencing ends here, but it can be noted that excellent general accounts of recent work have been given by Isaac (1984) in English, and by Roche (1980) in French.

Some general observations may be made about recent developments. First, looking back to the spurt of fieldwork in the early 1960s, one notes Desmond Clark's observation that modes of analysis of material did not keep up with advances in field techniques of recovery (Clark 1967). Clearly much attention has been paid to this in the last twenty years. Desmond Clark must have been much encouraged to find in Glynn Isaac – who joined him at Berkeley – a colleague who was happy to challenge theoretical issues not merely as an obligation, but with gusto.

Although many advances have been made in techniques of analysis, it remains true for the Lower Palaeolithic that only a very few archaeologists have been primarily concerned with theoretical work. Thus our changing framework has come about quite largely through advances in other areas of science and archaeology, to which palaeoanthropologists have reacted. Some important points can be summarized:

(i) The steady improvement in dating methods, starting with radio-carbon in the 1950s, potassium-argon in the 1960s, culminating with complementary methods such as palaeomagnetism and fission track in the 1970s and 1980s (for example, papers in Bishop and Miller 1972).

(ii) The criticisms of climatic sequence dating methods at the end of the 1950s, which led to far greater emphasis on stratigraphic principles (Bishop 1959; Flint 1959).

(iii) Demands for revisions of terminology and classification, tackled at conferences in 1963 and 1965, and leading to greater emphasis on formally defined entities (especially treated in Bishop and Clark 1967).

(iv) A resurgence of ethnographic work upon hunters and gatherers, with express formulation of theoretical positions (e.g. papers in *Man the Hunter*: Lee and Devore (1968); parallel studies of living primates, and social models derived from these (e.g. papers in Washburn 1961 and 1963).

(v) Much input (and exchange) of new ideas from the earth sciences and palacontology, with an emphasis on site formation processes, the new science of 'taphonomy' (e.g. papers in Behrensmeyer and Hill 1980).

(vi) Increasing stress on large multi-disciplinary projects, and research oriented towards investigating specific questions.

(vii) A series of papers treating specifically the theoretical problems of dealing with the Lower Palaeolithic (e.g. Isaac 1972a and b).

These developments were centred on the new field projects of the late 1960s and early 1970s. In those projects archaeology was now only the dominant partner to the extent that human behaviour remained its preserve. Two major conference proceedings of the 1970s make the point: only 4 out of 34 papers are archaeological in one, just 5 out of 50 in the other.

In so far as there is any common theoretical base for archaeological studies, it must normally go back to things that have been agreed; and in science this tends to mean conference decisions. In studies of human origins, however, specialists are too scarce to form obvious communities, and it tends to be the research group or department that is important. In the wider forum, archaeologists of human origins are too few to hammer out perceptible shared approaches. Recent conferences seem to have had less impact than those in the 1960s, and it may be that the currency has been devalued. The Burg Wartenstein conference of 1965 is outstanding as a meeting where underlying issues were discussed in depth (Bishop and Clark 1967).   .

The developments listed above have done much to shape the subject over the last decade. Even so, colossal contributions have been made from within archaeology. The general reworking of ideas embraced by the 'New Archaeology' or 'processual' archaeology has been strongly felt in the archaeology of human origins. Ultimately much of this can be traced back to the interest of the late David Clarke, as well as to the intellectual force of Glynn Isaac. It would be inappropriate to single out other archaeologists for special mention here, but an exception can be made for Glynn Isaac, as he has left us so recently and tragically early. Isaac's contribution has been uniquely wide ranging. He stood for many things, including precision in fieldwork, objective approaches to artefact studies, attempts to study ancient landscapes, and models of early hominid behaviour related to archaeology.

Isaac's social models of early hominid behaviour – 'home bases' and 'food sharing' – have stimulated much controversy, most of it useful to the development of ideas. Isaac's own views had clearly evolved beyond his original labels (e.g. Isaac 1984), and would no doubt have developed much further.

Recent years have brought many technical innovations of analysis, as well as intellectual advances. These include the refitting of stone artefacts (an old idea freshly applied), extensive experiments, and a general effort to track the past dynamics of the various components which end up making an archaeological site. There is of course no point in applying any technique past the point of rewarding returns. In the last few years there has been something of a reaction, a realization perhaps that resolution of analysis can easily be pursued beyond the resolution of the available data.

These feelings have manifested themselves in sharp debates on the one hand about general models and their basis in fact, on the other particularly about the nature and certainty of crucial associations. Do stone tools and bones belong together? Do baked clay, stones and hominids belong together? It is unfortunate that controversies have tended to turn on, and be discussed in terms of, individual points on individual sites. Far less attention has been paid to the mass of data acquired over the last thirty years, or to its general weight in telling us about early hominid adaptation.

Cross-disciplinary approaches have the disadvantage that they may distract from intensive scholarship in a single field. For example, models of evolution in general books of palaeoanthropology sometimes pay virtually no attention to dissenting evidence which plainly exists in the storehouse of Palaeolithic discoveries. This is hardly surprising, as there is still no general agreement as to how anthropology is conducted. At least in palaeoanthropology we have an agreed body of methods in (i) field investigation and (ii) basic post-excavation analyses. We are unlikely to get agreement about the investigation of complex behaviour until (or unless) we are all sure that behaviour was complex.

There is now a mood of reappraisal; sombre but not gloomy. Early hominid sites have been located in very few countries. The loss of one of these to research – Ethiopia in the throes of revolution and civil war – has hit studies of human evolution very hard. The oil recession of the 1970s also struck at the foundations of large-scale research (quite literally). Thus there has been an enforced phase of reconsideration, which has been perhaps more of a hiatus.

Why, one may ask, has no more been done to investigate early sites in other countries? What now of Algeria, Nigeria, Cameroun, Sudan or Malawi? In each case one may be assured that a few dedicated individuals are trying very hard to pursue research in the Old Stone Age, usually with very limited financial and logistic resources. Amongst those with the most slender chances of carrying out new fieldwork are the freshly established generation of indigenous African scholars, at least several of whom have a keen interest in the very early human past. To say, accurately, 'several' measures the scope of the research problem in a continent with over forty countries.

In one of his last papers Glynn Isaac stressed the need for a broadening or 'internationalization' of studies in human origins, so that Third World countries would be fully included (Isaac 1985). That need remains pressing. If Africa should falter in this, the claims of early European and Asian sites will become more and more prominent. In Africa, however, the research has established the experience and credentials which should see it through. Lessons hard learned have ensured that one cannot now bring forward a few 'tools' from a conglomerate and have them accepted as an early industry. In a real sense a discipline has been built on African soil, and until its tenets have been fully assimilated elsewhere, Africa will retain its massive lead in research into human origins.

3 Weaving the Fabric
of Stone Age Research in Southern Africa

JANETTE DEACON

'The history of any science is the most revealing approach that a newcomer can employ,' wrote Goodwin (1946). His approach to the history of archaeology in South Africa was initially to compile a commentary on publications up to the mid-1930s that dealt with the information sequentially (Goodwin 1935). About a decade later he up-dated the bibliography and enlarged the commentary 'to attempt some analysis of the interweaving elements of time, culture, man and area in the light of past research and publication' (Goodwin 1946: 10). He called it *The Loom of Prehistory* because 'we are now trying to weave these into a patterned fabric, selecting our threads, relating them one with another, and evolving a fabric which should provide the cloth from which something new can be made' (1946: 10–11). Forty years later, one still hopes to weave such a cloth by identifying some of the people, trends and events that have shaped Southern African Stone Age studies.

The geographic focus in this chapter is on South Africa and Namibia with reference to Botswana and Zimbabwe where appropriate. The emphasis is on the history of Stone Age studies in general prior to 1960, and thereafter on the Later Stone Age in particular. Bibliographic works such as the one by Holm (1966) and Summers (1971a) have up-dated Goodwin's lists and detailed reviews of Later Stone Age studies have been published this decade (J. Deacon 1984a; Parkington 1984). Instead of repeating the conclusions drawn, this paper focusses on the goals of researchers over the past century or more, rather than on the results of their work. In doing so, one inevitably draws attention to individuals and the differences between them. For example, archaeology in Southern Africa has been dominated by a relatively small section of the population, namely English-speaking people of European descent with educational links with Britain, America and, to a lesser extent, Germany and France. As a consequence, over 95 per cent of all archaeological publications on Southern Africa have been written in English (Holm 1966 and recent journal indices). University teachers had more influence than those who held museum or national monuments posts, who were in turn more influential than those who had no formal training, yet all were threads in the loom and played a part in changing the pursuit from one of amateur involvement to one which is fully professional. In drawing comparisons and commenting on their careers I do not mean to imply that some were better or worse than others. My purpose is to try to discern how and why trends developed and who nurtured them. Although seldom made explicit, the goals of the earliest collectors were to discover the range of Stone Age artefacts found in Southern Africa and to speculate about the people who made them. Once these basic parameters were known, the focus changed to describing the temporal relationships and regional variability of the industries or cultures and, latterly, to investigating social and environmental correlates. In hindsight we can see that progress was speeded up at times by the stimulus of visiting scholars or the vision of individuals, and at other times it was retarded by wars and economic factors, but without the abiding interest of archaeologists there would have been no progress at all. For most of the archaeologists mentioned here, studying the prehistory of Southern Africa was or still is not just a job, but the absorbing interest of a lifetime.

Archaeologists in Southern Africa and elsewhere are becoming increasingly aware of the influences on their work of the social milieu in which they live (Smith 1983; Trigger 1984; Parkington and Smith 1986), particularly in the wake of the banning of South African and Namibian archaeologists from the World Archaeological Congress in Southampton (Tobias 1985a). Archaeologists have been eager to publicize their work in international journals but up to now have been slow to do the same in academically less prestigious ways. The result is a gulf between what they believe about the past and what is believed by the general public. This gap must be bridged. Unfortunately, in the past the ruling white elite government has promoted the myth that prehistorically the country was thinly populated by recent arrivals from central and eastern Africa. This is reflected clearly in school history textbooks (Inskeep 1970; Smith 1983), but it has not been the belief of professional archaeologists whose research, paradoxically, has been funded by the same government that prescribes the school textbooks. This dichotomy between the goals and beliefs of professional archaeologists and the beliefs of other members of the society in which their work must be recognized. To stamp it all as 'colonial' (Trigger 1984: 362) is to overlook the significant differences in attitudes that have developed between those involved directly in archaeological research and the more varied community of the country as a whole.

Discovering the Stone Age heritage

The controlling models and paradigms of authors between 1869 and the early 1920s were essentially those of all amateur collectors and their overriding goal was simply to record the range of artefacts found and to compare them with those found in Europe. A note by George Busk (1869) records that he first saw stone 'spear or arrowheads' in 1855, dug up by Colonel J.H. Bowker near the mouth of the Great Fish River in the eastern Cape. Although Hewitt (1955) notes that Thomas Holden Bowker (fig. 3:1), brother of J.H. Bowker, had in fact made this first collection of stone tools in 1858 and not 1855, the date is nevertheless very close to that of similar discoveries in France and Britain (Daniel 1975). Both Bowker brothers were born in England and came to South Africa with the 1820 settlers as teenagers. As collectors, they were typical of the Victorian colonial antiquarians of their time. J.H. Bowker was a Fellow of the Linnaean Society and member of several other learned societies and butterflies were his particular passion. T.H. Bowker not only collected artefacts for himself, but also sent specimens to the Royal Artillery Museum in Woolwich and to the Albany Museum in Grahamstown, prompted in part by the surge of interest created by the contemporary discoveries of Boucher de Perthes and others.

Collections sent later to England by C.J. Busk and Sir Langham Dale were made use of by Lord Avebury (then Sir John Lubbock) in papers to the Anthropological and Ethnological Society of London (Lubbock 1869, 1870b), but the first published record on stone artefacts to appear in Southern Africa was by Dale in the *Cape Monthly Magazine* in 1870. Certainly by the 1870s stone tools were widely accepted as having been

3:1 *Thomas Holden Bowker (1808–85), South Africa's first stone artefact collector*

made by the ancestors of the indigenous San of Southern Africa and had been found throughout the Cape Colony and Natal.

The first *Proceedings* of the South African Philosophical Society (later the Royal Society of South Africa) were published in 1878 and it was suggested that an Ethnological Section be started 'to devote itself to the preservation of Bushman relics and other Bushman remains', but there was insufficient response from members and the idea was dropped. From the perspective of the 1980s it is disappointing that more interest was not shown for the 1870s are remarkable for the fact that it was during this decade that detailed testimonies were taken from San informants from the northern Cape (Bleek 1873, 1875; Lloyd 1889; Bleek and Lloyd 1911; Dunn 1931) and the Drakensberg (Orpen 1874). Thereafter it became increasingly rare to find San who remembered much about their traditional beliefs and artefacts although Kannemeyer (1890) gathered enough information for one of the few detailed descriptions of the use and making of stone tools ever published in Southern Africa.

Although many more people were involved in the collection and study of stone tools in France than in South Africa, De Mortillet's first classification of the French Palaeolithic appeared at about the same time as the first classification schemes for South Africa published by Gooch (1881) and Rickard (1881a, 1881b). Their use of European terms such as Palaeolithic and Neolithic reflected the assumption that the stone tools in Southern Africa had the same cultural origins as their European counterparts. Some British researchers did not agree (Goodwin 1946: 30) because hand-axes were sometimes found on the surface in South Africa, but papers by Penning (1886, 1898) and Péringuey and Corstophine (1900) demonstrated that they were to be found also in stratified river gravel deposits and some of the doubts about their antiquity were dispelled.

The Eurocentric attitude towards Southern African Stone Age studies persisted, perhaps because many authors were themselves recent immigrants. By contrast, excellent advice was given in 1905 by A.C. Haddon who visited South Africa as President of Section H of the British Association for the Advancement of Science. He advocated the dropping of terms such as Eolithic, Palaeolithic and Neolithic for Southern African materials, and advised that the geological context of finds be studied because this would help to establish age. He also has the distinction of indicating the need for legislation to protect archaeological sites. Haddon's advice was later to have considerable influence on the early work of Goodwin in the 1920s. Haddon may not have had great influence in the world of Oxbridge intellectuals (Leach 1984), but his common sense fortunately reached the colonies. Regrettably, the antiquities laws promulgated in 1911 and 1913 after the founding of the Union of South Africa in 1910 were inadequate protection against the sale and export of Stone Age artefacts (Gill 1926), and the situation was not rectified until the 1930s (Goodwin 1958).

Palaeolithic archaeology was not taught as a university subject much before the First World War and Goodwin's appointment in 1923 was the first for a professionally trained archaeologist in Southern Africa. However, interest was sufficient for the publication of several general books on the Stone Age in South Africa in the first decade of the twentieth century by specialists from other disciplines, for example, the geologist J.P. Johnson (1906, 1910a, 1910b) and L. Péringuey (1911), an entomologist. Péringuey, then Director of the South African Museum, used both local and European terms to describe material, but again there was no systematic attempt to place them in a time sequence based on geological context. Although he believed 'purely on antiquarian grounds' that there was a Palaeolithic period and a more recent one, 'unfortunately, neither geology nor palaeontology has been able to give us, so far, a clue to the possible age of the South African finds' (Péringuey 1911: 7). He acknowledged that many artefacts had been made by the San (and in fact he advocated this term rather than 'Bushmen'), but wondered whether bifacially worked Stillbay-type points that are similar to those made in the Fayum could not 'have been made on the spot by mariners wrecked or temporarily stranded, or by adventurers seeking pastures new' (Péringuey 1911: 84).

The problems that bothered Péringuey most in making these comparisons were the lack of dating evidence, the fact that the Stone Age lasted until the recent past in South Africa, and the absence of a Neolithic and Bronze Age in southern Africa (Péringuey 1911: 8), but he realized too that 'classifications are made to be unmade' (op. cit.) and proposed his as an interim measure. It was not only that there were no data on past climates in Southern Africa and that there were no absolute dating methods, but there was also very little interest in improving the situation. J.P. Johnson (1910b: 77) took the easy way out by saying that 'The prehistoric bush country was probably no different to the present' and although geologists did remark from time to time on the stratigraphic positions of various artefacts, the data were not correlated systematically because there was no one with the training, the time and the inclination to tackle the daunting task.

A man for the job

The 1920s and 1930s saw the growth of Stone Age archaeology as a subject in its own right in most of the western world. In Southern Africa it was nurtured and guided by A.J.H. Goodwin and C. Van Riet Lowe. Astley John Hilary Goodwin (fig. 3:2a, b, c) was born in December 1900 and died shortly before his 59th birthday (Malan 1959). He went to Cambridge soon after the end of the First World War and graduated with an honours degree in archaeology in 1922. His mentors were Miles Burkitt and A.C. Haddon so he was well versed in ethnological and archaeological method and theory. In 1923 he was appointed as a research assistant

3:2 *(a, b, c) A.J.H. Goodwin in c. 1918 and c. 1932 and in July 1959 at Burg Wartenstein*

in ethnology under Professor Radcliffe-Brown at the University of Cape Town to compile a survey and bibliography of information on all sub-Saharan African people, a task which he continued until 1926 and added to until about 1935. After the death of Péringuey in 1924, Goodwin was invited to sort through some of the South African Museum collections and realized 'the absolute necessity for evolving an entirely new cultural terminology for southern Africa' (Goodwin 1958: 25). His Cambridge training had taught him to assign tool types to recognized cultures or industries, but in the South African case he had to start from scratch. He worked systematically, placing the tools into typological groups (hand-axes, scrapers, etc.) and he then rearranged the material according to site and from this new arrangement was able to discern which tool types consistently occurred together. Relative dating was worked out from patination and rare instances of stratigraphic superimposition. From the perspective of the present day, it is perhaps difficult to appreciate the enormity of this task. The fact that the basic subdivisions still hold good is testimony to the care and perception of Goodwin's work, regardless of its theoretical underpinnings.

In 1924, Goodwin began corresponding with C. ('Peter') Van Riet Lowe, born in 1894, and a civil engineer working at that time in the Orange Free State (fig. 3:3). Goodwin remarked many years later that writing to Van Riet Lowe 'disciplined me to clarify and set down my own views and methods for a man I had not met and who had no access to my material . . . while I . . . had no access to the material he was finding or to

3:3 *Clarence 'Peter' Van Riet Lowe*

the sites he was trying to unravel' (Goodwin 1958: 27). The result of Goodwin's work with the museum collections, together with a substantial number of field trips and the field experience of Van Riet Lowe, Hewitt, Van Hoepen, Heese and others, led him to suggest a two-stage subdivision of the Stone Age. The Earlier Stone Age was typified by the Stellenbosch culture (equivalent to the Acheulian and Lower Palaeolithic in Europe) and the Later Stone Age by the Eastern, Smithfield and Pygmy industries which he saw as similar but by no means identical to the Middle and Upper Palaeolithic and Mesolithic of Europe. He presented this scheme at a meeting of the South African Association for the Advancement of Science in Oudtshoorn in 1925, but acceptance was postponed until the following year when the Association met in Pretoria (Goodwin 1926). In the interim, Goodwin wrote a Handbook to accompany the new displays at the South African Museum and wrote a series of newspaper articles entitled 'Stories in Stones' in which he set out his ideas and stressed that 'It seems necessary . . . to discard all European terms, and to confine ourselves to purely South African terms' (Goodwin 1958: 29). And again, 'We had been trying to describe giraffe in terms of camel, or eland in terms of elk. It was essential to create *de novo* an unbiased and fairly logical framework specifically suited to southern Africa' (*op. cit.*: 33).

Although Goodwin was intellectually committed to a Southern African terminology, it is interesting that he still believed that many of the industries came to the sub-continent with migrations of people from North Africa (Goodwin and Van Riet Lowe 1929). The term Middle Stone Age was introduced subsequently in 1927 at the instigation of Revd Neville Jones in Southern Rhodesia and Miss Maria Wilman in Kimberley and included the Eastern (Stillbay) culture of the earlier scheme. At the same time, the Later Stone Age term 'Pygmy' was replaced by 'Wilton', named after sites on a farm of the same name that had been excavated by Hewitt (1921). The other Later Stone Age industry, the Smithfield, was named after a town of the same name in the Orange Free State, and was subdivided into Smithfield A, B and C on the basis of patination and choice of raw material (see Goodwin and Van Riet Lowe 1929, J. Deacon 1984a and Parkington 1984 for more details).

The Stone Age Cultures of South Africa, the result of seven years' work and

3:4 From left: *Miles C. Burkitt, Mrs Peggy Burkitt, Mrs Winnie Goodwin and A.J.H. Goodwin at a cave near Tarkastad, Eastern Cape, in 1927*

a classic example of empiricism at its most useful, was written jointly by Goodwin and Van Riet Lowe (1929). It post-dated the publication of Burkitt's general and popular book (Burkitt 1928; Schrire *et al.* 1986), written while on a tour of Southern Africa (fig. 3:4), and it also post-dated Jones's book on the Stone Age in Southern Rhodesia (1926) which Goodwin regarded as 'a somewhat meagre skeleton . . . in the light of [Jones's] own subsequent work' (Goodwin 1946: 55). Neither Jones nor Burkitt had used the South African terms, but after 1929 Earlier, Middle and Later Stone Age were widely adopted, not only in South Africa but further afield in Africa and, subsequently, in India as well.

Goodwin had had high hopes for prehistoric studies in South Africa in the 1920s, but seems to have been discouraged both by the lack of funds and by the turn of events. Both he and Van Riet Lowe had approached the influential politician J.C. Smuts with ideas on government involvement in archaeology, but it was Goodwin's 'correspondence pupil', Van Riet Lowe, who was appointed as Director of the Bureau of Archaeology (later the Archaeological Survey) when Goodwin had hoped that he himself would be appointed as Director of an Institute of Prehistory attached to the South African Museum (Goodwin 1958). As Leach (1984) has remarked, the 'background' of anthropologists in Britain in the first few decades of the twentieth century had much to do with whether they 'got on' in university politics, their class status having precedence over academic ability and training. In Van Riet Lowe's case, he was fortunate in the status he achieved from having served in the First World War because Smuts had done the same. The two men saw a lot of each other when, after attending the centenary meeting of the British Association for the Advancement of Science in London in 1931, Van Riet Lowe returned to South Africa on the same ship as General Smuts and the two had 'long and serious discussions on archaeological subjects almost daily during the voyage' (Malan 1962: 40). After Van Riet Lowe established the Bureau in Johannesburg in 1935 and became Secretary of the Historical Monuments Commission, he and B.D. Malan, appointed as his assistant, were 'constantly in the field' (Malan 1962: 41), and Van Riet Lowe also visited many other African countries advising governments in Southern Rhodesia, Mozambique and Uganda. Goodwin, on the other hand, began teaching ethnology and archaeology at the University of Cape Town in the late 1920s (the first university courses in archaeology in sub-Saharan Africa) and excavated at Cape St Blaize and Oakhurst (Goodwin 1938). Mary Leakey (1984: 51) visited Goodwin at Oakhurst in 1935 and remembers that his excavation methods were 'way ahead of his time'.

Goodwin and Van Riet Lowe's 1929 synthesis aimed to study the distribution of Stone Age cultures in Southern Africa in relation to the geography and climate that may have affected them. This was on the assumption that 'We are dealing primarily with a migrant and evolving animal . . . capable of inventing and perpetuating his various reactions to environment, or modifying those reactions to meet certain needs' (Goodwin and Van Riet Lowe 1929: 1). This model incorporated both technological and environmental change as well as a theory of migration to explain changes through time. In the absence of data on past climates, they described briefly the physical geography of various regions, focussing on river valleys and mountain chains that were considered to have been barriers or highways along which prehistoric people would have migrated. The lack of palaeoenvironmental studies prevented a detailed correlation of environmental and cultural data, although it was assumed that if Earlier Stone Age tools were found in what is now a desert, then the climate must have been more favourable at that time. Their goal was essentially to construct a time-space framework with the expectation that migration and diffusion of people and ideas could be traced through similarities in the stone artefact assemblages.

The view of Stone Age people as the helpless recipients of successive waves of innovation from Europe, the font of knowledge and invention, is again typical of research elsewhere at this time (Trigger 1984), even amongst British prehistorians (J.G.D. Clark 1966). Goodwin and Van Riet Lowe (1929: 3) saw Africa as 'a pocket from which nothing tangible returns', the Sahara acting as a significant barrier preventing the movement of cultures from south to north, but allowing 'higher' cultures to pass from Europe to south of the Sahara. Impey (1926), a medical doctor, even claimed that a 50,000-year-old wooden bridge had been found across a swamp somewhere in Africa, proving that 'Grimaldi Man' had migrated from Europe to South Africa. Amusing as this may be, J.G.D. Clark in his *World Prehistory* still thought of sub-Saharan Africa as a cultural backwater nearly fifty years later (Clark 1971: 67), a view resulting from his own inadequate knowledge rather than a fair reflection of the conclusions of Southern African archaeologists. Just as the classification of the Taung australopithecine took a long time to be accepted after Dart's announcement in 1925, amongst other reasons because of its 'provincial origins' (Howells 1985: 22), so the colonialist attitude of denigration of things non-

3:5 From left: *A.J.H. Goodwin, Mrs Harper Kelley, Harper Kelley, Abbé Breuil, H. Fleure and Mr Garfitt amongst the Fish Hoek sand dunes near Peer's Cave in 1929*

European persisted in British academic circles well into the 1970s. The sin, as Howells (1985: 24) phrased it, 'seems to have been mere inattention.'

After 1929, research had to fill in the gaps in several directions, particularly in respect of past climates and the dating and distribution of industries used in supporting the migration model. Interest in past climates was stimulated by the claimed link between northern hemisphere glacials and African pluvials, but it was used more as a relative dating tool than to explain changes in stone tool manufacture or population distributions. Leakey (1929) identified four pluvials from geological deposits in eastern Africa, and Van Riet Lowe (1929: 679) and Smuts (1932) were quick to apply the scheme in South Africa, encouraged in 1929 by visits from Louis Leakey (who drove from Nairobi to Johannesburg) and the Abbé Henri Breuil (fig. 3:5). Van Riet Lowe worked later with the Geological Survey on the mapping and interpretation of the Vaal River terrace deposits and described them firmly within the pluvial model. The stone artefact assemblages, each showing some technological difference in successive river terraces, were placed into a relative dating framework that was linked with sea level changes and the major period of rifting to East Africa (Söhnge *et al.* 1937). For the next twenty-five years, archaeology students at the University of Cape Town were taught the intricacies of the Vaal River sequence, which now hardly merits mention, and learned to identify terraces and to distinguish between rolled and 'fresh' artefacts, and those that were *in situ* or not. This strong geological focus was to influence many of the students in their later careers, in particular R.J. Mason, G.Ll. Isaac, P.B. Beaumont and H.J. Deacon. For many years it was the only relative dating scheme available. Unfortunately the pluvial scheme was flawed and ought never to have been exported from East Africa. Du Toit (1947: 40), an eminent and much respected geologist, appeared to have little faith in the ability of archaeologists to deal with geological problems when he assessed the field evidence for the pluvials and commented: 'prehistorians have a flair for embroidering their knowledge, with speculation about the derivation of cultures and techniques and such like, as mutable almost as the climatic oscillations that form the subject of these tentative remarks.' One may think these were hard words, but H.B.S. Cooke (1957) and Flint (1959a, b) later discredited the pluvial scheme entirely.

The migration model needed two kinds of data: distribution of items of material culture that could be mapped to show the routes taken by incoming people, and dating that would fix the origin and ultimate destination of the item or culture. Goodwin's study of the bored stones of South

Africa tried to do both, but without the benefit of an absolute dating method (Goodwin 1947: 2). He had begun collecting data in the 1920s, but other more pressing work intervened and it was not until military duties during the Second World War limited fieldwork opportunities that he took up the study again, inspired in part by Major Myers, an Egyptologist (*op. cit.*: 3). The patterning that he saw led him to conclude that geographical features had played a major part in determining migration routes of Later Stone Age people. In none of his other papers is Goodwin quite so explicit about his goal. He calls it a 'fundamentally statistical approach, which provides an ethnological tool as certain as that of geology in the earlier prehistoric field. ... It depends fundamentally upon deductions or logical judgments, made from available data, while speculation ... must not be permitted to affect the main issues of the survey' (Goodwin 1947: 4). His premise was that it should be possible to trace migration routes from one focal area to another using a typology of bored stones (Goodwin 1947: 108). He assumed at first that he would be discovering tribal or hunting areas, but soon realized that even if these were what the patterning represented, they were neither static nor stable, overlapping one another from time to time 'probably in relation to the waxing and waning of tribal strength' (Goodwin 1947: 115). In his opinion, the results showed that the 'complex of migrational routes revealed was logical and consistent. Each path was directly related to, and governed by, geographical factors. ... It is the logic of these routes that most decidedly proves the existence of types *per se*' (*op. cit.*: 116).

Apart from limiting fieldwork and publication funds, the aftermath of the Second World War had another marked effect on archaeology: the change of government in 1948 inhibited research and contact with other African countries. Paradoxically, the limitation of research and publication funds had a positive effect on Goodwin. From the mid-1940s, his energies were directed towards the establishment of the South African Archaeological Society and the editorship of the *South African Archaeological Bulletin*. Although his editorials in the first ten or more years are peppered with comments on the poor financial state of the Society, he worked tirelessly to write articles of general interest for the (mostly amateur) members and to encourage non-professionals to contribute articles. The *Bulletin* has remained the only South African journal devoted entirely to prehistory and was for many years the only regular archaeological journal south of the Sahara. Even so, the Society has only 900 members resident in Southern Africa out of a total membership of 1,200.

When Afrikaner nationalism strengthened and apartheid became entrenched after 1948, government interference was evident, apparently because of the threat posed by archaeological findings to biblical beliefs of creation (Goodwin 1952: 53) and to evidence showing that the country had been occupied well in advance of the arrival of European colonists (Smith 1983). The first problems arose in 1952. The first Pan-African Congress on Prehistory was held in Nairobi in 1947 and 22 archaeologists, geologists and physical anthropologists from Southern Africa attended comprising about one-third of all the delegates. The South African delegation was flown by military aircraft to Nairobi by special arrangement with the then Prime Minister, J.C. Smuts, and an invitation was extended to the congress to hold its next meeting in Johannesburg with encouragement from Smuts. Unfortunately his party lost the election in 1948 and the new Nationalist government informed Van Riet Lowe, after many arrangements had been made, that it was 'inconvenient' for the meeting to be held in South Africa after all. In an Editorial in the *South African Archaeological Bulletin* Goodwin remarked, 'We have the materials, we have the will, we have the men; we only lack the essential support of our own Government in this particular instance, which ill accords with their generous and continued support to our subject through many other channels' (Goodwin 1950: 2). The congress was rescheduled in Algiers at short notice and never again had the opportunity of meeting south of the Zambezi. In Algiers, Malan and Van Riet Lowe, Assistant Secretary and Vice President respectively, were unable to attend, and no other South African delegates participated. Van Riet Lowe continued to serve as a Vice President until his death in 1956 and thereafter it was the physical anthropologists, R.A. Dart and P.V. Tobias, who served as office bearers. From 1977, South African passport holders have been barred from entering the countries where Pan-African Congresses have been held and have therefore not been able to co-operate on an official level with their colleagues in other African countries.

Where Goodwin had been the academic prehistorian and teacher, Van Riet Lowe was the public relations man with what contemporaries have described as tremendous enthusiasm and drive (Malan 1962: 42). Although Van Riet Lowe may have published more papers than Goodwin, it is Goodwin's contribution to the subject that has been the more lasting, both in terms of the students he taught and of the general introductory texts that he wrote. His *Method in Prehistory*, a South African Archaeological Society Handbook, was until 1986 the only book published on this topic with a Southern African focus (Goodwin 1953). In it, Goodwin's remarks on theory show the unmistakeable influence of V. Gordon Childe whose writings he greatly admired.

Neither Goodwin nor Van Riet Lowe followed up their 1929 joint publication with a similar overview and the next major synthesis appeared thirty years later. J. Desmond Clark, appointed to the Rhodes Livingstone Museum in 1938, wrote what must have been one of African archaeology's best sellers. With twenty years' experience, he summarized the data base for both cultural and environmental information from southern Africa (Clark 1959a) and has remarked that this was the book he most enjoyed writing (Clark 1986: 187). By the mid-1950s the classification scheme had been expanded to include the First and Second Intermediate stages, radiocarbon dating had been introduced and had made a considerable impact, more sites had been excavated and a good start had been made on accumulating palynological and other palaeoenvironmental data. Clark wove a fine cloth from the enthnographic and archaeological threads, developing what he considered to be the all-important ecological approach to prehistory inherited from Grahame Clark (Clark 1986: 187).

The first serious questioning of the Stone Age terminology surfaced with the publication of R.J. Mason's *Prehistory of the Transvaal* in 1962, and later in 1965 at the Wenner-Gren conference on Background to Evolution in Africa where dissatisfaction focussed on the definitions rather than on the goals and aims. Despite the fact that the focus in the USA was beginning to shift from descriptions of artefacts to explanations of processes, this was not apparent at Burg Wartenstein where theory was hardly mentioned. Inskeep (1967a: 559) put it frankly when he wrote 'What we are trying to sort out today is our inheritance from our predecessors.' In Southern Africa the reaction was to replace many of the old cultural and industrial terms with new local ones, but without re-evaluating the definitions and meaning of the units themselves. This was most apparent in Zimbabwe (Cooke *et al.* 1966). In South Africa the desire to tidy up the terminology led Sampson (1970, 1972), who had been appointed to investigate sites in the Smithfield area along the Orange River that were to be destroyed by the H.F.

Verwoerd Dam project, to propose a series of phases to replace Van Riet Lowe's subdivisions, basing the phases on stratigraphic principles and radiocarbon dates. He later proposed a new classification scheme for Southern Africa within a series of (Industrial) Complexes (Sampson 1974). In the eastern Cape by contrast, the Wilton name site was re-excavated and the 8,000-year sequence was described as a single evolving tool-making tradition rather than as a succession of occupations by people with different traditions (J. Deacon 1972). These rather different interpretations reflect in part the legacy of a discontinuous sequence in the Smithfield area and a relatively continuous one in the eastern Cape as demonstrated by the distribution of radiocarbon dates for the Smithfield and the Wilton (J. Deacon 1974).

The professionalization of archaeology in the 1960s

Archaeology in South Africa had a relatively low profile before the 1960s. In over thirty years of teaching, Goodwin supervised only one doctoral student, R.J. Mason, and was instrumental in arranging professional archaeological employment for only three of his students: B.D. Malan in the 1930s, Mason in the 1940s and P.B. Beaumont in the 1950s, all in the Transvaal under the wing of the Historical Monuments Commission and Archaeological Survey. This dearth of graduate students was not unique to South Africa and was largely the result of economic circumstances – first during the depression in the 1930s and then during the Second World War – but it meant that after the death of Van Riet Lowe in 1956 and of Goodwin in 1959 there were few locally trained professional archaeologists to replace them (see comments by Goodwin 1954: 100). Goodwin's post was filled most ably in 1960 by R.R. Inskeep (fig. 3:6) from Cambridge and the department subsequently attracted graduates from Cambridge, Yale and Berkeley. B.D. Malan took over Van Riet Lowe's post as the Director of the Archaeological Survey, but when this was disbanded in 1962, Malan became Secretary of the Historical Monuments Commission in Cape Town and R.J. Mason joined the staff of the University of the Witwatersrand and was later appointed Director of the Archaeological Research Unit where the Survey collections are now housed. The disbanding of the Archaeological Survey as a government-funded body was a major loss and it was never adequately replaced either by the National Monuments Council or by the Archaeological Research Unit at the University of the Witwatersrand. Absence of a central organization of this kind has meant that rescue operations, such as the one by Sampson along the middle Orange River before the building of the H.F. Verwoerd Dam, had to be financed and staffed on an *ad hoc* basis. By 1972, however, there were professional archaeologists at most major museums in South Africa and teaching departments at the universities of Cape Town, Fort Hare, Pretoria, Stellenbosch, UNISA and the Witwatersrand. Most of these positions were filled by South African graduates, the majority having graduated in the 1960s. With an expanding job market and better research funds available after 1970, more graduates were able to study further. In 1986 there were about the same number of PhDs from South African archaeology departments as there were from British and American universities, but there were many more archaeologists with doctorates in university posts than in museum ones (table 3:1).

The impression one gets of the organization of archaeology in southern Africa prior to 1960 is that the heart of the subject was seen by both professionals and amateurs alike to rest with the amateurs, or at least with people not employed full-time nor formally educated as archaeologists. This is clear in the titles of articles published in the *Bulletin* and in the books and articles that professionals wrote. Amateurs were the authors of about 50 per cent of the papers published in the *Bulletin* before 1960. By the 1970s the percentage was about 10 per cent. When Inskeep arrived in Cape Town in 1960 one of his first tasks was an assessment of the role of archaeology in museums and he made it known that the number of posts at universities and at provincial and state museums was woefully inadequate (Inskeep 1961a, 1963). His hard-hitting comments bore fruit and by 1970 there were 6 university posts (*vs* 1 in 1960), 10 museum posts (*vs* 2 in 1960) and 1 National Monuments post (*vs* 3 in 1960, including the Archaeological Survey), all filled by university graduates with courses in archaeology (Editorial 1970: 84). In 1987 there were nearly 60 professional posts throughout the country, including temporary research assistantships (table 3:2), about equally divided between universities and museums. This exponential expansion was no accident. It was the result of the determined effort of Inskeep and others to see archaeology recognized officially as a profession rather than, as he put it, a bloodless blood sport (Inskeep 1961a: 225). The success of the campaign was helped by the fact that it coincided with a period of economic boom at Southern African universities and museums.

Goodwin (1946: 91) wrote that, 'It is first and always essential to appreciate that prehistory is not, and can never be, a Science ... the material upon which our evidence is based is of such a nature that it cannot be expected to yield absolute truth.' It was the injection of scientific method in the 1960s that changed the attitudes of Southern African archaeologists and widened the gulf between the empirical methods used in historically orientated research by amateurs and professionals alike, and the

Table 3:1 *The number of professional archaeologists with PhD degrees in full-time employment as archaeologists in South Africa and Namibia in 1970 and 1987, classified by primary research interest and place of employment.*

Research interest	Museums		Universities		National Monuments	
	1970	1987	1970	1987	1970	1987
Stone Age	1	—	—	9	—	—
Iron Age	—	2	1	4	—	—
Archaeozoology	—	2	—	1	—	—
Archaeometry	—	—	—	2	—	—

Note: in 1987, of the 20 archaeologists with PhDs, 3 are from British universities, 6 are from American universities and 11 are from South African universities. In addition to those listed above, there are 4 PhDs (one South African) who are not presently employed as full-time archaeologists.

Table 3:2. *Number of professionally trained archaeologists in full-time employment as archaeologists in South Africa and Namibia.*

Date	Museums	Universities	National Monuments
1930	—	1	—
1960	2	1	3
1970	10	6	1
1987	28	30	—

deductive methods based on anthropological and ecological theory used by more recent graduates. Amateurs found it increasingly difficult to adapt and their contribution has waned accordingly. Useful as the amateur contribution has been, it had a chaotic effect on Stone Age studies with an eclectic group of people, each trained in a different profession and working from common sense or casual instruction, each formulating a different way of describing what was found. This is seen most clearly in Inskeep's (1967a) review paper on the Later Stone Age where he found it impossible to compare results from published excavations and collections because each author had a different set of terms and definitions. Without instruction at university level, it was difficult for the few professionals to teach others their methods or to instil a sense of professionalism amongst the scattered archaeological community. A colleague once remarked that it is odd that people expect to be able to learn archaeology in their spare time, but no one expects to learn heart surgery or architecture on the same basis.

For archaeology to come of age it had to throw off the amateur tag, yet maintain good relations with the general public. This has been an ongoing but sometimes difficult process in the past twenty-five years and was high-lighted by changes to the National Monuments Act in the early 1970s. Pressure on the National Monuments Council led to the tightening up of antiquities laws, particularly those governing the collection of artefacts from prehistoric and historic sites. Rudner and Rudner (1973), both keen collectors who themselves made a valuable contribution to rock art, pottery and artefact distribution studies, felt very keenly that amateurs were being excluded and suggested ways in which the situation could be remedied. Comments on their paper were published with it and tend to polarize between those with formal education and employment as archaeologists and those without (Rudner and Rudner 1973). The issue has been only partially resolved and the conflict of interest will probably remain. The onus rests with the professionals to bridge the gap and publicize their findings to the general public.

The desire for professional status was an important impetus in the establishment of the Southern African Society for Quaternary Research (SASQUA) in 1969 and the Southern African Association of Archaeologists in 1970. Both have promoted research and interaction through their biennial meetings. My own impression is that barring South Africans from conferences in other countries has not affected the enthusiasm or the results of Stone Age research although it may have increased the provincialism of theory and explanations and may have lowered the credibility of important finds in the eyes of non-South African researchers. It is perhaps the credibility problem that will be the most damaging to the profession in the long term.

Broader perspectives in the 1970s and 1980s

The effect that social and political events have had on research goals in Later Stone Age studies is not as obvious as is the case in Iron Age research, but influences were felt and a few generalized observations can be made. First, compared with the 1960s, the financial support given to archaeological research now is generous in South Africa. Both government funded agencies, such as the Human Sciences Research Council (HSRC) and the Council for Scientific and Industrial Research (CSIR), as well as private corporations and mining houses, have been supportive even though archaeology does not generate financial rewards directly. Further impetus was

3:6   *R.R. Inskeep*

3:7 ▶*H.J. Deacon*
3:8   *John Parkington*

3:9 ▶*C. Garth Samp-
son at Haaskraal Pan in
the Zeekoei Valley,
1985.*

given by the establishment of the palynological laboratory at the University of the Orange Free State under E.M. van Zinderen Bakker and of the radiocarbon dating laboratory at the CSIR in Pretoria under J.C. Vogel. These developments had a demonstrable effect on employment opportunities and therefore on the amount of research that has been done.

Second, greater awareness of the role that archaeology can play in the construction of histories of indigenous people has certainly given an impetus to research on Khoikohoi herders, first begun in the late 1960s (Schweitzer 1970) and developed more recently by Humphreys (1972a), Avery (1976), Elphick (1977), Deacon *et al.* (1978), Robertshaw (1978), Sampson (1984, 1986), Smith (1986), Webley (1986) and others. Iron Age and historical archaeology, too, have expanded greatly since the mid-1970s and although there is an impression that Stone Age projects are not being given as much attention as in the past, an analysis of current interests amongst Southern African professional archaeologists shows an almost equal number of Stone Age as Iron Age specialists, with an additional three posts for historical archaeologists (table 3:3).

Third, the events that influenced the goals of Stone Age archaeologists of the 1970s and 1980s most profoundly did not take place in Southern Africa. They are known collectively as the 'new archaeology' and filtered through in classic diffusionist ways in the form of literature and visiting scholars. Flannery (1967) encapsulated the spirit of the new paradigm as an interest in 'the system behind the Indian and the artefact' and predicted that in the next decade 'we shall see general systems theory, game theory and locational analysis all applied successfully to American archaeology in spite of the loudest mutterings of the establishment.' Except in the case of game theory, these predictions could be applied equally appropriately to Southern Africa.

The new archaeology as advertised by Binford (1962), Flannery (1967) and others introduced anthropological rather than historical methods in the search for general laws of human behaviour and emphasized hypothesis testing and culture process rather than normative methods and culture history. Archaeologists in Southern Africa had deep culture-historical roots and many of the older generation of prehistorians found the new ideas esoteric (Summers 1971a: 26) and confusingly quantitative (Rudner 1979), as did their American counterparts (see Flannery 1967). Amongst the younger generation, the new paradigm was greeted enthusiastically and certainly changed the course of Later Stone Age research. Although the Burg Wartenstein meeting had stressed the need to tidy up terminology and increase the number of observations (Bishop and Clark 1967), this was not what the new archaeology ordered. Initially at least, environmental and ecological versions of the new approach took precedence on the one hand, and ways of objectively analysing artefacts were explored on the other. With the majority of active researchers educated in the natural rather than the social sciences, anthropological theory was not uppermost in their minds and systems theory was more appealing. In hindsight, it is odd that until the 1980s environmental and artefact studies were not deliberately integrated. The preoccupation was with what people ate and did rather than with the social reasons for their choices. The strong focus on environment and diet was encouraged by the Cambridge school (Higgs, Clark and Clarke) and its graduates (Inskeep, Parkington, Derricourt, Carter and others) and is seen most clearly in papers by Parkington (1972a) and Carter (1970, 1978). Yet, although the first detailed quantitative analyses of faunal (Hendey and Singer 1965; Brain 1969) and floral (Wells 1965) remains were done by South African graduates, it was the impetus given to faunal studies by the work of Klein (1972a, b, 1974, 1978, 1980, 1981, 1984) that has been most influential. His excavations and analyses of fauna from Nelson Bay Cave (Klein 1972a, b) were the first to show unequivocally that climatic change had influenced the distribution and extinction of Late Pleistocene/early Holocene larger mammals in the southern Cape.

The ecological focus of Later Stone Age studies in the 1960s and 1970s is most clearly developed in the work of H.J. Deacon (fig. 3:7), whose interest was primarily in adaptive changes through time in the eastern Cape, and J.E. Parkington, whose interest lay mainly in spatial variability in the western Cape. Through an excavation programme in the eastern

Table 3:3 *Primary research interests of professional archaeologists in South Africa and Namibia.*

Research interest	Museums		Universities		National Monuments	
	1970	1987	1970	1987	1970	1987
Stone Age	7	9	3	14	1	—
Iron Age	2	8	3	10	—	—
Zooarchaeology	1	8	—	1	—	—
Archaeometry	—	—	—	5	—	—
Historical archaeology	—	3	—	3*	—	—

* These individuals have interests in Stone Age and Iron Age research as well.
Note: Stone Age research includes rock art specialists.

Cape at Scott's Cave, Melkhoutboom, Springs and Highlands where plant food remains were exceptionally well preserved, Deacon was able to reconstruct an extinct Holocene subsistence system based on underground plant foods such as watsonia and hypoxis, with hunting providing supplementary protein (Deacon and Deacon 1963; H.J. Deacon 1969, 1972, 1976). The research coincided with and supported similar ethnographic observations made amongst present-day Kalahari San (Story 1958, 1964; Lee 1965, 1968; Silberbauer 1965; Yellen 1977). After summarizing the evidence for subsistence during the Holocene in Southern Africa as a whole, H.J. Deacon (1972) described the various levels of change that occurred in the archaeological record within a model of homeostatic plateaux to explain how climate, environmental factors and human subsistence and artefact systems interact. It is based on systems theory and an explicitly biological concept of positive and negative feedback (H.J. Deacon 1976: 78 ff). The goal was to examine the organization, subsistence and demography of Holocene hunter-gatherers and he saw this as permitting 'a view of the time depth of the adaptations shown by populations genetically related to the present-day Kalahari Bushmen in somewhat more diverse habitats' to test 'the degree to which such generalizations are meaningful' (H.J. Deacon 1976: 159). This interest in biological systems has led on to research on Quaternary palaeoenvironments (H.J. Deacon 1983b) and the evolution of Mediterranean-type ecosystems in general and the fynbos of the southern Cape in particular (H.J. Deacon 1983a; H.J. Deacon et al. 1983). It was the concept of integrating palaeoenvironmental data from as many different sources as possible that led to the bold research design adopted in the excavation of Boomplaas Cave in the southern Cape from 1974 to 1979 (H.J. Deacon 1979; H.J. Deacon et al. 1984). These data allowed the assumption that technological change coincided with climatic change to be tested and the results show the effect of climatic forcing on demography (Deacon et al. 1984; Deacon and Thackeray 1984).

Parkington (fig. 3:8) derived his model from Kalahari San ethnographic studies of the 1960s to investigate spatial variability in the form of seasonal movements in the western Cape during the Holocene and this has spawned a wide variety of studies all designed to identify season of occupation or movement between resource zones and to map spatial variability (Parkington and Poggenpoel 1971; Parkington 1972a, 1976, 1977, 1980; G. Avery 1977; Fletemeyer 1977; Robertshaw 1977; Buchanan et al. 1978; Mazel and Parkington 1978, 1981; Manhire et al. 1983; Klein 1984; Sealy and Van der Merwe 1986). His model has changed as various hypotheses have been tested and reformulated (compare Parkington 1972a with Parkington 1980), but it remains essentially an ecological approach with ethnographic analogues important in predictions and explanations. The addition of rock art as a component will have far-reaching implications because it could provide the database for exploring the archaeological manifestation of the San cognitive system in the western Cape (Yates et al. 1985). The potentials of such an approach have been outlined in a series of influential papers by Lewis-Williams (for example, 1982, 1984). Stimulated by Parkington's ideas, seasonal mobility models have also been applied in Namibia (Wadley 1979), Lesotho (Carter 1978), Natal (Cable 1984; Mazel 1983) and the Transvaal (Wadley 1984, 1986).

Alongside the environmental and dietary studies, there was a strong desire for objectivity in artefact analysis. This was motivated in part by the resolutions of the Burg Wartenstein conference that urged greater clarity in definitions and terminology (Clark et al. 1966), and in part by the stimulus of Mason (1957, 1962), Sackett (1966), D.L. Clarke (1968) and others who used statistical analyses in seductive ways to quantify interassemblage differences. Mason's pioneering use of statistical techniques in the quantification of change through time in the Transvaal Stone Age was innovative and typified the desire for objectivity by eschewing functional terms in favour of geometric ones. Other attempts used multivariate attributes (Parkington 1972b), metric attributes (J. Deacon 1972; H.J. Deacon 1976; Opperman 1978; Humphreys and Thackeray 1983) and detailed typological approaches (Sampson 1972; Wendt 1972), but all were essentially supportive of a technology-based culture-stratigraphic framework by seeking to quantify similarities and differences between assemblages. It was assumed that the assemblages that were grouped together in this way had some social significance (Sampson 1974) in much the same way as Goodwin (1947) had assumed that groups of bored stones of similar size reflected tribal groupings, but this assumption was based on hope rather than on sound ethnographic or anthropological analogues. The assumption needed to be investigated (Inskeep 1967). This was difficult to do, and the easy way out was to disregard the social correlates (for lack of evidence) and to see the statistically verified groupings as purely techno-logical units (Clark 1974; J. Deacon 1984b) that implied no social bonds between the people who made them except that ideas and techniques would have been communicated amongst people in regular contact with each other. Others, for example H.J. Deacon (1976: 172), thought that it may be possible to use stylistic variations of particular tool types to plot dialectal boundaries amongst contemporary groups if they had any long-term stability. The ethnographic research of Wiessner (1983) that showed different arrowhead designs correlated with language groupings amongst present-day !Kung in Botswana has therefore been timely. Sampson (1986) (fig. 3:9), taking up this issue amongst others in his Zeekoei Valley project, has attempted to map the distribution of particular San bands by examining in detail the decoration on potsherds found in a restricted area and assuming styles to be specific to individual potters. Such studies, where ethnography is providing specific models for archaeologists to test, suggest that a structuralist approach is gradually replacing the functionalist one.

The assumption of social correlates is most difficult to justify in cases where there is an obvious and relatively sudden change in technology through time at a particular site or within a region. However, not everyone has acknowledged or even questioned the fact that whereas ethnographic analogues could be used to explain differences in material culture between contemporary but geographically separate assemblages, no such analogues can be obtained for changes through time simply because the archaeological time span is unique in being so much longer than any that can be observed ethnographically (J. Deacon 1984b). Mason (1962), Sampson (1974) and Wymer (Singer and Wymer 1982), in dealing with both the Middle and Later Stone Ages, have tended to equate major changes through time with the movement of people in the tradition of Goodwin and Van Riet Lowe's migration model and the explanations given by Bordes and Bordes (1970) for variability in the Mousterian in France. By contrast, H.J. Deacon (1969, 1972, 1976), J. Deacon (1972, 1978), Humphreys (1972b), Parkington (1980) and Humphreys and Thackeray (1983) regard such changes as developments within the technological tradition, possibly as adaptive responses to changes in hunting patterns, availability of raw material, new tasks or social organization. Beaumont (1978) and J. Deacon (1984b) have also explored the possibility of recognizing general laws of technological change by comparing long-term stylistic variations to similar adjustments in modern technological systems (see also Spratt 1982). Where traditional artefact analyses have sought to quantify inter-site differences, these techno-logical models have aimed more at discovering general laws of technology and material culture by identifying recurrent patterns of style or fashion in stone tool manufacture. They ought to be widely applicable in Africa as a whole.

In addition to the broader issues discussed above, the last twenty years have seen the introduction of a wide range of archaeometric techniques inspired by the need for both dating and particularistic information on palaeoenvironments. Radiocarbon laboratories were established in Zimbabwe and in South Africa in the 1960s and have played a major role in the dating of sites and materials – the Pretoria laboratory alone has processed more than 4,000 dates – and a further dating facility has been opened recently at the University of the Witwatersrand. J.C. Vogel at the Pretoria laboratory has made a significant contribution in processing dates and to devising new dating and stable isotope techniques (Vogel 1978, 1983). His development of carbon isotope studies as an aid to the reconstruction of diet has allowed the seasonal mobility hypothesis to be tested independently of food remains and stone tools (Sealy and Van der Merwe 1986). Analyses of charcoal (H.J. Deacon et al. 1983), pollen (Van Zinderen Bakker 1967; Scott 1984), small mammal (D.M. Avery 1982), large mammal (Klein 1984) and bird remains (G. Avery 1977) as well as studies of sediments and geomorphological features (Butzer 1984; Vogel 1984) have been introduced and refined. In the wider context of Stone Age studies, these techniques have broadened the scope of palaeoenvironmental constructions to a degree that was probably unimagined thirty years ago. For this reason, the goals of Stone Age archaeologists have themselves broadened to encompass palaeoenvironmental issues, and thereby per-petuate the ecological paradigm. Microwear studies, on the other hand, have been used in the identification of use wear on stone tools to confirm previous assumptions about function (Binneman 1982, 1984). The design of such a research project has remained so far within the functionalist paradigm but has the potential to be useful in testing hypotheses generated by historical materialism to explore Stone Age ideology.

What next?

Southern Africa has an extraordinarily rich heritage of Stone Age materials. There are more excavated Later Stone Age sites, more ethnographic studies of hunter-gatherers and more full-time archaeologists in Southern Africa than in any other region in sub-Saharan Africa and there remains the potential for a significant contribution to be made to the long history of Later Stone Age people. To predict for Southern Africa, as Flannery did in 1967 for North America, what the future holds for archaeology in the next decade or so one would have to distinguish between what ought to be done in the public sphere and what will possibly be done on the academic front. We ought to push ourselves from the ivory tower and put a lot more energy into informing the general public of the results of archaeological research (Inskeep 1970). Maggs (Nisbet et al. 1984) has shown the way by co-authoring a primary school history textbook that includes a chapter on the Stone Age and the First South Africans. We need to attract a wider range of people to the subject and begin to break the virtual monopoly that white English-speaking people of European descent have in the present archaeological job-market, as has been done in Botswana and Zimbabwe. Professional standards have been established and now they need to be applied if we are to achieve public credibility and make our research socially relevant.

In the academic sphere, research will need to focus more on social and ideological explanations for variability than on palaeoenvironments. This was a goal of Goodwin's (1953: 12–15) too, but, like Childe, he did not have the data base (Tringham 1983: 98). Inskeep, amongst others, was aware of the difficulty of extracting social information from stone tools and saw his goal as the study of the evolution of Southern African society (Inskeep 1978: 86). Instead of using stone tools for this purpose, he saw patterns of resource utilization as reflecting changes in social organization (*op. cit.*: 80) as H.J. Deacon (1976) proposed for the eastern Cape. For some time, Stone Age archaeologists have felt intellectually dissatisfied with the methods of 'number-crunching' stone-tool analyses, fashionable in the 1960s and 1970s, that have become abstract, mechanical and lacking in social correlates. Metric and numerical analyses have served their purpose in placing limits on the range of variability to be expected and in enabling inter-site comparisons to be made. By focussing on the tools instead of the toolmakers, however, the humanity and creativity of the people who made the artefacts have been given less attention, making it seem as if they were the victims rather than the perpetrators of change. Southern African archaeologists are not alone in this dilemma of relevance (Dunnell 1982) and the time has come to integrate the various facets of archaeological research.

As a solution, Lewis-Williams, in an unpublished paper read at the Southern African Association of Archaeologists meeting in Grahamstown in 1985, challenged Stone Age researchers to place a moratorium on excavation until the theoretical issues have been resolved, declaring that the 'real spadework of archaeology is done in the study not in the field.' He has advocated historical materialism as a useful concept within which economic activities and ideology of extinct societies can be studied through material culture (Lewis-Williams 1982) and this is the direction that research may take in the next decade. (It is unlikely, though, that the moratorium on excavation will be taken seriously. Five colleagues to whom this paper was sent for comment all disagreed with Lewis-Williams on this point.) It will be an exacting challenge to see whether we can extract 'the beliefs behind the system behind the Indian and the artefact' without throwing away the achievements of the past century that have already identified the tool-maker, the tools and the environment in which they were made. As Wadley (1987) has suggested, the full mode of production for a Stone Age society can be constructed only when studies of the forces of production and the relations of production are integrated. The resurgence of interest in historical theory and methods that is in the air (Smith 1983: 47) will place greater emphasis on the motivations and actions of prehistoric people and their relationships with their contemporaries and this change in emphasis can only be welcomed. The dichotomy that has developed in Stone Age archaeology between the goals of social science on the one hand that would like to extend history and ethnology back in time, and the goals of the natural sciences on the other hand that examine environmental parameters and require experimentation with chemical and physical analyses, must be resolved because all these threads are needed in the loom if the fabric of Southern African society is to be woven with meaning and sensitivity.

Acknowledgement

I should like to thank Whitney Davis, H.J. Deacon, Martin Hall, Simon Hall, Ray Inskeep, Richard Klein, Aron Mazel, John Parkington, Peter Robertshaw, Andrew B. Smith, Anne Thackeray and Lyn Wadley whose comments have helped to improve this chapter.

4 'Hidden History':
Iron Age Archaeology in Southern Africa

MARTIN HALL

Past and present

One of the illusions of Southern African archaeology is that the past can be neutral; that artefacts will 'speak for themselves' and that archaeologists can discern a history of past communities that is 'scientifically' derived and free of bias. This notion has been challenged for other contexts and seems particularly inappropriate for a region where history has long been contested terrain. Early colonial settlers validated appropriation of the land through a reading of history; Afrikaaner nationalist historians have long justified segregation through the creation of ethnic histories; Liberal historians have obscured the relationship between capital accumulation and segregationist policies and African nationalist historians have begun to write histories that authenticate the nation (Cornevin 1980; Legassick 1980; Marks 1986a; Ranger 1979; Saul and Gelb 1981). Why should archaeology be above such processes?

In this review of the history of the archaeology of farming communities in Southern Africa (still known widely, if inappropriately, as the 'Iron Age'), I start from the premise that *all* readings of the past are intimately connected to the present. This is not to suggest that history is merely propaganda, or that archaeologists do not carefully assemble and weigh information before coming to reasoned conclusions. Certainly, there are examples of obvious distortion (particularly in interpretations of the major site of Great Zimbabwe), but by and large the tie between present and past is more subtle. The concerns of the present become the problems of history, and unarticulated assumptions about the nature of human society – 'common-sense' understandings of the present – become the links which connect fragmentary archaeological evidence. In addition, archaeologists working in Southern Africa have maintained strong connections with schools of thought in other parts of the world. As a result, historiography is a complex layering of propositions, assumptions and information and is often difficult to tease apart.

Colonial expansion and the right to domination

Complex as this historiography is, however, there is one focal point which links the earliest explorations with the most recent explanations. Early in the colonial expansion into the interior, travellers and settlers encountered the ruins of Great Zimbabwe (fig. 4:1), standing beneath the southern lip of the high plateau that divides the Limpopo and Zambezi river systems. Long the subject of Portuguese myth and romance, the overgrown and intricate architecture of the Hill Ruin (fig. 4:2), Great Enclosure and other buildings was described by Karl Mauch in 1872 (Burke 1969), and by other travellers,

4:1 *The Great Enclosure from the Hill, Great Zimbabwe*

4:2 *A doorway leading from the Western Enclosure on the Hill at Great Zimbabwe. This is the only original doorway surviving intact*

and caught the imagination of Cecil Rhodes (Garlake 1973, 1982; Summers 1971b). Rhodes had a clear sense of the political value of history. His imperial dream for Africa could gain legitimacy if he were seen to be re-establishing a long-lost Phoenician civilization (Garlake 1982, Hall 1984a). R.N. Hall, who had represented Rhodes's business interests in the United Kingdom, was put to work excavating the site, producing an extensive monograph which argued that Great Zimbabwe was the source of Solomon's gold before falling to 'Bantu degeneracy' (Hall 1905).

Hall's conclusions served settler ideology well. Great Zimbabwe stood as a monument to civilization in the Dark Continent; the necessity for those with superior ability to save the indigenous population from its own inability to rise above barbarism. The same theme was repeated in other precolonial histories. Thus Stow (1905: 233–5) believed that 'the seething mass of equatorial life' was hemmed in by Mediterranean civilization to the north, 'until amid internal heavings and internecine wars another storm wave rose which, beaten from the north, would naturally expend its fury in the opposite direction . . . until they came into contact with strange white faced men still more invincible than they had imagined themselves to be, against whom, with many minor fluctuations, the tidal wave of rude barbarism beat in vain.' A similar reading of the evidence was given by Stow's contemporary, Theal (1907: 56, 59).

Looking back over more than half a century, these early interpretations of the precolonial past look particularly distorted. However, they can be better understood if their ideological context is taken into account. Prior to the Second World War, the Southern African economy was dominated by the interests of agriculture and of mining capital. Droughts and stock disease in the late nineteenth century had made conditions for South African farmers difficult and recovery had been dependent on large state subsidies financed by mining taxes and, particularly, on controls to maintain supplies of cheap, coerced black labour. Thus although there had been capital investment in white farming, agriculture had feudal features: 'a tied, serf-like labour force on the white farms and a black agricultural sector that was kept in an underdeveloped and pre-capitalist state, so that it would not compete with white farmers and would instead serve as a source of cheap labour for white farms and mines' (Lipton 1986: 85). Southern Rhodesia had a similar agricultural economy and a rapidly increasing black population (Arrighi 1967). Mineowners were also faced with a shortage of black labour and the high costs of skilled white labour, maintained by government-enforced job reservation which satisfied the political demands of white labour interests. As mining returns diminished (with a fixed gold price and increasing costs of production), mineowners maintained profits by cutting real wages for unskilled black labour (Lipton 1986). For white interests in Southern Africa, then, talk of black civilization or progress were not merely an indulgence; such concepts struck at the heart of a labour policy which was vital to white interests.

This outlook conflicted markedly with the views of those in the mother country. During the last decades of the nineteenth century, Britain had continued to dominate international trade; major industries such as textiles, coal and shipbuilding continued to be highly profitable, as did massive overseas investments. Nevertheless, both aristocracy and bourgeoisie were acutely conscious of the threat of proletarian revolt. Nineteenth-century *laissez-faire* liberalism – the dominant economic philosophy in Southern Africa – was being replaced by policies of state intervention to correct poverty and co-opt the working class to bourgeois interests:

among the many members of the middle classes who were doubtful about the value and effectiveness of classic liberalism, but nervous about the swelling ranks of Labour, radicalism seemed a middle way between the dusty old world of the squires and the messianic aspirations of emancipated labour as represented by the small socialist groups. In short, it was a reassuring compromise, for radicalism preached intervention on the part of the State, but guaranteed order and free enterprise. (Bedarida 1979)

British interests drew analogies between their perception of the 'condition of England' and appropriate policies in the colonies. This was well expressed in an article published in London in 1897:

To us – to us, and not to others, a certain definite duty has been assigned. To carry light and civilization to the dark places of the world; to touch the mind of Asia and of Africa with the ethical ideas of Europe; to give to thronging millions, who would otherwise never know peace or security, these first conditions of human advance: constructive endeavour such as this forms part of the function which it is ours to discharge. (Quoted by Bedarida 1979: 145)

William Booth, the founder of the Salvation Army, pointed out that working-class England and Central Africa were similar in their poverty and degradation.

In consequence, R.N. Hall's claims for Great Zimbabwe, while fitting settler presuppositions perfectly, were anomalous in England, where they were published. Such doubts were reinforced by Hall's clear lack of technical skills. He openly admitted, and showed in his photographs and figures, that he had shovelled away tons of deposit with little regard to stratigraphy or context (Hall 1905). Professional archaeology in Europe had moved beyond such wanton vandalism, and academic sensibilities were bruised.

The response from London was a commission to an experienced archae-ologist, David Randall MacIver, to excavate at Great Zimbabwe and to test the veracity of the settler interpretation. MacIver sampled the site, as well as several other ruins in Southern Rhodesia. Although his sequence has since been reversed by radiocarbon dating, MacIver came to the conclusion that Great Zimbabwe was medieval in date, and 'Bantu' in origin. But his chronology was based more on the absence of evidence for high antiquity than on the discovery of *in situ* artefacts that proved more recent construc-tion, and his monograph added fuel to the controversy (MacIver 1906). Hall responded with an avalanche of text that reasserted Southern Rhodesia's claim to the lost goldfields of Ophir (Hall 1909).

In 1929, the British Association for the Advancement of Science again responded to the challenge of the settler interpretation of Great Zimbabwe, sending Gertrude Caton Thompson (who had recently won acclaim for her work in North Africa) to excavate at this and other sites. With the aid of two women assistants (one of whom was Kathleen Kenyon), Caton Thompson placed trenches that would test the stratigraphical relationship between stone walls and deposits, and excavated laterally one of the buildings that formed part of the Valley complex. Unlike MacIver, Caton Thompson was able to recover datable artefacts in unquestionable context, reporting to the Association's congress in Pretoria, and leaving open her sections for subsequent inspection by a committee of her peers (Caton Thompson 1931, 1983).

Caton Thompson's report, as well as her memoirs, show that she shared many of the racial prejudices of her times. But in contrast with the settler consensus, she was also open to the possibility of African achievement. The public interest in her report, evidenced by attendance at her public lectures in South Africa and comment in the press, showed that the Great Zimbabwe controversy was as sharp as it had been fifty years earlier. By her own admission, her conclusion to the Pretoria congress was provocative:

> I have tried to eliminate all theory and vague generalities incapable of proof. But I will allow myself one subjective observation. . . . It is inconceivable to me now I have studied the ruins how a theory of Semitic or civilized origin could ever have been foisted on an uncritical world. Every detail in the haphazard building, every detail in the plan, every detail in the contents apart from imports, appears to me to be typical African Bantu . . . you have here a mature civilization unsus-pected by all but a few students, showing national organization of a high kind, originality and amazing industry. It is a subject worthy of all the research South Africa can give it. South African students must be bred to pursue it. (Caton Thompson 1983: 131)

These remarks won the reaction she anticipated, particularly in her public clash with Raymond Dart, whose australopithicine discoveries had recently won international note. Before storming from the room Dart, according to the *Cape Times* of 3 August 1929, 'delivered remarks in a tone of awe-inspiring violence. . . . He spoke in an outburst of curiously unscientific indignation and charged the startled chairman . . . with having called upon none but the supporters of Miss Caton Thompson's theory.'

State repression, security in technique

The clash between settler opinion on the African past and MacIver and Caton Thompson's conclusions from their work in Southern Rhodesia set a theme that was to run through Southern African archaeology until the present day. On the one hand was a popular colonial consciousness, heavily influenced by the economy and ideology of domination. Opposed were a small group of archaeologists, whose methodological standards were drawn from the international scholastic community, but who were themselves also part of the dominating group. For the latter, this contradiction in their position was often accommodated in one of two ways: by avoiding the contested ground and researching less controversial periods of antiquity, or by retreating into highly technical analyses which effectively excluded all but the acolytes of the profession. In consequence, and despite the continued politicization of the Southern African past, Gertrude Caton Thompson was to remain virtually the only professional archaeologist to take to the public battlefield.

It is perhaps because of this contradiction that Caton Thompson's highly publicized conclusions only attracted limited attention to the archaeology of the immediately precolonial period. One writer whose work was to have a sustained impact was John Schofield. Schofield was an architect by training, and had been interested in the public buildings at Great Zimbabwe before Caton Thompson's expedition (Schofield 1926). After collaborating with Caton Thompson, Schofield turned his attention to ceramics, constructing a typological scheme for the subcontinent based largely on surface collections, but also attempting to build regional sequences from limited excavations (Schofield 1948). As with MacIver many years earlier, Schofield's scheme was to be up-ended by the radiocarbon chronology (for example, Maggs 1973). Nevertheless several of his categories, albeit refined and renamed, are still elements in currently accepted typological schemes; NC3 pottery, for instance, now dated to the first millennium AD, has been renamed at least twice (Huffman 1982; Maggs and Michael 1976). But although Schofield saw his task as the extension backwards in time of the current ethnographies, his typological categories were sanitized by numeration; labels such as 'NC2D', 'ST1' and 'NT1' were hardly likely to affront the settler consciousness.

Similarly, research at Mapungubwe – a site considered sufficiently promising for its purchase by the Union Government – was soon shrouded by technique and technical controversy. The first report on the site, edited by Leo Fouche (1937), was dominated by its technical appendices, while synthesis was impeded by the conflict between the interpretation of the ceramics as 'Bantu' (Schofield 1937) and Galloway's (1959) conclusion that the skeletal remains were 'Hottentot'. Subsequent research was not published for many years, and then demanded re-interpretation by its reviewers (Fagan 1970; Gardner 1963).

It was in this context that professional research on the Iron Age from within Southern Africa was first founded. In 1947 Keith Robinson and Roger Summers (fig. 4:3) were appointed to full-time posts by the Southern Rhodesian colonial government. Robinson had farmed in the territory and had a flair for fieldwork, while Summers had trained with Gordon Childe at London's Institute of Archaeology (Hall 1984a and b; Summers 1970). Their careful and systematic work was to lay the basis for a complex ceramic typology and their excavations at sites such as Khami (Robinson 1959), Great Zimbabwe (Robinson 1961; Summers 1961) and in the Nyanga area to the east of the country (Summers 1958) were to provide a solid basis for future syntheses. In addition, Summers was one of the first archaeologists of this period to place settlements within an environmental context (Summers 1967a). Although their use of ethnography was not to be without controversy (Ranger 1979) they, like others before them, avoided many potential clashes with settler ideology by using highly technical frameworks for conceptualizing and reporting their results. The 'Bantu Period', which had contained both the archaeology and ethnography which fell between the Stone Age and colonial settlement, was abandoned in favour of an adaptation of the three-age system that had seen such long service in Europe – the 'Iron Age' (Mason 1951, Summers 1950). Within this, cultural boxes were mapped out, defined by their ceramics and modelled consciously on Hawkes's scheme for Europe (Hawkes 1931; Summers 1950, 1967b). As in Schofield's work, labels were esoteric: 'Z2', 'Leopard's Kopje 1', 'M2' and so on (Summers 1967b).

But despite this technicism it is notable that, while a steady stream of Iron Age research continued through the 1950s and early 1960s in Southern Rhodesia and, for that matter, in Northern Rhodesia (for example, Clark 1974; Fagan, Phillipson and Daniels 1969; Phillipson 1968, 1970), very little comparable research was initiated south of the Limpopo, with the exception of an early study by Revil Mason (1951). In general syntheses of African prehistory (for example, Clark 1959a; Fagan 1965a; Oliver and Fagan 1975) South Africa remained unknown territory. This contrast was closely connected to the changing political circumstances of Southern Africa, and the different courses taken by the colonial administration of Southern Rhodesia and by the South African state.

As in many other parts of the world, the Second World War had brought changes in political economy. For South Africa's major metropolitan regions, the war stimulated massive industrial expansion

:3 *Roger Summers*
below) with Père
nciaux de Faveaux
uring an excursion of
e third Pan-African
Congress 1955

:4 *Revil Mason*
uring an excursion of
e third Pan-African
Congress, 1955

coupled with large-scale enrolment of white labour into the armed forces, together creating a shortage of skilled labour in the manufacturing sector. As a result, segregationalist policies were relaxed, permitting a substantial flow of black labour from the countryside to the cities (Lipton 1986).[1] The effect of the war economy was even more marked in Southern Rhodesia, which had had a very small industrial sector before the increase in external demand (Arrighi 1967).

But although the economic effects were similar, the administrative responses after the war were very different in the two countries. In South Africa, agriculture was still under-capitalized and heavily dependent on cheap black labour. In addition, there were still many whites unemployed in the cities. The coalition of these interests was the basis for the National Party election victory of 1948 and the extension of apartheid legislation, which sought to keep black labour in the countryside (Lipton 1986). Segregation was maintained by stringent security provisions: the Suppression of Communism Act of 1950, extensive police action against dissent, large political trials, the banning of opposition movements. In consequence the late 1950s, and particularly the 1960s, were a period in which effective opposition to white minority rule was crushed (Lodge 1983).

These policies were justified by a pervasive ideology, promoted through government publications and particularly through the syllabi of segregated schools and the philosophy of Bantu Education (Molteno 1983), in which a version of Southern African history played no small part. The nineteenth-century fable of barbaric, black hordes sweeping into the subcontinent at the same time as white settlers moved up from the Cape served to re-affirm white claims to the land (Hamilton 1982). Historic roots for 'ethnic groups' were invented by ethnographic extrapolation, justifying the claim that the Bantustans were natural homelands (Dubow in press).

It is still a matter of debate whether capital, and particularly manufacturing capital, benefited from apartheid policies in the 1950s and 1960s (compare Johnstone (1970) and Legassick (1975) with Lipton (1986)). However, despite the initial fears of capital, the National Party sought national industrial expansion after 1948, and particularly after the 1960 Sharpeville crisis, when the threat of sanctions and isolation began to become greater. For capital, the restrictions of apartheid and the high costs it placed on white labour were offset by the advantages of draconian state security and the suppression of black labour costs through influx control and the prohibition of unionization. The relationship between government and capital may well have been 'surly' (Lipton 1986: 285), but there can be no doubt about the substantial economic boom of the 1960s which blunted the abrasive edges of apartheid ideology. Apartheid was a comprehensive victory for the settler consciousness which Caton Thompson had encountered, and hardly an environment in which Iron Age research would be promoted.

In Southern Rhodesia, circumstances were at first different. In contrast with South Africa, white wages after the war were high and there was little unemployment. Initially, the National Party victory in the Union made capital interests fear the possibility of state control, and capital investment was diverted from South Africa to Southern Rhodesia, leading to a doubling of foreign investment between 1947 and 1949, and a doubling again by 1951 (Arrighi 1967). But the full potential of this capital growth was limited for the manufacturing sector by the decreasing productivity, and therefore low purchasing power, of the African peasantry. Government policies sought to correct this situation by moving from the concept of separate development towards the ideal of 'racial partnership', to be effected by such reforms as the recognition of black trade unions, increased expenditure on university education and agricultural reform: 'the constant factor noticeable in Government policies during the '50s was the creation of an African middle class and bourgeoisie by inducing more interracial competition' (Arrighi 1967: 53).

It was consistent with these circumstances that, in contrast with South Africa, Iron Age research should be actively promoted by the Southern Rhodesian colonial administration. In 1948, for instance, the governor of the colony, along with the trustees of the National Museums of Southern Rhodesia, the Commission for the Preservation of Natural and Historic Monuments and Relics and the Eastern Districts Regional Development Fund, launched an appeal for funds to investigate the archaeology of the eastern highlands which, although falling short of its target, had substantial support from the State Lottery, the Beit Railway Trust and the British South Africa Company (Summers 1958). Robinson's work at Khami was supported by the monuments commission (Robinson 1959), as were major excavations at Great Zimbabwe in 1957.

However, the development of the post-war political economy of Southern Rhodesia had not been without its contradictions. The dollar shortage had also promoted tobacco farming, which could now compete favourably with the American estates. In common with agricultural interests in South Africa, tobacco farmers needed land (appropriated from African peasants) and cheap migrant labour, and thus had interests that conflicted with manufacturing capital. Weakened by a decline in the post-war boom, the United Federal Party lost the 1962 election to the Rhodesian Front which, in 1965, broke from colonial control with the Unilateral Declaration of Independence (Arrighi 1967).

The accompanying ideological change was sharp, and had an immediate effect on Iron Age research. Rather than contributing to the development and stability of the black bourgeoisie, any suggestion of precolonial historical achievement was now seen as seditious. It was stated in the Rhodesian parliament, for instance, that archaeological work at Great Zimbabwe was directly furthering the cause of the black liberation movements (Garlake 1973), while the Rhodesian Front press was more outspoken:

In these days of deliberate subversion of civilised authority, the international New Liberalism attempts to mould all aspects of life including the sciences, to the glorification of the Negro. Archaeology, the study of antiquities, is a natural victim, for it can be used as a means of creating an artificial cultural respectability for Black nationalism and, accordingly, a justification of Black rule. Against all objective evidence, Zimbabwe is again being promoted as a Bantu achievement. (*Property and Finance Magazine*, November 1972; quoted by Frederikse 1982: 12)

In the face of such opinions from an establishment which had embraced South African techniques of state security, it is hardly surprising that leading archaeologists chose to leave the country.

Thus by the end of the 1960s – forty years after Gertrude Caton Thompson's pioneering work had captured the headlines – little had been achieved. A ceramic sequence had been established in Southern Rhodesia, but many years' work at Mapungubwe had yielded little and the rest of the Iron Age in South Africa was very poorly understood. In these circumstances, the pessimistic tone of Inskeep's general review is understandable:

we may say that historical evidence long ago pointed to penetration on the east side of South Africa, by Bantu-speakers, reaching as far south as the Transkei by the sixteenth century, and probably much earlier. . . . That we cannot at present speak in more precise terms about the prehistory of existing Bantu-speaking peoples is due rather to inadequacy of research than to improbability that the story could be written. (Inskeep 1969a: 39)

Thus the black majority of Southern Africa had been comprehensively alienated from their history; the 'silence' of which Shula Marks (1986a) has written, and which served the ideological needs of the South African and rebel Rhodesian governments so well.

Revival

But despite the comprehensive oppression of South African government policies, the idea of African studies, in which Iron Age archaeology played a part, was kept alive in the liberal universities of Cape Town and the Witwatersrand. Such research was further encouraged by the nationalist tide in other parts of the continent, by the independence granted to increasing numbers of former colonies through the 1960s, and by the 'discovery' of African history and its importance (Hall 1984a; Marks 1986a). At the University of the Witwatersrand, Revil Mason (fig. 4:4) turned back to his earlier interest in the Iron Age and began an extensive survey and excavation programme (Mason 1962, 1968, 1986). Mason was clear about the connection between past and present. As he told the South African Archaeological Society in his presidential address of 1966:

The archaeology of food and metal production and settlement in the South African interior is exceptionally important to the understanding of the changes that created South African society today . . . the South African Iron Age represents a technological phase crucial to the success of present day South African technology. Present day South Africa could not function without the technological skills of its Bantu-speaking population, skills which are not entirely due to imported Western technology, but are partly the behavioural inheritance from their Iron Age ancestors. (Mason 1967a: 8–9)

Mason felt that to understand the Iron Age was part of a necessary 'social reciprocity', without which 'South African society in its present form will not survive the unprecedented pressures to change that await us within the next few decades' (Mason 1967a: 17).

To the south, at the University of Cape Town, most archaeological interest had been in the Stone Age. But, after his appointment to the Department of Archaeology in 1960, Ray Inskeep increasingly saw the importance of Iron Age research development. In his editorials for the *South African Archaeological Bulletin* Inskeep called for more ethnographic work to provide a basis for Iron Age research (Inskeep 1961b), deplored the reduction in the status of the Archaeological Survey (Inskeep 1962a), and complained that the 'archaeology of Africa is floundering twenty years behind the times' (Inskeep 1964: 2). By 1967 he could welcome Mason's work in the Transvaal and Tim Maggs's extensive investigation of Iron Age settlement patterns on the southern Highveld (Maggs 1976a) (fig. 4:5), while commenting that, in comparison with Zambia and Rhodesia, Iron Age research was still much neglected (Inskeep 1967b).

But Mason and Inskeep's case was not to have much effect until the turn of the decade, when the nature of post-war South Africa began to change. By this time, increased mechanization, coupled with natural population increase, had eased the labour shortage in agriculture and started a demand for skilled labour. In the mining sector, the relaxation of the fixed gold price in 1970 (which had been $35 per ounce since 1934) dramatically increased production possibilities and further exacerbated the skilled labour shortage and the high price of job reservation. Similarly, manufacturing capital began to press for increased attention to education and training, to ease the shortage of skilled workers. White labour interests, which had been so influential in 1948, had also shifted; twenty years of National Party rule had resulted in a massive state bureaucracy and the upward movement of whites behind the shield of job reservation, largely solving the 'poor white' problem (Lipton 1986).

These changing interests, coupled with increased state revenues from the 1960s economic boom and the higher gold price, led to increased government expenditure on research, museums, public buildings, the arts, etc.: the cultural apparatus necessary to present the image of a 'modern state'. Professional archaeology, and particularly Iron Age research, benefitted markedly from this shift. In 1967 the government-funded Council for Scientific and Industrial Research had started a rock-art recording project and, more importantly, a radiocarbon dating laboratory (Inskeep 1967c). Departments of Archaeology were established at the Transvaal Museum (Pretoria) in 1969 and the Natal Museum (Pietermaritzburg) in 1972 (Inskeep 1969b; Summers 1972): both institutions were to be focal points for Iron Age research over the following years. Other museums, as well as university departments, were able to expand their staff and research facilities. By 1974, when the boom years ended and South Africa entered a severe economic recession, the professional basis for Iron Age research had been firmly established.

Naturally, the form that this surge of Iron Age research took continued earlier directions and concerns, while reflecting at the same time the paradigms dominant in international archaeology. Indeed, the connection with the theoretical and methodological issues dominant in other parts of the world was accentuated by the fact that a minority of those who now found professional employment in South Africa had been trained in the country: connections with British and American archaeology were particularly strong.

4:5 *A Highveld site after excavation*

In common with other countries, and continuing a concern which had been central to Robinson and Summers since the late 1940s, was the search for a firm chronology and a generally-accepted artefact sequence, based in this case on ceramic form and decoration. The establishment of the Pretoria radiocarbon laboratory had circumvented the need to depend on expensive determinations from foreign laboratories, and absolute dates for the Iron Age were obtained in ever-increasing numbers, as the periodic reviews of the radiocarbon chronology in the *Journal of African History* reveal (Hall and Vogel 1980; Maggs 1976b; Parkington and Hall 1987). The antiquity of the Iron Age south of the Limpopo – long suspected but never proved – was soon firmly established, and regional patterns of chronological variation were identified as well. As in other parts of the world, absolute dates sometimes reversed cause and effect relationships, demanding a radical revision of hypotheses. For instance, John Schofield's earlier ceramic sequence was upended (Maggs 1973, 1980c; Schofield 1948), and Mapungubwe, long believed to have been a spin-off from the early Zimbabwe state, was shown on the basis of an elaborate suite of radiocarbon dates rather to have been a precursor: a formative state system in itself (Hall and Vogel 1980). The sequence at Great Zimbabwe itself was shortened by several crucial centuries (Huffman and Vogel n.d.). Except for those whose preconceptions gave them no choice except that of rejecting the method of absolute dating (Hromnik 1981, Mallows 1984), the new Pretoria dates took the guesswork out of the Southern African Iron Age chronology.

The results of work on ceramic sequences were less unambiguous. Impressive as the radiometric skeleton was, there were still many hazy areas which allowed competing connections between ceramic groupings to be put forward. In addition, although dated sites were crucial to the emerging patterns, the majority of the evidence for Iron Age settlement still came from undatable surface ceramic assemblages, the affinities for which had to be drawn on typological grounds, and were therefore open to dispute. In addition – and again in common with archaeology in other parts of the world – there had been no thorough ethnographic study of the *meaning* of trends in ceramic decoration.

In this situation, schools of thought developed concerning the meaning of ceramic groupings which were based on subjective affinities with wider trends in archaeology (Hall 1984a). One approach had its roots in Childe's concept of 'culture'. Summers's typological scheme for Southern Rhodesia had depended on the isolation of ceramic types, characterizing 'boxes' delineated in time and space (Summers 1950, 1967b), and this same approach was pursued by Mason in the Transvaal (1962, 1986), Maggs in his sequence both on the southern Highveld (Maggs 1976a) and in the Thukela River basin (Maggs 1980a, 1980b, 1984a, 1984b, Maggs and Michael 1976) and Hall in Zululand (1981). Phillipson's general syntheses (1977a, 1985) were predicated on the same concept: typological 'boxes' were strung together in time and space to postulate linear sequences of population movement through time and space.

In contrast, Huffman brought to Southern African Iron Age studies the concept of the ceramic *tradition*, well established in American archaeology (Binford and Sabloff 1982, Hall 1984a). This approach demanded a far closer analysis of ceramic attributes, which could be summarized statistically and built into tree-like models which traced traditions through time and space (Huffman 1978, 1979, 1982). Although the ceramics that were the object of study often came from the same sites, the implications of finding traditions rather than cultures could be profound. This was evident from Huffman's first focus of research: a re-examination of Robinson's earlier (1959) sequence for south-western Zimbabwe. Instead of a local evolution of cultures, Huffman found a complex interplay of traditions, with a first millennium ceramic style truncated by a different set of motifs (Huffman 1974). Huffman and, later, Evers (1983) (using the same approach) went on to map out a complex set of ceramic traditions that acounted for much of the ceramic variability of the Southern African Iron Age (Huffman 1982). This general synthesis has many differences with the general schemes proposed by Phillipson (1977a, 1985), Maggs (1984a) and Mason (1986) and, although there has been considerable debate, both in the literature and informally, concerning the contradictions in the different schemes, it is probable that the fundamental methodological differences behind the two approaches make them irreconcilable.

The absence of ethnographic research into the meaning of material culture has led to differing interpretations of both ceramic cultures and traditions. Although some workers have left this question open, merely using ceramic affinity as a form of relative dating within the framework of absolute chronology, others have equated their archaeological units with historical or ethnographic collectivities. Maggs (1976c), for instance, linked his Type Z architecture of the southern Highveld with the expansion of specific Tswana lineages, and Iron Age settlement in part of the Drakensberg foothills with a specific, early nineteenth-century chiefdom (Maggs 1982a). Van der Merwe and Scully (1971) sought continuity through the full span of the second millennium in the eastern Transvaal, linking together ceramic assemblages and oral traditions. Mason (1986) has sought a more general equation between pottery going back to the fourth century AD and the broad 'Sotho-Tswana' group of chiefdoms. Such forms of interpretation preserve a connection with earlier patterns of Iron Age interpretation, such as Schofield's (1948) search for the 'tribes' of antiquity.

In contrast to these broad, socio-political interpretations, ceramic *traditions* have been interpreted far more narrowly. In an early paper,

4:6 *Oliver Davies at Moor Park, Estcourt, Natal 1972*

Huffman (1970) set out the case for a 'package' of Iron Age traits that included ceramics and language and which were brought into Southern Africa by the southerly migration of Iron Age farmers. He has since developed the argument that ceramics and languages were tightly related: necessarily linked as forms of communication. This has allowed him to see ceramic traditions as linguistic markers, indicating the origins, and subsequent dispersal, of specific languages (Huffman 1982). Thus the Kutama tradition has been linked with the spread of the Shona language into Zimbabwe (Huffman 1978), while the Moloko tradition likewise equated with the westward spread of the Sotho-Tswana languages (Evers 1983).

But although ceramics are the largest category of artefacts to occur on Southern African Iron Age sites, and have received extensive attention, other subjects have also been studied. The technology of iron production, for instance, has received attention from a number of workers: Mason (1986) and Maggs (1982b) have looked at mining techniques, Van der Merwe and Killick (1979) at smelting, Van der Merwe (1980) at the chemistry of iron production and Kussel (1974) and Friede and Steel (1977) have experimentally reconstructed technological processes. The direct reconstruction of early agriculture has proved more elusive, as there have been few excavated sites with good floral preservation: an important exception has been Shongweni Cave in Natal, from where plant remains have been closely studied by Davies (fig. 4:6) (1975). Faunas, in contrast, have often been more adequate, and considerable work has been done on early husbandry practices in the northern Transvaal (Voigt 1980, 1983; Voigt and Plug 1981) and Natal (Voigt 1984; Voigt and Von den Driesch 1984) and on the use by early farmers of wild faunas in regions such as the southern Highveld (Maggs 1976a) and the Transvaal Lowveld (Mason 1986).

Important also have been studies of early farming settlements themselves. One approach, which again has been consistent with general trends within archaeology, has been to seek explanation of settlement patterns in environmental and ecological terms. A pioneering analysis of this type was by Summers (1967a), who explored the influence of trypanosomiasis on the distribution of farming settlement in Zimbabwe. Maggs (1976a) set the distribution of Highveld settlements against the constraints of soils and climate, and went on to argue that environment had dictated the geography of the Iron Age on a subcontinental scale (Maggs 1980c, 1984a). Hall (1981), in contrast, took a far smaller area for study – coastal, valley and interfluvial environments in Zululand – and looked for more detailed patterns of settlement/resource correlation that could explain Iron Age settlement patterns.

A rather different approach to studying settlements has been developed by Tom Huffman and his colleagues at the University of the Witwatersrand. The view that ceramics were a form of language, and could be analysed as such, naturally pulled archaeology towards the techniques of structural linguistics. Additional structuralist influences have been Lewis-Williams's (1981a) work on Southern African rock art and Adam Kuper's (1980) analysis of settlement patterns revealed in the ethnographic data. The result has been an approach to archaeological settlements that reads them as 'cognitive systems': principals of structure that order the conception of the world (Huffman 1982). Huffman has suggested that one such cognitive system – the 'Bantu Cattle Pattern' – probably goes back to the earliest years of farming settlement. He has argued that an important cognitive transition took place with the emergence of hierarchical political systems at Mapungubwe in the twelfth century AD (Huffman 1982). At a more detailed level, this structuralist approach has allowed Huffman to put forward a close interpretation of the architecture of Great Zimbabwe (Huffman 1981, 1984a).

Thus by the early 1980s advances in the understanding of the Iron Age were marked, and the basis had been laid for a general synthesis. Rather than being the 'empty land' of government propaganda and apartheid education, it had now been demonstrated through a firm radiocarbon chronology that Southern Africa was first settled by farming communities by AD 200 (Maggs 1976b). By AD 1000 the subtropical lowlands of Mozambique and Zululand, the arid Limpopo valley and the eastern Transvaal, and the river valleys and basins of Natal and the Transkei were occupied by farmers who lived in villages, tended cattle, sheep and goats and grew a variety of crops, of which sorghum and millet were generally the most important. After AD 1000, the high grassland areas were settled as cattle became increasingly important in the economy. Swahili traders, who had been inching their way southwards along the Indian Ocean shoreline for some centuries, had begun to build trade links with the interior, providing the economic basis for a stratified society in the Limpopo Valley, based on the major site of Mapungubwe. By AD 1200, Mapungubwe was in decline and the centre of power had shifted northwards with the rise of the early Zimbabwe state. Based on the capital of Great Zimbabwe, which was supported by a network of regional centres, early Zimbabwe was able to contribute to the medieval world's voracious demand for gold, receiving in return beads, cloth and other exotic items of great local value. But by the early sixteenth century, when the Portuguese tried to capture the wealth of Southern Africa for themselves, the balance of power had shifted again, with competing kingdoms in the northern and southern areas of the Zimbabwe plateau – the capital of the latter being the site of Khami (Hall 1987).

This writing of the precolonial archaeology of the sub-continent, achieved largely within a decade, was a remarkable achievement. But accompanying the successes of conferences, meetings and academic publications was an equally remarkable contradiction. For the liberal germ, from which the florescence of Iron Age research has stemmed, had been outrage at the conscious distortion of history to form a part of apartheid ideology. And yet, with a few exceptions based on earlier work (for example, Garlake

1973; Inskeep 1969a; Mason 1967), there was no attempt made to make the new archaeological synthesis accessible either to challenge settler consciousness or to serve black nationalist aspirations. Indeed, Iron Age research had become highly specialized even within the field of professional archaeology and any understanding of how the complex ceramic typology fitted together was confined to a small inner circle.

The extent of the distance between professional archaeology and the wider community is evident in the failure of the new Iron Age synthesis – potentially one of the most politically significant branches of archaeology in the world – to make any political impact. School textbook, and popular, writers could claim not to understand the highly esoteric form in which results were presented, and continued to re-work apartheid history without challenge (Smith 1983; Stewart and Mazel 1986). Their preconceptions were reinforced by well publicized fringe writing which continued to resurrect the old nineteenth-century myths (for example, Hromnik 1981; Mallows 1984; Smith 1972).

More significant was the irrelevance of the new work in the revival of black nationalism. Almost a decade after the suppression and banning of the ANC and PAC, opposition had reformed after 1969 around the Black Consciousness movement (Gerhart 1978; Kane-Berman 1979; Lodge 1983). Through the South African Students Organization and the Black Peoples Convention, Black Consciousness gained a momentum which was further accelerated by the success of the nationalist guerrilla forces in the Rhodesian war, and by the collapse of Portuguese colonial rule in Angola and Mozambique in 1974, and was a significant political force by the time of the 1976 Soweto uprising.

Representing 'the coming of age, despite the institutions of apartheid, of a new African petty bourgeoisie' (Lodge 1983: 325), Black Consciousness emphasized the need for self-identity in order to counter the cultural impoverishment of colonialism and apartheid. It would be logical to expect that the new understanding of the Iron Age, directly contradicting apartheid history, would become important in Black Consciousness philosophy, but instead an abstract, utopian vision of the precolonial past developed. 'The fundamental aspects of pure African culture', wrote Steve Biko, which had survived the cultural onslaught of colonialism, included emphasis on the individual, communalism, and an ignorance of poverty: 'Thus in its entirety the African Culture spells us out as people particularly close to nature' (Biko 1978: 46). This return to 'merrie Africa' may have been due in part to the antipathy of Black Consciousness towards white liberals and liberal enterprises (Gerhart 1978), but it was also the result of the tight parcelling of archaeological information in a technical form that made it unintelligable beyond the profession. Thus the Black Consciousness intelligensia knew about Great Zimbabwe and held it as a symbol of black achievement, but were not aware of the results of Iron Age research south of the Limpopo.

This isolation of the results of Iron Age research from popular consciousness was due to several factors. First, the effectiveness of apartheid segregation made it difficult for academics – almost exclusively white and working in segregated research institutions and universities – to communicate the results of their work to the majority of the population. Second, Iron Age researchers in Southern Africa were still faced with an ideological contradiction, being part of the dominant minority while at the same time contesting its view of its history. And third (but by no means least importantly) archaeology in Southern Africa was part of a 'world system', with its practitioners looking outwards at international methodological and

theoretical concerns. Thus ecological case studies (Hall 1981), analysis of iron technology (fig. 4:7) (Van der Merwe 1980; Van der Merwe and Killick 1979) and structuralist models (Huffman 1981, 1984a), for example, were as much addresses to the general world of scholarship as they were contributions to the history of those whose history had been so systematically denied.

This last point is further expanded by comparison of the course of Iron Age research through the 1970s with new historical work over the same period. At root, both disciplines shared common concerns, particularly in seeking an understanding of the precolonial period. But whereas archaeology was, in general, dominated by positivism and the search for general laws of human behaviour (Trigger 1984), historians had been strongly influenced by 'revisionism', with its strong connections to structural Marxism. Historians of Southern Africa began to look for precapitalist social formations in Southern Africa (Bonner 1981; Hedges 1978; Slater 1976) and, for the postcolonial period, challenged conventional interpretations of the relationship between segregation and capital (Marks 1986a). Although historians and archaeologists of Southern Africa met in conferences and workshops (Lesotho in 1976, Pietermaritzburg in 1977 and Grahamstown in 1979), there were few connections of approach between the disciplines.

Crisis

The changing balance of power in South Africa through the 1970s, reflected in increasing labour unrest and the formation of independent black trade unions (Hindson 1984; Lodge 1983), and widespread revolt in 1976–7, has led in the 1980s to what Gramsci termed a 'crisis in hegemony' (Saul and Gelb 1981: 3).

4:7 Ethnoarchaeological fieldwork with iron-smelters in Malawi. N.J. van der Merwe in foreground

This political crisis within Southern Africa has coincided with a more general crisis within archaeology as a discipline. As Edmund Leach (1973) has caustically observed, changes in archaeological interpretations usually follow a decade behind shifts in cognate disciplines. Thus the early 1980s saw a revival in the application of Marxist theory to archaeology (Leone 1982; Spriggs 1984) and a linked concern with the social context of archaeological knowledge, spurred by campaigns for land rights in Australia and North America (Hodder 1983). Consequently, archaeologists in Southern Africa have had, in recent years, access to international revisionist theory (which their colleagues in cognate disciplines enjoyed some ten years earlier), coinciding with a regional political crisis.

The first major challenge to the archaeological concensus of the 1970s came in 1983. Over the preceeding decade professional archaeologists in the subcontinent had carefully nurtured the ideal of a community of scholars whose mutual academic connections overrode political boundaries. The original South African Association of Archaeologists had been renamed the Southern African Association of Archaeologists and members included virtually all professional workers in Zambia, Zimbabwe, Botswana, Lesotho, Swaziland, Mozambique and South Africa. However, at the 1983 conference in Gaborone, delegates from Mozambique forced a resolution seeking the condemnation by the Association of apartheid and other forms of discrimination. Although the majority of delegates, mostly from South Africa, were openly opposed to the racial policies of the South African government, they also had little taste for the explicit involvement of their discipline in the political arena. Although the contentious motion was not put to the vote, delegates from Mozambique and Zimbabwe resigned from the Association and many others left the meeting feeling that internationalist ideals were no longer attainable.

In the months that followed, the crisis within South Africa became openly apparent. The reformist National Party government, responding both to the changed interests of capital and to the political crisis, had installed a new constitution – a token concession to democracy (Lodge 1985). During 1983, formerly disparate civic associations, trade unions, educational groups and other organizations opposed to apartheid came together to form two massive national coalitions: the National Forum and the United Democratic Front (Barrell 1984; Dollie 1986). For a year the campaign against the government gained momentum, leading to the failure of the elections for the new 'Indian' and 'Coloured' parliaments and, from August 1984, violent clashes with state security forces in all the major metropolitan areas in South Africa (Bundy 1986). In response, security force powers were extended under regulations which, by June 1986 had become national. Tens of thousands were detained without trial and hundreds were killed in township clashes. Many came to believe that South Africa was in a state of civil war.

As a result of popular protest, and particularly in reaction to the heavily repressive state response, the African National Congress, which had been virtually destroyed inside the country in the 1960s, regained massive support (Lodge 1986). At the same time the United Democratic Front, with its non-racial policy and affiliate structure, offered whites opposed to the state a political home inside the country for the first time since the 1950s, while other campaigns – and particularly the lobby against compulsory military service – began to chip at entrenched white minority consciousness. Although it was clear that the South African government still had massive reserves of power, many whites came to believe that majority rule was inevitable and that the balance of power was shifting rapidly.

Archaeologists were as caught up as others in this crisis of hegemony and some began to examine the role of their work in contemporary social context. In this they were encouraged by the development of critique in archaeology as a whole, and spurred by the overwhelming international attention that was directed upon the South African crisis, which led to the exclusion of delegates from South Africa to the World Archaeological Congress, to be held in England in 1986. The results of this trend have been varied. In 1985, an Archaeological Awareness Workshop was formed, with some fifty members committed to making the results of research far more widely available. Others have become closely aligned with the Inkatha movement and its campaign for a Zulu nationalism which hides class differences through claim to a common national history and culture (Marks 1986b). Some have turned to research in historical archaeology as a means both of tracing the origins of oppression and of challenging white glorification of the colonial past. Although diverse, these approaches are unified in recognizing that the old archaeology will be inappropriate for the new South Africa that is emerging.

These new directions are evident in post-independence archaeology in other Southern African states. Great Zimbabwe had always been a powerful symbol for liberation movements and, following the nationalist victory, the site was reinterpreted to affirm an idealist vision of precolonial life (Mufuka 1983). Mufuka's work was stridently criticized for disregarding virtually all the archaeological evidence (Garlake 1984) but, given the firm alignment of public archaeology with white domination, the swing in interpretation to the opposite extreme was hardly surprising. More recently, major reinvestigation of Great Zimbabwe has begun, including the restoration of the site to fulfil its role as a premier national monument. In Mozambique, new models of fieldwork have been tried, in which local communities are consulted concerning the aims of research (Morais 1984). In addition, a perceived class bias in earlier research design has been challenged by concentrating on the archaeology of peasant settlement rather than elite residences – for example, in a re-investigation of the Zimbabwe-style site of Manyikeni (Morais and Sinclair 1980), earlier studied only as a royal enclave (Barker 1978; Garlake 1976). It is difficult at the moment to see clear trends in this 'contextualized' archaeology, but what is apparent is the conscious break with earlier practices.

Conclusion: archaeology as ideology

This review of Iron Age studies in Southern Africa shows a close relationship between the volume of work, the form of interpretations and political economy. From the first years of colonial penetration there were clashes between settlers, with their need for unskilled, cheap black labour, and cosmopolitan imperialists, aware of the need for contented proletariats. With the exception of the brief, post-war period in Southern Rhodesia this placed the aims of archaeological work in potential conflict with Southern African governments. In consequence, few resources for research were available. By the late 1960s the interests served by the South African government had begun to change and scientific and cultural research was promoted as part of the modernization of the state image. Iron Age work expanded rapidly, transforming knowledge of the precolonial period within a decade. But archaeology, as with all aspects of life in South Africa, was inexorably structured by apartheid and the new synthesis had little impact beyond a small, largely professional elite. For the black majority, caught up in the resurgence of nationalism and resistance, the precolonial period was still a 'hidden history'.

This history of research endeavour shows the pervasive influence of ideology – if ideology is taken to be the means whereby the contradictions within a social formation are obscured or redefined. This ideological role has been overt at times (for example, in Rhodes's need for a Phoenician presence, in the attacks on archaeology in the Rhodesian parliament, or in the *genre* of fringe writing that continues in the present) and more subtle at others (for instance, in the failure to provide resources for research, or in the persistent discovery of 'ethnicity' in the past). This relationship between archaeology and ideology is, of course, not unique to Southern Africa, as others have shown for other parts of Africa, Australia and North America.

But to make this point is not to argue that there is a tight, deterministic relationship between political economy and readings of precolonial history. As Althusser (1971) has shown, in the modern state ideologies are complex. In Southern Africa, different economic interests have been in competition throughout the present century, while archaeology has been injected with interpretations formed initially in other parts of the world. This has led to sustained and fundamental conflicts of interpretation within the profession, and differing views on the relationship between archaeology and wider society.

Taking this last point further, when have the tables been turned, giving to Iron Age research an active, if minor, role in reshaping political interests? Such could be the situation in a Gramscian 'crisis in hegemony' when the conflict of interests within the state provides a space for academic influence that would not otherwise be opened up. In general, the history of research in Southern Africa is of doors remaining firmly closed. Despite extensive publicity, Caton Thompson's work at Great Zimbabwe had little influence on settler consciousness, while editorial comment in the *South African Archaeological Bulletin* through the 1960s was a voice in the wilderness. The one exception was in Southern Rhodesia between 1947 and 1962, when manufacturing interests, temporarily holding political power and seeking to restructure the political economy of central Africa, could listen to, and be influenced by, the archaeological case for a rich precolonial history.

Notes

1 In summarizing aspects of the political economy of southern Africa, I have found it necessary to use some secondary sources, in particular Merle Lipton's (1986) examination of the relationship between capitalism and apartheid. In a less general review I would have had the opportunity to use more primary material, and to examine precise connections more closely. The material that Lipton presents is valuable, even though her conclusions are not sustained by her own evidence.

5 The Development of Archaeology in East Africa

PETER ROBERTSHAW

The history of East African archaeology is one of changing research priorities within a complex web of development. Academic training and the results of previous work have been the moving forces behind the establishment of research priorities, but the results obtained have often been used to serve ideological ends – the past as 'charter' or 'bad example' (Holl, this volume, quoting Wilk). Prior to 1950 archaeology in East Africa was virtually synonymous with Louis and Mary Leakey in Kenya and northern Tanzania and E.J. Wayland in Uganda. To dub these individuals and their archaeology as 'colonialist' is to misrepresent their attitudes, archaeological training and goals, as it would be likewise to subsume all the archaeology of recent years by indigenous archaeologists under the label 'nationalist'. This chapter therefore is an attempt to elucidate some of the complexities of the development of East African archaeology from a combination of what may be loosely termed archaeological and ideological perspectives. The geographical focus of this chapter is basically restricted within the modern boundaries of Kenya, Uganda and Tanzania. No attempt is made to chronicle excavations and important discoveries, rather the aim is to understand the ideas behind the excavations and the interpretations to which the discoveries gave rise. This is not to deny the fact that particular discoveries were instrumental in guiding the direction of future research, the most notable example of course being the discovery of 'Zinjanthropus' at Olduvai Gorge in 1959.

Before proceeding further it may be prudent to consider whether East African archaeology should be treated as a separate entity with its own developmental sequence, or whether the identification of an East African region is nothing more than a convenient editorial device to break up the continent into more manageable pieces. I believe that reading this chapter alongside others in the volume will indeed reveal that East African archaeology has a history of its own, but that this history articulates more or less closely through time with developments elsewhere in Africa and outside the continent. This latter point is scarcely surprising when one bears in mind the international forum provided at regular intervals by the Pan-African Congresses of Prehistory and Quaternary Studies. Indeed, it is remarkable the efforts to which archaeologists went in the first half of this century, given the generally appalling roads and hazards of flying, to visit each other's excavations and exchange ideas. For example Louis Leakey drove from Nairobi to Johannesburg and back in 1929, while Wayland regularly found the time and means to visit Leakey's sites.

It can be argued that in the last decade or two there has emerged not one but two East African archaeologies – one concerned with human origins (palaeoanthropology) and the other with later prehistory. The former is touched on mostly only in passing in this chapter since, on the one hand, it is discussed in depth in Gowlett's contribution and, on the other hand, it can be posited that to a large extent the study of our origins has transcended regional boundaries. A note of clarification is also required for my use of the term 'later prehistory' in this context. The archaeology of the coast is not prehistoric, in the sense that there are numerous documents describing the East African coast at various times in the past written by Arab travellers and others. It has been a common practice to divorce this archaeology from that of the interior (e.g. Merrick 1983). However, it is my intention to discuss this coastal research, albeit briefly, in the present chapter, and thus it is subsumed within the term 'later prehistory' when this is used to contrast with the study of human origins. This device is used to avoid both unnecessarily cumbersome phrases and that unfortunate term 'protohistory'.

Pioneers, pluvials and the organic model of prehistory

The first collections of stone tools in East Africa were made by the geologist J.W. Gregory, beginning in 1893 (Gregory 1896: 322–5). His collections and those of several others, notably C.W. Hobley (Dewey and Hobley 1925), were vaguely classed as 'Neolithic' (L.S.B. Leakey 1931: 3). In Tanzania a German, Hans Reck, excavated a fossil human skeleton at Olduvai in 1913 but without observing any stone artefacts, since his expectation had been that these would be made of flint (Reck 1914). Reck also investigated several burial mounds in the Ngorongoro Crater and visited the Iron Age sites at Engaruka (Reck 1926). However, it was E.J. Wayland's arrival to join the government service in Uganda in 1919 that was to set East African archaeology on the course that it was to follow for the next forty years or more.

Wayland, a geologist by profession and an archaeologist by avocation, served for twenty years as the Director of the Geological Survey of Uganda. Prior to the First World War he had worked in Ceylon where he had discovered stone tools in high-level Pleistocene gravels. The search for an explanation for these gravels led Wayland to the work of a meteorologist, Brooks, who argued that during glacial advances areas further south must have experienced wetter conditions (Brooks 1926). Thus, when Wayland, an indefatigable fieldworker, began to find stone artefacts in high gravel deposits in Uganda, he realized immediately the potential for establishing a sequence of archaeological industries (usually referred to at that time as 'cultures') tied to a sequence of pluvial episodes, correlated in turn with the European glacial sequence (Wayland 1924). The major purpose, of course, was to provide a method of relative dating to examine the question of contemporaneity between similar stone tool cultures found in both Europe and other parts of Africa. Using this framework Wayland boldly challenged orthodox views of the time by claiming not only that Uganda had been inhabited for as long as Europe but also that it was 'extremely probable that man originated in Africa' (Wayland, quoted in Van Riet Lowe 1952: 8). The oldest culture recognized by Wayland was the Kafuan, but the artefacts assigned to it were later shown to result from natural fracture of pebbles (Bishop 1959). Although outside his main sphere of interest, Wayland also made substantial contributions to Iron Age archaeology (Posnansky 1967a).

Louis Leakey (fig. 5:1), born in Kenya of missionary parents, began archaeological research in Kenya in 1926 with excavations in the Central Rift Valley, notably at Gamble's Cave. Fired with a passion for prehistory from boyhood, Leakey had studied archaeology and anthropology at Cambridge under A.C. Haddon and Miles Burkitt, and learnt much physical anthropology with the guidance of Sir Arthur Keith

(Cole 1975). Leakey was quick to apply Brooks's and Wayland's pluvial hypotheses, a task made easier by the pronounced high beach levels which are so common in the closed lake basins of the Central Rift. By 1929 Leakey had already succeeded in establishing 'a fairly complete cultural sequence' (L.S.B. Leakey 1929: 750). This sequence, for which a characteristic type series of tools was described for each culture, was tied to a palaeoclimatic sequence of pluvials linked in turn to the South African and European archaeological and climatic sequences (L.S.B. Leakey 1931). The archaeological sequence thus established for East Africa survived with only minor modifications for the next thirty-five years and parts of it are still considered to be valid nowadays (Ambrose 1984).

5:1 L.S.B. Leakey (bottom left) during excavations at Gamble's Cave.

The approach of Leakey and others working in East Africa during the first half of this century to the business of doing archaeology and accounting for culture change was remarkably similar to that espoused by contemporary Palaeolithic researchers, an approach which in recent years has often been categorized as 'normative' or 'straight' archaeology. The essence of this sort of archaeology as practised by Peyrony and others in France has been brilliantly captured by Sackett (1981); his analysis would fit the East African context equally well. Archaeology is here seen as a positivist discipline very closely akin to palaeontology, wherein cultures are conceived of in organic terms as being not unduly different from animal species. Thus, cultures are defined by the presence of *fossiles directeurs*, i.e. highly specific artefact types found in narrowly defined stratigraphic contexts. In the East African context this was relaxed so that cultures were usually defined on the basis of the co-occurrence of several distinctive tool-types. No allowance was made for the possibility of functionally different tool-kits being made by the same group of people at different sites; variability was to be accounted for by temporal differences or attribution to different groups of people. Moreover, the qualitative approach to the definition of cultures was unlikely to discern anything less than major changes in tool-making traditions. The organic approach to culture was reinforced by a tendency to identify particular human physical types (races in many instances) as the makers of particular cultures (see Leakey 1935), and also to assume the existence of a close correlation between archaeological and geological stratigraphy. As a consequence of the latter, it is not surprising that faunal remains discovered in archaeological contexts were viewed not as evidence of diet and rarely of palaeoenvironments, but as aids to dating the cultures with which they were associated.

Recognition of the organic model of culture embraced by Leakey permits an understanding not only of his approach to data collection and analysis but also of the manner in which he both named and interpreted the cultures he unearthed. Leakey very often applied the names of Western European industries to his East African cultures, a practice which Leakey's mentor, A.C. Haddon, described as 'rash and in every way undesirable' (quoted in Cole 1975: 69). However, in accordance with the organic model of culture, Leakey followed established zoological practices of nomenclature; thus any culture for which a European or a South African equivalent was known was accorded the same name, only prefixing the name Kenya (L.S.B. Leakey 1931: 27–8). Where no equivalent was known, a new name was used, as for example in the case of the Elmenteitan. Furthermore, Leakey (*ibid.*) insisted that 'the culture name used does not imply any date, or even of necessity a culture contact'. The classic example of this process of nomenclature is the culture, first recognized at Gamble's Cave, which Leakey (*ibid.*) named the Kenya Aurignacian after the European Upper Palaeolithic culture, since both were dominated by large backed blades and burins. Later, following research by others in North Africa, the name was changed to Kenya Capsian in recognition of the fact that similar assemblages existed nearer to East Africa than Europe (L.S.B. Leakey 1952a). More recently again, in line with the Burg-Wartenstein recommendations on nomenclature (see below), a local name, the Eburran industry, was substituted (Ambrose *et al.* 1980).

The organic model also provided the framework for the explanation of culture change. Basically such explanation involved the intuitive weighing of the relative merits of ideas of 'evolution' against 'diffusion'. This is well illustrated by some examples from *Stone Age Africa* (L.S.B. Leakey 1936): eleven distinct evolutionary stages of development of the 'Chelleo-Acheulean hand-axe culture' were recognized (p. 41); the Aurignacian and Levalloisian cultures were found in the same area at the beginning of the 'Gamblian Pluvial period', both were 'very highly evolved' – a case of 'parallel evolution' (p. 58) – and eventually they 'affected each other in such a way as to give rise to . . . the East African Stillbay culture' (p. 187); the Aurignacian culture 'evolved' in East Africa and then 'spread' north to become the North African Capsian (p. 187). Leakey was not alone in his evolutionary perspective (e.g. Wayland 1934a; Van Riet Lowe 1952a), though O'Brien (1939: 51–2) recognized the cultural variability that might result from different environments and varying raw materials. The organic model of culture had a tendency to breathe life into stone tools so that they could 'evolve' (Leakey *op. cit*, p. 183), give rise to 'hybrid cultures' (p. 186), and in the case of the Aurignacian become 'more virile' (p. 59). Concern with evolutionary sequences of stone tool industries was mirrored in the way other sorts of archaeological data were evaluated; for example Leakey (*op. cit.*, 152) limited his discussion of Tanzanian rock art to the elucidation of the sequence of 'styles' and made no attempt to examine the meaning of the art. Nevertheless, *Stone Age Africa* is a landmark publication

5:2 *Njoro River Cave at the time of excavation*

in African archaeology, for in it Leakey demonstrated the importance of linking regional sequences into a continent-wide overview.

Leakey's wholehearted embracing of the organic model of culture with its links to palaeontology, as well as the recognition of the importance of geomorphology to the construction of his culture-stratigraphic framework, may go a long way towards explaining the curious intellectual separation between his archaeological and ethnographic studies. On the rare occasions Leakey drew upon ethnographic analogy for archaeological explanation, he did so in the crude 'shotgun' manner characteristic of the time. On the other side of the coin, in his monumental ethnography of the Kikuyu written in the late 1930s (Leakey 1977), he never considers the role archaeology might play in deciphering Kikuyu history, stating instead that 'the study of their origins and development can be obtained only from their traditions' (*ibid.*, vol. I: 48). Ludwig Kohl-Larsen was another scientist who practised both cultural anthropology and archaeology but as two divorced disciplines. Kohl-Larsen led several major expeditions to the highlands of northern Tanzania in the 1930s (Kohl-Larsen 1943), but his important archaeological excavations at Mumba-Höhle and other sites received little attention until after his death in 1969 (Müller-Beck 1978–86; Mehlman 1979).

From 1934 onwards Louis Leakey devoted almost all his fieldwork energies to the search for fossil human ancestors and to the stone tools of the earliest time-ranges of prehistory. The mantle of later prehistory in Kenya fell upon Mary Leakey, who continued to refine Louis's cultural-stratigraphic framework. Perhaps more importantly, in the publications of her excavations at Hyrax Hill (M.D. Leakey 1945) and Njoro River Cave (fig. 5:2) (M.D. and L.S.B. Leakey 1950) she significantly raised the standard of excavation reports, not least by presenting quantitative details of the recovered assemblages.

In Uganda the late 1930s saw the first stirrings of doubt about the pluvial hypothesis that Louis Leakey had so ardently embraced. While the final demise of the hypothesis occurred only at the end of the 1950s (Cooke 1957, 1958; Flint 1959a), Wayland himself had always had nagging doubts (see e.g. Van Riet Lowe 1952a: 14) that must have been strengthened by Solomon's 1939 critique. J.D. Solomon had assisted Leakey in establishing the pluvial sequence in central Kenya, yet by 1939 he was of the opinion that 'the Pluvial Hypothesis rests on very slender foundations, and the writer is inclined to discard it completely as a basis for the classification of the African Quaternary. ... He is further of the opinion that there is no reliable material for the institution of Glacial-Pluvial correlations' (Solomon 1939: 41). Solomon was supported by the archaeologist O'Brien (1939: 292), who argued that 'the whole prehistoric complex in Uganda is different ... from that in Kenya–Tanganyika' (*op. cit.*, 294). O'Brien was perhaps the first East African archaeologist to give serious consideration to the role of environment and raw material in determining cultural patterning. He was also precocious in his thinking and in recognizing the ideological role of archaeology, ending his book thus:

> African Stone Age Man achieved his own, essentially African culture, built out of African materials, in an African environment to which that culture was especially and purposely suited. In that realisation lies, I believe, a promise of tremendous significance for the future of African archaeology and for the solution of racial and kindred anthropological problems in that continent. (O'Brien 1939: 295)

Colonial ideology and later prehistory

O'Brien's views are very different from those of Sonia Cole, whose importance for East African archaeology lay in her role as synthesizer and publicist. Cole's *Prehistory of East Africa* (1954, rev. ed. 1963) is even today the only major synthesis of the region's prehistory. After receiving some training in geology, Cole came to Kenya as a farmer's wife and soon became a stalwart helper on Leakey expeditions, eventually writing Louis's biography after his death (Cole 1975). Given this background it is no surprise that she embraced the pluvial hypothesis (though the revised edition was more guarded) and presented a lucid account in accordance with the organic model of prehistory discussed earlier. As the wife of a prominent white Kenyan farmer and the daughter of aristocracy it is also no surprise that she shared prevalent colonialist attitudes towards 'the natives' and used her writings to deny these people their past. However, as a synthesizer of prehistory she could hardly refute the fact that there was a past of considerable interest. To overcome this paradox she attempted to alienate ownership of the past from the present inhabitants of the region. This was done by contrasting a glorious Stone Age with a miserable later prehistoric period. Thus, in earliest times East Africa was 'a centre of evolutionary progress' and 'by no means the cultural backwater that it became later' (Cole 1964: 40). The 'cultural stagnation' that set in after the Stone Age was attributed to isolation and disease (*op. cit.*, 329), as well as the fact that the good climate made basic subsistence too easy to obtain and hence promoted 'lethargy' (*op. cit.*, 40). Cole indeed lamented that 'it is rather the fashion nowadays to make excuses for the negligible contributions to civilization made by the inhabitants of Africa other than Egypt' (*op. cit.*, 49). Therefore, Cole's prehistory could be seen to justify the white man's burden of colonialism and to excuse the servile conditions of cheap indigenous agricultural labour that was a cornerstone of the white farmer's prosperity (see also Hall, this volume). Other writers were far more blantantly racist than Cole in their interpretation of prehistory for these same ends (e.g. Wilson 1952, 1954).

The colonial encounter with the African was, however, rather more complex than the preceding sentences might suggest. For, although agricultural peoples were despised and degraded to excuse the expropriation of their land and their exploitation as cheap labour, many colonialists had a sneaking, if not open, admiration for the 'proud' pastoralists of the more arid regions, which held little or no potential for European farming methods. A highly romantic view of the Maasai and other pastoralists was common currency in colonial times and is still prevalent, as is obvious from coffee-table literature.

Thus, archaeological research into recent prehistory in the colonial era was motivated in large part by a desire to prove the validity of this view of the pastoral peoples by demonstrating that they were descended from more 'civilized' peoples to the north (e.g. Bolton 1927). Of course most of this work was entirely speculative, the 'lost tribes of Israel' being a regular feature. Indeed, much use was made of the Old Testament as a source on East African prehistory. This curious phenomenon may be understood if it is realized that these researches were the work of amateur *historians* with little or no appreciation of the assistance that archaeology might offer. Thus, the Bible was the only textual source to which they could turn. It must also be remembered that this was the time when the hyperdiffusionist views of Elliot Smith and Perry were enjoying wide publicity (Daniel 1962: 91–5). Therefore, for example, to see the Maasai as wandering Jews did not appear as ridiculous in the 1920s and 30s as it does nowadays. These studies were given a veneer of respectibility too by Louis Leakey's conclusion that the great majority of the skeletons from later prehistoric burials were of Caucasoid or Mediterranean stock and distinctly non-Negroid (L.S.B. Leakey 1935, 1945, 1950a; see Rightmire 1975). Beads made from semi-precious stones found at various central Kenyan sites were also considered as evidence of Mediterranean, probably Egyptian, contacts (L.S.B. Leakey 1931: 243: M.D. Leakey 1948; see Gow 1984). It was then but a small step to equate the Caucasoid physical type with the 'Hamitic' (Cushitic) language family and thence to show that 'Nilo-Hamitic' (Eastern Nilotic) speakers such as the Maasai were descendents of Hamitic peoples from north-eastern Africa who had intermarried with incoming Negroes (Cole 1954: 98).

The 'Hamitic myth', as it was later characterized (Sutton 1968: 96), was also used in the guise of 'Megalithic Cushites' (Murdock 1959: 196) or 'Azanians' (Huntingford 1933) to explain to colonialist satisfaction the presence of some rather impressive stone monuments and earthworks found through much of Kenya and northern Tanzania. All these sites were considered the handiwork of an 'Azanian civilization' forced south from the Horn of Africa in the eighth century AD by Islamic invaders, but (conveniently) disappearing in the fourteenth or fifteenth centuries (Hungtingford 1933). The name 'Azania' was the Greco-Roman term for the East African coast; thus the monuments of the coast were ascribed to the same light-skinned people as those of the interior (Murdock 1959: 205). Therefore, colonialist ideology was reinforced both by denying the indigenous peoples a claim to the more impressive monuments of both the interior and the coast, and by asserting that they were the work of Caucasoid people in contact with the civilized Mediterranean world. However, we should not think of these studies as nothing more than colonialist plots or propaganda. Diffusionism – not the extreme diffusionism of Elliot Smith but the more cautious 'modified diffusionism' of Gordon Childe – was the major explanatory framework for later European prehistory. Thus, a search for origins outside East Africa was entirely in keeping with the archaeological paradigms of the day. The racial correlations also had their roots in the prevalent pseudo-Darwinian sociology of the early decades of this century (MacGaffey 1966).

When Sonia Cole's *Prehistory of East Africa* was published in 1954 there could be no doubt that East African archaeology had come a remarkably long way in less than thirty years, thanks in no small measure to the tireless energy of Louis and Mary Leakey. A detailed cultural sequence had been established for the Stone Age, which was at least as long as the European sequence. This sequence had moreover been dated by reference to the pluvial hypothesis, tied in turn to the European glacial sequence, hence permitting questions of cultural diffusion and evolution to be examined from an apparently sound body of archaeological observations. Not only that but later prehistoric studies had also shown that peoples from or in contact with the Mediterranean world had been responsible for the achievements of the recent past, including not only stone monuments and earthworks but also the introduction of domestic animals and agriculture; so the righteousness of the white man's burden was given an archaeological seal of approval. Against this background the discovery in 1959 of 'Zinjanthropus' at Olduvai Gorge was a very just reward for all the Leakeys' hard work. However, the Mau Mau rebellion of the 1950s had already sounded a clear warning that major political changes were coming that would have repercussions, even for the seemingly esoteric subject of archaeology.

The winds of change

The achievement of independence by the East African states in the early 1960s had, as might be expected, little, if any, immediate impact upon the region's archaeology. More significant, at least in the short term, were the changes under way within archaeology and its sister disciplines. The first of these has already been mentioned – that is the demise of the pluvial hypothesis, which collapsed under a barrage of criticism around 1960. With it, of course, went the Stone Age chronology. However, rescue in the form of absolute dating methods was close at hand; Bed I at Olduvai was dated by the potassium-argon method in 1961 (L.S.B. Leakey *et. al.* 1961) and suddenly there was a million more years of prehistory awaiting discovery. Although radiocarbon dating had been invented in the 1940s, processing of archaeological dating samples from East Africa became routine only in the 1960s. The advent of radiocarbon dating meant not only an absolute chronology but also that archaeologists, freed from the requirements of relative dating through stratigraphic ordering, could now usefully excavate single-occupation open sites, the most common type of Neolithic and Early Iron Age sites.

These methodological developments were part of much broader upheavals in archaeology that were taking place outside East Africa, particularly in America. I refer, of course, to 'New Archaeology' and the attack upon 'normative' archaeology, to which the organic model could be deemed to belong. Archaeological theory has rarely, if ever, been debated within East African archaeology, except perhaps in the context of the recent arguments concerning the integrity of Plio-Pleistocene sites and the nature of early hominid diet and social organization (see Isaac 1983). East African archaeologists have generally eschewed discussion of theory and worked within the unspoken guidelines of normative archaeology in reconstructing the prehistory of the region. However, this does not mean that East Africanists were unaware of theoretical developments elsewhere and that the latter did not have any effect on the practice of archaeology within the region. Yet there was no attempt to import 'New Archaeology' wholesale into East Africa; much of the rhetoric of systems theory and of the need for establishing cross-cultural laws was shunned, as was the over-reliance on the hypothetico-deductive method. Instead there was new concern with faunal remains and that hoary old favourite, terminology and nomenclature, the latter perhaps more of a reaction against 'New Archaeology' than a response to it. Two major factors probably account for the lack of acceptance of 'New Archaeology' among East Africanists in the 1960s and early 1970s. The first was perhaps recognition of the fact that much of the region was still archaeological *terra incognita* and, therefore, the data simply did not exist nor would exist in the near future to address the sorts of sophisticated sociological hypotheses favoured by many of the 'New Archaeologists' in the mid-late 1960s. However, this argument is weakened when one remembers that 'New Archaeology' was often practised where good culture-stratigraphic frameworks were lacking and that this type of archaeology was never popular in the Perigord region of France, despite the excellence of the prehistoric framework for the region and the fact that Binford himself worked there. More fundamental was the simple fact that few, if any, of the growing numbers of archaeologists who found their way to East Africa from Europe or America had been trained by the main exponents of the 'New Archaeology'; many of them in fact had been taught by Desmond Clark at Berkeley, where they had learnt 'normative' archaeology but increasingly within an ecological paradigm that Clark pioneered in his synthesis of Southern African prehistory, in which he drew heavily upon ethnographic analogy (Clark 1959a).

Prior to the 1960s faunal remains from East African archaeological sites were studied by palaeontologists for palaeontological ends, archaeological interest being confined to their use as dating indicators. However, in the 1960s with the weakening of the organic model of prehistory and the growth of the ecological paradigm in archaeology, the role of diet and subsistence within human adaptational systems was seen as a valid field of study. Cattle bones were positively identified in association with a Later Stone Age lithic assemblage (Sutton 1966: 41), and it became common practice to retain and identify, both to species and body part, all the bones found in an excavation (e.g. Gifford-Gonzalez and Kimengich 1984). With large assemblages of faunal remains it was possible to reconstruct butchery practices and subsistence, and to generate informed hypotheses about patterns of seasonal land-use (Gifford *et al.* 1980; Marshall 1986).

The agony over the hierarchial classification of stone artefact assemblages and the question of appropriate nomenclature which was so central to the Burg-Wartenstein symposium of 1965 (Bishop and Clark 1967) was not simply a reaction to the 'New Archaeology' but represented also a new provincialism with complex roots. On the one hand, the collapse of the pluvial hypothesis as a means to relative dating and hence inter-regional comparisons had led to a new mood of caution, reinforced by concern at the onslaught on normative archaeology in the United States; on the other hand, the emergence of the new nation-states of Africa encouraged a provincial approach to the identification of industries, which perhaps satisfied the search for a national heritage that many of the newly independent countries were engaged in both in East Africa and elsewhere on the continent.

The Burg-Wartenstein recommendations on classification and nomenclature met with considerable sympathy and adherence among Africanist archaeologists, despite the fact that they were most difficult to apply in practice and failed to take adequate account of the effects of varying activity and deposition patterns on the composition of artefact assemblages (Parkington 1970). The imposition of the recommendations, if not to the letter then in spirit, upon the East African cultural sequence resulted not only in a revamping of the terminology but also in a rejection of the validity of many of the industries defined by Leakey (e.g. Sutton 1966: 38). In some instances, for example with the Elmenteitan, it seems that the baby was thrown out with the bathwater (Ambrose 1982: 128). This exercise was partly responsible for the great concern over the culture-stratigraphic framework for the Later Stone Age and Neolithic eras that has been evident in archaeological research in East Africa over the last twenty years (e.g. Cohen 1970; Nelson 1973; Bower et al. 1977; Bower and Nelson 1978; Ambrose 1982; Collett and Robertshaw 1983).

The 1960s saw not only changes in archaeological theory and method but also the emergence of African history as an academic discipline with obvious connections to archaeology. The rapid rise of African history was both a reaction to the colonialist denial of an indigenous African past and a conscious search for roots to bolster the pride of the newly independent states. However, the limited time-depth of oral traditions meant that much of the pre-colonial past was of necessity only accessible through archaeology. The period that mattered was the Iron Age, not the Stone Age upon which the Leakeys had expended so much effort. However, at independence the Iron Age consisted of little more than the lost tribes of Israel, the Azanian civilization and on the coast the 'Arab city' of Gedi (Kirkman 1954). Later prehistory and particularly the Iron Age were the gaps in our knowledge of the East African past that were most in need of filling, both to complement the new discipline of African history, including the advances being made in historical linguistics, and simply because almost all serious archaeological endeavour had until then focussed on the Stone Age. New work on the Iron Age was therefore a high priority to which the Antiquities Services of Uganda and Tanzania responded as best they could with the limited means at their disposal. However, the focus of archaeological research by the National Museum in Kenya (there being no Antiquities Service) remained, with the exception of the work of James Kirkman on coastal sites, on the beginnings of human culture. Indeed, in 1962 the Centre for Prehistory and Palaeontology came into being under Louis Leakey's guidance at what was then the Coryndon Museum in Nairobi (Cole 1975: 266). East Africa as the cradle of humankind was of course itself a strong international selling-point in the quest for research funding, and a matter of considerable pride for the governments of the region.

Although not unnaturally viewed with some suspicion as an organ of the former colonial power, the founding of the British Institute of History and Archaeology in East Africa (later the British Institute in Eastern Africa) in 1960, commissioned to study later archaeology and pre-colonial history, was something of a windfall for those keen to see serious study of the Iron Age. The idea of a British Institute in East Africa had first been publicly aired at the 1953 conference on African history held at the School of Oriental and African Studies in the University of London. The proposal was embraced with characteristic enthusiasm and

determination by Mortimer Wheeler in his capacity of Secretary to the British Academy. The successful foundation of the Institute followed intense lobbying, including a hectic tour of East Africa by Wheeler and Gervase Mathew to solicit the support of the colonial governments, during which they also found time both to survey the southern Somali coast and excavate at Kilwa. Wheeler was fascinated by the coastal monuments, but the potential of later archaeology in the interior was not forgotten (Wheeler 1970). With Louis Leakey's understandable initial reservations placated, the Institute came into existence in 1959 (Caton Thompson 1983: 261–3). While the Institute's long-serving director, Neville Chittick (fig. 5:3), studied the coastal settlements which he believed were founded by colonists from the Persian Gulf (e.g. Chittick 1984), work was rapidly begun also on the Iron Age of the interior aided by a substantial grant from the Astor Foundation. An active programme of fieldwork soon led to substantive results, including the demise of the 'Hamitic myth' in all its forms (Sutton 1973: 67–76). Publication was effected mainly through a special issue (Soper 1971) of the Institute's annual journal *Azania* founded in 1966 and now the main organ of publication for reports on the later archaeology of Eastern Africa.

5:3 Neville Chittick, for twenty years the Director of the British Institute in Eastern Africa, commencing excavations at Manda

Research directions of the last twenty years

Before discussing in greater detail the rise of nationalism within East African archaeology and concomitant developments in the training of indigenous archaeologists, it is worthwhile to reflect upon some of the research questions addressed by archaeologists to the study of later East African prehistory over the last twenty years. All these archaeologists were trained either in Europe or America, the main institutions involved being Cambridge, where Africanist students were predominantly taught by

Charles McBurney, the Palaeolithic specialist, and Grahame Clark, and Berkeley where Desmond Clark and later Glynn Isaac resided. Surprisingly perhaps, most of the American-trained archaeologists have focussed their research on the Neolithic and earlier periods, while the Europeans were drawn more to the Iron Age, partly no doubt because this was the main *raison d'être* of the British Institute.

For the terminal phases of the Stone Age in the post-Pleistocene – both those with and without evidence for food production – archaeological endeavour, as indicated earlier, has been mostly harnessed to the problem of establishing a reliable culture-stratigraphic framework. This effort has met with only limited success because, in part, the number of large well-dated artefact assemblages is still inadequate for the task. Indeed it is a common misconception that scores of foreign archaeologists flock to East Africa each year to dig. Given the competing attraction of Plio-Pleistocene deposits, the advances that have been made in our knowledge are attributable to probably less than a dozen individuals. Difficulties with the culture-stratigraphic framework are also explicable by its undoubted complexity, particularly for the period of Stone Age food-producers. After Nelson (1973, 1976) had shown the limitations of stone artefact assemblage analysis for this task, attention shifted to ceramics (Wandibba 1980). However, even here the fact that several distinctive 'wares' apparently co-existed in the same geographical area for several centuries suggested a patterning that was 'unusual in global perspective' (Bower and Nelson 1978: 564). A re-analysis of the relevant assemblages, few as they are, has produced a more 'traditional' answer (Collett and Robertshaw 1983), but one that is by no means universally accepted. The concern with establishing a cultural sequence prompted attempts to correlate archaeological industries with particular language families (Phillipson, 1977a: 82–4; Ambrose 1982) in order to explain the complexities of the present distribution of languages in East Africa, in which all four major African phyla are represented. Such exercises seem almost inevitably to invoke population movements, often over large distances, to account for the observed distributions (Robertshaw and Collett 1983: 292–3). These results are at odds with nationalist preceptions that would favour autochthonous development within the region. Support for the latter position may be claimed from the re-analysis of the later prehistoric human skeletal record which has both demonstrated the antiquity of the negroid physical type in East Africa (Gramly and Rightmire 1973; Bräuer 1980) and refuted the claims for the presence of 'Caucasoids' in the region (Rightmire 1975, 1984).

In recent years there has been an increasing tendency to undertake culture-stratigraphic studies for the terminal Stone Age within what might be termed a functional or ecological context (Gifford-Gonzalez 1984). Methodologically rigorous survey strategies (Bower *et al.* 1977; Barthelme 1985; Robertshaw in press) have been combined with analyses of excavated faunal assemblages (Gifford *et al.* 1980; Marshall 1986) so that regional subsistence and settlement patterns may be reconstructed (Ambrose 1984; Nelson *et al.* in prep; Robertshaw in press).

Iron Age studies have followed a somewhat different trajectory, in part due to the nature of the evidence and in part perhaps due to the fact that few researchers have actively studied both the Iron Age and preceding periods. An explanation of the latter phenomenon may reside in the observation made earlier that American-trained archaeologists have been drawn more to the Neolithic and earlier periods while Europeans have worked on the Iron Age. In the American university system archaeologists generally receive their training within anthropology departments, whereas their European counterparts are perhaps encouraged through an emphasis on *prehistory* to forge closer links with historians. Indeed archaeology at the University of Nairobi, itself established on the model of the British education system, is taught within the Department of History. Moreover, many, if not most, of the pioneers of precolonial East African history took their doctorates in the 1960s at British universities where they often established mutually beneficial ties with archaeologists.

Most Early Iron Age sites in East Africa contain ceramics and evidence for iron-smelting but lack faunal remains. Thus, studies of ceramics and iron technology have predominated, and they have generally been subsumed within a single explanatory framework – the expansion of the Bantu (Phillipson 1976, 1977a). The goal of the Bantu Studies Research Project (BSRP) of the British Institute carried out between 1965 and 1971 was the clarification of this expansion through the application of archaeology. Prior to the mid-1960s the primary sources of evidence about the origins and spread of the Bantu were linguistic. Thus, the BSRP was conceived as adding an archaeological dimension to the linguistic reconstruction; in particular Roland Oliver, then Professor of African History at the University of London and the driving force behind the creation of the BSRP, believed that the crucial contribution of archaeology would lie in the provision of radiocarbon dates so that the chronology and directions of Bantu expansion could be firmly established (Oliver 1966: 371). In 1966, when Oliver was writing, very little was known of the East African Iron Age in comparison with that of Zambia and Zimbabwe. Thus the BSRP was eventually undertaken as a series of area surveys, combined with small-scale excavations of selected sites, with the aim of establishing 'a framework of linked Iron Age sequences within East Africa' (Soper 1971: 1). The success of the BSRP is evident from the publications that resulted; indeed, Oliver (1979: 7) wrote that while the dominant contribution to the problem of Bantu expansion in 1965 was linguistics, ten years later it was that of archaeology. However, it could also be said that the outcome of the study of the Early Iron Age from this limited perspective was that rather scattered sites and their associated dates had the misfortune to be given exaggerated importance in grand explanatory designs (Posnansky 1967b; Schmidt 1975).

Archaeological manifestations of the later Iron Age – sites falling in the present millennium – are more varied, ranging from small farming settlements to salt-working sites (e.g. Sutton and Roberts 1968), the terraced villages and irrigation furrows of Engaruka in northern Tanzania (see Robertshaw 1986 and Sutton 1986 for references), and to the large sites, like Bigo and Ntusi in Uganda (Posnansky 1969; Lanning 1970), which some believe to have been the capitals of kingdoms. The sorts of information obtained from these sites and the hypotheses explored have varied accordingly. One feature that these sites do appear to hold in common is that they may often be linked, directly or indirectly, to oral traditions. The theoretical underpinnings of tying archaeology to oral tradition have been little explored in Africa (but see Schmidt 1978 and this volume). Too often there has been a lack of integrated research (Posnansky 1967b) with the result that archaeological findings have been used simply to support or deny the accuracy of the traditions, and to provide radiocarbon dates as a check on the historians' chronology derived from dynastic genealogies (e.g. Posnansky 1968). Nor have there been any attempts to use archaeological data in conjunction with oral traditions to explore the question of state formation in the inter-lacustrine region, despite the fact that sites relevant to this problem have been excavated. It seems that in this case senior historians have been satisfied with their own reconstructions (e.g. Oliver 1977) and have not goaded the archaeologists to action.

Despite its contemporaneity the Iron Age of the East African interior has always been treated as something separate from the archaeology of the coast. Mortimer Wheeler's dictum that one should start at the coast and progress inland and thus work from the 'known' to the unknown (Shinnie, this volume) has never been followed. There seem to be two major reasons why this apparently artificial coast/interior dichotomy has developed. The first is that very few coastal imports, apart from occasional glass beads and cowrie shells, have been found at sites in the interior, nor have any of the inland trading posts of the Swahili caravans, which are mentioned in nineteenth-century European explorers' accounts, been excavated. It is also probable that such long-distance caravans were not a feature of the trade prior to the late eighteenth or nineteenth century. Even at this late date there were no permanent trading posts in the interior, simply locations at which caravans would regularly camp. The second reason for the dichotomy would appear to be a distinct lack of interest by coastal archaeologists in the interior, other than as a reservoir of ivory and other resources to supply the Indian Ocean trade. For these archaeologists the coastal settlements were founded by colonists from the Persian Gulf (e.g. Chittick 1984), and were thus seaward-facing communities clinging to the edge of Africa with no knowledge of the interior beyond contact with the people who came to their settlements to barter for their trade goods. This model of coastal settlement, ascribing the impressive towns of the coast to the work of non-Africans, was not surprisingly anathema to the indigenous archaeology that was beginning to emerge in the late 1970s.

Indigenous archaeology

Far less emphasis was placed on the training of indigenous archaeologists in East Africa than in West Africa (Shaw 1976: 165) for reasons that are far from clear but no doubt include the fact that funds for East Africa were channelled into research on the origins of humankind. Moreover, the British Institute in Eastern Africa was never able to assume a major training role since its funding was specifically to be directed towards research, and its staff were discouraged from undertaking teaching commitments. Therefore, to the best of my knowledge, the first East African, apart from of course Louis Leakey, to obtain a doctorate in archaeology was J.C. Onyango-Abuje in 1977. Few others have followed in his footsteps: in 1986 those with doctorates comprise three Kenyans – one working in the National Museum and two in the University of Nairobi, two Tanzanians – one in the National Museum and one in the Antiquities Service, and one Ugandan currently working in Botswana. Archaeology teaching programmes exist at the Universities of Nairobi and Dar es Salaam; that at the latter was only recently established with substantial foreign funding. At neither university is there a separate department of archaeology; rather, archaeology is taught within the history department. Therefore, undergraduates receive training in both disciplines while specializing in their final year in archaeology. Close links are thus forged between archaeology and African history, while very little attention is paid to the natural and earth sciences. Therefore, it is not surprising that the products of this training have chosen to embark upon research into later prehistory, with its potential links to oral tradition and history, rather than the archaeology of early humankind, where the connections lie with geology, palaeontology and other sciences.

Osaga Odak, a Kenyan archaeologist, suggests a different answer to the question of why indigenous archaeologists have been drawn to later prehistory; he believes 'that there is no future for a discipline whose research findings cannot be applied to sociocultural development efforts. This has made it necessary for archaeology to participate in development through ensuring that peoples' culture and history are properly preserved for purposes of identity, self-confidence, and the like' (Odak 1980: 721). He then goes on to bemoan the fact that archaeological resources have been mostly expended on the Stone Age – 'this rather irrelevant effort' (op. cit.) – with the result that archaeology has had little impact on the Kenyan public, who view it as 'an occupation for foreigners with funds to throw away' (op. cit.). While Odak may have been deliberately provocative in the expression of his views, his basic sentiments may well hit the mark.

Recent archaeological research, much of it undertaken by the British Institute in Eastern Africa, has succeeded in reversing the colonial denial of an indigenous African past; this has been achieved by stressing autochthonous developments and by claiming an importance for East African prehistory on the world stage through arguing for a great antiquity for various innovations in the region. In the latter context the discoveries of early hominids and their artefacts at Olduvai Gorge and in the Lake Turkana region are, contra Odak, matters of considerable national pride in Tanzania and Kenya, with the name 'Leakey' being known in most households, and without the aid of television.

The 'Neolithic', both the term itself and what it signifies, has in many ways been central to the concerns of what might be dubbed 'nationalist archaeology'. Rightmire (1975) opened the door for the post-colonial reinterpretation of the 'Neolithic' when he debunked the idea of a Caucasoid physical type in the East African skeletal record. In addition, on the terminological front it had already been mooted that 'Neolithic' be abandoned as 'cumbersome' and 'subjective', in the 1960s trend of disposing with inappropriate European labels (Sutton 1966: 38). Kenyan reaction to these two papers well illustrates the points made in the previous paragraph. On the one hand Rightmire's results were applauded as further evidence that the East African 'Neolithic' was essentially indigenous in origin (Onyango-Abuje 1976; Onyango-Abuje and Wandibba 1979); on the other hand it was strongly argued that the term 'Neolithic' should be retained as it was used elsewhere in the Old World and there was no reason why Africa should be treated as something apart (Onyango-Abuje 1976: 16). Recently, the term 'Pastoral Neolithic' (Bower et al. 1977) has met with widespread favour in the region.

Nationalist sentiment towards the great antiquity of indigenous developments in East Africa was well served by claims for the presence of domestic stock in central Kenya by the sixth millennium BC (Bower and Nelson 1978), and possibly as early as the terminal Pleistocene (Nelson, pers. comm.). These claims met with ready acceptance (e.g. R.E. Leakey 1980: 6), despite the fact that most of the evidence has not yet been published. Claims for iron-smelting in the first millennium BC in the interlacustrine area (Schmidt 1978) and for the presence of pottery in the Early Holocene at various Rift Valley sites (Bower and Nelson 1978) have also been welcomed and have further encouraged the reaction against interpretations based upon ideas of migrations and diffusion (e.g. Lwanga-Lunyiigo 1976; Onyango-Abuje 1980). These developments have been repeated in the study of coastal archaeology in which a greater appreciation of the influence of the interior is evident (e.g. Nurse and Spear 1985). New work has suggested that the early coastal towns were not colonies of the Persian Gulf, but indigenous settlements, later Islamicised, founded to gain access to the burgeoning Indian Ocean trade of the ninth century AD (Allen 1981; Horton 1984). The Swahili people, long characterized as simply the result of miscegenation between Arabs and Africans, have thus been given a new identity and historical tradition (see e.g. Allen 1982; Nurse and Spear 1985).

Substantial achievements have been made by nationalist archaeology in East Africa within the last decade. Many of the theories that buttressed colonial ideology have been overturned and replaced by models emphasizing indigenous innovation and development. In using the term 'nationalist archaeology' I have not wished to imply that this archaeology is in some sense not 'true' archaeology; rather the purpose has been merely to emphasize the contrast with colonialist interpretations and to show how these new models have a relevance for the creation of historical pride in the East African peoples. Indeed the rise of nationalist archaeology has not involved any radical reorientation of archaeological method and theory – the eyes of the archaeologists have remained the same, it is merely the tint of the spectacles that has changed. Nor would it necessarily be correct to say that it is the nationalism which has motivated the research; rather it would appear to be the case that research priorities are established on the basis of previous work, predominantly upon academic interests, but that the archaeologists involved have not been slow in grasping the implications of their results for promoting nationalist perspectives about the past. These developments were not restricted to the discipline of archaeology; indeed they were part and parcel of a broader upheaval within the social sciences as a whole, detailed discussion of which is unfortunately not feasible within the restricted length of this chapter.

Most archaeologists now active in East Africa are products of the ecological functionalist archaeological schools of the 1960s and early 70s; they are, to use current jargon (e.g. Hodder 1986), processualists. The Marxist, structuralist and post-structuralist schools of archaeology have as yet no adherents, it seems, in East Africa. The region has, however, been used as an ethnographic testing-ground for the development of new approaches in archaeology and the study of material culture (e.g. Hodder 1982; Larick 1985; Moore 1986). These ethno-archaeological studies have had little impact or relevance to local archaeology. This is to be lamented since it promotes an image of western archaeological theory exploiting Africa's ethnographic wealth without any compensation in the form of better understanding of the continent's prehistory, beyond, that is, whatever might become the theoretical orthodoxy of the 1990s and thence applied to African archaeology. The development of ethno-archaeological studies of particular relevance to the understanding of East African prehistory is perhaps an important goal to which a handful of projects have begun to point the way (e.g. Ammerman et. al. 1978; Larick 1986; Mbae 1986; Robbins 1973; Sutton 1984). In this respect there would appear to be tremendous potential in conducting ethno-archaeological research in conjunction with historical and archaeological work in regions where one can demonstrate cultural/ethnic continuity from the prehistoric past to the present.

Summary

This brief review has examined the changing research priorities that have motivated archaeological work in East Africa over roughly the last sixty years. In the colonial period the few professional archaeologists working in the region devoted most of their attention to the establishment of a culture-stratigraphic framework for the Stone Age and the search for human ancestors. Later prehistory was left mainly to amateur historians, who sought the origins of the present inhabitants of East Africa in the Mediterranean world. Following independence in the early 1960s and the upsurge in the number of archaeologists working in East Africa, which resulted from the great expansion in the universities of Europe and America in the same period, much more professional effort was expended on later prehistory, particularly the Iron Age, though the study of human origins, not surprisingly, continued to attract attention. The training of indigenous archaeologists is a feature mostly of the last decade. While archaeological results have served to bolster dominant ideologies – both colonialist and nationalist – the character of the research undertaken has been moulded by changing paradigms within the discipline. An organic concept of culture, in which change was to be explained through diffusion or evolution, permeated Stone Age studies in the formative years of East African archaeology under the leadership of Louis Leakey. In the last couple of decades the organic model has given way to the ecological paradigm, but migration and diffusion have remained as important explanatory devices in Iron Age research. The major focus of a great deal of East African archaeology remains the construction of regional culture-stratigraphic sequences; that this should be the case after more than half a century of archaeological endeavour indicates how little we yet know about East African prehistory. We have literally hardly scratched the surface of the archaeological record.

Acknowledgements

This chapter was first presented to a staff seminar of the Department of History, University of Nairobi; I thank all the participants for their helpful comments. The subsequent revised version was read by Curtis Marean, Edward Steinhart and John Sutton, but these gentlemen should not be held responsible for the inadequacies of the final product.

6 Late Quaternary Archaeological Research in the Horn of Africa

STEVEN A. BRANDT & RODOLFO FATTOVICH

Introduction

The purpose of this chapter is to present an overview of the history of late Quaternary (Upper Pleistocene and Holocene) archaeological research in the Horn of Africa (Djibouti, Ethiopia and Somalia). The chapter is not meant to be an exhaustive review of the literature, but rather an objective and subjective outline of the development of archaeological thought on the later prehistory and early history of the Horn.

We have elected to concentrate upon three subjects which, we believe, clearly demonstrate the historical course of archaeology in the Horn: (1) the evolution of the Axumite kingdom; (2) the origins of food production; and (3) the later prehistory of hunter/gatherers.

The evolution of complex societies: the Axumite kingdom

The first western scholars to write about Ethiopia's past concerned themselves almost exclusively with the origins of the Axumite kingdom. For 300 years inquiry into Axumite origins was dominated by the question: Who were the people that founded the kingdom? Drawing essentially upon the little linguistic data available at the time, the German historian J. Ludolf published in 1691 that the Axumite kingdom was founded by the 'Habashat', a Semitic-speaking South Arabian tribe who migrated to northern Ethiopia in ancient times (Ludolf 1691). This proposed linguistic connection between Semitic-speaking peoples and the origins of Axum was to dominate intellectual thought until the present day.

After visiting Ethiopia in 1769 James Bruce (1790) speculated that the large 'storied' stelae of Axum were built by Ptolemaic Greeks rather than South Arabians, while the other ruins were of ancient Egyptian origin. H. Salt, who in 1805 conducted the first archaeological reconnaissance of Axum, also proposed that the stelae were built by Greek craftsmen employed by the Axumite kings (Salt 1814). Salt also argued against an exclusively South Arabian origin of the Axumite kingdom, claiming that Ge'ez (the ancient language of Ethiopia) and South Arabic were two separate languages derived from a common (?Hebraic) linguistic ancestor. The Habashat people therefore represented a combination of indigenous Africans and foreign emigrants. T. Lefèbvre (1845–54), a Frenchman who explored and recorded many ancient sites in northern Ethiopia between 1839 and 1843, suggested that the Axumite kingdom arose from contact between Greeks or Byzantine settlers and local Ethiopian populations. However, historians and philologists of the early 1800s were quick to reject hypotheses incorporating Greek and Egyptian influences. This was due in part to the linguists' dogma of a South Arabian origin, as well as the lack of any specific evidence to support a Greek or Egyptian presence.

The discovery by J. Halevy in 1869–70 of the ancient South Arabian civilizations of Saba and Ma'in, combined with Ethiopia's first professional excavations at Adulis, Yeha and Axum (Bent 1893), provided an important turning point in the study of Axumite origins. The South Arabian discoveries and their numerous South Arabic pre-Islamic inscriptions supplied for the first time data with which to compare Ethiopian discoveries. Bent drew upon these data to argue that his Ethiopian excavations of Sabean-like ruins and inscriptions pre-dating Axumite levels suggested a first millennium BC colonization of northern Ethiopia by South Arabians. These latter populations integrated, both physically and culturally, with the indigenous Ethiopians to form the Habashat people of Axum.

At the end of the nineteenth century E. Glaser, an Austrian epigraphist and historian, attempted to reconcile the linguistic evidence for South Arabian migrations with the new epigraphical and archaeological evidence from South Arabia and Ethiopia. He suggested that the Habashat were a South Arabian tribe who moved from the Hadramawt into the Horn in prehistoric times, becoming the most important Semitic-speaking people of the region (Glaser 1895). The Habashat soon came under control of the Sabeans who colonized Ethiopia during the first millennium BC. By the end of the first millennium BC the Habashat regained independence and founded the kingdom of Axum. Glaser's explanation for the origins of the Semitic-speaking peoples of Ethiopia gained wide acceptance and was to have long-standing influence on future studies.

Archaeological research into the origins of the Axumite kingdom increased substantially at the beginning of this century, with Italian and German archaeological missions largely responsible for a shift away from speculation to description and classification of archaeological finds. Coming on the heels of their country's military and poltical forays into Eritrea and northern Ethiopia, Italian archaeologists focussed upon: (1) the excavation of the ancient Axumite port of Adulis on the Eritrean coast (Paribeni 1907); and (2) a systematic geological, geographical and archaeological reconnaissance of the Eritrean plateau. The Italian investigations resulted in the documentation and description of virtually all surface monuments (Dainelli and Marinelli 1912).

The Deutsche-Aksum Expedition (Littmann et al. 1913) laid the foundation for all future studies of the material (especially architectural) remains of ancient northern Ethiopian complex societies. German research included a detailed study of the archaeological sites scattered along the route from Asmara to Axum as well as the first complete survey of Axum itself. The Deutsche-Aksum Expedition also recorded many South Arabic and Ge'ez inscriptions indicative of South Arabian (Sabean) occupation of the country prior to the rise of Axum. This prompted the Germans to accept uncritically the linguistics-based hypothesis that all basic features of Axumite society derived from earlier Near Eastern and/or South Arabian populations.

Four major syntheses of ancient Ethiopian history appeared in the 1920s (Kammerer 1926; Budge 1928; Conti Rossini 1928; Coulbeaux 1929). Arguably the most influential was Conti Rossini's *Storia d'Ethiopia*, which drew upon linguistic, philological, epigraphical, historical and archaeological data to produce a history of Ethiopia from the earliest times to the advent of the Salomonid dynasty in the fourteenth century AD. Conti Rossini (1928) argued that such 'civilized' features as food production and a state form of political organization were introduced into northern Ethiopia by South Arabian groups who colonized the region in the first millennium BC. The South Arabians first occupied the Red Sea coast from

Assab to Massawa in order to control the trade routes. Later they moved into the highlands, subduing the indigenous Cushitic farmers and pastoral populations.

The main body of the South Arabian colonizers, the Habashat, came from south-western Yemen, but during the second half of the first millennium BC came under the political control of the Sabean kingdom. By the end of the first millenium BC the Habashat had regained political control, and in collaboration with indigenous populations established autonomous kingdoms. The kingdoms gradually grew in wealth and power as Roman trade in the Red Sea and Indian Ocean expanded during the first centuries AD. By the end of the first century AD Axum was just one of many polities. However, during the second-third centuries AD Axum increased its power base by conquering neighbouring tribes and small kingdoms, expanding its dominion to include South Arabia and sending military expeditions as far north as Meroe. By the fourth century AD the process of state formation in northern Ethiopia was complete as Axum became the major intermediary in the trade between Rome and India.

The lack of archaeological research in northern Ethiopia between the 1920s and 1950s assured that Conti Rossini's speculative account of the rise of Axum remained essentially unchallenged (and untested) into the 1960s (and for some scholars still remains undisputed [e.g. Ricci 1984].

With the establishment of the French Ethiopian Archaeological Institute in 1952 and subsequent excavations of such sites as Matara, Yeha and Axum, archaeological emphasis shifted to the construction of culture-historic sequences. F. Anfray (1964, 1967, 1968) distinguished two main periods corresponding to different stages of state formation. The Pre-Axumite Period (c. 500 BC–AD 100), characterized by the appearance of the earliest urban settlements on the plateau, was further divided into two phases: (1) an 'Ethiopian-Sabean' phase (c. 500–300 BC) reflecting probable direct contact between indigenous Ethiopians and the kingdom of Saba, and a later 'Intermediate' phase (c. 300 BC–AD 100) where South Arabian influence was considerably less evident as an autochthonous Ethiopian culture began to emerge. Iron was also introduced into Ethiopia at this time. The Axumite Period (c. 100–1000) represented the florescence of the kingdom of Axum and was tentatively divided into two 'epochs', Axumite 1 (c. AD 100–400/500) and Axumite 2 (c. 600–800), each roughly corresponding to pre-Christian and Christian periods. In conclusion, Anfray argued that the Axumite kingdom owed its origins to contacts between indigenous African societies and small groups of South Arabian emigrants. South Arabian ethnic and cultural influence was gradually absorbed by local populations through acculturation. The local population also came under the influence of : (1) the kingdoms of Meroe and Achemenids in early Pre-Axumite times; (2) the Greek and Romans in late Pre-Axumite/early Axumite Periods: and (3) the Byzantines and Syrians during the later Axumite periods.

Additional support for Anfray's interpretation of the archaeological record came from new epigraphical and linguistic studies of pre-Axumite South Arabic inscriptions. Drewes (1962) suggested that an indigenous Semitic-speaking (Ge'ez) people were already living in Northern Ethiopia in the early 1st millennium BC. These people formed the basic ethnic and cultural stock for both the pre-Axumite and Axumite states, and were only minimally affected by Sabean influence in the mid-1st millennium BC. On epigraphical and archaeological grounds Schneider (1976) also argued that an autochthonous urban society was already in

6:1 *Excavations at Axum 1973. Neville Chittick in trench*

existence at the beginning of the 1st millennium BC. He emphasized that the roots of the Axumite civilization lay in Africa, not Southern Arabia.

In 1973 and 1974 N. Chittick of the British Institute in Eastern Africa directed excavations at Axum, with the purpose of shedding light on the age and functions of the monumental architecture (fig. 6:1). Preliminary results (Chittick 1974) indicated that the stelae, situated near the royal cemetery and part of a ceremonial centre, dated to no earlier than the first century AD. Such a late date has prompted Fattovich (in press) to suggest that the stelae are probably of African and not South Arabian origin.

Axumite research of a fundamentally different and historically important nature also occurred during the 1970s. Rather than being concerned exclusively with questions of population movement, description and/or culture history, archaeologists began initial explorations into the processes of northern Ethiopian state formation. In 1974 J. Michels (1979) conducted the first systematic archaeological survey of the Axumite region. Working under the assumption that the dynamics of Axumite society can be understood only in terms of a total picture of the settlement system (Michels 1979: 22), Michels undertook a stratified random sample survey of a 500 sq. km area of the Axum region, resulting in the complete coverage of 200 sq. km and the identification of 250 sites.

While a monograph on the results of the survey is nearing completion (J. Michels pers. comm.), preliminary analyses (Michels 1986) reveal eight distinct culture-historical phases dated by obsidian hydration to 700 BC–AD 1000. The spatial and temporal distribution of settlements argue for significant differences in site patterning. Michels suggests these differences reflect changes in the socio-political processes of state formation from the initial appearance of farming villages to the development of complex urban centres with monumental public works, social stratification, intensive agriculture and other aspects of complex societies:

> When fully analyzed, the data ought to very sensitively document shifts in agricultural strategy and alterations in the organization and distribu-

tion of population over the landscape. This will enable us to glimpse the economic, political, and demographic frameworks within which sites ... have undergone growth, modification, and ultimately, abandonment. (Michels 1979: 29)

K.W. Butzer's geo-archaeological research in 1973 represents another landmark study in our understanding of the evolution of Ethiopian complex societies. Drawing upon a preliminary analysis of alluviation and soil erosion in the Axumite area, Butzer (1981) concluded that the development of the Axumite kingdom into a major urban and commercial complex would not have been possible without the ameliorating climatic conditions and increased rainfall beginning in the first century A.D. that:

> vastly improved the surface and subsurface water supply, doubled the length of the growing season, and created an environment comparable to that of modern central Ethiopia – where two crops can be grown per annum without the aid of irrigation. This appears to explain how one of the marginal agricultural environments of Ethiopia was able to support the demographic base that made this far-flung commercial empire possible. (Butzer 1981: 491)

Butzer also suggested that a chance series of mutually reinforcing processes related to changes in access to raw materials, foreign relations, productivity, demography, socio-politics and a return to more arid conditions in the eighth century AD led to environmental degradation and the collapse of the Axumite kingdom.

Finally, mention must be made of the 1979 publication of Y. Kobishchanov's *Aksum*. The original publication, printed in Russian in 1966 (Kobishchanov 1966), was a detailed, wide-ranging review of Axumite economic and socio-political systems drawn essentially from epigraphic and other historical sources. Unfortunately the Russian edition guaranteed a very limited readership outside the Soviet Union, and as a result *Aksum* contributed little during the 1960s and 70s to Western scholars' thoughts on the evolution of the Axumite kingdom. However a revised edition was translated into English under the editorship of J. Michels (Kobishchanov 1979). Although not without its problems (Munro-Hay 1982), *Aksum* provides tantalizing, albeit speculative, hypotheses on the political, economic, social and ideological organization of the Axumite state. The potential for archaeologists to test these hypotheses remains perhaps the most important aspect of the book for archaeologists. As Michels (1979: 30) has stated: 'Kobishchanov has offered numerous tentative reconstructions that give focus to Axumite institutions, society, culture, and history. That focus can guide problem-oriented research for years to come.'

Unfortunately the political events of 1974 to the present effectively ended fieldwork in northern Ethiopia. In fact, all archaeological fieldwork in Ethiopia was suspended officially in 1982 by the Ethiopian government pending the establishment of new antiquities laws (and as of August 1988 archaeological fieldwork had still not resumed). Recent archaeological research into the development of northern Ethiopian complex societies has therefore focussed upon refinements and reassessments of previously excavated data. This has included further epigraphical investigations (e.g. Munro-Hay 1982) as well as efforts to document more fully the role of indigenous Ethiopian societies in the establishment of the Axumite kingdom (Fattovich 1977, 1978, 1980, 1982, 1984, in press).

The origins of food production

Investigations into the origins of food production in the Horn began in the early part of this century when scientists conducted research on the biogeographical origins and distribution of cultigens. Impressed by the quantity and diversity of domesticated cereals, spices, vegetables, drugs and oil plants, the Russian agronomist N. Vavilov (1926) proposed Ethiopia as one of the eight world centres of origin for cultivated plants. The biogeographer Carl Sauer (1952: 76) also considered Ethiopia to be one of the world's greatest and oldest centres of domestic seed plants'. Nevertheless, in spite of continuing interest amongst biogeographers and agronomists (Harlan 1969), archaeological inquiries into the origins of food production in the Horn have been surprisingly few.

Although P. Graziosi's 1935 excavations in Somalia (Graziosi 1940), may have yielded the first evidence of food production in the Horn (domesticated cattle and ovicaprids), it was not until 1954 that an archaeologist attempted to consider how and why food production arose in this region. Impressed by the numerous rock art sites depicting humped and humpless cattle, camels and ovicaprids in styles reminiscent of the Neolithic rock art of the Sahara and Nile Valley, J.D. Clark (1954: 330) suggested that pastoralism was the direct result of:

> a definite migration of peoples into the Horn of Africa during Late Stone Age times, bringing with them traits which link them with the Saharan Neolithic cultures, and with the Neolithic B group people of the Fayum. This migration took place during a period when climatic conditions were wetter than at the present time.

Although Clark did not address the question of agricultural origins, the cultural anthropologist G.P. Murdock, drawing largely upon ethnographic and linguistic data, postulated that some time prior to 5000 BP Eastern Sudanic-speaking 'Pre-Nilotes' introduced Sudanic agricultural practices (e.g. a sedentary lifestyle, animal husbandry and the use of hoes and digging sticks for cultivating sorghum, cotton, sesame and other crops) to the 'Bushmanoid' and 'Caucasoid Cushite' hunter-gatherers of western Ethiopia (Murdock 1959: 170, 181, 187). The 'Cushites' soon took it upon themselves to domesticate indigenous Ethiopian plants, and as a result of geographical isolation, three separate centres of Cushitic economy, language and culture evolved.

Like Clark, Murdock also regarded migration as the prime mover behind the origins of agriculture in the Horn. None the less, he was the first scholar to put forward the idea of independent invention and was the first to realize that the complexity and diversity of modern food-producing systems in the Horn demanded equally complex and diverse prehistoric origins. But perhaps the most important aspect of Murdock's work was that it stimulated considerable discussion and debate amongst archaeologists and other anthropologists (Stahl 1984).

In the 1960s and 70s, Clark expanded his pastoral model to incorporate hypotheses on the origins of agriculture in the Horn. Postulating that a mid-Holocene period of environmental desiccation forced Nubian 'C-Group' pastoralists to search for new grazing lands, Clark (1962) argued that as pastoralists moved south into the temperate Ethiopian highlands they introduced not only cattle pastoralism but possibly wheat and barley cultivation to the indigenous 'Afro-Mediterranean Cushite' and 'Negroid' hunter-gatherers. Clearly influenced by the writings of Murdock, Clark

(1967) later proposed that the increasingly arid conditions of the mid-Holocene forced 'Pre-Nilote' populations (Murdock 1959: 170) out of the lowlands of eastern Sudan and western Ethiopia on to the Ethiopian Plateau where they introduced farming to the hunter-gatherers of highland Ethiopia. These latter groups then took it upon themselves to cultivate such indigenous Ethiopian plants as 'noog' (*Guizotia abyssinica*) and 't'eff' (*Eragrostis teff*). Clark (1976; 1980) also hypothesized that by 3000 BP subsistence farming was the dominat mode of production across most of the Ethiopian highlands. Only the economies of the Afar Rift, the eastern highlands around Harar and northern Somalia were still based predominatly upon cattle pastoralism. Around 2500 BP Semitic-speaking populations from southern Arabia introduced dromedary camels and humped cattle (*Bos indicus*) into the Horn.

While all of Clark's models focus upon environmental change, coupled with primary diffusion, as primary causes of food production in the Horn, his interpretations of the effects of environmental change upon society have altered dramatically over the years. In the 1950s Clark viewed environmental change as a 'permissive factor' (Stahl 1984: 19) which allowed mobile pastoral populations to colonize new lands and introduce a better way of life to the indigenous hunting-gathering populations of the Horn. In his later writings, Clark perceived environmental change as a 'stress factor' (*ibid.*) whereby deteriorating environmental conditions created a climate of economic and social unrest, forcing people to move and/or take up a new mode of food production. This shift in interpretation was probably due to at least two factors: (1) new data on the timing and extent of Holocene climatic changes (e.g. Butzer *et. al.* 1972); and (2) recent hunter-gatherer studies which have questioned the notion that food production is intrinsically superior (e.g. Lee and DeVore 1968).

The historical linguist C. Ehret (1976, 1979) proposed a radically different model, arguing instead that Ethiopian agriculture, which evolved considerably earlier than other models suggested, owed little to developments outside the Horn. Drawing upon human demographic pressure as the prime mover for food production, Ehret suggested that by the end of the Pleistocene 'proto-Afroasiatic'-speaking peoples occupying north-eastern Africa were engaged in the intensive harvesting of wild cereals due to a severe food crisis brought about by demographic pressure. Intensive harvesting soon led to domestication, and by 7000 BP Omotic-speaking peoples were growing ensete in the southern highlands while 'proto-Cushites' were cultivating such indigenous cereals as t'eff and/or finger millet in the northern highlands. The proto-Cushites also raised humpless cattle and ovicaprids which, according to Ehret, diffused into the Horn after the establishment of agriculture. By 5000 BP the farmers of highland Ethiopia embraced Nile Valley wheat and barley as well as the plough and draft animals, while Southern Cushitic-speaking peoples migrated into southern Somalia from south-eastern Ethiopia with their livestock and (possibly) sorghum. A thousand years later, Northern and Central Cushitic-speaking cattle pastoralists established themselves in the Afar Rift and along the Red Sea, while Eastern Cushitic cattle pastoralists moved into the southern Afar and possiblly northern Somalia by 3000 BP.

Ehret's model represents a bold attempt at dealing with the historical complexities of prehistoric food production in the Horn. However his use of overpopulation as the causal explanation for Ethiopian food production suffers from the same theoretical and methodological problems (e.g. Cowgill 1979; Hassan 1981) which beset Cohen's (1977) original treatise. Furthermore, Ehret not surprisingly is concerned almost exclusively with the historical timing and geographic location of events rather than with their socio-political and economic effects.

Unfortunately, as is the case with virtually all aspects of archaeology in the Horn, the evidence to support or refute models concerned with the origins of food production is meagre. The surface finds suggestive of food production (e.g. Arkell 1954) provide little substantive information, while the few excavated sites funish only: (1) a few scraps of bone, horn and/or teeth tentatively identified as domesticated stock; and/or (2) sparse macrobotanical remains of cultigens (Clark and Williams 1978; Dombrowski 1971; Phillipson 1977b). Furthermore, J.C. Dombrowski's research in the highlands of north-central Ethiopia almost two decades ago still remains the only archaeological project to be devoted exclusively to investigating the origins of food production in the Horn (Dombrowski 1971).

In a recent review of the origins of food production in Ethiopia, S.A. Brandt (1984) criticized previously constructed models as being too culture-historically oriented and/or difficult (if not impossible) to test. He suggested that:

> Perhaps a more desirable avenue of research for the near future ... would be to develop research programs designed to investigate the processes involved in the transition from hunting/gathering to food production, and the concomitant social, demographic, and ecological effects of such a major economic change. Such programs would not require a vast understanding of Ethiopian culture-history (although they would certainly contribute to it) and could be limited to a geographical area small enough to be archaeologically testable. (Brandt 1984: 185).

To exemplify his position, Brandt constructed a model for the evolution of 'ensete' (*Ensete ventricosum*) cultivation, the most economically important cultigen of the Omotic and Eastern Cushitic speaking farmers of southern Ethiopia. He hypothesized that the hyper-aridity of the terminal Pleistocene resulted in major changes in hunter/gatherer adaptations, including the alteration of foraging tactics to allow for the greater utilization of ensete as a dependable, stress-relieving food supply. Once ensete was domesticated following a period of experimentation, a horticultural system based upon shifting cultivation and increased sedentariness evolved. As populations increased through the process of 'settling down' (Harris 1978), it became more difficult for groups to bud off and colonize new lands. This would have soon created new ecological, demographic and socio-political demands upon the land and people.

Brandt futher hypothesized that once domesticated animals were introduced into southern Ethiopia some time during the early to mid-Holocene, the use of domesticated animal manure to fertilize ensete fields would have arisen as a way to increase ensete yields without having to practise shifting cultivation. A more sedentary lifestyle, in addition to the need for a large labour force, would have resulted in significant population growth. This could have been partially offset by increasing ensete production as well as developing ways to postpone consumption and prevent surplus crop spoilage, such as the current system of storing fermented ensete in deep earthen pits.

In a similar vein, Brandt and Carder (1987) have recently advanced a model for the evolution of pastoralism in the Horn which focusses upon pastoral rock art. They postulate that postoralists and/or their products diffused into the Horn from northern Africa following a mid-Holocene period of environmental desiccation. After establishing a pattern of seasonal transhumance involving the movement of herds from highland to lowland pastures, pastoral populations increased in size and density, eventually coming into competition with already established highland farming communities for pasture and seasonal labour. Risk minimization strategies (Johnson 1982), including rituals, evolved to ensure co-operation and participation between these populations. The depiction of pastoral stock (i.e. humpless cattle [*Bos taurus*] and ovicaprids) in caves and shelters may have played an important role in such rituals.

With more favourable climatic conditions *c.* 2000 years ago, increased availability of resources would have resulted in a reduction in transhumance and the devolpment of more spatially focussed settlements. With an increase in both pastoral populations and their livestock, social mechanisms operating not only at an inter-regional scale but also at an intra-regional level would have become necessary. This would have resulted in an increase in the number and stylistic diversity of rock art sites as well as the spatial clustering of sites into ecologically distinct territories. Following a return to more arid conditions and a resulting increase in population pressure after 2000 BP, at least two possible risk minimization strategies would have become available: (1) the inclusion of horticulture in the pastoral subsistence base, resulting in the escalation of ritual behaviour at the local level and unparalleled diversity and increase in tribal symbols indicative of territoriality; and (2) the adoption of more drought-resistant livestock species such as camels and Zebu cattle, followed by pastoral expansion into more arid lands and a shift in rock art emphasis upon the latter species.

The later prehistory of hunter-gatherers

The first account of Stone Age sites in the Horn was published in 1882 when the French explorer G. Revoil reported the discovery of stone artifact scatters in north-eastern Somalia (Revoil 1882). Over the next three decades French, British and Italian explorers, scientists, colonial administrators and military personnel collected stone artefacts from numerous surface sites throughout the Horn (Clark 1954: 16–42). Many of these collections eventually found their way into European and African museums and universities where archaeologists described and classified them using prevalent European typologies (e.g. Breuil and Kelley 1936; Burkitt and Barrington Brown 1931; Jousseaume 1895; Puccioni 1936; Teilhard de Chardin 1930). Unfortunately virtually all of these collections are incomplete, selected samples lacking adequate provenience (Mussi 1974–5).

In 1929 Teilhard de Chardin and H. de Monfried, in the course of a survey of what is now eastern Ethiopia, conducted the first professional Stone Age archaeological excavation in the Horn (Teilhard de Chardin 1930). A few years later the Italian archaeologist P. Graziosi (fig. 6:2) undertook the first professional excavations in Somalia when he test-excavated a rock shelter at Buur Heybe in the southern part of the country and a small cave near the coastal town of Eyl in north-eastern Somalia (Graziosi 1940). Comparing their material with previous research in the Horn, East Africa and Europe, Teilhard de Chardin and Graziosi established the first, albeit tentative, Stone Age cultural sequences for the Horn.

Teilhard's excavations at Porc Epic cave near Dire Dawa in eastern Ethiopia yielded 'Micoquian bifaces' and other tools of 'Upper Palaeolithic' age, (Teilhard de Chardin 1930). Graziosi's excavations of Gogoshiis Qabe rock shelter at Buur Heybe, southern Somalia uncovered evidence for four

6:2 *Paolo Graziosi* (on left) *in Somalia 1935*

major culture-historic units spanning the Upper Pleistocene and Holocene. From earliest to latest these were: (1) 'Stillbay'; (2) 'Magosian'; (3) 'Eibian'; and (4) an unnamed 'degenerate' industry associated with pottery and rare domesticated fauna. By applying such terms as Stillbay and Magosian, Graziosi (1940) concluded that the Stone Age cultures of Somalia were similar technologically to other Southern and Eastern African industries (Goodwin and Van Riet Lowe 1929; Leakey 1931). However, Graziosi also argued that the Somali industries, although younger in age than the European Stone Age sequence, were essentially of local origin, changing gradually through transitional stages.

During the 1940s, British military personnel conducted the majority of Stone Age research in the Horn. Although this usually consisted of unsystematic sampling of surface occurences, some excavations and more planned surveys were undertaken (e.g. Clark 1954; Moysey 1943). In 1954 J.D. Clark published the influential *Prehistoric Cultures of the Horn of Africa*, the first major attempt to place the prehistory of the Horn of Africa into a regional and pan-African culture-historic/climatological framework.

Incorporating data from his own 1940s fieldwork in Ethiopia and Somalia as well as other investigators' research in the Horn, Clark (1954: 155) drew upon Southern African Stone age nomenclature to divide the later prehistory of the Horn into the 'Middle Stone Age' (MSA) and 'Later Stone Age' (LSA) (fig. 6:3). The MSA encompassed three 'culture complexes' (the 'Acheulio-Levalloisian', 'Levalloisian' and 'Somaliland Stillbay') while the LSA included two: the 'Doian' and 'Somaliland Wilton'. Transitional between the MSA and LSA were the 'Somaliland Magosian' and 'Hargeisan' complexes. Clark was never explicit about what distinguished MSA from LSA cultures, although his writings suggest technological and typological criteria: the MSA was characterized by prepared core technology and bifacial points, and the LSA was distinguished by blade technology and microliths.

Clark emphasized both the migration of hominid populations and

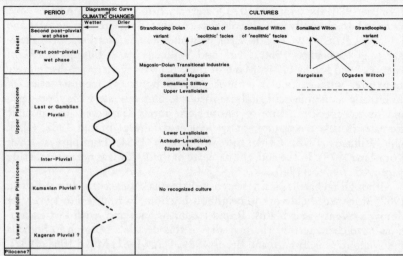

6:3 *J.D. Clark's culture-historic sequence for the Horn (after Clark 1954)*

localized adaptations as the most likely explanatory factors for prehistoric culture change in the Horn. The Stillbay, for example, was probably 'indicative of a northward migration of Stillbay stock into the Horn' (Clark 1954: 321). The Doian may have represented the southward migration of LSA populations from northern Africa. On the other hand, the Stillbay 'developed directly into the Magosian without any outside interference' (Clark 1954: 328). The Hargeisan showed 'typological similarities to the Upper Capsian of Tunisia', and owed its origin to the 'existence of a similar ecology and . . . a similar form of raw material rather than to any cultural connections' (Clark 1954: 329). Clark, like Graziosi, also considered the Stone Age industries of the Horn to be later in age than typologically equivalent industries in Europe.

Compared to the establishment of culture-historic sequences, Graziosi and Clark relegated little time and effort to the reconstruction of prehistoric settlement patterns of diet. However, Graziosi (1940) took the innovative step of analysing soil samples and faunal remains for information on past environments and human diets. Clark (1954: 362–7) also reported on the faunal samples from his excavations, but these were in the form of 'laundry lists' which had little interpretive value.

Although Clark never had time to conduct systematic settlement pattern studies, he did attempt to plot the distribution of known surface and excavated sites by culture complex and geographic region. Clark also hypothesized about the effects of climatic change upon prehistoric settlement patterns:

> the sites of the Somaliland Stillbay Culture which existed during the dry period at the end of the Upper Pleistocene, are confined very largely to the valleys of the bigger rivers or the large pans and springs, but the occupation of the Doian and Somaliland Wilton peoples on the other hand, who lived at the time of the 'Neolithic Wet Phase' . . . are extensively distributed throughout the plateau. (Clark 1954: 14)

During the 1950s and 1960s archaeologists conducted surprisingly little Stone Age archaeological research in the Horn. Those few projects (e.g. Bailloud 1965; Graziosi 1954) continued to focus upon the establishment of culture-historic sequences, doing little to alter the prevailing view that 'Abyssinia and the Somalilands constituted a blind alley into which there penetrated cultures whose centres were elsewhere' (Alimen 1957: 192).

In the 1970s the tempo of late Quaternary Ethiopian Stone Age research increased dramatically as archaeologists conducted research in the Afar and Ethiopian Rifts as well as the Ethiopian and Somali (South-eastern) Plateaux (e.g. Chavaillon 1980; Clark and Williams 1978; Phillipson 1977b; Wendorf and Schild 1974). Many of these projects were multi-disciplinary in nature, with particular emphasis placed upon the reconstruction of prehistoric economies and land-use patterns. Unfortunately the short-term and/or site-specific nature of the projects rarely translated into notable increases in palaeo-economic or settlement data (e.g. Brandt 1982; Clark and Williams 1978; Clark and Williamson 1984; Humphreys 1978; Kurashina 1978). In the end, the database of the 1970s was not substantially improved over the 1940s.

Although archaeological research in Ethiopia came to an abrupt halt in 1982, Stone Age fieldwork in neighbouring Somalia resumed in 1981 after almost a twenty-year hiatus. Rapid reconnaissance and small test excavations have characterized the majority of this decade's research in Somalia and Djibouti (e.g. Brandt and Brook 1984; Ferry 1981; Mussi 1984, 1987). However, in 1983 S.A. Brandt (1986, 1988) initiated the Buur Ecological and Archaeological Project (BEAP), a long-term multidisciplinary investigation of late Pleistocene/Holocene human adaptations in the inter-riverine region of southern Somalia.

BEAP represents a significant departure from previous Stone Age projects in the Horn. Rather than simply documenting late Quaternary hunter-gatherer variability and culture change in time and space, BEAP attempts to determine how and why hunter-gatherer systems changed. Using a deductive methodology, BEAP is designed to test a microeconomic model based on a cost-benefit analysis of human socio-territorial organization. The testing of such a model involves a long-term commitment to obtaining micro- to macro-regional data through such activities as: (1) the reconstruction of culture-historic sequences and palaeoeconomies from the excavation of a suite of sites; (2) a systematic regional survey of Stone Age settlement patterns and potential natural resources (e.g. edible plants, pottery clays and lithic sources); (3) ethnoarchaeological studies of artifact and site formation processes; and (4) detailed palaeoenvironmental investigations.

Summary

When we began this review we were determined not to force our narrative into pre-conceived 'periods' or 'phases' as some recent histories have done. However, after an examination of the literature we have concluded that late Quaternary archaeological research in the Horn has in fact passed through general stages of development, which in many ways parallel those recognized for New World archaeology (Willey and Sabloff 1980).

Archaeological research prior to the twentieth century (which for all intents and purposes meant Axumite archaeology) focussed essentially upon speculative thought on who the Axumite were and what languages they spoke. Those who engaged in such speculation were explorers, armchair linguists or historians obviously trained in fields other than archaeology. Emphasis was usually placed upon the migration of populations from South Arabia, Egypt or even Europe as the explanation for the rise of Axum, with indigenous Ethiopian populations playing little or no role in Axumite origins.

Towards the end of the nineteenth and into the twentieth century professionally trained European archaeologists introduced survey and excavation methods to the study of the Axumite kingdom. They tended to place particular emphasis upon the description and classification of artifacts and features, as did the few European prehistorians who analysed and classified stone artefacts from the Horn.

In the 1930s and 1940s archaeologists undertook the first Stone Age excavations. Particular attention was paid to stratigraphic excavations for the purposes of: (1) classifying cultures in time and space; and (2) reconstructing palaeoenvironments as a way of relatively dating cultures. Prehistoric archaeologists also began to question why cultures changed, focussing upon migration and environmental change as causal factors. As was common practice at this time in both the Old and the New World, archaeologists paid only lip service to questions of palaeoeconomy and settlement pattern.

During the 1950s and 1960s archaeologists initiated stratigraphic excavations and established culture-historic sequences at pre-Axumite and Axumite sites. Although the frequency of prehistoric archaeological field-work declined, these two decades witnessed a flurry of activity related to the building of models on the origins of food production. Most of these models focussed upon migration and/or diffusion brought about by climatic change as the prime mover. Attempts to correlate ethnographic 'races' with languages and socioeconomic (food producing) systems was another overriding, but ultimately fallacious (MacGaffey 1966: Trigger 1968: 8) concern at this time.

In the 1970s prehistorians organized multi-disciplinary field projects that emphasized: (1) the reconstruction of palaeoenvironments; (2) the establishment of radiometrically dated culture-historic sequences; and (3) the development of a 'palaeoeconomic approach' (Higgs 1972) to prehistory. When it came to explaining culture change, however, these projects made little theoretical headway as they failed to demonstrate (or in some cases even consider) why and how migration, diffusion, demographic pressure and/or environmental alterations actually caused culture change. Axumite research continued to concentrate upon the elucidation of culture-historic sequences and monumental remains, as well as the reevaluation of data pertaining to autochthonus northern Ethiopian societies and the rise of the Axumite kingdom (Anfray 1981). Michels's settlement pattern survey and Butzer's study of the effects of environmental change represented important supplements to the rich, albeit imprecise historical sources (Munro-Hay 1981) that heretofore provided the only data on the processes of Axumite state formation (Kobishchanov 1981).

In the 1980s Ethiopia closed down and Somalia opened up for archaeological research. In general, investigations in Djibouti and Somalia have focussed upon the description and chronological ordering of archaeological sites. However Stone Age studies are now under way in Somalia which promise to shed light not only on culture-history but also on processes of culture change.

Conclusions

Past archaeological research into the later prehistory and early history of the Horn of Africa was steeped in an inductive and 'normative' approach to inquiry where the goals were to: (1) establish artifact-defined 'cultures' across time and space; (2) place these cultures within a palaeoeconomic or historic perspective; and (3) then determine 'the significance of the evidence 'dug out of the soil' (Anfray 1981: 378). Given the dearth of archaeological research in the Horn where fewer than 50 prehistoric or Axumite sites have been excavated, these lines of inquiry must continue to form vital parts of research designs. However, it is imperative that archaeologists also utilize the other side of the coin of scientific method: deductive reasoning. We need to construct and carry out long-term, multi-disciplinary problem-oriented research projects designed explicity to test hypotheses that explain, rather than explain away, how and why cultural systems evolved. Such projects should be conducted at different scales of analysis, often (but not always) centring first upon the macro-region and then telescoping down to various spatial and temporal units of analysis including site-specific micro-scale studies (Brandt 1986).

The few processual studies conducted in the Horn (Brandt 1984, 1988; Brandt and Carder 1987; Butzer 1981) have used microeconomic and/or culture ecological models to explain culture change. While these models have their advantages and shortcomings (e.g. Keene 1983), archaeologists working in the Horn need to develop other testable models which consider political, economic, socioeconomic, ideological, symbolic and other factors in the search for an understanding of the processes of cultural change in the Horn.

The testing of processual models requires archaeologists to dedicate themselves to long-term research projects. Unfortunately the effects of European colonial underdevelopment of Africa in general (e.g. Rodney 1976) and the Horn in particular (e.g. Sbacchi 1985) have meant there is only a handful of professionally trained Djiboutian, Ethiopian and Somali archaeologists capable of conducting such projects, and little government money with which to finance research. This effectively means, at least for the immediate future, that western archaeologists will continue to perform the majority of late Quaternary archaeological research in the Horn.

Trigger (1980), Schmidt (1983) and Hall (1984) have recently commented on the ramifications of European and Euroamerican ideology upon archaeological research in Africa and America. They point out that archaeologists must be more sensitive to the local historical and/or ethnohistorical needs of the host country by developing associated archaeological projects and disseminating the results to the local populace. Archaeologists must also pay closer attention to possible racial or ethnocentric overtones in their work (e.g. South Arabian v. indigenous Ethiopian contributions to the rise of Axum, or the use of such typologies as primitive/civilized or literate/non-literate).

The resolution of this problem lies with the training of more indigenous archaeologists, either at African or non-African universities, and greater financial support from their respective governments and/or international donors. While it is important that these future archaeology students are trained in 'traditional' western archaeological method and theory, it is imperative that their training also includes a solid grounding in ethnohistory, social history, historic preservation and cultural resource management. These latter two fields will become particularly important as the urban centres of the Horn continue their rapid expansion. Historic preservation and cultural resource management may therefore represent a way (perhaps the only way outside of continued collaboration with foreign projects) of generating enough funds to conduct long-term archaeological projects. Only when the problems outlined in this review are resolved will archaeologists be able to make major contributions toward the understanding of late Quaternary cultural evolution in the Horn of Africa.

7 *Phases & Facies*
in the Archaeology of Central Africa

PIERRE DE MARET

Central Africa is archaeologically the least known part of the continent. However, research started there early and was in line with what was being accomplished in other areas. Considering the size and diversity of this region, the results obtained to date remain minimal and very scattered.

Midway between the Mediterranean and the Cape of Good Hope, and between West and East Africa, lies a major crossroads of the African past. Centred in the Zaïre/Congo basin, but touching those of the Niger, the Nile and the Zambezi, this gigantic junction of nearly 5,700,000sq. km – almost as large as West Africa outside the Sahara and the whole of East Africa – is the meeting-point of the principal cultural complexes of the continent. Although historically linked to their neighbours, the people of this region possess a great unity, if only because they are mostly Bantu-speakers. The boundaries of Central Africa are imprecise, but the region is usually considered to comprise Cameroon, southern Chad, the Central African Republic, Equatorial Guinea, Gabon, Congo, Zaïre, Angola, Rwanda and Burundi (fig. 7:1).

Research in Central Africa is hampered by thick vegetation, erosion and the rapid deterioration of archaeological remains. Inadequate roads and the vastness of the region have greatly restricted surveys and excavations.

During the colonial era, Central Africa was divided among nearly all the colonial powers, since the ten modern states which now exist result from the interaction between France, Belgium, Germany, Spain, Portugal and the United Kingdom. The Berlin Conference of 1884–5 was convened to defuse the crisis caused by the conflicting expansionist policies of these powers in this part of the world. Archaeologically the result was a dispersion of effort and a diversity of publications in numerous journals, which often had only limited circulation. However this diversity could provide an opportunity for comparison of the different colonial 'styles' of research, and so enable us to distinguish different phases and facies within the history of Central African archaeology itself. But we must recognize, unfortunately, that on the whole the colonial powers neglected scientific study of their Central African colonies to the benefit of other regions. Not having other colonies, only tiny Belgium concentrated all her efforts on the Belgian Congo, a country 77 times larger than herself. Although the idea is appealing, a comparative study of the different facies presented by colonial archaeology would not therefore have much significance for this chapter, since the comparisons should be made at the continental level. Like Central Africa itself, this chapter will focus on Zaïre where most research has been undertaken, comparisons being made with neighbouring countries whenever possible.

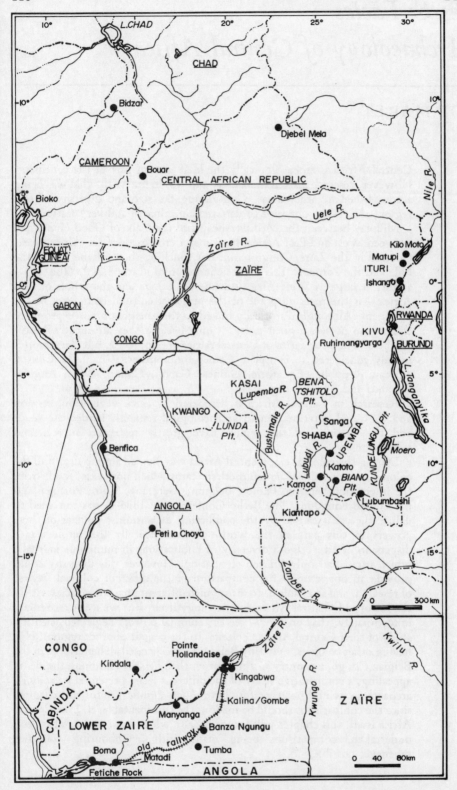

7:1 *Sites mentioned in this chapter*

Phase 1. African and European pioneers

The majority of the peoples of sub-Saharan Africa share with archaeologists a devotion to the past. Interest in the ancestors and the material relics of their existence must have started long before the arrival of the first Europeans. Oral traditions provide numerous examples of a relationship between material relics of the past and the history of a people. Anxious to install mythical lands within the topography of territory familiar to his audience, a narrator frequently made reference to particular places, for example the dwelling place of an ancient king. For recent times, these locations seem to be very precise, but for older periods, it is often an iconotrophic process, whereby a site is fed back into tradition (Vansina, 1985: 187). Accidental discoveries of ancient pottery, skeletons or smelting furnaces are thus integrated into a story.

Integration of the archaeological past into day-to-day living is also marked by the systematic conservation of chance discoveries of ancient objects. Some of these, like polished axes, pottery, bored stones, and cross-shaped copper ingots, are incorporated into rituals as a sort of metaphor of the ancestors. Thus, the first stone artefacts mentioned by European explorers were given to them by the local inhabitants. E.C. Hore (1882), a Master Mariner appointed to the 1877 London Missionary Society's expedition to Central Africa, was the first to receive two bored stones collected on the western shore of Lake Tanganyika by local people who considered them to be messages left by their ancestors. They were kept carefully in baskets or little huts. The great ritual importance of these bored stones has been recently described again in the region (Roberts 1984). Similarly Chief Gambari of the Mount Tenna region in the Uele gave Emin Pasha six beautiful polished axes of haematite and a hammerstone. In turn, the latter gave them to the famous naturalist and explorer, Schweinfurth, who published them (Schweinfurth 1884). Considered to be thunderbolts, these axes were preserved by the inhabitants of the region for numerous generations. H.M. Stanley brought back a similar tool which he received, probably from Emin Pasha, during his relief expedition of 1887–9.

As in other parts of the continent, the first evidence of the past to engage the attention of European explorers directly was rock art. Thus, in 1816 at the mouth of the River Congo, on the left bank, Tuckey observed a rock with engravings which he named 'Fetiche Rock' and of which he published a detailed description (Tuckey 1818).

The extraordinary infatuation for prehistoric research in Europe in the second part of the nineteenth century coincided with colonial expansion in Africa. Exploration of the world and the past was conceptually linked and, beginning in the preceding century, European antiquaries travelled to study ancient monuments in the classical world and in Egypt. Those who could not afford to travel initiated research on the antiquities of their own country (Daniel 1981b: 25). It is not surprising, in this context, that the attention of the first explorers was very soon drawn to stone artefacts, particularly abundant in certain regions. Thus, in 1885, the year of the Berlin Congress, Zboinski, an engineer engaged to study the layout of a railway project in Lower Zaïre, collected the first flaked stone tools from near the Zaïre River in southern Manyanga on the hills, denuded by severe erosion, where they are found in abundance. In announcing this discovery in 1887, Dupont, Director of the Royal Institute of Natural Sciences of Belgium, saw these artefacts as proof of the existence of a true Stone Age in these regions, extending to Mozambique and Angola, where Zboinski had also found artefacts (Dupont 1887a). Dupont (1887b) also insisted on what

he called 'the universal uniformity of features of this Stone Age', which
was in accord with the evolutionary theories of the time. These discoveries
were confirmed by those of another engineer, Cocheteux (1888–9), also in
Lower Zaïre, and then by Dupont himself, who made a study-tour to the
region in 1887 (Dupont 1889). Other discoveries were made during the
construction of the Matadi–Léopoldville, now Kinshasa, railway line
which took place between 1889 and 1898. New discoveries were also made
in the interior. In Uélé, in the north-east, Commander Christiaens
collected another polished axe (Stainier 1897a), while in the extreme south-
east in Katanga, now Shaba, two geologists noted interesting sites:
Diederich observed grinding grooves on the shores of Lake Moero (Stainier
1899: 12) while Cornet (1893) found a stone artefact site on the shores of
the Lubudi River. Cornet (1896) then drew up the first synthesis of
discoveries made in Lower Zaïre. He listed eighteen sites, some located
along the caravan route which runs along the river, and others to the south,
along the railway line. In addition to some observations on raw material,
Cornet wondered about the age of this material; he did not doubt its
prehistoric character, but considering that prehistory only ended in these
regions four centuries earlier, the problem was not solved. However, he
condluded, like Dupont, that this material belonged within the Neolithic,
despite the large size of the artefacts and the absence of polishing.

In 1897, in the context of the Brussels International Exhibition, an
exhibit devoted to the Independent State of Congo was opened at
Tervuren. King Léopold II wanted to impress upon Belgians the riches of
this country and the developments he had undertaken. He aimed to
convince reticent Belgians of all the profits that could be drawn from a
colony. Strangely enough, it was in the part devoted to the economic
wealth of Congo that, among the documents on geology, a display cabinet
was to be found devoted to prehistoric archaeology produced by two
geologists, Stainier and Cornet. In view of the mastery which the peoples
of Africa demonstrated in the working of metal, Stainier (1897b)
maintained in the exhibit catalogue that the Metal Age must be very
ancient, although impossible to date. Flaked stone tools were attributed to
the Pygmies, an idea which conformed to evolutionary theories which
made Pygmies and Bushmen 'contemporary ancestors'. In 1913, a South
African law forbidding export of archaeological remains still used the term
'Bushmen relics' (Goodwin 1946: 129). However, on the basis of the
available information it seemed difficult for Stainier 'to compare
chronologically the Stone Age of the Congo with the same period in
Europe, because the tool types found were also very different'.

In view of the success of the exhibit on the Congo, it was decided to keep
it at Tervuren as a permanent museum, and the artefacts exhibited there
constituted the beginnings of the collection of the 'Prehistoric
anthropology section', as it was first called. It is interesting to note the
course of research by plotting the number of stone artefacts catalogued in
the Tervuren collections each year from this date up to Congo's
independence (fig. 7:2).

Two years later, in January 1899, this new museum inaugurated a series
of publications devoted to human sciences with a work by Stainier
entitled: L'Age de la Pierre au Congo (The Stone Age of the Congo). A
synthesis of data from the whole country, it was the first book exclusively
devoted to the prehistory of sub-Saharan Africa. Stainier began by
enumerating the twenty-six sites known at the time. After giving their
precise locations, he outlined the circumstances of their discovery and drew
up a distribution map. Undoubtedly influenced by Cornet's hypothesis, he

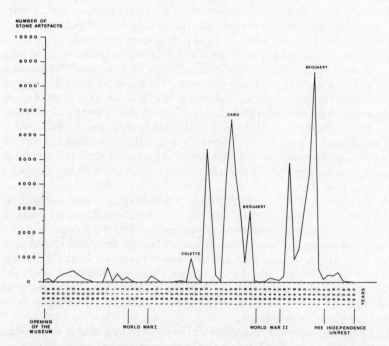

7:2 *The number of stone artefacts from Zaïre registered annually in the Prehistory Section of the Tervuren Museum from its opening to the independence of the Belgian Congo*

compared these finds with material, mostly Neolithic, discovered in Belgium. However, he remained very circumspect regarding a possible date since the material came from surface finds without associated fauna. He stressed the importance of research in caves and added: 'A long time will pass before extensive excavations show the nature of the African Quaternary and enable us to discover (human) remains of this period. Until this time, modesty would be fitting' (Stainier, 1899: 13–4, editor's translation).

For Stainier, the skill that he observed in the metallurgy was proof of its antiquity. This encouraged him to date the stone artefacts much earlier. He examined the different flaking techniques and judged them crude. Next, as a geologist, he identified the sources of the raw materials in Lower Zaïre. Typological study of the material led him to emphasize a particular type: Zole's ellipsoidal hatchet, a parallel-sided bifacial tool, characteristic of the Middle Stone Age/Late Stone Age of Central Africa. He also concluded that the sites were found close to the raw material sources, on prominent hills close to water. Finally, Stainier tried to place the artefacts in the context of what was known of the prehistory of Africa at that point. He emphasized the backwardness of the inhabitants as demonstrated by their prehistoric tool-kit. In conclusion, he hoped that systematic research would confirm that Africa was inhabited during the Stone Age as were other parts of the globe, as indeed the distribution of finds seemed to indicate. Whatever biases are evident, this book with its bibliography and photographic plates of great quality is an outstanding work.

An Italian engineer, Gariazzo, who participated in the construction of the Lower Zaïre railway, collected a great number of artefacts along the railway line, which he gave to the Antiquities Museum of Torino. Professor Taramelli (1902) studied this material for the International Anthropological and Prehistoric Archaeology Congress held in Paris in 1900. Taramelli had at that stage no knowledge of Stainier's study, but his ideas and conclusions were very close to Stainier's, confirming the great uniformity of the conceptual framework of European scholars at this time. For Taramelli, the most important question arising from the study of these African artefacts was to know whether they were the work of very old populations contemporary with prehistoric European cultures or if they were the work of surviving populations, like the Bushmen and Pygmies at a very rudimentary stage of development. However, Taramelli rejected evolutionary concepts when, following the lead of the great French prehistorian Mortillet who had already affirmed that 'Egypt's civilization came from Africa', he considered it likely that in this case the Palaeolithic and Neolithic levels were of considerable antiquity. This seemed to him to be confirmed not only by the skill which Africans showed in their iron-working but also by the fact that the diffusion of this metallurgy implied a very long Iron Age.

At the same period, Jacques (1901) in Belgium studied a new collection of 655 artefacts found around Tumba, also in Lower Zaïre, by Haas, a captain in the police force of the Independent State of the Congo. Using a typology proposed for Europe and America, Jacques described several new types of tools. He noted, contrary to Stainier's opinion, that the flaking was very fine. He also regretted that, until then, only beautiful pieces (*les belles pièces*) had been collected, because if finds had been gathered randomly, one would have expected the same quantity of cutting tools to have been found as in Europe.

In 1903, Jacques (1904) examined all the collections available in Belgium – nearly 3,000 pieces. For Jacques, the Pygmies were the first inhabitants of the forest and, if the end of the Stone Age did not date back more than five or six centuries, it could still have begun at the same time as in Europe. Unlike other researchers working in Africa, he refused, with much foresight, to date the artefacts on a purely typological basis. His discussion of the influence of raw materials on flaking techniques and artefact morphology is also very modern. However, the influence of evolutionary ideas is very clear in his conclusion. There he states that in all the countries of the world, evolution took the same course, but in some it was slower than in others. In Zaïre, the Stone Age was undoubtedly as recent as a few centuries ago, but everywhere the same needs created the same shapes and used the same materials. The problem of when the Stone Age began was yet unsolved.

The Tervuren archives attest to the passion for the collection of lithic artefacts and one is struck by the knowledge of prehistory and its specialist vocabulary shown by the officials of the Independent State, as well as by businessmen, engineers and servicemen. Fig. 7:2 shows that the Museum collections were regularly enriched with small donations of flaked tools, nearly all from Lower Zaïre, up to the beginning of the First World War. Many finds were made during major earthworks. The first stratigraphic observations were noted after 1900 but unfortunately they were often not brought to the attention of specialists (Colette 1935a). Just before the First World War, petroglyphs were noted in the Uélé, in the north of the country (Calonne-Beaufaict 1914) and Grenade (1910) wrote a first synthesis of the polished tools from Uélé.

Outside Zaïre, archaeological discoveries were noted in neighbouring French Congo, first by Dupont (1889: 372), who made a detour there during his trip to Lower Zaïre in 1887 in order to visit the copper mine (Dupont, 1889: 334–9), next by Regnault (1894) and Bel (1908). Other finds were reported in Gabon (Hamy 1897) and in Angola (Severo 1890; Delgado 1900–1; Choffat 1900–1; Leite de Vasconcelos 1913). There is a striking contrast with countries like Cameroon, Rwanda and Burundi where practically nothing was noted right up to the end of German domination after the First World War. In Cameroon only a few finds were made by German colonists between 1890 and 1912. These were mainly polished tools found in the eastern part of the country (Buisson 1935; Fourneau 1935).

We can consider this first phase of archaeological research in Central Africa to have ended with the First World War. Until then discoveries were mainly made accidentally by servicemen, explorers, missionaries, geologists and engineers. Even if it was only amateur research, interest in prehistory was very widespread. Under the influence of current thinking prehistorians looked to Africa for confirmation of general evolutionary models. African prehistory was simply a facies of European prehistory.

Phase 2. The inter-war years

After the First World War, research was still rather casual and guided by evolutionary ideas. However, the year 1925 marked a decisive turning-point in the development of archaeology in this part of the world. That year, Colette began the first systematic excavation and Menghin (1925) published a synthesis in the tradition of the cultural-historical school of Vienna. Based on a comparison between a collection of fifteen specimens belonging to his friend Crawford, the founder of *Antiquity*, and the artefacts stored in the museum and published up to that date, Menghin created the 'Tumbakultur', named after Tumba in the neighbourhood of which were found the richest collections. He saw in these surface assemblages a homogenous archaeological entity extending to the French Congo and to Angola. Typical tools were arrow-heads or spears, blades, axes and other bifacial tools. Menghin put forward the idea that the Tumbian was, at least in part, ancient and derived from the great hand-axe culture. There were no true polished axes, only rubbed axes. This material, which included some pottery in its younger phase, was regarded as not very ancient by Menghin because it was found at shallow depths and because it contained picks and choppers resembling the Campignien of Europe. In this very confused article, Menghin hesitates between two or three phases, with or without pottery and polished axes, and corresponding to matriarchal populations. Not realizing that the material was from different horizons and had been brought together by intense erosion, he made the Tumbian a new cultural stage, typical of recent Central African prehistory and of a 'pig-raiser-culture' (*schweinezuchterkultur*) of which he found evidence on the different continents (Menghin 1925, 1926; 1931).

In 1931 in his book *Weltgeschichte des Steinzeit*, Menghin dated the origin of the Tumbian culture and distinguished an ancient phase (*Fruhtumbien*), one more recent (*Spat-tumbien*) and a phase which marked the transition to the Neolithic (*Ubergangs-tumbien*). This book had a considerable impact and marked a significant point in world archaeology because here Menghin drew up the first synthesis of the Stone Age on a global level and suggested a reclassification of prehistoric cultures. The success of this work contributed to the spread of the usage of the term Tumbian throughout Africa. Applying archaeology to the works of Schmidt, Frobenius and Graebner, Menghin is particularly representative of the Austrian diffusionist school. The theories of this school were widely accepted in the Germanic world in the 1930s and earned Menghin the rectorship of the University of Vienna. His involvement in the national-socialist ideology led him to Argentina where he continued his research after the Second World

War, publishing, in particular, an article on the intercontinental correlations of the Tumbian of Africa (Menghin 1949)!

The contrast between Menghin and Colette, although they were
contemporaries, is remarkable. Colette was a postal employee and it is in
this capacity that he left for the Congo in 1924. As an amateur he had
already carried out archaeological research in Belgium and naturally continued his hobby in Africa. He was successively posted to Boma, Matadi,
Léopoldville and Kwamouth and discovered a series of prehistoric sites.
Most of these were surface findings, and due to the admixture of artefacts of
Palaeolithic and Neolithic types, it was impossible to classify them chronologically (Colette 1928), a problem Colette had previously encountered in
Europe (Colette 1933d). Were these two industries contemporaneous and
even quite recent in Central Africa? Furthermore only '*les belles pièces*' had
been collected so far and one wondered whether prehistoric man in Central
Africa did not know of tools that were commonly used in Europe. As
Colette himself stated, 'only geology and an absolutely rigorous method of
excavation and recording would produce new data ... in order to
corroborate or to refute these three theories' (Colette 1929). Thus, in order
to answer these questions Colette undertook the first systematic excavation
organized in Central Africa, at the Kalina Point in Léopoldville (Kinshasa)
(fig. 7:3). Between December 1925 and October 1926, Colette visited the
site 24 times and without any help carried out an excavation in 20 cm spits.
His discoveries engaged the interest of the provincial Vice-Governor and he
was able to organize an official excavation in April 1927 just before his
return to Europe. To help him six prisoners were put at his disposal. They
received a bonus if they showed him the artefacts before picking them up
(Colette 1928).

Colette was ahead of his time, and the quality of his excavation work and
analysis, combined with great care in interpretation, compel admiration.
Nobody is better placed than J.D. Clark (1971) to evaluate Colette's
contribution to the archaeology of Africa in general:

His very careful attention to stratigraphic controls, detailed recording of his finds and precise presentation of the results of his excavations set an example that has been followed by few who came after him. Indeed, his approach and methodology in respect to the archaeological occurrences was little different from that which is only now passing into general practice in this continent.

Colette published the stratigraphy of the site and the related stone industries in detail, elaborating his interpretation of the sequence in several papers published after his return to Belgium (Colette 1928, 1929, 1933a, 1933b, 1933d, 1935a, 1936a). Following Colette's premature death, Bequaert (1938) published his field notes and drawings.

Considering that the morphology of the artefacts alone was not sufficient basis to correlate these industries with the subdivision of the European palaeolithic, Colette decided to introduce new terms to be used provisionally as working tools, he stressed, until absolute proof of a synchronism between European and Central African prehistory was established. From the bottom level to the top he distinguished a Kalinian, a Djokocian, an Ndolian and a Léopoldian Neolithic. Each aggregate was well illustrated and defined on a quantitative basis. In this last respect Colette was very innovative; he provided an inventory of all stone tools and waste by levels and employed bar diagrams to compare the frequencies of stone artefacts and tools among the various levels (Colette 1933a). Furthermore, in 'Complexes et convergences en préhistoire' (Colette, 1935), a lengthy paper where he summarized his research on the prehistory of Central Africa, he calculated the variation in the size of tools from the Léopoldian, Djokocian and Kalinian and, using his training in the natural sciences, presented the results in cumulative and frequency curves. This use of statistics was a first for African, if not world prehistory. In the same paper one finds not only a summary of the history of archaeological research in Zaïre but also a survey of the most significant sites known throughout the country at that time.

As far as his general theoretical framework is concerned, we must add to Colette's merit that, even if he did not explicitly oppose the diffusionist thesis, he nevertheless stressed the phenomenon of typological convergence between artefacts of different ages, resulting from the use of polymorphic sandstone as raw material. He also carefully studied the process of patination of this material. All this led him to conclude that he was dealing with a complex of industries instead of a unique homogeneous industry. Nevertheless he remained very cautious in his conclusions, stressing the lack of stratigraphical, paleontological, faunal and floral data (Colette 1935).

Colette was also interested in a palaeoethnographic perspective using oral traditions to interpret Neolithic remains, mainly those from the northeastern part of the country, which he called the Uelian Neolithic from the Uele River (Colette 1933c, 1933e, 1935, 1936b). He was also precocious in his commentaries on the importance of termite activities (Colette 1936a). On returning to Europe in 1927 at the age of 26, Colette began his studies at the Free University of Brussels where he became a Doctor of Sciences. He was then, from July 1934 to his death in November 1936, the first head of the (Physical) Anthropology and Prehistory section of the Tervuren Museum. Unfortunately, although he benefited from official recognition, his work, published in Belgian reviews of limited circulation, had little impact on the scientists of his day and quickly sank into oblivion.

In contrast, Menghin's Tumbian was internationally successful and was adopted, in particular, in East Africa (O'Brien 1937; Leakey and Owen

1945) and in West Africa (Delcroix and Vaufrey 1939; Alimen 1955: 273–80). Colette never challenged Menghin's view. However, in 1930, Cipriani of the University of Florence made some stratigraphic observations during the construction of a reservoir in the western part of Kinshasa (Graziosi 1933; Cipriani archives). The depth at which artefacts were found here and their patination seemed to indicate a more ancient period than that attributed to the Tumbian by Menghin. Graziosi, therefore, arrived at the conclusion that the Tumbian grouped artefacts of very different periods and that the term should consequently be used in a geographical and not a chronological sense. However it seemed impossible for Graziozi to know, as Breuil suggested (1931), whether all the facies of the Tumbian were Neolithic.

Francis Cabu (fig. 7:4), a medical assistant, who had done some amateur archaeological research in Europe, notably in the south of France, tried for eight years to find prehistoric artefacts in stratigraphic contexts in the Kinshasa region. He finally found some objects in test-pits in the alluvial plain in the eastern part of the city. In order to acquire the means to carry out a large-scale excavation, he conceived of a drainage plan for all of this swampy area. In doing so, it was not great earth-moving that provided an opportunity for archaeological observations, but rather it was the desire to promote archaeological research that provoked major earthworks. With the help of the authorities who provided him with 210 labourers, he dug, in 1934 and 1935, 4 km of canals, one of which is still known as the 'Cabu trench'. They were excavated in successive levels of 30 cm, sometimes down to depths of 5 or 6 metres (fig. 7:5). The thousands of artefacts collected in this way convinced him (Cabu 1935a, b, c, d) of the fallacy of the Tumbian theory, which he vigorously attacked in his thesis (Cabu 1936b) and in a series of articles and conference papers (Cabu 1936a, 1944). He clearly perceived that the Tumbian resulted from racist thinking, according to which Central African peoples had only recently emerged from the prehistoric era. For Cabu, Central Africa's prehistory was, on the contrary, ancient and the Tumbian was only a superficial mixture of different industries. Cabu was right, but his ideas took a long time to gain recognition.

Although the records that Cabu left show numerous stratigraphic observations, they were never published in detail. Colette raised some doubts regarding the precision of the stratigraphic details, which was not surprising considering the extent of the work. Cabu can also be faulted for the absence of illustrations and detailed descriptions of the material in his too few publications.

Cabu also understood the prime importance of the press and through this medium gained the support of the colonial authorities, a move which seemed to have irritated some of his colleagues, who were not particularly in favour of this kind of publicity. Self-taught like Colette, he presented a thesis on his research at the University of Liège; then in 1936 he took charge of an official research expedition to Katanga, now Shaba. The work of this expedition resulted in the establishment of the Elizabethville Museum (Lubumbashi), of which Cabu became the curator. Cabu examined a series of prehistoric sites, but was particularly interested in the study of rock art in the Kiantapo Cave, where he started an excavation in 1937, and in bored stones, the Kwés so abundant in Shaba (Cabu 1937, 1938a, 1938b; Cabu and Vanden Branden 1938).

Cabu's opposition to the Tumbian and championing of the terminology proposed by Colette was echoed as early as 1938 in a survey published by the French prehistorian, Vayson de Pradenne (1938: 164). However, the

7:4 *F. Cabu at work in Kinshasa 1935*

7:5 *'Excavation' of Cabu's Canal in Kinshasa 1935*

Abbé Breuil, generally regarded as an authority at the time, had already begun to use the term Tumbian proposed by Menghin, while not sharing the latter's views that it belonged to the Upper Palaeolithic (Breuil 1931). During the Second World War, in 1941, Cabu went to the University of the Witwatersrand with 331 artefacts from Kasai and Shaba, a film and numerous photographs. He showed them particularly to Goodwin, Van Riet Lowe and Breuil. The last two wholly supported his point of view and voted to abandon the term Tumbian. 'For the first time are we now able to see the Congo not as the home of a single Stone Age Culture (the ill-conceived "Tumbian" of Oswald Menghin) but as a vast stage upon which man has practised his skill from the very dawn of the Pleistocene right up through the millennia to the present,' stated Van Riet Lowe (1944: 173). For Breuil also (1944: 159), the term Tumbian 'established on a museum table from artefacts chosen from uncertain contexts, should disappear to make room for vocabulary better adapted to typological and stratigraphic realities.' Breuil then proposed a nomenclature as much based on typology, as was his custom, as on patination. This nomenclature included, with some regional variations, a pebble-culture stage followed by a Kamoan with Abbevillian and archaic Acheulean stages comparable to the Stellenbosch of the Vaal. Next, Breuil distinguished an evolved Acheulean, three Kalinian stages and a Djokocian, these last two terms being used in homage to Colette. Next came two more advanced stages, for which he proposed the terms Lupemban (named from the Lupemba stream in Kasai) with its blades and 'armes de jet' and Tshitolian (named after the Bena Tshitolo, an ethnic group who lived on a plateau in Kasai), characterized by numerous arrow-points.

This period between the wars was also marked by the activities of another archaeologist, Maurits Bequaert, who was preferred over Cabu to succeed Colette as head of the Prehistory section of the Tervuren Museum in 1937. As a civil engineer Bequaert had spent twelve years in the Congo; then, aged 41, he returned, like Colette and Cabu, to university to study the history of art, archaeology and geology. In 1938 and 1939 he undertook a long excavation and survey expedition, which began with test-pits around Tumba and Thysville (Banza-Ngungu) in Lower Zaïre. He then concentrated on Kwango, but Kasai was the main focus of his trip. In fifteen days he carried out, in the district of Tshitolo, an excavation of 1,400 sq. m to a depth of 15 cm, and in one place to 30 cm. This only yielded about 700 stone artefacts (Bequaert and Mortelmans 1955). He also tested some of the caves of Bushimaie Valley (Herin 1977–8).

Bequaert never freed himself from his background as a public works engineer. He filled notebooks with meticulous topographic minutiae before he started to excavate, but recorded the actual excavation data much less efficiently. Curiously enough, although his expedition was instrumental in adding nearly 7,000 artefacts to the Tervuren Museum collections (cf. fig. 7:2), he published very little on this material, contenting himself with writing up general syntheses and catalogues from which quantitative data were missing, as was any discussion. He often preferred to publish surface collections made by the numerous amateurs active in the country rather than his own material.

For Bequaert, as for Cabu, Colette and their predecessors, the goal of research was to specify Africa's place in world prehistory and their curiosity, therefore, centered almost exclusively on the Stone Age. The more recent past of the indigenous populations was of no interest to them. The first non-prehistoric excavations were undertaken with the aim of studying the traces of the first evangelization of the kingdom of Kongo.

Hence, in 1913 research by a territorial administrator uncovered two tombs near a wooden cross and an old Portuguese cannon (Vandenhoute 1972–3: 192–3). Next, some missionaries undertook research in 1937 in the cemetery and ruins of a church in order to find the tomb of a Capuchin, Joris Van Geel, who had been killed there in 1652. The aim of this excavation was to collect information on his martyrdom with a view to pressing for his canonization. Learning that Bequaert was leading an archaeological expedition, they asked him to help them. In the church ruins 35 tombs were excavated but Van Geel's burial place was not found (Vandenhoute 1972–3).

It was also in response to amateurs that Bequaert excavated test-pits in the caves of the Bushimaie Valley, but the aim here was to find prehistoric remains, flaked stone tools or, even better, human skeletons. However, he found only pottery, probably of rather recent date, which he never published (Herin 1973; 1977–8).

It was in fact outside the Belgian Congo and from ethnologists that an interest in using archaeological research in order to understand the past of local populations and verify oral traditions was initiated. In this regard, Marcel Griaule and Jean-Paul Lebeuf carried out pioneering research in their 1936 expedition to the region south of Lake Chad. Their research on the so-called 'Sao civilization' and the associated terracotta figurines was to have a considerable impact in France and was to inspire new research on the archaeology of African peoples and ethnoarchaeology with, following Mauss, a marked interest in material culture (Lebeuf 1937; Griaule 1943).

In northern Cameroon, the rock engravings of Bidzar were examined in 1933 (Buisson 1933), while the first stone tools were noted in the English part of the country in 1923 (Migeod 1925). A series of sites, notably of Neolithic age located in the centre of the country, were recorded by amateurs, especially Buisson (1933, 1935), Fourneau (1935) and Jauze. Buisson (1933) had tested a small rock-shelter in the western part of the country as early as 1929. Jauze carried out a small dig at Obobogo in the embankment of a new road, which produced abundant pottery (Jauze 1944). Similarly, in the Central African Republic, geologists collected the first flaked tools in 1931, some of which were studied by Breuil (1933). An ethnographic study also mentions archaeological finds (Eboue 1933) and the existence of rock art at Djebel Mela in the extreme north-east of the country was noted in 1937 (Breuil 1937). Thereafter, the prehistory of this country fell into oblivion for nearly thirty years.

The situation was rather similar in the other French Equatorial African territories where research most often remained the work of amateurs making very occasional collections. In the area which was to become Gabon, it seems that after the first discovery forty-five years elapsed before, at the beginning of the 1930s, the French prehistorian Furon (1958: 313) and the geologist Babet (1931), followed later by Droux (1937), discovered a number of sites (Blankoff 1969). In the Congo, from 1927 to 1947, prehistoric research developed thanks mainly to the work of Lagotala (1933), Droux (1937, 1941) and the geologists Babet (1929, 1931, 1936) and Lombard (1930, 1931). Droux, an administrative officer, discovered the site of La Pointe Hollandaise during the dredging of the port of Brazzaville and also carried out the first excavation in the Kindala cave near Mfouati (Droux and Kelley 1939). From 1937 to 1947, Bergeaud (1937) held the post of prehistoric attaché at the Institute of Central African Studies, the first official post for an archaeologist in French Equatorial Africa. Bergeaud discovered numerous sites and, as a result of major construction works, was able to examine a series of sections at Brazzaville,

Pointe Noire and along the Zaïre River (Droux and Bergeaud 1937, 1939; Lanfranchi 1979: 180–207). All this research was the subject of essentially descriptive publication with very little in the way of hypothesis or interpretation. In Angola research between the wars was also confined to occasional collections of prehistoric artefacts which, on the basis of comparisons with Zaïre, were considered to be Tumbian (Serpa Pinto 1930, 1933; Dos Santos 1934; Mouta 1934) despite associations in some cases with iron objects. A Belgian geologist, Janmart, became Head of the Prospecting Department of the Companhia de Diamantes de Angola in 1937 and initiated, mainly after 1942, research on the prehistory of the province of Lunda in the north-east of the country.

In Rwanda the first prehistoric artefacts were found in 1921/2 by Salée (1924–5, 1926), a White Father. In Burundi it was only in 1926 that the first archaeological discoveries were made by Tristan (Salée 1927). Other finds were mentioned by Lebzelter in 1933, and in 1936 Mrs Boutakoff, whose husband was a geological prospector, made an inventory of a series of Middle Stone Age sites, some of which she attributed to the Sangoan. She systematically excavated the Ruhimangyargya Cave where she identified a Middle Stone Age level overlain by a microlithic level with hearths and pottery, which she considered to be associated with the lithic tools (Boutakoff 1937). Unfortunately, the only article that she devoted to this research, which she considered to be a preliminary publication, was never followed by a detailed report with sections and plans. As Mrs Boutakoff followed her husband to South America and as she had excavated the cave in its entirety, it will never be possible to work out the exact relationship between this Urewe-type pottery and the Later Stone Age material.

This period as a whole saw an increasing number of casual discoveries and a progressive institutionalization of research with the hiring, locally and in European institutions, of the first professional archaeologists and financing by the French and Belgian colonial authorities of the first expeditions. However, even for these professionals, excavation remained the exception rather than the rule and the essence of their interest was in debating classificatory and technological problems on the basis of collections, which most often were very selective and from surface contexts. The entity most characteristic of this approach was the Tumbian, the success of which must be linked to the diffusionist ideas of the time, but probably also to a more or less unconscious racial prejudice. This encouraged a perspective on the archaeology of Central Africa which conceived of a single invariant prehistoric past of no great antiquity. This conformed with the notion that Central Africa was inhabited by the most primitive of primitives. However, archaeologists eventually realized the importance of meticulous stratigraphic observations. From this perspective, as well as from that of quantitative analyses of artefacts, Colette's excavations at Kalina could have marked the beginning of a significant development in Central African archaeology, but this was prevented by his premature death. At the regional level, the terminology used in Zaïre served as a model for the neighbouring countries, while on a continental level it was the results of research in South Africa that served as a reference. Rare was the author who would risk suggesting a date for the different periods.

While the interest of archaeologists remained fixed on the Stone Age, the French ethnologists Griaule and Lebeuf began systematic excavations aimed at understanding the history of the ethnic groups living to the south of Lake Chad. As elsewhere, the discovery of objects of artistic value excited the imagination and served to facilitate research. However, this work was very advanced for its time because it was motivated neither by the fascination for ruins attributable to non-Africans nor by the discovery of gold artefacts as was the case elsewhere, but by real interest in the history of the people of the region and by the importance for science as a whole of testing historic and ethnographic data against those of archaeology.

Finally, the first examples of rock art were noted in different parts of Central Africa; here again, the direction of research was influenced by European trends.

Phase 3. From the Second World War to independence

The discussions on terminology were to culminate at the First Pan-African Congress of Prehistory held in Nairobi in 1947. L.S.B. Leakey (1952b) made himself the advocate for the Tumbian, while Cabu (1952) asked for the withdrawal of the term. As Leakey, who used the term, explained shortly before the Congress:

> In rejecting the names Kalinian and Djokocian in favour of the retention of the name Tumbian, I in no way wish to minimise the value of Dr Cabu's work and I believe that he will agree with me that the retention of the name Tumbian which is so essentially connected, in the minds of all prehistorians, with the Belgian Congo, cannot but be of advantage, seeing that the word conveys such a clear picture of Tumbian picks and lance heads to the minds of many students. (Leakey and Owen 1945)

Finally, it was recommended by the Congress that:

> In consideration of the agreement reached at the plenary session of the Congress between Dr Leakey and Dr F. Cabu, it is agreed to recommend that the term Sangoan be used as far as, and including, that portion of the Tumbian as described by Oswald Menghin to which Messrs. Collette [sic] and Cabu have applied the term Djokocian and Kalinian in the Congo Basin. It is similarly agreed that the term Sangoan be used as far as and including the Middle Tumbian as described in Dr L.S.B. Leakey's and Archdeacon Owen's paper of March 1945. It is further recommended that the term Kenya Lupemban be substituted for the Upper Tumbian of Kenya. (Leakey and Cole 1952: 8)

From an emotional point of view, in the atmosphere prevailing immediately after the war, and judging by the strong stand taken by Cabu in demanding the rejection of the Tumbian, we cannot refrain from thinking that its suppression was in part linked to its 'Germanic' origin. From a scientific point of view, this decision was perplexing because 'Tumbian' was solemnly replaced with 'Sangoan' and 'Lupemban', terms which at the time also referred to surface collections. Moreover, could the term Sangoan be applied correctly to the industries of the Congo/Zaïre basin? In any case, why prefer these terms to those of Colette which were defined on the basis of excavated assemblages found in a precise stratigraphic sequence and painstakingly differentiated by quantitative and typological analyses?

In Angola, from 1946 Janmart devoted more and more time to prehistoric research on the sections exposed by the extraction of diamonds. He published his first observations following the terminology proposed by Menghin (Janmart 1946a), then by Breuil, Cabu and Van Riet Lowe (Janmart 1946b). Leakey was then invited to visit the Lunda region and to study Janmart's collections. In line with the Nairobi resolution, Leakey (1949) proposed a sequence in which he distinguished five stages of Sangoan followed by Lupemban and a post-Lupemban. Leakey was followed by Breuil who decided to remain faithful, with regard to the study of the Angolan material, to the nomenclature that he had agreed upon with Cabu, while giving equivalents according to the resolutions of the 1947 Congress (Breuil and Janmart 1950). Finally in his last publication, Janmart (1953) used the terminology adopted in Nairobi, since, as he wrote in a hand-written dedication to Mortelmans 'the Tumbian has become taboo', but his support was not without reservations: 'I do not like the Nairobi terminology because it was, as far as the Congo Basin is concerned, the result of a compromise which is, at its best, an unscientific process' (Janmart 1953: 13–14).

During this period, research in Zaïre was developing. Arriving there for the first time in 1937, Georges Mortelmans and Lucien Cahen were engaged in the systematic geological description of Shaba. They became more and more interested in prehistory as a means of dating surface geological deposits. From 1940, Mortelmans dealt more directly with prehistory, which permitted him to specify the stratigraphic positions of different industries. Convalescing in South Africa in 1943, he met Breuil and Van Riet Lowe who inspired him with a passion for prehistory. He began by adopting Breuil's typology (Mortelmans 1947, 1952b, 1953) as did the other researchers working in Zaïre at the time – Anciaux de Faveaux (1955) and Bequaert (1952). From 1950 to 1952 the latter carried out a second large-scale archaeological expedition.

The request by Bequaert for funds for his expedition submitted to the Minister of the Colonies and preserved in the archives at Tervuren is very enlightening. For Bequaert, 'the study of the prehistory and the protohistory of the Belgian Congo and Rwanda-Burundi has arrived at the point where it is necessary to orientate ourselves towards the preparation of local and regional monographs. Consequently during excavations, the expedition will try to gather data to aid the resolution of a series of outstanding problems.' Examining the list of 'problems' for each province one notes that practically all are concerned with very local aspects of prehistory. Bequaert was obviously preoccupied with the Stone Age: only six out of forty-six problems for study fall outside the Stone Age. Among these, we note the study of Christian burial sites in Lower Zaïre, the study of the traces of European penetration to the sites of the ancient capitals of Kuba kings, and the process of the transition from the Stone Age to the Iron Age in Shaba. The funding was approved but, as was forseeable, for lack of time and the necessary cash the expedition was confined to Lower Zaïre, to Kinshasa and further east to Kwango. As during the preceding expedition, Bequaert spent an enormous amount of time in compiling topographic descriptions of sites before starting excavations. These gave rather disappointing results and the sections and plans available are very inadequate (Clist 1981–2: 34–6). Moreover, Bequaert never published the results of this work except in a few summary notes (Bequaert 1955, 1956; Bequaert and Mortelmans 1955).

This period was also notable for the activities of two Catholic missionaries, for whom, as for many of their colleagues, archaeology first represented a hobby, but progressively became almost a full-time activity. Anciaux de Faveaux (fig. 7:6), a doctor of chemistry, arrived in the Belgian Congo in 1930, and in 1941 started surveys and excavations on the Katangan high plateau of Kundelungu and Biano (Anciaux de Faveaux 1955). He produced evidence of an archaeological succession stretching

7:6   *Père Anciaux de Faveaux 1955*

7:7   *H. Van Moorsel supervising his excavation in the*
Kinshasa Plain 1956

from the Acheulean to the Late Stone Age. Although he followed the
nomenclature that Breuil continued to defend (Breuil and Janmart 1950),
he introduced several new terms for those assemblages which he considered
to be local facies.

   Hendrik van Moorsel (fig. 7:7), who taught at a middle school for
Africans in Kinshasa, also took an interest in the archaeology of the region
from 1938. With the help of his students he made observations and collections during development works in the town (Van Moorsel 1944, 1947,
1948). In 1948 he received a subsidy from the Institute for Scientific
Research in Central Africa and undertook a series of excavations, notably at
Kingabwa, on the banks of the Malabo (ex Stanley) Pool in Kinshasa. He
excavated artefacts from an Iron Age site which he identified as the
Ngombela town described in the seventeenth century by Capuchin
missionaries. These were also the first systematic excavations aimed at

understanding recent history in the Belgian Congo.

In the east of the country, an organic chemist turned geologist with a keen interest in Quaternary studies and the Stone Age, Jean de Heinzelin de Braucourt (1948), first studied a collection of stone artefacts made by a gold-mining engine at Kilo-Moto in Ituri. He attributed this material to the Tumbian in view of the diversity of the typological characteristics present. In 1950, he excavated at Ishango at the outlet of the Semliki River from Lake Edward. De Heinzelin excavated about 163 sq. m and brought to light an exceptionally rich sequence notable for both the number of layers and the preserved bone artefacts. He distinguished three Mesolithic industries, the most ancient being the Ishanguian, which in turn was divided into three stages on stratigraphic evidence and on the basis of the evolution of the characteristic bone harpoons. Above it, came a Mesolithic level without pottery, followed by one with pottery and a later Mesolithic stone industry that he compared to the Wilton. Finally, the upper level yielded tombs and the remains of an Iron Age village (Heinzelin de Braucourt 1957).

Although excavated by exposing a vertical face of the deposit, the Ishango excavation can be considered as the first truly modern excavation undertaken in Central Africa, with meticulous lithostratigraphic description, typological analysis and quantitative details of the lithic industry, inspired by the methods proposed by Bordes in France, as well as detailed and original study of the faunal and human remains. The only unexpected note was the mathematical analysis of groups of engraved lines on a long bone in which a quartz flake was hafted. Believing he had found a parallel with Egyptian arithmetic, and noting comparisons with Sudanese Neolithic harpoons, de Heinzelin suggested that certain cultural features from Mesolithic Central Africa spread as far as pre-dynastic Egypt. Such a relationship did not imply a migration. This hypothesis was echoed in models developed by Egyptologists, who were starting to admit an African rather than an Asian origin for Egyptian civilization.

Shell samples from Ishango produced the first two radiocarbon dates on Central African material. A result of $21,000 \pm 500$ bp (W–283) obtained for the Ishanguian seemed much too ancient. On the basis of global palaeo-climatic correlations, comparisons with the Khartoum Mesolithic, technological evolution and the speed of local geomorphological phenomena, de Heinzelin estimated that the real age was at least 10,000 years younger than the radiocarbon age. So began what we may call the radiocarbon revolution, which was to facilitate the development of an absolute chronology in an area where, lacking external correlations, it had been rare for anyone to dare to give an age to the industries.

In general, with an exception being made for de Heinzelin's excavation, this phase of Central African archaeology is characterized by a series of local developments made by researchers who continued to be more preoccupied with nomenclature than with excavation. They tried to find local evidence for a general sequence and drew up lists of tool-types, but these tools were rarely found during excavation and practically never illustrated. They hardly ever asked questions about the way of life of prehistoric peoples, the importance of raw materials or any reason for a modification of the tool-kit.

However, there was a growing tendency to correlate prehistoric industries with the climatic cycles of the African Quaternary, in particular with the pluvials and interpluvials that were considered to be the tropical equivalents of European glaciations and interglacials. Mortelmans, who had acquired an interest in prehistory in order to attempt to date recent geological deposits, played a major role in this development. After he defended his thesis on the geology of central Shaba in 1947, he became Professor of Geology at the University of Brussels and directed a large part of his work towards prehistory. Apart from his own observations, he studied the collections of other researchers, principally those gathered by Bequaert (Bequaert and Mortelmans 1955), Cabu and especially Van Moorsel. The stratigraphic, technological and typological study of this last collection led him to recognize the existence of facies both with and without 'armes' from the same levels (Mortelmans 1962: 158). Since the presence or absence of 'armes' was of major importance in Breuil's nomenclature, Mortelmans dissociated himself from this scheme of nomenclature. At the third Pan-African Congress held in Livingstone in 1955, where he organized an excursion to Katanga, Mortelmans abandoned the terminology inspired by Breuil and proposed a new nomenclature more in line with the resolutions of the first Pan-African Congress (Mortelmans 1957a). The desire to conform to this resolution must have influenced his decision, but he explained the changes by the fact that he realized more and more that these industries were part of a continuum. Later he elaborated this terminology by progressively including data from other regions and particularly the data collected during expeditions in 1957 and 1959 to Lower Zaïre as part of the preparations for the fourth Pan-African Congress. Mortelmans also strived to specify the stratigraphic and climatic context of the industries and in particular he stressed the influence of ecological factors. He claimed to study 'the industries themselves, by applying the most modern methods of statistical analysis recently established in France for the study of industrial complexes' (Mortelmans 1957b). However, he practically never published quantitative data; the reason for this, no doubt, is the fact that he hardly ever took part in an excavation.

Based on his detailed knowledge of the Lower Congo and Katanga industries, Mortelmans (1957b) stressed the differences between them in his general reviews on Central African prehistory. Beginning with the Sangoan, he distinguished a western and an eastern facies, within the Middle Stone Age, a dichotomy between the forest cultures of the west and the savannah cultures of the east where, he said, 'a great number of facies received names as varied as they were useless.' Mortelmans also considered that these tool-kits demonstrated by their variety a growing mastery of the environment – an evolution which was analogous to that observed in Europe. For more recent periods, he conceived of a Neolithic, probably of Saharan origin, which was confined to the north by the forest and was found at the northern edges of the rain forest, along the great rivers and in Upper Katanga and Lower Congo. In the south of the Congo Basin, in the absence of evidence of Neolithic culture, Mortelmans envisaged the persistence of Mesolithic culture until the arrival of metal. Similarly, the Stone Age did not suddenly cease with the appearance of Bantu invaders bearing iron during our era (Mortelmans 1957b). These views conformed to the paradigms of the time but the idea of linking the introduction of iron to the arrival of Bantu-speakers, even though expressed in general terms, was a new development in the world of archaeology.

We must also stress Mortelmans' interest in art, which he studied in Katanga (Mortelmans 1952a) and especially in Lower Zaïre, where he saw evidence of the first evangelization of the country (Mortelmans and Monteyne 1962). In presenting one of his final papers to the fourth Pan-African Congress of Prehistory, which he organized in 1959 in Léopoldville, he established the sequence of industries in the western Congo: the final Acheulean was followed by the Sangoan, which resulted from the evolution of certain Acheulean tools, often distinguished by their size, and which represented an adaptation to the forest environment, notably with numerous picks. The Sangoan then developed, with diversification in the tool-kit and technology, into the Lupembian complex which is divided into four phases. Then came the Tshitolian complex, after a transitional industry called the Lupembo-Tshitolian characterized by the disappearance of certain Lupembian types and the appearance of new ones, especially arrow-heads. With the Tshitolian which followed, the tool-kit became even smaller, with a great variety of arrow-heads, and, towards the end, the appearance of rare polished tools. Finally, numerous polished tools probably associated with crude pottery were ascribed to Colette's Leopoldian Neolithic.

Combining a solid geological training with a knowledge of the country that was far superior to that of his predecessors, gifted with great curiosity and a remarkable ability to synthesize data, Mortelmans made a decisive contribution to the evolution of archaeology after the Second World War. However his tendency to synthesize led him to neglect precise definitions, illustrated by examples, of the archaeological units which he had proposed. Thus, the major influence of his work in the long term seems to have been the exposure of archaeological research in Central Africa to the concepts and theoretical models in use in other parts of the continent. In this regard, the role of contacts established during the Pan-African Congress seems to have been of paramount importance in unifying research.

In Angola the research by Janmart, who died prematurely, was carried on by Clark, who adopted the nomenclature proposed by Mortelmans, adapting it to the local conditions. On the basis of stratigraphy, typology and technology, Clark distinguished four archaeological units: Sangoan/Lower Lupemban, Upper Lupemban, Lupembo-Tshitolian and Tshitolian. Unlike the results of many of his predecessors, these distinctions were backed by abundant illustrations, by precise descriptions and by the use of quantitative data (Clark 1963).

From 1953, Hiernaux, a medical doctor, devoted himself to archaeological work in Rwanda-Burundi and in Kivu as part of a research programme in physical anthropology undertaken by the Institute for Scientific Research in Central Africa (IRSAC). Several ancient iron-smelting sites with remains of brick furnaces and potsherds were thus discovered (Hiernaux and Maquet 1956). The associated pottery was soon seen to be the same as Dimple-Based pottery described from Kenya (Leakey, Owen and Leakey 1948). After further research, Hiernaux reached the conclusion that this pottery belonged to the first Iron Age peoples in Rwanda and in the other regions of East Africa where it had been discovered. The pottery appeared abruptly and therefore must have been brought, together with the iron, by immigrants who lived for a period with the last Stone Age people. The discovery by Nenquin (1959) in the collections of the prehistory section at the Tervuren Museum, where he had just replaced Bequaert as its head, of pottery from Kasai which Nenquin, Leakey and Hiernaux all agreed to be Dimple-Based, extended the region covered by this tradition to a large part of Central Africa.

Hiernaux (1962) first had the idea, in 1959, at the Pan-African Congress at Léopoldville, of linking this pottery with the enormous and relatively recent expansion of the Bantu linguistic group documented by Greenberg (1949). This idea was already in the air, for, as has been mentioned above, Mortelmans (1957b) had attributed the introduction of metallurgy to the Bantu. Clark (1959a: 21–2; 283) had also attributed to Bantu-speakers, migrating from East Africa, the introduction of the use of metal and food-production into South Africa. But the idea of linking Dimple-Based pottery and the beginning of metallurgy to Bantu migrations was Hiernaux's, though subsequently developed by Posnansky (1961).

Suddenly the Bantu had erupted on the African archaeological scene. Although, as Vansina has shown (1979, 1980), the problem of the origin and diffusion of Bantu languages had been debated for a long time by linguists and ethnologists, archaeologists had hardly bothered with the question. This link had been suggested at a moment when, at the time of independence of numerous states, an interest in precolonial history was developing. The School of Oriental and African Studies in London was to play a major role in this process. By incorporating the conclusions of the British linguist, Guthrie, historians stimulated research by numerous British archaeologists in East Africa and in the south of Central Africa. Once the coincidence of the arrival of Bantu and the beginning of metallurgy had been admitted, this relationship became the dominant paradigm in research devoted to the beginnings of the Iron Age.

In Central Africa, the Iron Age incited little interest before 1949 when van Moorsel started to excavate in Kinshasa and then Hiernaux began research in the east in 1953. The latter, appointed Rector of the Official University of Congo at Lubumbashi in 1956 initiated research on the archaeology of the recent past in Shaba. The existence of archaeological remains in the Upemba depression in the centre of the province had been noted as early as 1909. New finds were regularly made and sometimes offered to the Museum at Tervuren. In 1945, Cabu had even recorded about ten sites, in the course of exploration, but no excavations had been organized. Once again, it needed an ethnologist, Maesen of the Museum of Tervuren who, after a visit to the area, attended the third Pan-African Congress which in 1955 was being held at Livingstone. Here he met Hiernaux and drew his attention to the existence of these sites (Maret 1985a: 35–9). In 1957 the first excavations in the Upemba finally started, under the joint direction of Hiernaux and Nenquin. In the first year they excavated the Sanga site which was shown to be an extremely large cemetery of exceptional wealth (Nenquin 1963). The following year Hiernaux continued these excavations, then in 1959 undertook the excavation of Katoto (Hiernaux, Longrée, De Buyst 1971; Hiernaux, Maquet, De Buyst 1972). This work revealed the existence of groups of people whose skills in the working of metal, ivory and pottery attested to a very ancient, advanced culture in the centre of the continent. This newly-revealed wealth had a tremendous impact at the time, even more so as these cultures were isolated in time as well as space. Thus on the eve of independence, discoveries were made that demonstrated that the archaeo-logical wealth of Central Africa was not confined to the Stone Age.

Outside Zaïre, Lebeuf tirelessly pursued his research on the region to the south of Lake Chad, where he mixed ethnography and archaeology (Griaule and Lebeuf 1948, 1950; Lebeuf and Masson Detourbet 1950; Lebeuf 1962). In the British Cameroons, Jeffreys (1951) made a series of collections of large tools of flaked and polished basalt which he attributed to the Neolithic. In an article published in 1951, Nicolas stressed that, apart from research in northern Cameroon, all the other known artefacts from the country comprised surface collections and thus only a classification by technique was possible, all chronology being precluded. He also noted the immense hiatus that existed between the stone artefacts and the oldest oral tradition.

Immediately to the south of Cameroon, in the small Spanish colony of Equatorial Guinea, no research was done until a Spanish archaeologist,

Martinez Santa Olalla (1947), was sent there in 1946 on a brief expedition. He mainly described material discovered on the island of Fernando Poo (now Bioko) and mentioned, without giving any details, two sites on the mainland. From 1951, spurred on by a missionary, Martin, and in collaboration with the local authorities and the Ethnological Museum of Barcelona, research was undertaken on the island, where the population had remained at a Neolithic stage until the arrival of Europeans. This research permitted the establishment of a detailed sequence consisting of a pre-Neolithic stone industry, followed by a Neolithic where one could distinguish nine stages that Martin (1960, 1965) grouped into four principal phases. The evolution of the lithic tool-kit, of the pottery and of the areas inhabited was meticulously established. Only very limited excavations were undertaken, and most stratigraphic observations were made on the archaeological levels exposed by the sea. Two radiocarbon dates were obtained. A series of promising sites were also recorded by Perramon (1968) in Rio Muni itself. Equatorial Guinea's independence in 1968 and the installation of one of the worst dictatorships ever known in Africa put an end to this promising research, the results of which were only published in very condensed form.

The prehistory of the Central African Republic remained in oblivion for twenty years until 1955, when, during renewed geological exploration, the presence of flaked stone artefacts was noted in the alluvial deposits of several rivers (Berthoumieux and Delany 1957). Other geological expeditions continued to draw attention to archaeological discoveries in the years preceding independence (Bayle des Hermens 1975: 16–17).

In Gabon stone artefacts were also collected during exploration and construction work (Beauchène 1963; Blankoff 1969).

In the Congo, Le Roy, attaché of Prehistory at the Institute of Central African Studies, began in 1950 to study the deposits located previously in Brazzaville. He was particularly interested in establishing the stratigraphic positions of the industries (Le Roy 1950). In the north of the country, Bodoesse gave Breuil a collection of tools from a laterite quarry to study. Following his method, which combined typology with the degree of patination, Breuil distinguished Sangoan, lower Lupembian and Tshitolian artefacts (Breuil 1955a).

Finally, in Angola before independence in 1975, Santos Jr and Ervedosa (1970) excavated a shell midden at Benefica, immediately south of Luanda. In the centre of the country, a primary school teacher and, when the fancy took him, gold-digger Moura (1957) explored and dug some test-pits at the Feti la Choya site, considered by the Ovibundu as the place where, according to legend, Choya their first queen was buried. Afterwards, Childs (1964) collected some samples of wood from the lower level of one of the structures, which were dated at Yale.

In Rwanda-Burundi, still under Belgian mandate, Nenquin was invited in 1960 by J. Vansina, at the time head of the local centre of IRSAC, to excavate known royal sites in the hope of testing some of his views on the history of the area, his own study of the local oral traditions being almost complete (Nenquin 1967: 3). But on Nenquin's arrival this project appeared impossible due to the vastness of the sites and the very tense political climate. Thus, Nenquin resorted to Stone Age studies. He undertook surveys and excavated three sites in order to establish the stratigraphic ordering of the lithic industries. This enabled him to increase the number of known sites in the country to 127, on the basis of which he was able to write the first general and well-illustrated account of the prehistory of the region. It seemed particularly interesting to Nenquin that in this part of the continent one found industries which appeared to be intermediate between those of the Congo/Zaïre basin and those of East Africa (Nenquin 1967: 295–9).

Phase 4. Post-independence

Immediately following independence, the development of archaeological research was hampered not only by the ever-present problem of the natural environment, but also by a very difficult political situation, as all the states in the area suffered civil wars or *coups d'état*, if not both. In this context, institutionally sponsored archaeology virtually came to a halt. Faced with enormous socio-economic problems, the local authorities could not consider archaeology as a priority.

Former colonial institutions disappeared or underwent an identity crisis. In all of Central Africa, there was not one properly trained national to carry on research. Only a handful of European amateurs continued to do field-work wherever local conditions allowed. Such was the case in Gabon, a country that held very little interest for archaeologists during the colonial era, and became very prosperous after its independence. In 1961, expatriates created a Société Préhistorique et Protohistorique Gabonaise whose members included one of the French advisers to the Gabonese president who gave his support, and Blankoff (1969), who had formerly studied Zaïre's prehistory. This dynamic team of amateurs initiated many surveys, the results of which were published in a bulletin and several memoirs.

In Zaïre, at the beginning of the 1960s only two missionaries, Anciaux de Faveaux (1966) and van Moorsel, carried on their research but with meagre resources. The latter continued his study of the Kinshasa plain and, with the collaboration of a geomorphologist, De Ploey, he was able to work out the stratigraphy and the palaeoecological evolution of the region (De Ploey and van Moorsel 1963). In 1968, van Moorsel became curator of the Museum of Prehistory that he had started at the Lovanium University of Kinshasa and published an *Atlas de Préhistoire de la Plaine de Kinshasa*, in which thirty years of research were summarized, but which was mainly addressed to his students and secondary school pupils. It was the first attempt to incorporate prehistoric research into a school curriculum. Meanwhile, the critical situation prevailing in Zaïre led the archaeology department of what by then had been re-baptized the Royal Museum of Central Africa in Tervuren to launch an important research project on the Benue River in north-eastern Nigeria. This attempt at geographical diversification was not very successful and soon after, Daniel Cahen, a member of that team, had the opportunity to carry out two seasons of excavations in 1969 and 1970 at the site of Kamoa in Shaba in order to make a coherent interpretation of this Acheulean site, which Cabu had discovered thirty years earlier. These excavations enabled Cahen (1975) to outline, thanks to an interdisciplinary approach, a complete sequence from the Early Stone Age to the Late Iron Age.

Simultaneously on the initiative of the President of Zaïre and in co-operation with the Museum of Tervuren, the Institute of the National Museums of Zaïre (IMNZ) was created. At the same time an antiquities law was passed which required an official permit to be obtained for any excavation. Under the aegis of this new Institute and in collaboration with the Museum of Tervuren, both institutions having the same director, L. Cahen, a series of new research projects was organized. As far as archaeology was concerned the goal was to catch up with the progress that had been made in neighbouring countries like Uganda and Zambia. At the same time, a scheme to train Zaïrian archaeologists, both in the field and in European universities, was developed.

All the north and the north-east of Zaïre had been neglected archaeologically, but in 1972–3 Van Noten, who had replaced Nenquin at the head of the Prehistory section of the Museum of Tervuren, surveyed this region (Van Noten 1977–8). He discovered an important archaeological deposit in the Matupi Cave in Ituri. Study of the faunal remains (Van Neer 1981) from this site indicated that man exploited the savanna and neighbouring forests, but more importantly the deepest levels yielded examples of microlithic technology dating to about 40,000 bp (Van Noten 1977).

In 1968, a small symposium was held at Tervuren in order to discuss the excavations of Colette at Kalina and the nomenclature problems. The participants recognized the great value of his work and recommended new excavations at the site (Nenquin 1969; Clark 1971). Thus Cahen started new excavations at Kalina Point, now called Gombe Point, in 1973. This work clarified Colette's observations and six archaeological units were distinguished and dated. However, systematic efforts at refitting stone artefacts to each other brought to light the existence of important disturbances in the deposits, showing that the different archaeological units did not constitute homogeneous industries (Cahen 1976). This led Cahen (1978) to re-examine the whole problem of nomenclature and to conclude, perhaps over-pessimistically, that after the Acheulean it would be better to confine oneself to speaking of a 'Post-Acheulean Industrial Complex of Central Africa' within which any sub-division was very tentative. Cahen also proposed the withdrawal of all terms previously used. Archaeologists had come full circle, since this idea of a continuum evoked memories of the Tumbian.

Thus began a period of disillusionment for prehistorians and almost all research in Zaïre ceased. The situation was not much better in neighbouring countries where research was limited to some prospection. However, an official French body called the Office de la Recherche Scientifique et Technique d'Outre-Mer (ORSTOM) was excavating in Cameroon (Marliac 1975) and Congo (Emphoux 1965, 1970). More significant are the results obtained by Lanfranchi, a professor at the University of Brazzaville who, with some geomorphologists, attempted to resolve the issues raised by D. Cahen's excavations across the Zaïre River. Indeed, it is essential for the future of Stone Age research in this part of the continent to understand processes of disturbance of the deposits. Recently, the discovery of *in situ* prehistoric horizons has allowed a more optimistic outlook on the future of Stone Age research in Central Africa (Lanfranchi 1979, 1986).

The study of the Iron Age, which had been neglected, took off in the early 1970s. Research was problem-oriented. Two themes dominated, the first being the origin of the Iron Age, with a progressive shift in interest towards the beginning of food production, after it was realized that this period was probably the one related to Bantu expansion. Begun in Lower Zaïre, research extended northward to Gabon and Cameroon where linguists situated the Bantu homeland (Maret 1985b, 1986; Eggert 1984). The second area of interest was the potential contribution of archaeology to the history of the present-day people. Thus, new excavations were carried out in the Upemba Depression (Maret 1978). In Rwanda, some royal graves and a former capital were excavated, as well as numerous Early Iron Age brick furnace sites (Van Noten 1972, 1983; Van Grunderbeek *et al.* 1983).

At Tervuren, emphasis was placed on the interdisciplinary approach with the integration of a team of three professional archaeologists, a geomorphologist and a palynologist. Some research was also done in collaboration with the linguists from the Museum. During the 1970s this group carried out research in Zaïre, Rwanda and Burundi, resulting in a spectacular increase in radiocarbon dates (Maret *et al.* 1977; Van Noten 1982). North Cameroon was also an area where an ethnographic and historical approach was successfully added to a purely archaeological one. Besides Lebeuf and his co-workers, who were still active in the area, remarkable ethnoarchaeological research was accomplished by David on Fulani settlements and ceramics (David 1971; David and Hennig 1972). In the nearby Central African Republic, Vidal, an ethnologist by training, became interested in the megaliths around Bouar and invited archaeologists to study them (Vidal 1969; Bayle des Hermens 1975; David 1982).

The late 1960s and 1970s, a period which enjoyed some political stability and economic prosperity, saw the development in the former French and Belgian colonies of archaeological research by a new generation of professionals working from an interdisciplinary perspective. The interest in archaeology aroused in Central Africa, among both the authorities and intellectuals, resulted in the training of local African archaeologists. Unfortunately, the present financial crisis allows them to carry out their own work only rarely and leaves them very dependent on external financing, usually obtained by mounting joint expeditions with foreign archaeologists.

5. General conclusions

The history of archaeological research in Central Africa spans little more than a century. Despite the range of work that I have attempted to summarize in the preceding pages, we cannot help but find the results wanting. Nick David's remark (1981a) regarding the state of archaeology in north Central Africa, that it was an 'unknown region preserved', could in fact be applied to the whole area. Even if the environmental situation and the lack of visibility of many sites do not facilitate research, the poor state of research at present essentially results from human factors. Archaeology has been almost exclusively the work of amateurs who, in some cases, became professionals but without acquiring the right 'reflexes'. For a long time, *la belle pièce* and a mania for taxonomy were predominant; excavation was hardly ever considered. In this regard, it seems that those who had received training in the medical or natural sciences were more inclined to open up the ground than the geologists, missionaries and engineers.

Although Dr Hasse gave a prehistory course in the early 1950s at the Overseas Territories Institute in Antwerp to initiate future colonial administrators in this discipline, no Belgian university offered courses in African archaeology before Zaïre's independence. For those who know the ideological splits in Belgium, it is interesting to note that the Free University of Brussels, considered the most progressive, had as students Colette, Cabu, Mortelmans, de Heinzelin, Hiernaux, Blankoff, L. Cahen and D. Cahen. Apart from the University of Ghent where Bequaert, Nenquin, Van Noten and Stainier were trained, and the University of Liège which produced Anciaux de Faveau and Cabu (the latter defended his thesis there after having been a student at Brussels), the Free University of Brussels trained virtually all the archaeologists who worked in Zaïre. The Catholic University of Louvain, traditionally more conservative, trained not one. As this division was not linked to the existence of courses, it seems to indicate that a propensity for African archaeology corresponded to a certain liberal philosophy (in the Anglo-Saxon sense), although one should keep in mind the significant contributions to research made by numerous missionaries.

The isolation of researchers must be stressed, be it in Europe or Africa. In Belgium, it was only in 1934 that Colette became head of the Prehistory Department at Tervuren, and there was never more than one archaeologist at any time in this department up to the end of the 1960s. In Zaïre, only a few amateurs received support from the local authorities. However, at the first Pan-African Congress the official support given by the Belgian government to archaeology was cited as an example (Leakey and Cole 1952: 2). In this regard, the Second World War, which brought Mortelmans and Cabu into contact with Breuil and local researchers in South Africa, was very important. But it was especially the Pan-African Congresses of Prehistory, beginning in 1947, which made archaeologists in Central Africa more aware of what was going on elsewhere on the continent. From this point of view, just as Belgium had an intermediary role between France and the United Kingdom, so also Central Africa was subject to influence from both French researchers in West Africa and British researchers in East and South Africa. Apart from Breuil, the British influence seems to have been predominant, particularly because the French undertook little research in this part of their colonial empire.

Research was essentially focussed on prehistory. For the more recent periods, ethnologists first took the initiative by excavating in Cameroon. In Zaïre it was only with the end of the colonial era that interest developed in protohistory and the contribution that archaeology could make to the understanding of local history.

From a theoretical point of view, apart from the rather pointless discussions over nomenclature, the archaeologists hardly seemed to concern themselves with larger explanatory models. Even though it was in Central Africa that a link between the Iron Age and the Bantu expansion was first suggested and it was here that their homeland was said to be situated, there were practically no excavations designed to study these problems before the 1970s.

Contrary to the Anglo-Saxon tradition, publications on Central Africa were almost exclusively descriptive, the formation and discussion of hypotheses being exceptional. In terms of prehistory, the essense of the debate was whether to stress continuity or discontinuity in the nomenclature. Only more excavations and quantitative analyses of the material will enable progress in this field. The quantity of work accomplished is also in part a reflection of the quality of the available sites; from this point of view the poor conservation of organic remains and the mixing of deposits in open-air sites as well as rock shelters often make the work of prehistorians a thankless task.

Finally, the bulk of what has been accomplished is due to the efforts of a few individuals with very limited official support. In order to make any progress in the future, it is essential that the universities and museums of the countries concerned be given the means to bring together interdisciplinary teams, which will develop dynamic and concerted programmes of research.

8 Archaeology in Anglophone West Africa

FRANÇOIS J. KENSE

Introduction

A regional history of archaeology comprises two integral but distinct facets of the discipline. One reviews excavations and advances in methodology and the techniques of archaeological investigation. The other considers the 'social context' (Trigger 1984: 357) in which archaeologists operate. While the first focus is traditional for reviewing archaeology, changing social and political forces have been recognized in recent years as influences upon archaeological research. An 'anthropology of archaeology' is as important for evaluating reconstructions of the past as are chronometric dates and cultural sequences.

This chapter examines the development of archaeology in anglophone West Africa – the modern countries of The Gambia, Ghana, Liberia, Nigeria and Sierra Leone (fig. 8:1). This grouping is largely arbitrary beyond sharing English as a national language. Isolating these countries from the francophone states also reflects an Eurocentric perspective based on the colonial heritage. A full analysis of the context in which archaeology developed in this area is beyond the scope and resources of this paper. However, it is hoped that several important factors identified herein will receive further study.

This division does not refute or belittle the common cultural and political history of West Africa. Rather, it recognizes that archaeology arose from a peculiarly western curiosity about the past that was largely alien to Africans. Furthermore, as European traditions of archaeology varied, so too did the colonial archaeologies of the francophone and anglophone regions develop in different ways. Although Trigger's tripartite division of the social environment of archaeology into national, colonial and imperial orientations is important (Trigger 1984), it is also appropriate to recognize the diverse interest of the colonial powers which affected the development of archaeology in their respective territories.

One example of this difference is the absence in anglophone West Africa of a central institution such as the Institut Fondamental de l'Afrique Noire (IFAN). From its headquarters in Dakar, IFAN long served as the primary scientific agency for research, publication, and the storage and curation of collections. The Institute reflected French colonial policy of centralization and assimilation of its African territories within a single political (and ultimately socio-cultural) identity. It is appropriate that the first comprehensive summary of human responses to West African environments was Raymond Mauny's *Tableau géographique*, published in 1961 under the auspices of IFAN and integrating most relevant data from West Africa.

Britain administered its colonies as distinct and separate entities. This provided little incentive or opportunity for compiling comparative scientific information. Archaeologists worked largely in isolation and in ignorance of each other's research. Oliver Davies's *West Africa Before the*

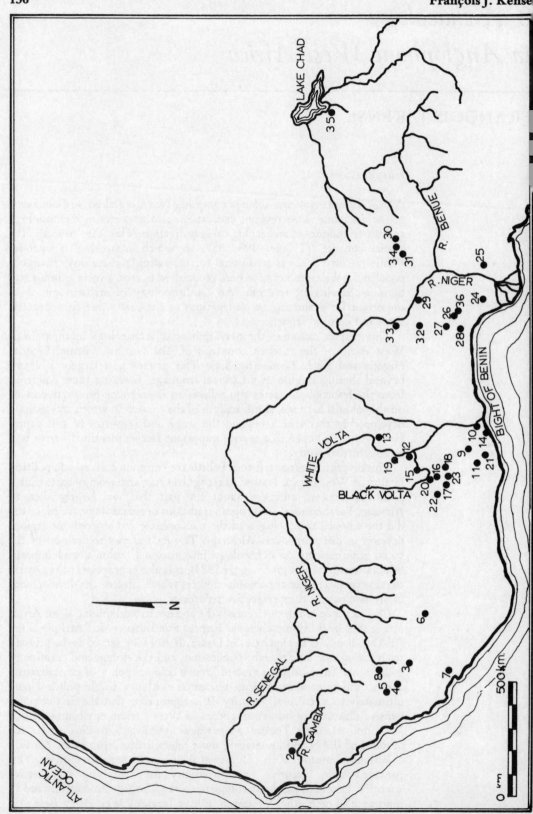

Europeans, published in 1967, although also a pioneering monograph, reflected a greater difficulty in presenting a sweeping overview of the anglophone areas in comparison with Mauny's review of the French Sudan.

Yet in spite of this basic difference between francophone and anglophone areas, West Africa as a whole has proved elusive to synthetic studies. No further studies, in either English or French, on a scale similar to those of Mauny and Davies have been published. This largely reflects, I think, a demographic and cultural pattern in West Africa that is more complex than those of eastern and southern Africa. The antiquity and density of its present-day population, the impact of long distance trade and of Islam, and the diversity of environmental zones have made West African societies unique in Africa. These factors possibly intimidated scholars from evaluating and interpreting evidence from neighbouring regions. It is ironic that many summaries of West African prehistory, as presented in major monographs, are often written by specialists in southern and eastern Africa (Clark 1970; Oliver and Fagan 1975; Phillipson 1985). Summaries by West African specialists of regional research are available, but not abundant (Anquandah 1982; Davies 1961a, 1964a; McIntosh and McIntosh 1981, 1983; Shaw 1945, 1963a, 1969a, 1972a, 1978, 1981a).

The scheme

The development of archaeology in anglophone West Africa can be subsumed within three stages. The initial stage spans the earliest recognition of archaeological materials to the arrival of the first professional archaeologists. The second stage begins in the late 1930s and lasts to independence (1957–64). Research during this period focussed on reconstructing culture history, with sporadic excavation. Education and problem-oriented archaeology characterizes the third stage which started in the 1960s. Africans trained during this decade are now active professionals. Their dominance of West African archaeology may well signify a second phase within this third stage; a phase in which indigenous archaeologists are responsible for initiating and sustaining independent research. Unfortunately, this last development has occurred only in Ghana and Nigeria. There are no trained archaeologists from the Gambia, Liberia or Sierra Leone.

Recognition of a past

In the present state of our information, it is impossible to offer any conjecture as to the age of these [stone age] implements. The depth at which they occur, and the absence of any tradition concerning them, prove no doubt that they are not of yesterday, but do not necessarily indicate any great antiquity. (Lubbock 1872: xcv)

Until recently, Europeans did not consider Africa to have had much of a history in the traditional sense. This attitude, which accorded Africa with a sense of timelessness, discouraged the growth of archaeology. To the European observer in the late nineteenth century, the African peoples represented a mirror of how Europeans once lived. While some groups were stone-using and nomadic, others used and made iron goods and engaged in long-distance trade. However, many aspects of material culture, viewed from a technological perspective, seemed surprisingly primitive.

Africa was seen as a 'cultural museum in which archaic cultural traditions ... continued ... without contributing to the main course of human progress' (Clark 1969: 181).

The concept of 'history' in African traditions also discouraged a more enlightened view. Most societies viewed the past and present as forming an uninterrupted continuum. Continuity between generations, emphasized through ancestral worship and kinship relationships, ensured that the present was understood largely through an identification with forebears. There was little allowance for change or innovation in either the cultures or the traditions of the African groups which colonials encountered.

Attention to an African past began in the late nineteenth century as part of a general desire to address universal cultural questions. The quote at the beginning of this section is one of the earliest references to archaeological material from West Africa (Lubbock 1872). These implements, perforated pebbles and 'thunderbolts' or 'God's axes', were recovered from the Gold Coast (now Ghana) littoral. The fellows of the Royal Anthropological Institute were intrigued by the similarity of these groundstone axes to ones known from Europe and India. The artefacts were not examined so much for what they indicated about the African past (see also Balfour 1903); instead, they were seen as a graphic example of human psychic unity and parallel development.

With the absence of professional archaeologists in West Africa until 1937, archaeology was the work of amateurs. In many cases archaeology was inadvertently pursued by geologists during their fieldwork. Many archaeological data, therefore, were contained in the records and publications of various Geological Surveys (see below). They provided a valuable source of information concerning the location of archaeological sites in areas poorly known to outsiders. Since the interests of geology, however, were distinct from those of archaeology, the archaeological data were usually random and incomplete. Nevertheless, they encouraged a greater appreciation of Africa's antiquity.

This period is best exemplified by three individuals who had a strong amateur interest in archaeology. Sir Albert Kitson, a Director of the Gold Coast Geological Survey, recorded customs and archaeological remains from both Nigeria and Ghana in the opening decades of this century. Although he published only sporadically (Kitson 1913, 1916), he did assemble a substantial collection of artefacts. Although some of the Ghanaian material remained in Ghana, much of it went to England (Shaw 1945: 470).

N.R. Junner, another Director of the Gold Coast Survey, made extensive observations on the elevations of river terraces and coastal shorelines (Junner 1939, 1940). This led to the recognition of climatic variation in West Africa and a preliminary appreciation of its importance for prehistory. Junner discovered numerous artefacts through his fieldwork and reported on many of these in his annual contributions to the *Geological Bulletin*. An important discovery made in 1931 was the network of trenches in the area of Manso and Akwatia (Braunholtz 1936: 469). Excavation of some of these trenches in 1934–5 yielded potsherds which, although in unstratified contexts, showed some stylistic variation with increasing depth below the surface. This evidence strengthened the recognition that there was indeed an African past, that it was of sufficient age to change over time, and that it was identifiable in the archaeological record. Junner's work is the first example of systematic excavation in Ghana. He excavated the trenches in Manso as part of a strategy to resolve an archaeological problem. Although Junner admitted that the Survey could not afford the time to continue the work, he was able to conclude that the trenches were pre-European and the pottery was quite distinct from present Asante wares (Braunholtz 1936: 472–4).

R.P. Wild, Inspector of Mines until 1937, contributed prolifically about archaeological finds to both local publications like the *Gold Coast Review* (which he founded) and the *Gold Coast Teachers' Journal* (1927a, 1927b, 1931 and 1935c) and to scientific journals like *Man* (1934, 1935a, 1935b and 1937). Wild was mainly interested in the history and the prehistory of the inhabitants of Asante region, since that was the location of most mining activities.

Although antiquities were encountered by geologists working elsewhere in West Africa or included in geological reports (e.g. Braunholtz 1926), there were seemingly fewer keen amateurs outside Ghana. One of the few reports on the geology of The Gambia to contain a brief description of stone circles and grinding hollows, which were observed during a two-month survey (Cooper 1927: 34–5), was in fact written by a member of the Gold Coast Geological Survey.

Archaeological investigation in The Gambia, however, was not entirely unknown. The impressive megaliths (or stone circles) of Senegambia excited the attention of explorers, travellers and historians for several centuries. These circles, so reminiscent of European monuments, were unexpected amongst a people who lived in huts of mud and thatch and professed to have no knowledge of the ruins. Preliminary investigations of several stone circles by Todd (1903) and Ozanne in the first decade of this century, were followed by excavations of some of the larger circles by Todd and Wolbach (1911) and later by Parker (1923). Considering the period in which these investigators were working, especially when one remembers contemporary research conclusions concerning Great Zimbabwe (e.g. Hall 1905), Todd and Wolbach took a very enlightened view of their work. This was possible largely because there was less political and social pressure on researchers from within the colony to demonstrate a foreign (i.e. non-African) origin for the ruins than there was in Southern Africa. An unattractive climate and low potential for large-scale farming in The Gambia discouraged settlement by outsiders, and prevented their need for legitimizing control. Instead, Todd and Wolbach noted similarities in the style and form of pottery and spearheads currently in use among neighbouring villages with a few antiquities collected from around the circles. They were interested in examining whether other articles and human bones excavated from the circles would also prove comparable (1911: 162). Although their method of analysing excavated human material is questionable, their conclusion that the circles were the product of African activity, albeit not by the present population, was significant. This interpretation has been vindicated by later archaeological work.

Although some interesting artefacts had been reported from Sierra Leone (Joyce 1909), and there had been a Monuments and Relics Commission there for some time, very little archaeological investigation occurred until the 1960s.

Geology was not the only form of enquiry that contributed to archaeology. Documentary histories written in the late nineteenth and early twentieth centuries contained valuable data pertaining to regional histories that might otherwise have been lost (Reeve 1912; Claridge 1915; Migeod 1926; Talbot 1926; Palmer 1936; Niven 1937; Gray 1940; Ward 1948). Unfortunately, historians usually recognized only a very limited historical span for West African cultures. Most paid only scant attention to, or completely ignored, the pre-European contact period. That 'the authentic history of the Gambia begins with the penetration of the Portuguese in the fifteenth century' (Southorn 1952: 15) was not an uncommon sentiment in many colonies. More ambitious writers, recognizing a far greater antiquity than a mere 400 years, were usually satisfied with conclusions made 'on the basis of scanty references in the writings of contemporary Greek and Carthaginian travellers' (McCulloch 1950: 7).

A second tradition of historiography, represented by the writings of educated Africans, was more sensitive to the past of indigenous societies (e.g. Reindorf 1895; Johnson 1921). These writers devoted considerable attention to oral traditions in the interpretation of pre-contact events. A drawback to their value as historical records, however, was the inability to verify the details independently and the limited context within which they could be evaluated. These problems also plagued later attempts at interpreting specific royal histories (e.g. Meyerowitz 1951, 1952). Nevertheless, some important frameworks for later archaeological research were suggested.

However, the group most responsible for studying West African societies, was the cadre of anthropologists who were active from the 1920s through to Independence. Many worked initially as government officials (e.g. Cardinall 1920; Rattray 1923, 1927; Nadel 1942); later, others were affiliated with various academic institutions (e.g. Forde 1951; Fortes and Evans-Pritchard 1940; Goody 1954, 1964). Their contribution to archaeology consisted of their study of cultural processes and the role of material culture within particular social systems. Although these anthropologists were only marginally concerned with the archaeology of the areas in which they worked they often recognized the potential of archaeological research (e.g. Rattray 1923).

The development of Nigerian archaeology was influenced most directly by art history. The finely crafted plaques, heads and statues in terracotta or 'bronze' had long excited public and scholarly imagination. The appearance of these materials in Europe, after large-scale plundering of Benin in 1897–8 and the pilfering from Ife by Frobenius a decade later, resulted in numerous scholarly descriptions and interpretations of their significance to Nigerian art (e.g. Pitt-Rivers 1900; Dalton 1903; Frobenius 1913; Braunholtz 1940; Fagg and Underwood 1949). Many of the famous pieces were discovered accidentally as construction increased during the first quarter of this century. The earliest known terracotta, later assigned to the 'Nok' tradition, from the Jos Plateau, was uncovered during tin-mining operations in 1928 (Fagg 1945b, 1962; Eyo and Willett 1980: 4), while the first cache of bronzes from the site of Igbo-Ukwu was uncovered in 1938.

Initially these pieces were studied as unique art forms, with little consideration given to their cultural affinities. Whether the technology was indigenous or introduced by Europeans was considered more important than determining the context in which they were produced. Although enlightened views concerning their significance were expressed (Meyerowitz and Meyerowitz 1939; Meyerowitz 1941a, 1941b, 1943), it was not until later that detailed archaeological work provided more plausible interpretations.

Kenneth Murray pioneered the struggle for preserving and conserving these materials. Seconded to the colonial government in 1927, he first reviewed the effects of education on traditional crafts and later taught art history (Eyo and Willett 1980: xi; National Commission for Museums and Monuments 1983: 10). Murray took a personal interest in Nigerian arts and started a substantial collection. He, and others such as the editor of *Nigeria*

Magazine (Shaw 1978: 13), urged the colonial government to initiate preventative action against the steady loss of antiquities (Murray 1939, 1941). This lobbying eventually resulted in the establishment of the Nigerian Antiquities Service in 1943 and in his appointment as Surveyor of Antiquities.

The pioneering professionals

the other chief difficulty of archaeological investigation in the Gold Coast, as perhaps might be expected . . . is the lack of any chronological framework or sequence of cultures into which discoveries can be fitted. (Shaw 1945: 470)

Braunholtz noted in 1936 that 'it is clear that there is here a large, interesting and almost untouched field awaiting the spade of the trained archaeologist' (1936: 474). His comment was applicable to all of anglophone West Africa. Within four years, two trained archaeologists were based in West Africa: Thurstan Shaw became a lecturer and part-time curator of the tiny museum at Achimota College in Ghana in 1937; Bernard Fagg went to Nigeria in 1939 as an Assistant District Officer with the Nigerian Administrative Service. The task confronting them was formidable and was not eased by the scepticism they faced from their peers at home. Shaw recalls Grahame Clark's response to one worker enthusing about his African work with, 'Rather peripheral, isn't it?' (Shaw, pers. comm.). Archaeology was not, however, the primary duty of these archaeologists in their early years; research had to be fitted within a busy schedule of other duties. Fagg's first excavation, at Rop Rock Shelter, took place in 1944 during his leave from colonial administration while Shaw took advantage of school breaks to undertake his research between 1937 and 1945 (Shaw, this volume).

The sites selected by Shaw and Fagg for excavation reflected their perception of the discipline and the major issues within it. In particular, as Cambridge-trained students of Miles Burkitt and peers of Desmond Clark and Charles McBurney, they were interested in Palaeolithic materials and lithic technology. However, the continuity between much of the observed archaeological record and the indigenous societies of West Africa was soon apparent to Shaw and Fagg. Whereas the West African data yielded little immediate evidence for the Early and Middle Stone Ages, it was clear that settled, agricultural and metal-using peoples had long occupied the region. Since much of this latter record was undocumented, it seemed an appropriate focus for their research.

The importance attributed to sheltered sites for retrieving archaeological data was shown by Shaw's choice of Bosumpra Cave (Shaw 1944) and Fagg's work at Rop Rock Shelter (Fagg 1945a). The evidence for a microlithic component at both sites had encouraged their examination. What proved to be surprising, however, was the presence of pottery fragments and ground-stone adzes or axes in association with the microliths. This new evidence suggested that the development of agriculture and technology in West Africa followed a different trajectory from Asia and Europe. Without clear means of dating their finds, however, the full significance of these early excavations remained unknown for some years.

This initial work in West Africa needs to be viewed within the context of research in Africa as a whole. Considerable interest in early hominids and hominoids from Africa was generated by the discoveries and gradual acceptance of the finds by Dart and Broom in South Africa between 1924 and 1947 (Tobias 1985b) and by Louis Leakey in East Africa after 1931. The strong interest of Leakey, and others like Van Riet Lowe and Goodwin in Southern Africa, in Stone Age cultures resulted in several studies proposing relative chronologies and sequences. Encouraging these interests was a belief in the relatively recent introduction of iron to Africa, rendering the later period of less archaeological significance. There were also possible political undertones in avoiding direct investigation of the Iron Age (Hall 1984a and this volume).

This bias in favour of Stone Age studies can be measured by the papers presented at the early Pan-African Congresses of Prehistory. While the importance of these congresses is discussed elsewhere in this volume, it is instructive to note that out of the 53 papers given in 1947, only 3 (Mauny, Arkell and Amer Bey) related to topics not concerning Pleistocene environments, geology, human palaeontology or Stone Age archaeology. The situation only became more balanced with the fourth Congress in 1959 (Léopoldville), when 18 papers, out of 40 published, concerned the post-Stone Age period. What did not increase as quickly, however, was the proportion of participants at the congresses who were involved in research in West Africa. In 1947, only 3 participants (out of 61 attending) worked in West Africa, and of these, only Fagg was from anglophone West Africa. In 1952 (Algeria), Fagg was joined by two English participants from Ghana – Oliver Davies and A.W. Lawrence. These three were also the only representatives from anglophone West Africa three years later. In 1959, there were 7 participants (out of 32) from all of West Africa. Only four (Davies, B.E.B. Fagg, W. Fagg and Frank Willett) were from anglophone areas. There were several reasons for this poor representation by anglophone West African researchers. Since most congresses were held in eastern or southern Africa, the cost of travel was certainly prohibitive. However, a more important factor was the slow rate at which an archaeological community developed in the anglophone areas. This was due largely to an absence of institutions committed to archaeological research prior to the 1950s.

Shaw began excavation of a mound at Dawu in Akwapim region in 1942. While the final report is not explicit on why this site was chosen for excavation, one major goal of the research was clearly to establish a coherent chronology at a time when chronometric techniques were unknown (see Shaw, this volume). This was accomplished in part by correlating the traditional historical sources about the site with material objects for which a calendrical association was possible. This information, in conjunction with a measurement for the rate of deposition, allowed Shaw to date the whole mound (Shaw 1961).

Two other major interests of the Dawu research were related to the dating issue. Shaw recognized the importance of those materials for which external sources could provide a calendrical reference. One of these was the clay tobacco pipe. Dawu is one of the first sites in West Africa from which pipes were excavated from controlled stratigraphic contexts. Since the evidence is quite strong that tobacco smoking was introduced from the New World, the pipe was interpreted as appearing in West Africa from the sixteenth century onwards (Shaw 1960; Ozanne 1969). The Dawu material provided a preliminary pipe sequence by style and form. Shaw's position that more acutely angled pipes reflected a later period of manufacture has been verified repeatedly from other sites in West Africa (York 1973; Afeku 1976; Boachie-Ansah 1986; Kense 1981). The other

8:2 *Oliver Davies on leave from Ghana in Windhoek, Namibia 1957*

class of material that interested Shaw was that made from metals. In particular, he believed non-ferrous objects to represent evidence for an indigenous network of trade links with surrounding areas for raw materials or finished products. Shaw renewed his work on cuprous artefacts in his later study of Nigerian material.

Oliver Davies (fig. 8:2) was appointed to the Archaeology Department at Legon in 1952. Davies, a classicist by training (pers. comm.), had done archaeology in Ireland and Natal. When Davies arrived at Legon, Shaw had been out of Ghana for six years and Lawrence was concentrating on historical material. Thus, Davies felt that since so little was known archaeologically about Ghana, it was necessary to address basic issues, and his geological interests, developed during his stay in Natal, strongly influenced his approach to research. He devoted considerable time to examining beach and river terraces in order to reconstruct the quaternary environment (Davies 1952, 1956, 1957a, 1959b and 1964a). He also concentrated on locating evidence for early hominids in West Africa and for the appearance of Early and Middle Stone Age materials (Davies 1956, 1957b, 1959a). These concerns are demonstrated in the chapters of his summary of West African prehistory (Davies 1967).

One of Davies's lasting contributions to the archaeology of Ghana was his ceaseless and untiring commitment to field survey. Davies was the first, and as yet only, archaeologist in West Africa to make an extensive survey of a single country; the results of this work were published later as *Ghana Field Notes* by the Department of Archaeology (1970, 1972 and 1976). In his surveys, Davies recorded the locations of hundreds of sites and features throughout Ghana, ranging from instances of a single flake or scattering of sherds to large multicomponent sites and abandoned villages. He relied heavily on the existence of road cuttings and gravel pits that dotted the countryside in the wake of road construction activities. These allowed him to make quick and comparative observations about regional geological characteristics and local stratigraphies.

Davies also engaged in excavation, although, preferring to work alone or with only minimal assistance, most of his excavations were modest in size (e.g. 1973). Nevertheless, one site proved to have major implications for the understanding of Ghanaian prehistory and was to redirect Davies's focus away from the Stone Age period. The road cutting at Ntereso in northern Ghana, where Davies excavated in 1962, revealed numerous ground-stone axes, flakes and barbed points and pottery. The site also included many of the enigmatic objects made from either stone or baked clay that Davies termed, somewhat confusingly, 'terracotta cigars'. He interpreted a major part of the site to represent a Neolithic phase in West Africa known as 'Kintampo' (Davies 1960, 1962, 1973, 1980), since the material at Ntereso was quite similar to that identified earlier from the Kintampo areas (Kitson 1916: 380), as well as from several other localities around Ghana (e.g. Christian's Village and Mole Park).

Davies also became more interested in the Iron Age after he identified iron in the upper levels of Ntereso. He believed that iron technology, as with several other major innovations, had diffused to West Africa from north of the Sahara Desert. He was very concerned, therefore, to demonstrate north–south links in the archaeological record (Davies 1961b, 1966a, 1966b). His interest in the so-called 'Gonja Red Painted Pottery' (Davies 1964b), for example, also reflected this concern.

At about this time, Fagg too became increasingly interested in materials from the later or post-Stone Age period. Realizing the need for conservation of the terracottas uncovered during tin-mining activities in the Jos Plateau, Fagg began to catalogue the material during the 1940s. This was partially in preparation for the establishment of Nigeria's first museum, opened at Jos in 1952. Additional pieces recovered at Nok in 1954 initiated a lengthy period of study of what was termed the Nok culture (Fagg 1962). As with the Kintampo in Ghana, the Nok culture was associated with the beginnings of more settled communities and the practice of food production. Unlike Kintampo, however (although Davies once claimed the contrary), the Nok peoples possessed a knowledge of iron metallurgy (Fagg 1969). This is not unexpected, since the dating of Nok sites has subsequently shown them to be about a millennium later in time than the Kintampo.

The archaeological material from Nok, and to a much lesser extent from Kintampo, also had political significance. They demonstrated to the world that Africa had achieved an excellence in technology and art in the past that rivalled developments anywhere in the world. These sentiments provided a great source of pride to West Africans and instilled the belief that they could excel again.

Building national infrastructures

Archaeology achieved a new level of professionalism in Ghana and Nigeria during the 1950s and 1960s. On the eve of independence the new governments were very receptive to nurturing an indigenous archaeology as one way of sustaining nationalist sentiments. Archaeology was supported in three principal ways. One method was a museum network responsible for conserving and preserving the national heritage. A key task of the newly created Nigerian Antiquities Service in 1943 was the development of a dispersed museum structure throughout Nigeria. The abundance and diversity of art works and other archaeological material from the various regions of Nigeria necessitated immediate care. This, in conjunction with strong ethnic feelings in each region, encouraged the growth of local repositories under a national umbrella. After the Esie Museum was opened in 1945 (Shaw 1978: 13), others followed at Jos (1952), Ife (1954) and Lagos (1957). Several more were opened in the 1960s. The National Antiquities Department was created by legislation in 1953 to succeed the Antiquities Service, B.E.B. Fagg becoming its Director.

In 1951, A.W. Lawrence (the brother of T.E. Lawrence) was appointed to positions in two newly created institutions in Ghana – as Curator and then Director of the National Museum of the Gold Coast and as Professor of Archaeology at University College, Legon. Lawrence had left the Chair of Classical Archaeology at Cambridge to assume the appointments in Ghana. Although his historical interests led him to study the numerous castles and forts along the Ghanaian coast (Lawrence 1963), Lawrence was responsible for creating a national museum and a department of archaeology. Although there were plans to establish regional museums, the building of the National Museum in Accra received priority and no other museums have yet been finished.

This museum development is closely associated with Ghana's first indigenous archaeologist, Richard Nunoo. Although never formally trained in archaeology, Nunoo apprenticed under Shaw for several years. He excavated in 1945/6 (Nunoo 1948) and continued to undertake sporadic research over the next dozen years (Nunoo 1959). But after he assumed the Directorship of the Ghana National Museum in 1961 (following a four-year term by H.D. Collings), Nunoo's active fieldwork was greatly reduced.

A second means of influencing indigenous archaeology was through supervisory agencies which could monitor, and potentially direct, the growth of archaeological research. In Ghana, this role was combined with that of the Museums and Monuments Board while in Nigeria it was the responsibility of the Department of Antiquities.

The third mechanism was to create university departments through which archaeology would be undertaken. In Ghana, the first appointment to the chair of the Department of Archaeology at Legon, following its administrative separation from the Museum, was Peter Shinnie, who held the post from 1957 to 1966. Shinnie was an Egyptologist by training, who had gone to Africa as Assistant Commissioner with the Sudan Antiquities Service in 1946 (Shinnie, this volume). Through his energies in setting up a library, a lab and work rooms at Legon, Shinnie established the department as a credible and functioning entity. He also played an important role (along with John Fage) in the creation of the Institute of African Studies at Legon (1961), serving as its director for the first year. Shinnie's knowledge of Arabic and Islam led him to focus his research on northern Ghana where he excavated at Yendi Dabari (Shinnie and Ozanne 1962), the first later Iron Age occupation to be examined in Ghana. Shinnie used oral and written traditions about the Dagomba to interpret the archaeology of this their first capital, while the historian Ivor Wilks investigated Arabic/Islamic influence in the north (Wilks 1961, 1962, 1968).

Although Nigeria was first to take adequate measures against the destruction of the archaeological record, it was much slower than Ghana to create an academic department. In 1963, the University of Ibadan appointed Thurstan Shaw as Professor of Archaeology within the Institute of African Studies. It was only in 1970 that Shaw succeeded, after some opposition (pers. comm.), in establishing a separate Department of Archaeology, where he served as its head until 1974 (Shaw, this volume). Ibadan produced Nigeria's first professional archaeologist, Ekpo Eyo, who, following some early excavations in Nigeria (Eyo 1965, 1972), completed his dissertation in 1974 (Eyo 1974). Eyo was until recently the Director of the National Commission for Museums and Monuments (formerly the Department of Antiquities).

The impact of the archaeology departments at Legon and Ibadan upon the archaeology of their respective countries was considerable. Throughout the 1960s and the first half of the 1970s, archaeological research was initiated in many areas hitherto unexamined. As governments embarked upon elaborate and costly economic development schemes, usually through the participation of international agencies, substantial amounts of funds became available with which to carry out archaeological surveys and excavations. Increased government financial support encouraged the appointment of a number of research fellows and lecturers from overseas, especially Great Britain. One of the staff at Legon was Paul Ozanne, who, besides excavating several sites in southern Ghana during the early 1960s (Ozanne 1962, 1965), made a major contribution to West African archaeology through his painstaking study of clay tobacco pipes, by which he established a pipe typology that accurately reflected changes in style and form through time (Ozanne 1966a, 1969).

In 1953, the Nigerian Department of Antiquities undertook small-scale excavations around the sacred groves of Ife (Shaw 1978: 147). It was hoped that some stratigraphic context could be determined for the many terracottas and bronzes hitherto found only accidentally. Most of the sites tested, unfortunately, were the result of secondary deposits and not very informative. Additional accidental discoveries of materials at Ita Yemoo (Ife) four years later led the department to prevent further destruction of the site by purchasing the land outright. Such a costly response by a government agency was not common.

Ita Yemoo was excavated in the 1957/8 and 1962/3 seasons by Frank Willett (Willett 1960b; Fagg and Willett 1962). Trained as a philologist and anthropologist at Oxford, Willett was seconded to the Department of Antiquities for two years when Nigeria requested a museum expert to help with the final preparations of the Lagos Museum (Willett, pers. comm.). Upon his arrival, he had been offered the opportunity to excavate at Old Oyo (Willett 1960a, 1962), and from 1958 to 1963, he was employed as Government Archaeologist and Curator of the Ife Museum. During his stay at Ife, Willett catalogued and organized the Ife material for display, as well as studied its significance (Willett 1967).

Although it had been known since 1938 that the village of Igbo-Ukwu in south-eastern Nigeria had yielded some remarkable bronzes, it was not until 1959 that systematic excavation of the site was commenced. Igbo-Ukwu actually consists of three adjacent sites, each the result of a different activity (Shaw 1970a: 257). One of the principal objectives of the excavation was to determine the age of the materials associated with each site. This aim reflected the continuing debate about the status of the Nigerian bronzes. Much of the material from Benin appeared to be of fairly recent manufacture and use. Although the Ife statues and heads were usually recovered from the ground, the symbolism and style of the pieces had many parallels with Benin and modern artwork from the area. The Ife material, therefore, was not suspected to be of significant antiquity. Since it also seemed logical that craftsmen obtained their raw metals through overseas trade, the view that the works in bronze and brass dated to the contact period of Europeans with West Africa was gaining credence. The evidence from Igbo-Ukwu challenged that interpretation (Shaw 1970a: 259–62). Although material for radiocarbon dating was poorly

8:3 *Richard York's excavations at New Buipe, Ghana 1966*

8:4 *Pottery found in the excavations at New Buipe*

preserved at the sites, three samples did produce dates in the ninth century AD. These clearly suggested that West Africans were working with non-ferrous technology well before the arrival of the Europeans six centuries later. In the face of some opposition to this interpretation (e.g. Lawal 1972, 1973), Shaw eloquently defended his position (Shaw 1975).

Two other individuals contributed to the archaeology of Nigeria during this period. Oliver Myers, an Egyptologist by training, excavated in the Ife area during the 1963/4 season (Myers 1967). William Fagg, older brother of Bernard Fagg, and Assistant Keeper of Ethnography with the British Museum, developed a keen interest in Nigerian art (Fagg 1958, 1963) and participated in a number of excavations. He was instrumental in bringing Nigerian works and craftsmanship to the attention of the international community (Kan, in Eyo and Willett 1980: xii).

An important boost for Ghanaian archaeology was the multi-disciplinary Volta Basin Research Project (VBRP), established in 1963 by the University of Ghana to undertake salvage studies in areas of the Volta Basin threatened with inundation by the building of the Akosombo Dam. The archaeological component of the project included extensive surveying, much of it carried out by Davies, and small-scale excavations at more than fifty sites (Calvocoressi and York 1971: 91–3; Davies 1971: 10–11). One of the largest sites found was New Buipe (fig. 8:3), which was extensively excavated and fully published (York 1973), making it one of the best known sites in Ghana. The site comprised several occupations, spanning two millennia, from the Late Stone Age period through to the eighteenth century. Indeed, it was the first documented site to demonstrate continuity, albeit broken, over such a time span. The New Buipe excavations also produced a preliminary but detailed ceramic typology for a region hitherto virtually unknown (fig. 8:4). Furthermore, the excavator, York, showed that the tobacco-pipe typology and sequence established by Ozanne for southern Ghana was applicable to at least a part of northern Ghana. York was interested in establishing some connection between the archaeological record of New Buipe and the arrival in the area of Gbanya speakers, who established the Gonja state during the seventeenth century; for York, and others who worked in the Volta Basin, recognized the importance of linking the archaeological record with the historical past in areas where the cultural links were not direct or obvious, an approach which Shinnie had applied to the Dagomba material.

During this period another project was also organized in response to the danger of site destruction. Plans for the creation of the Kainji Reservoir on the Niger River in western Nigeria resulted in both surveys and excavations in the endangered area (Breternitz 1968, 1969, 1975; Hartle 1970; Priddy 1970a, 1970b; Soper 1965; and Wade 1971). This salvage operation saw the participation of two archaeological teams, one from Colorado University and the other from the University of Ibadan. Although both groups made laudable attempts at examining as much as possible before the flooding, it is clear that considerably more work could have been undertaken (Breternitz 1975: 149; Shaw 1978: 96, this volume).

Meanwhile an ambitious excavation programme had been undertaken in Benin City by Graham Connah during the early 1960s. This yielded a large quantity of material, all of which had to be analysed and described. Connah was prudent to solicit assistance from others and the final monograph on the site included reports by a total of sixteen specialists (Connah 1975).

Archaeologists also began to take an increasing interest in the three 'weak sisters' of anglophone West Africa: The Gambia, Liberia and Sierra Leone. All the archaeological research in these countries has been

8:5 *Megalithic site at Kerbach, The Gambia*

undertaken by expatriates; there has been no development of an indigenous archaeological community. No systematic survey for sites in Sierra Leone was undertaken until 1961 (Newman 1966; Ozanne 1966b), while the first full-scale excavation was conducted by Carleton Coon and his wife at Yengema Cave in 1965 (Coon 1968). Several other archaeologists have worked in Sierra Leone over the last twenty years (Atherton 1969a; Decorse 1980, 1981). Most of Atherton's and Decorse's research has been on Late Stone Age materials and early economic subsistence patterns (Atherton 1979) though Atherton has more recently become involved with ethnoarchaeology and historical archaeology (Atherton 1983).

Atherton's long standing interest in the nature of cultural adaptations to forested and semi-forested environments (Atherton pers. comm.; 1979) led him to make a brief archaeological foray into neighbouring Liberia in 1968 (Atherton 1969b, 1970). A more comprehensive survey was carried out by a team from Boston University in 1973, under the direction of Creighton Gabel (Gabel, Borden and White 1975; Gabel 1976). Although sites were located ranging in age from Middle Stone Age occupations through to European contact times, research focussed on microlithic materials of the Late Stone Age. Unfortunately, archaeological research in Liberia has not been active over the past decade, severely limiting understanding of adaptation and change in a major environmental zone of West Africa.

Few insights into the cultures responsible for the stone circles in The Gambia (fig. 8:5) have been obtained since the early work of Todd and others. There was a brief survey in 1964/5 (Evans and Beale 1966), which was largely a recording exercise. Most of the significant research has been undertaken in Senegal (e.g. Thilman *et al.* 1980). The circles were apparently constructed during the present millennium, although differences in form may have some temporal significance. In 1977, Matthew Hill attempted to locate the habitation site of the builders of one particular stone circle by experimenting with magnetometry survey techniques (Hill 1981). Although this proved unsuccessful, his investigation of the circle located a human burial and artefacts. It is clear that most circles are associated with interments; whether this was their primary or only function remains to be determined through further research.

Local knowledge and problem-oriented research

From the late 1950s through to the mid-1960s a phenomenal increase had occurred in the number of archaeologists in West Africa, in the creation of new institutions and departments and in the availability of resources for supporting research. The following decade, however, saw the economic growth of many West African nations begin to level off in response to internal and international factors. As financial support dwindled, the archaeological community responded by refining research goals and data collecting strategies.

There was a growing awareness among archaeologists in both Nigeria and Ghana of the untapped wealth of information extant in oral, and occasionally written, traditions and in the cultural practices of the peoples of West Africa. While the traditions recorded political and social statements about the histories of particular peoples over several centuries at best, cultural practices reflected millennia of interaction with the environment. Moreover, these traditions were gradually being lost as the younger generation became less inclined to learn from or imitate its elders. Thus, it was crucial that these traditions be recorded. The study of traditional technologies was favoured by many archaeologists (for example, see Posnansky 1981: 79). The benefits to archaeology were obvious, especially if the study of oral traditions and ethnoarchaeology could be combined with direct archaeological research.

The West African Trade Project (WATP) was designed to do just that. Organized by Merrick Posnansky, who succeeded Shinnie as Professor of the Archaeology Department at Legon in 1967, the WATP was an ambitious scheme to address a number of archaeological concerns. First, it emphasized a regional study rather than the more traditional focus on a specific site. Thus, the project was designed to examine the growth and effect of trade patterns on several sites within a given area during the second millennium AD. Second, it used oral and written traditions, unique to particular ethnic groups, to establish the location of old and often abandoned sites and assist in the interpretation of their archaeological record. Third, the project encouraged examination of traditional cultural practices, such as iron-working, pottery, the building of mud houses and food storage. The feasibility of undertaking the WATP was made possible largely through Posnansky's ingenius use of his students. By encouraging students to return to their home communities, where difficulties of trust and language were more easily overcome, Posnansky was able to construct a rich database of information concerning oral traditions and ethnoarchaeological studies from a large part of Ghana (Posnansky 1971, 1972, 1973). Much of the data is regrettably not widely available, languishing as honour students' long essays or as unpublished PhD or MA theses at Legon. Fortunately, Shinnie has recently embarked on a series of publications (Effah Gyamfi 1985; Boachie-Ansah 1986; Crossland in prep.) through the University of Calgary that will bring this research to a wider readership.

A second major shift during the late 1960s and 1970s was towards a more 'problem-oriented' approach. By this phrase, I do not suggest that previous researchers were not concerned with archaeological problems. Rather I wish to emphasize an increasing recognition of the need for research strategies with explicit objectives, usually addressed at broader questions than those concerning a particular site or area and its culture history. Although there is certainly a need for the latter approach (minimally, to establish a local cultural sequence), it is a sign of a maturing discipline when more general issues are addressed through the archaeological record.

An early example of this broader approach was the work of Connah in north-eastern Nigeria. After a survey of the Lake Chad area in 1963, Connah carried out large-scale excavations of the Daima Mound. What was particularly significant in the final results of the Daima research was Connah's explicit interest in combining archaeological and historical data to interpret the changing relationship between human adaptations and the environment through time. Certainly Connah was not the first prehistorian to emphasize this approach nor is it clear that his own research was initially focussed on this; yet he has produced one of the few published studies from West Africa in which an ethnoarchaeological perspective was followed through (Connah 1981).

A similar approach was taken in the survey and excavation of the Begho area (Posnansky 1981: 77). The town of Begho was an important trading centre, located between the forest region to the south and the savanna lands to the north, through which large quantities of gold, slaves, kola, leather and metal goods passed from about the thirteenth century through to the early eighteenth century. Begho is the earliest urban centre known in Ghana and provides important clues to the effect of long-distance trade upon traditional subsistence-farming communities. The research strategy designed for use at Begho reflected a multi-facetted interest in the development and structure of the site – its demographic/ethnic settlement pattern, its economic activity areas and its access to, and use of, resources. However, there is as yet no comprehensive report on the findings at Begho, other than an MA thesis (Crossland in prep.) and some preliminary syntheses (Posnansky 1975, 1976; Crossland and Posnansky 1978) and reports (Posnansky 1979).

Most archaeological research in Ghana continues to focus on Late Stone Age and Iron Age occupations. Questions about the significance of Kintampo material encouraged the re-examination of the Kintampo K6 rock shelter (Rahtz and Flight 1974; Flight 1976) and the excavation of several sites across Ghana (Dombrowski 1976, 1980). More recent work (Gavua 1985; Stahl 1985a) has shown that, while our understanding of the economy of the Kintampo tradition is increasing, many questions remain to be answered by further excavation. Excavations at Daboya have produced the most northerly evidence for Kintampo material from an excavated site. While these excavations were focussed on the archaeological visibility of a significant social and political event known from historical data, the site also showed a continuous occupation for about three millennia (Kense 1981; Shinnie 1981; Shinnie and Kense n.d.).

An historical focus in Nigerian studies is evident from several 'History Research Schemes' undertaken from the late 1950s to the 1970s. The initial concern of the Yoruba Historical Research Scheme was to trace the migration route of the Yoruba from the Sudan. However, Willett insisted that it was first necessary to reconstruct Yoruba history in Nigeria and that the best means to achieve this was through archaeological dating of sites (Willett pers. comm.).

The involvement of specialists in the analysis of archaeological material also increased during this time. For example, metallurgists who studied the Nigerian "bronzes" dispelled a number of misconceptions about the technology and the temporal span represented by the art forms (Shaw, 1969b, 1970b; Willett and Fleming, 1976).

Indigenous archaeology

The emphasis upon education in the last two decades has resulted in the assumption of leadership by Africans of the archaeological communities in Nigeria and Ghana. Although Ghanaian and Nigerian archaeologists had held managerial positions in government for some time (e.g. Nunoo and Eyo), they were absent from such positions in the universities for another decade or more. This was partly due to the tardiness of departments in becoming teaching-oriented, particularly at the graduate level. Posnansky was mainly responsible for developing the teaching of archaeology at Legon between 1967 and 1976, using the WATP as an effective training vehicle for his students. Emphasis on instruction was also encouraged by his successor, John Sutton, and by Shaw and David at Ibadan. The introduction of archaeology at other Nigerian universities – Nsukka, Cross River – ensured that African archaeologists were trained to fill govern-mental and academic vacancies as they arose.

There has also been a diversification in the sorts of archaeological research undertaken. Many studies now focus on the researcher's own home area (e.g. Anozie 1979; Effah-Gyamfi 1985; Boachie-Ansah 1986), where the investigator's knowledge of local history and culture has helped to define the research questions and the type of data collected. James Anquandah, the first Ghanaian to occupy the chair at Legon, has spent several years examining the archaeology of the Ga-Dangme area of south-eastern Ghana (Anquandah 1982: 113–25). Many African archaeologists have also begun to work elsewhere in Africa. Bassey Wai Andah, who trained at Berkeley, excavated Stone Age sites in Upper Volta (now Burkina Faso) for his dissertation (Wai Ogosu (now Andah) 1973). He succeeded David as head of the Archaeology Department in Ibadan in 1978 and has written on diverse aspects of West African prehistory (Andah 1973, 1978, 1979a, 1979b, 1979c, 1979d). David Kiyaga-Mulindwa, a Ugandan, studied in Ghana and examined the earthworks in the Birim area (Kiyaga-Mulindwa 1976), while Francis Musonda from Zambia also studied in Ghana and examined local lithic material for his MA thesis (Musonda 1976). Colla-boration with foreign researchers has also been an important means for African archaeologists to circumvent recent economic constraints (e.g. Van Hamm and Anquandah 1986).

A major vehicle for improved communication between archaeologists in West Africa was the growth of newsletters and journals. In 1964 Shaw created the *West African Archaeological Newsletter* and was its editor until 1970. In that year he started the *West African Journal of Archaeology*, which continues, somewhat sporadically, to be published out of Nigeria, and was edited until recently by Bassey Andah. More local journals also appeared during this time, some devoted to archaeology (e.g. *Sankofa*, *Zaria Archaeological Notes*) and others with broader interests (e.g. *Liberian Studies Journal*, *Odu*, *Transactions of the Historical Society of Ghana*, *Ghana Notes and Queries*). All these publications provide a forum for the dissemination of results and discussion.

It is premature at present to summarize the significance of the present phase of archaeology or to evaluate its impact upon the theory and methodology of African research. Clearly, there have been changes in research objectives and interpretations. These are indicated in such recent publications as the special volume devoted to papers on 'Perspectives on West Africa's Past' (*West African Journal of Archaeology*, 1979) and the monograph on *Rediscovering Ghana's Past* (Anquandah 1982).

Conclusions

Archaeological research in anglophone West Africa has gradually matured, both theoretically and methodologically, over the past century. An amateur curiosity with isolated artefacts and enigmatic features was followed, in the 1940s through 1950s, with a drive to establish local chronologies and sequences. The cultural reconstructions now available for most regions of West Africa have enabled archaeologists to address increasingly complex questions. Recent research has concerned broader issues in archaeology – urbanism (e.g. McIntosh and McIntosh 1984), metallurgy (e.g. Pole 1975), agricultural beginnings (e.g. Sowuni 1985; Stahl 1985), trade patterns (e.g. Posnansky 1971; Kense n.d.) and Holocene climatic changes (e.g. Talbot and Deliberias 1977). Much of this work reflects the potential of West African data. More importantly, however, the issues discussed and the high calibre of those discussions were generated by the pioneering contributions of archaeologists like Shaw, Fagg, Davies, Willett and Posnansky. None the less, the development of West African archaeology is not complete. One area in particular that has not received adequate attention is conservation and salvage archaeology. Very few safeguards exist at present to cope with the continuous process of destruction of innumerable sites throughout West Africa. This is as much a problem of insufficient public awareness of the value of antiquities as it is of inadequate funding.

There exists also a reluctance to experiment with more advanced methods of exploration and analysis. Hill's use of a magnetometer in The Gambia is probably unique in West Africa (Hill n.d.). Although there were problems in its application, it is only by repeated experimentation with such tools that their use can be perfected. Techniques for probability surveying are also poorly developed in West Africa in comparison with other parts of the continent. Yet the terrain, vegetation cover and size of many areas in West Africa which are still unexplored warrant enhanced methods of determining site distribution and recovery. This is especially true for the forested areas in the south, where comparatively little excavation has occurred to date. The interest in specific culture histories, greatly influenced by the wealth of oral traditions, must not preclude the necessity for reconstructing the general cultural landscape and determining major processes of change.

The growth of West African archaeology has not been free of problems. A fundamental difficulty remains the lack of resources to support research. Although inadequate finance has been a major factor, lack of equipment and manpower has also been a drawback. The latter is particularly disturbing, since as the economy worsens, many promising students have turned to more lucrative forms of livelihood to support themselves and their families. For similar reasons, a number of trained Ghanaian archaeologists moved to Nigeria to take up higher-paid teaching posts. However, this trend has slowed and the department at Legon now has more Ghanaian staff than ever before. One immediate solution to the economic constraints faced by African archaeologists is for them to work in conjunction with foreign professionals. In spite of problems of communication, planning and

Acknowledgements

The writer extends his sincere thanks to those scholars who responded to the questionnaire he inflicted upon them in preparation for this chapter. Their highly informative responses were in many instances far richer in content than a summary chapter such as this can do justice to. The writer claims all responsibility for errors of interpretation concerning the views made available by the respondents.

This chapter makes no pretence to be a complete summary of the history of anglophone archaeology in West Africa. Many valuable contributions to the reconstruction of the West African past have not been discussed here; the intent of the paper has been to demonstrate the major developments in the changing character of archaeology in West Africa.

I am indebted to an anonymous reviewer for many helpful comments and suggestions in improving the contents of this chapter. I am also grateful to Peter Shinnie for his comments on an earlier draft and for his continuing to be a teacher and a friend.

And most importantly, I wish to thank both Ellen Bielawski, my wife, for her constant encouragement and support of this project and for her editorship of the manuscript, and my son, Connor, for his patience throughout the writing.

administration, joint projects are mutually beneficial. Those who reside outside West Africa should encourage such arrangements with scholars of the countries in which they wish to work. This enables the indigenous archaeological community to remain active and progressive and encourages foreign researchers to be sensitive to archaeological issues of concern – both public and academic – to the host country.

9 Changing Paradigms, Goals & Methods in the Archaeology of Francophone West Africa

PHILIP DE BARROS

The purpose of this chapter is to discuss the history of archaeology in francophone West Africa in terms of changing research orientations, methods and techniques. Summaries of current knowledge on West African archaeology are to be found in McIntosh and McIntosh (1983, 1984, 1986). Francophone West Africa is defined as coterminous with the boundaries of the colonial Afrique Occidentale Française plus Togo and thus excludes the Algerian Sahara and Tchad.

Until the 1960s, the history of archaeology in francophone West Africa was primarily the work of the French. A brief historical overview of French archaeology is thus necessary to serve as a frame of reference for developments in West Africa.

A brief historical overview of French archaeology

While a comprehensive history of French archaeology has yet to be written, Sackett (1981) and Audouze and Leroi-Gourhan (1981) have dealt with some of the basic themes. The following summary is derived from their work.

. After the heroic epoch (1840–70), marked by the recognition of Boucher de Perthes' evidence for the antiquity of man (Daniel 1975), French archaeology developed along four main lines: prehistoric and classical archaeology, Egyptology and Orientalism, each pursuing its own separate course (Audouze and Leroi-Gourhan 1981: 170). Only prehistoric and classical archaeology are directly relevant to the present discussion.

FRENCH PREHISTORIC ARCHAEOLOGY

French prehistoric archaeology deals primarily with the Stone Age and can be divided into three main periods.

A *Pioneer* or *Formative Period* (1870–c. 1900) was marked by strong influences from both the natural and social sciences. Basic concepts of stratigraphy and temporal sequence were taken straight from geology and palaeontology and a 'palaeontological' perspective was borrowed from cultural anthropology. The unilineal evolutionism of the nineteenth century became its paradigm. Just as nineteenth-century cultural anthropology tended to have little basis in field research, archaeology during this period rested only marginally on technological, typological or stratigraphic reality (Sackett 1981: 86).

The *Traditional Period* (c. 1900–c. 1950) was characterized by a dismissal of palaeontological considerations and a narrow focus on artefact classification and time-space systematics. Archaeological cultures could be identified by certain *fossiles directeurs*. Such index fossils often took on normative characteristics, summarizing major morphological themes

155

(*ibid.*: 89; see Binford [1972: 195–207; 244–94] for a discussion of the normative view *v*. a multivariate, systemic approach to archaeology). Prehistory was dominated by an organic model of culture change derived from palaeontology which emphasized a one-to-one correspondence between archaeological and natural stratigraphic units and the basically invariate nature of cultural (read palaeontological) complexes (Sackett 1981: 90). The chief result was that assemblage variability and artefact provenance within a designated cultural unit were ignored. Important variation that did exist was interpreted phylogenetically and contemporary cultural traditions were often assigned to different biological evolutionary lines or races (*ibid.*: 90–3). A major exception to this trend was the relatively refined stratigraphic control and degree of artefact recovery of Denis Peyrony (1933).

The *Post-War Period* (post *c.* 1950) was marked by the Bordesian revolution in prehistoric lithic analysis, which recognized the totality of assemblage variability and introduced quantitative assemblage characterization and comparison, replacing the qualitative *fossiles directeurs*. However, Bordes' revolution was one of method, not theory. In the famous debate with Binford (1973), Bordes (1973) rejected functional interpretations of Mousterian variability in favour of stylistic differences representing different cultural traditions (Audouze and Leroi-Gourhan 1981: 172). This period also witnessed the development of refined stratigraphic excavation, an emphasis on artefact context, and an approach to stone tool analysis that emphasized the morphological contributions attributable to raw material, reduction techniques, and tool use (*ibid*: 172–3). This ultimately led to a recognition of the importance of functional variability (Sackett 1981: 96).

FRENCH CLASSICAL ARCHAEOLOGY AND LATER PREHISTORY

French classical archaeology, following in the European tradition, was linked primarily to the discipline of history. Although it subscribed to Lucien Fèbvre's *histoire totale*, excavation techniques lagged behind and Wheeler's excavation methods were not introduced into France until the late 1950s by Courbin (1963). French overseas excavations (outside of sub-Saharan Africa) received more support than those at home, but they often consisted of huge, well funded projects of monumental sites which produced massive quantities of data but did not lead to significant improvements in methodology (Audouze and Leroi-Gourhan 1981: 173). The historical orientation of French classical archaeology, as well as French medieval archaeology which developed in the 1950s under de Boüard (1975), exercised a major influence on the direction of later prehistoric and Iron Age archaeological research in francophone Africa.

Later prehistory developed unevenly. After the pioneering work of Dechelette prior to the First World War, little was accomplished until around 1960, and then by only a few scholars: G. Bailloud and J. Arnal for the Neolithic, and J.–J. Hatt, J. Audibert and J.–P. Millotte for the Age of Metals (Audouze and Leroi-Gourhan 1981: 173–4). Archaeologists were absorbed by the task of developing time-space systematics (culture history) and little attention was paid to methodological problems. Most studies emphasized a comparison of cultural traits oriented by a diffusionist explanatory paradigm (*ibid.*).

FRENCH ARCHAEOLOGY TODAY

For the most part French archaeology is a science of observation (Audouze and Leroi-Gourhan 1981: 174) which emphasizes exacting data recovery, spatial (contextual) analysis, the study of artefact/feature behavioural correlates, and rigorous artefact description and classification (*ibid*.: 174–82). This has been accompanied by Gardin's (1970, 1971) emphasis on computerized data banks and statistical analysis. The last two decades have also witnessed a growing interest in multidisciplinary studies, the ecological approach, and the use of sophisticated technology in artefact analysis. With classical (and medieval) archaeology, there has been an important shift to the urban periphery and to an emphasis on socio-economics, reflecting a parallel shift in French historical studies. Anglo-American influence has been important in the fields of environmental studies, archaeometry, ethnoarchaeology and socio-economic explanations of culture change (Audouze and Leroi-Gourhan 1981: 182).

Francophone West African archaeology

NINETEENTH-CENTURY BEGINNINGS

This period is characterized primarily by the collection of surface artefacts by merchants, soldiers, explorers and scientists who sent their finds to France for study by those who had never set foot in West Africa. As a result, artefact analysis and interpretation directly reflected developments in France. Perhaps the earliest published article was by de Beaufort (1851) who described finds from the Senegal Valley. Most publications consisted of artefact descriptions accompanied by comparisons with European artefact traditions and occasionally other West African finds. A great many were devoted to polished or ground stone objects regarded as Neolithic, such as axes and perforated stones, locally called thunderstones (*kwes, sokpe, nyame akuma*). Speculation regarding the possible racial affiliations of stone tool industries was a dominant theme (see Verneau 1905). Once the colonization of the continent was underway, a few superficial excavations took place in Senegal, Mali and Guinea that were, with one notable exception, either never published or were simply noted in colonial archives or briefly summarized by post-1900 excavators.

Many artefact collections were sent to the Musée d'Ethnographie du Trocadéro in Paris, founded in 1878. Its first director was Dr Ernest T. Hamy (1842–1909) and its first Anthropology Chair was occupied by Dr Raymond Verneau. Dr Hamy was trained in anatomy but later became an ardent prehistorian. He helped to start the journal *L'Anthropologie* in 1890 and helped sponsor Fernand Foureau's expeditions to the Sahara (1870s–90s) and Lt Louis Desplagnes' excavations in the French Sudan (Mali) between 1901 and 1904 (Obayemi 1969). He also wrote several papers on artefact collections from West Africa between 1883 and 1907. The most important concerned excavations at Kakimbon Rock Shelter near Conakry (Guinea). Conducted sporadically between 1893 and 1899, they represent the first officially sponsored excavations in French West Africa (Joire 1952: 297–301). Laurent Mouth, a public works foreman, reported his excavations (1899) and sent artefacts to Dr Hamy for analysis, who presented his findings to the twelfth International Congress of Anthropology and Prehistoric Archaeology in Paris in 1900. Dr Hamy (1902) described the stone tools, noted associations between raw materials and tool types, and described three cultural stages shown in cross-section: a recent layer overlying two Neolithic levels. The earliest Neolithic level was aceramic. He compared the different lithic assemblages to those found in Europe and eastern Senegal and interpreted the earlier material as the product of different peoples who occupied the area prior to the arrival of present-day populations. He also suggested the site was once used as a lithic workshop.

Hamy's paper led to a resolution which recognized the importance of West African archaeology and encouraged the Kakimbon excavations as a way of learning about African populations (Congrès international d'Anthropologie 1900: 602).

AVOCATIONAL COLONIAL ARCHAEOLOGY (1900 – c. 1940)

The French colonial regime solidified in the form of Afrique Occidentale Française with its capital in Dakar. During this period, archaeology was conducted by colonial administrators, military officers, civil servants and technical personnel (usually geologists). With few exceptions, these individuals were neither historians nor trained archaeologists. Artefact collections were primarily surface finds obtained during military, scientific and mining expeditions or those accidentally uncovered during various colonial construction projects. Most collections were sent to France.

Before 1916, articles on West African archaeology appeared in such metropolitan journals as the *Bulletin du Muséum d'histoire naturelle* and *L'Anthropologie*. Many were written by Dr Hamy, and his successor, Dr Verneau, an ethnologist, as well by those linked to the colonial regime in Dakar (e.g., Hamy 1904; Duchemin 1905; Crova 1909; de Zeltner 1913a). The year 1916 marked the creation of what would be the *Bulletin du Comité d'Etudes historiques et scientifiques de l'Afrique Occidentale Française* (1916–38), devoted to studies of France's West African territories. Most contributors were colonial officials, such as Pierre Laforgue (administrator), Dr Pierre Jouenne (physician), Henri Hubert (geologist) and various military officials.

In general, archaeology did not receive official encouragement. When Labouret (1932) published an outline for colonial officials for the writing of district monographs, neither prehistory nor archaeology was included. Most excavations were private ventures done during officials' spare time. Occasionally, major funding was obtained in Europe for scientific missions from such organizations as the *Académie des Inscriptions et Belles Lettres*, which sponsored Desplagnes' excavations of tumuli in Mali and those of Bonnel de Mézières at Koumbi Saleh (Obayemi 1969). Due to poor site visibility and the relatively poor quality of stone tools, relatively little fieldwork was done in the savanna and forest regions (Mauny 1953a: 861).

Fieldwork and Analytical Techniques

Fieldwork and analytical techniques during this period were not well developed and often did not reflect more sophisticated practices used in France. This was largely due to the participants' lack of professional training and was typical of colonial archaeology throughout the African continent.

Field methods were often rudimentary at best. Surface collections were basically grab samples from sites whose locations were often crudely mapped. As a result, collections sent back to France were often not representative of site contents in either a qualitative or quantitative sense (see also de Maret, this volume). Joire (1952: 351–2) notes that all Stone

Age assemblages from Guinea up to that time had been collected by amateurs and that no professional archaeologist had ever visited a Guinean prehistoric site. The same could be said for most of French West Africa.

Excavations often consisted of a few test-pits. ('*petits sondages*') dug to relatively superficial depths ('*à petite profondeur*') and reports consisted primarily of a partial description of finds with little or no description of methodology (see Thilmans *et al.* 1980: 14–25; Mauny 1961a: 95–8). Mauny (1961a: 97) notes with some bitterness that Lt Desplagnes' (1907, 1951) excavation of the large El-Oualadji tumulus near Macina (Mali) was the only such tumulus excavation to be published between 1900 and 1950 whose artefacts were still available for analysis! Drawings, if present, consisted primarily of crude plan and occasional section drawings of tombs or megaliths or highly simplified, reconstructed stratigraphic sections (e.g. Chapelle and Monod 1937). Even in the late 1930s, many reports included no stratigraphic information at all (Renoux 1937). Artefact provenance, if mentioned, was generally by gross stratigraphic unit, though artefact depths were occasionally given. While this lack of stratigraphic control was partially a reflection of the state of French archaeology, which generally equated cultural units with natural stratigraphic levels (see above), the practice of archaeology by untrained amateurs frequently led to excavations that were only a step above pothunting. In the case of the engraved stones at Tondidarou (Mali), the site was destroyed with parts shipped off to France or cut up and placed in the gardens of colonial officials (Mauny 1961a: 129–34). Similar examples could be drawn from the annals of anglophone colonial archaeology as well.

As in France, lithic analysis was basically descriptive and emphasized raw material, tool shape and dimensions, basic technological attributes (polish, retouch), accompanied by illustrations. Stone tool typologies were based primarily on qualitative morphological differences and presumed function (Crova 1909; Hubert, Laforgue and Vanelsche 1921; Hubert 1922; Laforgue 1924; Y. . . . 1933). Interpretations of past behaviour were generally limited to basic statements about subsistence and degree of sedentism (e.g. Verneau 1920: 362–3).

Collections were compared with those from neighbouring regions and/or from Europe and assigned to gross time periods similar to ones used in France (divisions of the Palaeolithic, Neolithic, Age of Metals). In view of the paucity of stratigraphic data, this is not surprising. In fact, the combination of amateur archaeology and the prevailing phylogenetic model of cultural change whose stages were represented by *fossiles directeurs* led Laforgue and Mauny (1938: 541) to conclude that their study of Stone Age deposits from the Cape Verde peninsula near Dakar had contributed nothing new ('*aucun élément nouveau*') to our knowledge of West African prehistory.

Ceramic analysis was limited to very brief descriptions. In a few instances, space was devoted to decorative techniques (Hubert *et al.* 1921) and these were sometimes compared briefly with those of other areas (Gaillard 1923: 633–6). To my knowledge, no formal ceramic typologies were developed. The well preserved faunal material from the Sahara was sometimes described (Y. . . 1933), but floral data were generally ignored. No metallurgical analyses were undertaken. Such trends reflected similar tendencies in France.

Human skeletal remains with skulls were of considerable interest for the light they might shed on past races (Hamy 1907; Gaden and Verneau 1920: 532–43; Boule and Vallois 1932) and diffusionist explanations of sub-Saharan African civilization (see below). Several authors made attempts to

assign racial affiliations (Negro v. Hamitic or Berber) to Saharan and
Sahelian settlements based on their lithic assemblages (Modat 1919;
Verneau 1920: 364–6) or rock art subjects (Chapelle and Monod 1937).
Some authors also attempted to assign ethnic affiliations to ceramic
decorative types (Hubert et al. 1921). More so than in France, this
preoccupation with racial and ethnic identities was typical of this period.
This was due to the focus on the external origins of African civilization, a
view which served as a convenient justification for colonialism and the
'white man's burden'. Attempts to make ethnic identifications were linked
to the clear continuity between the African past and present.

The Senegambian Megalithic sites fascinated colonial archaeologists, but
most excavations were superficial and provided little useful information
about artefact assemblages or the nature of the associated burials (Thilmans
et al. 1980: 14–23). Dr Jouenne (1918, 1920, 1930) devoted much time to
their study, but his writings often lacked coherence and he was convinced
that such sites were vestiges of a pervasive sun cult.

Despite their lack of professional training, some colonial archaeologists
produced thoughtful and original work. Laforgue (1925) reviewed
knowledge about the Stone Age in French West Africa, providing a
distribution map of Palaeolithic and Neolithic sites. He noted the lack of
stratigraphic data, the need for multidisciplinary studies of the environment, and attempted to infer past lifeways from the available site and
artefactual data (ibid.: 159–63). He also commented on stone tool lithic
reduction techniques. Hubert (1925), a geologist, argued against polished
stone tool classifications based on probable function as deduced from
general morphology. He proposed a classification system based on
dimensional measurements and ratios, scatter diagrams, artefact profiles,
sections, and edge angles, the extent and nature of grinding or polish, the
degree of weathering, rock type, and probable artefact function(s).
Unfortunately, his approach was generally ignored. One of the few to
follow Hubert's suggestions, Théodore Monod (1937, 1938) also
inventoried Saharan rock art sites and prepared a manual for colonial
administrators interested in recording and studying such sites.

The Diffusionist Explanatory Paradigm and European Ethnocentrism

This period was dominated by preoccupations with external origins for
Black African civilization, a focus that stemmed from European cultural
ethnocentrism and sense of racial superiority and the diffusionist
explanatory paradigm. Africa was declared to have no history of its own
(Fage 1980: 51–3) and obvious signs of civilization must have come from
the exterior. During the early part of the century, this view was abetted by
the British hyperdiffusionism espoused by Elliot Smith and W.J. Perry
which saw all civilization emanating from Eqypt. Later, it was exemplified
by Seligman's (1930) Hamitic hypothesis which stated that Black African
civilizations were entirely attributable to the influence of the white race.
This view remained a force well into the 1950s and beyond (Fage
1980: 57–8).

Desplagnes (1906: 544–6) hypothesized that Sudanic peoples were
derived from a mixture of Negritos, Ethiopian blacks descended from
Neolithic Sudanic peoples of Hamitic origin, red peoples of semitic-
Sumerian and Berber descent, and negroes and pastoral invaders from the
south and east led by a few families of Mongolian origin! Later, Neel
(1913: 441–2) argued that the soapstone statues of the Kissi region in

9:1 *Maurice Delafosse, at about 40 years of age (c. 1910)*

Guinea were due to Phoenician influence.

Maurice Delafosse (1900) marshalled a wide range of ethnographic and ethnohistorical data from the Ivory Coast to argue that the influence of Egyptian civilization had penetrated to the West African coast. He suggested that the Lobi stone ruins of Upper Volta were of Phoenician or Egyptian origin (Mauny 1957: 19) and he argued (1912: 22–5; 1924: 494) that the Kingdom of Ghana was founded and ruled by Judeo-Syrians from the fourth to eighth centuries AD. Near the end of his life he concluded that the Phoenicians had much more direct influence on West Africa than the Egyptians (Delafosse 1922).

Stone tool industries were also seen to exhibit northern influence (Laforgue 1923) or northern origin (Laforgue and Mauny 1938). Even the Tumbien Neolithic, which Delcroix and Vaufrey (1939: 312) described as ranging from the Congo to Guinea, was interpreted in terms of Egyptian and North African influences.

It is perhaps worth noting that much of the archaeological research of this period took place in the arid Sahel and Sahara once occupied by sedentary populations. Aside from stimulating an interest in climatic change and associated population movements (Hubert 1920, Chudeau 1921), the absence of such populations in the modern era provided fertile ground for the development of diffusionist explanatory schemes.

Maurice Delafosse and the Study of West African Town Sites

While the view that Africa had no history led most archaeologists to concentrate on the African Stone Age until the late 1950s (Posnansky 1982: 348), this was not entirely the case in French West Africa. This was due to Arab texts which described the various towns and capitals of the Ghana, Mali and Songhai Empires. Thanks primarily to Delafosse, such writings became known to colonial administrators and Africanists.

Delafosse (1870–1926), a Frenchman schooled in Oriental Languages, spent nearly seventeen years as a colonial official in the Ivory Coast, Mali, and Upper Volta between 1894 and 1909 and again in 1916–17 in Dakar (fig. 9:1). He took a great interest in local African populations and gathered invaluable ethnographic and linguistic data which was ultimately incorporated into several important works (L. Delafosse 1976). He translated Kati's *Tarikh el-Fettâch* with the help of his father-in-law, Octave Houdas (1913), who had also translated the *Tarikh es-Soudan* (1900) (see L. Delafosse 1976: 293). His three-volume *Haut-Sénégal-Niger* (1912) presented a detailed account of the Ghana, Mali and Songhai empires. Delafosse also understood the importance of interesting the public in France's African colonies and their indigenous populations (Labouret 1931: xiii) leading to the publication of *Les Noirs de l'Afrique* (1922) and *Civilizations négro-africaines* (1925). Delafosse's works represent the first syntheses of African history and archaeology.

The works of Delafosse were important for French West African archaeology for several reasons. First, Delafosse's writings, encouragement and guidance led such Africanists as Bonnel de Mézières (1920) and colonial administrators such as Vidal (1923a, 1923b) and Gaillard (1923) to seek out and excavate what were thought to be the capitals of Ghana (Koumbi Saleh) and Mali (Niani) and other sites described by the Arabs. Delafosse (1924) then wrote a synthesis of their findings. Other Africanists and historians, such as Monteil (1929), l'Abbé Breuil (1931) and Urvoy (1936), continued in his footsteps. This preoccupation with towns mentioned by the Arabs would continue to be the focus of much Iron Age research until the 1960s and beyond.

Second, Delafosse and Houdas's translations of Arab texts were accompanied by an uncritical acceptance of the self-serving, Arab view of the Sudan which interpreted the flowering of black civilization as the result of Arab (Islamic) influence. As a result, certain issues, such as the possibility of a local brass industry in the Sahel, were ignored simply because they had not been mentioned by the Arabs (cf. Vanacker 1979: 174).

Third, the strong influence of Delafosse and later historians insured that archaeology in francophone West Africa would develop as an adjunct to the discipline of history as was the case for both classical and medieval archaeology in France.

Finally, Delafosse's pioneering works helped popularize the already existing view that sought foreign origins for much of Black African civilization. But note that Delafosse was also a humanist who believed that Black Africans were a capable people whose 'backwardness' was due to their isolation from the Mediterranean world (Delafosse 1931: xxv–xxxiii).

MAUNY AND IFAN, OR SYNTHESIS AND STRUCTURE
(*c.* 1940–*c.* 1960)

The year 1938 marked the creation of the Institut Français d'Afrique Noire (IFAN) and the first year in Dakar of the young civil servant, Raymond Mauny (fig. 9:2). The creation of IFAN meant that French West Africa had its own research institute. In 1941, an Archaeology-Prehistory section was created and artefacts were now curated in Dakar instead of France. This led to the building of the first archaeological and historical museum on the island of Gorée (1954) with other museums to follow in Abomey, Abidjan, Bamako, then Niamey and Dakar. Most important, the appearance of IFAN resulted in the presence of two devoted professionals, Raymond Mauny in Dakar (1938–62) and Georges Szumowski in Bamako (1951–6).

Although Mauny had been trained in law and administration, he quickly focussed his interests on archaeology (Laforgue and Mauny 1938). In 1947, he was named head of the Archaeology-Prehistory Division where he remained until his departure in 1962. In addition to his IFAN duties (protection of sites and monuments, education of the public through

9:2 *Raymond Mauny in Austria 1965*

conferences, articles, museum displays and amateur associations), he found time to write his *thèse d'Etat* based on over fifteen years of archival and field research (Brasseur 1981: 2). During this same period, he wrote over 220 articles on African archaeology, ethnography, linguistics, physical anthropology, history and geomorphology, not to mention numerous book reviews and papers delivered at conferences all over the world.

Perhaps Mauny's greatest contribution was his synthetic vision. Between 1947 and 1961, Mauny wrote a series of articles which summarized current archaeological knowledge for most of the West African colonies (e.g., Corbeil, Mauny and Charbonnier 1948; Mauny 1949, 1950a, 1957; Mauny and Hallemans 1957), leaving Guinea to Joire (1952) and the Ivory Coast until after he had left Africa for the Sorbonne (Mauny 1972). Other synthetic articles dealt with the origin of copper and iron metallurgy (1951a, 1952), ceramic analysis (1951b), trans-Saharan contacts (1947), the locations of Ghana (Koumbi Saleh) and Awdaghost (1950b, 1951c), the archaeology of Gao (1951d), the domesticated plants of West Africa (1953b), rock art (1954), bone tools (Mauny and Monod 1957), and human skeletal remains (1961b).

His thesis, entitled *Tableau géographique de l'Ouest Africain au Moyen Age* (Mauny 1961a), was a synthesis of both substantive results and historical and archaeological method, and provided the basic archival groundwork and inspiration for much of the archaeology performed in subsequent decades (Bernus *et al.* 1984: 8). It was also important for its multidisciplinary focus which utilized historical documents, archaeology, ethnography, and geography for the reconstruction of the history and past lifeways of sub-Saharan African populations.

Mauny recognized that serious archaeological research was just beginning and urged a programme of site inventory and stratigraphic excavation (Mauny 1953a: 861–2). He saw the need for more sophisticated lithic analysis (1955a: 620), the identification of chronological markers, including ceramic types (Mauny 1961a: 59–60), and recognized the utility of metallurgical analysis (*ibid.*: 312) and aerial photography (*ibid.*: 63). He was the first to publish radiocarbon dates from francophone West Africa (*ibid.*: 63–4).

Ironically, this period was marked by only modest improvements in archaeological method and technique. Due to limited means and lack of formal field training, many of Mauny's excavations tended to lack stratigraphic care (Raimbault 1981: 17). At Koumbi Saleh (Thomassey and Mauny 1951, 1956), however, careful excavation revealed the presence of at least two occupation levels. In Mali, the archaeologist at IFAN-Bamako, George Szumowski (1956), performed the first stratigraphic rock-shelter excavations in that country and was probably the first to screen excavated deposits. He also provided more detail on excavation plans, cross-sections and artefact provenance than was seen in earlier studies. His work with the Macina tumuli (Szumowski 1957), however, consisted primarily of numerous test-pits. Overall, it is not surprising that progress was limited since major changes in France were just getting under way in the 1950s and 1960s as Courbin introduced Wheeler's excavation techniques into classical archaeology (Audouze and Leroi-Gourhan 1981: 173).

Lithic analysis in francophone West Africa was not affected by the Bordesian revolution (see Vaufrey 1953; Szumowski 1956; Lambert 1961) until the 1960s, and ceramic analysis, while providing for more rigorous descriptions of form, decorative technique and probable manufacturing procedure (e.g., Szumowski 1956; Mauny 1951b), was not vigorously pursued as a chronological tool. Raimbault (1981: 17) notes that many of the ceramics excavated by Mauny in Mali between 1950 and 1955 were never systematically studied. While more refined cultural chronologies, which went beyond such labels as Neolithic or Iron Age, were attempted (e.g., Mauny 1952), the use of radiocarbon dating was just beginning in West Africa and the utility of ceramic tobacco pipes as chronological markers had not yet been fully recognized (Daget and Ligers 1962).

Finally, the diffusionist paradigm was still operative and explanations for Black African civilization tended to rely on external influences, for example Mauny's (1947, 1952) discussions of Berber influence on Black Africa via a trans-Saharan chariot route and the diffusion of metal technology from North Africa. Vaufrey (1953: 137–8) continued to affirm that sub-Saharan Africa was basically a cultural backwater. However, the first cracks appeared as Joire (1952: 356–65) argued against a northern origin for the Tumbien Neolithic, and Person (1961: 7) opted for a local origin for the Kissi soapstone statues.

The 1960s – from French to francophone archaeology

This decade witnessed important changes in African education systems and significant shifts in research orientations and methods whose impact were not fully felt until the 1970s. It also saw the emergence of major research by non-French scholars.

The late 1950s saw the collapse of *Afrique Occidentale Française* leading to independence for all of francophone West Africa by 1960. With independence came the demand and the need for the study of African history. First courses, then degree programmes were created at the new universities in Dakar and then Abidjan. The emphasis on African history led to greater interest in the study of oral traditions (Fage 1980: 63; Mauny 1962). In 1965, African francophone countries adopted a new history and geography programme for secondary schools that replaced the colonial 'Nos ancêtres les Gaulois' approach. In 1966, UNESCO launched the writing of a general history of Africa (Fage *op. cit.*).

It was during the 1960s that the debate first raged between Cheikh Anta Diop and European Africanists regarding the antiquity and geographical distribution of Black African civilization and the role of Black Africans in

9:3 *Aerial view of the town site of Tegdaoust (Maurita-nia), excavated under the direction of Jean Devisse and Serge and Denise Robert during the 1960s*

the rise of Egyptian civilization (e.g., C.A. Diop 1955, 1960a, 1960b, 1962, 1967; Mauny 1960; L.-M. Diop 1968; Lhote 1970). For the first time, an African was seriously challenging European diffusionist explanations of African advances. The discovery of first millennium BC iron-working in Nigeria (Fagan 1965b) brought the first tangible archaeological evidence that sub-Saharan African civilization was much older than once believed, and by the early 1970s the diffusionist paradigm was seriously questioned (Flight 1976).

This first decade of independence also witnessed the launching of major excavations at Tegdaoust/Awdaghost (fig. 9:3) in 1962 by Jean Devisse, professor of medieval history at the University of Dakar (Robert *et al.* 1970; Vanacker 1979; Devisse *et al.* 1983). Other major studies begun during the 1960s include Filipowiak's (1979) study of Niani, the alleged early capital of Mali, and Bedaux's (1972) study of the Tellem. Except for Niani, most work was undertaken in the countries of the Sahel. The presence of Polish (Filipowiak), Dutch (Bedaux) and American (Munson at Tichitt) researchers augured well for the future of francophone West African archaeology which until then had developed in relative isolation, often to its methodological detriment (Devisse 1981: 6; Raimbault 1981: 18). It is worth noting, however, that Munson (1971: 123–34) insisted upon a diffusionist explanation for the introduction of plant cultivation in West Africa, despite botanical evidence suggesting a sorghum domesticate of local origin (Shaw 1972b: 154).

The most important change in research orientation and methodology involved a gradual shift from a preoccupation with artefacts to an emphasis on the spatial and contextual association of artefacts and structures within the various stratigraphic layers (Raimbault 1981: 18). This change had begun in France a decade earlier with the seminal work of Leroi-Gourhan (1950a, 1950b) on what would become known as 'ethnographic excavations', but it took the arrival of numerous professional archaeologists to effect the change in West Africa. Mauny continued his role as the grand synthesizer and continued to ask many of the right questions (Mauny 1964a, 1970, 1972), but he alone could not reorient archaeological method and theory. Parallel to these developments was the recognition that well planned, well financed, long-term studies of a series of sites (if not a region) were required in order to understand fully a past society's subsistence, habitat and technology (Raimbault 1981). This growing interest in the study of societies in their environmental context reflected developments in France (Audouze and Leroi–Gourhan 1981: 178–82), which would reach fruition in Africa in the late 1970s.

One manifestation of the shift in emphasis to contextual analysis was joint geomorphological and archaeological studies undertaken in the late 1960s (Guillot and Descamps 1969; Chamard, Guitat and Thilmans 1970; Linares de Sapir 1971). These studies paid much attention to stratigraphy, artefact provenance and the drawing and analysis of soil profiles. Descamps (1981: 147) notes, however, that it was not until the end of the 1960s that excavated material from Neolithic sites in Senegal was regularly screened, thus permitting a serious analysis of lithic industries and their associated reduction techniques.

Artefact distributional studies also made their appearance. The primary goal was to determine cultural boundaries or zones of influence, following the pattern developed for the French Neolithic by Arnal, Bailloud and Riquet (1960). Using ceramic design and bone harpoon typologies, Gallay (1966) delineated regional ceramic provinces which showed that bone harpoons are not associated with wavy-line pottery in the Azouad area of Mali. Less sophisticated distributional studies were done using Neolithic stone tools (Huard, Massip and Rosso 1968; Hébrard, Hugot and Thilmans 1970) and rock art (Huard and Allard-Huard 1978).

A relatively complex ceramic typology was developed by Lambert (1965) that classified Mauritanian pottery by decorative type and associated variation in form, surface treatment, paste, and wall thickness. The avowed purpose was to provide a descriptive typology for future comparisons using the French ceramic study of Arnal et al. (1960) as the model. This period also saw the development of two radiocarbon-dated cultural sequences based primarily on changes in ceramic attributes (see Linares de Sapir 1971; Munson 1971). The latter study represented one of the first attempts to establish a regional chronology based on ceramic seriation in francophone West Africa; unfortunately, methodological problems led to relatively unsatisfactory results (McIntosh and McIntosh 1986: 421–2). Another seminal study was the ethnoarchaeological investigation of Sarakolle pottery production and exchange conducted in 1965 by Gallay (1970). His call for the dating of homogenous ceramic assemblages in stratigraphic contexts and the use of ethnoarchaeology for understanding the context of archaeological ceramics has become a model for francophone West Africa (see Mêtinhoué and Adande 1984). In fact, it would not be inappropriate to suggest that such research in Africa (including work by Bernus and Gouletquer in 1976) helped to stimulate French interest in ethnoarchaeological studies.

In lithic analysis, Tixier's (1963, 1967) detailed typological studies in North Africa, which were based on knowledge gained from experimental flint-knapping, had a significant impact on typological analysis in the Sahara (see Camps 1979: 78–107) and served as a basis for later statistical analyses done by Clark (1976b) and Smith (1976) in Niger. However, aside from Tixier's influence on Saharan archaeology, Bordesian cumulative graph analysis was seldom used. There were a few attempts to derive or distinguish types based on statistical analysis (Guillot and Descamps 1969; Fontaine 1967), but Hugot (1966: 43), the director of IFAN from 1962 to 1970, expressed distrust of statistically derived types. While the need to adapt terminology to the sub-Saharan African context was recognized, European terms, such as Mauny's (1972) use of the term Mesoneolithic were slow to disappear.

The 1960s also witnessed the first serious geochemical analyses of metal ores and objects. Lambert's (1972) inventory, classification and statistical and chemical analyses of copper objects from Mauritania was the first of its kind in francophone West Africa. Linares de Sapir's (1971) work in Senegal was a fine example of a multi-disciplinary study which developed a cultural sequence based on multiple sites using a combination of ceramic, ecological (shellfish and animal bone), technological (iron), and microenvironmental data.

FROM HISTORICAL PARTICULARISM TO REGIONAL AND PROCESSUAL STUDIES

During both the 1960s and 1970s, many projects were initiated which focussed on town sites: Tegdaoust, Azugi, and Koumbi Saleh (Mauretania), Niani (Guinea), Jenne-jeno and Gao (Mali), and Azelik and Marandet (Niger). As McIntosh and McIntosh (1984: 85) note, research was initially prompted by reference to them in Arab texts. In many instances (Tegdaoust, Koumbi Saleh, Azugi), the primary research goal was the confirmation of this simple fact (see Robert and Robert 1972: 214). Excavation and analytical efforts frequently focussed on architectural features and imported artefacts that would help confirm the Arab texts, particularly with regard to trans-Saharan trade, while local industries, pre-urban levels and the urban periphery tended to get short shrift (McIntosh and McIntosh 1984: 76; but see Vanacker 1979; Robert-Chaleix 1983). In short, the basic thrust was site-specific, particularistic and descriptive.

In the late 1970s, a major shift occurred, which is perhaps best exemplified by studies at Jenne-jeno by Roderick and Susan McIntosh (1980a, 1981, 1983, 1984). The new approach concentrates on the inter-relationship and interdependence of the town and its hinterland settlements and on the mechanisms of urban growth and cultural change. Their regional and processual approach oriented towards urban origins and growth inevitably meant significant departures from the particularistic research design and methods of the past: a change of focus in which sites are viewed in the context of their natural and cultural environment; a need for regional chronological control leading to a regional ceramic sequence; the importance of formal sampling techniques in both regional survey and site excavation; and the need for both vertical and horizontal (spatial) control in excavation (McIntosh and McIntosh 1984: 79–84) (fig. 9:4). Their emphasis on the use of flotation for floral remains was also a first. Earlier studies tended to neglect important aspects of the regional environment and, with the exception of Filipowiak's (1979) study of Niani, often paid little attention to hinterland settlements. Chronological control tended to focus on radiocarbon dating and cross-dating using imported objects, with little effort spent on developing a regional ceramic chronology.

Concurrent to the Jenne-jeno study was the salvage project in the Agades Basin conducted by the French research groups, CNRS and ORSTOM (see Bernus and Gouletquer 1976; Poncet *et al.* 1983; Bernus *et al.* 1984; Paris 1984; Grébénart 1985). Although sampling strategies were relatively opportunistic and a detailed regional ceramic chronology has yet to be

9:4 *Excavations at the site of Jenne-jeno under the direction of Rod and Susan McIntosh, late 1970s*

developed, their focus was definitely regional. Excellent environmental studies were undertaken and the project implemented a successful inter-disciplinary study, particularly in its integration of human geography, metallurgical studies, archaeology, ethnoarchaeology and ethnography (see Bernus and Gouletquer 1976; Chauveau 1984). The project's contributions to an understanding of the origins and evolution of West African metallurgy have been substantial.

Another important multi-disciplinary, regional study which emphasized the environmental context of past human settlement in the Malian Sahara was conducted by Nicole Petit-Maire and her research group from the Laboratoire de Géologie du Quaternaire of CNRS (Petit-Maire *et al*. 1983). A wealth of geological, sedimentological, and climatological data was collected in conjunction with well preserved faunal, floral, and human remains associated with sedentary sites dating from 10,000 to 3500 BP. The results of this study complement earlier work along the western Atlantic coast of northern Mauritania and the Spanish Sahara (Petit-Maire 1979a).

Both the Agades Basin and Mali studies directly reflected the growing emphasis in French archaeology on ecological and environmental variables for both site specific and regional studies in later prehistory, which Audouze and Leroi–Gourhan (1981: 182) feel was due to the influence of British and American archaeology (see Smith 1974, Andah 1978, and later studies by Polet 1981, Rivallain 1983, and Camara and Dubosqc 1984).

Other major regional studies include those of de Barros (1985, 1986, 1988), Goucher (1983, 1984), and Holl (1985a, 1985b). De Barros used a quantitative, chronologically controlled, regional approach to the study of iron-working in the Bassar region of northern Togo that involved a combination of opportunistic and probability sampling, regional ceramic seriation, and the determination of changing levels of iron production. The goal was to study the effects of the rise of both small- and large-scale iron-working on demography, settlement patterns, specialization, trade, and political centralization. Goucher's study focussed on the technology of Bassar iron production and its impact on progressive deforestation as revealed through historical documents, ethnographic sources, and slag analysis. More recently, she has pursued an ethnoarchaeological approach through the study and filming of Bassar iron-smelting. Holl's work deals with the dynamics of agro-pastoral subsistence during the Neolithic and later trends towards state formation in the Dhar Tichitt region. Regional studies undertaken by Marchal (1981), Quéchon and Roset (1974) and Roset (1983), as well as Posnansky and de Barros's (1980) broad-scale Togo survey, are also of interest (Bower 1986: 31–2).

The 1980s have also seen an emphasis on the study of major metal-working centres (de Barros and Goucher *supra*; Kiéthéga 1983; the Agades Basin study; Echard 1983) and on the interaction between technology and environment (Goucher 1981; Haaland 1980; Lévy-Luxereau 1983). With increased emphasis on the later Iron Age, ethnoarchaeological studies have become increasingly popular (e.g., Raimbault 1980; Rivallain 1981; Adande and Mêtinhoué 1982; Pétrequin and Pétrequin 1984; Goucher *supra*).

Following Gallay (1966), J.-P. Maitre (1979) has demonstrated through careful ceramic typologies that Camps's (1974) 'Saharo-Sudanese Neo-lithic' was actually composed of many separate regional traditions. However, the recent trend in Senegal (Thilmans and Ravisé 1980: 126–34) of linking ceramic traditions ('*familles céramiques*') to specific ethnic or cultural groups poses problems (see Crossland and Posnansky 1978).

Another trend places an emphasis on site inventories. In 1967, Guitat (1972a) proposed an inventory project for the Neolithic sites of West Africa, noting the destruction caused by rapid urbanization. Guitat (1972b) and Ravisé (1975) followed up on this project for the western Sahel. In Senegal, such inventories have also been collected for protohistoric sites grouped within four archaeological provinces: coastal shell middens, Senegal River sites, megaliths and tumuli (Martin and Becker 1974; Thilmans *et al*. 1980: 11–12). In general, site inventory has become a major priority of most francophone West African nations. It is viewed as a tool for prioritizing the funding of both salvage and research projects, for time-space systematics, and for opening up new avenues of research.

Other research includes work by Bedaux *et al*. (1978), Gallay *et al*. (1981), Bedaux and Lange (1983), Thilmans and Ravisé (1980), and Chenorkian (1982), as well as detailed studies of human skeletal remains and burial practices by Thilmans *et al*. (1980) and Paris (1984). Finally,

Derefaka (1980) has used statistics to develop a typology of baskets. ·

Implicit in the above discussion is a major trend which began in the previous decade – the internationalization of archaeology in francophone West Africa. Aside from the French and francophone Africans, Swiss (Gallay), Polish (Filipowiak), Dutch (Bedaux), Anglo-American (Munson, Clark, Smith, Posnansky, the McIntoshes, Goucher, and de Barros), anglophone African (Andah, Derefaka) and Central African (Holl) archaeologists have also made important contributions.

THE EMERGENCE OF AFRICAN NATIONAL PRIORITIES

During the 1970s universities and history departments were created in Togo, Benin, Niger and Burkina Faso. Archaeological studies ceased to be centred in Dakar and the Sahelian belt as research proceeded in the coastal states of Ivory Coast, Benin, and Togo as well as in Burkina Faso. Only Guinea seemed out of step (but see Diallo 1971; Boriskovsky and Soloviev 1978). By 1981, most archaeological research institutes and history departments, including IFAN–Dakar, were partially or fully Africanized. African archaeologists and interested administrators watched as numerous foreign-sponsored projects took place while nationals struggled to find funds for even modest studies of single sites. In France, people like Raymond Mauny (1964b) and Jean Devisse (1981: 6) struggled to convince the French government and public of the importance of African history and archaeology and the need for structural reform. Their efforts ultimately resulted in the Valbonne Colloquium, a turning point in the archaeology of francophone West Africa (Groslier 1981).

At Valbonne, French Africanists and representatives from the francophone African countries met to discuss the priorities, problems and perspectives of archaeological research. Despite budget limitations, it was recognized that archaeology could make important contributions to the study of the cultural heritage of African peoples. It was also recognized that African archaeologists must keep abreast of advances in method and theory outside the continent. While recognizing the importance of prehistory, it was felt that emphasis should be placed on more recent history whose ties to the present would interest the public. Certain common objectives and desires were noted: a systematic site inventory to determine salvage priorities and to establish a series of cultural provinces linked to geographical/ecological zones; co-ordination between the various foreign research groups and the host government and project evaluation prior to funding; multi-disciplinary studies; formation, training and retraining of African personnel, including the need for an African Archaeological newsletter, *Nouvelles de l'Archéologie* (created in 1980); and site-protective legislation. France was asked for flexible modes of financial aid and help from professional archaeologists sensitive to African culture. Foreign researchers were welcomed but they were asked to train host-country nationals, publish quickly and leave copies of their work in Africa.

A study of various national priorities (Lame 1978; Camara 1985; Sidibe 1981; Raimbault 1981; Gado 1981; Kiéthéga 1981, 1987 personal communication; Mêtinhoué and Adande 1987, personal communications; Kuevi 1985; CNRS 1978) indicates other concerns: a desire to spread research projects over the different regions of the nation; a concern for chronology; and a growing interest in ethnographic *cum* archaeological and ethnoarchaeological studies inspired by the need to record the details of local crafts and technologies and local histories before they disappear. There is also a strong feeling that foreign researchers should focus on national research priorities which emphasize substantive results as opposed to the confirmation of popular theories. Of relevance here is Trigger and Glover's (1981: 136) observation that the current neoevolutionary/ecological approach so popular in the western world may be no more relevant to legitimate African concerns than were the earlier unilinear evolutionary and diffusionist views. There is also concern about the tendency of some foreign researchers to make hasty conclusions or to generalize beyond the limits of the site or region studied (see also Posnansky 1981: 78).

A study of current problems faced by African archaeology (cf. *supra*; Posnansky 1981; Shaw 1981b; David 1985) shows insufficient funding to be a critical problem. It results in insufficient work and storage space, laboratory equipment and field vehicles, insufficient documentation (maps, aerial photos, subscription to journals), a paucity of trained lab and museum technicians, and a lack of funds for salvage archaeology, for radiocarbon dating, and for the publishing of student theses. The necessary specialists for multi-disciplinary studies are often lacking and there are few funds to pay such specialists (see Devisse 1983: 24).

These problems are not strictly a matter of African budgetary priorities. Soustelle (1975: 22–3, 35) has documented the relative paucity of modern labs, libraries, professional archaeologists and professorships, and departments of archaeology in France itself and notes that much more is spent on archaeological research in other European countries. Moreover, the private funding of academic research is not encouraged through tax incentives, while legislation designed to protect or salvage sites endangered by development is poorly developed (*ibid.*: 45, 99). Thus, it is not surprising that archaeology has a low priority both in French aid programmes and in national budgets or that provisions for salvage are rarely made in development projects. Hopefully, the Agades Basin salvage programme is the trend of the future.

Another serious problem, noted by Posnansky (1982: 355), is the bureaucratization of archaeology. In the ministries and research institutes archaeologists become *fonctionnaires* who have a difficult time obtaining more than two weeks in the field at a time, once or twice a year. At the universities, the requirements for promotion (publication, theses) and the lack of funds force most researchers to limit their investigations to small-scale studies situated close to the capital (Gado 1981: 33). Such studies are often limited to a few test-pits, a couple of radiocarbon dates, a summary of relevant oral traditions, and the description of artefacts.

Training is also a critical problem. David (1985) has expressed the view that some African archaeologists educated abroad have not been given the kind of supervision and guidance needed to ensure their proper training. His comments suggest it is a problem of individuals but, for francophone Africa at least, it is also a structural problem. In the French university system, there are serious administrative and statutory obstacles to leading a mixed career that combines both research and teaching, including the absence of sabbatical leave (Soustelle 1975: 22). An African student may receive excellent classroom teaching but struggle to find adequate field and laboratory training (*ibid.*: 58). This situation is aggravated by the general academic split between prehistory and later historical periods. In particular, medieval or Iron Age archaeologists trained in France are often poorly prepared for the kind of fieldwork they may encounter in West Africa (Devisse 1983: 24).

THEORETICAL AND METHODOLOGICAL PERSPECTIVES

With some exceptions (Cleuziou *et al.* 1973; Cleuziou and Demoule 1980), present French archaeology tends to focus on careful data collection with an emphasis on the cultural historical approach and the reconstruction of past lifeways (ethnographic excavations). Audouze and Leroi–Gourhan (1981: 174) describe it as primarily '*une science d'observation*'. Archaeology in francophone West Africa generally reflects these trends. In his introduction to a series of articles on francophone archaeology in West Africa, Devisse (1981: 5) affirms that '*sans l'histoire, l'anthropologie culturelle ...* [et] *l'archéologie ne serait qu'une science de laboratoire satisfaisante pour les seuls initiés.*' In short, archaeology is viewed primarily as an historical science as opposed to an anthropological one. Devisse (*ibid.*) stresses the danger of forming hypotheses and constructing explanatory models before they have been extensively confirmed by the data (see also Gallay 1984: 5). He makes the interesting observation that the need for models or '*problèmatique*', very acceptable to the Anglo-saxon mind, becomes quickly dangerous in '*régions de culture "française"*' where there is the constant temptation to treat the working hypothesis as fact (Devisse 1981: 8ff). Only the use of multiple working hypotheses is acceptable (*ibid.*: 5), an approach rigorously applied by Gallay (Gallay *et al.* 1981) in a recent study of Senegambian megaliths.

One consequence of this reticence to generalize has been the current emphasis on site inventory and description and the relatively few in-depth regional studies which address questions of culture change. As a result most artefact typologies are descriptive, historical types associated with a particular site or small group of sites. Regional ceramic sequences based on typological or attribute seriation have thus far been developed primarily by Anglo-Americans (Munson 1971; McIntosh and McIntosh 1980; de Barros 1985). Although Tixier's (1963, 1967, Tixier *et al.* 1980) achievements in lithic typology, assemblage analysis and reduction techniques have had an important influence on Saharan archaeology, sophisticated analytical approaches to lithic assemblages in francophone West Africa are uncommon. The continued emphasis on a cultural historical approach may also explain why formal smapling techniques are rarely employed, particularly in regional survey. Taking a continental view, Posnansky (1982: 354) goes further and notes that 'the descriptive, cultural-historical nature of much of African archaeology has perhaps led to its failure to influence archaeological thought significantly.'

Yet, this theoretical and methodological polemic perhaps misses the point. As Devisse (1981: 5) emphasizes, Africans themselves are first and foremost deeply concerned about reconstructing their history(ies) and reaffirming and expanding their cultural heritage; the testing of neoevolutionary/adaptive models is of secondary interest. In this light, the emphasis on site inventory and chronology (see Saliège *et al.* 1980) has its *raison d'être*. Perhaps the best approach is one that strikes a balance between history and anthropology, between the substantive and the theoretical, and between site inventory, site-specific studies, and in-depth regional studies. Due to the prohibitive costs of regional research, however, most research will depend upon external financing. It is to be hoped that such studies will contribute to the advancement of both historical and anthropological issues and stress the integration and training of African archaeologists.

Acknowledgements

I wish to thank Susan Keech McIntosh and Rod McIntosh for many useful discussions. Special thanks also go to my anonymous 'West Africanist' reviewer and to Merrick Posnansky who provided valuable constructive criticism.

10 Soldiers & Bureaucrats: The Early History of Prehistoric Archaeology in the Maghreb

PETER J. SHEPPARD

Introduction

Archaeological research, indeed scientific research of any kind, is often dominated at any given time by one, or at most a small number of research problems. These may often challenge, or at least be difficult to fit within, the currently accepted theory or method of explanation (Kuhn 1972), thus requiring the development of new theory and research methods. The best review of the history of archaeological research in a particular geographical area can often be accomplished by examining the development through time of the dominant research problems and the fieldwork, theory and methodology developed to resolve those problems. Using this approach, the first fifty years of prehistoric archaeological research in the Maghreb (Morocco, Tunisia and Algeria: fig. 10:1) will be examined, focussing primarily on research in Eastern Algeria and Tunisia.

There are very few systematic reviews of the history of North African archaeology. Colette Roubet has produced the best summary of early research (Roubet 1979) with a focus on the work of Raymond Vaufrey and Marcellin Boule. She has also reviewed the development of professional archaeological training in Algiers and the development of the Centre Algérien de Recherches Anthropologiques, Préhistoriques et Ethno-graphiques (CRAPE) during the late 1940s and 1950s (Roubet *et al.* 1981: 29–33). Historical details can also be found in the overviews of North African prehistory by Camps (1974), Balout (1955) and Vaufrey (1955), and in the introduction to the epipalaeolithic lithic typology by Tixier (1963). The only review of the history of North African archaeology in English, with emphasis on the Capsian, is found in Sheppard (1987).

10:1 The Maghreb showing locations discussed in the text

The archaeology of the Maghreb was strongly influenced by developments taking place in France. The early archaeology of the area was carried out primarily by avocational archaeologists, generally doctors, military personnel and bureaucrats sent out from France to provide services and

0   100   200 kilometres

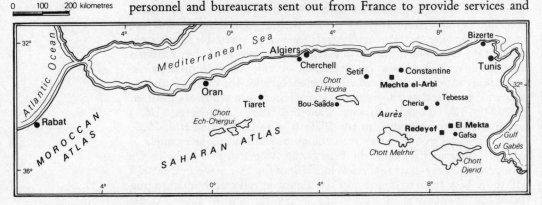

173

administration in areas that were either under French control (Morocco and Tunisia) or were being actively colonized (Algeria). These individuals maintained close ties with the archaeological and anthropological societies of France and often published their results in journals such as *L'Anthropologie*, whose editor, Marcellin Boule, had a strong interest in North African prehistory. There also developed quite quickly a set of very active archaeological and geographical societies in North Africa. Algeria, in particular, supported in the 1920s at least three societies with a strong archaeological focus: La Société de Géographie et d'Archéologie de la Province d'Oran, La Société Archéologique de Constantine and La Société de Préhistoire de Tébessa.

The archaeologists of the Maghreb, as with most Old World prehistorians in the early part of this century, generally attempted to fit their data into the space/time framework of the French Palaeolithic and to employ the excavation techniques and analytical approaches used in France. As was often the case elsewhere, this resulted in some mis-interpretation and controversy over data that did not quite fit the accepted scheme. There is also evidence to suggest a desire on the part of some local Maghreb archaeologists to interpret data in such a way as to make discoveries which might rival those from the south-west of France. For example, during the early part of this century local North African archaeologists suggested that the large blade industry which they were finding in Eastern Algeria and Tunisia was the predecessor of the European Aurignacian.

The major focus of research and controversy during the first fifty years, beginning *circa* 1890, of Maghreb archaeology was the nature of the industry which we know today as the Capsian and its relation to the French Aurignacian, which it resembled in its blade component. The fundamental questions asked were: (1) how old is the Capsian? and (2) did the Aurignacian derive from North Africa?

The development of the argument over the origin of the Aurignacian reflects, in part, the general shift at the turn of the century away from evolutionary thinking and an interest in what de Mortillet termed 'paléoethnologie' (de Mortillet 1882) toward a concern for the documentation of local sequences and the use of diffusion as an explanatory concept. In France during the first half of the twentieth century, most archaeologists followed the theoretical and methodological model provided by palaeontology and geology, and concentrated their efforts on the description of sequences and the development of chronology (Sackett 1981). The application of the methods of empirical science in the description of regional sequences was the first order of business; explanation could only proceed upon a firm chronological foundation. However, it seems to have been generally expected, especially by people such as Henri Breuil, that the French chronology and typology would be generally applicable throughout much of the Old World. In North America, the same descriptive concerns were important; however the influence of cultural anthropology on archaeology may have imparted a greater concern for the study of process, which for most anthropologists at that time meant the study of diffusion. Thanks to the Logan Museum (Beloit College: Wisconsin, USA) expeditions to the Maghreb in the 1920s (Collie 1928; Pond *et al.* 1928, 1938), the history of Maghreb archaeology provides a unique example of the early application of both the French and American paradigms to the same problem. In reviewing the development of the 'Aurignacian Debate' I will show how the development of the argument reflected both changing theoretical orientations in archaeology in general, and to some extent, divergent approaches in North American and French archaeology.

Early research

The first mention of stone tool-bearing sites in the vicinity of Tebessa in Eastern Algeria appeared in the journal of the Société Archéologique de Constantine in 1894. Duprat (1894: 549) made the important observation that the sites north of the town of Tebessa produced small tools, while those immediately to the south produced large-blade tools. This distinction, although subsequently ignored in the polemic of the early twentieth century, persists today in the distinction made between the Typical Capsian and Upper Capsian facies of the Capsian industry (see review in Lubell, Sheppard and Jackes 1984).

Immediately after Duprat's report, little work seems to have been carried out on the prehistory of east central Algeria and southern Tunisia. Research was developing, however, along the coast in the vicinity of Algiers and Oran, leading the Dean of North African Prehistory, Paul Pallary, to write in 1905 his 'Instructions pour les recherches préhistoriques dans le Nord-Ouest de l'Afrique' (Pallary 1909), in which he outlined what was known of the area's prehistory, postulated a relationship between the coastal industries of North Africa and Iberia, and discussed what he felt were important research directions. Pallary had been undertaking research in the coastal caves and shelters since 1890 (Roubet 1979) recovering Palaeolithic and Neolithic assemblages. Amongst this material were some small assemblages containing numerous microlithic tools (notably backed and pointed bladelets), few geometrics and no pottery or polished stone. Pallary noted that this material was similar to that recovered by his friend M. Louis Siret in Spain and published by Henri and Louis Siret in *Les premiers Ages du Métal dans le sud-est de l'Espagne* (H. and L. Siret 1887). To indicate this similarity Pallary named the North African coastal microlithic industry the *Ibéro-Maurusien*. Based upon the 'warm' fauna associated with this industry Pallary (1909: 46) thought that it must follow the palaeolithic Magdalenian with its 'cold' fauna and therefore bridge the period between the Palaeolithic and the Neolithic. The use of fauna as a method of dating by comparison with the European sequence became a standard approach in the Maghreb. Unfortunately the comparison of African and European fauna was not as simple as it seemed. The full glacial fauna of North Africa bore little resemblance to that of Europe.

Pallary continued his work along the western coast of Algeria; however, in the early years of this century the focus of research shifted east to the Constantine Plain and the region of Tebessa and southern Tunisia, where the Capsian industry was being investigated and defined. Although work continued in a sporadic fashion on the Iberomaurusian it is only with the development of radiocarbon dating which showed that this industry is final Palaeolithic in age (*c*. 20,000 − 9000 BP) that interest was revived in the Iberomaurusian (Brahimi 1970; Close 1977).

The Aurignacian Debate

The study of the prehistory of eastern Algeria and Tunisia did not effectively begin until 1909 when Jacques de Morgan, a very well known Near Eastern and Egyptian archaeologist, published, along with his colleagues the French prehistorian Dr L. Capitan and P. Boudy, a resident of Gafsa, the results of an archaeological survey conducted in the areas of Gafsa and Rédeyef in southern Tunisia. De Morgan reported stratified assemblages of stone tools which he called Capsian, after the Roman name for Gafsa. The stratigraphically lower assemblages contained large backed blades, burins and thick scrapers; while the upper or younger assemblages were described as more refined, containing backed bladelets, small scrapers, fragments of engraved ostrich egg shell, and polished bone tools (de Morgan *et al.* 1910: 273). De Morgan noted that much of this material resembled the French Aurignacian, the systematics of which had been recently worked out by Breuil (1905, 1912).

De Morgan was one of the last of the nineteenth-century evolutionists. Rather than explaining these assemblage similarities in terms of the diffusion of ideas or movement of peoples, he invoked independent development. In a very clear statement of the evolutionary, or what was then often called the 'palaeoethnological' point of view, de Morgan stated:

> It seems difficult to accept that in the Palaeolithic period the same industry was spread by diffusion in Western Europe and North Africa; it would appear more rational to assume that, in the two countries, the same causes have led to the same effects and it is a result of similarities of life imposed by nature that these people have developed similar industries. Moreover, we do not know if the Capsian is contemporaneous with the Aurignacian. (De Morgan *et al.* 1910: 117; author's translation)

Although de Morgan believed the Capsian took the place in North Africa of the European Upper Palaeolithic he saw no reason to invoke connections between the two because, as he stated, similar circumstances could produce similar effects. Rather than follow the European subdivision of the Aurignacian, de Morgan proposed a subdivision of the Capsian based upon the stratified assemblages excavated by Boudy from the rock shelters of Rédeyef. The more refined material was named *Capsien Supérieur* and he called the crude assemblage dominated by large tools *Capsien Inférieur*. This division essentially mirrors that of the modern Upper Capsian and Typical Capsian. The chronostratigraphic relationship inferred in 1910 remained associated with the Capsian until the late 1960s.

De Morgan's perceptive statement was immediately challenged by those who rejected the importance of independent development and saw similarity in archaeological industries as evidence of direct contact and/or diffusion of ideas. Still another group of French archaeologists, led ultimately by Raymond Vaufrey, wished to put any attempt at explanation or the search for origins on the back burner. Instead they adopted the theory and method of geology and palaeontology which had been so successful in ordering geological material in time and space and constructing the Alpine glacial sequence. For these people, the development of chronology and the definition and description of sequences was of primary concern; speculation on origins was to be delayed until 'all the evidence was in'.

THE DIFFUSIONISTS

Those who might loosely be called the diffusionists were predominantly avocational North African archaeologists; however, the opening shot for the diffusionist· argument was fired by the French archaeologist Dr L. Capitan. In the 1910 serial article (published in several installments from 1910 to 1911) written with de Morgan, Capitan disagreed with his co-author. Capitan took the position that the similarity between the Aurignacian and the Capsian must signify some form of relationship, most probably an exchange of ideas or people across a Mediterranean land bridge (de Morgan *et al*. 1911: 226). This position was further strengthened by Breuil's pronouncement, in his famous article 'Les Subdivisions du Paléolithique supérieur et leur signification' that the Capsian was clearly Middle Aurignacian and may have influenced the development of the French Aurignacian by way of Spain (Breuil 1912: 183). Of course Pallary had already suggested a relationship between Spain and North Africa, but one which followed chronologically the industries of the Upper Palaeolithic. After these illustrious beginnings it is understandable that the soldiers and bureaucrats, who formed the numerous archaeological and historical societies of the Maghreb, rushed to support the diffusionist argument and to discover Breuil's three stages of the Aurignacian in North Africa. It is probable that they wished to demonstrate that the Maghreb material was comparable to, and therefore as important as, the exciting finds coming out of the Palaeolithic caves of south-west France, and that North Africa might possibly be the original fountain from which the French developments sprang.

These early Maghreb archaeologists can certainly be excused on methodological grounds for wanting to correlate North African material with that from France, for by doing so they could provide themselves with a chronology. Like American archaeologists, workers in the Maghreb had few large stratified sites which could provide the basis for a relative chronology, let alone a chronology tied to geological events such as that being developed in France. In North Africa, as in North America, there were numerous small open-air sites which were generally assumed to be stratigraphically homogeneous. In central and southern Algeria and Tunisia these small mounds were called *escargotières* because they were primarily composed of land snail shell and ash (cf. Gobert 1937). By studying the stone tool assemblages found in these sites and comparing them to the European sequence, the North African workers hoped to develop their own regional sequence.

Foremost among these workers was Albert Debruge, a civil servant in the city of Constantine, capital of the eastern province of Algeria. Debruge was an active member of the Constantine Archaeological Society and it fell upon him in 1912 to excavate, for the Society, the site of Mechta El Arbi 50 kilometres west of Constantine. The site had previously (1907) been tested by the then vice-president of the Society, Gustave Mercier. Work was subsequently carried out by Debruge in 1914 and 1923. Debruge reported a lithic industry totally lacking in burins and geometric microliths and exhibiting what he thought were Mousterian affinities. He attributed the bone industry which had no affinity with European materials to intrusive Neolithic burials (Debruge and Mercier 1912: 304). Debruge subsequently made Mechta the type site for his *Aurignacien Ancien* (Debruge 1923: 55). During the various excavations, eight to ten adult and a similar number of sub-adult human skeletons were recovered and initially studied by the French anthropologist Dr Bertholon. Bertholon concluded that these skulls were Neanderthaloid (Mercier and Debruge 1912), thereby supporting the Palaeolithic age of the *escargotière*. Following the publication of this analysis, considerable disagreement arose in the French anthropological establishment as to the exact affinity of the skulls. Some felt that they exhibited 'Neanderthaloid' traits while others felt that the signs of tooth avulsion indicated a Neolithic age. They all concurred, however, that the skulls were definitely not those of Neanderthals (Mercier 1915; Pond *et al*. 1928). By so concluding, the French establishment refuted one possible line of evidence demonstrating the proposed North African ancestry of the Aurignacian. Although the skeletal evidence was of dubious value to the North African diffusionists, they could still, in the first quarter of the century, point to the similarity between French and North African tool assemblages as evidence for a relationship. However even this argument was becoming increasingly tenuous.

Although Debruge found very few geometrics in the central Algerian sites, as he moved east into the area of Tebessa he encountered sites with many more. The numerous geometrics in the sites of the Tebessa region clearly posed a problem for the 'Aurignacian school' since they were not often found in the French Aurignacian but rather in the post-Palaeolithic Tardenoisian (Coutil 1912). This led Debruge to adopt a more cautious stand on the Tebessa assemblages (Debruge 1923). Such caution, however, was not exercised by his friend Maurice Reygasse, *Administrateur Principal* of the *Commune Mixte* of Tebessa and the most active archaeologist in that region. From 1917 on, Reygasse divided the Capsian of the Tebessa region into three *civilizations Aurignaciennes* (Reygasse 1920: 515), the last of these being the *Tardenoisien le plus pur*. For Reygasse the abundance of geometrics beginning in his middle Aurignacian only demonstrated the development of geometrics in North Africa prior to the French Tardenoisian. He concluded that the richness of the Maghreb Aurignacian only confirmed the African origin of the Aurignacian in general (1922: 194–203). This position was of course difficult to refute without some method of dating sites, but some important work along these lines was being undertaken by Dr E.G. Gobert beginning in 1910 in Tunisia.

THE ARGUMENT AGAINST THE AURIGNACIAN CONNECTION

One of the foremost avocational archaeologists working in the Maghreb was Dr E.G. Gobert, a medical doctor attached to the hospital in Gafsa in south Tunisia. Gobert continued the work begun by de Morgan and his interest in 'paléoethnologie' seems to have been inspired by the de Morgan model. Gobert followed the view held by de Morgan that the assemblages coming from the *escargotières* and rock shelters should be called Capsian and that they bore no necessary relationship to the French Aurignacian (Gobert 1910: 595). Working within the geological paradigm of French archaeology, Gobert began to systematically excavate sites and develop a regional chronology based on rock shelter stratigraphy and inter-assemblage comparison. One of his most important observations, made as early as 1910, was that virtually all Capsian sites in southern Tunisia contained geometric microliths when the deposits were screened. As noted above, such elegant microlithic forms were not found in good Aurignacian context in France, but were instead associated with post-Pleistocene *Tardenoisien* or Mesolithic deposits. Therefore, if one were to use geometrics as a *fossil directeur*, the Capsian deposits should all be Holocene in age. Gobert (1910) attributed the extreme rarity of geometrics in the sites excavated by Debruge to poor excavation techniques. When used, sifting screens were generally employed in an unsystematic manner by most archaeologists working in the Maghreb. Gobert was specifically objecting to Debruge's use of large-mesh gravel screens which were set up on an angle. He was sure this technique would not recover geometrics, thereby increasing the Aurignacian character of the assemblages. In retrospect, it does seem probable that many of the sites excavated by Debruge on the Constantine plain did contain very few geometrics. In 1952, during the Pan-African Conference, Lionel Balout re-opened Mechta el Arbi from which Debruge had reported only a few segments. Balout also failed to find any geometric microliths (Balout 1955: 380). At least one aspect of the

Aurignacian debate does seem to have been fuelled by true regional variation in the Capsian.

In addition to the evidence provided by the microliths, Gobert argued that the fauna recovered from Capsian sites was a warm fauna containing zebra, ox, antelope and ostrich, and since this assemblage was not any different from the fauna associated with Neolithic sites, it seemed probable that the Capsian was not much older (Gobert 1910: 595). This argument was countered by the diffusionists who invoked a less severe climate for North Africa during the Upper Palaeolithic, due to its more southerly latitude.

THE LOGAN MUSEUM EXPEDITIONS

It was into this atmosphere of controversy that the Logan Museum launched its North African programme of research. Both the museum's director, Dr George Collie, and Alonzo Pond the expedition field director, were members of the French Prehistoric Society and were aware of the controversy. However, their entry into North African research was through contacts with Maghreb avocational archaeologists of the diffusionist school, and this naturally influenced the position taken by the Americans. Pond was first introduced to North African prehistory while attending the 1924 International Congress of Anthropologists at Toulouse, France, where Maurice Reygasse gave a paper on materials from *escargotières* around Tebessa. During the following summer of 1925, Pond and Collie visited Reygasse in Tebessa and studied sites in the area before going to Constantine. There Pond and Reygasse joined the 'Franco-American Expedition' on its trip south to Tammanrasset in the Hoggar mountains of the central Sahara. During this trip of over 2,800 kilometres, a large number of archaeological sites were located and a great quantity of artefacts collected. On the return trip, Pond and Reygasse left the motor-car expedition at Ain Salah and proceeded north-west by camel, conducting archaeological and ethnographic research as they travelled 500 kilometres to the railroad at Figuig on the desert edge (Pond *et al.* 1928).

This general survey was so productive that Collie and Dr Frank G. Logan (the Logan Museum's benefactor) decided to conduct further studies in North Africa, and in 1926, they signed a five-year research permit with the Algerian government. As a result, in the fall of 1926, Pond returned to North Africa, and with the official guidance of M.A. Debruge, began excavation at Mechta el Arbi (fig. 10:2). The results of this work were published in 1928. In 1927, work was conducted on the Mediterranean coast; in 1929 in eastern Algeria and finally in 1930, Pond, along with a contingent of fourteen American students, conducted a three-month campaign of excavation on the southern edge of the Constantine plain near Canrobert (Ain Beidha region).

The research methods used during these expeditions were a model for the time. Intensive field survey was followed by surface collection, and the accurate measurement and plotting of the sites on topographic maps. Each site was given an identifying number, and by the end of the 1930 season, 73 sites had been located and collections taken. As a general rule, sites were excavated by running 3 metre-wide trenches from the edge into the summit of the mound. The initial 15 centimetres of the deposit was excavated as a unit, and any artefacts found were placed with the surface collection. After this, a 3 by 2-metre pit was excavated to sterile soil at the outer edge of the trench. The balance of the trench was then excavated in arbitrary levels, the thickness of which depended on the thickness of the mound. All of the

10:2 *General view of the site of Mechta el Arbi during the Logan Museum excavations in 1926, showing the main excavation unit*

deposit was screened through gravel screens of one-centimetre mesh set on an angle in the same manner as those employed by Debruge (fig. 10:3). Although some material was necessarily missed using this procedure, examination of the reports and my own study of the collections (Sheppard 1984) has revealed no systematic bias against microlithic forms.

In addition to the careful quantitative study of all the stone tools recovered, the Logan Museum expeditions were exceptional for their time in that they recovered and undertook detailed identification of faunal and human remains, conducted studies of modern snail populations, noted such features as hearths and saved charcoal samples from them (fig. 10:4). Fifty years later it has been possible to obtain reasonable radiocarbon dates on charcoal which was collected in 1930 from Site 12 (Sheppard 1984). This careful approach to artefact recovery is best summed up in Pond's own words:

> Any published account of the work done on any site which does not include a quantitative record of *All* the material collected and a description of the classification types or terms used which will enable the general student to grasp the significance of the collection in its relation to other collections is practically useless. *ALL* the data are necessary, and those data often considered too commonplace to mention by the local investigator are frequently of greatest importance in giving their study its proper place. (Pond *et al.* 1938: 162).

Although this statement was directed to the study of stone tools, it also captures the spirit that led to the collection of other types of data, which were either generally ignored, or only casually collected by many other workers in North Africa. The standards of research and publication set by Pond were unfortunately not equalled by North African archaeologists for another twenty years.

Although the research methods of the Logan Museum expeditions were exceptional, it seems that both Pond and Collie did not have enough first-hand familiarity with the French Aurignacian, or other North African material, to enable them to see significant differences between the two. There were, however, differences between Pond and Collie in the degree of significance they attributed to the apparent similarity between the

10:3 *Excavation at Mechta el Arbi 1926 showing the use of vertical screens and arbitrary levels. M.A. Debruge seated in the foreground*

10:4 *Skull of an infant in situ at Mechta el Arbi 1926 resting in the snail shell and ash matrix characteristic of all Capsian escargotière*

Maghrebian and European industries. Collie appears to have had a strong theoretical interest in the Aurignacian, resulting in his support of fieldwork by the Logan Museum in both France and North Africa and publication, in 1928, of a general survey of the Aurignacian entitled 'The Aurignacians and their culture'. In this volume, Collie makes a detailed argument for a relationship between the North African material and the French Aurignacian based upon the skeletal, faunal, geological, and stone tool evidence. He argued that the Mechta el Arbi human skeletal remains were intermediate between Neanderthals and the Cro Magnons, the latter being associated with the French Aurignacian. Collie felt this supported the hypothesis that the Aurignacian was developed in North Africa by a human form which probably pre-dated the development of Cro Magnons (Collie, 1928: 4, 9, 14, 28). This intermediate form then carried the Aurignacian culture to Europe via a land bridge from Tunisia through Sicily and Italy. As evidence, he cited what he believed to be early Aurignacian skeletons with 'Negroid' characteristics found in the Grimaldi Caves in Italy. Collie admitted that there was no evidence for a Pleistocene land bridge across the Mediterranean; however he noted the evidence for bridges in earlier periods and suggested that it would be reasonable to assume their presence during the 'Late Palaeolithic' (Collie 1928: 14, 73).

As noted previously, the faunal material from the Maghreb sites contained species characteristic of a warm climate (e.g. zebra, elephant, giraffe, gazelle) which contrasted with the cold fauna associated with the European Aurignacian (e.g. horse, reindeer, *Bos* species) (Collie 1928: 20). The differences in these fauna suggested to some authors that the Maghreb materials were more recent than the European Aurignacian. Collie, however, explained the differences by invoking a milder climate in North Africa during the European Glacial period. In addition, Collie believed that the European Aurignacian dated to the very end of the Würm Glacial or to the Early Holocene. Prior to this time, during the height of the Glacial, he felt that Europe was basically uninhabitable. Therefore, North Africa provided a suitable environment for the early development of the Aurignacian during the Würm Glacial prior to the diffusion of the Aurignacian to Europe at the end of the Glacial. All of these arguments were of course subsidiary to the main contention that the stone tools found in the North African shell mounds were identical in form to those found in European Aurignacian deposits. Collie expressed this best when he stated: 'There are enormous quantities of palaeolithic utensils in North Africa and so many of them bear such close resemblance to European types that the old time explanation of parallelism of cultures does not suffice; only contacts, more or less direct, can explain the likenesses found' (Collie 1928: 73). Any important differences between the lithic assemblages of Europe and North Africa, such as the often considerable abundance of geometric microliths in the latter, were simply assumed by Collie to reflect either divergence after the movement to Europe or the advanced features of the original culture in Africa (Collie 1928: 45). Although Collie did describe the Aurignacian tool types, he did not attempt any detailed numerical comparison of North African and French assemblages. A careful study of any of the reports shows that the similarity between these assemblages is based primarily on the presence in both of large-backed blades. To summarize Collie's position, it is apparent that regardless of the poor chronology and limited data, Collie thought that he had a rather compelling argument for the origin in North Africa of the spectacular French Upper Palaeolithic developments.

If we can characterize Collie as the grand theoretician, Pond was much more the careful, methodical field-worker concerned with the practical problems of describing and comparing archaeological assemblages. In the 1928 report on Mechta el Arbi, Pond attempts to compare the materials from the site with the published material from France. With hindsight it is obvious that many of the similarities pointed out by Pond are not really important attributes of the Aurignacian, and Pond himself notes that many forms, and especially the bone tool industry, bear little or no resemblance to the published Aurignacian (Pond *et al.* 1928: 58). In addition, the appended report by Alfred Romer on the human skeletal material concludes that the crania from Mechta el Arbi are not related to either Neanderthal or Cro Magnon, and that they are likely ancestors of the modern North African types. Although evidence seemed to be pointing away from any Aurignacian connection, Pond was still faced with the basic archaeological problem of what level of assemblage similarity, or dissimilarity, must exist before two assemblages are considered to be members of the same or different archaeological cultures. In France the use of type fossils which were characteristic of particular time frames was the primary method of assigning an assemblage to an established time/space unit. This method was quite successful because many of the forms used were stylistically unique. Pond made some use of this approach, but he insisted on full assemblage comparison, comparing all the different classes of tool types and lithic waste that he had defined in the North African assemblages. It is probable that this use of full assemblage comparison was influenced by the American anthropological approach to cultural comparison using detailed trait lists, as practised by Boas and Kroeber. This approach, although quite admirable from a modern archaeological point of view, led in the North African case to an over-weighting of the more mundane aspects of the lithic assemblage which often have few useful stylistic characteristics, and correspondingly less attention to very useful temporal indicators such as microlithic geometrics. As noted above, geometric forms are often quite abundant in the Capsian, and were recovered by Pond, but they are quite rare (if not absent) in most French Aurignacian assemblages. Today the presence of the geometrics would generally indicate a Mesolithic age; however when it came to classification Pond was a 'lumper' not a 'splitter'; he preferred to focus on similarities rather than differences. In the preface to the final report on the Logan Museum expeditions (Pond *et al.* 1938) Pond sets out his methodological position as follows:

> The purpose of the science of prehistory is to answer the problems concerning man's origin, his migrations and distribution over the earth and the relation of groups in different parts of the world to those in other parts. To do this the data must be well organized and thoroughly correlated. Such correlation is facilitated by recognizing the *similarities first* and not by encumbering the science with a complicated nomenclature which emphasizes minor differences. (Pond *et al.* 1938: 5)

For Pond the use of the term 'Capsian' was an encumbrance which was, on methodological grounds, an improper use of scientific nomenclature, the Capsian resembled the Aurignacian and therefore it should be called Aurignacian. For Pond this need not imply any direct relationship. It seems clear that as the work progressed Pond realized that there was no connection with the European Aurignacian but he refrained from directly contradicting his employer Dr Collie. This is not to suggest, however, that Pond did not have any concern with the sort of theorizing undertaken by Collie. Pond did not make many explicit statements concerning European/African relationships but he did advance a complementary hypothesis concerning the migration routes of early man from southern into northern Africa and Europe. Based upon his study of museum collections in Italy and his reading of a study of the Italian Palaeolithic by Raymond Vaufrey (1928) and citing Louis B. Leakey, Pond hypothesized that man likely originated in Africa and entered Europe via the Nile valley and the Near East or by way of the Sahara and Spain. Pond's study of the Italian material had convinced him that Collie's 1928 hypothesis of movement of the Aurignacian across a land bridge from Tunisia to Italy was not supported by the stone tools coming from Italian sites. It was, however, the study of this same material which was to lead Vaufrey to work in North Africa and refute fairly conclusively the Aurignacian/Capsian connection.

The refutation by Vaufrey

Raymond Vaufrey (fig. 10:5) was, in the 1920s, a student of Marcellin Boule, then director of the Institute de Paléontologie Humaine in Paris and editor of the journal *L'Anthropologie*. Boule had a strong interest in palaeontological evidence for Pleistocene land bridges across the Mediterranean and he sent Vaufrey first to Italy and then, beginning in 1927, to North Africa to study both the faunal and artefactual evidence for such connections. As noted by Pond, Vaufrey quite quickly demonstrated in his thesis the lack of evidence for an Italian/Tunisian land bridge and he then went on to do a comparative study of the archaeological materials from southern Tunisia and eastern Algeria, often with the collaboration of Dr Gobert. During the course of a series of expeditions between 1931 and 1933, Vaufrey tested a large number of sites throughout this region (Vaufrey 1955: 5). Although the area excavated was often very small, Vaufrey insisted upon the screening of all deposits and the excavation of the unit down to sterile soil or bedrock (Roubet 1979: 29). The resulting collection was then selected with bias in favour of formal retouched tools. Upon his return to Paris in 1933, he published an article in *L'Anthropologie* entitled 'Notes sur le Capsien' (Vaufrey 1933a) in which he laid out what became the standard interpretation of the Capsian for the next thirty years.

In the 1933 report, Vaufrey discussed his work at numerous sites in Tunisia (El Mekta, Redéyef Table sud, Lala, Ain Sendes) and at Ain Rhilane an Algerian site near the Algerian/Tunisian border east of Tebessa. Vaufrey described the contents of the various Capsian industries, set up a relative chronology and demonstrated the lack of validity, on typological and geological grounds, of the Aurignacian hypothesis.

Vaufrey divided the Capsian into *Capsien supérieur, Capsien typique* and *Néolithique de Tradition Capsienne*. The Typical Capsian was represented by the industries from El Mekta and Redéyef. The El Mekta material consisted of numerous large backed blades, lateral burins, endscrapers and backed bladelets plus a very small number of geometric microliths (segments predominating) and over 50 microburins. The assemblage from Redéyef contained fewer of the large pieces but had many geometrics and microburins. It was felt to be either more evolved, or a local variant, or perhaps to represent horizontal variation within the site (Vaufrey 1933a: 470). The bone industry of both sites was represented by a few fragmentary pieces. In each of these sites Vaufrey pointed out the constant presence of 'les microburins du type "tardenoisien"' (1933a: 466). Vaufrey divided the Upper Capsian into two facies, the *'Intergétulo-néolithique'* of Tunisia (1933a: 474), and the *'Capsien supérieur typique'* which predominated in Algeria. The major characteristic of both facies was the

10:5 *Raymond Vaufrey in the main Choumovitch Trench at Abri 402, a Capsian site near Moulares. Djebel Bou-Dinar in the distance*

marked reduction in the number of large tools (backed blades, burins) (1933a: 477) and a great increase in the number and variety of microlithic tools, especially geometrics. What distinguished the facies, however, was primarily the type of geometrics found. In the '*Intergétulo-néolithique*' as represented by Lala, elongated scalene triangles dominated and truncations were frequent, while the '*supérieur typique*' was characterized by 'true geometric microliths' (1933a: 477), such as triangles and equilateral trapezes. Both industries contained a more varied and abundant bone industry than that found in the *Capsien typique*.

The final stage of the Capsian, the '*Néolithique de Tradition Capsienne*' (NTC) was characterized by the complete disappearance of most *Capsien typique* elements, a reduction of the number of geometric forms, and the introduction of bifacial points (1933a: 478). Vaufrey placed these three industries in a chronological sequence based upon reduction in the number of large tools and increase in the microlithic forms.

In a footnote to the 1933 article, Vaufrey stated that Gobert had found the NTC over the '*Intergétulo-néolithique*' at Redéyef and that his own work at Relilai had shown the *Capsien supérieur* overlying the *Capsien typique* (1933a: 480); 1933b: 648–649). In addition to establishing a chronology, Vaufrey argued that the presence of geometrics, and especially the presence of microburins in all stages, cemented the Capsian into a homogeneous block which could not be older than final Upper Palaeolithic:

> From a typological viewpoint, the Capsian appears to us as an industry of a Mesolithic character or at least final Palaeolithic, and one cannot contemplate making it the ancestor of the Aurignacian. (Vaufrey 1933a: 481; author's translation).

The presence of microburins was considered by Vaufrey to be a firm indicator of the manufacture of geometrics, since the use of the microburin technique for manufacturing geometrics had been amply demonstrated (Siret 1924), specifically so for the Capsian by Vignard (1934). Therefore, although some sites such as El Mekta might have very few geometrics, the presence of microburins 'du type Tardenoisien' (over 50 at El Mekta) indicated geometric manufacture, whether the geometrics were found or not.

Aside from demonstrating the *'Tardenoisien'* typological affinities of the Capsian, Vaufrey made the important observation that none of the Capsian sites were found in the old wadi alluvium, but rather resting upon it. This suggested a relatively recent geological age. When considered together these arguments virtually destroyed the theory of the African origin of the Aurignacian, and in 1937 Breuil (1937) conceded that such a theory should be abandoned. However, until the development of radiocarbon dating, Vaufrey battled sporadic revivals of the old idea (Lacorre 1949; Vaufrey 1955) although these were generally ignored.

In addition to defining the industries and providing a temporal framework, Vaufrey formalized knowledge concerning the geographical distribution of the Capsian. He noted that the *Capsien typique* was confined to the region south of Tebessa (1933a: 649) (Algeria/Tunisia), while the *Capsien supérieur* spread beyond that region throughout the Constantine plains as far as Sétif and south of the Coastal Atlas down to the large *chotts* marking the northern edge of the Sahara (1933a: 459). This is essentially, with some extensions on the borders, the distribution known today (Camps 1974: 117).

In the years following 1933 Vaufrey continued to investigate the Capsian but his interest now focussed on the portable and rock art of the Maghreb. Using the portable art recovered from his excavations in Capsian sites, Vaufrey attempted to develop a chronology for the rock art and investigate the relationship between the Capsian and neighbouring regions, notably Egypt and Spain (Roubet 1979: 42–6). It is also at this time that Vaufrey noted the resemblance between the Neolithic of Capsian Tradition and many other industries throughout Africa, leading him to postulate, along with his mentor M. Boule, a spread of the NTC throughout Africa.

From this period during the 1930s the number of avocational archaeologists working in the Maghreb increased dramatically with a small number (including G. Souville, G. and H. Camps, J. Tixier, H.J. Hugot, R. de Bayle des Hermens) being trained professionally at the University and Bardo Museum in Algiers by Lionel Balout who replaced Maurice Reygasse in 1947 as the instructor in prehistory (Roubet *et al.* 1981). These archaeologists have since made major contributions to our knowledge of the Capsian and the general prehistory of North Africa although much of their work can be seen as an amplification and refinement of the pioneering work of Vaufrey. The major problem which had animated North African research was resolved by Vaufrey and the following period has been, in the terms of Thomas Kuhn (1972), one of normal science during which the details of the new understanding were worked out. One of the most outstanding achievements of this period was the production by Jacques Tixier in 1963 of a tool typology for the Maghreb epipalaeolithic which is perhaps the best available lithic typology for a particular area and period. This typology together with the excellent bone tool typology developed by Henriette Camps-Fabrer (1966) allowed for the systematic study and comparison of the large number of excavated sites and for the production for the first time of very detailed site reports such as that published on Medjez II by Camps-Fabrer (1975). These methodological developments together with the increasing number of radiocarbon dates, which definitely placed the Capsian in the Holocene with the coastal Iberomaurusian preceeding it, enabled Gabriel Camps to write a synthesis of the prehistory of North Africa (Camps 1974) which has replaced the earlier works of Vaufrey (1955) and Balout (1955).

Since independence the amount of prehistoric research conducted in North Africa has declined. The majority of the archaeologists involved in prehistoric research have moved to take up positions in French institutions leaving few prehistorians in the former North African colonies, although the major research centre in Algiers (Centre du Recherches Anthropologiques, Préhistoriques et Ethnographiques) is still active. Some research by French and other foreign archaeologists, notably Danilo Grébéuart (1976), David Lubell (Lubell et al. 1975, Lubell et al. 1976, Lubell et al. 1984) and Colette Roubet (1979), has been carried out. However it has not been possible to develop on-going programmes of research. The difficulties of funding modern archaeology and the quantity and wide variety of historic and proto-historic sites which have a more immediate interest for the people of North Africa have resulted in less attention being paid to prehistory by North African archaeologists.

Acknowledgements

This work was supported by Social Sciences and Humanities Research Council of Canada grants to David Lubell (University of Alberta) and by SHRC post-doctoral grants to the author. Many thanks to David Lubell for providing me with the opportunity to conduct research on the Capsian and for assistance and advice on the preparation of this article. Figure 10:1 was prepared by Cartographic Services Department of Alberta, with funding provided by an SSHRC grant to David Lubell. I wish to thank especially Mr Alonzo Pond of Minocqua Wisconsin (USA) for providing me with both inspiration and photographs of the Mechta el Arbi Excavations. Mr Pond, who died at Christmas 1986, was one of the last of the early pioneers of North African archaeology, and a truly remarkable man. I would also like to acknowledge the assistance of Michael Trababulski (Madison, Wisconsin) whose interest in the photographic record of archaeology in North Africa in the 1920s and 30s. Finally I would like to thank Deborah Ross for her editorial assistance and Maxine Kleindienst for her support of my North African research.

Conclusion

In summary one can see at least three major themes reflected in the history of research on the Capsian. These are: (1) general shifts in social theory, (2) development and divergence of national archaeological traditions, and (3) conflict between colonial avocational archaeologists and metropolitan professional archaeologists. The debate began with the pronouncements of a nineteenth-century evolutionist who believed in the potential for independent development. The reaction in the early twentieth century to nineteenth-century evolutionism was a demand for less grand theorizing and more data. However, even data collection needed some guiding paradigm and for North American archaeologists working out of anthropology departments, diffusion and trait comparison became the major theoretical and methodological tools. This was the approach taken by the Logan Museum expeditions. In France the reaction to nineteenth-century evolutionism led archaeologists to search for more and better data and to adopt a geological theoretical framework and its most useful tool, the type fossil concept. When this approach was applied to the North African data, it produced a synthesis completely at odds with the diffusionist theory of the Americans, and the intellectual aspirations of the avocational archaeologists who made up the North African prehistoric societies. The Capsian was shown to be neither contemporaneous with, nor the source of, the Aurignacian. Once this problem was resolved, the way was prepared for a new generation to apply new methodology (e.g. systematic typology using the Bordian approach) and techniques (e.g. radiocarbon dating) to elaboration of the scheme developed by Vaufrey.

11 *A Personal Memoir*

J. DESMOND CLARK

With hindsight one can divide the history of African archaeology into three periods of development: the pioneer, the formative and the modern behavioural and actualistic period (from *c*. 1960 to the present). *The pioneer period* lasted from the beginning of the 1850s to 60s up to around 1930. By the late 1920s a number of amateurs and a very few professionals had produced a wealth of cultural remains but with very little evidence of age. By 1930, therefore, it was possible for the Abbé Breuil (probably the only archaeologist at that time to know both the North and South African material) to publish his overview of African prehistory – the first ever to be undertaken (Breuil 1930a). The following year Maurice Reygasse (1931) published his monograph on the prehistory of North Africa, though, in effect, it was largely restricted to Algeria. At the other end of the continent, Miles Burkitt had published *South Africa's Past in Stone and Paint* (1928) and John Goodwin and 'Peter' Van Riet Lowe in 1929 published their epoch-making volume 'The Stone Age Cultures of South Africa' – the work that laid the foundation for the ordering of cultural entities and terminology still in current use south of the Sahara (Goodwin and Van Riet Lowe 1929).

Starting later than the pioneer work in both north-west and south Africa was that begun by Louis Leakey in the late 1920s in the Kenya Rift Valley which, in 1931, culminated in the publication of *The Stone Age Cultures of Kenya Colony* (Leakey 1931). For the first time this showed both the great richness and the potential for archaeological research that exist in the East African Rift Valley. Interest everywhere centred on the Stone Age. In Europe this was where the interest lay and in Africa, where stone tools were prolific, it was believed that the Iron Age south of the Sahara was of recent date so that little or no attention was given to it except for Great Zimbabwe and the related ruin sites. Most white Africans thought the origins of these were exotic or, at least, enigmatic in spite of the excellent research by Randal MacIver (1906) and Gertrude Caton Thompson (1931) which clearly demostrated their cultural association with the ancestors of the Shona-speaking peoples of the region.

If these and other works brought the 'pioneer period' to an end, the introduction of a more scientific approach to recovering, dating and interpreting the context and distribution of cultural remains initiated the next phase of archaeological activity which can conveniently be called *the formative period*. This lasted from about 1930 to *c*. 1960 and was a period in which, in spite of the disruption of the Second World War, a growing number of professionally trained archaeologists began to work in different parts of the continent from such bases in Africa as universities, museums or government antiquities departments. At this time, most of Africa was under some kind of colonial administration so that the archaeologists who began the first systematic investigations were citizens of and received their training in France, Britain, Belgium, Portugal and, to a lesser extent, South

Africa. This was a time when archaeologists were just beginning (though there had been some notable exceptions much earlier (Johnson 1905, 1907a and b; Pallary 1907a and b)) to associate geologists and palaeontologists with their investigations in an attempt to place their discoveries into a relative framework of stratigraphical and geomorphological history and, where fossil faunal remains were also present, to try to date these within the broad divisions of Quaternary time. A good example of such an attempt is Louis Leakey's *Stone Age Africa*, the published version (1936a) of his Munro Lectures delivered in Edinburgh the same year. This was the first publication in English dealing with the continent as a whole that emphasized the need to study the palaeo-environments, climate and associated biota as a means of providing a chronological framework. The archaeological emphasis was still and for a long time would so remain, on the technological and typological characteristics of the Stone Age assemblages. The behavioural implications behind changes in the natural habitat and in technology through time were not, as yet, a subject for serious investigation and, if referred to at all, remained still in the realm of subjective speculation. None the less, *Stone Age Africa* was a milestone. At least, I believe it to have been, for it showed that the record of past human activity in Africa needs to be examined, not only at the regionally specific level, but broadly also on a continent-wide basis. In this way, regional manifestations in their context can be correlated and compared so that better understanding of the overall processes of adaptation and causes of transition can be attempted.

The formative period from the 1930s to the 1960s saw a considerable increase in the number of systematic excavations of cave and rock-shelter sites and some significant work on open sites. Among the former must be noted John Goodwin's excavation of the Oakhurst Shelter at George (1938) on the South African south coast which gave the first good Later Stone Age stratified coastal sequence with Peer's Cave, Fishoek, giving the Middle and Later Stone Age sequence (Keith 1931: 126–40). This was also the time of the first systematic survey of a river valley system with its contained cultural and faunal assemblages. Carried out in the 1930s by two geologists from the South African Geological Survey and 'Peter' Van Riet Lowe, in the middle and lower reaches of the Vaal River (Söhnge, Visser and Van Riet Lowe 1937), this survey provided a geomorphological framework for relative dating of the artefact assemblages that was further tied into a framework of changing climates first proposed by E.J. Wayland in Uganda in the 1920s (Wayland 1929, 1934a). Wayland was Director of the Geological Survey there and in the Western Rift, in the very long sequence of sediments preserved in the deep trough, he found evidence that appeared to show times when there was appreciably more rain with full lakes and eroding rivers and other times when the sediments suggested arid conditions. The first were called 'pluvials' and the second 'interpluvials' and these were given an inferred correlation with the glacial/interglacial periods in Europe. At the same time, Erik Nilsson (1940) was recovering similar episodes of rising and falling lakes in the Nakuru/Naivasha basins of the Kenya Rift. Louis Leakey adopted the pluvial/interpluvial hypothesis and gave names to the pluvials and wet phases after localities in the Eastern and Western Rifts. Probably in view of the fact that there was no better way of dating cultural assemblages, this hypothesis of climatic change was adopted from one end of the continent to the other and it became the fashion to find water-worn 'pebble tools' in high-level, residual gravel spreads and, if they were flaked only from one side, to label them 'Kafuan' or, if from both faces, 'Oldowan' after the basal industry in the Olduvai

Gorge. The Oldowan sequence, still without rival for completeness in stratigraphic history and cultural and faunal evolution for much of the earlier part of human history, was the subject of investigation by Louis Leakey and his team from 1931 onwards and appeared also to confirm the pluvial/interpluvial hypothesis.

It is surprising that it took some twenty-five years to expose the flaw in the evidence on which the pluvial hypothesis was based, especially since Leakey himself had drawn attention to the significant earth movements that could be clearly documented, in particular in the East African Rift system. It was not until Basil Cooke (1958) and Dick Flint (1959b) showed that, since earth movements could cause lakes to appear and disappear and divert rivers, or cause them to flow in the opposite direction, East Africa, one of the more unstable regions of the world, was not the best place on which to establish a framework of climatic history for the continent. Flint (1959b) put the final nail in the coffin of the pluvial/interpluvial climatic framework when he said,

I conclude that climate as a primary basis of any stratigraphic scheme is unreliable. This conclusion . . . does not constitute an attack on the reality of climatic change in East Africa, for such change seems truly to have occurred. It seeks only to re-establish climate in the secondary position in which it properly belongs in any stratigraphic scheme. . . . The three entities concerned – rock units, faunal zones and cultural materials – constitute, as a group, a reasonable basis from which can emerge broad correlation that will inspire confidence. (Flint 1959b)

This is the basis on which field research and correlation is undertaken today but with much greater confidence in the chronological framework since this is now based on various radiometric and isotopic dating techniques that provide ages in terms of years before the present.

The importance of radiocarbon dating, potassium-argon (Evernden and Curtis 1965) and the palaeo-magnetic reversal chronology (Cox 1972; Dalrymple 1972), as well as of other methods – thermo-luminescence, uranium-series and electron spin resonance dating – have released the prehistorian so that he may now try to interpret what a homogenous assemblage of artefacts in sealed context can say about the activities of the human group that made and used them.

I first arrived in Africa at the beginning of January 1938 and, after a brief stay at the Cape to meet John Goodwin, I took the train to Livingstone in Northern Rhodesia (now Zambia) (Clark 1986). I was interested in the Stone Age where the emphasis lay throughout the continent at that time and, due to the teaching of Miles Burkitt and Grahame Clark at Cambridge, stone artefacts were something that I believed I was equipped to investigate. At Livingstone, the Zambezi was literally on my doorstep and the Victoria Falls only six miles away. With the Vaal River survey as a model, I set out to try to establish a similar sequence for this part of the Zambezi valley that could be conveniently fitted into a pluvial/interpluvial framework. This was the first fieldwork I undertook on my own, to be aided shortly after by Frank Dixey, who did the geology, and Basil Cooke who described fossil elephant remains that I had found in sediments cut through by a canal dug to provide water for the first hydro-electric plant at the Falls. As with so many things in Africa, one had to relearn much of what one had accepted in Europe. With a great deal of walking, survey and mostly small-scale excavation, the Zambezi succession was established (Clark 1950). The sites and collections were visited and examined by several

11:1 *Louis Leakey and Desmond Clark at the opening of the Field Museum, Victoria Falls 1955*

prehistorians of note – the Abbé Breuil, Teilhard de Chardin, Van Riet Lowe, Neville Jones, the geologists H.B. Maufe, Frank Dixey, Geoffrey Bond, Basil Cooke and Dick Flint, and by a number more prehistorians and others at the third Pan-African Congress on Prehistory held in Livingstone in 1955 (fig. 11.1). Clearly, the last word has not been said but neither has the sequence as yet been seriously questioned. Indeed, one wonders why today anyone would want to question it since it has no particular value beyond the geomorphological and stratigraphic relationships as all the artefact assemblages, other than those of the Later Stone Age, are in secondary context and those that are quite fresh and unabraded eroding from the scarps of orange, Kalahari-type sands that flank the broad valley in this part of the Zambezi's course, are likely to have been moved vertically by soil fauna and hydrothermal action.

My contract with the Museum Trustees stipulated that I should do three-, later two and a half-year tours of duty in Northern Rhodesia, after which we were entitled to six months' leave back in Britain. This was quite invaluable since one was, in fact, living on one's resources archaeologically as there was no one to talk archaeology to nearer than Bulawayo, Cape Town or Nairobi and minimal library resources. These leaves enabled one to catch up on what had been going on in European archaeology during the previous three years and to recharge the archaeological batteries, so to speak. We used to look for a furnished cottage somewhere not too far from Cambridge and spend the time discussing, reading and working up reports on my African fieldwork. Cambridge, through Grahame Clark, Miles Burkitt and Charles McBurney, has been an important influence on the progress of archaeology in English-speaking parts of the African continent and, since the 1920s, had produced professionals like John Goodwin, Louis Leakey, Thurstan Shaw, Bernard Fagg, myself and a number of others who were responsible for starting systematic research in previously unknown regions and in shaping the directions that prehistory took during the formative years from the 1930s to the 1960s.

In the 1930s and 1940s we were still more concerned with the typology and less with the technology of the artefacts. We were, I suppose, at best still collectors and some remained so to the end. Many of the artefacts were fine examples of the stone-knapping craft – Acheulian hand-axes and cleavers, Levallois flakes, Middle Stone Age bifacial and unifacial points, and, *par excellence* if you lived in the Belgian Congo or worked in the Lake Victoria basin, the fine, long, Middle Stone Age lanceolates that are some of the finest examples of stone craft among Pleistocene humans. I remember Keith Robinson's telling me, when he gave me for the Rhodes-Livingstone Museum a collection of 'Magosian' artefacts we had made together from a site on the south, (Southern Rhodesian (Zimbabwean)), side of the Zambezi that, when he showed them to Neville Jones in Bulawayo, Jones said, 'Surely you are not intending to give that [a fine bifacial point] to Clark?'

Although the collections formed an important part of our lives it was for what they could tell us about technology, variation and the importance of raw material in affecting form. None the less, for some it was the context in which they occurred that was of overriding importance. Neville Jones is a good example of this. The pioneer prehistorian of Southern Rhodesia (now Zimbabwe), he started as a missionary and amateur archaeologist at Tiger Kloof in the northern Cape in 1920. Later he transferred to Matabeleland where he was responsible for finding most of the now classic sites and where later, as Keeper of Prehistory at the Bulawayo Museum, he carried out a number of significant excavations, mostly in caves in the Matopo Hills, at such sites as Bambata, Nswatugi, Madiliyangwa (Jones 1949) so that when Bond, Summers and Cooke began their systematic work in the 1950s, the main framework of the Stone Age succession had been reasonably well established.

Neville Jones was also called upon to direct, with John Schofield, the pioneer of southern African prehistoric ceramics, the excavations at the sacred hill-top settlement and sanctuary of Mapungubwe in the Limpopo Valley. Mapungubwe Volume I (Fouché 1937) is one of the finer examples of a site report from that time. With Great Zimbabwe, Mapungubwe, because of the rich grave goods, ceramics and stone work, remained more or less alone among Iron Age studies at this time mainly, I suspect, because anything Iron Age was thought of as being recent and likely to be related to the present-day Bantu-speaking population who were thought by most whites in Southern Africa to be not very innovative or exciting. I recall Neville Jones's telling me with disgust how the middens at Mapungubwe and Bambandyanalo could not be very old as it was possible, after breaking through a crust (possibly of compacted ash from burned cow dung), to collect a bottle full of the stinking gas that was released from the underlying horizon. Radiocarbon dating, which came at a time when the indigenous African populations were beginning to take an interest in their own past, showed us the unexpected antiquity of the beginning of the Iron Age and so gave research into this time range such stimulus that there are today more professionals working on Iron Age than on Stone Age sites. This is particularly so in the Black African nations because it is part of their direct cultural heritage. But, in general also, Iron Age studies have developed because so much more is preserved than at Stone Age sites – whole settlements with many features and much archaeological material – and also because, through the medium of ethno-archaeology, it is possible to use the ethnographic, written and oral historic records to reconstruct the social and economic way of life of the former inhabitants as this is demonstrated by the continuity of cultural traits and of the biota in habitats that have affected the way the human populations organized their lives.

When I arrived in Africa there were only two or three professional archaeologists in the whole of the continent south of the Sahara, who were separated by hundreds of miles and met only on rare occasions. So we all worked, or tended to work, in watertight compartments, so to speak. The danger of this is that one's own material tends to assume greater significance than it really deserves, if it is not looked at within a broader spectrum. Louis Leakey recognized the importance of this and, in 1947, brought together in Nairobi for the first time prehistorians, Quaternary geologists, human and animal palaeontologists, all actively working in the continent. The Pan-African Congress on Prehistory and Quaternary Studies, as it came to be called, was a milestone in prehistoric research in the continent as it broke down the geographical barriers and provided a forum for exchange of information about recent discoveries and research as well as for informal discussions, the establishment of collaborative research projects and the opportunity to visit the sites and examine collections on which the regional sequences had been built up. I cannot stress enough the significance of these early congresses (Clark 1980a). By the late 1960s they had begun to be more specifically archaeological and, with other outlets for the human palaeontologists and geologists due to the greater ease and speed of air travel, there has latterly, unfortunately, been less input from the natural sciences. In compensation, whereas in 1971 in Addis Ababa, Neville Chittick in his purple suit had to argue persuasively for separate sections on Iron Age and historic archaeology, today the weight of contributions from participants is on the later stages of the cultural past.

These Congresses saw some epoch-making releases of new discoveries and new concepts and theory of meaning. In Nairobi we were given in 1947 the first-hand account of the unique Atlantic coast sequence at Sidi Abderrahman, Morocco, from Camille Arambourg; the stratigraphy for the Aterian in Morocco from Armand Ruhlmann and from Sir Wilfrid LeGros Clark the vindication of the South African Australopithecines as representing the earliest known stage of hominid evolution. In 1955, in Livingstone, Raymond Dart released the evidence for his 'Osteodontokeratic' culture based on the first complete analysis of any African faunal assemblage; Louis Leakey presented the evidence for the driving of animals by *Homo erectus* into swampy streambeds and their subsequent butchery in Upper Bed II times at Olduvai at the sites of BK II and SHK II, dated to around 1.1 million years ago. He followed this up in 1959 at Léopoldville by announcing the discovery and producing the first early hominid remains from Olduvai – the robust Australopithecine *Zinjanthropus boisei*. Moreover, some of us were given the opportunity to handle the specimen. As Philip Tobias (who, at the same conference gave one of the most exciting presentations I have ever heard concerning an early fossil and its interpretation, namely about the Kanam mandible fragment) said at the Ancestors Conference in 1984 in New York, the possibility of mishap to the aeroplane or transit damage to the specimens was considered of little or no account in those days so that the first thing a discoverer ever did was to fly with the specimens to make comparisons with others of the same kind and to discuss the characteristics with colleagues.

If the Pan-African Congresses got people talking to each other, they also helped to make new, or to cement old friendships which, so far as I am concerned, have lasted in some cases for nearly forty years. As a young archaeologist it was a privilege to be able to meet some of the pioneers of African palaeo-anthropology: Maurice Reygasse and Dr E. Gobert from the Maghreb, pioneers of Algerian and Tunisian (Gobert 1950) prehistory respectively; and, of course, Lionel Balout who organized the second Pan-African Congress and shaped the course of Algerian archaeology for some fifteen years (Balout 1955); Robert Broom in his stiff butterfly collar and frock coat, the discoverer of the first adult Australopithecines and of both gracile and robust forms; E.J. Wayland fresh from his excavation in the M–N horizon of the 100-ft terrace of the Kagera at Nsongesi; Alex du

Toit, the great South African geologist, one of the first supporters of Wegener on plate tectonics; and Ralph von Koenigswald who, although he never worked in Africa, attended the Livingstone Congress in the course of studying the South African fossils; Mlle Henriette Alimen, as spritely as any of us in the Mauretanian desert in 1967 and the pioneer geologist working with Pleistocene cultural sequences in north-west Africa, who in 1957 wrote *The Prehistory of Africa* which was the most up to date and widely used overview of what we knew about African Stone Age prehistory at that time; Professor Pericot Garcia from Barcelona who made one feel that life was for living and attended every Pan-African Congress up to the time of his death in 1977 and was instrumental in saving the fifth Congress by arranging for it to be held in the Canary Islands in 1963; Theodore Monod, in his seventies and burned as brown as a Berber, who met us in the middle of the Mauretanian Adrar in 1967 after a camel safari of several hundred kilometres, in the course of which he discovered, in a deflated dune valley, the E1 Bayed Vendredi site with superb Acheulian, Aterian and Neolithic assemblages; Father Anciaux de Faveaux, that most lovable of men with his long snow-white beard (Père Noël), who pioneered prehistoric research in the Katanga (now Kabwe) province of the Belgian Congo (Zaïre); Pierre Biberson who did the definitive work on the archaeology of the Moroccan Atlantic coastal sequence, and his colleagues Lecointre and Marçais; the Abbé Roche, the excavator of Taforalt and Temara Caves that have thrown new light on the antiquity of the Mechta-Afalou population of north-west Africa; A.J. Arkell who, as the first Commissioner for Archaeology in the Anglo-Egyptian Sudan, gave us the Khartoum Mesolithic and Neolithic complexes; the geologists Jean de Heinzelin and Georges Mortelmans who were largely responsible for establishing the Quaternary cultural sequence in Zaïre, and Jean Janmart, chief geologist for the Diamond Company of Angola, who was the first to investigate the deeply buried sequence through the sands of Kalahari-type exposed in the huge open-cast diamond workings in north-eastern Angola; Bernard Fagg, whose investigations on the Jos Plateau in Nigeria gave us, with Geoffrey Bond, the first stratified evidence of Earlier and Middle Stone Age cultures in West Africa and, in particular, the first knowledge of the remarkable terracotta figurines of the Nok culture, the earliest iron-smelting society known so far from the savannas south of the Sahara; Oliver Davies who never missed a conference if he could avoid it and has now, regrettably, disappeared from the scene in tragic circumstances, travelled in his own Land-Rover through the whole of British and French West Africa more extensively than anyone, before or since, and left a record of Stone Age prehistory there that has not received as much recognition as it deserves, perhaps because of the generally informal nature of West African artefacts themselves, more often than not in quartz or some metamorphosed rock; Sonia Cole, who added distinction to any group of archaeologists. Trained as a geologist, she early acquired an interest in archaeology, working with Louis and Mary Leakey in Kenya and Tanzania, with Bill Bishop in Uganda and with me in northern Malawi. She was the author of the first general account of the prehistory of East Africa (Cole 1954) and was an experienced editor of at least two Pan-African Congress Proceedings and more than one or two doctoral dissertations; Charles McBurney, who never attended a Pan-African Congress but whose books *The Stone Age of Northern Africa* (1960) and *The Haua Fteah (Cyrenaica)* (1967) are landmark studies for the prehistory of the northern part of the continent.

All these and many more, including, of course, a number of my still

active contemporaries, have left an indelible record of their discoveries on
the history of archaeology in Africa. I always regret never having been able
to meet Jean Colette (1933a, 1935) who, in 1926, introduced quantitative
analysis to African prehistory through his excavations at Kalina Point (now
Gombe) at Kinshasa but whose histograms and polygraphs are long
forgotten because the realization of the significance of quantitative studies
for archaeology lay still some twenty years or more in the future. I did
know Francis Cabu (Cabu 1952), however, a large, weighty man with a
white, mane-like shock of hair, who introduced the Abbé Breuil and Peter
Van Riet Lowe to the cultural sequence in the Belgian Congo and, in
particular, at Lupemba in the Katanga, showed them the stratigraphically
and typologically distinctive succession of evolving later Pleistocene
industries to which the Abbé gave the names of *Lupemban* and *Tshitolian*
(Breuil 1944).

The 1940s and 1950s were a time when we were all very terminology-
conscious. It was realized that, while there were many terms in use, the
precise nature of the assemblages they purported to describe had often never
been defined or had been described from mixed assemblages of different
ages – the *S'Baïkien* of Algeria was one such, the *Tumbian* of the Congo
basin another. The second calls to mind the chequered record of nomenclature in the Belgian Congo/Zaïre which is still in need of further classification. Another controversial term is *Sangoan*. The characteristic artefacts
were discovered first in 1920 by E.J. Wayland on the hills overlooking
Sango Bay on Lake Victoria. They were crude core-axes and pick-like forms
and subsequently many other such assemblages were found, most often in
secondary context and appearing to be associated more generally with
regions of higher rainfall and more closed vegetation habitats. The Sangoan
is still known only from two or three sealed occurrences e.g. Pomongwe
and Bambata Caves in Zimbabwe and Kalambo Falls in Zambia. Faunal
associations are minimal but it is hoped that the new site of Simbi on the
Winam Gulf, Lake Victoria, which has fauna associated, will help to show
whether the Sangoan is a time-restricted industrial entity or whether it is a
time-transgressive expression of technological adaptation to a more closed
and wooded environment.

Some archaeologists, with whom I was fortunate to be able to meet
although at all too infrequent intervals, were an important influence on
how I looked at the material which I was finding in Northern Rhodesia. I
nearly said '*my* Zambian material' for there was quite a possessive trait
apparent among prehistorians in the southern part of Africa at that time. In
fact it is still a trait among prehistorians today as can be seen when one hears
such expressions as 'my Neanderthals', 'my Acheulian' or, indeed, 'my
site': Among those who contributed most to my thinking I would mention
John Goodwin who gave South Africa and, later, much of the continent
south of the Sahara, the terminology and nomenclature still in general use
today. John was a gentle man and a fine prehistorian who was one of the
first to look at southern African prehistory through the eyes of a
geographer. He was also one of the first to make use of the ethnographic
record, in particular that of the KhoiSan people at the Cape, and he
established a methodology and a problem-orientated approach to attempts
at understanding the meaning of technological variability. His long-time
associate 'Peter' Van Riet Lowe, an engineer turned professional archaeologist, was a very different, more extraverted person with a vivid
personality and tremendous enthusiasm who had the ability to interest the
public in the antiquity of humankind in South Africa and also captured the
ear of General Jan Smuts with the result that the South African Archaeo-

logical Survey was set up in 1935 and was a major influence in the recording, investigation and protection of archaeological sites and antiquities in that country. Apart from the Vaal and the Earlier Stone Age, one of Peter's main interests was the Later Stone Age 'Smithfield' of the Orange Free State where in 1927 he met the last of the Free state 'Bushmen' (Goodwin and Van Riet Lowe 1929: 180–1), who was able to show him how to strike blades from a core, and trim them into end- and side-scrapers and spoke of how they were used. Alas, the time had not yet come when archaeologists recorded in minute detail manufacturing techniques of modern stone-workers. Another of Peter's interests was the rock art – the superb paintings and engravings that are the unsurpassed record of a vanished people. His was a strong personality and when he and Louis Leakey, an equally strong and even more influential individual, were together the sparks began to fly, perhaps aggravated by Peter's work with E.J. Wayland on the Kagera River – in Uganda but adjacent to Kenya – that resulted in the *Prehistory of Uganda* volume (Van Riet Lowe 1952a).

The Abbé Breuil was the unchallenged doyen of world, let alone African archaeology and he was a major influence on South African and Maghrebian prehistory. I knew him relatively well and learned much from him about typologies, *fossiles directeurs* and rock-painting traditions and techniques. The Acheulian was thought of then as a kind of slowly evolving techno-complex the intricacies of which had been established in the Abbé's interpretation of the very complex geomorphological sequence in the Somme Valley in northern France. Accordingly, it was expected by some that the eight or more stages of the Acheulian identified there would also be found elsewhere in the world. They were looked for on the Vaal and I well remember the Abbé's telling me that, with his eyes closed and by merely *feeling* the bifaces from the Zambezi that I showed him, he could tell me which stage of Acheulian they represented. On another occasion, at the Algiers Congress in 1952, when the Abbé, who had been President of the 1947 Congress, was proposed for a second term, I put forward the suggestion that it was customary, was it not, at international congresses, to elect a new President at each Congress? The Abbé turned on me and said, 'Well, *who* would you suggest?' I retired defeated but we remained good friends. In those days, when pronouncements were made by an expert, they were all too often *ex cathedra* and not to be questioned. The Abbé was probably at his best when he was examining, tracing and speaking about rock art, as can be seen from the magnificent volumes on the French and north Spanish rock art or from those that later reproduce his work on the paintings in the Brandberg and Erongo Mountains in Namibia.

One of the most skilled and careful excavators of the late 1920s and 1930s was Gertrude Caton Thompson and her work in the Fayum (1934) with Eleanor Gardner and later in Kharga Oasis (1952) are examples of the finest studies of open localities to have been carried out at that time anywhere in the world. These are thorough, problem-orientated studies that set out the evidence and discuss alternative interpretations. They will remain sources of basic data that are essential evidence for all future research in these places. Kharga Oasis is a model that I long held up to myself as one to aspire to. It is true that it lacked much of the quantitative data that began to be universally adopted by the mid 1950s but it is, at the same time, free of the clutter of irrelevant measurements and other facts that are not infrequently to be found in assemblage analyses, then as well as later, where knowledge of technological processes of stone-working is lacking and evidences of use-wear become available only later from controlled experimentation.

Louis and Mary Leakey were as great an influence on my own research in

Zambia and elsewhere as anyone I have known. A combination of Louis's enthusiasm, knowledge that what he had found was much better and more interesting than anything anyone else had discovered, and his uncanny way – bred, I suspect, of persistence in the search – of finding the significant sites – 'Leakey's Luck', as he called it – together with the methodical care and meticulous excavation techniques that Mary introduced to exploration of the earlier Pleistocene activity areas, provided me with the stimulus and challenge to investigate further the savanna woodlands of south-central Africa. Mary's excavation in the 1940s at Olorgesailie of Acheulian occurrences in fine-grained sediments where minimal disturbance prior to burial had preserved distribution patterns on land surfaces that could be used to understand associations between artefacts and fauna and thus provide clues to at least one of the activities that took place there, was pioneer research that laid the basis for what is now the usual way such single-context sites are excavated. Such techniques certainly paid dividends at Kalambo Falls which we discovered in 1953 and which was one of the very few sites where plant remains, including much wood, are preserved in waterlogged deposits in association with a series of finely made and evolved Acheulian bifaces and other artefacts on occupation horizons between 100,000 and 200,000 years old (figs. 11:2 and 3). The botanical record preserved here shows the antiquity of the *Brachystegia-Julbernardia* woodland in this part of south-central Africa (Clark 1969).

Since the days in 1939 of the Mumbwa Caves excavation (Clark 1942), I have, in particular, been interested in trying to understand the ecological relationship of the human group whose cultural remains one was uncovering with their habitat and the plant and animal resources they made use of. At that time it was often impossible to make much headway since present-day faunal distribution and animal species' behaviour were largely unstudied and since the only living hunter/gatherers in Zambia were only contacted in the 1950s (Clark 1951). Long-range extrapolation of Kalahari San behaviour from such general works as Schapera's *Khoisan Peoples* (1930) gave us at best only general indications of seasonal use of selected plant and animal resources and settlement patterning. By the 1950s, pollen analysis and identification of carbonized plant remains and fossil fauna – though the latter was, unfortunately, in general scrappy and lacked the rich assemblages of the East African Rift – were beginning to help in the reconstruction of palaeo-environments in south-central Africa. The deep troughs of Lakes Tanganyika and Malawi do not, however, seem to have attracted settlement round the shores as did the shallow lakes of the East African Rift System and only in the north-east does the Malawi Rift provide evidence for earliest Pleistocene occupation extending back at least 300,000 years and possibly even substantially further. The Chiwondo Formation fauna is also the only important Plio-Pleistocene faunal record in south-central Africa and is significant as a connecting link between the faunas of that time in East and South Africa.

The period between the late 1930s and the 1960s, interrupted by war service in the Horn, was one of regular fieldwork for me in Northern Rhodesia, Nyasaland and Angola and often entailed long walks through the bush when one could get to know one's African companions and learn from them much about the plants and animals that were their constant companions and some of the techniques and devices used to acquire their food. Especially valuable was the knowledge of how wild resources were made use of – a variety of plants, game animals, insects, honey – so that when linked to the botanical evidence from excavated sites, like that from Kalambo Falls, it was possible to develop a model (Clark 1980b) for hunter-

11:2 *Members of the excavation 'team', Kalambo Falls 1963* Standing right to left: *Charles Keller, Sue Butlin, Desmond Clark;* sitting: *Maxine Kleindienst, Barbara Anthony, Betty Clark;* reclining: *John W.D. Clark*

11:3 *Excavations on Acheulian occupation surface (B2/59/5) at Kalambo Falls. Note wood and other plant material preserved by waterlogging*

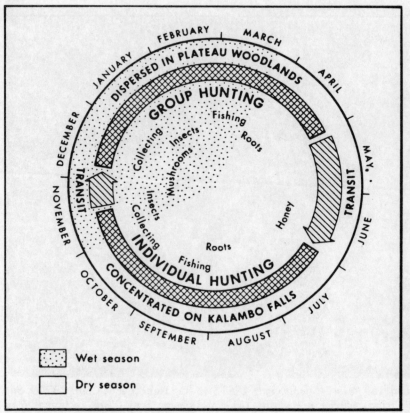

11:4 *A model for prehistoric hunter-gatherer subsistence and seasonal movement at the Kalambo Falls, Zambia (from Clark 1980b)*

gatherers' use of the resources in the Kalambo Basin and adjacent parts of the plateau at different seasons of the year (fig. 11:4).

Then, as now, we were to a great extent restricted in our concepts of how to interpret archaeological and palaeontological evidence. The moulding of the ways in which we view this evidence, which we acquired in our formative years at the university and later, has been a restraining influence. 'There is no horizon too high or too distant that one cannot get beyond it,' is true enough but, with the limited visibility we had then, we were all too prone to see what we had been taught and expected to see. The classic example of all time is, of course, that of Piltdown – accepted because that is what anthropologists expected to find. Dart's Taung child was rejected because it possessed features quite contrary to popular conceptions of the time; besides, it came from Africa, the last place in which early twentieth-century scientists would expect to find an early ancestor of humanity. Similarly, any human fossil found – Broken Hill (Kabwe), for example – was seen as an extinct off-shoot from the direct hominid line. The new technological and typological manifestations attendant upon the change from Earlier, to Middle, to Later Stone Ages, were seen as evidence for the appearance of new waves of immigrant peoples who replaced the older stock because they were possessed of superior intelligence and equipment. There were few who saw the possibility that such changes might be the outcome, in the case of contemporary or successive industries, of different adaptive processes in different ecological situations, or, again, of the transmission of improved technological and strategic practices by stimulus diffusion that need have little or nothing to do with ethnic replacements. Again the belief, bolstered by descriptions of Khoi-San sub-fossil

11:5 *Desmond Clark on eroded Aterian site, Adrar Bous 1970*

and fossil remains in Stone Age contexts in eastern Africa far to the north of their known historic distribution, together with the supposed late arrival of Iron Age cultures into southern Africa, were taken to confirm also the late arrival of the negroid peoples who brought food-producing culture to these parts. Yet another example of preconceptions producing skewed interpretations was the belief that appeared to be confirmed by a few radiocarbon dates, that the Middle Stone Age in Africa was contemporary, not with the Middle Palaeolithic of Europe and Asia, but with the Upper Palaeolithic there. Since also it was the custom to think of modern humans and the Upper Palaeolithic as indivisible, the implication was that Africa was a backwater where Middle Palaeolithic flake technology persisted as did the Archaic *Homo sapiens* populations that made it. This chimaera, of course, was finally dispelled as a result of a flood of new radiocarbon dates in reliable contexts and the evidence coming from the coastal caves in South Africa (Vogel and Beaumont 1972).

It took the recovery of primary cultural assemblages of Oldowan and Acheulian bifaces from excavated 'living-floors' at such sites as Olduvai Gorge, for a general recognition that there was a substantial component of 'small tools' in an Oldowan or Acheulian occurrence. At Ternifine in Algeria, it had been thought that these small implements were of Later Stone Age date and had fallen down through the sediments; in coastal Morocco, the small tool component of the 'Pebble Culture' complex was only found when the piles of smaller gravel ingredients in the quarries were searched. In the Vaal, the core/choppers and small artefacts in the massive calcrete that sealed the 'Older Gravels' of the 100-ft high terrace at Holpan (Van Riet Lowe 1953), were believed to be Later Stone Age and so the whole duracrust was considered to be late. Possibly it is indeed so but, at the time of the later investigation in 1961 (Mason 1967b) no small tools had ever been found with pre-Acheulian assemblages except at Olduvai and these had not been published; the locality is worth re-examination, therefore.

One thing Africa taught me is to try to keep an open mind when looking for possible explanations for a set of phenomena. There must always remain some kind of bias but time spent in Africa in the bush with local companions learning about plant and animal behaviour does provide one with a broader understanding of the innumerable choices open for adoption and the many ingenious ways the human population chose to exploit and exist on its resources.

In the 1960s, we were still much concerned with technology, typology and terminology. This last, of course, is based on definition but, in African archaeology in general, definitions left much to be desired. Most artefact entities had never been properly defined and, in consequence, terms in common use were often applied loosely or even incorrectly. In an attempt to draw attention to this and so to the need to introduce a greater degree of order into the way in which prehistorians defined and grouped their material remains and employed the hierarchy of terms in common usage, a three-week symposium of geologists, palaeontologists and archaeologists met in 1965 under the auspices of the Wenner-Gren Foundation to review the more precise knowledge of palaeoenvironments, plant and animal species and stratified cultural entities that had resulted from the increased activity of the previous ten years. This relatively thorough review resulted in a general stock-taking for the archaeologists and the volume *Background to Evolution in Africa* (Bishop and Clark 1967). In the discussion on analytical procedures and terminology in regard to the study of Stone Age industries, the symposium participants made a number of recommendations designed to produce greater precision but, at the same time, to retain an element of fluidity in matters of definition and terminology in African prehistory. These definitions are those in general use today though we are now less concerned with terminology than with the socio-economic implications of our excavated occurrences. This volume does emphasize the behavioural and adaptive aspects of palaeo-anthropological research and that in order to 'be effective these studies require the active participation of anthropologists and natural scientists in a diversity of disciplines in order to promote temporal frameworks and an appreciation of situation, association and context' (Howell 1967: 919).

By the 1960s there had taken place a fundamental change in excavation methods and in the ways in which we looked at our material and tried to understand its behavioural implications. The methods of recovery of assemblage distribution patterns and features by 'horizontal excavation' of minimally disturbed hominid activity areas, was now the normal way to set about investigation of earlier hominid activity areas in the open. The distribution pattern of stones and bones has a story to tell but the problem now is to interpret it correctly. The naive conclusion that concentrations of stone implements and bones were the result of hominid activity soon gave rise to a range of actualistic and experimental studies that were based upon the premise of uniformitarianism. These are experiments to show how

11:6 *Glynn Isaac at Ngodingodi camp, Ituri Forest, September 1985*

fluvial activity can concentrate and disperse materials in a stream; in the ways in which bones become incorporated, broken and dispersed and in ways of distinguishing between the different agents – geological, animal or human – that were responsible: the new science of taphonomy as it is called. There also followed experiments in the manufacture of stone artefacts using different kinds of rocks; in the study of the reduction process giving a more realistic understanding of intention behind the debitage and end-products; experiments in using these artefacts and, by study of the modification present on the edges of utilised pieces, of the manner of use and the material they were used on. These and other such studies are providing the controls that enable the prehistorian to narrow down possible interpretations.

New methods of survey and excavation and a greater reliance on collaboration with other scientists in team studies which, from the 1960s onwards, became the invariable way of conducting studies of Plio-Pleistocene hominid localities, resulted in a greatly increased amount of information concerning the palaeo-climate and environment and the geography of the palaeo-terrain favoured by the hominids. The extraction of increasingly precise and extended information from such sites is one part of trying to identify early hominid patterns of behaviour. Another lies in the use of present-day analogy, in particular that of great ape behaviour, especially the chimpanzee (Goodall 1986; Fossey 1983). As knowledge of chimpanzee social organization, aggression, feeding habits and tool-use expand, so we can see that in the chimpanzee there is preserved a living record of immediately pre-human behaviour that we can now see is likely to have been closer to that of the first tool-making hominids than is this to the behaviour of present-day surviving hunter-gatherers. The ethno-archaeological studies of the latter (Lee and DeVore 1968) – of their existing and abandoned camps, their foraging tactics, social groupings and use of resources – are also another invaluable source of comparative data when used cautiously and with a view to trying to identify common patterns of process (Yellen 1977).

The 1960s and the years that followed saw an increasing number of African nationals becoming professional archaeologists, trained mostly at universities overseas – in Europe, the United States or India. There are, however, still far too few trained people working in universities, musuems or antiquities services in the Black African countries. Some are lucky in having colleagues close at hand with whom they can interact but mostly they are on their own and are in as much need of regular dialogue and opportunities to visit with others as we were during colonial times. This is, I believe, still a major problem and it needs to be overcome because of the stimulus that regular interaction can give to the serious scholar.

In the advocacy of these new approaches and methods one man stands out above all others, namely Glynn Llewelyn Isaac (fig. 11:6) whose untimely death in 1985 took from palaeo-anthropology an original thinker and leader who was unsurpassed in his ability to bring together scholars from a host of different disciplines and sciences to help unravel the record of human behavioural evolution – a record that is today more relevant and important for us to understand than ever before. Glynn advocated an holistic approach and the need to try and identify territorial ranges of early hominid groups and to look not only at the concentrations that have been the invariable focus of investigation but at the 'scatters between the patches' as he called them, for, when patches and scatters are regarded as a single entity, they could provide the clue to understanding how, when and why hominids used and moved across the landscape (Isaac 1980). Whereas it used to be the custom, and often still is, to propound and defend against all comers an explanation of a set of cultural phenomena, Glynn taught us to look for alternative models, or explanations, the basis for which is to be found in the observation of present-day processes, animals and environments. As knowledge and understanding develop so the alternatives can be narrowed down. Today, therefore, this is the way that behavioural reconstructions are approached.

Glynn opened up a dialogue with the world of science and if future archaeology is to develop as it should, it must continue to expand its association with natural scientists and others interested in common problems of human life-ways in the past. In this, as in everything else, I am an optimist and believe that there is every indication that there is a growing body of informed archaeologists and others working in Africa today so that, in another twenty years, the horizons will be even more expanded and we will, with greater certainty, be able to trace the record of human origins and cultural evolution in that continent that not only gave us humanity but, if present indications are confirmed, Modern Man also.

12 *A Personal Memoir*

THURSTAN SHAW

I do not often write in the first person, but I suppose a personal memoir has to be so written. As one of the things I have been asked to write about is 'the influences that have guided your work', I ought to begin with my formative archaeological influences before I went to Africa.

Archaeological influences

I grew up in the middle of Devon, and went to Blundell's School, Tiverton. There, at the age of fifteen I was recommended by my history teacher to read Breasted's *Ancient Times* one school holidays. I can still remember the thrill which reading that book gave me; it opened up a hitherto undreamed-of world. I longed to take part in an archaeological excavation, but saw no prospect of such good fortune coming my way. Then, a year or so later, I heard about the excavations that had been conducted by Dorothy Liddell on behalf of the newly formed Devon Archaeological Exploration Society at Hembury Fort, which was only fifteen miles from my home. Volunteers from the Society were welcome on the excavation. I joined the Society, and took part in the 1932 Hembury Fort excavations, and in subsequent seasons there also. That was my initiation into excavation, and I could not have had better teachers: Dorothy Liddell herself was very good to me, but perhaps I learnt more real 'dirt archaeology', including how to use a trowel, from the digging foreman, W.E.V Young – who became a lifelong friend. Along with Dorothy Liddell he had come from the 'Keiller team', who had been excavating Windmill Hill and were beginning the investigation of Avebury itself, with the young Stuart Piggott also recruited to this outfit. Will Young was to the Keiller team what Wedlake was to the Wheeler firm, but is less well known because he did not have a Wheeler to promote and publicize his merits, although there is a fine tribute to him at the very beginning of her 'Acknowledgments' in Isobel Smith's Avebury book (Smith 1965). Thus I became associated with 'the Keiller school' of British archaeology of the day, in rivalry with 'the Wheeler school' – a rivalry amusingly illustrated by one of Stuart Piggott's cartoons recently reproduced in an *Antiquity* editorial (vol. LX 1986: 3). On one occasion a party of us from Hembury went over to Maiden Castle to see the flamboyant Wheeler's excavations there and indulged in criticisms of his methods! How could you possibly correctly interpret the section in a trench only 2 ft wide? Later in my career. I came to appreciate Wheeler's contribution better, and adopted some of his methods, although I found him one of the two vainest men I have met in my life. It was an exciting period in British prehistory: the Neolithic was 'opening up', and there was a general feeling of discovery.

Following my reading of Breasted's *Ancient Times* I thought that archaeology could only be pursued through excavation. I was disabused of this mistaken idea by a fortunate accident. I lived near Exeter, and had heard tell that there were 'underground passages' under the city. This fired my imagination and I wanted to know more, so I enquired at the Information Bureau. 'Yes,' they said, 'there are indeed underground passages. There's an article about them in that magazine on the rack over there, called *The Proceedings of the Devon Archaeological Exploration Society*. You can take it if you like.' This was Volume I of those *Proceedings*, and the article on the 'underground passages' explained that they were a medieval water conduit system – through which I subsequently crawled. However, more important for me was an article on 'Surface hunting' (Moysey 1930). This demonstrated how, simply by walking over the surface of ploughed fields and scanning the ground with a sharp eye, it was possible to find Neolithic flint implements – and sometimes, other ancient things as well. At the first opportunity I was out searching the ploughed field nearest to my home – and found two pieces of flint. These had to be imports, because the nearest natural flint was twenty-five miles away. This was a tremendous advantage in 'learning flints', because every piece picked up was a prehistoric artefact – apart, that is, from a couple of gun-flints I found. When I later transferred my hunting onto chalkland and other areas where flint occurs naturally, I had none of the difficulty in distinguishing artefacts from natural flints which those who learn in such areas sometimes have. In these days of systematic 'field-walking', such surface-collecting would be regarded as not only crude and primitive, but as also damaging the available evidence. However, it is always easy to be critical by means of hindsight, and at least I did keep everything I collected, and not just the implements and *belles pièces*, and, after washing each specimen, marked it with a number which was entered in a notebook recording the field it came from.

Two other people working at Hembury were Aileen Henderson (later to become Lady Fox) and Mary Nicol (later to become Mrs Louis Leakey) and the latter has testified to the excellence of the training we received under Miss Liddell and Will Young. Mary was beginning her association with Louis at this time, and it was through her that I met him. One day he brought a great block of flint to Hembury and gave a demonstration of flint-knapping, which was the beginning of my own efforts in that direction. It was not meeting Louis Leakey that determined my going to Africa, it merely helped to confirm an already-growing desire to work in that continent. This was largely the result of my father's interest in the Church Missionary Society and the experience of meeting and talking to a succession of African clergymen who used to come and stay in my home.

Because at school I had obtained Credits in Latin and Greek in the old 'School Certificate' examination, I was automatically drafted into the Classical Sixth – and made to drop mathematics, in which I had obtained higher marks than in the classical subjects. I have regretted this all my life, as also the decline in my competence in French. Instead I spent the next three years, very badly taught as I realize now, poring over classical texts and wasting time doing the juggling tricks known as composing Latin and Greek verses. I found some pleasure in Homer, and some intellectual excitement in the philosophy of Plato – although this was taught as a linguistic study and with no reference to later philosophical ideas. An even greater dreariness prevailed over my first two years at Cambridge taking Part I of the Classical Tripos. (In those days there was no Part I Archaeology and Anthropology Tripos.) During all this time my delight was to escape from my official studies into archaeology. At Cambridge I used sometimes to go with Charles Leaf in his fast car out into the fens to help him dig some site. In the vacations I spent all the time I could on activities with the

Devon Archaeological Exploration Society and on field-walking in my home and neighbouring parishes. Here I was lucky, as it was an area of Neolithic/Early Bronze Age occupation and some fields were very prolific. I added quite a few Bronze Age barrows to the Ordanance Survey map. Some forty years later, one of these barrows was excavated and Lady Fox kindly sent me a copy of the excavation report (Pollard and Russell 1969). In it the remark was made that in order to solve some of the problems raised it was necessary to discover the settlement site. On reading this, I immediately felt I knew, from the flint scatters I had found and recorded, where the settlement site was. During one of my leaves from West Africa I arranged to meet Lady Fox on site and showed it to her.

When it came to choosing what I should read for Part II of the Tripos, I had no doubt as to what I wanted that to be. Changing to Archaeology and Anthropology (specializing in Archaeology) was like stepping out of a rudderless canoe on a sluggish stream of treacle under an overcast sky into a pulsating disco with psychedelic lights flashing and thrills every other moment. Dear old Sir Ellis Minns was the Disney Professor, and I found his lectures dull and boring, as also Chadwick's, but the real prehistoric stuff, from Miles Burkitt, Toty de Navarro and Grahame Clark, was exciting, deeply satisfying, and well taught. There were five of us doing the Archaeology option: Betty Raven, daughter of the Master of Christ's, Charles McBurney, Terence Powell and Rainbird Clarke; Glyn Daniel was a year ahead of us, working on his PhD, and already prowling around like some grey eminence. Charles Phillips was in Selwyn, although he did not do much teaching, but sometimes took one or two of us along with his buddy Grahame Clark to visit a site in the fens. On one such occasion I remember listening fascinated to the two of them plotting the removal of Miles Burkitt!

At the end of that wonderful last year at Cambridge, in fulfilment of my desire to work in Africa, I was appointed to the staff of Achimota College in the Gold Coast. In those days there were no universities between North and South Africa, and Achimota College was the nearest thing to one in Black Africa; external London degrees were taken. Before taking up my appointment there, I was sent for a postgraduate year to the London University Institute of Education, to take a Teacher's Diploma and the Colonial Education Course at the time. I sometimes used to sneak away to Malinowski's seminars at nearby LSE!

Early days in Africa

I sailed from Liverpool on the Elder Dempster boat MV *Accra* on 1 September 1937, with everything on board arranged in full colonial style: only whites in the First Class, dressing for dinner every night and no air-conditioning! Takoradi was the only harbour in the Gold Coast in those days, recently built, but as there was then no coast road through to Accra, we landed there by surf-boat and 'mammy-chair'. The latter was a box which could seat four persons, who were slung up from the deck by the ship's derrick, swung out over the side and lowered onto a surf-boat below, rising and falling some ten feet on the swell; not many people got tipped in the sea. The surf-boat then took one the mile to the beach, riding the last hundred yards on a wave as on a giant surf-board.

At Achimota College, in addition to my teaching duties, I was in charge of the Anthropology Museum. This gave me a little time, and a little (very little) money to embark on an investigation of the archaeology of the country. I began keeping a systematic sites and finds register, which I handed over to Richard Nunoo when I left the country. From the Gold Coast Survey Department I obtained some specially printed maps of the country, with topographical and other details all printed in grey, for recording the locations of these sites and finds. I travelled as widely as I could during the vacations, but such travel was not a simple matter in those days. Many roads were dry-season only, there was only one major road-bridge in the country: other river-crossings had to be made by ferries or dry-season brushwood bridges; there were only 18 miles of tarred road; no hotels and no petrol pumps. There were government 'rest houses', usually consisting of a roof and walls only with no furniture, and a caretaker who supplied water and firewood. Everything else you had to take with you; vehicles were not as reliable then as now, so with overloading and appalling roads, breakdowns were to be expected. Petrol you also had to take with you, contained in wooden boxes each holding two 4-gallon tins, with enough to last from one Public Works Department store to the next. There was no road between Accra and Kumasi, instead you had to spend a whole day in the train. All these conditions were made much worse during the war, particularly by petrol rationing. Although I did spend Christmas 1937 in Gambaga, a post-war professor at the University of Ghana once idiotically asked me why I hadn't done more work in Northern Ghana, showing he had no inkling of what conditions had been like during those years.

Archaeological aims: Stage 1

I suppose at the beginning I had two principal aims, which in fact fed into each other. The first was to gather, as systematically as possible, all the archaeological evidence already obtainable which I could lay my hands on. The second was to create, and increase as widely as possible, an awareness of the 'archaeological dimension'. These two aims contributed to each other inasmuch as the more archaeological evidence there was to present and disseminate, the greater was likely to be the archaeological awareness: and the greater the archaeological awareness among people throughout the country, the more information about finds and sites was likely to come in.

Although the Gold Coast at the time was an almost virgin territory archaeologically and no trained archaeologist had worked there, nevertheless there was a certain amount of data to start from. Before leaving England I had discovered that the Gold Coast Geological Survey had a London headquarters in Cornwall Gardens, and that they had a large collection of stone implements which their field officers had collected and deposited there. Accordingly I paid this collection a number of visits, and made notes and drawings of its contents; this was where I first made the acquaintance of the hatched sandstone rubbers which Oliver Davies (1962) later christened, with resulting confusion, 'terracotta cigars', and which came to be recognized as a characteristic artefact of the 'Kintampo culture'. Altogether, the Geological Survey were very useful in the initial stages, and the Director was helpful – although he took umbrage when I had remarked (in print) that not much archaeological work had been done so far in the Gold Coast; he took this as an adverse reflection on his department. I paid another visit, to the Gold Coast headquaters of the Geological Survey, at Ankobra Juction (which could only be reached by rail), and studied the collection of stone implements they had there. The Geological Survey had also recorded a number of earthwork entrenchments in the Central

Province and dug into them; the finds had been presented to the British Museum, and Braunholtz had written a note about them in *Antiquity* (Braunholtz 1936). He had kindly shown me this material in the British Museum. There was also a Mines Inspector, Capt. R.P. Wild, who had in the course of his work collected stone implements, pottery and other artefacts from the hills around Obuasi, the Akwatia diamond diggings and other mining areas. He had written quite a lot about these finds in the *Gold Coast Review* and the *Gold Coast Teachers' Journal*, which had quite excellently begun the process of my second aim, to make such things widely known and recognized. He retired three months after I arrived in the country, but before he left I managed to make a special journey to visit him and pick his brains.

The dissemination of 'archaeological awareness' was pursued by the displays in the museum, by talks and lectures to schools, clubs and societies, groups of teachers and teachers' colleges, and by articles in the press and local magazines; and when Radio Accra came into being, by broadcast talks. The museum was the only one of its kind in the country, it was open to the public as well as to students, and everyone who visited the college paid a visit to the museum, so I think it had quite an influence. People were encouraged to report sites and finds to the museum, and to donate specimens to it, where they would be proudly displayed with the name of the donor. I think this policy of pursuing archaeological awareness, helped as it was later by the results of excavations, did in the end serve to create the necessary interest which resulted in 1957 in the foundation of the National Museum in Accra and the Department of Archaeology at Legon (Calvocoressi and York 1971: 87), the first in a Black African university. In the 1930s and 1940s it was not a matter of urging the importance of archaeology in what it could contribute to a sense of identity in an emerging nation, and the way it assists in giving a people a sense of its roots – all that came later. Rather, it was simply a matter of demonstrating that the archaeology was *there*, and that it was a form of study which could throw light on the unwritten past. Once these things had been appreciated, the importance of archaeology in the process of nation-building became much more readily self-evident.

Archaeological aims: stage 2

The collection of as much archaeological data as possible was, of course, not an end in itself; it was merely a step towards understanding as much as possible about the past of the country. The next step towards the latter goal was to try to establish a cultural sequence and a chronological framework for the prehistoric past. There are methods nowadays by which, given the resources, such an aim can be achieved for a new area relatively quickly. But I realized that with the very limited resources at my disposal, working in virtually virgin archaeological territory, with the logistical difficulties the circumstances imposed, in days before radiocarbon dating was even dreamed of – such an aim had to be regarded as a very long-term one, and one which presented formidable obstacles. Where to begin?

The dating problem was crucial, and gave me much anxious thought, of a kind that would seem absurd and unnecessary nowadays. My knowledge of European archaeology had taught me that most of the dating there depended on 'cross-cultural' imports: cultures were dated by the presence of objects imported from the civilizations of the Middle East which had their own dating from literary or inscriptional sources. That is putting it

crudely, but that was the basis of the system; and on it was erected a whole
house of cards, which was ultimately blown down by the winds of
radiocarbon dating. Nevertheless, at the time it was the best that could be
done. How could this be applied to West Africa? It might work for the last
five hundred years, by means of recognizable and dateable European
imports after the arrival of Europeans on the West African coast; but what
of times earlier than that, which I personally was more interested in than in
the last few centuries? In north-west Europe the system of cross-cultural
dating had worked, after a fashion, even if it was too far away from the
Middle East to have many direct imports, because of connections with
intervening areas; it worked on a sort of domino-chain principle. But in
Africa virtually nothing was known of the archaeology of the areas
between the West African countries and, say, Egypt. So one felt one was
completely groping about in the dark for dates. In fact, the received
wisdom of the day among anthropologists was to derive anything of skill,
culture or interest in sub-Saharan Africa from Egypt, by a process of
diffusion (Seligman 1930; Shaw 1963b: 23 and refs.; Shaw 1984: 7–8 and
refs) – but there were no reliable dates attached to these suppositions.
Frobenius had indeed attached dates to his supposed Greek colonization of
Ife, but this was pure speculation based on the 'naturalism' of the Ife
sculptural style (Frobenius 1913 vol. 1: 349 ff.).

For the period in Europe too remote for cross-cultural dating to work,
time-scales had been worked out in terms of glacial, interglacial and
postglacial events. But in Africa there had been no ice ages! Leakey had
been adducing evidence for 'pluvial' periods in East Africa, saying they
corresponded to the glacials of northern Europe; others said there were two
pluvials for each glacial – but nobody really knew, it was a theoretical
construction. So where, in West Africa, did we go from there – 'there'
being a sort of limbo without chronology? Another shortcoming of such
archaeological knowledge as we had at that time was that, apart from
the objects dug out of the Central Province earthwork entrenchments by
the Geological Survey, all our specimens had either been collected from the
surface, pulled casually out of roadside cuttings or handed in from mine-
workings without any exact provenance recorded. For example, ground-
stone axes (*nyame akuma*) were plentiful, but I wanted to know what was
the rest of the lithic and non-lithic material culture of their makers.

It seemed to me that excavation alone could provide the associations I
was looking for, and that by revealing some stratification it would at least
give some relative dating for that particular area. The search, then, was for
sites which might have a reasonable depth of stratigraphy and which might
therefore yield some associations not known before, as well as a succession
of artefacts. Where could I find a site on which to make this beginning?
Such open sites as I had seen nearly always appeared to have very little depth
of deposit. What about caves and rock shelters? In theory they should be
promising for my purpose, so I set about finding some.

Excavations

In fact, the first excavation I carried out, in the first twelve months I was in
the Gold Coast, was not in an attempt to solve any of these problems, but
was in the nature of a rescue excavation. I discovered an area on the
Achimota College farm with a scatter of iron slag and pieces of furnace wall
and tuyères. Farming activity was eroding the slope, so I decided to excavate while there was still a chance of recovering something undisturbed. In

this I was lucky, and was able to uncover the base of a furnace, with a large plug of slag in the bottom, so that the form of the furnace was clear. However, there were no other associated finds, there was no radiocarbon or TL dating in those days, so it remained undated.

The rock shelters I found were at the back of the Kwahu scarp, in Voltaian sandstone, and I selected one for excavation that looked as if it might have some depth of deposit. In this I was not disappointed, as there was nearly 2 metres of it at the deepest point. The upper layer, averaging about 45 cm thick, contained abundant pottery, a couple of stone rubbers, two fragments of iron-smelting tuyères and a small piece of iron slag. Everything below this was a fairly homogenous deposit containing a much smaller quantity of pottery, of poorer quality and quite a different type, stone rubbers, ground-stone axes, hammerstones, small biconically pierced quartz stones, and an abundant microlithic industry almost entirely in milky or translucent quartz – very different from the nice Beer flint I was accustomed to in Devon (Shaw 1944). So here at last (in 1940, not 1943 as misprinted in Shaw 1944: 1) was one set of associations established: the lithic industry that went with the ground-stone axes was microlithic in character, and we had the pottery that went with both. In Europe I had been accustomed to thinking of microliths as Mesolithic, but clearly here in West Africa was a very different type of situation. In the forty-six years since that excavation this association has been demonstrated over and over again in West Africa, until it has become a commonplace (although in addition an earlier aceramic phase has been established), but at the time it seemed startling. The excavation also showed that the small biconically perforated pebbles, which were already well known in south-eastern Ghana from chance and surface finds, belonged to the same material culture kit and were of 'Stone Age' date, and not later, as I had until then suspected. It had also been established that an 'Iron Age' deposit overlay a 'Stone Age' one, although it was not clear whether this was a direct succession without a break, or whether there had been an interval of time between the two occupations.

The excavation was not much more than a trial trench, dug in 1 ft level spits from the back of the shelter to the front and down the talus. I had returned on a later occasion and started to dig another trench beside the first in stratigraphical layers, but wartime exigencies caused me to be recalled to the College when I had only just started. In the course of the 1960s and 1970s the 'Kintampo culture' came to be increasingly defined, and dated to the mid-second millennium BC onwards. There was some puzzlement because the Abetifi industry, while having some elements in common with the Kintampo culture, nevertheless did not really seem to fit in. Andrew Smith found the solution when he did some further excavation in the cave in 1974 and discovered from the radiocarbon dates he obtained that the Abetifi industry was some 2000 years older (Smith 1975). F.B. Musonda excavated other rock shelters in the area, some of which I had previously inspected, but the contents of these, while mostly recognizable as of 'Late Stone Age' facies, appeared to be less distinctive than either Abetifi or the Kintampo culture; all the radiocarbon dates were said to be contaminated as they were placed in the present millennium (Musonda 1976).

In the next couple of years the time I was able to give to archaeology was devoted to the museum, to the 'dissemination of archaeological awareness' aim, and to writing up the Abetifi excavation report; this included doing all the drawings, and a fair amount of research in the Cape Town University library into all that I could lay my hands on concerning archaeology in Africa, especially West Africa. This was during a leave spent in Cape Town, where John Goodwin was very good to me and my wife. I had many archaeological discussions with him, and he was very kind in driving us round to various archaeological sites in the Cape. He even flew a kite about the possibility of my joining him on the staff of the Department of Archaeology at Cape Town University. In many ways this was an enormously attractive offer, but even in those days, before the South African colour-bar system had been given its present name, elevated into a theological and political philosophy, and refined into the existing execrable instrument of oppression, I could not square it with my conscience to become part of a system where blacks were officially treated as third-class citizens simply because of their skin-colour. On this leave I also met the Belgian archaeologist Dr François Cabu, who had brought with him a fantastic collection of stone tools from the Congo. On a subsequent South African leave I was able to travel to Johannesburg and meet Van Riet Lowe. In addition I met the Abbé Breuil, and heard and saw him expounding all that he thought he could infer from the patina and state of wear of Acheulian implements from the Vaal River gravels. On that leave I also travelled to what was then Southern Rhodesia and spent a very happy and memorable day among the ruins of Great Zimbabwe. From there I went on to Livingstone to glean all I could from the Rhodes-Livingstone Institute, and to meet Desmond Clark, the first of many happy meetings over the last forty-five years.

In 1942, with the wartime restrictions on travel and the difficulty of going very far afield either to excavate or to do reconnaissance and survey, I was looking for another site not too far away that would be likely to give some depth of stratigraphy and thereby contribute to a cultural sequence and a chronological framework, even if only relative and of local validity, of the sort I was seeking to establish. From reports of the Geological Survey I had taken note of the existence of a number of large mounds in north-eastern Akuapem, not too far from Achimota. The present inhabitants said they did not know the origin of these mounds and that they were there when their ancestors first arrived in the area more than a hundred years before. It was not clear from superficial examination, nor from the work that the Geological Survey had done on a couple of them, whether these mounds were the remains of some structure, were of funerary character, settlement mounds of a tell-like nature, or accumulations of rubbish, in fact middens. In any case, they promised a deep stratigraphy. I put a trench in one of them, in a village called Dawu (fig. 12.1), from top to bottom, all 25 ft of it, and was therefore involved with the problem of shoring – a situation of which I had had no previous experience. However, we managed to accomplish it, and fortunately no one was killed when we took the shoring out; this was the most difficult part, and one worker did have a narrow squeak. Nowadays everyone would be wearing industrial helmets, but in those days they were unheard-of. Anyway, we established that the mound was a midden, and we recovered vast quantities of archaeological material, including half a million potsherds, all of which we kept, and from which we were able to establish a local pottery sequence (Shaw 1961).

The excavation demonstrated for the first time how useful as a dating marker the presence of indigenously made clay smoking pipes could be; for they occurred in the top half of the mound but not in the bottom half. I placed their inception at about AD 1600, but it now seems probable that that was too early by about 50 years. The oral traditions available to me suggested that the accumulation of the midden ceased about AD 1800, suggesting a beginning of the mound around AD 1400. Thus I was led to suppose a slower rate of accumulation than later appeared to be the case,

12:1 *Thurstan Shaw at Dawu, Ghana 1942. Photo taken by a visitor on a Sunday when no digging was taking place*

with the mound beginning in the later part of the sixteenth century and ending towards the end of the eighteenth (Shaw 1962). One of the most interesting group of finds consisted of the broken pieces of clay brass-casting moulds. I have not heard of comparable finds from any other archaeological excavation in West Africa, but they will turn up one day. How wonderful it would be if someone could find the discarded rubbish from the brass-casters' workshops in Igbo-Ukwu, Ife, Benin or other brass-casting centres. It could settle a lot of arguments!

As a result of a conversation with Dr Margaret Read, in which I think I expounded my views on the need for increasing archaeological awareness in Africa, and the need for a pamphlet to do for African archaeology what Godfrey Wilson and Monica Hunter had done for African anthropology in their *The Study of African Society* (1942), she suggested that I should write such a pamphlet. Daryll Forde, Director of the International African Institute, also encouraged me, and published the result of my efforts as a Memorandum of the Institute (Shaw 1946). Some of what I wrote in it is a reminder of the conditions of the time, when I think I am right in saying that there were less than half-a-dozen trained archaeologists in the whole of British colonial Africa (Louis and Mary Leakey in Kenya, Desmond Clark in Northern Rhodesia, Bernard Fagg in Nigeria, and myself in the Gold Coast):

It is important that Government officials, miners, farmers, educated Africans and others should have sufficient knowledge to enable them to observe and record archaeological material on the spot, thus preserving data for others' interpretation as well as their own. . . . Interest in archaeology is spreading ever more widely, but the difference between a vague antiquarianism and the scientific principles by which modern archaeology achieves its results is not always fully appreciated.

Exit from the Gold Coast

In 1944 my wife was invalided home, and had a ghastly six-week wartime voyage with our two infant children, who, contrary to all the received medical wisdom of the time, had been born in West Africa. I followed a year later, and for a few years was too preoccupied with establishing a home and livelihood in England and bringing up five children for much archaeology. As soon as I got back, I went to my old teachers in Cambridge to see what prospect there might be of an archaeological job in the UK, but Grahame Clark was not very helpful. (It was reported to me later that he said of my tentative approach to him: 'Shaw expected us to find him a job.') By now, Miles Burkitt had been disappointed in his ambition to hold the Disney Chair of Archaeology at Cambridge, and devoted a lot of his time and energy to his work on the County Council and being Chairman of its Education Committee. He was anxious to recruit me to its service – in which he was initially successful; later I joined the Cambridge Institute of Education. Nevertheless, the need to publish the Dawu excavation report pressed on my conscience, and in 1953 I managed to return to Ghana to work on the materials. I found them all intact, in spite of attempts to throw away all the plain pottery! Cockroaches had done their best to make a meal of some of the labels, but fortunately no crucial ones. Back home I eventually managed to get the report written, and it was published with assistance from the newly established Department of Archaeology in the University of Ghana. As an experiment, in the publication I showed the stratigraphical distribution of different classes of artefacts and the different classes of pottery against a background of a mini-section of the mound. This was designed to be an immediately comprehensible graphical representation in place of using histograms. Not many reviewers thought the experiment a success!

West Africa again

In 1958 I was invited by Bernard Fagg, Director of the Nigerian Department of Antiquities, to come to Nigeria to excavate the site of Igbo-Ukwu. I did so in 1959–60 and the spectacular results are well known. I always find directing an excavation an anxious business, with so many decisions to take, large and small, and I am daily frightened of taking a wrong decision or failing to notice something with the result that precious, irreplaceable evidence is destroyed. That is so even under the most favourable circumstances, but Igbo-Ukwu was far and away the most nerve-wracking excavation I have undertaken. This was partly because I very soon realized that I was into something unique and important, partly because of the hazards of the physical circumstances under which the excavation was undertaken. For the first reason I was naturally anxious to employ the soundest and most sophisticated excavation techniques possible, while the second so often militated against this. A European officer of the Antiquities Department was supposed to have fixed up all the necessary permissions to dig and come to agreed terms of compensation, arranged quarters for me to stay in, and generally made it possible for me to start excavating straight away. He came for a day-and-half and then left, with nothing settled. I spent the next fortnight of my precious time off from Cambridge bargaining over all these things before reaching final agreement – and then only by the bluff of loading up the lorry and saying I was going to go and excavate elsewhere. Initially I had the assistance of Malam Liman Ciroma, Nigeria's first graduate in archaeology, and no one could wish for a stauncher assistant or a nicer companion; but for a great deal of the time he was called away to other duties, including those connected with supervising Nigeria's first general election. When he was not there, there was no one with real excavation experience and training: two museum technicians acted as finds recorders and interpreters, and a full-time job of it they had. The anxiety to see that no mistakes were being made in the recording and labelling; only one camera, and that sticking; fourteen miles to go at the end of every day's digging to get water; the actual work done by locally recreited labourers who had never before worked on an archaeological excavation, plus two Antiquities Department labourers who had had some experience; interference with the excavation at night in spite of the appointment of a night watchman; attempt in the night after the first bronze was discovered to steal it from under my bed; dysentry most of the time – all these things increased one's anxieties that some mistake might occur. Sometimes one had to make a choice between what was archaeologically desirable and what was physically practicable. One of the hardest things in these circumstances is professional loneliness; you have no one with whom to discuss and share the decisions that have to be taken and the interpretations that have to be made. Anyway, at the end of three months the excavations came to an end, we didn't lose any of the finds, and I do not think any important evidence went unobserved or unrecorded.

While I was excavating at Igbo-Ukwu, the Commission on Higher Education in Nigeria was travelling round the country on the fact-finding part of its mission, preparatory to making recommendations and writing a report. Sir Eric Ashby was the Chairman, and Kenneth Dike, the Professor of History at Ibadan, was a member. The latter had asked me to call on him on my way from Lagos to Igbo-Ukwu, which I did. He told me that when he was a research student in London he had come across my pamphlet on *The Study of Africa's Past*, and that this had been an absolute eye-opener to him, at a time when he was despairing of achieving any great time-depth in uncovering the continent's past by conventional historical methods. When the Commission was in Enugu he visited the excavations at Igbo-Ukwu, and brought Sir Eric Ashby with him. He had tried to get a Department of Archaeology established at Ibadan, but had been unsuccessful. Later, when he was Vice-Chancellor and Institutes of African Studies had become fashionable and money had been made available for them, he wrote into the establishment of the Ibadan Institute of African Studies Research Professorships in Linguistics and Archaeology. I was picked for the latter job, but I understood from the beginning that the research was to be regarded as building up the foundations for a teaching department.

The University of Ibadan

Since I had left Ghana, the founding of the Department of Archaeology in
the University of Ghana at Legon had made possible systematic archaeological fieldwork on a scale that had been impossible for me during the
war. Oliver Davies trekked over the length and breadth of the land,
examining exposures and collecting stone implements. This enabled him to
create a cultural sequence and a relative chronological framework for the
Stone Age. Never mind that I always felt sceptical about his scheme and
that few archaeologists accept it nowadays (Allsworth-Jones forthcoming),
Davies was a pioneer in producing *a* scheme. The building of the
Akosombo Dam, flooding a large area of the country, offered an
opportunity to stake the claims of archaeology in the area before it was too
late. The opportunity was seized, and field archaeologists were appointed
for the purpose (York *et al*. 1967). All this meant real progress.

Things took a rather different turn in Nigeria, and progress was more in
the direction of museums and a government Department of Antiquities.
This was partly because the moving spirits in this development were a
government Education Officer and an art teacher, partly because Nigeria's
wealth of artistic heritage tended to make archaeology art-oriented.
Bernard Fagg, who had excavated the Rop rock shelter during the war,
was later appointed to the department and investigated the Stone Age
occurrences on the Jos Plateau and surrounding area, as well as 'the Nok
culture' whose remarkable terracotta figurines turned up in tin-workings.

In my inaugural lecture at Ibadan, I felt it appropriate to quote the words
of an American anthropologist written three or four years before, to the
effect that the spade of the archaeologist had 'thus far lifted perhaps an
ounce of earth on the Niger for every ton carefully sifted on the Nile'
(Murdock 1959: 73). I commented:

> This fairly sums up the situation for us in Nigeria. We are at the stage
> when we are aware of the archaeological wealth and interest of the
> country, but when comparatively little excavation has been done. We
> have some knowledge of certain cultures and we know about certain
> centres and areas of activity in the past but there are great gaps in our
> knowledge both in time and space so that there are large hiatuses in the
> sequence. (Shaw 1963b: 19)

A dozen years later I wrote:

> This paucity of accumulated research carries certain consequences. It
> means that whereas in those parts of the world with a longer history of
> archaeological research, it is possible to make considerable advances by
> the analysis of material already published or in museums, and on the
> basis of established cultural sequences and chronological frameworks, in
> most parts of Africa these sequences and frameworks are only now being
> established and the top priority remains to go out into the field and
> excavate and obtain the necessary primary data. In Europe there was a
> mass of archaeological material in museums for the twentieth-century
> archaeologists to get to work on. In Africa there is nothing like that. In
> the archaeologically older parts of the world, too, interest has moved on
> from concern with 'What happened', since this is now largely estab-
> lished, to concern with 'How it happened', that is, to the dynamics of
> cultural change; fieldwork tends to be formulated to discover the
> answers to questions posed in these terms. In Africa we now have to
> have both sets of problems in mind in formulating field research

programmes, to try, at the same time, to find out both what happened and how and why it happened. (Shaw 1976: 159)

Fieldwork and research

This is not the place to give a detailed account of the fieldwork and research I carried out during this period. It was logical to do further work at Igbo-Ukwu, and I am convinced that there is still a lot more to be found there, and there remains a need to uncover the sites and remains of activities of the lower strata of the society which gave birth to the spectacular finds. They only represent a stone or two from the top of a social pyramid: this apex will not be properly understood until we have much greater knowledge of the mass of humbler stones supporting it.

One had become much more ecological in one's approach, and I wanted to know more about the way of life of the early occupants of the forest. There were those who declared that the forest environment was never mastered until people had iron tools; I did not believe this, reasoning partly by analogy with New Guinea and the Amazon forest, partly from the finding of so many ground-stone axes in the forest. So I conducted quite an extensive search for a cave or rock shelter in the forest, the excavation of which might give the answers. I eventually found what I was looking for at Iwo Eleru (fig. 12:2) and the resulting excavation did indeed provide a lot of answers – including some unexpected ones!

I became involved in one piece of fieldwork which for me was time-consuming and unrewarding. The building of the Kainji Dam offered an opportunity to do systematic archaeological work in the area to be flooded such as had been done in Ghana under the Volta Basin Research Project – but the opportunity was not taken. This was really the duty of the Government Department of Antiquities, but when the Antiquities Commission realized that the Department was falling down on the job, they asked me to pick up the pieces and do what I could – although they provided no finance for the purpose, so I became involved at short notice in raising funds and other resources and organizing what fieldwork I could arrange. I managed to get a vehicle out of Unesco, and persuaded a University of Colorado team, frustrated in its plans to work in Algeria, to switch their attention to Nigeria. I knew that taking on this commitment was likely to be difficult and unenjoyable, but under the circumstances I could not refuse. There were two reasons why the Department of Antiquities had been almost criminally inactive in the matter. The then director was not an archaeologist but an artist, and his predecessor, who was an archaeologist, had sent one of his field archaeologists to carry out a survey but the report that resulted was a two-edged weapon. On the one hand, its identification of sites was a great time-saver when we came to plan excavations with a minimum of time available; on the other, in the course of that survey, not a single trial trench was sunk and the director, on the basis of surface indications alone, declared that there was nothing of archaeological importance in the Kainji area; no art objects had been found! When I was trying to raise money and resources from official and other bodies, I kept on having these conclusions quoted at me. The whole situation also put me in an invidious and anomalous position *vis-à-vis* the archaeologists of the Antiquities Department whom I persuaded to work in the area.

The American university team had its troubles among its members, and also fell out with another American archaeologist who was a refugee from Biafra and whom I recruited to the Kainji campaign, so that he had to

12:2 *The excavations of Iwo Eleru: Thurstan Shaw encasing in plaster some of the bones of Iwo Eleru Man (at the time the oldest recognizably negroid skeleton yet found)*

transfer to a more distant site! My experience of foreign archaeological teams in Nigeria was that they seemed liable to internal dissension. I paid two visits to Tervuren while on leave to persuade a Belgian team to come to Nigeria to investigate the large urban site of Biepi, said to be the capital of the powerful but rather elusive mediaeval 'Empire of Kwararofa'; Nigeria did not at the time have the resources to tackle a site of this kind. The Belgian team was partly from the Tervuren Museum, partly from the University of Gent. One day I had a telegram at Ibadan saying that they were in trouble, could I please come and sort it out. When I eventually arrived I found that all work was at a standstill and that the two Belgian parties were literally not speaking to each other; although encamped together, they were taking all their meals separately. The trouble was partly a clash of personalities and the arrogance of youth, partly because the museum party were feeling frustrated at not finding art objects to put in their museum show cases. So I had to play the role of peace-maker!

The Department of Archaeology at Ibadan

Although doing research was more pleasurable and less arduous, I knew that I had a priority to get a teaching Department of Archaeology off the ground. This was an arduous and time-consuming process because it meant so many consultations and so much boring committee work. (It always astonished me to find there exists a class of 'committee professors', who seem to *enjoy* it, whereas I was always champing at the bit to get away to do some 'real' work.) The greatest support for the idea of a Department of Archaeology came from the Faculty of Arts, and in particular the Department of History. This was understandable, but it was an embrace which had to be gently resisted; some would have preferred a sub-Department of Archaeology within the History Department. This blandishment had to be fought off, not for reasons of empire-building self-aggrandisement, but because it would have resulted in the wrong sort of archaeology. Many historians do not understand the difference between history and archaeology, that its data and its methods are different, that its questions and answers are different. Especially where historians' raw material runs out a few centuries back, they wish to pirate the results of archaeology to their own purposes; this can be dangerous (Shaw 1981b: 115–18).

I had been anxious that anthropology should be associated with archaeology, but the time was not ripe. For too many at Ibadan at the time, 'anthropology' was still a dirty word, signifying 'the study of primitive people and their quaint customs'. When I talked to the Dean of the Faculty of the Social Sciences about this, about the relationship of anthropology and archaeology, that the latter might be regarded as 'palaeoanthropology', he did not know what I was talking about; he himself was a Scandinavian urban sociologist. So it was clear that the Faculty of the Social Sciences would not be a happy home for the Department of Archaeology. I am delighted that things have so far changed that the department is now the Department of Archaeology and Anthropology. I had found the scientists much the most understanding of what we were trying to do in archaeology and about the way we went to work. So I proposed that the new department should be in the Faculty of Science. This startled a lot of people, but so it came to be. Among other things it meant it was easier to establish a palynology laboratory within the department which I was keen to do.

Retrospect

Looking back from the perspective of half a century, one is tempted to regard the achievements of fifty years ago as small, and even as crude and simplistic. However, if one puts them in the context of the meagre financial resources, the comparatively little amount of time available, and the impossibility of much travelling, they do not appear so exiguous in proportion to those resources. I think that such resources as were available were deployed to good advantage and with a selection of strategic targets. As for being crude and simplistic, it is always easy, in the light of the development of new techniques, to be wise with hindsight. I do not think that what was done fell short of the better archaeological practices of the day. At any rate, I can vouch for the fact that the Abetifi Cave was excavated with a sounder technique than the digging I had observed two or three years previously in Kent's Cavern! Just as one can see in Europe the protracted transition from an interested, amateur antiquarianism to a professional, scientific

archaeology, so I think one can see this change taking place much more abruptly in West Africa, like other changes; and perhaps the significant date for this is around 1935.

Others (Calvocoressi and York 1971) have testified, too, to the fact that the attempt to arouse and intensify archaeological awareness was more successful than it seemed at the time, since it led to the founding of the Department of Archaeology in the University of Ghana – a step pregnant for the birth of more widespread systematic archaeological research and teaching. As far as my own later work is concerned, I consider that the setting up of the Department of Archaeology in the University of Ibadan, together with the founding of the *West African Journal of Archaeology*, were more important than any of my own archaeological discoveries. They represent the ploughing and sowing of a new field, which now, to my great joy, is beginning to produce a rich harvest.

12:3 *Thurstan Shaw being installed as Onuna Ekwulu-Ora of Igbo-Ukwu ('The mouthpiece which speaks on behalf of Igbo-Ukwu')*

13 *A Personal Memoir*

P.L. SHINNIE

My entry to African archaeology was markedly different from that of the two other 'elder statesmen' who contribute memoirs here. They are products of that leading school of archaeology at Cambridge and can be presumed to have had proper training in archaeological techniques and artefact study. I had none of this – my early interests were entirely in Egyptology, beginning in my early teens, and I had anticipated a career which would be largely based on the study of ancient Egyptian texts. I went to Oxford in 1934 with the intention of making myself competent to do this, but soon found that the text-bound study, which is what most British Egyptology was then, seemed too limiting and I began to think that fieldwork would be a more satisfying way of studying the past of Egypt. The rest of Africa was not then of interest to me, nor was much known about it, at least in those parts of Oxford academic life with which I was involved. My course of study – reading of texts in Ancient Egyptian and Coptic – provided no training for a fieldworker and in those days it was generally considered that an ability to read hieroglyphs was adequate training for excavating a site in Egypt. Things have changed for the better now but traces of this attitude are still to be found.

I sensed, without much knowledge, that other training was necessary if I was to become an archaeologist, even of Ancient Egypt, rather than a 'straight line' Egyptologist, and managed to learn something of excavation by joining Mortimer Wheeler's work at Maiden Castle in the years 1934 to 1938. No formal instruction was ever given but by watching and listening and the occasional informal demonstration I, and many others, learned, and Maiden Castle became a training ground for a whole generation of British archaeologists. Work at weekends during term with the Oxford University Archaeological Society was also useful and several senior members of the university gave up time to help and instruct undergraduates. During this time I also managed to fit in attendance at lectures on Comparative Ethnography given in the Pitt-Rivers Museum and a series on map-making and surveying given by a distinguished former member of the Survey of India who was reputed in his time in India to have re-mapped the sub-continent and moved it, cartographically, several miles further west.

My intention was still to work in Egyptology but with a somewhat wider view of the nature of the subject than was held by my teacher, Battiscombe Gunn, one of the great Egyptologists of the time. Gunn would almost certainly have said that for his study of Ancient Egypt, texts and tomb paintings would provide the most important evidence. He did not consider the study of artefacts very necessary and though he sent me to the Ashmolean Museum to copy inscriptions on funerary stelae he never suggested that I look at the rich collection of other Egyptian objects exhibited there.

There were excavators in Egypt with other ideas and I had the good fortune to meet and be influenced by two men, who without formal

221

qualifications in Egyptology were doing interesting and important field work. These were John Pendlebury and Oliver Myers and had the war not come, in which John Pendlebury died in Crete, I would probably have gone to join him in excavations at Tell el Amarna. The influence of both these two strengthened me in my resolve to try and become a fieldworker.

This early training in Egyptology and a short pre-war period as an Assistant Keeper looking after the Egyptian and Near Eastern collections of the Ashmolean Museum at Oxford have had an influence on my attitudes towards African archaeology and have biased me very strongly in favour of periods where there is some evidence, either from written or oral sources, for historical events. All my work, whether in the Nile Valley or in sub-Saharan African, has dealt with these later periods and I have come increasingly to consider myself almost as much a historian as an archaeologist. Prehistory, except for the period of the beginning of agriculture, particularly in the Nile Valley, has been of much less interest and I lack any expertise in the study of stone implements on which so much prehistory depends and in which many of my colleagues have developed great skill. I find the use of the word prehistory as a synonym for archaeology uncomfortable and I in no way consider myself a prehistorian, though I often work on problems where historical sources are scanty and the techniques for learning about the past are virtually the same as those of the prehistorians.

This humanistic background has also strongly influenced my approach to many archaeological problems and my general attitude to the discipline and has prejudiced me in favour of an area approach (specialization by area) where knowledge of the territory, the modern people and their customs and language have seemed to me as important as knowing the ancient artefacts, rather than, as is increasingly popular now, a topic approach where the researcher moves around the world pursuing the study of a single topic. I have also found myself unhappy with and out of sympathy with many aspects of the 'new' – now not so new – archaeology, though much of this may be reaction to the jargon in which many of its supporters write, rather than objection to the aims themselves, with many of which I am in agreement, and I consider that though often overstated the aims of this school have brought a refreshing new image to archaeology – a pity that this freshness is often spoiled by the way in which its exponents express themselves.

The implication in much of the writing of the new school that older archaeologists only dug sites because they were there and never formulated hypotheses to prove or disprove and never had a 'research design' is just not true. These ideas may not have been expressed in an as explicit a way as is now usual but they were certainly there. The new techniques, scientific aids, and increasing awareness of what new evidence is available for the reconstruction of the past are excellent. I am well aware of how much material from my own excavations was unstudied through my ignorance of what could be obtained from it and I have little doubt that young archaeologists are far better trained in the theory of archaeology and more aware of the ancillary aids to which the archaeologist can look. But I have also found many of them woefully ignorant of such basic knowledge as, for example, how to lay out a cutting, process a photograph or make a map.

The coming of the war interrupted my career and as I was a reserve officer in the Royal Air Force I was called up even before the declaration of war. I served in the RAF until after VE day, both on flying and intelligence duties, and was fortunate enough to be in several areas where I had opportunities to see ancient monuments: North Africa (Algeria and

Tunisia, where I spent several months at Carthage), Italy and Greece. One activity in which I took particular pride whilst serving with a photographic intelligence unit was the production of a set of annotated air photographs of Italian towns with the major monuments marked on them. The two volumes into which these photographs were made up were distributed to all Allied squadrons with instructions that efforts were to be made during operations to avoid damaging any of the monuments which I had marked on the photographs.

After the end of the war in Europe I remained in south-east Italy for some time awaiting posting home and during that time was able to save many air photographs with valuable archaeological information on them from destruction. In this I was joined by the late John Bradford to whom I gave help in initiating the investigation of early sites in Apulia which he was later to develop into a full-scale project.

After the war I went back to the Ashmolean for a short while and also had the opportunity to work for one season with Leonard Woolley at Tell el Atshana in south-east Turkey. With my training in the precision of Wheeler's excavations, the neat geometrical layout and emphasis on the observation of stratification and its recording with careful measured drawings, I was surprised at the apparently casual way in which a major Near Eastern excavation was undertaken.

Although the Ashmolean Museum was a splendid place in which to work and the intellectual climate of Oxford encouraging, I was still hoping for a job in which I could do fieldwork, preferably in the Nile Valley or the Near East. Egypt seemed no longer a possibility since Egyptians were replacing foreigners in all the posts in the inspectorate of the Egyptian Antiquities Service and the days in which a freelance excavator, raising his own funds each year and paying himself a salary from them, were over. My problem was solved by the creation of the post of Assistant Commissioner for Archaeology in the Sudan. I was appointed to this and arrived in Africa in December 1946, not my first visit as I had come to Cairo earlier that year on the way back from Turkey with Woolley.

Although I was now in Africa I did not consider myself an Africanist and was both ignorant of and indifferent to all that part of the continent to south and west. I regarded myself as an archaeologist of the Nile Valley with a strong background in Egyptology and realized that for the archaeology of the northern Sudan, where traces of Ancient Egypt were many, this was a great advantage.

I worked as assistant to A.J. Arkell who held the post of Commissioner for Archaeology and Anthropology and was responsible not only for the ancient monuments of the country but also for archaeological, ethnographical and natural history museum collections as well as for supervising any anthropological work that might be done. The Sudan government had done much to encourage social anthropology studies in the south of the country and the work of Evans-Pritchard and Nadel as well as that by some of the political officers such as P.P. Howell and B. Lewis, as well as many less professionally trained ones, owed much to this encouragement. I do not remember much of this work being carried out whilst I was Arkell's assistant and when I succeeded him the word anthropology was removed from the title of my post although I became a member of the Anthropological Board which gave permits for research and exercised supervision.

Arkell was an inspiring man to work for and his knowledge after twenty-five years of the Sudan was immense – he had started as an Assistant District Commissioner immediately after coming out of the First World War as a pilot with an MC. He spoke, as did all members of the Sudan

Political Service, fluent Arabic and impressed on me the need to do the same, and he had served in many parts of the country, particularly Darfur, where his main interest lay, before being appointed as the government's first full-time archaeologist.

The main emphasis in those days was on conservation of monuments and looking after the museum collections, though Arkell had found time, and a small amount of money, to carry out a rescue excavation in Khartoum which had provided the first evidence for an early pottery-making, probably non-agricultural, society, dated to c. 3500 BC. This is described in his book *Early Khartoum* where he coined the term Khartoum Mesolithic to describe the material he had found, perhaps a rather unfortunate name but one that dies hard.

Soon after my arrival I was taken by Arkell on a journey northwards along the Nile to visit the main monuments, inspect the guards, and when possible arrange for repairs, etc. On this journey I saw many ancient Egyptian sites but also a number which though owing something to Egyptian civilization were of a distinct style which could only be called Sudanese. These were the sites of Meroitic (c. 750 BC–AD 350) and medieval (c. AD 650–1400) times and I realized for the first time that the Sudan had an ancient cultural tradition of its own and that a study of these sites would be rewarding.

I did not especially think of these cultures as being African – of course they were in Africa and so by definition African, as is Egypt, but I was more aware of other influences – Egyptian and Graeco-Roman in Meroitic times and Byzantine and Coptic for the medieval. I did not see, nor do I now, that they had contact with other parts of Africa nor do I see influences from those other parts as contributing to what are distinctly cultures of the Nile Valley.

I succeeded Arkell in 1948 after his retirement from the Sudan to become a lecturer in the Department of Egyptology at University College, London. I was now free to start my own research programme, and although busy with administration and care of monuments I considered that the Government Antiquities Service should be seen to be carrying out research as well as conservation. The opportunity came when the Egypt Exploration Society, which had been working in the years before the war on several Pharaonic sites in the northern Sudan, wished to re-start at the site of Amara West and found that they had no field director. H.W. Fairman, who had directed in the immediate pre-war years, had been appointed to the Chair of Egyptology at Liverpool University and was unable to continue fieldwork. It was proposed that the excavation should be continued as a joint one of the Sudan Government and the Society and I became field director and thus had an excavation of my own for the first time.

The excavation consisted, in the main, of removing unstratified deposits of wind-blown sand from within the ruins of a Pharaonic Egyptian town which had been an important administrative and religious centre until its abandonment in c. 1000 BC. There had been no subsequent occupation. After two seasons (1948–9 and 1949–50) the Egypt Exploration Society decided that they had done what they wanted at the site and moved the focus of their work to Egypt.

The result of this excavation at Amara was to strengthen my opinion that I wanted to use excavation as a means of investigating the Sudan's past, and although much interested in Ancient Egypt and its role in the Sudan I saw a need to study those periods in which the Sudan had developed a unique culture of its own. At this time I was particularly interested in the medieval culture of the part of the country known as Nubia – at a time when it had been Christian and had developed a distinctive art and architecture, had writing in its own language, Old Nubian, and in particular a distinctive pottery which, owing something to Coptic Egypt and perhaps Sassanian Iran, was recognizably different and unique.

The standing monuments, mostly churches, had been studied and two catalogues of sites had been published (Somers Clarke, 1912 and Monneret de Villard, 1935/1957), and considerable surface collections of sherds had been made, largely by Arkell, but there had been no excavations and there were no criteria for dating any of the material other than knowing that it lay between the seventh and fifteenth centuries AD, these dates being provided by the Christian iconography frequent on the sherds and the historical knowledge of the dates when Christianity existed in the area. Different styles, particularly of pottery, could be observed but only a stratigraphic excavation could provide a relative chronology from which in time an exact chronology could be derived.

Funds and technical resources were extremely modest but Amara West and Arkell's work had established that the Antiquities Service could and should excavate and government were willing to allow a small sum for the purpose – in 1950 this amount was three hundred Sudanese pounds (approximately sterling £330) together with an air ticket to bring one assistant from England. Consideration of choice of site led me to Soba, a site which was almost certainly that of the capital of the medieval state of Alwa, the most southerly of the kingdoms of Christian Nubia.

Reasons for the choice of site were, first, that surface observations of the many mounds suggested that stratigraphic evidence would be found – not always the case in the Nile Valley, as Amara West had shown; second, that though little was known of the more northerly sites even less was known about Soba; and third, that it was only about 22 km from Khartoum and logistic problems would be easy. Finally, a minor consideration at that time, being near to Khartoum the site was in some danger, not at that time from building (as is now the case) but from random surface collecting and occasional digging by weekend visitors. A small-scale excavation was carried out in the winters of 1950–1 and 1951–2 using methods I had learnt from Wheeler and which were then rare, or unknown, in the Nile Valley. Strict attention was paid to stratigraphy and what is, probably, the first drawn stratigraphic section from the Nile Valley was published with the report (Shinnie 1955). In addition there were ethnographic observations of local pottery-making and of the construction and decay of modern mud-brick houses whose construction was similar to the medieval ones. These observations and the brief notes on them that were published seemed to me, then, a normal part of the archaeologist's work where he was in areas where old techniques were still being practised, and I did not think that one day such studies would be dignified with a name of their own and be promoted to be a sub-discipline of archaeology as 'ethnoarchaeology'.

If I am pleased to think that, in a small way, I pioneered better excavation methods and ethnographic observation I am ashamed of the total absorption in the retrieval of artefacts and study of architecture. At that time I had virtually no understanding of what information could be obtained from zoological and botanical materials and I remember throwing away animal bones as being of no use. It is certain that prehistorians of the early 1950s would not have been so cavalier and they would not have ignored potential information about subsistence, climate, etc. It may be, as I considered at the time, that at such a comparatively short time ago as the *floruit* of Soba, which traditionally came to an end in 1504, the climate, vegetation and subsistence pattern would have been the same as now – but this is not self-evident and needs to be demonstrated. Here was a weakness in a humanist training and I much hope that the new excavations at Soba carried out by the British Institute in Eastern Africa have made good my deficiencies. I certainly, wisely, left plenty of the site unexcavated and I am pleased to see from the reports so far available that the standard of excavation has improved greatly since my time.

It should be remembered that at this time radiocarbon dating was barely known – I had heard of it for the first time when Braidwood described the technique at the International Prehistoric Congress in Zürich in 1951. Very few samples were being accepted and it was far from certain that the technique would be useful for sites with such a recent history as Soba. That any improvement of the very generalized dates known for the period was made was due to the fortunate find of a large hoard of imported Syrian glass which was studied and published for me by D.B. Harden (Harden in Shinnie 1955) and this, together with a few pieces of Egyptian glazed pottery, was able to give some closer dating for the main pottery types than had been possible before.

Subsequent years in the Sudan were busy with excavations (Tanqasi – Shinnie 1954 – and Ghazali – Shinnie and Chittick 1961), travels round the country inspecting sites, and campaigning, unsuccessfully, for the building of a proper museum. My interests were still primarily concerned with the archaeology of the Nile Valley from c. 1000 BC on, but a visit to Darfur in company with O.G.S. Crawford and on another occasion on which I also went into Chad with Glen Balfour-Paul, then Resident, Geneina, had shown me something of the potential and importance of areas away from the river.

At this time, also, I managed to arrange for a number of publications. An annual report had been published for some years in pamphlet form and I had continued the format originally started by Grabham (Government Geologist and responsible as Secretary of the Archaeological and Museums Board for many years) and added an Arabic version so as to give it wider readership. In addition the journal KUSH, to be the annual of the Antiquities Service, was started in 1953 and three volumes appeared during my term of office. I also continued the Occasional Paper series which Arkell had started with his paper on the Old Stone Age (Arkell 1949). I used this series of papers to publish an account by O.G.S. Crawford of his survey (Crawford 1961) and my excavations at Soba (Shinnie 1955) and Ghazali (Shinnie and Chittick 1961) as well as the diary of Linant de Bellefonds (M. Shinnie 1958). To my knowledge there have been no further issues of this series. At a more popular level I started to issue a series of pamphlets – 'Museum Pamphlets' – which were intended for a wider public and to be issued in Arabic as well as English. This series has been continued.

These years in which I had been working in the Sudan saw many developments in African archaeology, particularly its prehistory, and the series of conferences which Louis Leakey had initiated in Nairobi in 1947 became an important meeting-place for those with common interests. The emphasis was, and still is, heavily Stone Age and I did not feel comfortable in the company of specialists in stone tools and early man. I did go to the conference held in Algiers in 1952 but felt that the interests of most of the participants were not mine – though I met A.W. Lawrence who had recently resigned the chair of Classical Archaeology at Cambridge to become the first Professor of Archaeology in what was then the University College of the Gold Coast. We found much in common in the later archaeology of Algeria and Tunisia but little did I think that six years later I would succeed him in what had by then become Ghana.

An incident that occurred on the post-conference tour from Algiers to Tunis – where we visited Carthage – typified for me the gulf between prehistorians and historically orientated archaeologists. On the way back from Tunis by motor coach we came, in the hills of Algeria, to the beautiful ruined Roman town of Djemila – a superb ruin set in superb country. While all the rest of us went to see the ruins Louis Leakey, who had been, along with the Abbé Breuil, a dominant figure in the conference providing fascinating information on his recent discoveries, sat in the coach with his hands before his eyes and said that he would not visit the site as he could not allow anything to distract him from thinking about the Old Stone Age.

The approach of Sudan independence brought all this work to an end and in 1954 I left the country on the Sudanization of my post. I was succeeded by the distinguished French Egyptologist Jean Vercoutter on the grounds that a Frenchman, being 'neutral' in the political issues then facing the Sudan, was acceptable in a post that was technically 'Sudanized'. Returning to Britain, I spent a short period back at the Ashmolean Museum, made a trip to the Island of Socotra to make an archaeological survey (Shinnie 1960a), and was then offered the post of Director of Antiquities in Uganda. Although my training and interests did not well equip me for this I accepted it, since there seemed no alternative, and I went there in December 1957. I do not think I made a success of my time in Uganda – I knew nothing of its archaeology before I went there, there was not much to know, nor did I feel any great interest in it. Very little archaeological investigation had been made there, although a start had been made by Wayland and O'Brien in studying the Stone Age and some collections, which I was not competent to assess, had been made. Kenneth Marshal, who had worked with me at Soba a few years earlier, had held a post as an archaeologist attached to the Geological Survey for a short time and had also made collections. For the Iron Age, which was to be my main interest, a number of earthwork sites were known. Some had been described and E.C. Lanning, then a District Officer, had begun a study of them and the associated pottery. There was a considerable amount of oral tradition associated with these earthworks and the peoples said to have made them, and after travelling round much of Uganda, except for Karamoja where I was refused entry on the grounds of disturbances there, I decided that the research part of my job should be to investigate one of the earthworks and establish the pottery styles associated with it to use as a basis for further work which Lanning had already begun.

The best known and the biggest of these earthworks was the one known as Bigo and here in the summer of 1957 I carried out an excavation – my first in sub-Saharan Africa and the first on an Iron Age site in Uganda (Shinnie 1960b). The results were not spectacular but they did for the first time show something of the structure of the earthwork and provide a sample of the pottery used by its builders. Chronology still depended on dates calculated from the oral traditions and although radiocarbon dating was now an established technique there were few laboratories accepting samples and I certainly did not know how to set about getting such samples, nor how to raise the necessary funds to pay for laboratory dating.

There was obviously going to be a problem in establishing a chronology for the Iron Age in East Africa away from the coast and the lack of any imports amongst the material found at Bigo made it impossible to do any cross-dating – though in principle this could be done if future excavations found dateable exotic pieces. Wheeler had said to me when I was first considering going to Uganda, 'One starts from the coast with objects of known date and then works inland.' This was fine in theory but I was tied to Uganda and it would only be with the founding of the British Institute in Eastern Africa that such cross-territorial approaches could be used. Even now, and with additional work at Bigo by Posnansky (1969), very little more is known.

Although reasonably satisfied with the work at Bigo, I did not feel that the archaeology of Uganda was going to be of great interest to me, and the complicated administrative arrangements by which I was part of the government and responsible to the Minister of Education while the museum, in which archaeological collections were housed, was controlled by an independent group of Trustees, proved more uncomfortable than I cared for. It was with some relief that I moved to Ghana as head of the Department of Archaeology in what was then the University College of Ghana, arriving in Febuary 1958 a little less than a year after Ghana's independence.

My time in Uganda had forced me to pay some attention to the archaeology of sub-Saharan Africa, and this was at a time when the subject was becoming of increasing interest to the scholarly world and in both east and west Africa work was starting and appointments being made. The University College of Ghana had had a department of archaeology, the first in 'black' Africa, since 1951 and in A.W. Lawrence had a distinguished scholar as its head. The first plans were being made for what was to become the British Institute in Eastern Africa and my appointment to Uganda and Neville Chittick's to Tanganyika were part of this new activity. This went hand in hand with new work in African history and, at least as far as Anglophone Africa was concerned, the two conferences held at the School of Oriental and African Studies of London University in 1953 and 1957 (I was present at the latter) marked the interest now being taken in African studies.

Arriving in Ghana early in 1958 I found the department suffering from the effects of separation from the Ghana Museum. Lawrence had been Professor of Archaeology and Director of the Museum and had made use of the rather good building at the university to house the collections until the museum was built. My appointment was only to the university and the museum was now an independent organization with its own director (H.D. Collings) and a government-appointed board. This suited me well and since the implication – never, I think, clearly stated – was that the university department was to be primarily for research rather than teaching, I set about developing it for that purpose. Funds were comparatively easy to get in those days and I was able to establish a library (only two books when I arrived!), a conservation laboratory, and a photographic dark-room, and to increase the amount of transport.

Oliver Davies, also a member of the department, was busy roaming Ghana and neighbouring countries mainly investigating Stone Age sites, and Seth Owusu, a Ghanaian research fellow, was involved in studying material from his own excavations. So in considering what research projects I should undertake it became obvious that I should concentrate on what I was most competent to do – the Iron Age of the area. It soon appeared to me that one of the least known aspects of the archaeology of West Africa was the nature of the various states that had been established from early medieval times along the critical region of the northern savanna.

In the reading that I was now, for the first time, doing into the history of West Africa these states seemed of importance for the development of not only the society of the savanna but also of the more thickly vegetated areas to the south, since it was through these Western Sudanic kingdoms that trade had passed both north and south. I considered that a university department need not confine itself to the archaeology of the country in which it was located and since my interest was still largely focussed on the Sudan and adjoining areas my first two investigations were both into the Sahel to look at the evidence for two of these states and to consider whether an excavation in either of them would be appropriate. The first journey, in March 1969, in conjunction with David Bivar, then of the Nigerian Antiquities Department, was to Borno to examine sites of the Kanuri state (Bivar and Shinnie 1962). The other, in December of the same year, was into southern Mauretania together with Pat Carter, recently arrived as Chief Technician to my department, to visit the site of Kumbi Saleh, often considered to have been the capital of Ancient Ghana. At that time, soon after Ghana's independence, there was much interest in the ancient state from which the former Gold Coast had taken its new name. Direct connection seemed unlikely but the emotional tie was real and I thought that excavation at Kumbi Saleh would satisfy several requirements. It would enable me to work in a physical environment which I found agreeable and under conditions where my past experience in the Sudan would be relevant, it would increase knowledge of an important period in West African history, and it would be popular in Ghana.

These were good reasons to start an excavation at Kumbi Saleh to continue earlier work by French archaeologists, and it is likely that but for an outside event a project would have started there in 1962. The outside event was the decision to build the Aswan High Dam in Egypt with the resultant flooding of much of Nubia. As soon as this happened and an appeal was made world-wide for archaeological help to salvage the monuments, I proposed that Ghana should participate in the international effort and send an expedition to the Sudan. This proposal was well received in Ghana at the highest level of government and special funds were provided which made it possible to carry out three seasons, from 1961 to 1964, of excavations at the medieval Nubian town of Debeira West in Sudanese Nubia (Shinnie and Shinnie 1978) (figs. 13:1 and 13:2). Debeira was chosen because my own interest suggested that there was a site which would provide material for an understanding of medieval village life and it was also the largest and possibly the most important of those Nubian sites which had not already been allocated to other expeditions.

During these years African studies were at their height and the University of Ghana (as it now was) played an important part in this development by creating an Institute of African Studies in 1959. I had been active in establishing this Institute and became acting director for its first two years until Thomas Hodgkin was appointed substantive director in 1961.

Going to Ghana at a time when African studies were developing very fast made a profound difference to my view of the importance of the continent and not only caused me to realize that parts of Africa other than the Nile Valley were of interest but also helped me to appreciate that the past of Africa could only be understood if those from different disciplines were to work together.

In the late 1950s and 1960s views about the need for multi-disciplinary research were being widely discussed, and even if there was more often lip-service to the ideal than practical achievement, there was at least some attempt to produce results in this way, and the University of Ghana's institute was founded for this purpose. I note, looking through old papers, that I had been groping towards this view and had started to move away from a purely old-fashioned artefact-obsessed archaeology as an aim in itself.

13:1   *Peter Shinnie and Adu Boahen (University of Ghana) at Debeira West, Sudan, 1961*

13:2   *Debeira West medieval village after excavation 1963*

Even in the early 1950s I had written a paper for the Sudan government urging the integration of archaeology, social anthropology, ethnography and linguistics in a research effort to throw light on the Sudan's history before 1821, the date at which historians at that time usually began to take an interest. My paper fell flat and the British officials then responsible for setting the intellectual climate of government and of the new University College were not sympathetic.

Ghana gave much more of an opportunity to express my views and put some of them into practice, and the early appointments to the Institute of African Studies whilst I was director reflect this. Of the first appointments one, Kwabena Nketia, was a scholar who quickly made an international reputation as an ethno-musicologist, two were linguists and one a historian with a strong multi-disciplinary bent (Ivor Wilks).

Although teaching was not the first consideration in developing the department of archaeology it was not ignored, and before there was a programme in archaeology lectures were given for the history department. In my opinion archaeology was not an appropriate subject for a first degree and the teaching programme in archaeology began with a course for a post-graduate diploma – my successors have changed this policy and shown me to be wrong and for some years undergraduate courses have been offered with success. For the earlier years I still think there was good reason to teach only at post-graduate level and it gives me great satisfaction that my first student in Ghana, James Anquandah, should now be the head of the department.

The archaeology of Ghana was not neglected and in 1960 I excavated at Yendi Dabari in northern Ghana (Shinnie and Ozanne 1962) (fig. 13:3). This excavation again reflected my interest in historical problems and was intended to provide dated material for the first time in this part of Ghana. Yendi Dabari, 'ruined Yendi', had been the site of the capital of the Dagomba kingdom since about AD 1500 until the move, under military pressure, to the present site at Yendi further to the east in the early eighteenth century. Approximate dates for this event and for the founding of the town were known by calculating average lengths of reign for each Ya-Na (king of Dagomba), the names and order of succession of whom were traditionally remembered.

The work in Nubia had got me back into the Sudan and I was now able to consider a project which had been in my mind for a long time. This was to excavate at Meroe – the capital of an independent Sudanese state during an important formative period and the centre of a distinct culture. It was a large urban site, occupied for at least a thousand years, and I hoped that its excavation would provide answers to chronological, social and environmental questions at the largest and most important site in the country. Starting in 1965 as a project of the University of Ghana, it was in subsequent years more conveniently carried out from the University of Khartoum after I had been invited there in 1966, and after 1970 from the University of Calgary, where I came to be head of department (in what was then the only department of archaeology in North America) for my first four years and subsequently to teach over a much wider range of archaeology than I had anticipated. From Calgary I was able to carry out more extensive fieldwork than would have been possible from either Khartoum or Ghana and I was also able to bring students from both Sudan and Ghana to Canada to work for higher degrees.

The start of a major excavation, though still only modestly financed, which was intended to be continued for many years made it possible to plan to investigate a number of topics. Though these were stated in the first

13:3 *Peter and Margaret Shinnie at Yendi Dabari, Ghana 1960*

application for non-university funds, made to the British Academy in 1966, arrival in Canada and the much more rigorous system for requesting financial aid made me think carefully about the aims of the work and provide a detailed research plan.

The general outlines of Meroitic archaeology and history were known, and had been described in a general work I had written on the topic (Shinnie 1967) but there was no stratigraphic control of the full range of artefacts, particularly pottery, and the nature of domestic occupation and subsistence in the important southern area of the Meroitic state, where the capital lay, was not known.

The town of Meroe with its deep deposits – in one place 10 metres deep – seemed likely to provide this information and the work was planned to include study not only of artefacts but also of zoological and botanical remains and to take full advantage of the possibilities of radiocarbon dating. It was also part of the plan that the aims of the excavation should be not only descriptive, as most of my published results had been, but that an attempt should be made to explain the nature of Meroitic culture and society.

Full-scale excavations started in 1966 after a preliminary season in 1965 when the site was carefully examined, a map made, and plans developed for subsequent work, and was continued every winter until I went to Calgary in 1970. From the University of Khartoum where, deliberately, there was then little undergraduate teaching of archaeology, it was easy to find time for fieldwork and four seasons were undertaken between 1966 and 1970. After moving to Canada, though funding was more plentiful, time off during the winter was more difficult, and it was only by careful use of sabbaticals and vacations that several seasons were possible (figs. 13:4

13:4 *Peter Shinnie and Kathleen Robertson at Meroe, Sudan 1976*

and 13:5). By 1976 this possibility had come to an end and though much work remained to be done only one further field season was possible, in 1983–4 after my retirement.

I was also in the Sudan in the latter part of 1979 pursuing another interest of mine, the Nubian language. I had long been interested in Nubian as part of my concern with the culture of the Nubians in medieval times. The language of that time, Old Nubian, known then from rather few documents – the number has increased dramatically during the last fifteen years as a result of excavations at Qasr Ibrim – was not very well known and I thought that a new study of the present Mahas dialect of Nubian, a direct descendant of Old Nubian, would be useful in developing

knowledge of the earlier stage of the language. To do this I stayed for several weeks in the village of Mishakeila, near the third Nile cataract, as the guest of the father of Dr Ali Osman who had studied with me in Khartoum and Calgary. The material collected is to form the basis of a study of the language which Ali Osman and I intend to publish.

13:5 *Excavations in progress at Meroe 1976*

The problem of how to find time in the busy schedule of a Canadian university, with its academic year from September to April, to do fieldwork in those parts of the world where climate makes it possible only to work from about November to March is a considerable one and has certainly reduced the amount of field activities in many parts of Africa. It was mainly this matter of how to find time to work in the field that caused me to switch my activities back to Ghana. Although there was plenty still to do at Meroe, the end of the 1976 season marked a reasonable stage at which to close the main excavation – evidence had been obtained to attempt to answer most of the questions which had been asked at the beginning, and it was necessary to start on the publication.

In looking for an area in which I could work during the university summer vacation it seemed obvious that Ghana was the most appropriate. Not only had I worked and lived there previously but climatic conditions made it possible to work in the northern part of the country even during the rainy season (June-September). My interest in periods for which there was some known history led me to consider Gonja, one of several chiefly states of northern Ghana for which considerable historical detail was known – both from oral tradition consciously preserved, as in Dagomba, for state purposes, but also from a document written in Arabic, probably in the early eighteenth century and commonly known as the 'Gonja Chronicle'.

There were a number of archaeological and historical problems that might be solved if a suitable site could be found and in 1977 I organized a survey in western Gonja primarily to examine sites known to be associated with the history and traditions of the Gonja people. As a result of this survey, Daboya, on the west bank of the White Volta River, was chosen for excavation and after the first season there had shown an unusual depth of deposit going back to early in the first millennium BC. Work was continued for three further seasons. The project was concluded in early 1985 with excavation of four small sites in the western part of the state in the hope of finding material to compare with that from Daboya.

Much of 1985 was concerned with the preparing of the publication of Daboya in collaboration with F.J. Kense, originally a graduate student and later colleague, and in making plans for a new project in Ghana to look for sites of early Asante occupation before the founding of Kumasi at the end of the seventeenth century. And now as I write in Kumasi two seasons of investigation at Asantemanso – claimed to be the place from which the Asante people came – have just been completed with rather surprising results since the radiocarbon dates strongly suggest that the site had been occupied as early as the twelfth century AD.

14 *Egyptology & Archaeology: An African Perspective*

DAVID O'CONNOR

I Culture and environment: their impact on Egyptology

A THE NATURE OF EGYPTIAN ARCHAEOLOGICAL REMAINS

Egyptology is the study of the textual and archaeological material generated by the Egyptians of the 'Pharaonic' period, running from *c*. 3100 BC to Alexander's conquest of Egypt, then a Persian province, in 332 BC (Trigger *et al.* 1983). Traditionally, Egyptological subject matter also includes the latter phases of Egyptian 'prehistory', of roughly 4500 to 3100 BC, (Trigger 1983) but does not run back into Palaeolithic times and, on the other end of the time-scale, has only a marginal involvement with the so-called 'Graeco-Roman' period, let alone the important monuments and rich history of Coptic and Islamic Egypt. Even within this comparatively narrow time-frame of 'Pharaonic' and 'later prehistoric' Egypt, however, a varied and complex archaeology came to occupy the 1360 kilometres of the Egyptian Nile Valley as well as its desert fringes.

Cemetery and settlement sites were represented in great abundance and both types might include very large, monumentally scaled pyramids and temples, their size emphasized by the still striking cliché that Khufu's 'Great Pyramid' at Giza could absorb within its over 75 million cubic feet bulk 'the cathedrals of Florence, Milan and St. Peters at Rome, as well as ... Westminster Abbey and St. Paul's Cathedral' (Edwards 1985: 97). Other archaeological data reflecting human activity were quarries, mines and specialized settlements beyond the flood plain, and – on the latter – irrigation basins (natural, but artificially enhanced), communication canals, river harbours, field systems and the like (Baines and Malek 1980) all of course less likely to survive well as compared to sites in the desert. The better preserved sites and the larger museum collections display an almost staggeringly rich array of art-forms and artefacts: abundant statuary, some colossal; reliefs and frescoes that, in some cases, cover hundreds of square feet of wall space (Smith 1958; 1981); innumerable materials used in daily life, such as clothing, jewellery, agricultural and industrial implements, weapons and furniture (Hayes 1953, 1959) and a multitude of religious items, many made exclusively for funerary use (Spencer 1982) but others intended for temples, chapels, domestic shrines and even magical practices. Durable materials, combined with an arid climate, make much of this material very well preserved, in this respect more akin to ethnographic rather than archaeological collections.

Texts are a vital and ubiquitous feature of Pharaonic archaeology, the onset of which is conventionally marked by the first appearance of writing. Many are, from our viewpoint, conventional in type, occurring in ink on papyrus or ostraca, or inscribed upon the walls of temples and tombs; but others occur on a surprising range of artefacts – often (and sometimes lengthily) on statuary and coffins, but also on mud-sealings, containers,

236

seals, furniture and implements. Quite apart from the general question of the relationship between textual and archaeological data (discussed below), this circumstance has a special impact on Egyptological research, including archaeology. Texts themselves are archaeological as well as philological data, the latter requiring in part the same kinds of typological, chronological and contextual analyses as are applied to the former. Moreover, while most Egyptian structures, graves and objects are not directly associated with texts, the association is common enough that the dating and interpretation of a specific structure, archaeological matrix or artefact (the results, by extension, being applicable to related or similar matrices and artefacts not directly associated with texts) is sometimes as dependent upon the associated text as upon more purely archaeological attributes.

Time-depth further increases the complexity of both Pharaonic and prehistoric archaeological remains, while a significant difference in the method of 'periodizing' the two broad phases has had a perceptible effect upon the role of archaeology in Egyptological research. The prehistoric phase might better be called 'preliterate' and, because of the absence of texts, its subdivisions into periods follow closely and consistently the changing typology of artefacts, especially pottery, as well as of art-forms and architecture (Trigger 1983: 21–40; Kaiser 1957). However, Pharaonic archaeology is sub-divided chronologically *not* by reference to changing typologies, but rather to the dynasty or period to which a specific archaeological assemblage is linked by associated textual material. How typological change is to be interpreted in historical or cultural terms is of course already a complex question, but for Pharaonic material this arbitrary chronological convention has complicated the problem, and perhaps contributed to Egyptological reluctance to make use of archaeological data for such purposes (Kemp 1976: 281–9).

On the positive side, this method of periodization provides Pharaonic archaeology with a framework of absolute dates (von Beckerath 1975; Krauss 1985), useful for measuring rates of archaeologically manifest change and for comparisons with other ancient cultures. Moreover, there are important if generalized correlations between the archaeological and historical records; if art-history be considered an aspect of archaeology, there are significant variations in the style and content of art-forms that can be linked with recorded political and socio-economic change; monumentally scaled structures diminish in number and size in the disturbed 'Intermediate Periods'; and certain types of artefacts are characteristic of some broadly defined historical periods.

On the negative side, typological change often does *not* bear an obvious relationship to textually documented political and social change, although archaeological change always demands explanation, which in turn may open up aspects of the historical picture not well documented in surviving texts. However, the arbitrary chronological scheme described above tends to mask this major feature of Pharaonic archaeology; and in any case analysis of the correlation between archaeological and textual data is a demanding and delicate exercise (cf. e.g. O'Connor 1974). For these and other reasons, much data already recovered (at considerable trouble and expense over nearly a century of controlled excavations) has fallen into a virtual limbo so far as the analytically based reconstruction of Egyptian history and society is concerned. Moreover, in these circumstances, the aims and the strategies of future efforts to recover additional archaeological data become hard to define.

B ENVIRONMENT AND ITS LOCATIONAL EFFECTS

Prehistoric and Pharaonic archaeological remains reveal a distinctive locational patterning, which is essentially a variable of the interaction between the ancient culture and its environment. This, in turn, in combination with later environmental and human factors, had a major impact on the survivability of archaeological remains, and their accessibility to the modern archaeologist.

In the Pharaonic period, as today, Egypt was a long, narrow oasis, perennially watered and annually inundated by the Nile and flanked by arid, rainless deserts; in the later prehistoric period environmental conditions were only marginally better (Butzer 1976: 13, 26–7). As a result, settlements were almost entirely confined to the flood plain (reaching an average width of 19.2 kilometres in Upper and Middle Egypt, and of a maximum 248 kilometres across the Delta) although there was, in certain areas, a deeper penetration of what are now desert zones in the prehistoric period (cf. e.g. Fairservis 1971–2). On each side of the flood plain, between it and the cliffs of the Nile gorge, extends a relatively narrow band of low desert, uninundated and hence sterile. A few specialized or peripheral settlements were located on the low desert, but much commoner, in Upper and Middle Egypt, were cemeteries of both the lower and upper classes, attracted by the convenient access combined with freedom from the destructive effects of surface or sub-surface water and of agriculture. Into the cliffs of the gorge the elite also had tunnel-like tombs cut and often decorated with frescoes or reliefs. In the broader Delta many cemeteries were perforce located on the flood plain, preferring (like settlements) the numerous expanses of higher lying ground known as turtle-backs (Butzer 1976: 22–5; Bietak 1975: 49 ff).

C THE SURVIVAL AND ACCESSIBILITY OF
ARCHAEOLOGICAL REMAINS

The environmental and locational factors described had an obvious effect on archaeological survival and accessibility. Towns and villages, palaces, fortresses and often even temples were built of sun-dried mud brick (Spencer 1979). Their remains, sometimes in the form of stratified tells or town-mounds well known elsewhere in the Near East and parts of Africa (e.g. Kemp 1977; Bietak 1979a; Jeffreys 1985) were partially eroded by the annual inundation and gradually engulfed – either entirely or in part – by a steadily rising flood plain. Many are now located not only below ground level, but within a permanent water table located not far below plain surface. Stone-built temples and stone architectural elements from palaces and houses survive better, but are engulfed by the same processes. In some regions, moreover, major shifts in the Nile channels have totally eliminated archaeological sites, at least down to some specific depth (Butzer 1976: 33–6; Jeffreys 1985: 48–51, 57–8).

In contrast, survivability was much higher on the low desert, especially for the subterranean burial pits and chambers. Many tombs of several socioeconomic strata had mud-brick superstructures, of which substantial parts or at least significant traces often survive, although wind erosion and flash floods from desert storms have often caused severe or total denudation. Pyramids, funerary temples and elite superstructures, if built of stone, and the rock-cut cliff tombs were virtually impregnable to environmental denudation. However, wind-deposited sand, advancing dunes and in some areas rock falls and scree slopes could, to varying degrees, overlie cemeteries and reduce access to them (Butzer 1961).

Human as well as environmental factors naturally also affected survivability and accessibility. Temples and more mundane structures might be razed in antiquity so that their materials could be re-used elsewhere (e.g. Goedicke 1971; Redford 1984: 63–71, 227–31), a process continuing into recent times; in 1881, for example, Petrie reported of the ruins of a large pyramid at Abu Rawash that: 'The monument was being quarried for stone – he was told that while the Nile was high, three hundred camel-loads a day would be carted off' (Drower 1985: 42). On the flood plain agriculture must have often adversely affected archaeological remains, most specifically but not solely by the demolishing of town mounds so that their nitrogen-rich soil could be used as fertilizer when, relatively recently, agriculture became more intensive (Kees 1961: 180, 189, 229, 291). Low desert cemeteries and sites were affected most substantially by repeated plundering.

Today, environmental and human processes affecting archaeology have become, for Egypt, uniquely combined. Over the decades the irrigation system has been gradually improved, and now depends on a vast reservoir created by the Aswan Dam. The river no longer floods and the flood plain has ceased to rise, but the impact of the new system upon the water-table, a greatly increased rate of salinization and atmospheric pollution caused by increased traffic and industrialization is having adverse effects upon standing monuments and archaeological sites. In addition, industrial and agricultural development and a rapidly increasing population is compelling expansion onto surviving river plain sites and into the low desert.

Environmental change and the tension between development and preservation is inevitable, but their impact upon Egyptian archaeology has not been ignored. An extensive and international community of Egyptologists has long publicized such problems (e.g. the Philae problem: Wilson 1964: 126) and Egypt has a long-standing committment to exploring and preserving its past. Since 1858, it can be credited with 'the first National Service of Antiquities . . . [and] the creation of the first National Museum in the Near East, and the birth of a conscience about the export of antiquities from Near Eastern lands' (Daniel 1981b: 72; Reid 1985). The Antiquities Organization today assigns a high priority to the security and conservation of archaeological sites and these issues, as well as the illicit trade in antiquities, receive considerable coverage in the Egyptian press. Nevertheless, archaeology in Egypt faces a major challenge because of these problems.

D THE SHAPING OF EGYPTOLOGY

Discussion of the environmental and human variables sketched above leads us to two important points about the past and future of Egyptology and archaeology in Egypt. First, when serious archaeology began in Egypt it was, because of prevailing scholarly and cultural values, predisposed towards the exploration of monumental sites and cemeteries and this attitude was naturally intensified by the better survival and accessibility of cemeteries and monumental funerary sites on the low desert and in the cliffs, and of a few major stone temples on the flood plain. The urban and village sites typical of the flood plain were less well preserved and less accessible, so settlement archaeology was of much less interest, becoming so minimal over an extended period that leading scholars argued that Egypt, for much of its history, was a 'civilization without cities', a theory now convincingly refuted (Kemp 1977; Bietak 1979a).

Settlement sites may well have attracted greater attention if their

excavation had yielded large amounts of archival texts, a significant factor
encouraging the early exploration of Mesopotamian town mounds
(Oppenheim 1964:; 228ff.; Saggs 1962: 22ff.) Egypt certainly once
produced the same rich panoply of political, economic, social and legal texts
as Mesopotamia, but the latter were incised on clay tablets, the former
written in ink on papyrus and ostraca (Černy 1952; Helck 1980). Archival
texts typically occur in settlements on the flood plain; clay survives
comparatively well, the other materials do not. There *is* abundant Egyptian
textual material from the cemeteries and better preserved temples, but this
is concerned primarily with religious concepts and rituals. Embedded
within it is a historical record that is of value, but one heavily distorted by
ideological factors inherent in the religious contexts for which these texts
were intended (Hornung 1966).

This brings us to a second point. For the prehistoric period we are totally
dependent on archaeological data for reconstructing all aspects of society
and its history at that time; but both interpretation and new recovery of
data need to be much more sophisticated than has been the case until
relatively recently. In Pharaonic archaeology a related but different problem
exists. Some aspects of Egypt's political, social and economic history can be
reconstructed by reference to textual and archaeological data derived from
cemeteries and temples; but the major core of textual information would
have been the archival sources (Donadoni 1963) which have largely
disappeared. The real challenge, then, is to explore the degree to which not
only cemetery but more especially settlement-site archaeology can fill the
vast gap caused by the destruction of the archival record. Salvage
archaeology and the conservation of sites and monuments are critical issues;
but success in these areas will be of limited value if social and economic
history, and the increased recovery and correllated study of the relevant
textual and archaeological data relevant to them, do not become much
more part of the Egyptological main stream than they have been.

II   Egyptian archaeology: the past and the future

A   THE STATUS OF EGYPTOLOGICAL STUDIES

Archaeology in Egypt, as elsewhere, is focussed upon the excavation of sites
and monuments and the study of the architecture, artefacts and other
materials thus revealed, within the context of the strata that enfold them.
The history and the future of Egyptian archaeology, however, can only be
understood if the other principal areas of Egyptological research –
philology, epigraphy and art history – are taken into account.

The issues involved are best brought into focus by a brief overview of the
status of Egyptological studies in the past and today; to what areas of
research and other activity have Egyptologists been devoting their efforts,
and in what proportions? A crude but revealing answer is provided by some
comparative statistics, based on two comprehensive bibliographical
records, dating to 1924 and 1981 respectively (Pratt 1925; Zonhoven 1985)
(table 14:1). The samples differ somewhat in their nature, the former
reflecting Egyptological publication over the preceding century, the latter
the published output of a single year; the statistics derived from them are
based on different units of measurement; and the statistics themselves are
only a rough indicator of the proportions of effort allotted to different areas

Table 14:1

Category of published research		Percentage of entire publication in terms of pages (1924) or entries (1981)	
		1924	1981
Language and texts		15.5	19.1
History and religion	Based mainly on textual study	17.2	10.8
Society and culture		3.5	5.5
Art		2.0	4.6
Archaeology, including field epigraphy and field reports		33.2	27.2

of research. Nevertheless, even with these qualifications in mind, the resulting picture provides a good basis for discussion (post-Pharaonic material has been excluded from discussion, but still counts as specific proportions of the published material being analysed).

The first points to emerge are a striking stability in scholarly attention over the entire history of Egyptology, with only relatively little proportional change, and a first slight but increasing dominance of language, texts and textually based studies over archaeology (1924: 38.2/ 33.2 per cent; 1981: 40.0/27.2 per cent). This dominance is the more evident when it is realized that both epigraphic and archaeological fieldwork are included under archaeology (and in practice cannot always be easily separated). To some extent this imbalance is historically determined (see below), but environmental impact is also evident. Within textually based studies, the emphasis on history and religion and the relatively slight attention to society and culture (including government, law and economics) reflects the discrepancy between the more frequent and better preserved 'monumental texts' from stone-built temples and dry low desert sites on the one hand, and the rarity of archival texts, typically located in flood plain sites, on the other (O'Connor 1983: 185–8).

Environmental factors are also at work within the archaeology category, as further analysis shows (table 14:2). In this case, the 1924 and 1981 sources can be supplemented by a comprehensive summary of all archaeological and epigraphic fieldwork dedicated to prehistoric and pharaonic sites in 1981–2 (Leclant 1983). In table 14:2 the percentages are of the number of pages or entries covering fieldwork *only*. (All figures are in percentages.)

Table 14:2

Publication	Monumental Funerary (inc. funerary temples)	Archaeology Temples (non-funerary)	Non-monumental archaeology		Survey
			Cemetery	Settlement	
1924	34.1	20.7	30.5	13.4	1.0
1981	36.2	13.0	8.7	23.2	15.9
1982	34.6	17.9	11.5	17.9	17.9
Averages	34.9	17.2 (1924)	30.5	13.4	1.0
		(1981, 82)	10.1	20.5	16.9

Again, note marked stability so far as monumental archaeology is concerned, the excavation, study and epigraphic recording of monumental sites maintaining a steady average of about 52 per cent throughout the history of Egyptology. So far as environment is concerned, such monumental sites are, as we have seen, the better preserved, and hence a more attractive component of the archaeology. Non-monumental archaeology however, has certainly not been neglected, holding about 46 per cent of scholarly attention over time; and within this category there have been significant shifts, which reveal an early effect of environment lessening because of intellectual change, a re-defining of scholarly aims. In 1924 cemetery archaeology (i.e., better preserved low desert sites) was dominant, representing almost 75 per cent of non-monumental archaeology; but by 1981 and 1982 it held only about 25 per cent. Settlement archaeology has increased substantially in recent times, in part indicating an increased interest in the less accessible flood plain sites, as has survey, indicating a greater interest in the regional mapping of both sites and *in situ* texts.

As the preceding remarks make clear, the status of Egyptological studies – and of archaeology within them – depends not only on environmental, but also on intellectual and historical factors, and it is to these that we should now turn.

B THE HISTORY OF EGYPTIAN ARCHAEOLOGY

Several excellent narrative histories of Egyptology are readily available (e.g. Fagan 1977; Bratton 1967; Wilson 1964; cf. also O'Connor and Silverman 1979), so discussion here can be brief. However, it should be noted that, in terms of intellectual analysis – analysis of the changing or enduring foci of scholarly attention (and prejudice) and related methodological stability or change – these histories do not go very deep. The 'intellectual history' of Egyptology remains to be written; but, at the least, a coherent impression of it amongst Egyptologists today is of importance for future developments in the discipline, as I shall argue further below.

The earliest scholarly and public interest about Egypt in Europe (the Arabic sources appear to have hardly been explored) was stimulated by the publications of various visitors to Egypt through the fourteenth to eighteenth centuries, culminating in the publication from 1809 to 1813 of the *Description de l'Egypte* (Greener 1966: 21–102; Fagan 1977: 32–81). This comprehensive description of Egypt, old and new, prepared by the *savants* accompanying Napoleon's invasion of Egypt (1798–1801), vastly increased the written and pictorial information available on Egyptian antiquity, a subject of great interest to a scholarly world that had long been involved in a keen but critical study of exotic cultures, the ancient past and the origins of religion (Hazard 1964). Egypt held a special place within this study, and in the public interest; in the seventeenth and eighteenth centuries the wise Egyptian as much as the Mohammedan Arab and Chinese Sage had become a prominent type figure in intellectual debate (*ibid.*: 27–40) while – on the public side – one of the earliest archaeological best-sellers was to be Wilkinson's lively *Manners and Customs of the Ancient Egyptians* (1837) (Wilson 1964: 31–2).

Champollion's decipherment of the Egyptian system of hieroglyphic writing (1822) (Pope 1975: 60–84) gave Egyptology the basis it needed to become a scholarly discipline, and throughout the nineteenth century the significant achievements were in philology and epigraphy. While scholars in Europe published grammars, dictionaries and historical and cultural studies based on the texts, major epigraphic expeditions (Champollion and Rossellini 1828–9; Lepsius 1824–5) copied and published standing monuments and extant documents in rich detail. Egypt, under the Europe-oriented rule of Mohamed 'Ali and his successors, was much more accessible to Europeans than before; but archaeology as such was hindered by the elementary state of this discipline in general (Daniel 1981b: 13–79), and specifically in Egypt by the great emphasis placed on the discovery of new monuments and texts and the unscientific recovery of art works and artefacts for European museums and private collectors. The worst excesses were brought under control by the establishment of an Egyptian Antiquities Organization and National Museum (1858), led for many years by Auguste Mariette; but scientific archaeology, in the modern sense, was not introduced until the 1880s (Wilson 1964: 21–158; Fagan 1977: 97–359).

Our picture of this last development is perhaps over-dominated by the undoubtedly extraordinary figure of Flinders Petrie (whose Egyptian excavations began in 1880) (Drower 1985). The American, George A. Reisner – whose fieldwork began nineteen years later – was also a key figure (Wilson 1964: 144–69; Dunham 1958) while the contributions in both method and theory of other early archaeologists such as Ludwig Borchardt (Dawson and Uphill 1972: 33–4) still await full assessment. Controlled excavation was now established as an ideal, as philological expertise already was, and from this point two interrelated developments characterized Egyptology throughout three-quarters of the twentieth century. Professionally staffed academic departments and museum collections gradually proliferated while archaeological and epigraphic fieldwork in Egypt increased dramatically, with a significant hiatus from 1940 to 1960 followed by a marked revival since then. Today, there are approximately 130 significant Egyptological centres, mostly in Egypt, Europe and North America but extending as far afield as South America, the Soviet Union, Japan and Australia (Karig 1984). The amount of fieldwork carried out has been very great, although public attention has naturally been dominated by the more spectacular discoveries, such as Tutankhamun's tomb, or sites such as the great pyramids of Giza.

These developments generated a complex structural background, in terms of support, organization and funding, which is not irrelevant to the history of Egyptology and its future. The Egyptian Antiquities Organization has always played a major role in fieldwork, albeit often linked to the accessibility or conservation of monuments or to salvage archaeology; and Egyptian universities have become increasingly more active in field research. On the whole, despite some occasional vicissitudes, successive Egyptian governments have been, and continue to be supportive of foreign archaeological activity, which today is perhaps at a higher level than ever before. The researchers involved are generated by the Egyptological centres noted above, but in significantly different ways. Some governments, for example, have long supported specific research institutes in Cairo (French, German, Austrian and others), through which a great deal of fieldwork is organized and published. In other cases, we find private societies, supported by consortiums of universities, museums and other institutions and providing a rather different kind of organization through which fieldwork is structured; typical here, but not unique, are the United Kingdom, the United States and Canada. While drawing on private support, these societies, like the institutes and individual investigators, depend significantly on government funding, naturally affected by a variety of criteria and circumstances. Beyond even these lies the influential if diffuse area of public opinion, whether of Egypt itself with a natural concern for its cultural heritage, or globally, where modern communications and changing educational emphases continually reinforce an already strong interest in ancient Egypt.

C AUX ARMES, CITOYEN!

Periodically, and with good reason, the alarm has been sounded about the status of Egyptian archaeology, both as a physical entity and a discipline. On the whole, both the Egyptian authorities and Egyptologists have responded well to such alarms, as in the successful international salvage campaign for Nubia, carried out in the 1960s under the aegis of Unesco and the Egyptian and Sudanese governments. Nevertheless, urgent issues remain, serious enough to prompt a leading Egyptologist to exclaim recently that in urging more salvage archaeology and a greater role for archaeological studies in Egyptology he felt he was 'acting the part of a prophet in a Classical tragedy, seeing disaster but inspiring no belief' (Bietak 1979b: 159).

Two points are fundamentally important. First, there is an evident need for much expanded conservation and salvage archaeology, for all kinds of sites are being damaged or obliterated by increasing development as well as environmental factors. This need is widely recognized (cf. Grimal 1981; Bietak 1979b) and a concrete plan for an Egypt-wide archaeological survey (supplemented by selective excavation) has been sketched out (Smith 1985). There are certainly serious problems of funding and organization involved in such ambitious schemes, but a major expansion of salvage archaeology is called for, perhaps combining some national co-ordination and centralization with existing field projects.

The successful Nubian salvage campaign of the 1960s is both analogy and example, but it was smaller-scale and more dramatically worthy of funds than the needs of Egyptian archaeology today. It also raises the second, more intellectual issue noted above, for while the Nubian salvage campaign generated enhanced and new interpretations of the Palaeolithic and post-Pharaonic periods in that region (Egyptology Titles, 1971–9, 'African Connections'; Zonhoven 1983 et seq. 'Nubian studies') similarly innovative developments have not, as yet, occurred in the study of the later prehistoric and Pharaonic periods in Nubia. The potential for such exists, but is underexploited; might we not encounter the same problem, on a larger scale, in Egypt proper? In other words, emergency excavation and survey may temporarily stimulate archaeology in Egypt, but they alone will not provide it with an increased importance and momentum.

Intellectual change within Egyptology is essential if society and culture are to receive the attention their importance in prehistoric and Pharaonic Egypt justifies. This in turn requires much increased exploitation of the archaeology of settlements and lower order cemeteries, since the relevant textual data are either relatively abundant but only peripherally relevant ('monumental' texts) or directly relevant but are (and will always be), relatively rare (archival texts). The intellectual shifts required are best brought about by persuasion and example, which are already underway, although their efforts will probably be only slowly felt. The analysis of economic, legal and other questions is becoming increasingly sophisticated (e.g. Janssen 1975); models and interpretive methods derived from anthropology are being judiciously integrated into the more traditional modes of inquiry, which remain necessary and valuable (e.g. Trigger 1979; Janssen 1975; O'Connor 1987c); and it is being demonstrated that archaeological data can illuminate important aspects of prehistoric and Pharaonic history and society for which textual information is slight or non-existent (e.g. Kemp 1981; Janssen 1983; Tietze, 1985, 1986).

Another potentially productive way of influencing Egyptological attitudes and priorities is a deeper probing of the discipline's intellectual roots. As the data quoted above indicate, Egyptological preoccupations have been remarkably stable; even today, one observer notes: 'textual exegesis dominates history, prosography and genealogy are the main springs in the study of local history, art history is regarded as the major component in evaluating the development of material culture' (Kemp 1983: 355). These circumstances raise questions Egyptologists should explore and answer; how did such circumstances come about, are these preoccupations sufficient for the fullest possible understanding of prehistoric and Pharaonic Egypt, what new kinds of approaches might be developed?

We can easily see that philological analysis was historically favoured to dominate archaeology in Egyptology. Philology was an already highly developed discipline by the time the hieroglyphs were deciphered (1822), as was the textually based study of ancient history and religion (Hazard 1964), and Egyptological philology developed rapidly and became firmly established. Archaeology was a rawer, newer discipline and its development within Egyptology was also biased by the environmental and historical factors already described. Intellectual analysis in the future, however, should proceed to deeper, if more difficult levels than these. The difficulty arises from the complex issues raised; what was the prevailing scholarly ambience, what were general social and cultural prejudices from generation to generation and how did they specifically affect Egyptology? Equally important, and as difficult to explore, are the individual motives, strategies and preoccupations of the influential, leading Egyptologists – philologists and archaeologists – of each generation. Unfortunately, detailed biographies are rare, and tend to focus on narrative and the evocation of character rather than the drier area of intellectual analysis. For example, a recent biography of Petrie (fig. 14:1) is both historically excellent and warmly human in its delineation of character (Drower 1985), but important questions remain to be answered on the intellectual side. What exactly was the nature of Petrie's formidable, if flawed, intelligence and vision, that made him the only Egyptologist referred to in a famous historiographical essay of 1946 (Collingwood 1963: 264) and caused a leading statistication to remark recently:

> Petrie should be ranked with the great applied mathematicians of the nineteenth century. He makes use of many sophisticated statistical ideas which, it seems . . . he must have invented for himself; and his writings also contain what must surely be the first fully developed 'mathematical model' (a mechanical analogue of his sequencing process) in the literature of archaeology (Kendall 1971: 214)

What can be asked about Petrie can equally well be asked about other leading figures, who are less served biographically.

More specifically, important questions need to be answered about the history of Egyptian archaeology itself. Junior partner though it was, archaeology made a promising start as an alternative means of reconstructing and interpreting Egyptian society and its evolution. Petrie argued vigorously on behalf of this view; and Reisner (fig. 14:2) developed several stimulating reconstructions of segments of Egyptian society on the basis of archaeological data (Reisner 1923, 1932, 1942). Yet their

14:1 *Flinders Petrie*

14:2 *George A. Reisner*

technically very able students, who continued to carry out much fieldwork, did not significantly expand upon these early efforts at socio-economic and historical analysis. Why this should be requires investigation, but in part may be due to the fact that most were museum curators, focussed upon the accumulation and documentation of archaeological data, rather than its interpretation in the broad social and historical framework. The latter remained the primary concern of the university world, which continued to be dominated by philogists. More recently, one may ask why the excavation of lower order cemeteries has declined, and so little effort has been made to analyse the historical and socio-economic implications of already published, non-elite funerary archaeology. In part, the answer may be that socio-economic analysis has attracted only small numbers of Egyptologists until recently. Finally, as we have seen, archaeological survey and settlement archaeology are increasing in Egypt; but the purposes and aims of expansion in these areas – apart from that of pure salvage and increased documentation – have not as yet been articulated clearly.

One should stress that these questions are as relevant to prehistoric as to Pharaonic archaeology, for prehistoric studies are undergoing a marked revival in Egypt (Egyptology Titles 1971–9, 'Prehistory of Egypt'; Zonhoven 1985, 'Prehistoric cultures'). Moreover, the increasing sophistication of archaeology naturally and inevitably encourages the development of specialist prehistorians, which in turn raises the problem of maintaining productive interraction between prehistoric and Pharaonic archaeologists respectively. Egyptian prehistory and history is a continuum, a vital fact not to be lost sight of amidst the continuing development of different disciplines.

III Egyptian archaeology: an African perspective

Egyptian archaeology, and Egyptology as a whole, has a significance extending well beyond the Egyptian Nile Valley itself. In later prehistoric and even more in Pharaonic times Egypt was in contact with a wide range of peoples and cultures in the eastern Mediterranean, the Near East and north-east Africa. These contacts are important in themselves but, equally significant, throughout this vast area Egypt is one of a few well known and comparatively highly developed cultures that are paradigms, models against which the evolution of the other known cultures of the regions involved is measured. In this volume, it is most appropriate to focus on north-east Africa, where the relationships and comparisons with Egypt are the least clearly defined, and where we shall see again emerge – now from a somewhat different perspective – crucial issues about Egyptian archaeology which have been discussed above.

A THE ROMANTIC PERIPHERY

Broadly speaking there are two approaches to the study of Egypt in Africa. One might reasonably be called 'romantic' because it places much less restraint on intuition and imagination than the other, more sober approach; it is also peripheral in that much of the evidence it employs ultimately fails to meet the test of accuracy or of scholarly reasonableness, and hence cannot bear the heavy speculative weight it carries. The romantic approach can take two common forms. In one, Egyptian civilization is seen radiating out throughout much of Africa (indeed, of the world, in the more extreme versions of diffusionism) (Daniel 1981: 115, 149–50). In the other, it is argued that the evidence of physical anthropology (directly and indirectly reconstructable by a variety of means) shows that the Egyptians were 'unquestionably amongst the black races'; and that further the similarities between Egyptian language and culture and those of other, more recent African groups are so strong that 'Egyptian antiquity is to African culture what Graeco-Roman antiquity is to Western culture' (Diop 1981, esp. 49).

For the most part, neither concept – diffusionist or Africanist – can survive critical scrutiny. Leclant's critique of the evidence for wide-spread Egyptian contact throughout Africa still stands (Leclant 1972) and the Africanist view is vigorously propounded in the recent Unesco *History of Africa* (Diop 1981), only to be implicitly contradicted by many of the chapters within the same volume (Mokhtar 1981). Yet, the romantic school of thought should not be neglected. Its proponents are sincere and enthusiastic and have roused considerable public interest, so historically it is of some importance – witness the inclusion in the Unesco volume noted above. Moreover, its existence stimulates us to think out more carefully and clearly our ideas about the relationship between Egyptian archaeology and that of Africa in general; and perhaps to see whether traditional or existing scholarly attitudes to the question do not in fact merit re-examination and change.

B 'THE OVERSHADOWING COLOSSUS'

This quotation (Adams 1977: 669) brings into focus the really major questions about prehistoric and Pharaonic Egypt in the context of north-east Africa. What really was the nature of interactions between Egypt and other entities throughout this vast region, which may be roughly described as a trapezoid defined by Cyrenaica, the northern half of the Republic of the Sudan and the African shore of the Red Sea (Clark 1982)? Further, how do these entities – and many others, yet to be discovered – compare with Egypt in terms of political, socio-economic and general cultural development? It is fair to say that the prevalent view about both questions takes it that Egypt was the vastly superior element, the 'colossus' amongst pigmies; and it is indeed clear that in significant ways Egypt was more 'highly' developed than the other cultures of north-east Africa. Yet it is also possible to argue on reasonable grounds that the cultural contrast is drawn too sharply and that Ägypto-African relations were often much more of a dynamic, two-way process than might appear from the current literature. Naturally, the interpretation of non-Egyptian archaeological remains is deeply involved in discussion of this issue, but ultimately we must return also to a question already raised: just how well do we understand ancient Egypt itself as a social organism, and what is the present role and future potential of archaeology in that understanding?

There are several reasons why Egypt came to dominate our thinking about north-east African archaeology. Not only was Egypt's material culture striking and, in a sense, always known to scholarship (e.g. Herodotus *c.* 450 BC) but Egyptologists themselves played a key role in the delineation of north-east African archaeology in general. Soon after hieroglyphs had been translated (1822) Egyptologists, with the help of Egyptian depictions of distinctively 'African' peoples, were identifying in the texts inhabited regions clearly located in Africa (Gauthier 1925–31) and later Egyptologists led in the discovery of archaeological remains outside of the Egyptian Nile Valley. Important standing monuments along the Nubian Nile (First to Sixth Cataracts) were first published in detail by Egyptologists (Champollion 1835–45, 1844; Rossellini 1832–44; Lepsius

1849–59, 1897–1913) and in the early decades of the twentieth century the identification of several important indigenous cultural phases along the Nubian Nile was due to Egyptologists, especially G. Reisner but also others (Adams 1977: 71–7). Egyptologists continue to be, on occasion, deeply involved in Nubian archaeology (*ibid.* 77–87) and only relatively recently have prehistorians and other scholars of non-Egyptological disciplines become more active in this field.

Even today, the archaeological map of north-east Africa tends to reflect the archaeological interest or disinterest of Egyptologists in the past. For late prehistoric and Pharaonic times, the Nubian Nile and, to a much lesser extent, the flanking deserts and the northern Butana are well on the way to comprehensive mapping, but the west remains enigmatic and, to the east, entities such as Punt (and probably many others) remain archaeologically unknown, documented only through Egyptian texts and scenes. West of Egypt proper the oases are increasingly becoming better known, but the eastern desert – except for obvious traces of Egyptian activity – remains unmapped, although there is good reason to believe a substantial indigenous people, the nomadic Medjayu (Bietak 1982) occupied much of its southern reaches (cf. generally, Leclant 1950, 1951, 1953, 1955, 1962 *et seq.*; Shinnie, P.L., *et al.*, 1972 *et seq.*). Further west, the Libyans of Cyrenaica, known from texts to have been long in contact with Egypt and of quite critical importance to it in the late second and earlier first millennia BC, remain archaeologically unknown (Ösing 1980; O'Connor 1987c).

In these circumstances, it is not surprising that, both directly and indirectly, Egyptologists have strongly influenced our ideas about cultural evolution throughout north-east Africa and, in particular, have reinforced the idea of Egypt's dominant cultural position throughout the region. Egyptological predilections emerge both in subtle and in more obvious ways. Much of the earlier literature was marked by an outright prejudice against 'Africans' as distinct from Egyptians – a phenomena of course widespread at the time. This has long disappeared, but contributed perhaps to the still fairly low level of attention paid to Ägypto-African relations as compared to Egyptian contacts with the Near East. When comparisons are drawn, they tend to overlook significant details that subtly soften the abruptness of the differences between Egypt and north-east African entities. It is certainly true, for example, that those of the Nubian Nile adopted literacy relatively late, had 'court cultures' of much less elaboration and, for a long period, compared unfavourably with Egypt in technology. Yet it is important to note that Nubians (the Kerma culture) were making use of literacy by 1700 BC (Kemp 1983: 173–4) were well aware by then of the value of advanced technology (Bonnet 1986) and that the tumulus tomb of one of their most powerful rulers at the time while occupying – at 63.6 per cent of a hectare (Reisner 1923: 136) – an area much less than say that occupied by the *average* royal pyramid of the Old Kingdom (1.35 hectares), compares much more impressively with the *late* Old Kingdom and the Middle Kingdom pyramids, respectively occupying on average 62.3 per cent and 99.8 per cent of a hectare. Of course, pyramids are much higher and bulkier than tumuli, but the point is that the fine shading of the detail softens the apparent sharpness of contrast in the picture of Ägypto-African relations.

However, by far the most powerful support for the idea of Egyptian cultural and, to a great extent, political dominance has been the ancient Egyptian evidence itself. The history of Egypt's foreign relations is perforce drawn from the better preserved and frequently studied 'monumental' texts and pictures from temples and tombs. These are heavily biased, subordinating historical details and reality to the assertion that the gods had assigned Egypt an immeasurable political and cultural domination over *all* foreigners (Hornung 1966; O'Connor 1983: 186, 188–202). So far as the Near East is concerned, the relatively well known archaeology of the latter, as well as the literacy of several of its cultures, have enabled scholars to assess accurately the cross-cultural comparison with Egypt. Even while the general bias of the Egyptian sources is realized, it is much harder for Egyptologists to find this balance so far as the non-literate, less well-known cultures of north-east Africa are concerned.

Typically, therefore, we find Ägypto-African relations of relatively slight importance in general historical discussions. Thus, in the magisterial *Cambridge Ancient History* Egyptian contacts with Syria and Palestine receive specific and extended attention, while relations with Africa are, for the most part, subsumed into the narrative describing Egypt's own history (Edwards *et al.* 1971, 1973, 1975). More recently, contributors to the *Cambridge History of Africa* (vol. I) (Clark 1982) and to the *Unesco History of Africa* (vol. II) (Mokhtar 1981) have naturally provided greater coverage on entities outside of Egypt and noted some of their possible internal dynamics, but continue, to a large extent, to treat them as part of Egypt's story. Naturally enough, even scholars of a disciplinary background other than Egyptology and more receptive to assessing non-Egyptian cultures on their own merits, are still strongly influenced by the secondary historical literature produced by Egyptologists. Adams, for example, sees the ancient Nubians as an 'external proletariat', very much in the political, economic and ideological shadow of Egypt, 'the overshadowing colossus to the north' (Adams 1977: 668–9), while Trigger – in a work significantly entitled, *Nubia Under the Pharaohs* – displays, like Adams, sensitivity to Nubian achievements, but sees much of their history in terms of the 'increasingly efficient but also ... increasingly costly exploitation of Nubia' by Egypt (Trigger 1976: 149–51).

Yet, Egyptian sources permit us to hold a different view, stressing more the internal developmental strength of various African entities, as well as greater externally oriented initiatives on their part. The conquest of Egypt by a Kushite state in *c.* 750 BC (Kitchen 1986: 363–98; Trigger 1976: 138–48; Adams 1977: 246–93) is an extraordinary phenomenon, demanding analysis of Kushite cohesion and organization as much as of Egyptian fragmentation; while earlier the whole pattern of Egyptian government may have been strongly affected by Libyan modes of governance as a result of intense interaction with Libyans through the late second and early first millennia BC (Leahy 1985; O'Connor 1987c). Going back to more remote times, the prevailing scholarly view would be that, in the later third and earlier second millennia BC, Lower and Upper Nubia were crammed with a series of relatively small indigenous political units, fairly easy to dominate and subdue; but it is possible to argue that the better known Nubian entities were in fact much larger and more dynamic and aggressive, and were concentrated not merely along a larger part of the Nubian Nile than normally envisaged but extended out into the Butana and adjoining regions (O'Connor 1987a, 1987b). The available archaeological data can fit both the narrower and more expansive theories, perhaps even favouring the latter more. The massive Egyptian fortresses in Lower Nubia then become a realistic defence against comparatively powerful Nubians rather than 'examples of the material hypertrophy which is characteristic of Egyptian civilization' (Adams 1977: 187) while the Kerma culture of Upper Nubia grows to a more significant power, in keeping with increasingly complex and rich archaeological data that are being recovered about it (Bonnet 1986).

Ultimately, however, in considering the place of Egypt in north-east African archaeology in general, we come back to our starting point. Our picture of Egypt's cultural superiority and recurrent political dominance is derived not only from the directly relevant textual and archaeological data (which, I have argued, are in fact subject to a more qualified interpretation), but also from a general impression that Egypt, for much of its history, was a highly cohesive and sophisticated socio-political entity. Yet this view, like that of Ägypto-African relations, is strongly coloured by traditional scholarly interest in history and religion as conveyed through biased 'monumental' texts and in the archaeology of monumental sites. In the more traditional view, the unstable and contractive 'Intermediate Periods' of Egyptian history are aberrations, deviations from a more normal pattern of strong centrality and cultural unity; yet, alternatively, the 'Intermediate Periods' might be seen as overt expressions of an underlying instability masked but still present and potent in more outwardly stable periods.

In this alternative view Egypt loses none of its unique cultural qualities, but its political and military strengths are not so disproportionately greater than those of other Nilotic kingdoms further up stream (Kemp 1983: 123; Trigger 1976: 149). Egypt then competes with these for territory or influence on more equal terms, and displays – probably as do its rival kingdoms – major fluctuations in internal stability. Which of these two views is closer to reality depends upon the reconstruction, in so far as is possible, of the dynamics of social and economic processes in the different periods of Egyptian history. And, as noted above, this in turn requires in Egyptology much greater recovery and analysis of settlement and lower-order cemetery archaeology, in conjunction with substantial shifts in intellectual attitudes.

15 *Oral Traditions, Archaeology & History: A Short Reflective History*

PETER R. SCHMIDT

The use of oral traditions as part of the direct historical approach in African archaeology has become a popular method in the history of Iron Age cultures. The reasons for this are threefold. African societies for the most part have experienced severe culture change only during the last century, thus offering more intact historical systems of thought than many other world areas where industrialization has a longer history; literacy in many African societies is mostly a development of this century, a phenomenon that immediately causes the African archaeologist to look to indigenous history that has not previously been recorded, as well as to oral accounts recorded by the educated elite, missionaries, travellers and administrators; and, the richness of oral traditions about specific places and events in history has inevitably enticed historical archaeologists to use such sources in locating and in explicating the function and meaning of sites. The environment for the use of oral traditions, then, has been particularly ideal and conducive in Africa. This is the case particularly in areas of Africa where there are state systems with well developed and well preserved historiographies.

In cultural contexts where there are deep genealogies and mechanisms for preserving oral traditions there arose three decades ago an interest in bringing together oral traditions with archaeological investigations into the past. The propinquity of centralized states with long genealogies to centres of higher education in Uganda, Ghana and Nigeria has led to a fuller development of this perspective in these areas. The first experiments with archaeology and oral traditions, particularly in Uganda, gave rise to a rather heady optimism about the potentials of wedding archaeology with information derived from oral histories and oral traditions. This sanguine perspective flourished during the 1960s under the elegant pleas by Vansina to formulate an interdisciplinary approach that used archaeology, oral traditions, historical linguistics and other ethnographic data in African history (Vansina 1965; 1967). In the absence of written records for a pre-nineteenth-century history, this appeal seemed to offer hope for the construction of a more complex African historiography.

Vansina unquestionably provided the earliest, best reasoned justification for the use of oral traditions with archaeology. Among the early examples he cited was Posnansky's excavation of an Ankole capital site at Bweyorere, with the observation that archaeology had verified traditions for two successive capitals on that one site (Vansina 1967: 72). We will later examine the Bweyorere report to see what results inspired that initial endorsement. It is apparent from the other examples provided by Vansina that several categories of oral traditions are considered most useful. For example, oral traditions in the interlacustrine region (fig. 15:1) often relate the location of former capital sites and royal tombs and can be used to fix such sites on the landscape. Oral traditions as a locational device have long been recognized, especially in East Africa (Oliver 1959). Vansina also

15:1 *The interlacustrine region with nineteenth-century kingdom boundaries noted in Uganda. Sites mentioned in the text and associated with oral traditions appear as a circle*

noted that oral traditions may not be exactly correct in their specific attributions of a site's antiquity, though they may have a kind of facility for pointing out ancient places. Finally, the question of migrations, still a matter of fascination in African archaeology, is also thought to be a subject to which both archaeology and oral traditions can be applied. But there is often considerable distance between these ideal views and the methodologies that have been proposed and tested over the last three decades. It is now time to reflect on the history of such experiments to see if we have developed a clearer view of the potentials and pitfalls of oral traditions as adjunct information in archaeological inquiry.

Oral history

The use of oral traditions with archaeology takes place at a different level of complexity than working with oral histories, which are direct historical recollections provided by informants. Oral histories, while subject to various cultural and memory transformations, are easier to cross check among informants who were also witnesses to the same events or processes.

But when the oral histories have been compiled by amateurs and by ethnographers interested in different theoretical and substantive problems they are less certain to be reliable sources, especially for historical analogies that demand specific material and spatial observations. At a general level oral histories can be used to reconstruct historical subsistence practices and other aspects of the economy. They are also invaluable in the ethnoarchaeology of religious and ritual practices, particularly in tracing out changes in symbolic values that have accompanied culture change in the historical era. Past settlement patterns have been reconstructed in Southern Africa by the use of oral histories, oral traditions and older ethnographic accounts (Maggs 1976c). Similarly, Huffman has used oral histories (along with oral traditions and myth) and ethnographic data collected by other investigators to abstract symbolic values associated with the organization of southern Bantu royal compounds (Huffman 1981, 1984b, 1986a, 1986b).

Huffman's observations based on these diverse sources show that in much of Bantu-speaking Africa there were powerful political and economic ramifications to the control over symbolic space. This observation compels us to recognize that interpretations of symbolic space are central to understanding power relationships between different social and economic groups. In Kenya Linda Donley-Reid's (1984) ingenious work on symbolic space in Lamu houses has employed oral histories of various Swahili houses to uncover heretofore imperfectly understood ritual and symbolic space and artefacts; this illuminates the cultural meaning of archaeological features that would otherwise appear to be anomalous. The use of direct oral testimony has significant potential to elicit ritual information and symbolic meanings that are central to understanding the structure of communities and obtaining insights into recent African worldviews. This is particularly true in Nigeria. For example, at Isoya, south of Ife, Eluyemi's (1977) research indicates that the structural layout of this community is determined by symbolic, ritual and religious space. The Dogon immediately come to mind as another African culture in which cosmology is central to the structuring of subsistence practices, community layout and the architectural configurations of individual compounds. Clearly, the correlates between the material and ideological world are rich and varied. Oral histories, in conjunction with ethnoarchaeology, hold much promise for the more thorough investigation of these phenomena, as well as better understanding of pre-industrial technologies.

The use of oral histories has been an important component in the investigation of Iron Age industrial life in Africa. Historians and archaeologists of Africa have used oral testimony of former iron-smelters to obtain information on the location of smelting and forging sites, the types and locations of resource used, the rituals surrounding such industrial activity, and the chronological ordering of different technological areas (Soper and Golden 1969; Schmidt 1978; Shinnie and Haaland 1985; Goucher 1984; De Barros 1985). However useful such oral history is in setting the background to the ethnotechnology, such information is also subject to significant distortions. There is often a wide gap between the idealized oral accounts and actual behaviour. If not checked against actual technological behaviour, such information can significantly mislead investigators and lead to confused and distorted reconstructions of technologies. Second-hand accounts, that is, accounts of those who have observed but who have not participated in technological systems, are unreliable and contain very little accurate technological information (Schmidt and Childs, forthcoming).

Oral traditions

The most common applications of oral traditions in African archaeology have been their use to locate sites of archaeological interest (Schmidt 1983a; Atherton 1983). This approach has also incorporated explanations of site history and site function (e.g. Sutton and Roberts 1968; Scully 1969, 1979; ten Raa 1969; Soper 1979). Its utility varies widely from culture to culture and sometimes provides accurate functional information that is not attached to any chronology (Sutton 1973). The most dominant school of thought, dating from the 1950s in East Africa, is the verification approach. This rubric describes a perspective that prevails both in the use of ethnohistorical data in African archaeology (which I see as a part of historical archaeology), but also in the use of historical data in historical archaeology as is currently practised in North America (Schmidt 1983a). The verification approach seeks to affirm or verify by archaeological means the accuracy and validity of oral traditions that comment upon the antiquity or function of sites in Africa. In the North American context, it is manifest in the attempts by many historical archaeologists to provide redundant evidence for phenomena that are already well known in the historical literature.

In the history of African archaeology there is the inherent assumption that the oral traditions are the data to be verified by the archaeological evidence. This view derives from the still dominant attitude that oral traditions are *ipso facto* the more unreliable or questionable of the two data sets. This may or may not be true, depending on the complexity of the oral evidence and the history of transformation in the archaeological data. There are no *a priori* relative strengths or weaknesses in the various data. Each data set presents a different perspective in what develops into a dialectical exchange between the two that grows as analysis deepens.

As in western historical archaeology, when there is a more complex historiography attached to sites, then a richer and more precise interpretation of the archaeological data will also result. In an African context it often takes years of historical and ethnographic investigation to gather together and synthesize the different pieces of information that are interrelated and that illuminate an historical problem. Over the last several decades it has become abundantly clear that in-depth field research, not research dependent solely upon the collections of oral traditions by other scholars, provides the kind of evidence adequate to the task of figuring out the interrelationships of oral traditions and archaeological evidence.

I have reviewed elsewhere some of the major approaches and research characteristic of the above-mentioned approaches, so for the purposes of brevity I refer the reader to that review (Schmidt 1983a). Here I want to focus on several case studies that are seminal in terms of understanding the history of the use of oral traditions and archaeology in East Africa. Not only are they important for understanding the genesis of thinking that brings the two forms of evidence together, but they also provide background to similar work that has occurred in West Africa. In particular I want to trace the history of efforts to correlate oral traditions with archaeology at Bigo, the famous earthworks site in western Uganda. The Bigo experiment, as I will call it, is perhaps the most important early attempt to use oral traditions and archaeology together in Africa. It has been used as an ideal model by a subsequent generation of Africanists interested in constructing a history richer than that available strictly through archaeology. Bigo has also been used as an example of the potential of oral traditions to illuminate the political histories of so-called royal sites. Precisely because Bigo does not stand alone, it is important to review derivative and related work, such as that conducted during the following decade in Buhaya.

Bigo

A history of the use of oral traditions and archaeology naturally turns first to the question of the Bacwezi and their putative association with the extensive and enormous earthworks in western Uganda known as Bigo. This case study is unquestionably the best known attempt to mesh oral evidence with archaeological data and it is also the most popular example in terms of the widespread acceptance of its validity and its subsequent integration into the historical literature of East Africa. Because the Bigo case is so widely accepted as a model of the potentialities of using oral traditions with archaeology, it is appropriate that its history be examined. Are the archaeological data adequate to support the generalizations and conclusions that have emanated from the Bigo research? Are the oral traditions that are supposedly related to the site properly evaluated and tied to the germane archaeological evidence? And, are the oral traditions used by both historians and archaeologists equal to the task to which they are put, both substantively and interpretatively?

I have previously commented in summary fashion on the authenticity of the oral traditions and the adequacy of the archaeological evidence (Schmidt 1983a). It is necessary to re-evaluate the evidence and its attendant conclusions because of the importance Bigo has assumed in African historiography and because research there apparently established the efficacy of early attempts to wed oral traditions with archaeology.

Bigo is located just south of the Katonga River in Mawogola, once a district in the western part of the former kingdom of Buganda and part of a larger region called Bwera. Bigo is a massive complex of earthworks, made up of mounds and trenches – some dug into bedrock – that run for up to 10 km in length (fig. 15:2). The site has long attracted the interest of antiquarians, amateur historians, historians and archaeologists. It is the largest of three apparently related sites, all located along the southern bank of the Katonga River and stretching along 15 km of it. Moreover, the well known 'Bacwezi' sites of Masaka Hill (c. 25 km WNW) and Mubende Hill (c. 50 km NNW) are located within a region closely associated with Bacwezi oral traditions.

Mubende Hill has long been known in Ugandan oral traditions and ritual life as the former residence of Ndahura, the first of the so-called Bacwezi kings, while Masaka Hill is known as one of the residences of Wamara, the most powerful and also the last of the Bacwezi. Bigo bya Mugenyi, according to some interpretations, takes its name from one of the minor Bacwezi deities, Mugenyi, who is Wamara's nephew (Nyakatura 1973; Fisher 1970). The question that is so central to Bigo and these other sites is whether or not the Bacwezi constitute a real political dynasty or if the mythologies surrounding the Bacwezi are a symbolic rendering of processes of opposition and resistance by indigenous peoples to outsiders (see Schmidt 1978; Berger 1981). Later dynastic linkages with the alleged Bacwezi dynasty are clearly part of a process of legitimization that is so central to the acceptance of political domination of outsider groups.

The genesis of western thought about the Bacwezi is well summarized by Berger (1981) as being derived from the racist Hamitic hypothesis (see Robertshaw, this volume), which in this case was perpetrated by Sir Harry Johnston who along with many others saw the pale-skinned

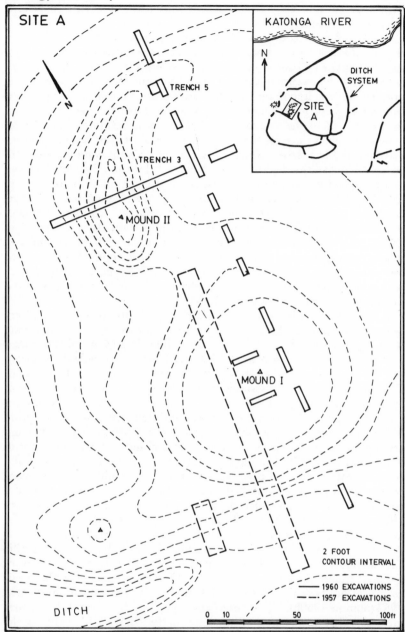

5:2 *Plan view of Posnansky's 1960 and Shinnie's 1957 excavations in the central enclosure of Bigo. The box in the upper right of the figure depicts only the inner system of ditches. Mound II is the alleged crescent-shaped mound that is used to interpret the site as a royal capital (from Posnansky 1968)*

Bacwezi as coming from the north as a real, live political dynasty. Debate has long raged about whether the Bacwezi should be seen as an historical dynasty or as deities in a religious, symbolic mythology (e.g. Oliver 1953; Wrigley 1958; Posnansky 1966; Schmidt 1978; Berger 1981). I have in my previous work also stressed the history of the multiple roles played by influential Bacwezi leaders, particularly in religious, social and political life. An important observation, though, is that the Bacwezi in some areas such as Buhaya are associated with the earliest iron production (Schmidt 1978). There is also evidence that points to the pre-Bahinda and pre-Babito practice of Bacwezi spirit mediumship by political and social authorities. This being the case, it is easy to see how the first European observers could

have reduced this variety of multiple authority to a strictly histori-
cal/political phenomenon.

There is also the additional observation that the sacred sites of western
Buganda (which became a part of Buganda only in the nineteenth century),
such as Masaka Hill and Mubende Hill, remained important Bacwezi cult
centres into the twentieth century. The Mubende Hill cult centre and its
priestess were so important that they were protected during war between
Buganda and Bunyoro (Berger 1981). More importantly, the cult played an
important role in the Bunyoro rituals of royal installation. This process
closely resembles the roles that the former ruling clans of Bacwezi descent
played in the installation rituals of Kiziba and Kiamutwara kingdoms in
Buhaya. The political legitimacy of the later Babito and Bahinda dynasties
clearly depended upon the protection and patronization of the Bacwezi in
this context. The incorporation of Bacwezi ritual authorities into royal
ritual points to the ideological necessity of a Bacwezi identity for the later
dynasties. The longevity and continuity of important Bacwezi shrines in
Bwera also resemble the situation in Kiamutwara kingdom, Buhaya,
where a sacred Bacwezi cult centre associated with iron-making remained
indepedent of Bahinda authority until the late seventeenth century, at
which time the Bahinda dynasty finally moved to occupy the site and
incorporate its oral traditions as its own.

A close look at Bigo and its associated oral traditions reveals that very
little of substance can be turned up to document its supposed connection
with the Bacwezi. Apart from its name, Bigo bya Mugenyi, possibly a
reference to one of the Bacwezi deities (or a Ganda mythological figure),
the site has no direct connection with the oral traditions of the Bacwezi.
The absence of any direct association with Bacwezi tradition is not only an
embarrassing observation for East African historiography, but also an
interesting commentary on the obsession of certain historians to find proof
of Bacwezi origins for the elaborate earthworks of Bigo. The underlying
assumptions here are that the Bacwezi 'dynasty' and its extensive empire of
Kitara was a centralized and highly organized state system. The large and
complex earthworks of Bigo, it was reasoned, could only have been
constructed by a well organized labour force under the supervision of a
centralized state system such as the Bacwezi (Posnansky 1969; Berger
1981); since the Bacwezi were 'known' as the only pre-Babito state in the
area, the Bigo earthworks must have been made by the Bacwezi.

This reification of the Bacwezi as a definite political dynasty with specific
sites attributed to it is one of the cornerstones of East African historiography. Archaeological involvement with the question of a 'Bacwezi'
central authority at Bigo began with Peter Shinnie's investigations there in
1957 (Shinnie 1960b). The archaeological goals at Bigo from the very first
were to verify the general chronology of the Bacwezi 'dynasty' as the
predecessor to the Babito dynasty, which was thought to begin in approximately the fifteenth century in the area. So, the Bigo investigations fall
clearly within the verification school. But verification of what kinds of oral
traditions? The answer to that question is best obtained by tracing out the
origins of the claims and evidence that attach the Bacwezi to Bigo bya
Mugenyi.

The story starts in 1909 with the publication of a two-page article in the
Uganda Official Gazette entitled 'Ancient Forts'. While the author is not
identified, we learn from a later article by Wayland (1934b) that it was
written by a former District Commissioner named D.L. Baines. It is
important to observe that Baines's first oral history is derived from
Buganda, which never had effective control over the Bwera region in which

Bigo is located until the colonial era: 'The most generally accepted tradition amongst the Baganda attributes the construction of this place to the 'stranger' (Mugenyi) a personage who is supposed to have entered Uganda from the north soon after Kintu's time, roughly 600 years ago' (Baines 1909: 138). Baines's account also includes Banyoro oral tradition that claims that a Bunyoro chief named Nalubongoya erected the fortifications as a precaution against attempts by the Banyoro to recover the royal cattle that he had stolen. Finally, Baines cites a third oral tradition that he claims was challenged by the Baganda: 'a chief of Mawogola by name "Mugenyi" erected it as protection against the raids of the people of Ankole' (*ibid.*).

In none of these poorly attributed accounts do we find any specific reference to the Bacwezi. The seminal work of Père J.L. Gorju (1920) on interlacustrine societies repeated the Baines account and presented a confident interpretation that the Mugenyi of Bigo was the Mucwezi figure of that name. But Gorju failed to offer any further evidence that affirmed that there were oral traditions about the Bigo site. The next major account of Bigo and its alleged oral traditions was made by E.J. Wayland (1934b). He reprinted the 1909 *Gazette* article and a 1921 report compiled by a geologist, A.D. Combe, who had been sent out to Bigo to investigate the possibility that mining had taken place there and at the nearby sites. Wayland wisely observed that 'a quarter of a century has not added much to our knowledge of the Biggo and nothing to the identity of the "Mugenyi" ' (Wayland 1934b: 25). Through the use of Combe's report, Wayland introduced the idea that there was a link between the more southern site of Ntusi (with dams but no entrenchments) and Bigo, as well as the proposition that Ntusi was a large settlement and a distribution centre. But most important was Combe's idea that 'probably the entrenchments at Biggo were constructed as forts, against the invasion of a raiding tribe or faction from the North, to protect the Ntusi encampment' (Wayland 1934b: 24).

Wayland's article was immediately answered by 'The Riddle of Biggo', a compilation of recollections by J.M. Gray (1935). One of Gray's first accounts was that 'one of the many traditions regarding the earthworks is that their constructor, Mugenyi, was buried there' (Gray 1935: 229). This supposed oral tradition lacked attribution and has never been verified by subsequent investigators. Most peculiar, perhaps, is Gray's undocumented assertion that there are many tales associated with Bigo. Certainly the published evidence up to this point indicates a paucity of Bacwezi oral traditions, and a bias toward the Ganda side. The absence of pre-eighteenth-century Ganda association with the area and the fact that the Mugenyi of Ganda oral traditions is an altogether different character from that of Bunyoro cast doubt upon whether the few, mostly Ganda traditions compiled to the mid-1930s are germane to the Bacwezi question. Gray went on to discuss some other traditions, such as Apolo Kagwa's reference to one of the early kings of Buganda having lived there. Kiwanuka (1971) has dismissed this as a reference to the Bigo earthworks site and has explained the location of the Bigo site mentioned in Ganda traditions.

One of the traditions cited by Gray, who references a 1923 *Munno* (a Ugandan newspaper) article, is about a Muziba prince (from the Haya state to the south) who recovered some stolen royal cattle at the neighbouring site of Kagago during the sixth Bunyoro reign. Gray was unable to confirm the Nabulungoya (sic?)[1] story first related by Baines. Most important, though, is his reference to Gorju (1920), whom he used to support the idea that the proper translation of the name, Biggo bya Mugenyi, is 'the forts of Mugenyi' rather than 'the forts of the stranger'. He also cited Bikunya (1927) on Bunyoro history as making the same point. Still, there is no further evidence for any association of Bigo with Bacwezi oral traditions. In fact, Gray remarks, 'Mugenyi was one of these Bacwezi, but, apart from his name, tradition does not associate him with the regions of Biggo and does not picture him as a fighting man. Mwenge in Toro District is commonly assigned as the portion of the country over which he ruled' (Gray 1935: 232).

Even though the evidence was overwhelmingly against the conclusion that the Bigo earthworks could be attributed to the Bacwezi, that did not deter Gray from concluding that 'Alone of all the traditional rulers of the land, the Bacwezi, of whom Mugenyi was one, seems to fit in with the evidence afforded by the earthworks themselves' (Gray 1935: 233). This failure to acknowledge the paucity of evidence on behalf of the Bacwezi linked to Bigo gave birth paradoxically to a conclusion that was the opposite of what the available evidence seemed to indicate. We will see that it is Gray's conclusion, not any oral traditions, that forms the principal foundation for subsequent interpretations.

Gray's position was instrumental in setting the scene for the transformation of the Bacwezi from a religious/political phenomenon to an historical dynasty located at Bigo. By the late 1950s a half century had elapsed without serious inquiry into the matter of putative Bacwezi association with the Bigo earthworks. By this time, the transformational process was well under way. In 1953 Oliver introduced the idea that archaeology could be an important part of the investigation into the antiquity of the Bacwezi 'capital' sites: 'the earlier Bachwezi capitals . . . if found and excavated along with sites in Bwera and Mubende, would surely add a wealth of material evidence to support and qualify the allegations of traditions (Oliver 1953: 137). At this point we must examine closely Oliver's argument to understand the foundation of his later conclusions. Evidently he was able to preview a pre-publication copy of A.G. Katate and L. Kamungugunu's work on the traditional history of Ankole, later published in 1955. He accepted this synthetic account's contention that a character named Ruyanga (elsewhere referred to as Ruhanga) was one of the Bacwezi, even though he is not mentioned elsewhere in interlacustrine oral traditions as one of the Bacwezi. Most important, perhaps, was Oliver's unattributed contention that, 'Ruyanga ruled from Kishozi, from the north bank of the Katonga, opposite Bigo' (Oliver 1953: 136). The point to take note of here is that Oliver appears to identify Kishozi with Bigo on the basis of geographical proximity. The attribution of Ruyanga as Bacwezi is highly contentious; but simply because Bigo is nearby the dubious capital of Ruyanga does not *ipso facto* make Bigo the Bacwezi capital.

By 1959 Oliver was firmly committed to the idea that the Bacwezi were not only an historical dynasty, but were also the makers of Bigo (Oliver 1959). However, there was no documented oral evidence to support this conclusion – only arguments based on geographical proximity. Unfortunately no one stepped forward to challenge this construct. Instead, Oliver grew more confident in his position, and the non-existent data became more concrete once archaeological data became available.

Shinnie had excavated at Bigo in 1957 (fig. 15:3) expressly to throw light on the historical problems connecting with the 'legends', but he modestly concluded that after his excavations 'we are no nearer to solving the Bachwezi problem' (Shinnie 1960b: 27). Posnansky's excavations of 1960, though unpublished when Oliver wrote his chapter for the 1963 *Oxford History of East Africa*, seem to have caused a significant shift in Oliver's position. He began to claim that many versions of oral traditions

15:3 *Excavation in progress at Bigo, Uganda 1957*

had identified Bigo as the Bacwezi capital: 'According to tradition, the last capital centre of the last of the Chwezi kings was in the celebrated entrenched earthwork site at Bigo on the Katonga river' (Oliver 1963: 181).[2] Though there was no specific oral tradition cited to support this claim, the undisclosed archaeological evidence was called upon to bolster it, to wit: 'Recent archaeological investigations have tended to confirm the traditional evidence that Bigo was the seat of a Hima dynasty' (Oliver 1963: 181). Thus, a speculative construct began to grow and expand, taking on more detail and historical veracity from the archaeological data. Interpretations of undisclosed archaeological features were developed to support the idea that Bigo was a royal site: 'The original layout of the central embankments was almost certainly similar to that of the typical orirembo or royal town, of the early Hinda kings of Ankole' (Oliver 1963: 182).

Surprisingly, still no one questioned the authenticity of the alleged oral accounts, the supposed tales linking the Bacwezi to Bigo. The confident tone of Oliver's hypothetical construct, born out of Gray's contradictory conclusions of a quarter century earlier, gained in popularity because Oliver apparently had the physical confirmation that his speculations were accurate historical interpretation.

Posnansky's excavations at Bigo in 1960 (fig. 15:4) were carried out over a six-week period, during which time he excavated a prodigious number of trenches in four separate locales. While the results were later published in 1969 (Posnansky 1969), the final report was preceded by an important article titled 'Kingship, archaeology and historical myth' (Posnansky 1966).

15:4 *The Bigo earth-works 1960*

Posnansky, accepting the interpretations of oral 'evidence' made by his eminent colleague, concluded that 'on the basis of the tradition, (I) would date the Bigo culture at 1350–1500 AD and would also accept the correlation of the Bigo culture with the Bacwezi' (Posnansky 1966: 4). It is important to realize that Posnansky's reference is to the Bigo culture – which includes sites such as Ntusi and the Bigo earthworks among others – rather than to the Bigo site proper. But the key argument remained, that Bigo was the capital site of the Bacwezi dynasty. In this interpretation Posnansky apparently relied on Oliver's earlier (1963) suggestion that the layout of the site resembled a royal enclosure:

> At the centre of Bigo an enclosure bank, originally more than ten feet high and now partly destroyed, has been interpreted as a royal enclosure (orirembo) of the type that survived in Ankole, Rwanda and Karagwe until the nineteenth century. This supports the further suggestion that Bigo was the capital of this state. (Posnansky 1966: 5)

At this time Posnansky also introduced three of four radiocarbon dates obtained from Bigo that 'reinforce the view that the occupation period was short and provide a date for that occupation of around 1350–1500 AD. The date is identical to that for the Bacwezi worked out from the traditional history' (*ibid.*) We will later look at the radiocarbon dates to see if their interpretation can be accepted.

In 1969 Posnansky published 'Bigo bya Mugenyi' (Posnansky 1969), which repeats many of the interpretations previously made by Oliver, thus reaffirming Oliver's original position. That article is the keystone to the entire interpretative structure; hence it merits review. Posnansky's goals at Bigo were diverse and wide-ranging. He was chiefly concerned with

15:5 *Merrick Posnansky c. 1960*

documenting the structural sequence of construction at Bigo and his excavation strategy was aimed at obtaining this kind of chronological evidence. Most excavations were concentrated in a central enclosure that contained two mounds, no. I being round and flat, and no. II being very slightly crescent-shaped and higher.

Shinnie had previously found evidence for post holes under mound I, but without indication of a structural pattern. Posnansky found that there had been settlement at Bigo prior to the construction of the ditch system and mounds; this he called Bigo I, while the later period he called Bigo II. While structural evidence was found under mound I, it was absent under mound II, which he felt was built before mound I. Mound II (the putative royal enclosure) had been partially destroyed, he felt, by the construction of mound I, but as we will see there is reason to question this. The reasoning ran that had mound II not been partially removed, then it would have been crescent-shaped. Even though structural evidence from mound II was virtually absent, Posnansky concluded that 'Mound II is interpreted as being the ekyikari enclosure at the centre of a royal village, or orurembo' (Posnansky 1969: 135). No specific structural evidence is cited to substantiate this general interpretation, based on projected mound shape.

Let us now consider the radiocarbon dates, which are the crux of the chronological argument in so far as historical associations are concerned. The first, GXO 516, came from charcoal on the old ground level under mound II, the putative royal enclosure: AD 1505 ± 70; the second, GXO 517, came from a depression in a trench north-east of mound II: AD 1450 ± 300; GXO 518 came from the lowest infill of the ditch at site D: no date is given except the comment that it is less than 200 years at 2 standard deviations, or, something on the order perhaps of AD 1800 ± about 80 or 90?; and finally, GXO 519, obtained from the matrix of mound II, the alleged royal enclosure: AD 1570 ± 90.

The GXO 518 date, not cited, creates the first question. The excavator dismisses it on the grounds that it is contaminated and/or washed down from above, rather than a date for a recently deepened ditch. There is no apparent reason to accept either of the first two options over the last. The recent date very probably documents recent activity on the site. It is highly probable, given the other more substantial oral histories about successive use of the site during the last 300 years, that the site has been used and reused many times by a number of different groups over the last several hundred years. Here was an opportunity to look more closely at the non-Bacwezi oral traditions to see if this apparent anomaly could be explained. Let us summarize the other dates at a 95 per cent level of confidence:

GXO 516: AD 1365–1645: calibrated, AD 1395–1510
GXO 517: 850–present
GXO 519: AD 1390–1750: calibrated, AD 1395–1660

The interpretative conclusions derived from these dates are both perplexing and perhaps influenced by Oliver's prior assumption that the Bacwezi should be dated to the fifteenth century, if not earlier. Posnansky says that 'the main period of Bigo's history can be assigned to a period around AD 1290–1575. This is a conclusion that agrees fairly well with previous estimates based on oral traditions in which Bigo is ascribed to the Bacwezi dynasty as forbears of Uganda's hereditary monarchies' (Posnansky 1969: 135). In the three years following the 1966 article there was a shift from AD 1350–1500 to AD 1290–1575 in the interpretation of the dates, but no explanation for the change. It is not clear how the AD 1290–1575 range is obtained. The younger date is the GXO 516 date plus 1 standard deviation, but there is no reason given for the selection of AD 1290 as the older range. The dates show a range of 850 to present, with GXO 516 and 519 ranging from AD 1365 to 1750 at a 95 per cent level of confidence and AD 1435–1660 at a 65 per cent level of confidence. This puts Bigo plainly in the fifteenth to seventeenth centuries, too late by Oliver's reasoning. When the GXO 517 and 518 dates are included, the conclusion is further weighted toward the younger side.

Although the general interpretation of these results suggests that Bigo is connected with Bacwezi tales, Posnansky (fig. 15:5) maintains a judicious balance in his final appraisal, an appraisal that deserves close attention: 'there are no descriptive accounts about the site itself and many of the traditions would appear to have been invented later to explain the presence of such earthworks' (Posnansky 1969: 143). This final assessment by Posnansky isolates several of the major problems with the Bigo oral data and it shows that at the end Posnansky agreed that there are no oral traditions that ascribe Bigo to the Bacwezi, let alone to a Bacwezi dynasty. So, the archaeological attempt to verify the alleged Bacwezi oral traditions was fraught with problems from its inception. It was based on a false premise derived from a distorted and seriously misrepresented body of oral traditions. Posnansky acted out of a genuine concern to advance the cause of archaeology and history in East Africa. In the end he expressed grave doubts, but the pre-publication interpretation of his data associated him with interpretative positions about which he harboured significant reservations. The Bigo excavations hardly offered Oliver the proof for which he was looking. If anything, they have introduced much more profound questions about the reliability of the putative oral traditions about Bigo. Given the history toward fabrication, substitution, and manipulation of the so-called oral traditions about the Bacwezi at Bigo, we must reject such alleged oral traditions until reasonable scholarly attribution is forthcoming.

Subsequent experiments in verification

Posnansky's pioneering and important work with oral traditions and archaeology in Uganda began in 1959 with a variation on the verification approach applied to excavations at the Bweyorere capital site in Ankole. His goals were explicit and straightforward. He wanted 'to ascertain whether the traditions are a reliable guide for archaeology in Uganda' (Posnansky 1968: 165). The Bweyorere site presented a complex diachronic settlement history in terms of the associated oral traditions – mostly derived from a translation of Katate's royal history of Ankole. Those royal oral traditions claimed that the site had been occupied in at least three different generations, possibly four. It was probable that three kings had sucessively occupied the site during the later eighteenth and early nineteenth centuries and once twelve generations ago. Posnansky recognized that the later occupation period would be difficult to sub-divide by archaeological criteria.

The most specific oral traditions concerned the second (possibly the third according to another account) royal to occupy the site, approximately at the beginning of the nineteenth century. This king was said to have been murdered by his brother and his body subsequently burned in his palace by his sister. Posnansky's appraisal of the excavations was that there were two main occupation periods – which generally agrees with the oral traditions. Moreover, he found evidence for a large burned structure, which he attributed to the murdered and cremated king, Karara. While he found the radiocarbon dates rather ambiguous, they appear to jibe with the oral traditions. GXO 520 came from a post hole and appears to date the earliest occupation: AD 1640 ± 95. The second, Y-1394, was derived from a structure that dated to AD 1820 ± 80 and corresponds to the later phase of the second, multi-generation occupation.[3]

In the latter case we are not told if the date is associated with the burned structure, but it appears that the dating of structural evidence at Bweyorere affirms the general outline of the oral traditions about the settlement of this royal site. These results gave rise to Vansina's hopeful assessment in the mid-1960s and they certainly suggest that other such sites, especially those with more time-restricted settlement histories and with detailed oral traditions, would lend themselves to archaeological investigations. Clearly, the value of oral traditions in such contexts are directly related to specific details about a king's reign that may have direct archaeological corrolaries, such as the burned palace of Karara. Posnansky's initial success at Bweyorere, then, was an important one for the verification approach in East Africa, one that should not be overshadowed by Bigo.

While Posnansky was able to bring together published oral traditions and archaeological data at Bweyorere, similar research in the same culture zone using published accounts has not fared as well and proves the adage about the necessity of first hand, in-depth research. The capital site of the former kingdom of Karagwe in north-west Tanzania was the focus of test excavations in 1970. Unable readily to locate local informants, I relied on the published accounts of Israel Katoke on Karagwe's royal history. Katoke, using a manuscript written by a local historian, noted that the father of the famous king Rumanyika was a widely renowned iron-worker (Katoke 1969, 1975). This king, Ndagara, is reckoned to have ruled from the Bweranyange capital site during the second quarter of the nineteenth century. The oral traditions, according to Katoke, claim that this king manufactured iron on the capital site:

> His 'scientific' curiosity especially about what lay under the earth's surface and what happened to his departed ancestors led him to dig an underground ditch or tunnel, hoping that he would finally reach the centre of the earth where he would find his departed relations. Soon after digging a few yards he discovered that his project was a fruitless effort so he decided to abandon it. Even so, he directed his talents to something else, the forging and manufacturing of metal works. ... Ndagara's decision to embark on this elaborate project was also precipitated by the awareness of the iron deposit in Karagwe. He dug a horse-shoe shaped

ditch at the rear of the royal enclosure which he used as a workshop. He smelted iron from special stones 'obutare' and forged iron from which he made the now famed metal objects. (Katoke 1969: 108)

A quick walk-over of the Bweranyange site reveals that there is indeed a large shaft in the southern part of the site and that adze marks can be seen in the exposed iron stone of the shaft walls. From the deeper shaft there is a serpentine, semi-circular barrow (the horse-shoe shaped pit?) that apparently followed a vein of iron ore. One problem with this 'oral tradition' is that its source is not revealed. Furthermore, it may be a reworked account that attributes the shaft, horse-shoe shaped pit, and iron artefacts to Ndagara because he is tied to other oral traditions regarding iron-working.

The 'testimony' has the tone of a rationalized attempt to explain obvious features by attributing them to Ndagara. This points out some of the problems of working with second-hand accounts. The Bweranyange test excavations, however, did show that the centre of the site, perhaps in the centre of the royal compound, was a locus of iron-forging. The excavations also revealed that the shaft with its contiguous semi-circular pit was indeed an iron-ore mine. Most interesting, though, was that the bottom of the shaft had received a child burial, with a large riveted iron pot laid across its pelvis. We cannot attribute these activities to Ndagara on the basis of the published oral traditions, but the Bweranyange excavations point to the fact that iron-working took place in the royal compound and that iron-mining occurred on site. The issue of Ndagara and his possible association with such features will remain unclear as long as there are not more definitive oral traditions with clear-cut attributions.

The application of the verification approach to Ugandan sites has been followed by similar research in West Africa. Let us turn to several selected case studies that illustrate this experimental approach. In all of Africa, the most significant and truly grand earthworks are found in Benin City, Nigeria. These earthworks, a veritable mazeway, extend over a linear distance of some 16,000 km (Darling 1984). Benin has been a focus of historical and archaeological research for several decades, most notably by G. Connah and P.J. Darling. Prominent among the research goals at Benin has been the attempt to correlate oral traditions with the history of the town walls. Connah (1975) exclusively used the already published oral traditions that claim that Benin was founded in the mid-fifteenth century by Oba Oguola. Connah obtained a radiocarbon date of AD 1305 ± 105 for the inner city wall and a date of AD 1340 ± 105 for a pottery pavement that he attributed to the reconstruction of the palace, which also occurred during the mid-fifteenth-century according to some interpretations of the oral traditions. The radiometric dates fall within the attributed period at a 95 per cent level of confidence, but they appear too early at a 65 per cent level of confidence. According to others such as Willet (1960b), the reign of the Oba Oguola dates to the late fourteenth century, an interpretation more in accord with the findings of Connah. Clearly, the variability of interpretations over the chronological character of the oral traditions influences the overall synthetic chronological interpretations and points to the necessity of a great plenitude of radiometric dates and ceramic sequences from a variety of structural features attributed to various periods of Benin history.

The complexity of the Benin City site is overwhelming, and it has continued to evade better dating by archaeologists (Darling 1984). Darling, for example, projects from his study of Benin that its origins may well lie in the first millennium AD or even earlier. Darling in his documentation of the earthworks paid close attention to oral traditions and oral histories about the walls, but does little with them to try to illuminate the history of the structures, nor do the oral traditions provide sufficient specific detail to be helpful.

If the research at Benin has not yielded the kind of results hoped for, it is partly the result of the absence of a well reasoned research design to deal with the oral traditions. This is not the case with the research of Susan and Roderick McIntosh, who have also been influenced by the teaching of Merrick Posnansky. The McIntoshes have concentrated their attention on the history and prehistory of Jenne-jeno, the community that was the predecessor to Jenne in Mali. The McIntoshes have employed both recorded oral traditions along with oral traditions that they have collected themselves. These they juxtapose against the conventional ethnohistory touching on Jenne as written by early Arab and European observers.

The interpretations of ethnohistories hold that Jenne was founded in the Islamic era, no earlier than the thirteenth century (McIntosh and McIntosh 1980a: 55–9; 1980b). However, indigenous oral traditions as recorded in documents such as the *Ta'rikh es Sudan* claim that Jenne-jeno or Zorobo, just to the south of the later city, was founded by the eighth century AD. Regardless of the ethnic diversity in the region, the McIntoshes found that the accounts that they collected corroborated the accounts recorded much earlier. The excavations of Jenne-jeno are important not only for establishing the much earlier incidence of trade in the inland Niger delta, but also because they definitively show that Jenne-jeno had developed into an urban centre between AD 400 and 900. (McIntosh and McIntosh 1980a, 1980b).[4] This generally confirms the validity of the oral traditions of the founding of this early urban centre and it illustrates Vansina's observation that such oral traditions are often not exactly correct but that they do correctly focus on the considerable antiquity of certain places – in this case more accurately than the written accounts by outsiders.

There are a host of other experiments in West Africa that have attempted to use oral traditions in one variety or another of the verification approach, many of them inspired directly or indirectly by Posnansky's teaching and research. Keteku's research at Akwamu Amanfoso (Old Akwamu) at Nyanawase, Ghana, for example, focusses on the reputed capital site of the Akwamu kingdom (Keteku 1978, 1984). Keteku's excavations provide a set of dates that have large standard deviations and fall predominantly in the range of late eighteenth to mid-nineteenth centuries. Given that most samples are obtained from strata without tobacco pipes, the interpretations of these dates are suspect (McIntosh and McIntosh 1986). They contradict Ozanne's earlier research at the same site, based on tobacco-pipe sequences as well as documentary and oral tradition, that indicated that the queen's quarter had been abandoned by 1660, or about seventy years earlier than the rest of the town (*ibid.*; Ozanne 1971). Keteku's dates when viewed at two standard deviations fall between 1460 and 1950, concordant with the more precise evidence offered by Ozanne.

From verification to synthesis

As a concluding vignette to this essay, I want to discuss the history of methodology in oral tradition by turning to my own research in Buhaya, north-west Tanzania. I do this for several reasons. I have already pointed out that this research also touches on the Bacwezi, but that the results lead us to very different methods and conclusions (Schmidt 1978; 1983b). While the research began at the end of the 1960s with a verification approach in mind, it has evolved to one in which a structural, symbolic approach has utility in sorting out the function and meaning of certain oral traditions. It is hoped that this example might show the way for similar approaches in other African cultures to which its application may be appropriate. When I conducted initial oral tradition research in 1969–70, I was working within the same set of assumptions that guided Posnansky at Bigo, i.e. that the Bacwezi were a pre-Babito and pre-Hinda dynasty. But the realities of oral traditions in the kingdom of Kiamutwara soon caused me to shift away from this perspective and to acknowledge Bacwezi oral traditions as a body of oral literature that was exceedingly ancient and subject to periodic manipulations by groups vying for power and legitimacy.

One of the key observations resulting from the Haya research is that oral traditions held by social groups that claim descent from the Bacwezi are central to unlocking the riddle of sites associated with the Bacwezi. In particular, it became clear through the testimony of the oral traditions themselves that such groups were associated with iron-working, rain-making and fertility. All of these characteristics are woven together as a part of an ideological system that surrounds iron-working and control of the political economy based on iron production. Political power was closely tied to association and identity with the symbolism, myth and ritual surrounding the productive economy based on iron production (Schmidt 1983b). In addition, those groups who were recognized as legitimate were those who practised the Bacwezi religion and maintained Bacwezi oral traditions. These observations led, inevitably, to the recognition that the Bacwezi should not be taken literally as a political dynasty, but that Bacwezi-led groups were social-economic entities that maintained political power by virtue of their control over a religious system that incorporated the symbolism of fertility associated with iron production.

Legitimacy is the central concept that arises out of the Haya studies. Those groups that occupied space that was identified with Bacwezi symbols and myth could gain control over the productive economy and political power and authority. Thus, the key attributes for sorting out Bacwezi oral traditions and their material correlates lie in: (1) identification of social groups that claim Bacwezi descent and are associated with iron-working; (2) the location of sacred sites revered by such groups and attributed to Bacwezi gods and/or aetiological events; and (3) the symbolic association of iron and fertility with such sacred sites. The conclusions of this research pose contradictions to the Bacwezi/Bigo construct, for it sees the Bacwezi phenomenon as an ancient process in which history, myth and symbol were manipulated by social groups as a means to power (control over iron-working) and political legitimacy.

This conclusion was affirmed by archaeological investigations at the Rugomora Mahe site, where an early Iron Age forge dating to c. 500 BC (uncalibrated) was located by oral traditions associated with a huge shrine tree named Kaijja, meaning the place of the forge. The tree was linked with oral traditions about an iron tower that was allegedly built by Rugomora Mahe, the first and only Bahinda king to occupy the site. The ancient forge and the traditions about its use in building the iron tower were clearly not Bahinda phenomena. Rather, they were aspects of the cultural landscape that had been appropriated by the Bahinda in their attempt to wrest power from the Bacwezi clans. Structural analysis of the oral traditions further revealed that Bacwezi mythemes had been integrated into the Bahinda royal traditions, a process that was parallel to the Hinda co-opting the aetiological myth for iron and their occupation of the sacred site that once belonged to the Bayango clan, those of Bacwezi descent who were iron-workers and rain-makers.

Bahinda occupation of the site occurred twelve generations ago, or approximately AD 1650 to 1675 if we reckon 25–27 years to a generation. Archaeological evidence from the central ritual area in the site, attributed to the death rituals commemorating king Rugomora Mahe, also affirms the genealogical evidence. There is a remarkably tight fit among genealogical evidence, oral traditions about function of the central area, the structure of archaeological features, and radiometric dating. Two highly stratified pit features located in the ritual zone where the king's burial hut (for his jawbone) was located were dated to AD 1645 ± 120 and AD 1700 ± 100. At a level of confidence of 65 per cent, the dates range from AD 1525 to 1800. While the large standard deviations show some of the difficulties of working with radiocarbon dating on more recent sites, it is non the less significant that the dates straddle the time period that we would normally assign on genealogical grounds.

Bahinda dynastic occupation of the ancient Bayango/Bacwezi shrine marked a major turning point in the history of Kiamutwara kingdom. The Kaiija shrine was symbolic space intimately linked with the productive economy controlled by the Bacwezi clans. How long the Bacwezi clans had controlled the Kaiija shrine is an open question, but there is every reason to believe that clans such as the Bayango date to the earliest period of occupation along the Lake Victoria shore. It is certainly more than coincidence that the site of the early Iron Age forge was still remembered and specifically pointed out in the oral traditions. Part of the process of continuity in its preservation undoubtedly rests with the maintenance of the shrine as a sacred, symbolic place over several millennia. The oral evidence points to continuity of use and importance over time. The fact that the Bacwezi are consistently associated with shrines that date to the early Iron Age in Buhaya shows either that they indeed are an ancient religious/political phenomenon on the landscape or that they, too, co-opted such sites from older social groups in the region. The latter seems unlikely, for the oral histories suggest that the Bacwezi clans are the most ancient residents of the area along the lake shore, an area that has been continuously occupied over the last 2000 years.

The fact that the Kaiija shrine is such an important part of the symbolic system surrounding fertility and iron-working is another major element in our attempts to understand the Bacwezi of Bwera, Uganda. Iron-smelting is a reproductive process in which the smelting furnace is metaphorically represented as a woman. Fertility is symbolically linked to Bahaya iron-smelting when the iron-smelters act out the role of ritual officials who bless women and their iron hoes to insure their fertility. Wedding songs sung to the furnace during iron-smelting celebrate its symbolic impregnation by the sexually hot smelters, and ritual medicines used in the furnace ensure its fertility. Human fecundity and iron production are closely woven together in a symbolic system that is particularly richly developed at the Kaiija shrine tree (Schmidt 1983a; 1983b). There the iron tower is the central metaphor. Surrounding place names show that it is a beating phallus that prepares the way for sexual intercourse by stimulating the production of vaginal fluid (*ibid.*).

The iron tower as phallus is an interpretation suggested by the local place names themselves. But it is only a part of a much more complex ritual and symbolic system that encompasses all of iron-working and Bacwezi myth. We must also remember that in Buhaya one of the chief figures of the Bacwezi pantheon, Irungu, is the patron spirit for iron-working. His domain extends to the hinterlands where iron ore, clays and charcoal are obtained as well as where iron-smelting often took place.

I now want to turn to a final consideration of the value of the experiment at Bigo. There is no question that Posnansky's conceptualization of the problem was sound, in so far as one may give credence to the verification approach. Even though there was no conjunction between oral evidence and the archaeological data, the approach and the hope that it offered to those studying the recent prehistory of Africa cannot be denied. Posnansky has acknowledged that much more work needs to be done at Bigo to sort out the occupational history of the site. I agree with that assessment with the provisos given above, but hasten to add that much more attention should be paid to the later oral traditions that claim that there were a number of periods of use on the site. More careful attention to these variants may help to build a more complex use history that is not locked into the preoccupation of proving the presence of a Bacwezi dynasty.

The Bigo experiment has stimulated further experiments in developing methodologies that bring together oral traditions and archaeology.[5] The Buhaya research had its genesis in this approach, even though it has taken a very different direction. Van Noten's research with the royal tombs of Rwanda is also derived from the same intellectual tradition. One of the anomalies that has arisen out of Van Noten's investigation of the Rwanda royal tombs is the discovery of early Iron Age pottery in the excavations of two tombs (Van Noten 1972). It was Van Noten's goal to verify by archaeology the oral traditions for the royal house of Rwanda. Previously recorded oral traditions were used to locate the royal burial sites, but in most cases Van Noten found no burials. The traditional tomb of Mutara I – dated by oral traditions to 1648 – was associated with early Iron Age pottery and radiocarbon dated to 230 BC (Maret *et al*. 1977). And, the royal grave of Mutara II was also found to contain early Iron Age pottery and was dated to the mid-third century AD (Van Noten 1972). These findings are no surprise, for Van Noten's results parallel the Buhaya research. The empty tombs located in ancient places are important because they illustrate a process by which a dynasty gains and affirms its legitimacy through identity with ancient places – a process that creates the illusion of continuity with the past. This often involves control over sacred, symbolic space that has been revered and associated with ruling groups since ancient times. We see this explicitly expressed in Rugomora's appropriation of Kaiija shrine and the myth of the iron tower.

If we have learned anything of importance in this endeavour to marry oral traditions with archaeology, it is the lesson that oral traditions often identify processes of transformation, and are symbolic renderings of historical manipulations that mask changes in political and economic power. This is an important realization, but it also demands that we set aside literal and facile treatments of oral traditions, that we embark upon much more serious collection of oral histories and traditions in the field, and that we submit the evidence to rigorous analysis. One of the hopes of the future is the application of structural and symbolic analysis to oral traditions because such analyses, especially with genealogically articulated oral traditions, allow us to isolate periods of major change. As oral histories often touch on political history, ritual history, economic history, and religious history we have the hope of diagnosing when change is coeval in two or more of these domains of history. Such change, once documented, can then be related to the archaeological record to see if it corresponds to change in access to economic resources, technology, settlement patterns, political centres, ritual centres and subsistence.

Notes

1 Baines spelled it Nalubongoya. Gray does not make clear why he changed the spelling if the oral tradition could not be verified.
2 None of the four sources Oliver cites, e.g. K.W., Nyakatura, Katate and Kamagungunu, and Gorju, specifically support this claim.
3 At a 95 per cent level of confidence the two dates range (uncalibrated) between AD 1450 to 1830 and 1660 to present. This overlap does admit the possibility that only one occupation was dated.
4 The urban development phase has now been refined to AD 300–800, during which time a city wall was built, copper appeared (AD 400), and gold appeared (AD 800) (McIntosh and McIntosh 1986).
5 I am personally indebted to Merrick Posnansky for his inspirational teaching in the field of oral traditions and archaeology. I had the good fortune to study at Makerere University during 1966 when he was actively engaged in this early research.

16 *The Study of Rock Art in Africa*

WHITNEY DAVIS

No short review could survey all aspects of a century of research on African rock art or what is currently believed about rock art throughout Africa (see Willcox 1984; Smith 1982: 397–400; Camps 1982: 608–11; Striedter 1984; Phillipson 1977a: 268–90; Lewis-Williams 1983a). Instead, a few representative and influential studies have been chosen here to illustrate different assumptions guiding the collection, organization and interpretation of evidence and to typify the approaches of different scholars, schools or moments in the intellectual development of research. A comprehensive documentation of all contributions can be found in several bibliographies (Gaskin 1965; Striedter 1983: 264–87; Davis 1979; Vinnicombe 1976: 369–78; Willcox 1984: 267–79).

1 The exploratory reports

Rock pictures were observed by Europeans in Southern Africa as early as the middle of the eighteenth century (Rudner and Rudner 1970: 245–68) and in North Africa, the Sahara and the Nile Valley at least by the middle of the nineteenth (see comprehensive review in Flamand 1921). By the turn of this century, many casual reports had accumulated, reflecting the penetration of the continent by colonial administrators and adventurers, commercial and military expeditions, and scientific surveys.

Despite their ephemerality, the earliest exploratory reports set the tone for later work. The weathered appearance, alien style and exotic subjects of rock pictures immediately suggested their probable antiquity and possible associations with vanished peoples. These conclusions naturally fuelled further exploration and the interest of historians.

Almost as soon as rock pictures were reported, they were described as 'art'. Whether regarded as 'primitive' or surprisingly accomplished, with the exception of geometric symbols most images were evaluated qualitatively in European aesthetic terms. Reflecting the conventions of western art, observers singled out the purely graphic and compositional features of individual striking images and copied them as self-sufficient wholes. An early metaphor was repeated well into the twentieth century: the rock art of Africa was a prehistoric 'art gallery' or 'museum', where pictures are displayed for our aesthetic contemplation – and, by implication, that of their makers – and value is attached to the visible surface qualities of a finished artefact. Even when recognized as ancient and alien, rather than being felt as irrevocably distant rock pictures evoked a more romantic antiquarianism: a modern observer could look directly into the world of the past. Like the people or the resources of Africa, the past of the continent was initially felt to be unproblematically available to the European consciousness.

Reports of the discovery of rock pictures gradually attracted the notice of scholars with a professional interest or background in history, archaeology or the arts. Some, like Henri Breuil, had studied prehistoric arts elsewhere; some, like Walter Battiss in Southern Africa, were professional artists; some, like Hans Winkler in the deserts of Egypt, were ethnographers; some, like Maurice Reygasse in the Sahara, were archaeologists; some, like Leo Frobenius, were independent scholar-adventurers with theories to prove. Along with a number of amateurs able to devote their leisure to recording rock art, these writers synthesized a mass of casual reports, followed up on superficial explorations and opened new territories, developed methods of recording still in use today, examined particular issues (e.g., rock patination), and put forward the first systematic chronologies and attributions.

2 North Africa and the Sahara: criteria for a typology and chronology

Building from the pioneering descriptions of E.E.F. Gautier (1904) and motif-typological approach of F. de Zeltner (1913b), G.-B.-M. Flamand's monumental *Pierres écrites (Hadjrat-Mektoubat)* (1921) summarized all previous research on North African engravings and included a long excursus on rock art traditions around the world. The distribution of engravings was surveyed and indexed by locale. The core of the work was, first, a sophisticated analysis of '*le facies*' of engravings (their morphology, including patina, technique, and, less clearly, style or '*l'esthétique*'), based on many dozens of examples and illustrated mostly by line-sketches. Flamand paid microscopic attention to the way engravings were made (e.g., the depth, direction, and cross-section of incisions), extracting inferences about the step-by-step procedures – by implication, the schemata and conventions – of the engravers. No comparably detailed technical study has ever appeared again in the study of African rock art.

Second, although not the first to propose it, Flamand articulated what became the standard classification of North African engraving as belonging to 'prehistoric', 'Libyco-Berber' and 'modern' (Arab) groups. First justified on epigraphic and iconographic grounds, Flamand's classification also noted many technical differences between engravings belonging to the different groups. Flamand felt that from the prehistoric to the historic periods rock-engraving deteriorated from a realistic to a schematic style.

Third, Flamand remarked many stylistic and iconographic parallels between North African engravings and Gerzean (Nagada II/III) pottery decoration and early dynastic carved ivories, palettes, and small-scale sculpture in Egypt (c. 4500–3100 BC). The Egyptian connection continued to occupy a major place in the study of North African rock art (see Smith 1968: 16–20).

An early entry in the series of publications Frobenius and his expeditions were to offer over the next quarter-century, Frobenius and Obermaier's *Hadschra Maktuba* (1925) focussed on engravings in Algeria. In its emphasis on '*Stilgeschichte, Kulturkreise und Geistigkeit*' (history of style, culture-areas and spirituality), Frobenius' later 'culture-morphological' work – like *Ekade Ektab* (1937), on the Libyan Fezzan – moved away from the descriptive empiricism and relatively cautious typologies espoused by Obermaier in 1925. Obermaier followed Flamand's periodization and soberly considered North African rock art in comparison to south-western European evidence and 'in the light of prehistoric research'. He extracted inferences from the engravings about the climate, fauna, and human populations of the region (see fig. 16:1).

In grouping engravings into manageable sets, Frobenius and Obermaier, like Flamand, made considerable use of a stylistic measure of 'naturalism', ranging engravings as very schematic, '*halbnaturalistisch*', quite naturalistic, etc., on a continuous scale. Although very popular in later writing, the anchors of this scale – non-figuration at one end and illusion at the other? – were never clearly specified. They derived as much from the experience of modern art in Europe – photography and Realism, Impressionism, abstraction – as much as from any general logical or psychological consider- ations (although see Solignac 1928: 12–16; Lefèbvre 1967): the naturalistic was that which a modern observer judges to be an evocatively faithful impression or illusion of a subject produced by an artist attending to 'reality'. In an important later article, Obermaier (1931) insisted on the correlation between 'naturalism' and an early (post-Pleistocene, pre- Libyco-Berber) date for some engravings; the measure of naturalism took on an archaeological as well as aesthetic sense.

Unlike Flamand's work, *Hadschra Maktuba* included many photographs of rock art in context and watercolour copies of whole surfaces, but, like Flamand, Frobenius and Obermaier also prepared tables presenting examples of individual motifs brought together from separate sites as morphologically similar. In this procedure, prehistorians may have intended to do for rock pictures what typologists had been doing with stone tools – finding similarity-sets within certain collections of artefacts and positing 'cultures', 'traditions' or 'styles' as their source. With few exceptions, the measurement of similarity was conducted intuitively.

Later empirical work in northern Africa was dominated by French prehistorians applying the lessons of Flamand and Frobenius and Obermaier. New finds were continually published (e.g., Reygasse 1935; Chasseloup-Laubat 1938). For the western Sahara, in his major synthetic study Theodore Monod (1938) attempted to correlate different motif-types (e.g., chariots, personnages with javelins and shields) with other traits of the engravings (e.g., 7 types of technique, 6 types of patination), hoping to isolate regularities, but ultimately concluded that 'more than patina, technique, and style, the content of the rock art material remains the most important element for establishing a classification' (p. 128). Since the desired classification was chronological and culture-historical, the subject- matter of rock pictures would have to be partitioned into distinct groups (one phase or epoch from the next), and the images themselves would probably have to be regarded as documentary. As Monod himself later recognized (1963), both of these background assumptions proved to be very troublesome.

Although Flamand, Reygasse and Obermaier regarded the earliest 'naturalistic' engravings as post-Pleistocene (Neolithic), the convictions of Herbert Kühn (1927) and Breuil (1931), two principal authorities on ice- age art, were sufficient for many scholars to hold to a Palaeolithic date (see Smith 1968: 8). Obermaier (1931) based his argument largely on recognizing the 'domesticated' animals of Neolithic times among these engravings, but his emblems of domestication – discs between the horns of the rams, collars and neck-ornaments on various animals – have been found in depictions of wild fauna as well (Huard and Massip 1964); despite Monod's hopes, iconography would not necessarily provide clear-cut dates. Raymond Vaufrey (1936, 1938, 1939), very suspicious of purely sty- listic dating, linked engravings of bovids, human beings, and *spirales* with the 'Neolithic of Capsian tradition', an industry associated in the main non-stratigraphically but almost exclusively with these images in several locales in the southern Maghreb and exhibiting parallels with predynastic and dynastic Egyptian cultures. On this basis Vaufrey dated the engravings to 4500–3000 BC at the earliest; they reflected 'borrowing' from Egypt by the populations of the Sahara – '*c'est le "fait colonial"* ' or 'colonial effect' (1938: 29).

Measures of relative naturalism, motif-types and trans-regional similarity provided the scaffolding for the archaeology of rock art: with Vaufrey's tentative chronology in mind, Mauny (1955b), Butzer (1958), and especially Henri Lhote (1959) clearly distinguished between engravings of the *Bubalus* and polychrome paintings of the 'bovidian pastoralist' styles as successive periods of prehistoric rock art. The older *Bubalus* phase was characterized by the 'naturalistic' representation of rams with 'discs' between the horns (Huard 1961; Lhote 1964), giraffe and other large wild fauna, especially the extinct *Bubalus antiquus* (*Homoïceras antiquus*) (a giant wild bovid) (fig. 16:1). Later discoveries again pushed the earliest date for this 'hunters' art', at least in the Tadrart Acacus (south-west Libya), to as early as 9000 BC (Mori 1974). The bovidians of the fifth-third millennia BC (Mori 1965; Van Noten 1978) depicted cattle, evidently fully domesticated, and a variety of social and economic activities. In the 'historic' periods, a horse or chariot (fig. 16:2) and a camel group were comfortably distinguished (Lhote 1953; Mauny 1955; Camps and Gast 1982).

As Monod, Lhote and other writers insisted, not all features or phases of all of these four major style-periods could be found everywhere in North Africa and the Sahara. Studying the paintings of Tassili, Lhote (1959) inserted an intermediate prehistoric style-period, the 'Round Head', a 'symbolic' style characterized by giant human figures with rounded, often featureless heads. In all, he identified 16 'stages' and 30 'styles' at Tassili (see Monod 1963: 183). Although some prehistorians associated different styles with different Neolithic traditions (see Smith 1982: 399), at Tibesti Paul Huard (1960) found them to be evolutionarily continuous, recognizing an 'archaic phase' of incipiently bovidian art quite close to the engraving of the preceding 'Neolithic hunters' (see also Fuchs 1957), and at Oued Djerat (Tassili) Lhote (1975) did not recognize any break between engravings of the *Bubalus* and bovidian pastoralist periods. Even at the present time the overall picture of Saharan development (Striedter 1984) is complicated by different and sometimes conflicting regional chronologies; the lack of well confirmed absolute dates or archaeological associations means it is always possible to reshuffle or even invert certain sequences (see, for instance, important re-evaluations by Muzzolini and Kolmer (1982, 1983)).

3 The Nile Valley: constituting an independent culture-historical record

Early on, some engravings found on the Nile cliffs or in the wadis and nearby deserts of the Nile Valley were recognized as predating the Egyptian dynastic period (De Morgan 1896: 162–4; Schweinfurth 1912), even as 'Palaeolithic' (Capart 1905: 206), leading to an uneasy division of labour in the study of north-eastern African rock art.

Some engravings could be used as evidence of Pharaonic history, written, in Egyptology, largely on textual rather than material grounds. These engravings had been produced by expeditions of Egyptian soldiers and workmen and were often accompanied by Egyptian inscriptions. Examined

16:1 *Engravings of the* Bubalus *period, Sahara-Atlas (Er-Richa, Ain Sfasafa, Ksar el-Ahmar) (after Kuper 1978)*

16:2 *Engravings of the horse or chariot period, Tassili-n-Ajjer (Oued Djerat) (after Kuper 1978)*

by epigraphers committed to the Egyptological paradigm (Spiegelberg 1921, Černý 1947, Goyon 1957), this material was integrated
unproblematically into their narrative of Egyptian history.

However, other pictures might be novel evidence of the pre- and proto-
dynastic periods (e.g., Green 1903; Cottevieille-Giraudet 1931; Scharff
1942; Massoulard 1949: 91–106), not well known through ordinary
documentary sources, or even evidence of otherwise unknown early
populations. Possibly they provided a glimpse of cultures which were
eclipsed by Egyptian civilization and occluded by the Egyptological
narrative. As with other aspects of north-east African archaeology, the
study of rock art became increasingly independent of Egyptology. This
development was not without tension or contradiction and has not yet been
resolved.

Although prehistorians working in North Africa perceived connections
between rock art in the Sahara and in the Nile Valley (Vaufrey 1938), due to
gaps in communication and the isolation of Egyptology this insight was not
followed up systematically until the 1960s (Huard 1964; Donadoni 1964;
Leclant 1973; Huard and Leclant 1980). Rock art in the Nile Valley was set
apart from the rest of northern Africa, 'though it is doubtful that this
distinction can be justified on any grounds except geographical
convenience' (Smith 1968: 4).

For Egyptologists, the rock art of the Nile Valley was known chiefly
through the work of Hans Winkler and J.H. Dunbar – an ethnographer
and a prehistorian who insisted on the antiquity of some engravings and
their usefulness in reconstructing pre-Pharaonic cultural history. Dunbar
(1934, 1941) recorded many engravings in lower Nubia (see fig. 16:3).
Winkler (1939) associated the rock art of Gebel Uweinat, 600 km due west
of Wadi Halfa, already well known to some scholars (e.g., Newbold 1928;
Kamal el-Dine and Breuil 1928), with the predynastic art of the Nile
Valley, recalling parallels noted by several writers, like Breuil (1931)
(although see Van Noten 1978: 32–3). Whereas Egyptologists, committed
to Herodotos' famous dictum that Egypt was the 'gift of the Nile', had
traditionally focussed on the cultivated river-valley, Dunbar and Winkler
expanded the range of important evidence substantially south and west – a
development which exerted a strong influence on the later work of non-
Egyptological prehistorians in north-eastern Africa (e.g., Butzer 1958;
Trigger 1965; McHugh 1975). However, this achievement was not
immediately seen as implying the need for a culture-history of north-east
Africa truly alternative to that based on Egyptian texts and official images.

Winkler's principal interest (1934, 1937, 1938–9) was in the subject-
matter of engravings in the eastern and western deserts of southern Upper
Egypt. He outlined what could be learned from engravings about the dress,
weapons, physical characteristics and daily life – the *Völkerbewegungen* or
folkways – of prehistoric populations, in the tradition of German
ethnological connoisseurship pioneered in the Nile Valley by the Africanist
Felix von Luschan (1897, 1922), adopted by Egyptological art historians
(e.g., Klebs 1915), and attempted elsewhere by other scholars of rock art.
Concluding that the engravings depicted the folkways of several different
ethnic groups, Winkler produced an influential reconstruction with its
own internal consistency. Although he participated in archaeological
re-connaissance (Bagnold 1939, see McHugh 1975), the material record of
prehistoric life in the Egyptian 'deserts' was still too meagre to provide any
real test of his culture-historical inferences. He used archaeological data
about rock-pictures – superimposition, patination – only to work out the
spatial and temporal interrelations of the groups already identified by an

16:3 *Engraving of cattle pastoralist period, fourth–second millennium BC, Nubia (Sayala) (after Resch 1967)*

ethnological analysis.

Arab, 'Blemmyan' and Coptic pictures and signs (1938: 10–17) could be distinguished from dynastic Egyptian and from 'undatable early, predynastic, and prehistoric pictures'. Winkler (1937) initially identified five different ethnic groups as authors of the undatable drawings, later (1938) collapsed into four. Commonly depicting the elephant and giraffe, hunted with nets, traps, and a big C-shaped bow, the 'earliest hunters' worked in a 'coarse' but technically accomplished style (see Huard 1965; Huard and Leclant 1980). They were displaced by 'autochthonous mountain-dwellers', inhabiting the uplands for several millennia, a Hamitic cattle-breeding people related to the 'Amratians' of the valley who in the 'deserts' gradually evolved distinctive folkways. Rhotert (1952) later suggested that these Hamites moved further into the Sahara, where their contact with indigenous hunters who had produced the *Bubalus* engravings gave rise to the 'bovidian pastoral' painting (see also Butzer 1958; Huard 1964; Huard and Leclant 1980). Winkler's desert Hamites were 'separated by the police of a strong, well-organized state' (1939: 19) which grew up in the valley itself. This state was the achievement of a third group whose drawings could be seen in the desert, 'early Nile-dwellers' who plied the river in boats with standards like those depicted on predynastic Gerzean pottery, evidently in contact with a fourth group, 'eastern invaders' – probably 'Mesopotamian foreigners' – who used a high-prowed, straight-hulled boat. Presumably in the late predynastic period, the mountain-dwellers, Nile-dwellers and invaders lived contemporaneously (1938: 35) (fig. 16:3). Later, Winkler (1939: 34–5) added a new fifth group, 'Oasis dwellers' of the Dakhleh depression, sharing the resources of the north-west desert with the hunters.

Although the various shifts in Winkler's attributions were perhaps a sign of their insecurity, his culture-history was largely consistent with the rather tendentious account of the early development of Egypt promoted by Flinders Petrie and Henri Frankfort (see Hoffman 1979). His 'eastern invaders' played the part of Petrie's 'dynastic race' or Frankfort's incoming Mesopotamian culture-heroes. In rock art, Winkler saw the main evidence for the 'invasion' in the alleged difference between Nile and sea-faring vessels. (However, his detailed attempt (in 1938: 35–9) to describe these boat-types was so complex that later specialists (e.g., Engelmayer 1965) chose to abandon the distinction, athough it has had a countinuing life in Egyptology.) With Childe's (1934) stress on an indigenous 'Neolithic revolution', the dynastic race hypothesis lost favour; invaders became assimilated to Nile-dwellers, whose engravings Winkler assigned to the Egyptian predynastic period as the work of Gerzean (Nagada II–III) people, a conclusion later confirmed by archaeological associations (Bietak and Engelmayer 1963). The other groups had a much more shadowy existence in Winkler's narrative, perhaps because they did not appear at all in Egyptological evidence and hardly at all in other archaeological evidence: it was therefore to Winkler's credit that he attempted to write the 'earliest hunters' and nomadic pastoralists into the history of north-east Africa.

Winkler made less sense of depictions of fauna. For example, rather surprisingly, elephants and giraffe appeared in the engravings of *all* of his groups, including 'cattle-breeders' and 'invaders'. Implicitly avoiding Winkler's four- or five-fold ethnological classification, Dunbar (1941) suggested a single successive sequence from the depiction of large game (hunters) to cattle and boats (agriculturalists) (fig. 16:3) to Pharaonic and later themes. Presumably one people gradually changing its way of life made all the drawings.

Dunbar fixed a time-range for the hunter's game pictures as convincing as Winkler's Gerzean date for cattle-and-boat pictures. The level of the Nile flood had apparently fallen since Palaeolithic times. Following Sandford and Arkell (1933), Dunbar systematically plotted the relation of engravings to river level throughout lower Nubia (1941: pl. 26). Among other results, finding 'not a single elephant under the Upper Sebilian (water-) line' (high on the rocks and assessed at 7000 BC), this ingenious analysis suggested hunters could have been working as early as the late Palaeolithic period and certainly during the earliest predynastic (1941: 34). As the river-level fell, drawings appeared lower on the cliffs. This 'stratigraphic method' required tuning but has been confirmed in general (see Davis 1977, and compare Fock *et al.* 1980); seventh-millennium dates were later obtained for high-elevation engravings at Abka near Wadi Halfa (Myers 1958; Davis 1985a).

With the final publication of Frobenius' Upper Egyptian and Libyan material, collected in 1926 and 1933–5 (Rhotert 1952; Červíček 1974), with its additional evidence for 'nomadic pastoralism' (see also Rhotert and Kuper 1981), and explorations in the Nubian deserts (Resch 1963, 1967, 1969), it became clear that the history of rock art in north-eastern Africa was more complex than Winkler or Dunbar had imagined. Almost all regions of Egypt, Libya, and Nubia – once savannah, later desert or semi-desert – had been inhabited or traversed by image-making peoples. Prehistoric archaeology stimulated by the Nubian salvage campaign amply supported this view. Several expeditions each produced a *corpus* of rock-drawings (e.g., Almagro Basch and Almagro Gorbea 1968); in particular,

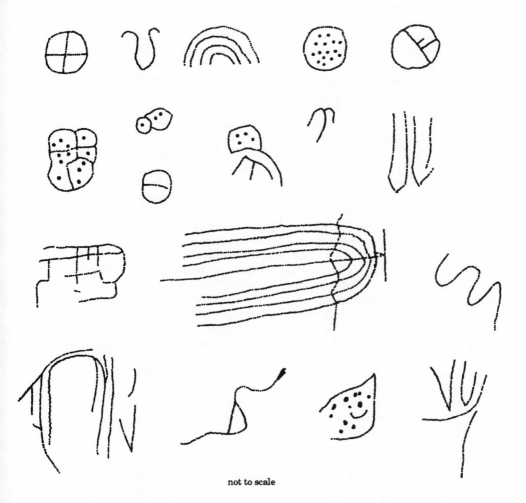

not to scale

16:4 *Abstract engravings, c. 7000–6000 BC, Nubia (Abka/ Wadi Halfa) (after Myers 1958)*

many associations were observed between Neolithic 'A-Group' assemblages and rock drawings near the second cataract (Hellström 1970) (fig. 16:4), filling in the fuzzy period between the late Palaeolithic and settled Pharaonic/C-Group agriculturalism in the valley. By the late 1960s, a complete culture-history based on rock art and other material evidence could be proposed confidently (Trigger 1969; Červíček 1974) – a history relatively well-integrated with Egyptological history but providing an independent record of *Völkerbewegungen* in north-eastern Africa. Winkler's and Dunbar's vision of an historical ethnology based on rock art was apparently tantalizingly within reach.

4 Sub-Saharan Africa: the continuity and discontinuity of traditions

In comparison with the north, the rock art of sub-Saharan Africa was accessible in relatively excellent copies. Tongue (1909) published watercolour copies of many compositions. The final publication of George W. Stow's copies of the 1870s (Bleek ed. 1930) attracted a good deal of attention. By 1952, paintings in over fifteen hundred localities in South

Africa had been noted (Van Riet Lowe 1952b). Willcox (1956) was perhaps the first investigator to use colour photography to record rock paintings, and in a special technique refined to an extraordinary level of accuracy and accomplishment Pager (1971) used oil-based paints to colour black-and-white photographs of rock paintings.

On the basis of such rich and relatively accessible evidence, scholars in Southern Africa devised elaborate classifications of the zones and phases of rock art production. However, some of the more notorious failures of this enterprise led, by the late 1950s, to a more marked withdrawal from this traditional empirical project in sub-Saharan studies than elsewhere.

In *South Africa's Past in Stone and Paint* (1928), Miles Burkitt synthesized contemporary knowledge of the distribution of southern rock art (see Schrire *et al.* 1986). Burkitt's ambition to introduce specialists and the public to Southern Africa's rich rock art was largely successful; despite its flaws, including the obvious superficiality of his site inspections and the haste with which the book was written, his approach had an enormous influence on later investigators. He stressed the 'archaeological' study of 'typology' (stylistic classification) and 'stratigraphy' (sequences based on superimposition), treating a rock picture as an archaeologist would treat a stone tool or other artefact. This conceptualization of the appropriate means of proceeding was not significantly challenged until the 1970s, when some writers began to doubt that rock pictures, as images or texts, could have the same status in an archaeological narrative as other artefacts (see below, sections 5 and 6). Burkitt's most basic typological and stratigraphical distinction between a 'red'-coloured group of paintings in southern Zimbabwe (with three successive phases) and the naturalistic polychrome animal paintings of Natal has withstood the test of time (Phillipson 1977a: 268–90). Burkitt took both sequences to evolve from a simple or crude through an accomplished ('wonderful', 'vigorous and attractive') to an ossified ('hard and angular') manner, judgments indebted to the organic theories of stylistic development promoted by historians of Graeco-Roman art. Although tending toward seeing rock art as ritual or magical in function and meaning, Burkitt's conclusion at this level was largely empty: rock art was 'the result of an innate artistic tendency in the people, a something intensely personal and, as it were, extra and not essentially necessary to the actual business of living' (p. 110). Nothing further was said about this 'tendency', this 'something'. The conclusion sat awkwardly with Burkitt's own archaeological approach – for other artefacts had definite and specifiable functions, meanings and values in technological, social and cultural contexts – but nothing was done to remedy the contradiction unitl ethnographic analogies led, in the 1970s, to hypotheses about the iconographic meaning and cultural significance of rock art (see below, section 6).

Other students focussed on sequencing within a particular territory or at a single site. For example, following the work of Péringuey (e.g., 1907–9), Wilman's (1933) classification of engravings was based solely on iconographic and stylistic criteria. The 'classical' engravings of Botswana and the northern Cape Province principally depicted wild fauna and evolved from a simple 'pitting' technique through a 'furrowed outline' to partly or wholly 'filled-in outline' drawing (fig. 16:5), regarded as the aesthetic apogee of the style. Later drawings were mostly seen as 'imitations' or degenerations of the classical technique (for considerably refined and detailed investigation of the engravings, see Fock 1979; Fock and Fock 1984).

Burkitt's student A.J.H. Goodwin (1936) founded his more elaborate

16:5 *Engraving in 'classical' style, northern Cape Province (after Wilman 1933)*

classification on superimposition and 'comparative patination'. At a single locality he identified eleven successive styles of mostly 'classical' engraving. However, the differences in incising technique or subject-matter were not especially marked one style from the next. For this reason, Goodwin regarded his phases as an uninterrupted 'locality tradition' in which a prime desideratum was to 'imitate and emulate the older artists' (p. 207). This view was largely shared by Clarence Van Riet Lowe (1936, 1952), although his sequences and Goodwin's did not correspond exactly. For both scholars, the artists were 'Bushmen' whose ways of life had slowly changed.

By the late 1930s, rock art in Zimbabwe, South Africa and Namibia had been partitioned into several separate zones, each with an internal evolutionary development and a clearly preferred period of florescence. This model (see further Willcox 1956, 1963), a rather conservative 'art history' of rock art, did not easily admit interruptions or outside influences in the sequences.

After a visit to South Africa in 1929, Henri Breuil (1930b) published a brief comparison of 'Bushman' painting with Palaeolithic cave art (see also Dart 1925; Schapera 1925). He suggested that the southern paintings represented the 'prolongation of our European palaeolithic art through thousands of years down to the most recent times' (p. 151), and identified possible intermediaries in the art of the Spanish Levant and of North Africa, the Sahara and Libya, in some respects 'indistinguishable' from southern pictures. This north-to-south pan-African diffusion, even with its obviously Eurocentric bias, seemed initially admissible to many scholars working at both ends of the continent (e.g., Graziosi 1942: 273–85; Rhotert 1952: 121–5 – although he preferred an Asian origin for North African engraving; Willcox 1963: 52–3; but compare Monod 1963: 186–7; Lhote 1964; Smith 1968: 12–13).

Later Breuil's analysis took a more extreme turn. Working from 1942 to 1948 in Zimbabwe, South Africa and Namibia as a member of Van Riet Lowe's Archaeological Survey, he published five volumes of copies and descriptions (from 1955 to 1966). The first, the famous *White Lady of the Brandberg* (1955b), presented an important group of paintings in the Brandberg first discovered in 1917. For Breuil, ' "this is no Bushman painting: this is Great Art" ' (p. 7); specifically, the 'White Lady' painting

– although in reality an image neither of a white nor of a female – exhibited for him a number of 'foreign influences' (pp. 9–12). Although few if any of these interpretations are accepted now, and many were regarded sceptically by Van Riet Lowe and other archaeologists, in the principal 'lady' Breuil and his collaborator Mary Boyle saw similarities with the 'girl bull-fighters' of the frescoes at Knossos in Crete; 'her face is clearly of the best Mediterranean type with a straight nose' (p. 21). They quoted both Minoan and Egyptian parallels for other details of the 'procession' depicted in the painting, and here and elsewhere also found depicted 'a number of typical Europeans, mostly Semitic' (p. 14, and compare 1957: 5; 1966: 7). All of these paintings with 'foreign influence' seemed 'more static' than the naturalistic 'Bushman' paintings of animals Breuil had studied previously.

Breuil believed (1947, 1949, 1966) that the paintings might be dated through their foreign associations and that the prehistory of Southern Africa could be reconstructed on their evidence. He suggested that a 'Nilotic' people of 'remote, possibly Libyan, origin' between 4500 and 3000 BC moved into the Aegean, Nile Valley, and by land through the inner Sahara into south-western Africa, practising an art descended from European cave-painting. Although Breuil occasionally wrote of an 'invasion', evidently he regarded the whole process as a slow 'infiltration'. According to his theory, the foreign groups encountered and 'combined their creative work' with indigenous peoples. If Breuil's account was correct, then the rock art of Southern Africa was not the work of a single people, was not recent in origin, and was not a single slowly evolving 'tradition' but a complex palimpsest of discontinuities and influences exerted by 'no one country alone'.

However, Breuil's views at this level were generally disregarded by archaeologists working in sub-Saharan Africa, in part because Breuil could not produce independent evidence for any of his claims and in part because the underlying evolutionist, diffusionist and racist assumptions of some archaeological work in Africa in general were coming under considerable criticism. Despite the professional criticism of Breuil's work, his publications were enormously important in stimulating public interest in Southern African rock art.

Other writers apart from Breuil also saw elements other than the purely 'Bushman' in the rock art of Southern Africa. Whether it was foreign to Southern Africa or not, Frobenius (1931) described the 'wedge style' of rock painting in southern Zimbabwe and the Transvaal – the trace, he proposed, of the 'Erythraean' culture with a sophisticated tradition in the decoration of monuments – as markedly different from naturalistic images further south, attributed to 'Bushmen' and the product of a distinct *Kulturkreis* (culture-area) with its own spiritual unity. The artist Walter Battiss (1948), a protégé of Breuil, regarded the 'classical' naturalistic animal paintings of Cape Province and Natal as the work of an unknown prehistoric people. Only the later paintings, 'romantic' compositions with many human figures, were the work of 'Bushmen' – 'a different art' (see fig. 16:6).

Despite their differences over the cultural attribution and affiliation of the rock art they were studying, and controversy concerning the interpretation of details depicted in images as indigenous or foreign to sub-Saharan Africa, it is important to note that in practice Burkitt, Van Riet Lowe, Goodwin, Breuil, Frobenius and Battiss all recognized many of the same varations in the rock art of Southern Africa – between the Brandberg and the Drakensberg, between 'static' and 'naturalistic' styles, between engraving and painting – but construed the archaeological significance of

0 centimeters 20

6:6 *Rock painting depicting men and eland, southern San, Drakensberg Mountains (Barkly East) after Lewis-Williams 1981a)*

these variations very differently depending on their background views about chronological and cultural correlations. Despite Breuil's authority, many archaeologists – tempered by the caution of Van Riet Lowe and others – did not accept his stronger diffusionary arguments. However, like Breuil, on the basis of superimposition, coloration, drawing technique, and other criteria they continued to partition the material into elaborate sequences of as many as a dozen separate phases (e.g., L.S.B. Leakey 1950b; Cooke 1955; Goodall 1957; Lee and Woodhouse 1970; M. Leakey 1983). As few confirmations for the relative dates proposed were available, the method was largely self-sustaining, justified by the organicist assumptions first adopted by Burkitt.

By the late 1950s, the whole project began to collapse at least in part under the very weight of the unwieldy classifications it had generated. Later investigators could not fit new discoveries easily into the stylistic or chronological classifications proposed by earlier investigators; thus, for instance, in Tanzania Odner (1971) and Masao (1976) put forward analyses in which they attempted but failed to accommodate the classifications of L.S.B. Leakey for that area (1950) – and such problems of accommodation and calibration were extremely common. Most of the major disenchantments with the classificatory projects and their underlying methods were directly or indirectly registered by 1971 in a special issue of the *South African Journal of Science* devoted to rock art (Schoonrad ed. 1971), a volume marking a turning-point in the study of rock art in Africa (see further below, sections 5 and 6). Here, a number of investigators stressed the need for neutral terminologies in stylistic analysis, for comprehensive quantitative analysis of the frequency of techniques and themes, and for focussed study of the totality of rock art at a single site. These interests were a natural refinement of the individual empirical achievements of Wilman (1933), Goodwin (1936), and Van Riet Lowe (e.g., 1937), and still embodied the classificatory method of analysis. In one highly sophisticated project, the Focks (Fock 1979; Fock and Fock 1984) examined the micro-distribution of techniques and themes of engraving at two major engraving sites in the northern Cape. They developed a finely tuned version of Wilman's (1933) analysis of 'classical' engravings, permitting fine distinctions among engravings at a single site (compare Scherz 1970–86). When matched against palaeo-environmental and archaeological data of other sorts, the micro-distributions might be seen to reflect changing climates, patterns of material life, and so forth (see also Butzer *et al.* 1979; Fock *et al.* 1980; Manhire *et al.* 1983; Smits 1983).

In two major contributions, A.R. Willcox's suspicion of the 'subjective jargon of art criticism' and detailed knowledge of variations in rock art throughout Southern Africa led him to doubt the feasibility of universal classifications (1956: 46, 59; 1963: 54). Simplifying and rationalizing the work of his predecessors, he presented a reconciliation of competing views about the continuities and discontinuities in southern rock art (and in 1984 extended his approach to the accumulating central African evidence as well). In his review and analysis of 1963, 'indirectly' descended from European Palaeolithic, eastern Spanish, North African and Saharan art, rock painting in Southern Africa was the work of later Stone Age (Wilton/Smithfield) 'Bushman' hunter-gatherers – this cultural association was by now archaeologically confirmed – and could be divided into two clearly recognizable zones. The first zone comprises monochromes and 'unshaded polychromes' in southern Zimbabwe and further south (Willcox's Zones 1 + 3), and the second zone the naturalistic shaded polychromes, sometimes using foreshortening (Willcox's Zone 2) (Willcox 1963: 6, 40). In Willcox's analysis, as was usual in rock art studies in Africa, engraving is quite distinct (Zone 4), although regarded as produced by the same people who produced the paintings moving freely in wide territories. Within both zones, production exhibited an evolution from simplicity to complexity in technical skill, in the use of colour, modelling, foreshortening, and in composition, with a final regression or deterioration (Willcox 1963: 38, 52).

Based on some earlier observations and attempts at classification (e.g., Culwick 1931; L.S.B. Leakey 1936, 1950b), between the 1950s and the late 1970s a relatively clear picture emerged of what Clark (1959b) called the 'Central African Schematic Art Group', that is, of rock art around Lake Victoria, in Zaïre, Angola and Mozambique, and in Zambia (fig. 16:7) and Tanzania (see especially Mortelmans 1952a; Chaplin 1959, 1974; Summers ed. 1959; Phillipson 1972; Lindgren and Schoffeleers 1978; Masao 1979; M. Leakey 1983). Perhaps because of the fragmented colonial and political history of Central Africa, no synthesis comparable to Willcox's (1963) for Southern Africa appeared until the regional prehistoric synthesis of Phillipson (1977a) and the review of previous investigation by Willcox (1984: 75–125). Within this separate, broad central African province of sub-Saharan rock art, investigators working in several countries and in several languages distinguished a number of later Stone Age and Iron Age traditions, on stylistic grounds (the vocabulary deriving ultimately from Burkitt, Wilman and Van Riet Lowe) or on the basis of archaeological and cultural associations. Because of the archaeological expertise of many of the investigators, learning from the difficulties of mentors like Breuil and Van Riet Lowe, and because of some controls introduced by a few possible archaeological associations between rock art and identifiable assemblages (e.g., Clark 1958; Inskeep 1962b), the account of rock art chronology and cultural affiliation in Central Africa, particularly in Zambia and Tanzania, has withstood the test of time and is gradually being filled in (Phillipson 1977a; Willcox 1984: 75–125). Very regrettably I cannot consider this important research in detail. It represents the vigorous continuity of the

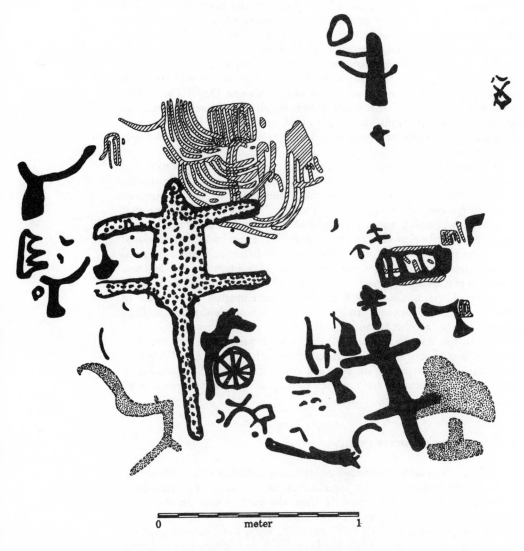

■ white ▨ faded white/buff ▨ red/purple

6:7 *Rock paintings f 'Central African chematic Art Group', Zambia (Chaingo) fter Phillipson 1976b)*

archaeologically cautious branch of the empirical programme. Despite some assertions, very little headway was made with problems of interpretation, especially regarding the non-figurative rock art of this broad region (although see Lindgren and Schoffeleers 1978; Willcox 1984: 108).

With the increasing recognition of the regional distinctiveness and importance of the Central African rock art traditions, and based on the early dates for the painted stones from Apollo XI Cave, Namibia, *c.* 27,500 BP (Wendt 1976; Thackeray 1983), a fragmentary engraved slab from Wonderwerk Cave in the Northern Cape, *c.* 10,000 BP (Thackeray *et al.* 1981), and other evidence (see Butzer *et al.* 1979; Thackeray 1983; Willcox 1984: 231–7), including the claim that the rock art of Tanzania may date as early as 40,000 BP or before (Anati 1985: 54), it now seems less plausible to derive sub-Saharan rock art, directly or indirectly, from the Franco-Cantabrian or northern African traditions. The Upper Paleolithic and late Stone Age cultures in the two broad regions north and south of the

15 degrees north parallel seem to have developed independent indigenous artistic traditions. Current interest now focusses on the problems of using art diagnostically to identify Upper Paleolithic or late Stone Age techno-cultural complexes, the presence of anatomically and/or cognitively modern humanity (*Homo sapiens sapiens*), or social organization of a certain socio-economic, ritual or other complexity. Is rock art or art-making in general essentially or necessarily associated with the Upper Paleolithic, with modern man, or with social groups requiring internal and external ideological identifications? If so, does rock art therefore help us archae-ologically to identify continuities and discontinuities in human biology, demography, society and culture?

In the study of Southern African rock art, the stylistic classification and the stylistic history assumed that image-making has internal rhythms of its own – progressing, for instance, from simplicity to complexity, or developing from 'schematism' to 'naturalism'. However, the hope that such rhythms (which might be identified with extraordinary precision in the micro-distribution of features at individual sites) could be correlated with other rhythms of prehistoric life was never definitively borne out until a better understanding of how rock art was actually integrated into and was actually a precipitate of functioning social and cultural organizations could be achieved. As traditionally formulated, the empirical programme in Southern African rock art studies did not promise this understanding. Therefore the accumulation of data about possible continuities and discontinuities was always somewhat detached from a culture-historical or anthropological perspective, in marked contrast, for example, to Winkler's ethnohistorical perspective on the rock art of the Nile Valley (section 3). These issues are certainly too complex to pass off in a few sentences, and I turn to them now in some detail.

5 The empirical programme

The *sine qua non* of a knowledge of style and sequence was a substantial *corpus* of rock pictures. At least in publishing copies and photographs and in recording sites, empirical research from the early 1920s on was very successful in establishing this corpus (see variously the comprehensive publications of Hellström 1970, Lhote 1975, 1979, Lefèbvre and Lefèbvre 1967, Pager 1971, Scherz 1970–86, Fock 1979, in addition to the several volumes of *Die afrikanischen Felsbilder* (Graz: Akademische Druck- und Verlagsanstalt)).

However, finding a uniform descriptive vocabulary or set of metrics proved more elusive. Partly because of intrinsic characteristics of graphic representation itself (Davis 1985b: 7), standardization of terms was certainly never achieved. Empiricists usually regarded this difficulty as due to 'subjective' elements in description – eliminated, supposedly, by being more 'scientific', for example, by using colour-charts or exact measure-ments. The ideal of an empirical science of rock art was largely derived from contemporary archaeology.

Some stronger 'theoretical' policing was sometimes required to buttress this ideal. For instance, from the 1940s on, diffusionist and culture-evolu-tionist assumptions gradually lost favour, to be replaced by more interest in local traditions. An emerging division between 'hard', increasingly quantitative analysis and 'soft', art-critical analysis paralleled the general schism between 'scientific' archaeology and 'humanistic' history and criti-cism. However, few explicit methodological arguments were published in rock art studies until the 1970s and 1980s.

In practice, empirical description depended upon several distinctions. The influential stylistic distinction between 'schematic' and 'naturalistic' images was the basis of chronological discriminations and proposals about the relative importance of animal and human figurations in rock art, but was not clearly defined. The technical distinction between engraving and painting was used to identify zones of image-making or different authors. It was never clear whether the differences were due to intrinsic character-istics of the media or real differences in date, author, intention, or use (see further Smith 1968: 4–6; Lewis-Williams 1983a: 36; Lewis-Williams and Loubser 1986: 259). Finally, many qualitative distinctions about images – described as anything from 'crude' or 'degenerate' to 'beautiful' and 'sophisticated' – seemed to be based on modern criteria and tastes. Little systematic work was published on original conventions of representation, perhaps partly because the apparatus of iconological (Panofsky 1939) or semiotic (Morris 1938) theory was not well known in archaeology in general (see further Striedter 1983; Davis 1984, 1985b).

Despite the tendentiousness of these various stylistic, technical, quantita-tive, and qualitative distinctions, in the first stage of the empirical programme all (or nearly all) pictures in a *corpus* were sorted into groups on their basis. In so far as the distinctions had been accepted *a priori* or estab-lished through 'observation', the classification was real. However, it was also clear in advance that each individual picture was different from the next in some respects. *Some* kind of classification could always be obtained. Therefore the second stage of analysis required a specification of what the groups – for convenience, usually called 'styles' – represented in chrono-logical, cultural or other terms. If no correlation could be proposed, the classification, however elegant, had to be discarded and another attempted. The problem, of course, was that in the virtual absence of independent evidence, chronological and other correlations could not be established easily.

Three correlations were at the heart of the empirical programme. First, different styles should be correlated with different dates of production, an idea leading to an understandable obsession with possible independent means of dating rock pictures (see further Smith 1968: 8–9, 25–7; Lewis-Williams 1983a: 26–31). Flamand (1921), Wilman (1933), Dalloni (1936), Dunbar (1941), Červiček (1973), and many others published detailed and often sceptical studies of rock patination and patterns of superimposition as evidence of relative age. Although suggestive, processes of weathering were too complex to be definitive. Superimposition was definitive – the lower image is 'older' than the upper – but usually rather limited. No measure of the actual time-lag could be obtained and patterns of super-imposition at different sites could be quite varied. A palimpsest might even be regarded as a single self-contained conventional composition. The verdict on these means of dating was therefore always highly qualified. Although rare, dates could also be obtained by associating rock pictures with covering deposits or nearby archaeological assemblages. Evaluated critically and used where possible, these associations often provided only generalized cultural rather than precise chronological information. Relative *or* absolute dates applied only to those pictures for which they had been worked out. Pictures elsewhere or whole 'styles' were tied in inferentially on the dubious premise that similarity (often of only a few traits) implied contemporaneity.

Second, styles should be correlated with anthropological or historical 'cultures', themselves the subject of controversial indentifications. At least when they were first proposed, some of these cultures, like Winkler's 'autochthonous mountain-dwellers', existed largely on the evidence of rock pictures anyway. Others, like the Neolithic of Capsian tradition, the Nagada II/III, or the Wilton/Smithfield, were well known through other evidence. It was tempting to align a style or zone of rock art with such a well established entity. Although the correlations were sometimes not exact, a lack of fit could be explained on an *ad hoc* basis. For example, predynastic artefacts were not found everywhere in the deserts, Winkler's 'Nile-dwellers' left their images – but perhaps these people only made drawings at some desert locales; Wilton/Smithfield tool-industries had greater antiquity than many were prepared to admit for existing rock paintings – but perhaps earlier paintings in Southern Africa had not survived. The very possibility of making one-to-one style-to-culture correlations was rarely questioned. They were encouraged by entrenched assumptions, like simple psychologies (e.g., since hunters tend to observe the details of their prey, their art must be 'naturalistic') or doctrines of the 'functional coherence' of culture (if social life is an internally consistent set of customs and expressions, then different-looking images cannot belong to the same culture and cannot be in contradiction with any of its other expressions).

The third type of correlation to some degree conflicted with the first two. Here, an overarching evolutionary or historical narrative was produced to make sense of the whole mosaic of different styles identified in a classification. Sometimes these histories were supported by other evidence. However, many also depended upon strong, self-fulfilling assumptions: if 'schematic' precedes 'naturalistic' in the general evolution of representational ability, then schematic rock-drawings evolved into naturalistic. No consistent theory of the causes, rates, or characteristics of stylistic constancy or change was ever worked out. (In this, the study of rock art was no different from mainstream art history; however, it was remarkable that no explicit use was made of the work of Riegl, Wölfflin, and others – a reflection of the early separation of archaeology and art history.) Furthermore, these narratives were only as convincing as the individual dates or cultural attributions for each discriminable style. There were too few of these to inspire confidence among dirt archaeologists.

The paltriness of the actual results gradually demoralized the empirical programme as normally expressed. Although important evidence for dating and other problems continued to be published (McHugh 1975; Wendt 1976), for some areas of Africa even by the early 1970s knowledge of variability in rock art was not much further advanced than it had been initially (see Willcox 1968). Furthermore, since the theoretical vulnerability of the distinctions and correlations was easily exposed, all but the most laconic documentation could be dismissed as 'mere speculation' – the criticism most dreaded by empiricists. The gap between the study of rock art and archaeology (post-Childe), anthropology (post-Radcliffe-Brown), and art history (post-Panofsky) became more evident. Many prehistorians who were not specialists in rock art were highly critical of the whole programme. 'As far as prehistory is concerned, and quite apart from questions of aesthetics, we have very little if anything to learn from the pictographs of the Sahara Desert that we cannot learn as easily, more cheaply and with much greater certainty by the systematic and thorough investigation of other kinds of evidence' (Cabot Briggs 1958: 15–17, 38). Art historians rarely paid attention at all. (For other histories and evaluations of the empirical programme of research, see Lewis-Williams 1983b; Lewis-Williams and Loubser 1986: 254–62.) The solution to the sluggishness of research seemed to be in a sense to make a virtue of 'mere specula-tion', and, of course, 'speculation' – that is, theoretical hypotheses about and interpretations of rock art – had always implicitly or sometimes even explicitly been part of the empirical study of rock art; the final section is devoted to this question (below, 6).

The integration of the empirical study of rock art into African archae-ology proceeded haphazardly. Although Breuil (e.g., 1955) and Frobenius (e.g., 1931) had proposed cultural histories for various regions of Africa at least in part based on rock art, these accounts were largely disregarded by professional archaeologists for reasons we have noted. Rock art sites were sometimes accorded a separate chapter in regional prehistoric syntheses, as part of the 'archaeological' remains of the region, by archaeologists who had personally worked with rock art (e.g., Trigger 1965; Clark 1954; Phillipson 1977a), but in other syntheses (e.g., McIntosh and McIntosh 1983; Sampson 1974) rock art played virtually no role, usually because the lack of dates and associations for images were judged to render them useless for archaeological purposes.

Students of rock art, as we have seen, hoped to effect correlations between their styles or sequences of rock art and other, 'real' chronological, cultural, or evolutionary entities and phases. In practice this hope was hardly ever borne out unless archaeologists already had independent evidence for the existence of these entities and phases – in which case, as Cabot Briggs hinted (1958: 15–17, 38), the evidence of rock art was simply superfluous.

Although this chapter has not taken up these matters at all, for somewhat parallel reasons rock art did not much figure either in the social anthropology or the art history of African cultures. Both of these disciplines were significantly intertwined in the interpretation of African art-objects, and perhaps because in part they required a rich cultural context for analysis, they looked to archaeology to provide the appropriate evidence. There are currently good prospects for an anthropological and art historical analysis of rock art as empirical archaeology becomes more influenced by anthropological and hermeneutic concerns (e.g., Hodder ed. 1987).

Reading the other way around, rock art studies were integrated into African archaeology in so far as the empirical and classificatory interests of prehistorians, from Burkitt onwards, were generalized to cover the evidence of rock art in addition to other artefacts. The comprehensive publications of Lhote (1975), Camps and Gast (1982), Hellström (1970), Fock (1979), and others were modelled on the systematic excavation reports, site surveys, detailed typologies of tool industries, and other protocols of Egyptologists and Africanist prehistorians, although they were sometimes cross-fertilized by the favoured mode of presentation of art historians, the documentary exhibition catalogue and the interpretative essay. Several of these *corpora* were explicitly designed to provide archae-ological information about palaeoenvironmental, palaeodemographic and comparable questions. They were used in reconstructions of prehistoric paleoculture (e.g., Butzer *et al*. 1979; Manhire *et al*. 1983). The archae-ological professionalization of rock art studies was never and is not now complete. Many archaeologists were primarily interested in fundamental problems of the African techno-complexes in which rock art studies could play only a subsidiary role. Among amateur students of rock art, although Burkitt's early 'archaeological' descriptions of style and sequence were well received, in part because they suited *a priori* assumptions about art and about Africa, the more complex, technical, and professional methods of modern archaeology tended to be resisted, paralleling the resistance to anthropological or art historical interpretation in a professional sense.

Yet it would be too easy simply to conclude that rock art studies failed to be integrated into the mainstream of African archaeology, anthropology and art history simply because of the poor archaeological contexts of the material and the less-than-professional interests and training of many investigators. After all, rock pictures did have contexts like any other material evidence, and although often they could not be dated or attributed using stratigraphic means this did not imply that they never could be dated or attributed. By now, many groups of rock pictures are as well anchored to cultures at particular points in their social development as many other classes of artefact. Moreover, many investigators were careful, critical, and comprehensive and the base of evidence for archaeological, anthropological and art historical inference is by now as good as or better than that for many other classes of artefact. The real difficulties apparently cut deeper. In so far as archaeologists were deeply committed to the view that artefacts could be made to speak directly about the world of the past, it was not clear that rock art could or should *in principle* be integrated into an archaeological analysis. The 'new archaeology' did serve to problematize archaeologists' understandings of how the artefact was tied to some past history of production and use – and we might go so far as to say that the crisis in archaeology precipitated by the 'new archaeology' had *always* figured in the study of rock art. A rock picture could not be integrated into *any* archaeological analysis until its status as a unique kind of archaeological evidence was clarified: and no *a priori* expectations about the nature, function, or symbolic significance of either works of art or other ordinary archaeological artefacts were likely to be generalizable to the case. The empirical programme did not have its own archaeologically plausible 'theory' of the production of rock art.

6 Theoretical frameworks

The operating 'theory' of empirical research consisted in its favourite distinctions and correlations (above, section 5). Moreover, already by the beginning of the century a certain interpretation of rock art had been proposed and implicitly accepted.

In considering its mode of representing its objects, most writers on African rock art asserted that art depicted aspects of the artist's immediate world, such as the activities of his daily life or what he saw around him. Its mode of depiction was realistic or naturalistic. The latter specification was often qualified by the ambiguous terms 'schematic', 'conceptual', or 'conventionalized', as somewhat *ad hoc* allowances for the artist's 'lack of skill in depiction' or for the image's 'distortion' of what we would really be able to see if we were there. But despite the 'conventionalization', it was believed the image did indeed depict something really there to be seen. Although some pictures might be illustrations of contemporary fables (e.g., Bleek 1932), even here they could be taken as documents for the very existence and content of these fables – what they really contained.

If these assertions were accepted, then most rock pictures could be used as archaeological evidence for aspects of prehistoric life. They became *archaeological* evidence by virtue of an interpretation of their *symbolic and aesthetic* qualities. Some individual reconstructions of prehistoric life tended to be somewhat *ad hoc*, partly because interpreters naturally focussed on the most puzzling details of images from a modern point of view, and attempted to locate specific and often specialized denotations, and partly because to make sense of an image an interpreter necessarily had to assume things about the image-maker's world which were not in fact directly represented in the image itself. On the basis of various strategies for turning images into archaeological documents, and using a substantial enough *corpus*, remarkably detailed reconstructions of prehistoric ecology (e.g., Butzer 1958), material life and culture (e.g., Camps and Gast 1982; Manhire *et al.* 1985), social organization (e.g., Tschudi 1955), demographic history and movement (e.g., Cooke 1965), or religion (e.g., Joleaud 1934; Goodall 1962) were attempted. But if the straightforwardly depictional functions and documentary status of rock pictures were denied or regarded as only part of the story, on whatever internal, empirical or theoretical grounds (for which see below), then these reconstructions became tendentious (for examples, see Lewis-Williams 1985; Lewis-Williams and Loubser 1986). It was never particularly clear whether *other* archaeological evidence would or should count as a confirmation or disconfirmation of what a rock picture was thought to depict, whether the evidence of rock pictures – just because they had directly intentional and communicative elements – should be regarded as specially privileged, or whether the Romantic emphasis on their 'aesthetic' elements could be reconciled with the archaeological desire to regard them as direct unmediated precipitates of real aspects of life.

Did the documentary status of rock pictures exhaust the possibilities of their function and meaning as well? For some writers, rock pictures had actually served their *makers* as records or commemorations. This economical suggestion at least had the virtue of self-consistency and of eliminating worries about the subtle purposes of prehistoric artists.

However, despite their empiricism most writers were committed to further *a priori* specifications of the function of rock art – the well-known 'magical' and 'aesthetic' interpretations (see generally Ucko and Rosenfeld 1967). Taken up from Frazer by anthropologists like Henry Balfour (1909), the interpretation of early images as hunting or fertility magic was applied to African rock art just as to any other (Brentjes 1969 for a particularly strong statement). In western (especially Romantic) aesthetics, 'art for art's sake' included the terrible, fanciful, symbolic and abstract, but for students of rock art (e.g., Cooke 1969; Rudner and Rudner 1970) it implied no more than the artist's pleasure in drawing. Although pleasure may depend upon completion, success or reward, no further anthropological analysis of aesthetic pleasure was presented. These two specifications of function could be combined (magic required skilled depiction) or mutually exclusive (aesthetic sensibility went beyond material needs). With status and function specified in this way, meaning took care of itself; once again empirical writers found nothing further to say about it (Clegg 1982). Prehistoric people drew pictures on rocks for the direct magical benefit or simple aesthetic pleasure of representing their world, and this is what their work meant to them.

However, the empiricist's favourite interpretations did not fit the facts as they were gradually revealed archaeologically and ethnographically. As spadework became increasingly penetrating, an independent portrait of prehistoric life was puzzled out. Ultimately it became clear that the figurative and material records did not completely match up in the way required by the Frazerian or Romantic interpretations.

One compelling demonstration, by archaeologists in Southern Africa (Maggs 1967b; Vinnicombe 1967, 1972a, b; Smits 1971), showed quantitatively that rock painters did not depict animals in proportion to their material significance in daily life, as understood by archaeological examination of faunal remains, but concentrated on a few species, like the eland. Similarly, rock drawings in the Nile Valley focussed on a few canonical themes not necessarily representative of prehistoric and predynastic daily life. As well as being a fatal blow to the Frazerian view, the statistics suggested that rock art was not simply or straightforwardly but rather *selectively* documentary – or perhaps not documentary at all.

Reorientation of research was stimulated by a systematic collection of data, as in comprehensive surveys of individual regions (e.g., Pager 1971), tabulations of technical and environmental information (e.g., Hellström 1970), various distributional studies (Maggs 1967b), and sophisticated 'internal' analysis. For the other side of the equation, regional archaeologies and reliable ethnographies were matched critically against the 'record' of rock art.

Many writers on rock art had initially aligned themselves with empirical (and later with 'scientific') archaeology in construing the rock picture as an 'artefact' rather than as (also) an 'image' or 'text'. The artefact was regarded as the fossil of something which really occurred, in this case, something really seen or experienced by the maker – as *the impress or imprint of the Real*. In the 1960s and 70s, the 'New Archaeology' called for testable hypotheses about the generation of the present evidence by past behaviours, usually understood as materially adaptive. As some prehistorians recognized (e.g., Monod 1963: 181; Smith 1968: 32), behaviour could be very complex: at least as studied in the humanities, an 'image' or 'text' – no more and no less than *a representation of the Real* – had to be approached cautiously, on the look-out for metaphor, satire, propaganda, fantasy, or downright *mis*representation for rhetorical, ideological, or other purposes. If rock art could not be easily used as evidence for prehistoric material life, as such, perhaps it could be used as evidence for 'ideology', however that was in turn thought to have a place in human affairs.

The old problem of the 'meaning of the art', as it was often phrased, now had a renewed urgency. Artists had some 'motivation' for selectively representing aspects of their environment, 'aesthetically charged' for some specifiable reason (Davis 1984: 16–18). 'Motivation' implied an active choice of subject-matter and style, rather than the passive registration and instinctive performance attributed to prehistoric artists in earlier 'innatist' literature (Lewis-Williams 1982: 429–30). Formerly connected by the simple 'psychological' theory that artists drew what they knew about what they saw, now some explicit anthropological theory was required to connect the artistic and material records. This theory would at least in part be an account of an artist's 'meaning', that is, a specific, selective cultural preference and social convention in producing a representation.

For *la pensée sauvage*, Lévi-Strauss (1966) claimed, certain animals were less important materially than 'good to think', an idea partly developed (e.g., in 1962) as a critique of Malinowski's 'empirical' account of the selection of totemic designations. The preponderance of eland in San paintings might therefore be explained by examining how and where the animal figured in San belief-systems. Returning to nineteenth-century 'ethnographies' of the vanishing southern San and, with increasing confidence in the reliability of the analogy (see especially Lewis-Williams and Biesele 1978), to the contemporary ethnography of the Kalahari San, Vinnicombe (1972b, 1976) reviewed San beliefs about the interconnection of supernatural, animal and human powers, and Lewis-Williams (1981a) explored San trance performance. They proposed that a rock painting

16:8 *Rock paint-ings depicting trance dancers, southern San, Drakensberg Moun-tains (Barkly East) (after Lewis-Williams 1981a)*

might directly depict or metaphorically represent the transcendental events of rain-making rituals or the union of man and animal in trance-dance, in all of which the eland figured as a 'central or key symbol' whereby the San represented ('thought') truths of their natural and social world (see also Vinnicombe 1975; Lewis-Williams ed. 1983) (figs. 16:6, 16:8).

As elsewhere in archaeology, ethnographic analogy had to be approached cautiously. Surprisingly early dates for rock art throughout Africa were being obtained (Myers 1958; Davis 1977, 1985a; Mori 1974; Wendt 1976; Butzer *et al.* 1979; Fock *et al.* 1980; Thackeray 1983). Although traditions of rock art apparently exhibited some stability throughout long periods, were the ancient contexts of production at all like the modern? Could modern ethnography tell us anything about the deep past? Moreover, some authorities were not convinced that the authors of the drawings had really been identified. Whether *ad hoc* or systematic, ethnographic analogies and associations (e.g., Culwick 1931; de Ganay 1940; Lhote 1952a; Dieterlen 1966; Lindgren and Schoffeleers 1978; Lewis-Williams 1981), assumptions of continuity between past and present (Lewis-Williams 1984), and so forth, therefore had to be adopted as explicit heuristic and sometimes frankly speculative devices. In the absence of independent evidence, their test was their power to produce consistent and comprehensive accounts of as many features of images as possible (see Lewis-Williams 1983b, 1983c).

Stress on the symbolic connotations of images was necessarily accom-panied by an interest in symbolic conventions. Some of these could be inter-preted in the light of ethnographic data (e.g., Lewis-Williams 1981b). In other instances, only an internal 'syntactic' analysis might be possible. This analysis identified pairings and polarities of figures sufficiently constant to be regarded as conventionally meaningful, or subtle differences between and among images to be regarded as significant (see further Davis 1984: 14–16, 1985b: 5–6). The somewhat modest success of syntactic analysis reflects the difficulty of any purely formal/structural analysis, as pioneered by the *Strukturforscher* or structural-formalists in art history and by Lévi-Strauss and his followers in anthropology. Style could be regarded as a set of conventions of representation and expression, but little work on the basic character of style in rock art had been conducted since the writing of Flamand (1921) and Burkitt (1928). Enthusiasm for the pursuit of iconographic meanings enabled rock art studies to catch up with the traditional iconological manoeuvres of modern art history, as formulated by Panofsky (1939), but often promoted an artificial distinction between content ('the meaning') and form. At the present time it is still not clear why rock artists drew in the way that they did, that is, how they established and secured 'meaning' in and by formal conventions of representation and expression. Recent systematic study from a linguistic-semiotic point of view (e.g., Striedter 1976, 1983) promises some help with this matter. The syntactic (formal), semantic (iconographic), and pragmatic (functional or contextual) aspects of a rock picture will be considered simultaneously and as mutually interdependent.

One important result of interpretation based on ethnographic analogy was the conclusion that a 'picture' need not depict real things in the real world of the artist, straightforwardly recorded by him. Davis (1984) suggested that rock art represented *problematic* aspects of the world, requiring the artist's skill with conventions of 'naturalism' and of metaphor to make them fully intelligible to viewers in the first place. Throughout Africa, rock pictures tended to represent ritually significant events, out-of-the-ordinary phenomena, and adaptively significant local realities, for which prehistoric peoples had probably evolved penetrating classifications. Moreover, if the grammar and meaning of these sign-systems were ever to be understood, it was not sufficient to group pictures in 'styles' on the basis of a few similarities or a single diagnostic trait (Smith 1968: 26–7). The siting of rock-pictures, their characteristics as a 'functioning whole assemblage', and their interrelation throughout a site or territory required re-evaluation (e.g., Butzer *et al.* 1979; Manhire *et al.* 1983), paralleling recent work by anthropologists on the 'figurative system' of Palaeolithic cave painting or the rock art of Australia and by archaeologists on the significance of spatio-temporal distributions. Intentionally or not, rock pictures might 'signpost' a natural or social territory – a domain of resource management, travels, economic exchanges, ritual occurrences, or social self-consciousness.

With some conception of symbolic connotation and convention, it seemed possible to approach the cultural context and significance of rock art. Pursuing a line of thinking derived from Durkheim and Radcliffe-Brown, Vinnicombe suggested that rock painting contributed to 'creating a feeling of cohesion and security in the face of uncertainty' fundamental to the survival of society (1972: 198, 202). Citing structural-Marxist theory, Lewis-Williams argued that the several metaphors explored in rock painting and decoded in his iconographic analysis were 'intrinsic to the conceptual framework which made belief in the medicine men's symbolic work possible'; since trance-dance had 'direct economic and social consequences', painting might be regarded as due 'in the last instance' to infrastructural determinants (1982: 431, 438). Partly in order to avoid the reductionist tone of some functionalist and Marxist reasoning, some stress has also been placed on the constitutive role or causal efficacy of image-making. In 1968, Smith (p. 32) recalled Meyer Schapiro's (1950: 294) famous remarks on the 'ideological construction' or mediations of art, that is, a style's 'complex imaginative transposition' of social and economic realities. Signs stand in a referential but in Saussure's word a 'sliding', oblique and metonymic-metaphoric, relation to the signified; for some writers, what could be symbolically signified was just 'the limit of the world' of the sign-user (Striedter 1976: 50, after Wittgenstein). Individ-

Acknowledgements

In preparing this chapter I have greatly benefitted from the advice of many colleagues. Although they will not always agree with my selections or point of view, for their assistance and critical scrutiny I thank in particular E. Anati, K.W. Butzer, G. Camps, J.D. Clark, H. Deacon, J. Deacon, J.D. Lewis-Williams, the late H. Pager, P. Robertshaw, K.H. Striedter, and A.R. Willcox. The work was supported by the Society of Fellows, Harvard University, and could not have been completed without the magnificent facilities of the Tozzer Library of Anthropology at Harvard University and the Anthropology Library of the University of California at Berkeley.

uals, groups and classes, and societies are constructed by and through networks of representation (e.g., Biesele 1983; Davis 1984, 1986); attending to the conventions of rock art is attending to how a culture knows the world. In all of this research, 'in essence "functional" in its attempt to confront causality' (Biesele. 1983: 54), rock art was seen as having a central role in the production and reproduction of society.

Although the study of rock art has been viewed suspiciously by archaeologists and historians, it has awakened public interest in the African past. The importance of this contribution cannot be overestimated. That rock art might substantially complement the record of tools, settlements, chronicles or oral tradition has sustained most serious scholarly interest. Although with less precision than a taxonomist, iconographer or semiotician would wish, a century of research has catalogued and classified variability in African rock art in a multitude of dimensions. The ambition to transform a catalogue of variability into an archaeology of production and meaning has met with less success so far. It is not clear how complex, mediated, and oblique images can be used reliably as traces, indices, symptoms, or expressions of history, or what kind of history – of material life, of *thought about* this life? – might be revealed. These uncertainties are not unique to the study of rock art but reflect general tensions in art history and now in contemporary archaeology as well.

17 *West African Archaeology: Colonialism & Nationalism*

AUGUSTIN HOLL

I   Aims and purposes

There is no doubt that African archaeology, as well as anthropology, is a child of the colonial enterprise which succeeded in sharing the African 'cake' shortly after the Berlin Congress (1884–5). If we define archaeology narrowly as the study of material evidence surviving from the past, it is thus an analysis of the tangible and visible products and achievements of extinct communities. It has been shaped as an academic discipline in Africa by its role in either supporting or countering dominant assumptions concerning African history. This paper is about these conflicting paradigms, by the examination of which we will try to understand how archaeological knowledge was produced, used and manipulated to fit various interests and assumptions. Changing truths, theories and explanations in archaeology are often interpreted by professional archaeologists as signs of progress in the discipline. This comfortable attitude has been challenged by many scientists and scholars; Kuhn (1970), for instance, has convincingly argued that paradigmatic changes in scientific explanations result from complexes of interacting factors, not only reducible to progress in interpretation:

> What occurs during a scientific revolution is not fully reducible to a reinterpretation of individual and stable data. In the first place, the data are not equivocally stable. More important, the process by which either the individual or the community makes the transition from one theory to another is not one that resembles interpretation. . . . Given a paradigm, interpretation of data is central to the enterprise that explores it. This enterprise can only articulate a paradigm, not correct it. Paradigms are not corrigible by normal science at all. (Kuhn 1970: 121)

If we consider 'explanation' roughly as a re-statement of something (be it an event, a theory, a doctrine, etc.) in terms of current interests and assumptions, which satisfies because it appeals to a particular worldview and thereby supersedes older or rival sets of ideas (Piggott 1981, Wilk 1985, Hall 1984b), it is clear that the great values of studying the history of archaeology are two: we will be in a position to realize, first, that archaeology is not simply a straightforward record of discoveries, and, second, that it is a record of findings mixed with social and ideological assumptions – 'forgery and the refusal of established archaeologists to regard their work historically' (Daniel 1981c: 13). In this regard, the reconstruction of the archaeological past must be considered neither as an unattainable 'past-in-itself' nor as a series of 'pasts-as-known', but mainly as dependent upon the archaeologists' minds and the intellectual framework within which their aims and purposes are conceived. The past can therefore serve multiple purposes: it can be 'past as charter' or 'past as bad example' (Wilk 1985: 319); thus, far from being an escape from the present, the past assumes specific roles in the present in social and political spheres. As members of a discipline committed to studying the past, archaeologists assert firmly that there is a connection between past and present and that this feature is relevant and important.

According to both Wilk (1985: 319) and Hall (1984b), there is no need for archaeologists to be defensive about explicitly or implicitly drawing on their personal, cultural and political experience in their professional work:

> I think we should drop the pretense of absolute objectivity. Further, I suggest that drawing on present experience and interests is hardly 'unscientific' and that it strengthens, rather than weakens, our work. The connection between present and past is a source of power, the power to offer legitimacy or attack. . . . Rather than condemning those who 'pervert' the past to their own political purposes, we should acknowledge that there is *no* neutral, value-free, or non-political past – that if we take the present out of the past we are left with a dry empty husk. (Wilk 1985: 319).

Archaeologists all over the world, and especially in Africa, are faced with the challenge of taking full responsibility for the important power they wield in interpreting the past. In this chapter I will discuss paradigms of West African archaeology during the colonial period, the reinterpretation which occurred with the rise of African nationalism, and, finally, the place of archaeological knowledge in modern West Africa.

II Archaeology and colonialism

After a long struggle with late medieval and clerical obscurantism, prehistory and archaeology finally came into existence during the second half of the nineteenth century all over Europe as a self-conscious and separate discipline devoted to the study of man's past (Daniel 1962, Laming-Emperaire 1964). Let us assume that during that exciting period archaeology and prehistory progressively acquired the status of 'science'. As perceptively demonstrated by Mayr (1982) in his book devoted to the growth of biological thought, the essence of science is the continuing process of problem-solving in the quest for an understanding and explanation of the world in which we live. A history of science is foremost a history of the problems of science and their solutions or attempted solutions; it is also a history of the development of the principles that form the conceptual framework of science (Mayr 1982: 1).

Colonial proselytism was based on the assumption of African backwardness, so that, ideologically, self-expressed aims of colonialism included a '*mission civilisatrice*' or 'white man's burden', aimed at bringing the achievements of civilization to African peoples living in an endemic state of Lockian 'ware'. All the components of the colonial enterprise – armies, medical services, civil administration, missionaries, etc., – participated in varying degrees in this task.

Who produced the earliest archaeological knowledge of West Africa? How was it produced and what was its explanatory framework? My discussion of these topics will be heavily biased in favour of French literature with which I am more familiar; also, the vast majority of West African countries were colonized by France. However, references to data in English will be considered where appropriate.

The earliest research reports dealing with archaeological information on West Africa were published between 1870 and 1900 (Breuil 1899, Burton and Cameron 1883, Hamy 1877, Lubbock 1870a, b, Maxwell 1898, Mouth 1899). Laforgue (1925, 1936) and Mauny (1968) have published lists of references from the colonial period: it appears that in 1925 there were only 80 published papers, rising to 220 by 1936 and 840 by 1968. Before 1940, all archaeological information was contained in short papers, which dealt with the description of surface finds of artefacts and sites. At that time, the colonial powers were engaged in surveying their new territories; powerful expeditions were often organized. Many expeditions headed by army officers crossed the Sahara from the north to the south (Mission Foureau-Lamy in 1905) and from the west to the east, from Dakar to Djibouti. In this process of 'pacification', the participants recorded various kinds of information about peoples, languages, customs, geography, geology, traditions and archaeological finds. Thus, it is logical enough that the earliest archaeological reports from West Africa were written by army and medical officers, civil administrative officers, school teachers and priests, many of them being 'enlightened amateurs'.

The majority of the earliest reports were concerned with stone artefacts collected at random. These data were used to create typological charts similar to French ones, in order to build an approximate time-scale. Another major concern was with monuments and impressive buildings: the data collected were used to locate ancient political centres and the capital cities of West African medieval empires mentioned in the Arabic historical record (see McIntosh and McIntosh 1983, Delafosse 1916).

During this early colonial period the situation of archaeology and prehistory in France was changing rapidly (Laming-Emperaire 1964), as these disciplines had not yet been fully integrated into academia. In 1866 the first International Congress of Archaeology and Prehistoric Anthropology was organized at Neuchâtel and in the next year at Paris, followed in 1876 by the creation of the Ecole anthropologique de Paris and by the foundation of a chair of historical geography at the Collège de France in 1892. At the same time, lectures on prehistoric man were delivered at the Musée d'histoire naturelle and specialized scholarly journals were created: L'Anthropologie in 1872, L'Homme préhistorique in 1884. However, archaeology and prehistory were still entrenched in the practice of 'enlightened amateurs'; it was only in 1927–8 that these disciplines entered the university cursus – through a certificate of ethnology including lectures on prehistory in the faculties of letters and sciences of the University of Paris Sorbonne. It is one of the basic features of French archaeology and prehistory that that part of it dealing with physical anthropology, palaeontology, geology and related disciplines is hosted in faculties of science; the other part dealing with more recent societies is associated with letters, fine arts and social sciences.

Many of the people who actively participated in colonialism played an important role in the emergence of French archaeology as a self-contained discipline. T. Hamy, who was a medical officer in West Africa, published about twelve papers between 1877 and 1907, and edited several volumes in the series Matériaux pour servir à l'histoire de l'Homme from 1864. He was also the editor of the journal La Revue d'ethnographie in 1890 (Mauny 1968, Laming-Emperaire 1964). Delafosse was the governor-general of the French colonies of West Africa. Thus, from his administrative position it was his duty to enforce French colonial policy. Delafosse was not exactly an archaeologist, but he employed a wealth of archaeological data to explain the process of the peopling of West Africa. His publications (Delafosse 1900, 1912, 1916) are therefore one of the best illustrations of the colonial attitude towards the West African past.

2 PROBLEMS AND EXPLANATORY FRAMEWORK

The colonial period lasted in West Africa from about 1850 to approximately 1960. In terms of archaeology, this period can be divided into two parts: the earlier – from the beginning to about 1950 – and the later – from 1950 to 1960. The first Pan-African Congress organized by L.S.B. Leakey and held in Nairobi in 1947 can be considered as the major event which brought about genuine change in the nature of archaeological investigation in Africa. During that meeting, a visit to the excavations at Olorgesailie convinced all the participants that it was possible to recover the 'occupation floors' of early human sites, whereas most African archaeologists had been fully convinced previously that, due to the tropical climate, archaeological data were always mixed so that it was useless to dig carefully; surface collection of artefacts and a desperate search for stratigraphy had in general been the only techniques used up to that date. Consequently discussion in West African archaeology had been focussed on the problems of the origins of particular technological complexes of artefacts.

We have already noted the foundation of a chair of historical geography at the Collège de France in 1892; this event occurred only two years after the publication of F. Ratzel's three volumes of *Völkerkunde* and ten years after *Anthropogeographie*. The occurrence is not coincidental since German scholarship has had a tremendous impact on French scholarship; all the major books of German scholars were quickly translated into French, some of them unfortunately with mistakes (Zwernemann 1982). Ratzel was the founder of cultural-historical studies in anthropology; he argued that only real historical descent explained the similarity of form of objects found at places hundreds or thousands of kilometres apart. He promoted a theory of culture contact – the 'migration theory' – according to which the driving forces behind dynamic historical processes are migrations. Ratzel published classifications of African peoples based on both their cultural achievements and their economies. The former includes, from the top to the bottom, the Arabs and Nubians, Ethiopians, Berbers, peoples of the Sahara, peoples of the Central Sudan, Fulani and the 'dark' peoples of Western Sudan (Zwernemann 1982: 29). According to Ratzel, where older cultural traits point to outside Africa, they point east; thus, iron, cattle, pigs, chickens, the cultivation of millets, the vertical loom and the simple bow came from the east (*ibid.*).

In this atmosphere, the most appealing archaeological research problem was that of the origin of peoples, their races and their position in the hierarchy, which had civilization at the top – equated of course with European industrial societies – and savagery at the bottom. This concept is crudely explicit in the preface written by Bordes and Bordes to the posthumous book of R. Vaufrey (1969), *Préhistoire de l'Afrique*, vol. II: 'many of the ideas he [Vaufrey] has presented have been welcomed and successful, especially that of "Africa as a backward continent", an idea which has been borrowed by other specialists' (Bordes and Bordes in Vaufrey 1969: 5).

African 'backwardness' was one of the major assumptions of colonialism, but this idea was contradicted by some archaeological findings. If

Africans were as backward as was thought, how could one explain the presence of some stone tools similar to European and Near Eastern specimens, how explain the presence of unexpected monumental buildings, how explain the presence of fine art and divine kingship, etc.? That was the dilemma of colonial archaeology. The answer was offered by the German cultural-historical school of anthropology: all these achievements may have occurred as a result of diffusion and migrations. Ratzel and Frobenius (1911, 1912, 1923, 1933) offered the explanatory framework; Delafosse (1900, 1912, 1916), Desplagnes (1907), Mauny (1952, 1953c), Palmer (1931), De Pedrals (1948, 1950) among many others, used that framework to explain culture changes in West Africa's past. The titles of some of their publications are quite explicit, for instance Delafosse's paper published in 1912 is entitled 'Sur les traces probables de la civilization égyptienne et d'hommes de race blanche à la Côte-d'Ivoire' ('On the probable traces of Egyptian civilization and men of white race on the Ivory Coast'). According to colonial archaeology – summarized in De Pedrals (1950) – the West African medieval empires of Ghana and Songhai were founded by immigrants from the Near East: Jews, Yemenites, Arabs; the Ghana ruling dynasty was founded by a group of Jews, the Bani Israel, because divine kingship was basically a 'Hamitic feature'; the burial mounds of the inland Niger delta were also built by Jews. According to Robin (1939), a place called Kala in the inland Niger delta, containing groups of burial mounds, was the settlement of 'Pharaouni' (see De Pedrals 1950: 78), the chief of a white people ruling blacks with the help of *You Houzou*, a creature with superhuman strength. Robin discovered that the name *You Houzou* could well be the phoneme *z* which in the Djerma language becomes *dy* or *dj*; he thus considered the name to be a variant of *Jew*. These powerful immigrants introduced the art of digging deep wells, iron metallurgy and, finally, complex social organization; they were always rulers and belonged to the elite. According to De Pedrals (1950: 85), from Ethiopia in the east to Gambia in the west, and in what was called 'French Sudan', there existed a Hamitic complex, 'the exact image of that part of the Ethiopian-Israelite genealogical chart in which there is no place for black people . . . the [racial] type of the earliest invaders was absorbed in the black mass more quickly and radically elsewhere than it was in Nubia and Abyssinia.' The presence of groups of white people everywhere in West Africa was considered as a precondition for cultural evolution and technological change – 'it seems that we owe to those movements of peoples iron metallurgy' (De Pedrals 1950: 112). Much evidence from material culture, such as the use of stone as building material and the erection of megaliths (Palmer 1931), was seen as proof of migrations of peoples and diffusion of culture traits from the Nile Valley and Egypt. The 'white man's burden' was therefore validated; colonial systems had to continue the onerous task of their white forerunners and bring yet again the light of civilization to 'backward' Africa.

In the 1950s a slight change occurred in the colonial archaeological milieu. Professional archaeologists began to take up appointments in various research institutions; the first museums were founded in Ghana and Nigeria (Shaw 1978); IFAN (Institut français d'Afrique noire) was founded in Dakar (Senegal) and published a journal from 1939 in place of the *Bulletin du Comité d'études historiques et scientifiques de l'Afrique occidentale française* (1918–38). The first Pan-African Congress of Prehistory and related disciplines which took place in Nairobi in 1947 and the second one in Algiers in 1952 gave these professionals the opportunity to compare and contrast their methods and results. The resolutions of these congresses aimed to achieve methodological clarification and a common terminology.

However, major research problems of the pioneer stage of West African archaeology were not completely abandoned – 'raciology' was still a focal point of investigation as was the problem of the origins of different stone tool complexes, the Levallois technique, blade technology, microlithic complexes, pottery, food production, metallurgy, and so on. But change was manifest mainly in the greater emphasis on archaeological artefacts, on the description of sites and finds, and on typology, but with only very brief discussions of origins. The construction of chronological charts was the main aim of these professional archaeologists. Monumental textbooks on African prehistory were published in the 1950s (Alimen 1955, Balout 1955, Vaufrey 1955). References to Frobenius and his associates of the cultural-historical school all but disappeared from the literature. However, some research topics were still couched in crude diffusionist terms. This was the case with problems related to the emergence of iron technology in West Africa. According to Mauny (1952, 1953), iron technology diffused from Charthaginian North Africa through contacts with proto-Berbers in West Africa. Mauny's discussion is in fact very similar to the arguments of the cultural-historical school (Zwernemann 1982: 50). He first considered the technological complexity of the process of iron production and manufacture of iron implements; then, he stated that technological processes are such complex phenomena that a repeated independent invention is very improbable; consequently iron technology was developed elsewhere and diffused to West Africa.

Some interesting patterns emerge from this short and biased review of archaeology and prehistory in the colonial period. First of all, the sociological milieu of archaeologists was a very narrow one; they were soldiers, teachers and civil servants who were obliged in their daily tasks to enforce colonial ideology. Second, there were differences in emphasis in explaining the significance of archaeological data uncovered; simple soldiers, primary school teachers and clerks published descriptions of sites and the finds, but some of them were obliged to send their excavation reports to their superiors (Waterlot 1909). Those belonging to the colonial elite (Robin 1939, Delafosse 1900, De Pedrals 1950, Maes 1924, Lucas 1931) – military and medical officers and high-ranking civil servants – used to interpret archaeological data in terms of the historical precedence and superiority of white peoples over black natives, thus reinforcing their '*mission civilisatrice*'. Therefore, in varying degrees, archaeological knowledge participated in the colonial enterprise of political domination and economic exploitation.

III Archaeology and nationalism

During the colonial period there were no indigenous African archaeologists; however, all the professional archaeologists working in West Africa were not always in agreement with the dominant diffusionist paradigm. Lhote (1952b), for instance, disagreed with Mauny (1952, 1953) on the emergence of iron technology in West Africa, and considered it to be the outcome of local development. Nevertheless, what may be considered as a revisionist conception of archaeological knowledge was initiated by scholars other than archaeologists; these were novelists, poets, historians and sociologists who met in French universities when they were students in the years following 1920. They were political activists, fighting for the freedom of Africa and against the dominant colonial paternalism and manipulation of the knowledge which was the main subject of their studies. The problem faced by these pioneers was how to restore African dignity. For some like Cheikh Anta Diop and T. Obenga, the major issue was to study the African past in order to identify the assumptions and biases of the dominant colonial rhetoric and thereby to create the basis for an African revival. The Senegalian scholar, Ch. Anta Diop, can be considered as the most prominent proponent of the use of archaeological knowledge, along with linguistics and history, to create a coherent body of ideas congruent with an African radical nationalism. Shaw (1978: 11–12) is certainly right when he writes that the advocacy of Egyptian diffusionism by colonial administrators was enthusiatically espoused by African writers also, but the global project of Anta Diop (1960b, 1967, 1977, 1979) was more complex than the simple restatement of earlier ideas.

The major purpose of Anta Diop's studies was to fight against cultural alienation (Anta Diop 1979: 4); he noticed that the whole body of 'scientific' statements on Africa's past in the 1950s was utilitarian and pragmatic in the sense that it was used to enforce colonial dominance; thereby the natives were deprived of any aptitude for cultural achievement. In order to create national self-consciousness, Africans had to study their past critically. This was done in three major steps. The first was to establish Ancient Egypt firmly as the cradle of almost every black African people. The second was to demonstrate the true nature of the links between a sample of African peoples and linguistic groups with Pharaonic Egypt while ascertaining the 'negritude' of the latter's peoples. And the third was to consider Pharaonic Egypt as a centre of civilization which exerted a tremendous influence upon Ancient Greece and consequently upon the whole western world.

1 ANCIENT EGYPT AS THE CRADLE OF BLACK AFRICANS

This idea was quite an old one (Shaw 1978, Delafosse 1900, Obenga 1973). Ancient Egypt is a part of Africa, which has seen a glorious and great civilization, thus, as noted by Shaw (1978: 11), it gives added lustre to African pride to trace cultural and even physical ancestry to that source. During the colonial period, this argument was used to support the idea of African inability to achieve a high degree of 'civilization' without external influence. With the same information, Anta Diop by using three categories of data argued that Ancient Egypt was the cradle of black Africans. Ethnological data, including discussions on totemism, circumcision, kingship, cosmology, social organization and matriarchy, were used to show the existence of general similarities in the structures, as well as in the mental templates, of Pharaonic societies and the vast majority of black societies (Anta Diop 1979: 204–19). Historical data gathered from classical Greek travellers and the works of historians were then used to demonstrate the close connection between Egypt and Meroitic Sudan, the very early achievement of civilization in Nilotic Sudan, and the rise in power of the Meroitic dynasty of Piankhi, Shabaka and Sabataka at Napata in Upper Egypt. Finally, linguistic data were employed to attest the genetic relationship between Pharaonic Egyptian and Negro-African languages (Diop 1977, 1979: 335). According to Anta Diop, this large body of data is in itself sufficient to ascertain beyond any doubt the reality of Ancient Egypt as the cradle of African peoples.

2 THE PEOPLING OF AFRICA FROM THE NILE VALLEY

As the cradle of almost all African negroes, Ancient Egypt and the Nile

Valley had witnessed several waves of migrations which radiated all over the continent. According to Anta Diop (1979: 377–403), the Kara from southern Sudan and Upper Oubangui, the Kare-Kare from north-eastern Nigeria, the Yoruba of south-eastern Nigeria, the Fulani, the Poular (ancient Toucouleurs), the Serer, the Zulu, etc., originated from the Nile Valley. Archaeological data are used to trace the routes of migrations. The burial mounds of the inland Niger delta are interpreted as a West African version of the pyramids of the Nile Valley (Diop 1979: 349) and the distribution of the megaliths of Senegal, Gambia and Mali are considered as markers of the migrations of the Serer from the Nile Valley to the Atlantic coast of West Africa. In this regard, the Malian site of Tundi-Daro was a subject of debate. The site is a field of megaliths located at the base of a red sandstone hill which has been interpreted as representing the material manifestation of an agrarian ritual. For Maes (1924), these stones had been erected by Carthaginians because

> for he who knows the psychology of negroes, one can surely ascertain that this undertaking was not executed by the representatives of the negro race because it represents a considerable amount of effort, without any immediate usefulness and bearing no relation to the regular require-ments of feeding and reproduction; the only functions which are really appealing to the negro. (Maes 1924: 31; translation mine)

However, for Anta Diop (1979: 398–9), this field of megaliths is further support for his hypothesis concerning the migration route of the Serers who still worship such stones. Negroes left the Nile Valley because of overpopulation and social crisis, and penetrated deeper into the continent. Their adaptation to the different ecological conditions they met on their way brought about changes in technological equipment and scientific knowledge; some features vital along the Nile but of no use elsewhere were abandoned and later forgotten (Diop 1979: 351).

3 ANCIENT EGYPT AS THE MOTHER OF CIVILIZATION

Ancient Egypt was the centre in which civilization developed and whence it radiated all over the world. This great cultural achievement was realized by black Africans who invented social complexity, kinship, monotheism, mathematics, science, writing, architecture, monumental art, etc. (Diop 1979: 411). Many of the great philosophers and scientists of Ancient Greece were trained by Egyptians: Pythagoras, Thales, Solon, Archimedes, Erathosthenes and many others made the trip to Egypt, where science was esoteric and secret. In Greece, science lay in the public domain where it was progressively integrated into the material world. Eventually, according to what we may refer to as Anta Diop's syllogism, Ancient Egypt brought civilization to the entire world. As Ancient Egypt was inhabited by negroes, it was negroes who brought civilization to humankind. Anta Diop thus asserts that black peoples must assume this glorious past, impose it as an unmistakable fact and, in continuity with Ancient Egypt, they must revive their national pride in order to reconquer their rightful place in the modern world.

In summary, Anta Diop's thesis is the most radical and complete in African French-speaking scholarship; developed to combat colonial scientific imperialism, it succeeded in demonstrating the weaknesses of the colonial rhetoric. The diffusionist paradigm was strengthened; only some of its directions were reversed. Instead of being a mere recipient of culture traits, Africa was shown to have played an important role in the dissemination of several culture traits to Europe.

Other researchers have followed the same tracks, but on a smaller scale (Obenga 1973). As far as archaeology is concerned, Diop (1968) and Andah (1980, 1979c, d) used archaeological data to combat diffusionist ideas of the colonial period. However, Andah avoids as far as possible the new kind of dogmatism, instilled by the pioneering research of Anta Diop, which is now very fashionable in many West African Francophone universities. According to this new attitude,

> Almost everything attests that in the beginning, in remote prehistory, during the Upper Palaeolithic, negroes were predominant. They kept this predominance in civilization and in technological and military superiority all through the millennia of history. (Diop 1967: 11)

Surprisingly enough, West African-trained archaeologists did not always adhere to this extreme nationalism; the knowledge gained from archaeology was used by some as 'charter' or good example. For example, Opoku-Gyamfi (1975) employed archaeological knowledge of the emergence of food-producing economies in northern Ghana to advocate self-sufficiency in food production in the modern context:

> The agricultural revolution which was initiated brought wealth to the majority of the Kintampo industrial people. Wealth which we see reflected in their finely-made stone bracelets, rasps and their art. The 'Kintampo culture' was indeed a unique phenomenon in Ghana's rise to prosperity. The tradition was really 'Ghanaian' although it derived inspiration from outside. That they were able to feed much of Ghana with the limited tools at their disposal, is a mark of great cultural achievement which we must all be proud of. (Opoku-Gyamfi 1975: 82)

In national and local newspapers, many other minor authors appeal to historical connections between present-day peoples and vanished populations, whose material remains are located in their respective national boundaries, as 'charter' for their opinions and actions.

IV Archaeology in modern West Africa

Present-day African archaeology can be safely characterized as international. Research is carried out by scholars from all over the world. The situation in Europe and Northern America is very different: in those continents, it is not easy for a researcher from another country to undertake fieldwork. The African situation thus favours a plurality of research problems, methods and techniques. However the other side of the coin is that only a very few West African countries have institutional structures adequate for archaeological research. Archaeology is expensive, and many West African countries are still 'fighting for survival'; nevertheless almost every country has an embryo of archaeology, either as departments of archaeology in universities, antiquities services and museums in 'wealthy' countries such as Nigeria, Ghana and Senegal, or subsumed within departments of history in almost all the Francophane countries. Institutes of human sciences have been created recently in Mali, Niger and Cameroon.

1 ARCHAEOLOGY AND SOCIETY

Almost every West African country aims to create national and regional museums. Some already have a National Museum (Mauritania, Mali, Niger, Ghana, Nigeria). However, the problem of regional museums is very difficult to solve: first, there is a lack of trained personnel; second, archaeological investigations are concentrated in various regions while others are devoid of any archaeological finds, though local art and folklore may easily fill the empty cases. The major problem is certainly the final one: due to the relative weakness of the new 'national' consciousness, many political leaders are afraid to emphasize regional traditions and customs which may be considered threats to the search for 'national unity'. There seems to be a confusion between ethnic consciousness and 'tribalism'. This specific feature of many African countries will probably be solved in the near future; in the meantime, regional museums will stay mostly in the planning stage. Some countries like Nigeria have succeeded in this particular undertaking and are thus a good example for many other West African countries.

The interest of the general public in archaeology varies from one country to another, dependent partly on the general level of education, the strength of real or assumed historical connections between present-day peoples inhabiting a specific area and the archaeological findings from the same area. For example, in northern Cameroon, where I am engaged in a field project, I had the opportunity to discuss my work with citizens from Kousseri, a town located only 15 kilometres from the mound I am excavating. They were suspicious of my account of the aims of my research; indeed they were deeply amazed by the fact that I had travelled from so far only to collect broken pots which are without any 'practical' benefit (i.e. in terms of material profit); they proposed that I purchase new pots in the market. They believed that I had some secret reasons for my work; in fact they were fully convinced that I was digging for antiquities in order to sell them at a profit in France. This example from my own experience is representative of the attitude of many average citizens in that part of Cameroon. The attitude of educated people is totally different; they are fully aware of the historical implications of archaeological research and are always ready to give some help to the desperate archaeologist, even if they still picture him or her as an 'old bearded man' living in another world – an image that I do not fit. Slowly but surely archaeology is gaining the support of West African peoples; this wider support places additional pressures on achaeologists who have to search for an equilibrium between their own specific research problems and the local people's implicit desire to possess on their land, the most ancient finds, the most beautiful material culture, and the origin of the major achievements of civilization.

2 CURRENT TRENDS IN WEST AFRICAN ARCHAEOLOGY

This basic contradiction in the purpose of archaeological research is not unique to West Africa, nor to archaeology; it is a tension imbedded in every scientific endeavour. Present-day West African archaeology is characterized by multi-disciplinary research, or at least multi-disciplinary perspectives, with the goal of understanding and explaining West African cultural dynamics. However, there are differences between the dominant space-time analytical framework which characterizes the research tradition of the Francophone countries and continental Europe (Tillet 1983, Treinen-Claustre 1982, Kuper 1978, Bernus and Bernus 1972, Paris 1984, Poncet et al. 1983, Petit-Maire 1979b, Petit-Maire and Riser 1984, Vernet 1984, Lebeuf 1969, Lebeuf et al. 1980, Amblard 1984, Devisse et al. 1983, Thilmans et al. 1980, Thilmans and Ravise 1980, Roubet et al.

1981, etc.) and the predominantly anthropological and systems-oriented research procedure mostly favoured by Anglophone archaeologists (McIntosh and McIntosh 1980a, 1983, Andah 1979c, d, Connah 1981, Holl 1983a, 1985a, b, 1986a, b, Stahl 1985a, b, 1986, Nzewunwa 1980, Warnier 1985, etc.). Thus, problems of culture change and transformation are investigated using different research procedures and techniques. Arguments about racial attribution of material culture remains are out of fashion. A case study will be useful to measure the radical change which has occurred in West African archaeology; for this I shall use what was until recently an archaeological 'terra incognita' in south-western Cameroon, an area usually called the 'western grassfields'. Fieldwork conducted there (Warnier 1984, 1985, Warnier and Fowler 1979, Rowlands 1986) has shed new light on the current debate over West African iron metallurgy.

There is a large amount of literature on the origins of iron technology in West Africa (see Holl 1983b, 1986a, McIntosh and McIntosh 1983). Two main traditions coexist: one, initiated by Leo Frobenius and the German cultural-historical school of anthropology, is composed of various kinds of diffusionist theories, while the other argues for local evolution. The simplistic nature of the arguments mobilized in this long-standing debate is misleading. Indeed, the analytical level of the discussions is too general and far too often a matter of faith, for it is obvious that iron technology is a complex system of interactions between societies, environments, technical knowledge and social demands. According to Rustad (1980: 232), it is clear that iron technology must be broken down into its components to permit valid comparisons. Since these components may take different forms, the question 'Did iron technology diffuse?' is both too broad and too vague. Many of the components of iron technology could have diffused independently, while others may have been invented locally, for example, to deal with the specific nature of the local iron ore. The appropriate line of thought is thus to begin with specific traits which are amenable to comparison on technological, economic and social levels. A systems approach tries to bridge the gap between static archaeological data and the dynamics of past societies from which these data derive. The research project on the west Cameroon grassfields was carried out from this perspective.

Until recently, the archaeology of this area was known only from notes on surface finds of stone tools published by Jeffreys (1951). Even if scholars suspected the existence of very ancient settlements, the consensus was that the area was inhabited only quite recently by waves of migrants coming from the north-east. However, archaeological surveys and excavations begun in 1974 have shown that rock shelters in the region have been inhabited since 9000 BP (Warnier 1984, 1985, De Maret 1980, 1982, Essomba 1986, David 1981b) and that iron technology was practised from about the third or fourth century AD. Furthermore, Warnier (1984, 1985) believes that the high-altitude savanna that comprises the Cameroon grassfields is mainly a product of long-term human interference with the environment.

Archaeological surveys have shown that the production of iron artefacts in the grassfields took place within the context of a long-distance trade network controlled by regional centres. In this centre/periphery set of relations, iron tools were exchanged for palm oil from the south and cotton and textiles from northern Nigeria. The results of this fieldwork (Warnier and Fowler 1979, Rowlands 1986) show that the nature of the iron-working sites, the technologies used and the scale of production contradict the colonial stereotype according to which African peoples lacked any kind of technological skill and initiative, a stereotype which had been given credibility by the fact that at the time of colonial contact, the Germans observed only very small-scale smelting furnaces. In fact, three different types of smelting furnaces are now known to have existed: a low cylindrical furnace which appears to have been the earliest and the most widespread form, in use from the third to the seventeenth century; a larger 'clump' furnace, in use during the seventeenth to nineteenth centuries; then, another form of small bowl furnace similar to the first, which survived as the dominant means of indigenous iron production until the 1940s. The technology of 'clump' furnaces was a response to the intensification of long-distance trade, the emergence of social stratification and an energy crisis. During this period intensive production of iron implements resulted in deforestation which in turn encouraged technological advances. This highly intensive system could only be maintained with a sustained demand; the introduction of mass-produced European iron implements during the nineteenth century, as well as the effects of the slave trade, resulted in the collapse of the whole system, to be replaced by the use of small bowl furnaces in which European iron and slag from earlier periods were smelted. The most likely explanation of this change is the failure of the local economic system to compete with the increasing quantity of imported European ingots and hoe blanks in the late nineteenth century.

The available evidence suggests that 'incorporation into European trading networks has served to break the complexity of existing local exchange networks and relations of production and probably to move local populations into more self-sufficient strategies of resource procurement' (Rowlands 1986: 6). And, more important, it appears that it is larger regional systems that were thus destabilized, resulting in increased warfare at the end of the nineteenth century when colonial powers began to take total control of Africa. Therefore, it is not surprising that they found disturbed social and economic systems (Holl 1979). This case study is interesting in that it shows how in some situations what appeared as African 'backwardness' may have been an artefact of the colonial powers themselves.

Epilogue

Archaeology seeks to learn about past cultures from the fragmentary remains of the products of human activity. West African archaeology, as well as African archaeology in general, has witnessed impressive progress in the last two decades. In this paper, I have reviewed some of the major paradigms of West African archaeology during the colonial period and during the emergence of African nationalism. The task of unravelling man's past makes heavy demands on multidisciplinary resources; consequently it is extremely costly for technical and financial reasons. It may be very distasteful for professional archaeologists engaged in exciting research, but we cannot avoid the question any longer: what is the relevance of archaeology in modern West Africa?

> Or, more specifically, . . . is archaeology sufficiently relevant to warrant the diversion of funds and of potentially productive men, skill, materials and land. Does prehistory really mean enough to us today to support such large claims on social resources? (Clark 1968: 251)

This problem is particularly dramatic for many West African countries which are still fighting for their survival in very difficult social and economic situations. Many important archaeological findings are tied to specific regional settings; yet, due to the artificial nature of the boundaries of modern African states, and the dominant emphasis on 'National Unity', any expression of local particularity or ethnic consciousness may often be misunderstood, and deemed a threat to national unity.

I should like to emphasize the humanistic value of archaeology, which appeals to individuals as members of societies and as individuals. 'Archaeology finds complete justification if it enriches the experience of men and helps them to live more abundantly as heirs of all ages and brothers to one another' (Clark 1968: 264). Archaeological experience shows that cultural achievement is a complex combination of interacting processes, both within and beyond any spatio-temporal cultural unit. If we want to build a true world of humanity, we must consider all the levels of human interaction composed as they are of a hierarchy of components. At the bottom is the individual, who belongs to a family, a corporate group, a culture and an ethnic group. All these components are included in various types of social groupings (bands, chiefdoms, states, empires, etc.), among which the modern 'nation-state' is only one among many. At the top of the hierarchy, I am inclined to place the vague 'Mankind', which for some admittedly is meaningless. Archaeology must be a school of tolerance; it tries to understand the basic features of human nature:

> One of the most potent factors in social integration is history. If people are to be led to feel themselves members of a world society, one way of helping them to do so is to stimulate a consciousness of world history. In other words, the unit of history has to be expanded from the parochial to the universal, from the history of nation or civilization to that of the world. (Clark 1968: 261)

A history of archaeology in this regard is the history of how archaeologists have explained variations in human cultural achievements. It is the responsibility of archaeologists to be well aware of the power resting in their hands; they have to create 'a frame of mind, a vivid consciousness of belonging to a world society, transcending, but also comprehending regional and even national loyalties' (Clark 1968: 266).

18 *The History of African Archaeology in World Perspective*

BRUCE G. TRIGGER

I have read the foregoing chapters, which provide the first comprehensive survey of the history of African archaeology, with much pleasure and profit. It is now my responsibility to comment on them and set them into a perspective of world archaeology. This is far from a routine assignment. Some of the chapters (Deacon, Robertshaw, Kense) constitute a compelling challenge to abandon my division of African archaeology into colonialist and nationalist types (Trigger 1984). Other contributors seem to find this distinction useful and Holl has even invented a similar one. I am therefore encouraged to refine rather than abandon these concepts. At the same time I will set them into a broader context by arguing that they are not the only important variables when it comes to describing the history of African archaeology.

After a long period of positivist certainty, western archaeologists, like many other social scientists, have been increasingly embracing a relativist theory of knowledge. As a result of direct or indirect exposure to the writings of Thomas Kuhn, Herbert Marcuse, Jürgen Habermas, Paul Feyerabend and Barry Barnes, few archaeologists believe any longer that objective knowledge of the past can be gained simply by applying sound techniques of analysis to an adequate corpus of data. Instead it is maintained that the questions archaeologists ask and the answers they are predisposed to accept are influenced, often unconsciously, by the opinions and beliefs that they bring to their research. To some degree this position, which I believe is correct, is shared by all the contributors to this volume. I certainly have no quarrel with the Marxist claim that groups construct ideologies to promote their economic and political interests, either by making exploitation appear to be part of the natural rather than the social realm or by claiming that in some way it is altruistic. Some hyper-relativists go further and assert that archaeological interpretations are nothing more than a reflection of subjective factors, thereby often unwittingly reducing archaeological data to being merely a stimulus for fantasy or a source of propaganda for various good and bad causes. While none of these papers espouses this extreme position, Holl's comes the closest to it. Although hyper-relativism is intellectually challenging, its principal effect is to undermine an independent role for archaeology as a source of insight into human history and behaviour and to reduce the social sciences to the same level as works of fiction or political advocacy (which lack systematization and verifiability, although they may provide significant insights into human behaviour). It seems to me that the case studies presented in this volume strongly contradict a hyper-relativist view of archaeological interpretation. While African archaeology has been powerfully influenced by its social and political milieu, its often unanticipated findings have altered entrenched interpretations of African history. Because of this, archaeology has played a significant role in helping to promote the decolonization of Africa. It is more than a passive reflection of social, political, and economic conditions, but must be seen as a discipline that plays an active role in helping to bring about social changes. One of the questions that I will consider in more detail is how and on what basis archaeology plays this role.

African archaeology began in a colonial setting. It was first practised by European visitors and settlers and the earliest interpretations of archaeological data reflected the understandings and prejudices that these people brought with them from Europe as they were modified to accord with the economic and political conditions in which they found themselves. Many of these situations favoured views of the past that saw Africans as incapable of self-improvement and attributed any evidence of advanced cultures to the actions of civilized colonists who had come from elsewhere in prehistoric times. Yet, as these studies dramatically illustrate, there was not one colonial view of Africa, but many. While Cecil Rhodes and the white settlers of Rhodesia had vested interests in portraying the local Bantu as incapable of improvement, colonial administrators were often predisposed to be more receptive to evidence that native people could benefit from development programmes (Hall, Barros). Likewise, in the 1960s, as part of a nationalist effort to present an image of South Africa as a modern nation, its white-minority government promoted the development of professional archaeology that soon produced evidence that contradicted cherished Afrikaner claims about the late migration of the Bantu into the country from the north (Hall). Despite the Eurocentric bias of most colonial archaeology, some French settlers in Algeria were prepared to claim their adopted country as the place of origin for the Aurignacian culture (Sheppard). There is abundant evidence that public opinion, or decisions by people in a position of authority, influence the availability of funding for archaeological research, the questions that archaeologists ask, the extent to which archaeological findings are communicated to particular groups, and the level of proof that is required to substantiate a particular argument. Social status may also determine the sort of archaeological research that an individual does and how the results of this research are published, as Holl has shown was the case during the colonization of French West Africa. Yet it is abundantly clear that there is no simple connection between social conditions and the precise manner in which archaeological research is carried out and archaeological findings are interpreted. More generally, as Hall observes, there is no 'tight, deterministic relationship between political economy and readings of precolonial history'. Concepts such as colonialist and nationalist archaeology are generic ones rather than labels for specific approaches to the past. Within each category there is much room for variation and even for overlap.

Archaeological interpretation is also influenced by available data, which in the case of Africa were very limited until recent decades. Few philosophers of science are still prepared to defend the proposition that historical and archaeological data are objectively given and independent of the interpretations that are offered of them. It has been demonstrated that even basic classificatory units are dependent on theory and that the kinds of data that are collected and the way in which they are studied are influenced by stereotypes. It is also possible, as Davis and Sheppard have shown, for the same data to be interpreted in many different ways, especially in the absence of adequate chronological controls. Yet information concerning subsistence patterns or levels of cultural development reached in particular regions at particular times and about the kinds of connections that may or may not have existed between different regions, once established, may exert a firm constraint on what is known about the past.

Third, archaeological interpretation is influenced by the analytical techniques that are available and by currently accepted standards of practice. Because, until recently, all professional archaeologists, including those born in Africa, have been trained abroad, the influence of metropolitan models has been especially strong. Even in the post-colonial era rival metropolitan approaches continue to produce significant differences in African archaeology, as, for example, between the culture-historical models favoured in former French West Africa and the ecological-anthropological ones adopted in Ghana and Nigeria (Holl, Barros). These aspects of colonial archaeology have their origins in social contexts that often are remote from those found in colonial situations and may unwittingly have led archaeologists to carry out research that was contrary in its orientation to colonial ideology. One of the most important objectives of the history of African archaeology must be to determine the relationship between archaeology as it developed in Europe and North America and the situational interests that were generated by specific colonial contexts. The most effective way to study the relationship between African and world archaeology is to examine how successive metropolitan paradigms have influenced archaeology in Africa.

Except in Egypt, where they started several decades earlier, serious studies of African archaeology began in the last decades of the nineteenth century, which was also the era of most active colonization. In Europe this period witnessed the slow transition between unilinear evolutionary anthropology and the newly developing culture-historical anthropology. Already by the 1860s, unilinear evolutionism had fallen under the racist influence of social Darwinism, especially as it was represented in the writings of Sir John Lubbock. In Lubbock's global scheme the failure of non-European races to advance culturally could be attributed to their lack of biological capacity; in terms of which Africans, for various political and economic reasons, had long been ranked low. This view continued to influence some studies of African archaeology into the early twentieth century, especially in areas where French intellectual influence was strong (Maret).

Culture-historical anthropology began in Germany in the 1880s with the work of Friedrich Ratzel. It interpreted cultural similarities as evidence of cultural connections that resulted from diffusion and migrations. Ethnologists found diffusionism a more expedient theory to explain away the evidence of cultural development in Africa, which took the form of large-scale iron-working, highly productive agriculture, urban centres, monumental architecture, centralized kingdoms, and highly developed art (Holl, Barros). Diffusionists argued that all of these traits originated outside of Africa and had been brought there by prehistoric white colonists, whose creative abilities had ultimately been destroyed as a result of miscegenation with blacks. Anthropologists zealously applied this theory to explain the ethnographic record. Light-skinned Hamitic pastoralists were assigned a leading role in transmitting traits of higher culture from the Near East into black Africa.

This same explanation was applied to various archaeological finds that were made throughout Africa. In the 1890s the explorer J.T. Bent drew upon earlier Portuguese speculations to suggest that the stone ruins of Zimbabwe were the remains of a Semitic gold-mining colony dating from biblical times; a theory that long remained popular with white settlers. Until well into the twentieth century burial mounds in West Africa and rock art in Southern Africa were attributed to Near Eastern and European influences, not only by amateurs but also in some cases by professional

European archaeologists (Barros, Hall). Likewise, impressive stone monuments, earthworks, and other evidence of advanced culture in East Africa were assigned to Hamitic (Azanian or Megalithic Cushite) invaders from the north-east (Robertshaw). Even Palaeolithic Africa was regarded (except by E.J. Wayland and a few others) as a cul-de-sac whose development was influenced by waves of more advanced culture coming from the north and where cultures survived long after they became extinct in Europe. This conclusion was supported despite the fact that Darwin long before had identified Africa as the likely cradle of humanity. It was also generally maintained that Africans had begun to work iron quite recently, although X. Stainier argued that their technological expertise suggested that the African Iron Age had begun long ago.

Diffusionism as applied to African prehistory was an ethnological theory created in the absence of any detailed archaeological or historical record. It was used to interpret archaeological data mainly by amateur archaeologists and almost invariably in the absence of adequate cultural chronologies. The only exception was Egypt, for which a culture-chronology was already available. On the basis of limited evidence Egyptian civilization was interpreted as resulting from Near Eastern influences being imposed on a primitive African 'substratum', in marked contrast to earlier Enlightenment speculations that it had originated in the Sudan. As O'Connor points out, Egypt's relations with neighbouring African groups, in so far as they were considered at all, were seen as those of a colonizing power dealing with a primitive hinterland, a view that seemed all the more convincing because it accorded with the Ancient Egyptian ideal of their cultural supremacy. The Ancient Egyptians, like the Phoenicians, Carthaginians, Southern Arabians, and at second hand the Hamites, were treated as prototypes of the civilizing role that nineteenth- and early twentieth-century Europeans saw themselves playing in Africa.

Yet by the beginning of the twentieth century culture-historical archaeology was sufficiently developed to refute many of these claims, although it was derived from the same anthropological paradigm and shared the same biases as did diffusionist ethnology. While it took over a century for a feebly developed archaeology to refute the Moundbuilder myth in North America (finally achieved by Cyrus Thomas in 1894), Gertrude Caton-Thompson was able in one season of excavations to provide irrefutable stratigraphic evidence that the stone ruins of Zimbabwe dated from the Christian era and had been built by the Bantu, not Phoenicians. Hereafter amateur archaeologists and white settler regimes might refuse to accept her interpretations but no professional archaeologist did. Hall may be correct that Thompson's findings accorded with the interests of colonial administrators, who also supported Iron Age research in Rhodesia in the 1940s and 1950s. Yet it seems to me that the more development-oriented interests of administrators would have inclined them towards a benevolent neutrality with respect to archaeological findings, rather than to become promoters of a pro-Bantu archaeology, as Rhodes and white settlers had been partisans of a 'white settler' Zimbabwe. The more substantial basis for Caton-Thompson's discoveries was the new level of technical expertise that archaeologists had achieved with respect to excavation techniques, particularly stratigraphy. While Richard Hall had interpreted the 'Bantu' pottery at Zimbabwe as evidence of an epigonal occupation of the site and David Randall-MacIver had found no evidence that people other than Bantu had lived there, Caton-Thompson was able to demonstrate that a Bantu presence preceded as well as was contemporary with the building of Zimbabwe and to date the sequence by means of trade goods. The same stratigraphic procedures provided the basis for the growing understanding of the Iron Age in Zimbabwe after the Second World War.

In the first half of the twentieth century similar stratigraphic methods promoted an understanding of Stone Age sequences in eastern, southern, and central Africa and began to reveal the distinctiveness of many of the cultures that were being identified (Robertshaw, Hall, Maret). In East Africa Louis and Mary Leakey discovered typologically more primitive Palaeolithic stone tool assemblages than had been found anywhere else in the world and were able to demonstrate stratigraphically that these Oldowan assemblages ante-dated the more familiar Lower Palaeolithic cultures found in Africa, Europe and Asia. In the 1950s and 1960s spectacular early hominid finds and the geochronometric establishment of the unexpected antiquity of these assemblages strongly supported Darwin's claim that humanity had evolved in Africa and made East Africa the key area for the study of this process. European and American archaeologists now saw Africa as offering an opportunity to investigate the remote origins of all human beings, including Europeans, which was impossible in their own countries. At the same time radiocarbon and potassium-argon dating established that successive Palaeolithic cultures were at least as old as similar ones found in Europe, thereby confirming the importance of Africa as a centre of cultural as well as biological development throughout the Stone Age. In textbooks of world archaeology published in the 1960s and 1970s Africa was no longer described as having been a backwater throughout the whole of human history. Instead it was featured as a focal point of progress, especially in early Palaeolithic times. Yet many of these same textbooks continued to treat Africa in recent millennia as a continent that (except for Egypt) had remained retarded and marginal by comparison with Europe, Asia, and the tropical parts of the New World.

While culture-historical archaeologists shared the same pessimism about human creativity and the same reliance on diffusion and migration to explain cultural change as did culture-historical ethnologists, the growing control that they gained over cultural chronologies revealed the inadequacies of many ethnological speculations about African prehistory. In particular, they demonstrated the falseness of many claims about the backward nature of African cultures and their inability to change without external stimuli. A colonial mentality may have retarded the development of archaeological research (through the belief that there was nothing to study) and predisposed many archaeologists to attribute changes to outside influences. It did not, however, preclude archaeological research that challenged these stereotypes in fundamental ways and altered the significance of African prehistory in relation to world archaeology.

The next major trend to influence African archaeology was increasing attention to functional interpretations of archaeological data. Although European archaeologists had been interested in the relationship between cultures and their natural environment since the 1840s, a functional approach became more important in the 1930s with Cyril Fox's geographical analyses, Gordon Childe's economic explanations, and Grahame Clark's studies of subsistence economies and exchange. Clark's work had an especially important impact on African archaeology as a result of the many Cambridge-trained archaeologists who worked there, beginning with J. Desmond Clark and Thurstan Shaw, who had come to Africa in the 1930s. Both of them started with culture-historical studies of the late Stone Age. This choice of period generally seems to have reflected the belief that iron had been introduced only recently into Africa and perhaps that Stone Age studies were less controversial than Iron Age ones (see also Maret). Yet, after the Second World War, they and other archaeologists such as Jean de Heinzelin in the Belgian Congo, paid increasing attention to changing patterns of hunter-gathering and the development of food production; thereby establishing a trend that has become increasingly prominent in African archaeological research (Clark, Deacon, Brandt and Fattovich). At the same time the Leakeys began to move in a similar direction with their trend-setting excavations of Palaeo-lithic 'occupation floors'. This research, which included palaeoenviron-mental reconstructions and studies of plant and animal behaviour, drew attention to dynamic, adaptive capacities in African cultures that had hitherto been ignored. Efforts to understand changing subsistence patterns also caused archaeologists to study traditional African cultures and enhanced the appreciation of their richness and flexibility. While ecological approaches in the 1960s tended to interpret cultural changes more as automatic ecosystematic responses than as voluntaristic human behaviour, the result was to add a new dimension to African culture history that stressed cultures as functioning systems. This in turn laid the basis for understanding prehistory in terms not only of diffusion and migration but also of the internal transformation of cultures.

By the 1960s three new factors began to influence the development of African archaeology. Throughout most of the continent a rapid movement towards decolonization had produced a growing interest in the peoples of Africa. Historians, encouraged by Basil Davidson, sought to transcend the narrow limits of colonial history. This encouraged a growing interest in oral traditions, historical linguistics, and archaeological data, which could help them to do this. At the same time African scholars began to search for a past in which they could take pride, even if in the case of Cheikh Anta Diop this amounted to little more than a restatement of the ethnologist Grafton Elliot Smith's Egyptocentric diffusionism, with the ancient Egyptians firmly identified as Africans, and hence blacks. Diop's work outside of Egypt, like that of Elliot Smith, was based not on archaeological evidence but on ethnography and speculative history. Second, a growing number of professionally trained archaeologists began to be employed in museums, universities, and research centres in different parts of Africa. Knowing the latest techniques of archaeology, they started to elaborate cultural chronologies, where these were lacking or deficient, and to investigate ecological and other problems. Partly influenced by the political 'winds of change' and partly challenged by the unknown, many archaeolo-gists began to turn their attention to the Iron Age and the early historic period in the final years of colonial regimes. It is significant that after the Second World War major progress was made in elaborating Iron Age chronologies in Rhodesia and South Africa, despite the very different regimes that were in power in these countries. Archaeologists studying late prehistoric states in Uganda and West Africa also began to tackle the very difficult problems involved in integrating archaeological data and oral traditions (Schmidt); while the correlation of historical linguistics and archaeological data centred pre-eminently on the reconstruction of prehistoric Bantu migrations (Maret).

The third influence on archaeology at this period, especially in anglophone Africa, was the New (or Processual) Archaeology, which developed in the United States in the early 1960s out of the cultural evolutionary and settlement approaches that had influenced American archaeology in the previous decade. Knowledge of the New Archaeology was transmitted to archaeologists working in Africa not only through the literature but also by an increasing number of American archaeologists who did fieldwork there beginning in the 1960s. British-trained archaeologists who were employed in North American universities, in particular Desmond Clark, Glynn Isaac, Merrick Posnansky and Peter Shinnie, played a sensitive role in transmitting new ideas to their African colleagues. Although the New Archaeology was rarely accepted as a programme, except among younger archaeologists in South Africa, its strong emphasis on understanding changes within cultural systems and its rejection of diffusion and migration as satisfactory explanations of change helped to reinforce trends already under way in African archaeology that stressed creativity in African cultures. Its desire to study whole cultural systems also legitimized and encouraged interest in a broadening spectrum of features of late prehistoric African cultures, including mining, trade, metallurgy, urbanism, social hierarchies, the development of states, and religious traditions. Continuing studies of subsistence patterns provided evidence of the unsuspected antiquity and diversity of food production throughout much of Africa and confirmed earlier predictions by Nicolay Vavilov and others that Africa had been a major centre of plant domestication. Growing evidence was produced of the indigenous elaboration of metallurgy, the early development of long-distance exchange, and the indigenous growth of urban centres in West Africa and along the coast of the Indian Ocean. Hitherto these centres either had been believed not to exist in precolonial times or were attributed to Arab colonists (Barros, Robertshaw). These discoveries created a new and a more positive image of precolonial African history that accorded with and helped to reinforce the hope for the future that accompanied the decolonization of Africa.

Yet despite the New Archaeology's emphasis on internal change and the contributions that its methodology made to creating a more positive understanding of African history, it is clear that this effect was not inherent in the New Archaeology as it was conceived and practised in the United States. In North America the New Archaeology revealed the inherent capacity of prehistoric native cultures for innovation, in opposition to the culture-historical paradigm which attributed most changes to diffusion and migration. Yet because the New Archaeology saw its goal as being to produce universal generalizations about human behaviour and evolutionary changes, the implications of its findings for understanding North American native history went largely unnoticed by archaeologists, although they were later picked up by ethnohistorians (Trigger 1985). Despite its close ties to ethnology the New Archaeology remained as remote from native people and their concerns as culture-historical archaeology had been. As a small minority of the total population, native North Americans are of relatively little concern to most North Americans. Under these circumstances archaeologists have preferred to risk confrontation with native people over a variety of issues rather than to try to make archaeology of interest to them. Instead the New Archaeology has sought to justify itself by producing generalizations that applied to white American society. In Africa the New Archaeology encouraged and provided many of the techniques necessary to investigate a broader range of behaviour in prehistoric times than had been attempted previously. Yet because nationalism had created a growing interest in the history of the continent as a whole and its specific regions, these findings were applied to producing specific historical interpretations rather than evolutionary generalizations. Under these circumstances the New Archaeology helped to enrich the study of the history of Africa and its peoples.

We may therefore conclude that the New Archaeology allowed a wider range of human behaviour to be inferred from the archaeological record but the use that was made of these findings depended on specific social circumstances. In Africa, the techniques of New Archaeology, while drawing archaeology and anthropology closer together, helped to create a new African history that principally aimed at understanding what happened to particular peoples and regions at specific times. In North America the New Archaeology aimed at producing evolutionary generalizations. Thus, while the New Archaeology played an important role in encouraging the development of new techniques to interpret archaeological data, the use that was made of those techniques depended on the social milieu.

The last two decades have seen an intensification of trends in African archaeology that were already evident in the late colonial period. Much of the indigenous archaeological effort is expended on studying recent prehistory, which generally means the Iron Age. Yet, although the Palaeolithic period is of more interest to foreign archaeologists, African archaeologists also take pride in the unique antiquity of the archaeological record on their continent and its relevance for understanding human origins. Despite the nationalistic bias of much contemporary archaeology there is no more unity to the study of African prehistory now than there was in the past. Egyptology, with its continuing dedication to epigraphy and art history, maintains a methodological as well as an interpretive isolation from the rest of African archaeology. This reflects a perpetuation of its original modelling on classical rather than on prehistoric archaeology as well as modern Egypt's ambiguity about its role as an African or a Near Eastern nation. Across the rest of Africa differences in archaeological practice correlate with the size and resources of specific countries, their colonial heritage (as documented by Holl for British and French West Africa), and the cultural policies of different regimes (see, for example, Hall on Mozambique). The most developed versions of nationalist archaeology are found in the larger states of West Africa, where universities have established departments of archaeology to train the staff needed for work in this region. The most striking contrast is between the archaeology of these countries and that of South Africa.

South Africa has a large number of professional archaeologists (especially in relation to the size of its white population) and has invested heavily in archaeology since the 1960s. Close contacts are maintained with professional archaeologists in Europe and America and the training of archaeologists within South Africa conforms to the pattern of these countries. The research carried out by South African archaeologists has likewise achieved a high technical standard and in some fields has won international recognition for pioneering new methods of analysis. South African archaeologists keep abreast of the most recent developments in archaeology, as evidenced in the chapters by Davis, Deacon and Hall, which note and reflect the influences of relativism and neo-Marxism that are not yet evident elsewhere in Africa. In spite of this South African archaeology remains the most colonial of all African archaeologies. As the creation of a white minority intelligentsia, its relationship to the majority of South Africans remains highly ambiguous. The findings of South African archaeologists flatly contradict cherished European myths about a late Bantu arrival which still play a major role in government propaganda. Yet, as Hall points out, these findings are generally expressed in an arcane vocabulary and in the past they have not been communicated in a comprehensible manner to either the black majority or white minority of South Africans. The dominant strategy seems to have been to buy government support and freedom to carry out research at the cost of maintaining political neutrality and apparent irrelevance to social issues. At the same time South African archaeology takes pride in being a branch of world archaeology that is able, like American archaeology, to produce evolutionary generalizations that promote a general understanding of human behaviour. In this respect at least, the relationship of archaeology to the majority of South Africans is not different in kind from that of American archaeology to a much smaller number of native Americans. In both the United States and South Africa prehistoric archaeology remains caught up in problems of internal colonialism long after each country has become independent. Yet, as the contradictions in South African society grow deeper, this pose becomes ever more difficult for South African archaeologists to maintain. A group of them are now engaged in trying to communicate archaeological findings to black schoolchildren (Taylor 1988).

In West Africa archaeology is less well funded than in South Africa, but at least in some of the more populous countries a significant infrastructure has been created for teaching and research, in which West African rather than expatriate archaeologists play a leading role. These archaeologists are interested in the precolonial history of their countries and of the region as a whole. They address problems of ethnic origins and prehistoric economic, social, and cultural development. Many students carry out research in their home territories that combines oral traditions and ethnographic data with archaeology by means of ethnoarchaeology and the direct historic approach. The archaeology that is practised in Nigeria and Ghana is simultaneously intensely anthropological and intensely historical, even though in the universities it has avoided institutional affiliations with documentary history, which is seen as using different methods to study the past (Kense). While archaeology remains much more closely affiliated with history departments in the countries of former French West Africa, growing involvement with researchers from many different parts of the world is promoting an internationalization of archaeological methods (Barros).

Throughout West Africa problems arise as to how archaeological research should serve regional, national and local or ethnic goals. Sites of historical importance have become the focus of special study and preservation and museums are being developed as centres of public education. In some situations it is feared that by strengthening local loyalties archaeology may weaken national ones; in others this contradiction is not regarded as a serious issue. Political control of archaeological research and interpretation has been indirect and achieved through the allocation of funding where it has occurred at all. Above all, the general goal of strengthening pride in West Africa's precolonial achievements is one that is not seen, by West Africans or outsiders, as creating a contradiction between 'objective' or 'scientific' canons of archaeological research and serving social and political ends. Archaeology is providing West Africa with a far more detailed, dynamic and exciting past than did Diop's ethnographically based speculations. West African archaeologists take pride in their research and believe that, by enhancing respect for their past, they are playing a significant role in the economic and social development of their region.

This survey indicates that African archaeology has been influenced by the successive major trends that have shaped the interpretation of archaeological data in Europe and America. This openness to metropolitan influences is perhaps especially characteristic of colonial archaeologies, but also seems to be a feature of archaeology worldwide (Trigger 1986). Yet it is equally clear that the development of African archaeology has been, and

continues to be, influenced in many complex and subtle ways by social and
political conditions in Africa. Many of these chapters demonstrate how
European and North American approaches to archaeological analysis have
been modified by local conditions when they are applied in Africa. The final
question that must be addressed is whether changes in archaeological
interpretation represent merely shifts in fashion (each addressing certain
issues, while ignoring others), or the results of archaeological studies are in
some way cumulative and lead to irreversible changes in a scientific
understanding of African prehistory.

It is clear that archaeology played a significant role in refuting colonial
mythology about Africans and their past. The culture-historical approach,
although based on the same diffusionist views as many of the speculations
that attributed significant cultural change in Africa to external influences,
definitively refuted many of the latter speculations. Since then empirical
studies of chronology, subsistence patterns, technology, exchange, and
social and political organization have provided evidence of cultural change
and creativity that has consistently dispelled the view that in precolonial
times Africa was culturally stagnant and retarded. In addition to
documenting earlier stages of cultural development than have been
identified anywhere else, archaeology has demonstrated that in later times
Africa was as culturally dynamic as any other major region of the world.
While stereotypes have influenced the problems that archaeologists have
been prepared to study and even what answers they have regarded as
credible, a growing corpus of information about African prehistory has
been collected that now imposes severe limitations on what it is possible for
professional archaeologists to believe about African prehistory. This
increasing awareness of changes in the course of African prehistory, which
now complements an awareness of cultural continuities, is clearly in accord
with, and to some degree has been stimulated by, the social conditions
surrounding decolonization and independence. Yet empirical evidence
indicates that these findings are more than socially induced fantasies. Proof
of this is found in professional archaeology's refutation of static views of the
past in South Africa as well as in the rest of the continent. Conversely
archaeology has produced evidence that refutes major aspects of Diop's
nationalistic theories no less than the racist stereotypes of Lepsius and
Seligman. The chief impact of African archaeology is its empirical data that,
especially in recent years, have compelled both Africans and non-Africans to
rethink how they regard the history of that continent and its peoples.

I agree with Holl and others that archaeology has a political and cultural
role to play, whether it wishes to or not. What is important, however, is
the manner in which it plays that role. While not refuting the importance
of relativism, archaeological findings have the power to restrain fantasy, if
sufficient data are collected and they are analysed in a scientifically rigorous
fashion. Popular myths or political restraint may preclude a scientific
analysis or the public acceptance of the findings derived by such methods.
Yet the history of African archaeology as documented in this volume
demonstrates the ability of archaeological findings to triumph over
colonialist myths based on misinterpreted ethnography, as well as to refute
the well intentioned but equally imaginative claims of the negritude
movement, as represented by the work of Diop and his followers. The most
constructive contribution that archaeology can make to African development is to determine as precisely and objectively as possible what happened
in the past. The results produced so far indicate that this is an endeavour
worthy of support by all those who are concerned with Africa's future as
well as its past. The long-term influence that is gained by archaeology in

this manner is different from and clearly superior to the short-term power derived from consciously striving to serve propagandistic ends.

Studying the history of archaeology reveals much that is crucial about the nature of the discipline and justifies R.G. Collingwood's (1939:132) observation that 'no historical problem should be studied without studying ... the history of historical thought about it.' These chapters and the history of archaeology generally reveal that while social, political and cultural biases preclude an ultra-positivist approach to archaeological interpretation, archaeologists must equally discount the currently popular but highly enervating hyper-relativist view that data play no significant role in what they say about the past. This is fortunate, since it is only in this way that archaeologists can avoid abandoning themselves to the production of political propaganda or play a role that is different from writing novels. The present study is of particular interest because it offers the first detailed account of the history of archaeology for a region that has seen European colonization followed by decolonization. It stands as a record of the exogenous forces that brought African archaeology into being. The next account of the history of African archaeology will no doubt be written mainly by archaeologists who are to a much greater degree than the present authors an integral part of Africa's cultural traditions and who will chronicle the further integration of archaeology into those traditions and of those traditions into archaeology.

Bibliography

ADAMS, W. (1977), *Nubia. Corridor to Africa*, Harmondsworth: Allen Lane Penguin Books. #DOC

ADANDE, A. and MÊTINHOUÉ, G. (1982), 'Potières et poterie de Sè: une enquête historique et technologique dans le Mono béninois', *Le Courrier de la Recherche au Bénin* 2: 1–55. #PB

AFEKU, J.K. (1976), 'A study of smoking pipes from Begho', unpublished M.A. thesis: University of Ghana. #FJK

ALIMEN, H. (1955), *Préhistoire de l'Afrique*, Paris: Editions Boubée. #PM #AH

ALIMEN, H. (1957), *The Prehistory of Africa*, London: Hutchinson. #JDC #SAB

ALLEN, J.DE V. (1981), 'Swahili culture and the nature of east coast settlement', *International Journal of African Historical Studies* 14: 306–34. #PR

ALLEN, J. DE V. (1982), 'Traditional history and African literature: the Swahili case', *Journal of African History* 23: 227–36. #PR

ALLSWORTH–JONES, P. (forthcoming), 'Sangoan and Middle Stone Age in Ghana: a reconsideration'. #TS

ALMAGRO BASCH, MARTIN, and ALMAGRO GORBEA, MARTIN (1968), *Estudios de art rupestre nubio I.* Madrid: Ministerio de Asuntos Eteriores. *Memorias de la Mission arqueologica Española en Egipto* 10. #WD

ALTHUSSER, L. (1971), 'Ideology and ideological state apparatuses (notes towards an investigation)', in *Lenin and Philosophy and Other Essays*: 121–73, London: New Left Books. #MH

AMBLARD, SYLVIE (1984), *Tichitt-Walata: civilisation et industrie lithique*, Paris: Editions Recherches sur les civilisations, A.D.P.F. #AH

AMBROSE, S.H. (1982), 'Archaeology and linguistic reconstructions of history in East Africa', in Ehret, C. and Posnansky, M. (eds), *The Archaeological and Linguistic Reconstruction of African History*: 104–57, Berkeley and Los Angeles: University of California Press. #PR

AMBROSE, S.H. (1984), 'The introduction of pastoral adaptations to the Highlands of East Africa', in Clark, J.D. and Brandt, S.A. (eds), *From Hunters to Farmers: The Causes and Consequences of Food Production in Africa*: 212–39. Berkeley and Los Angeles: University of California Press. #PR

AMBROSE, S.H., HIVERNEL, F. and NELSON, C.M. (1980), 'The taxonomic status of the Kenya Capsian', in Leakey. R.E. and Ogot, B.A. (eds), *Proceedings of the 8th Pan-African Congress of Prehistory and Quaternary Studies, Nairobi, September 1977*: 248–52. Nairobi: The International Louis Leakey Memorial Institute for African Prehistory. #PR

AMMERMAN, A.J., GIFFORD, D.P. and VOORRIPS, A. (1978), 'Towards an evaluation of sampling strategies: simulated excavations of a Kenyan pastoralist site', in Hodder, I. (ed.), *Simulation Studies in Archaeology*: 123–32. Cambridge: Cambridge University Press. #PR

ANATI, EMMANUEL (1985), 'The rock art of Tanzania and the east African sequence', *Bollettino del Centro Camuno di Studi Preistorici* 23: 15–68. #WD

ANCIAUX DE FAVEAUX, A. (1955), *Gisements et industries préhistoriques des hauts plateaux katangais*, Académie Royale des Sciences Coloniales, Classe des Sciences Naturelles et Médicales, Nouvelle série, II, 2, Brussels. #PM

ANCIAUX DE FAVEAUX, A. (1966), 'Evolution parallèle de deux ou plusieurs techniques au paléolithique ancien et moyen sur les hauts plateaux katangais. Fouilles 1960 et 1961', *Atti del VI Congresso Internazionale delle Scienze Preistoriche e Protostoriche* III: 230–5. #PM

ANDAH, BASSEY W. (1973), 'Archaeological reconnaissance of Upper Volta', unpublished PhD thesis: University of California, Berkeley. #FJK

ANDAH, BASSEY W. (1978), 'Excavations at Rim, Upper Volta', *West African Journal of Archaeology* 8: 75–138. #FJK #PB

ANDAH, BASSEY W. (1979a), 'The quaternary of the Guinea region of West Africa: an assessment of the geomorphic evidence', *West African Journal of Archaeology* 9: 9–46. #FJK

ANDAH, BASSEY W. (1979b), 'The early palaeolithic in West Africa: the case of Asokrochona coastal region of Accra', *West African Journal of Archaeology* 9: 47–85. #FJK

ANDAH, BASSEY W. (1979c), 'The Later Stone Age and Neolithic of Upper Volta viewed in a West African context', *West African Journal of Archaeology* 9: 88–117. #FJK #AH

ANDAH, BASSEY W. (1979d), 'Iron Age beginnings in West Africa: reflections and suggestions', *West African Journal of Archaeology* 9: 135–50. #FJK #AH

ANDAH, BASSEY W. (1980), 'L'Afrique de l'Ouest avant le VIIe siècle', in Mokhtar, G (ed.). *Histoire générale de l'Afrique; II: L'Afrique ancienne*: 641–71. Paris: Unesco. #AH

ANDRÉ, R. (1882), 'Die steinzeits Afrikas', *Globus* 41: 185–90. #PR

ANFRAY, F. (1964), 'Notre connaissance du passé ethiopienne d'après les travaux archéologiques recentes', *Journal of Semantic Studies* 9: 247–9. #SAB

ANFRAY, F. (1967), 'Matara', *Annales d'Ethiopie* 7: 33–53. #SAB

ANFRAY, F. (1968), 'Aspects de l'archéologie ethiopienne', *Journal of African History* 9: 345–66. #SAB

ANFRAY, F. (1981), 'The civilization of Aksum from the first to the seventh century', in Mokhtar, G. (ed.), *General History of Africa II: Ancient Civilizations of Africa*: 362–80. Berkeley: University of California Press. #SAB

ANOZIE, F.N. (1979), 'Early iron technology in Igboland (Lejja and Umandu), *West African Journal of Archaeology* 9: 119–34. #FJK

ANQUANDAH, James (1982), *Rediscovering Ghana's Past*, Accra: Sedco/Longman. #FJK

ANTOINE, M. (1935), 'Aperçu sommaire sur les industries lithiques du Maroc Central', *Bull. de la S.P.M.* 4: 29–49; and *Bull. Archéol.* 1930–31 (Paris 1935): 623–36. #JAJG

ANTOINE, M. (1948), 'La préhistoire du Maroc atlantique et ses incertitudes', *Vol. jubil. de la Soc. des Sc. nat. du Maroc, 1945*: 361–89. #JAJG

ARAMBOURG, C. (1952), 'The African Pleistocene mammals', in Leakey, L.S.B. and Cole, S. (eds), *Proceedings of the Pan-African Congress on Prehistory, Nairobi 1947*: 18–25. Oxford: Basil Blackwell. #JAJG

ARAMBOURG, C. (1955), 'Le gisement de Ternifine et l'Atlanthropus', *Bulletin de la Société Préhistorique Française* 52: 90–5. #JAJG

ARKELL, A.J. (1949), *The Old Stone Age in the Anglo-Egyptian Sudan*, Sudan Antiquities Service Occasional Papers No. 1. Khartoum. #JAJG #PLS

ARKELL, A.J. (1954), 'Four occupation sites at Agordat', *Kush* 2: 33–62. #SAB

ARNAL, J., BAILLOUD, G. and RIQUET, R. (1960), 'Les styles céramiques du Néolithique français', *Préhistoire* 14: 1–208. Paris: Presses Universitaires de France. #PB

ARRIGHI, G. (1967), *The Political Economy of Rhodesia*, The Hague: Mouton. #MH

ATHERTON, JOHN H. (1969a), 'The Later Stone Age of Sierra Leone', unpublished PhD thesis: University of Oregon, Eugene. #FJK

ATHERTON, JOHN H. (1969b), 'Archaeology in Liberia: problems and possibilities', *West African Archaeological Newsletter* 11: 19–21. #FJK

ATHERTON, JOHN H. (1970), 'Liberian Prehistory', *Liberian Studies Journal* 3: 83–111. #FJK

ATHERTON, JOHN H. (1972a), 'Protohistoric habitation sites in northeastern Sierra Leone', *Bulletin de la Société Royale Belge d'Anthropologie et de Préhistoire* 83: 5–17. #FJK

ATHERTON, JOHN H. (1972b), 'Excavations at Kamabai and Yagala Rock Shelters, Sierra Leone', *West African Journal of Archaeology* 2: 39–74. #FJK

ATHERTON, JOHN H. (1979), 'Early economies of Sierra Leone and Liberia: archaeological and historical reflections', in Dorjahn, V.R. and Isaac, B.L. (eds), *Essays on the Economic Anthropology of Sierra Leone and Liberia*, Philadelphia: Institute for Liberian Studies. #FJK

ATHERTON, JOHN H. (1980), 'Speculations on functions of some prehistoric archaeological materials from Sierra Leone', in Swartz, B.K. and Dumett, R.A. (eds), *West African Cultural Dynamics*: 259–75. The Hague: Mouton. #FJK

ATHERTON, JOHN H. (1983), 'Ethnoarchaeology in Africa', *African Archaeological Review* 1: 75–104. #FJK #PRS

ATHERTON, JOHN H. (1984), 'La Préhistoire de la Sierra Leone', *L'Anthropologie* 88(2): 245–61. #FJK

AUDOUZE, F. and LEROI-GOURHAN, A. (1981), 'France: a continental insularity', *World Archaeology* 13: 170–89. #PB

AVERY, D.M. (1982), 'Micromammals as palaeoenvironmental indicators and an interpretation of the late Quaternary in the southern Cape Province, South Africa', *Annals of the South African Museum* 85: 183–374. #JD

AVERY, G. (1976), 'A systematic investigation of open station shell midden sites along the south-western Cape coast', unpublished MA thesis: University of Cape Town. #JD

AVERY, G. (1977), 'Report on the marine bird remains from the Paternoster midden', *South African Archaeological Bulletin* 32: 74–6. #JD

BABET, V. (1929), *Étude géologique de la zone du chemin de fer Congo-Océan et de la région minière du Niari et du Djoué*, Paris: Larose. #PM

BABET, V. (1931), 'Présentation de pièces d'industries lithiques au Congo', *Bulletin de la Société Préhistorique Française* 28(6): 287–8. #PM

BABET, V. (1936), 'Note préliminaire sur un atelier de pierres taillées à Brazzaville (Afrique Equatoriale Française), *Bulletin de la Société Préhistorique Française* 33(2): 153–4. #PM

BAGNOLD, R.A. *et al.* (1939), 'An expedition to the Gilf Kebir and 'Uweinat', *Geographical Journal* 93: 281–313. #WD

BAILLOUD, G. (1965), 'Les gisements paléolithiques de Melka-Kunturé (Choa)', *Cahiers de l'Institut Ethiopien d'Archéologie* 1. #SAB

BAINES, D.L. (1909), 'Ancient Forts', *Official Uganda Gazette* 15 May: 137–8. #PRS

BAINES, J. and MALEK, J. (1980), *Atlas of Ancient Egypt*, New York: NY Facts on File Publications. #DOC

BALFOUR, HENRY (1903), ' "Thunderbolt" celts from Benin', *Man* 3: 182–3, #FJK

BALFOUR, HENRY (1909), 'Introduction', in Tongue, H., *Bushman Paintings*, Oxford: Clarendon Press. #WD

BALOUT, L. (1955), *Préhistoire de l'Afrique du Nord, essai de chronologie*. Paris: Arts et Métiers Graphiques. #JAJG #PJS #JDC #AH

BALOUT, L., BIBERSON, P. and TIXÌER, J. (1967), 'L'Acheuléen de Ternifine, gisement de l'Atlanthrope', *L'Anthropologie* 71: 217–35. #JAJG

BARBETTI, M., CLARK, J.D., WILLIAMS, F.M. and WILLIAMS, M.A.J. (1980), 'Palaeomagnetism and the search for very ancient fireplaces in Africa', *Anthropologie (Brno)* 18: 299–304. #JAJG

BARBOUR, G. (1957), 'Obituary, Neville Jones', in Clark, J.D. and Cole, S. (eds), *Prehistory: Third Panafrican Congress, 1955.*: xxviii. London: Chatto & Windus. #JAJG

BARKER, G. (1978), 'Economic models for the Manekweni zimbabwe, Mozambique', *Azania* 13: 71–100. #MH

BARRELL, H. (1984), 'The United Democratic Front and National Forum: their emergence, composition and trends', *South African Review* 2: 6–20. #MH

BARROS, P. DE (1985), 'The Bassar: large-scale iron producers of the West African savanna', PhD thesis: U.C.L.A. Ann Arbor: University Microfilms. #PB #PRS

BARROS, P. DE (1986), 'Bassar: a quantified, chronologically controlled, regional approach to a traditional iron production centre in West Africa', *Africa* 56: 148–74. #PB

BARROS, P. DE (1988), 'Societal repercussions of the rise of large-scale traditional iron production: a West ·African example', *African Archaeological Review* 6 (in press). #PB

BARTHELME, J.W. (1985), *Fisher-hunters and Neolithic pastoralists in East Turkana, Kenya*, Oxford: BAR International Series 254. #PR

BATTISS, WALTER (1948), '*The Artists of the Rocks*, Pretoria: Red Fawn Press. #WD

BAYLE DES HERMENS, R. DE (1975), *Recherche préhistorique en République Centrafricaine*, Nanterre: Labethno. #PM

BEAUCHÈNE, G. DE (1963), 'La préhistoire du Gabon', *Objets et Mondes* 3(1): 3–16. #PM

BEAUFORT, DE (1851), 'Recherches archéologiques', *Bulletin de la Société des Antiquaires de l'Ouest*. #PB

BEAUMONT, P.B. (1978), 'Border Cave', unpublished MA thesis: University of Cape Town. #JD

BEDARIDA, F. (1979), *A Social History of England 1851–1975*, London: Methuen. #MH

BEDAUX, R. (1972), 'Tellem, reconnaissance archéologique d'une culture de l'ouest africain au Moyen Age: recherches architectoniques', *Journal de la Société des Africanistes* 42: 103–85. #PB

BEDAUX, R. and LANGE, A.G. (1983), 'Tellem, reconnaissance archéologique d'une culture de l'ouest africain au Moyen-Age: la poterie', *Journal des Africanistes* 53: 5–60. #PB

BEDAUX, R., CONSTANDSE-WESTERMANN, T.S., HACQUEBORD, L., LANGE, A.G. and VAN DER WAALS, J.D. (1978), 'Recherches archéologiques dans le Delta Interieur du Niger', *Palaeohistoria* 20: 92–220. #PB

BEHRENSMEYER, A.K. (1970), 'Preliminary geological interpretation of a new hominid site in the Lake Rudolf Basin', *Nature* 226: 225–6. #JAJG

BEHRENSMEYER, A.K. and HILL, A. (1980), *Fossils in the Making: Vertebrate Taphonomy and Paleoecology*, Chicago: University of Chicago Press. #JAJG

BEL, J.–M. (1908), 'Rapport sur une mission au Congo français (1906–1907)', *Nouvelles archives des missions scientifiques* 6, Imprimerie Nationale, Paris. #PM

BENT, T. (1893), *The Sacred City of the Ethiopians*, London: Longmans, Green. #SAB

BEQUAERT, M. (1938), *Les fouilles de Jean Colette à Kalina*, Tervuren: Annales du Musée du Congo Belge, Série 1, Anthropologie et Préhistoire, 1–2. #PM

BEQUAERT, M. (1952), 'La préhistoire du Congo Belge', *Encyclopédie du Congo Belge* 1, Brussels: 45–77. #PM

BEQUAERT, M. (1955), 'Fouilles à Dinga (Congo Belge)', in Balout, L. (ed.), *Congrès Panafricain de Préhistoire. Actes de la IIe Session, Alger 1952*: 347–53. Paris: Arts et Métiers Graphiques. #PM

BEQUAERT, M. (1956), 'Recherches archéologiques au 1952', *Crónica del IV Congreso Internacional de Ciencias Prehistóricas y Protohistóricas, Madrid 1954*: 29–45. Zaragosa. #PM

BEQUAERT, M. and MORTELMANS, G. (1955), *Le Tshitolien dans le bassin du Congo*, Académie Royale des Sciences Coloniales, Classe des Sciences Naturelles et Médicales, Nouvelle série, II–5, Brussels. #PM

BERGEAUD, G. (1937), 'La préhistoire en Afrique Equatoriale Française', *Bulletin de la Société des Recherches Congolaises* 23: 163–70. #PM

BERGER, I. (1981), *Religion and Resistence: East African Kingdoms in the Precolonial Period*, Tervuren: Musée Royal de l'Afrique Centrale. #PRS

BERNUS, E. and BERNUS, S. (1972), *Du sel et des dattes. Introduction a l'étude de la communauté d'In Gall, Tegiddan Tesemt*, Niamey, Études nigériennes no. 37. #AH

BERNUS, E., BERNUS, S., CRESSIER, P., GOULETQUER, P.-L. and PONCET, Y. (1984), 'La région d'In Gall – Teggidda N Tesemt (Niger). Programme Archéologique d'Urgence 1977–1981, Vol. 1: Introduction: methodologie-environnements', *Études Nigériennes* 48. Niamey: Institut de Recherches en Sciences Humaines. #PB

BERNUS, S. and GOULETQUER, P. (1976), 'Du cuivre au sel. Recherches ethno-archéologiques sur la région d'Azélik (campagnes 1973–1975)', *Journal des Africanistes* 46: 7–68. #PB

BERSU, G. (1940), 'Excavations at Little Woodbury, Wiltshire, Part I: the settlement as revealed by excavation', *Proceedings of the Prehistoric Society* 6: 30–111. #JAJG

BERTHOUMIEUX, G. and DELANY, F. (1957), 'Mission diamant dans l'ouest Oubangui', *Bulletin de la Direction des Mines et de la Géologie* 77–91. #PM

BIBERSON, P. (1961a), *Le cadre paléogeographique de la préhistoire du Maroc atlantique*. Rabat: Publications du Service des Antiquités du Maroc, Fascicule 16. #JAJG

BIBERSON, P. (1961b), *Le Paléolithique inferieur du Maroc atlantique*, Rabat: Publications du Service des Antiquités du Maroc, Fascicule 17. #JAJG

BIESELE, MEGAN (1983), 'Interpretation in rock art and folklore: communication systems in evolutionary perspective', *South African Archaeological Society Goodwin Series* 4: 54–60. #WD

BIETAK, M. (1975), *Tell el-Dab'a II*, Wien: Hermann Böhlaus Nachf. #DOC

BIETAK, M. (1979a), 'Urban archaeology and the "town problem" in ancient Egypt', in Weeks, K. (ed.), *Egyptology and the Social Sciences*: 97–144. American University in Cairo Press. #DOC

BIETAK, M. (1979b), 'The present state of Egyptian archaeology', *Journal of Egyptian Archaeology* 65: 156–60, #DOC

BIETAK, M. (1982), 'Pfannengräber', Helck, W. und Westendorf W. (herausgeb.) *Lexikon der Ägyptologie, Band IV*. Wiesbadan: 999–1004. #DOC

BIETAK, MANFRED and ENGELMAYER, REINHOLD (1963), *Eine frühdynastische Abri-Siedlung mit Felsbilden aus Sayala-Nubien*, Vienna: Österreichische Akad. d. Wissensch. *Denkschriften (Phil.-Hist. Kl.)*. #WD

BIKO, S. (1978), 'Some African culture concepts', in: *I write what I like*, London: Bowerdon Press. #MH

BIKUNYA, PETERO (1927), *Ky'Abakama ba bunyoro*, London: Sheldon Press. #PRS

BINFORD, L.R. (1962), 'Archaeology as anthropology', *American Antiquity* 28: 217–25. #JD

BINFORD, L.R. (1972), *An Archaeological Perspective*, New York: Seminar Press. #PB

BINFORD, L.R. (1973), 'Interassemblage variability: the Mousterian and the "functional" argument', in Renfrew, C. (ed.), *The Explanation of Culture Change*: 227–54. London: Duckworth. #PB

BINFORD, L. and SABLOFF, J. (1982), 'Paradigms, systematics and archaeology', *Journal of Anthropological Research* 38: 137–53. #MH

BINNEMAN, J.N.F. (1982), 'Mikrogebruikstekene op steenwerktuie: eksperimentele waarnemings en 'n studie van werktuie afkomsting van Boomplaasgrot', unpublished MA thesis: University of Stellenbosch. #JD

BINNEMAN, J.N.F. (1984), 'Mapping and interpreting wear traces on stone implements: a case study from Boomplaas Cave', in Hall, M.J., Avery, G., Avery, D.M., Wilson, M.L. and Humphreys, A.J.B. (eds), *Frontiers: Southern African Archaeology Today*: 143–51. Oxford: British Archaeological Reports International Series 207. #JD

BISHOP, W.W. (1959), 'Kafu stratigraphy and Kafuan artefacts', *South Africa Journal of Science* 55: 117–21. #JAJG #PR

BISHOP, W.W. (1978), 'Geological framework of the Kilombe Acheulian site, Kenya', in Bishop, W.W. (ed.), *Geological Background to Fossil Man*: 329–36. Edinburgh: Scottish Academic Press. #JAJG

BISHOP, W.W. and CLARK, J.D. (eds) (1967), *Background to Evolution in Africa*, Chicago: University of Chicago Press. #JAJG #JD #PR #JDC

BISHOP, W.W., HILL, A. and PICKFORD, M. (1978), 'Chesowanja: a revised geological interpretation', in Bishop, W.W. (ed.), *Geological Background to Fossil Man*: 309–27. Edinburgh: Scottish Academic Press. #JAJG

BISHOP, W.W. and MILLER, J.A. (eds) (1972), *Calibration of Hominoid Evolution*, Edinburgh: Scottish Academic Press. #JAJG

BISHOP, W.W., PICKFORD, M. and HILL, A. (1975), 'New evidence regarding the Quaternary geology, archaeology, and hominids of Chesowanja, Kenya', *Nature* 258: 204–8. #JAJG

BIVAR, A.D.H. AND SHINNIE, P.L. (1962), 'Old Kanuri Capitals', *Journal of African History* 3: 1–10. #PLS

BLANKOFF, B. (1969), L'état des recherches préhistoriques au Gabon', *Actes du Premier Colloque International d'Archéologie Africaine, Fort-Lamy, 1966*: 62–80. Fort-Lamy, Institut National Tchadien pour les Sciences Humaines. #PM

BLEEK, D.F. (ed.) (1930), George W. Stow, *Rock Paintings in South Africa*, London: Methuen. #WD

BLEEK, D.F. (1932), 'A survey of our present knowledge of rock-paintings in South Africa', *South African Journal of Science* 29: 72–83. #WD

BLEEK, W.H.I. (1873), *Report of Dr. Bleek concerning his Researches into the Bushman language and customs*, Presented to the Honourable House of Assembly by command of his Excellency the Governor. Cape Town: House of Assembly, #JD

BLEEK, W.H.I. (1875), *A Brief Account of Bushman Folk-lore and Other Texts*, Second Report concerning Bushman Researches presented to both Houses of Parliament of the Cape of Good Hope. Cape Town: Juta #JD

BLEEK, W.H.I. and LLOYD, L.C. (1911), *Specimens of Bushman Folklore*, London: Allen. #JD

BOACHIE–ANSAH, J. (1986), *An Archaeological Contribution to the History of Wenchi*, African Occasional Papers, No. 3. Calgary. #FJK

BOLTON, C.L. (1927), 'On the origin of various tribes of Kenya and Uganda other than Bantu. (A reply to Mr C.C. Luck's essay on the origin of the Masai, Journal for August 1926)', *Journal of the East African and Ugandan Natural History Society* no. 28: 11–19. #PR

BONNEL DE MÉZIÈRES, A. (1920), 'Recherches sur l'emplacement de Ghana et de Takrour', *Mémoires de l'Académie des Inscriptions et Belles Lettres* 14: 227–73. #PB

BONNER, P. (1981), 'The dynamics of late eighteenth century northern Nguni society – some hypotheses', in Peires, J. (ed.), *Before and after Shaka. Papers in Nguni History*: 74–81. Grahamstown. #MH

BONNET, C. (1986), *Kerma. Territoire et Métropole*, Institut français d'Archéologie oriental du Caire. Bibliothèque générale 9. #DOC

BORDES, F. (1973), 'On the chronology and the contemporaneity of different palaeolithic cultures in France', in Renfrew, C. (ed.), *The Explanation of Culture Change*: 217–26. London: Duckworth. #PB

BORDES, F. and BORDES, D. de S. (1970), 'The significance of variability in Palaeolithic assemblages', *World Archaeology* 2: 61–73. #JD

BORISKOVSKY, P.I. and SOLOVIEV, V.V. (1978), 'New data on the Stone Age of Guinea', *West African Journal of Archaeology* 8: 51–74. #PB

BOSWELL, P.G.H. (1935), 'Human remains from Kanam and Kanjera, Kenya Colony', *Nature* 135: 371. #JAJG

BOÜARD, M. DE (1975), *Manuel d'archéologie médiévale, de la fouille à l'histoire*, Paris: SEDES. #PB

BOULE, M. and VALLOIS, H. (1932), *L'homme fossile d'Asselar (Sahara)*. Paris: Masson. #PB

BOULE, M. and VALLOIS, H.V. (1957), *Fossil Men*, translated from the 4th French edition by Michael Bullock, London: Thames & Hudson. #JAJG

BOURCART, J. (1943), 'Le géologie du Quaternaire en Maroc', *La Révue scientifique* 3224: 311–36. #JAJG

BOUTAKOFF, I. (1937), 'Premières explorations méthodiques de gisements de l'âge de la pierre au Ruanda-Urundi. Abris sous roche, ateliers et stations en plein air (communication préliminaire)', *Institut Royal Colonial Belge, Bulletin des Séances* 8(1): 179–201. #PM

BOVIER–LAPIERRE, P. (1925), 'Le Paléolithique stratifie des environs du Caire', *L'Anthropologie* 35: 37–54. #JAJG

BOWER, J. (1986), 'A survey of surveys: aspects of surface archaeology in sub-Saharan Africa', *African Archaeological Review* 4: 21–40. #PB

BOWER, J.R.F., NELSON, C.M., WAIBEL, A.F. and WANDIBBA, S. (1977), 'The University of Massachusetts' Later Stone Age/Pastoral "Neolithic" comparative study in central Kenya: an overview', *Azania* 12: 119–46. #PR

BOWER, J.R.F. and NELSON, C.M. (1978), 'Early pottery and pastoral cultures of the Central Rift Valley, Kenya', *Man* (N.S.) 13: 554–66. #PR

BRAHIMI, C. (1970), 'L'Ibéromaurusien Littoral de la Région d'Alger', *Mémoire du Centre de Recherches Anthropologiques, Préhistoriques et Ethnographiques,*' No. 13. Paris: Arts et Métiers Graphiques. #PJS

BRAIN, C.K. (1969), 'Faunal remains from the Bushman Rock Shelter, eastern. Transvaal', *South African Archaeological Bulletin* 24: 52–5. #JD

BRAIN, C.K. (1970), 'New finds at the Swartkrans australopithecine site', *Nature* 225: 1112–19. #JAJG

BRAIN, C.K. (1978), 'Some aspects of the South African Australopithecine sites and their bone accumulations', in Jolly, C. (ed.), *Early Hominids of Africa*: 131–61. London: Duckworth. #JAJG

BRANDT, S.A. (1982), 'A Late Quaternary cultural/environmental sequence from Lake Besaka, Southern Afar, Ethiopia', unpublished PhD thesis: University of California, Berkeley. #SAB

BRANDT, S.A (1984), 'New perspectives on the origins of food production in Ethiopia', in Clark, J.D. and Brandt, S.A. (eds), *From Hunters to Farmers: The Causes and Consequences of Food Production in Africa*: 173–90. Berkeley: University of California Press. #SAB

BRANDT, S.A. (1986), 'The Upper Pleistocene and early Holocene prehistory of the Horn of Africa', *African Archaeological Review* 4: 41–82. #SAB

BRANDT, S.A. (1988), 'Early Holocene mortuary practices and hunter-gatherer adaptations in Southern Somalia', *World Archaeology*, 20: 40–56. #SAB

BRANDT, S.A. and BROOK, G.A. (1984), 'Archaeological and paleoenvironmental research in Northern Somalia', *Current Anthropology* 25: 119–21. #SAB

BRANDT, S.A. and CARDER, N. (1987), 'Pastoral rock art in the Horn of Africa: making sense of udder chaos', *World Archaeology* 19: 194–213.

BRASSEUR, G. (1981), 'Raymond Mauny', in *2000 ans d'histoire africaine: le sol, la parole et l'écrit: Mélanges en hommage à Raymond Mauny*, Vol. 1: 1–3. Paris: Société française d'Histoire d'Outre-Mer. #PB

BRATTON, F. (1967), *A History of Egyptian Archaeology*, London: Robert Hale. #DOC

BRAUER, G. (1980), 'Human skeletal remains from Mumba Rock Shelter, Northern Tanzania', *American Journal of Physical Anthropology* 52: 71–84. #PR

BRAUNHOLTZ, H.J. (1926), 'Stone implements of palaeolithic and neolithic type from Nigeria', *Geological Survey of Nigeria, Occasional Paper* No. 4. Lagos. #FJK

BRAUNHOLTZ, H.J. (1936), 'Archaeology in the Gold Coast', *Antiquity* 10: 469–74. #FJK #TS

BRAUNHOLTZ, H.J. (1940), 'A bronze head from Ife, Nigeria', *British Museum Quarterly* 14: 75–7. #FJK

BREASTED, J.H. (1927), *Ancient Times*, London: Ginn & Co. #TS

BRENTJES, BURCHARD (1969), *African Rock Art*, London: Dent. #WD

BRETERNITZ, DAVID (1968), 'Interim report of the University of Colorado-Kainji Rescue Archaeology Project', *West African Archaeological Newsletter* 10: 30–42. #FJK

BRETERNITZ, DAVID (1969), 'Rescue archaeology at the Kainji Dam, northern Nigeria', *Current Anthropology* 10: 136. #FJK

BRETERNITZ, DAVID (1975), 'Rescue archaeology in the Kainji reservoir area, 1968', *West African Journal of Archaeology* 5: 91–151. #FJK

BREUIL, H. (1899), 'Compte rendu des travaux de MM. Mouth et Roux près Konakry (Guinée française)', *Congrès de l'Association française pour l'avancement des sciences*: 286–7. #AH

BREUIL, H. (1905), 'Essai de stratigraphie des depots de l'âge du Renne', *Comptes Rendues Congrès Préhistoriques Français. Periquex*: 74–80. #PJS

BREUIL, H. (1912), 'Les Subdivisions du Paléolithique supérieur et leur signification', *Congrès International d'Anthropologie et d'Archéologie Préhistoriques. Comptes rendu de la XIVeme Session*: 165–240. Geneva. #PJS

BREUIL, H. (1930a) *L'Afrique préhistorique*, Cahiers d'Art, 5e Année Nos 8–9: 449–500. #JAJG #JDC

BREUIL, H. (1930b), 'Premières impressions de voyage sur la préhistoire sud-Africaine, *L'Anthropologie* 40: 209–23. #JAJG

BREUIL, H. (1930c), 'The palaeolithic art of north-eastern Spain and the art of the Bushmen – a comparison', *Man* 30: 149–51. #WD

BREUIL, H. (1931), 'L'Afrique préhistorique', in Frobenius, L. and Breuil, H., *Afrique*: 449–82. Paris: Editions Cahiers d'Art. #PM #PB

BREUIL H. (1933), 'Pierres taillées venant du plateau de Mouka, Oubangui-Chari (Afrique Equatoriale Française)', *L'Anthropologie* 43: 222–3. #PM

BREUIL, H. (1934), 'Peintures rupestres préhistoriques du Harrar (Abyssinie)', *L'Anthropologie* 44: 473–83. #WD

BREUIL, H. (1937), *Les subdivisions de Paléolithique supérieur et leur signification*, 2eme edition, Paris: Lagny. #PJS

BREUIL, H. (1944), 'La paléolithique au Congo Belge d'après les recherches du Docteur Cabu', *Transactions of the Royal Society of South Africa* 30: 143–60. #JAJG #PM #JDC

BREUIL, H. (1952), 'Raised marine beaches around the African continent and their relation to Stone Age cultures', in Leakey, L.S.B. and Cole, S. (eds), *Proceedings of the Pan-African Congress on Prehistory, Nairobi 1947*: 91–3. Oxford: Basil Blackwell. #JAJG

BREUIL, H. (1955a), 'Un gisement de l'âge de la pierre à Fort-Rousset (Oubangui–Chari)', *Journal de la Société des Africanistes* 25: 7–11. #PM

BREUIL, H. (1955b), *The White Lady of the Brandberg*, London: Trianon Press. *Rock paintings of southern Africa* 1. #WD

BREUIL, H. (1957), *Philipp Cave*. London: Breuil Publications/Collins. *RPSA* 2. #WD

BREUIL, H. (1966), *Southern Rhodesia: The District of Fort Victoria and Other Sites*. Clairvaux: Singer-Polignac Foundation. *RPSA* 5. #WD

BREUIL, H. and JANMART, J. (1950), *Les limons et graviers de l'Angola du Nord-Est et leur contenu archéologique*, Diamang, Publicações Culturais, no. 5. Lisbon: Museu do Dundo. #PM

BREUIL, H. and KELLEY, H. (1936), 'Documents préhistoriques recueillés par la Mission du Bourg de Bozas en Abyssinie', *Journal de la Société des Africanistes* IV. #SAB

BROOKS, C.E.P. (1926), *Climate through the Ages*, London: Ernest Benn. #PR

BROOM, R. (1936), 'A new fossil anthropoid skull from South Africa', *Nature* 138: 486–8. #JAJG

BROOM, R. (1937), 'Discovery of a lower molar of *Australopithecus*', *Nature* 140: 681–2. #JAJG

BROOM, R. (1938), 'More discoveries of *Australopithecus*', *Nature* 141: 828–9. #JAJG

BROOM, R. (1950), *Finding the Missing Link*. London: Watts & Co. #JAJG

BROOM, R. and ROBINSON, J.T. (1949), 'A new type of fossil man', *Nature* 322. #JAJG

BROOM, R. and SCHEPERS, G.W.H. (1946), *The South African Fossil Ape-man: the Australopithecinae*, Pretoria: Transvaal Museum Memoir 2. #JAJG

BROWN, F.H. (1969), 'Observations on the stratigraphy and radiometric age of the "Omo" beds, lower Omo basin, southern Ethiopia', *Quaternaria* 11: 7–14. #JAJG

BRUCE, J. (1790), *Travels to Discover the Source of the Nile*, Edinburgh: G.G.J. & J. Robinson #SAB

BRUEL, G. (1937), 'Lettre de M. l'Administrateur en Chef Bruel relative aux dessins rupestres du djebel Méla', *Bulletin de la Société de Recherches Congolaises*, 23: 181–2. #PM

BUCHANAN, W.F., HALL, S.L., HENDERSON, J., OLIVIER, A., PETTIGREW, J.M., PARKINGTON, J.E. and ROBERTSHAW, P.T. (1978), 'Coastal shell middens in the Paternoster area, south-western Cape', *South African Archaeological Bulletin* 33: 89–93. #JD

BUDGE, E.A.W. (1928), *A History of Ethiopia, Nubia and Abyssinia*, London: Methuen & Co. #SAB

BUISSON, E.–M. (1933), 'Matériaux pour servir à la préhistoire du Cameroun', *Bulletin de la Société Préhistorique Française* 30(6): 335–48. #PM

BUISSON, E.–M, (1935), 'La préhistoire au Cameroun', *Congrès Préhistorique de France, Compte-rendu de la onzième session, Périquez, 1934*: 182–3. Société Préhistorique Française, Paris. #PM

BUNDY, C. (1986), 'Street sociology and pavement politics', Paper presented at conference on the Western Cape, Centre for African Studies, University of Cape Town. #MH

BUNN, H., HARRIS, J.W.K., ISAAC, G.Ll., KAUFULU, Z., KROLL, E., SCHICK, K., TOTH, N. and BEHRENSMEYER, A.K. (1980), 'FxJj 50: an early Pleistocene site in northern Kenya', *World Archaeology* 12: 109–36. #JAJG

BURKE, E.E. (ed.) (1969), *The Journals of Carl Mauch: His Travels in the Transvaal and Rhodesia 1869–1872*, Harare: National Archives. #MH

BURKITT, M.C. (1921), *Prehistory: A Study of Early Cultures in Europe and the Mediterranean Basin*, Cambridge: Cambridge University Press. #JAJG

BURKITT, M.C. (1927a), 'Archaeological methods', *South African Journal of Science* 24: 496–501. #JAJG

BURKITT, M.C. (1927b), 'Note on Stapleton and Hewitt, Stone implements from Howieson's Poort', *South African Journal of Science* 24: 587. #JAJG

BURKITT, M.C. (1928), *South Africa's Past in Stone and Paint*, Cambridge: Cambridge University Press. #JAJG #JD #JDC #WD #PR

BURKITT, M.C. and BARRINGTON BROWN, C. (1931), 'Stone implements from British Somaliland, *Man* 31: 157–9. #SAB

BURTON, R.F. and CAMERON, V.L. (1883), 'On stone implements from Gold Coast, West Africa', *Journal of the Anthropological Institute of Great Britain and Ireland* 12: 449–54. #AH

BUSK, G. (1869), 'Stone antiquities found in Africa', *Transactions of the International Congress on Prehistoric Archaeology, London 1868*, London. #JD

BUTZER, KARL W. (1958). *Studien zum vor- und frühgeschichtlichen Landschaftswandels der Sahara*. Mainz: Akademie d. Wissensch. u.d. Lit. *Abhandlungen (Math-Naturwissensch. Kl.)* 1958. #WD

BUTZER, K.W. (1961), 'Archäologische Fundstellen Ober – und Mittelägyptens in ihrer geologischen Landschaft', *Mitteilungen des Deutschen Archäologischen Instituts Abitelung Kairo* 17: 54–68. #DOC

BUTZER, K.W. (1976), *Early Hydraulic Civilization in Egypt. A Study in Cultural Ecology*, University of Chicago Press. #DOC

BUTZER, K.W. (1981), 'Rise and fall of Axum, Ethiopia: a geo-archaeological interpretation', *American Antiquity* 46: 471–95. #SAB

BUTZER, K.W. (1982), 'The palaeo-ecology of the African continent: the physical environment of Africa from the earliest geological to Later Stone Age times', in Clark, J.D. (ed.), *The Cambridge History of Africa Volume 1: From the earliest times to circa 500 BC*: 1–69. Cambridge: Cambridge University Press. #JAJG

BUTZER, K.W. (1984), 'Archeogeology and Quaternary environment in the interior of southern Africa', in Klein, R.G. (ed.), *Southern African Prehistory and Paleoenvironments*: 1–64. Rotterdam: Balkema. #JD

BUTZER, K.W., FOCK, G.J., SCOTT, L. and STUCKENRATH, R. (1979), 'Dating and context of rock engravings in southern Africa', *Science* 203: 1201–14. #WD

BUTZER, K.W., ISAAC, G.L., RICHARDSON, J.L. and WASHBOURN-KAMAU, C. (1972), 'Radiocarbon dating of East African lake levels', *Science* 175: 1069–76. #SAB

CABLE, C. (1984), *Economy and Technology in the Late Stone Age of Southern Natal*, Oxford: British Archaeological Reports International Series 201. #JD

CABOT BRIGGS, LLOYD (1958), *The Living Races of the Sahara*, Cambridge, Mass.: Peabody Museum, *Papers of the Peabody Museum of American Archaeology and Ethnology*. 28, no. 2. #WD

CABU, F. (1935a), 'À propos de ma contribution à l'étude de la préhistoire africaine', *Bulletin du Cercle Zoologique Congolais* 12: 98–106. #PM

CABU, F. (1935b), 'Considérations sur la stratigraphie des gisements pléistocènes à outillage paléolithique de la région de Léopoldville', *Bulletin de la Société Royale Belge d'Anthropologie et de Préhistoire* 50: 269–81. #PM

CABU, F. (1935c), 'Note préliminaire sur l'altération des outils archéologiques provenant de mes fouilles de Léopoldville, Congo Belge', *Bulletin de la Société Royale Belge d'Anthropologie et de Préhistoire* 50: 384–7. #PM

CABU, F. (1935d), 'Les industries préhistoriques de la cuvette centrale, congolaise et leurs rapports avec la préhistoire générale', *Bulletin de la Société Royale Belge d'Anthropologie et de Préhistoire* 50: 399–411. #PM

CABU, F. (1936a), 'L'âge de la pierre taillée dans la cuvette Centre-Africaine', *XVIe Congrès International d'Anthropologie et d'Archéologie Préhistorique, Bruxelles, 1935*: 449–58. #PM

CABU, F. (1936b), 'La préhistoire congolaise', unpublished PhD thesis: Université de Liège. #PM

CABU, F. (1937), 'Rapports de fouilles, mars-avril 1937', typescript. #PM

CABU, F. (1938a), 'Premières notes d'ensemble de la Mission de recherches préhistoriques au Katanga (Congo Belge)', *Bulletin de la Société Préhistorique Française* 35(4): 172–86. #PM

CABU, F. (1938b), 'Haches polies du Katanga', *Le Katanga illustré*, 7: 3. #PM

CABU, F. (1944), 'Données antérieures à 1931 et données actuelles sur la Préhistoire congolaise au Pléistocène', *Bulletin* de l'Association Congolaise des Anciens Étudiants de l'Université de Liège 2: 24–34. #PM

CABU, F. (1952), 'Some aspects of the Stone Age in the Belgian Congo', in Leakey, L.S.B. (ed.), *Proceedings of the Pan African Congress on Prehistory, Nairobi 1947*: 195–201, Oxford: Basil Blackwell. #PM #JDC

CABU, F. and VANDEN BRANDE, M. (1938), 'Contribution à l'étude de la répartition des Kwés au Katanga', Tervuren: *Annales du Musée du Congo Belge*. #PM

CAHEN, D. (1975), 'Le site archéologique de la Kamoa (Région du Shaba, République du Zaire). De l'âge de la pierre ancien à l'âge du fer', Tervuren: *Annales du Musée Royal de l'Afrique Centrale*. #JAJG #PM

CAHEN, D. (1976), 'Nouvelles fouilles à la Pointe de la Gombe (ex-Pointe de Kalina), Kinshasa, Zaïre', *L'Anthropologie* 80(4): 573–602. #PM

CAHEN, D. (1978), 'Vers une revision de la nomenclature des industries préhistoriques de l'Afrique Centrale', *L'Anthropologie* 82(1): 5–36. #PM

CALONNE–BEAUFAICT, A. DE (1914), 'Les graffiti du mont Ngundu', *Revue d'Ethnographie et de Sociologie* 3–4: 109–17. #PM

CALVOCORESSI, D.S. and YORK, R.N. (1971), 'The state of archaeological research in Ghana', *West African Journal of Archaeology* 1: 87–103. #FJK #TS

CAMARA, A. (1985), 'La recherche préhistorique et protohistorique au Sénégal', 1er Congrès A.C.S., Dakar. Comité Scientifique 3, Document de Travail 2. Mimeographed, 5 p. #PB

CAMARA, A. and DUBOSCQ, B. (1984), 'Le gisement préhistorique de Sansande, Basse Vallée de la Falémé, Sénégal: approche typologique et stratigraphique', *L' Anthropologie* 88: 377–402. #PB

CAMPS, G. (1974), *Les civilisations préhistoriques de l'Afrique du Nord et du Sahara*, Paris: Doin Editeurs. #PJS #PB

CAMPS, G. (1979), *Manuel de recherche préhistorique*, Paris: Doin Editeurs. #PB

CAMPS, G. (1982), 'Beginnings of pastoralism and cultivation in northwest Africa and the Sahara', in Clark, J.D. (ed.), *The Cambridge History of Africa. Vol. 1: From earliest times to c. 500 BC*: 548–623, Cambridge: Cambridge University Press. #WD

CAMPS, G. and GAST, M. (1982), *Les chars préhistoriques du Sahara: archéologie et typologie*, Aix-en-Provence: Université de Provence. *Actes du Coll. de Sénanque*. #WD

CAMPS–FABRER, H. (1966), 'Matière et Arts Mobilier dans la Préhistoire Nord-Africain et Sahariene', *Mémoire du Centre de Recherches Anthropologiques, Préhistoriques et Ethnographiques*, No. 5. Paris: Arts et Métiers Graphiques. #PJS

CAMPS-FABRER, H. (1975), *Un Gisement Capsien de Faciès Sétifien, Medjez II, El Eulma (Algérie)*, Paris: Editions du C.N.R.S. #PJS

CAPART, JEAN (1905), *L'art primitif en Egypte*, Brussels: H. Grevel. #WD

CARDINALL, A.W. (1920), *The Natives of the Northern Territories of the Gold Coast*, London: G. Routledge & Sons. #FJK

CARNEY, J., HILL, A., MILLER, J.A. and WALKER, A. (1971), 'Late Australopithecine from Baringo District, Kenya', *Nature* 230: 509–14. #JAJG

CARTAILHAC, E. (1892), 'L'âge de la pierre en Afrique. 1. Egypte', *L'Anthropologie* 2: 405–25. #JAJG

CARTER, P.L. (1970), 'Late Stone Age exploitation patterns in southern Natal', *South African Archaeological Bulletin* 25: 55–8. #JD

CARTER, P.L. (1978), 'The prehistory of eastern Lesotho', unpublished PhD thesis: University of Cambridge. #JD

CATON THOMPSON, G. (1931), *The Zimbabwe Culture. Ruins and Reactions*, Oxford: Clarendon Press. #MH #JDC

CATON THOMPSON, G. (1934), 'Recent discoveries in Kharga Oasis, Egypt', *Proceedings of the 1st Congress of Prehistoric and Protohistoric Sciences, London 1932*: 74. London: Oxford University Press. #JAJG

CATON THOMPSON, G. (1946), 'The Levalloisian industries of Egypt', *Proceedings of the Prehistoric Society* 12: 57–120. #JAJG

CATON THOMPSON, G. (1983), *Mixed Memoirs*, Gateshead: Paradigm Press. #MH #PR

CATON THOMPSON, G. and GARDNER, E.W. (1934), *The Desert Fayum*, 2 vols London: Royal Anthropological Institute. #JAJG #JDC

CATON THOMPSON, G. and GARDNER, E.W. (1952), *Kharga Oasis in Prehistory*, London: Athlone Press. #JAJG #JDC

ČERNY, J. (1947), 'Graffiti at the Wadi el-Allaki', *Journal of Egyptian Archaeology* 33: 52–7. #WD

ČERNY, J. (1952), *Paper and Books in Ancient Egypt*, London: H.K. Lewis & Co. #DOC

ČERVIČEK, PAVEL (1973), 'Datierung der nordafrikanischen Felsbilder durch die Patina', *IPEK* 23: 82–7. #WD

ČERVIČEK, PAVEL (1974), *Felsbilder des Nord-Etbai, Oberägyptens, und Unternubiens: Ergebnisse der VIII. DIAFE nach Ägypten 1926*, Wiesbaden: Steiner. *Veröff. des Frobenius-Institut, Ergebnisse der Frobenius-Expeditionen* 16. #WD

ČERVIČEK, PAVEL (1978), 'Notes on the chronology of the Nubian rock art to the end of the Bronze Age', in *Études nubiennes: colloque de Chantilly 1975*: 35–56. Cairo: Institut Français d'archéologie orientale. *Bibliothèque d'Études* 77. #WD

CHAMARD, P., GUITAT, R. and THILMANS, G. (1970), 'Le lac holocène et le gisement néolithique de l'Oum Arouaba (Adrar de Mauritanie)', *Bulletin de l'Institut Fondamental d'Afrique Noire* (B) 32: 688–740. #PB

CHAMPOLLION, J.F. (1835–45), *Monuments de l'Égypte et de la Nubie*, Paris: #DOC

CHAMPOLLION, J.F. (1844), *Monuments de l'Égypte et de la Nubie. Notices descriptives*, Paris: #DOC

CHANTRE, E. (1908), 'L'âge de la pierre dans la Berberie orientale, Tripolitaine et Tunisie', *37e Congrès Association française pour l'Avancement des Sciences, Clermont Ferrand*, 2e partie: 686–8. #JAJG

CHAPELLE, J. and MONOD, T. (1937), 'Notes sur la grande sépulture d'El-Mretti (Mauritanie)', *Bulletin du Comité d'Études historiques et scientifiques de l'A.O.F.* 20: 507–21. #PB

CHAPLIN, J.H. (1959), 'The Munwa Stream rock engravings', *South African Archaeological Bulletin* 14: 28–34. #WD

CHAPLIN, J.H. (1974), 'The prehistoric rock art of the Lake Victoria region', *Azania* 9: 1–50. #WD

CHASSELOUP–LAUBAT, F. de (1938), *Art rupestre au Hoggar (Haut Mertoutek)*, Paris: Librarie Plon. #WD

CHAUVEAU, J.-P. (1984), 'Une entreprise interdisciplinaire dans le domaine de la métallurgie africaine', *Cahiers d'Études africaines* 95 (24–3): 371–6. #PB

CHAVAILLON, J. (1970), 'Découverte d'un niveau Oldowayen dans la basse vallée de l'Omo (Ethiopie)', *C.R. Soc. Préhist. Franç.* 1: 7–11. #JAJG

CHAVAILLON, J. (1971), 'État actuel de la préhistoire ancienne dans la vallée de l'Omo (Ethiopie)', *Archeologia* 38: 33–43. #JAJG

CHAVAILLON, J. (1973), 'Chronologie des niveaux paléolithiques de Melka Kunturé (Ethiopie)', *C.R. Acad. Sc., Paris*, 276, Série D, 1533–6. #JAJG

CHAVAILLON, J. (1976a), 'Evidence for the technical practices of early Pleistocene hominids, Shungura Formation, Lower Omo Valley, Ethiopia', in Coppens, Y., Howell, F.C. Isaac, G.Ll. and Leakey, R.E.F. (eds), *Earliest Man and Environments in the Lake Rudolf Basin: Stratigraphy, Paleoecology and Evolution*: 565–73. Chicago: University of Chicago Press. #JAJG

CHAVAILLON, J. (1976b), 'Les habitats acheuléens de Melka-Kontouré', *Proceedings of the Panafrican Congress of Prehistory and Quaternary Studies, 7th Session*: 57–61. Addis Ababa. #JAJG

CHAVAILLON, J. (1980), 'Chronologie archéologique de Melka-Kunturé, Ethiopie (fouilles 1972–1976)', in Leakey, R.E. and Ogot, B.A. (eds), *Proceedings of the 8th Panafrican Congress of Prehistory and Quaternary Studies*: 200–1. Nairobi: The International Louis Leakey Memorial Institute for African Prehistory. #JAJG #SAB

CHAVAILLON, J., CHAVAILLON. N., HOURS, F. and PIPERNO, M. (1978), 'Le début et la fin de l'Acheuléen a Melka-Konturé: methodologie pour l'étude des changements de civilisations', *Bulletin de la Société Préhistorique Française* 75: 105–15. #JAJG

CHAVAILLON, N. (1979), 'Les habitats oldowayens de Melka-Kontouré', *Proceedings of the Panafrican Congress of Prehistory and Quaternary Studies, 7th Session*: 61–3. Addis Ababa. #JAJG

CHENORKIAN, R. (1982), 'Les fouilles de l'amas coquiller de Songon Dagbe', *Annales de l'Université d'Abidjan* (Série 1, Histoire) 10: 5–40. #PB

CHILDE, V. GORDON (1934), *New Light on the Most Ancient East*, rev. edn, London: Kegan Paul. #WD

CHILDS, G.M. (1964), 'The kingdom of Wambu (Huambo), a tentative chronology', *Journal of African History* 5: 367–79. #PM

CHITTICK, H.N. (1974), 'Excavations at Aksum, 1973–74: a preliminary report', *Azania* 9: 159–205. #SAB

CHITTICK, H.N. (1984), *Manda: Excavations at an Island Port on the Kenya Coast*, Nairobi: British Institute in Eastern Africa Memoir no. 9. #PR

CHOFFAT, P. (1900–1), 'Echantillons de roches du district du Mossamedes', *Communicações da Direcção dos Serviços Geológicos de Portugal* 4: 190–4. #PM

CHMIELEWSKI, W. (1968), 'Early and Middle Palaeolithic sites near Arkin, Sudan', in Wendorf, F. (ed.), *The Prehistory of Nubia*, Dallas: Southern Methodist University Press. #JAJG

CHUDEAU, R. (1921), 'Le problème du dessèchement en Afrique occidentale', *Bulletin du Comité d'Études historiques et scientifiques de l'A.O.F.* 4: 353–69. #PB

CIPRIANI, L. (n.d.), Archives de la section de préhistoire et d'archéologie du Musée Royal de l'Afrique Centrale, Dossier no. 185. #PM

CLARIDGE, W.W. (1915), *A History of the Gold Coast and Ashanti*, London: John Murray. #FJK

CLARK, J.D. (1942), 'Further excavations (1939) at the Mumbwa Caves, Northern Rhodesia', *Transactions of the Royal Society of South Africa* 29: 133–201. #JDC

CLARK, J.D. (1950), *The Stone Age Cultures of Northern Rhodesia*, Claremont, Cape: South African Archaeological Society. #JDC

CLARK, J.D. (1951), 'The Bushmen hunters of the Barotse forests', *Northern Rhodesia Journal* 3: 56–65. #JDC

CLARK, J.D. (1952), 'Recent prehistoric research in the Somalilands', in Leakey, L.S.B. and Cole, S. (eds), *Proceedings of the Pan-African Congress on Prehistory, Nairobi 1947*: 146–64. Oxford: Basil Blackwell. #JAJG

CLARK, J.D. (1954), *The Prehistoric Cultures of the Horn of Africa*, Cambridge: Cambridge University Press. #JAJG #SAB #WD

CLARK, J.D. (1958), 'The Chifubwa Stream rock shelter, Solwezi, northern Rhodesia', *South African Archaeological Bulletin* 13: 21–4. #WD

CLARK, J.D. (1959a), *The Prehistory of Southern Africa*, Harmondsworth: Penguin. #JAJG #JD #MH #PR #PM

CLARK, J.D. (1959b), 'The rock paintings of Northern Rhodesia and Nyasaland', in Summers, R. (ed.), *Prehistoric*

Rock Art of the Federation of Rhodesia and Nyasaland: 163:220. Salisbury: National Publications Trust. #WD

CLARK, J.D. (1962), 'The spread of food production in sub-Saharan Africa', *Journal of African History* 3: 211–28. #SAB

CLARK, J.D. (1963), *Prehistoric Cultures of Northeast Angola and their Significance in Tropical Africa*, Diamang, Publicacoes Culturais, no. 62. Lisbon: Museu do Dundo. #PM

CLARK, J.D. (1965a), 'Prehistory', in Lystad, R.A. (ed.), *The African World*: 11–39. New York: F.A. Praeger. #PR

CLARK, J.D. (1965b), 'Changing trends and developing values in African prehistory', *African Affairs* (Special issue: proceedings of the 1964 conference); 76–95. #PR

CLARK, J.D. (1967a), 'Introduction to Part III: B. Sub-Saharan Africa', in Bishop, W.W. and Clark, J.D. (eds), *Background to Evolution in Africa*: 413–16. Chicago: University of Chicago Press. #JAJG

CLARK, J.D. (1967b), 'The problem of Neolithic culture in sub-Saharan Africa', in Bishop, W.W. and Clark, J.D. (eds), *Background to Evolution in Africa*: 601–27. Chicago: University of Chicago Press. #SAB

CLARK, J.D. (1969), *Kalambo Falls Prehistoric Site, Vol. I: the geology, palaeoecology and detailed stratigraphy of the excavations*, with contributions by G.H. Cole, E.G. Haldemann, M.R. Kleindienst and E.M. van Zinderen Bakker. Cambridge: Cambridge University Press. #JAJG #JDC

CLARK, J.D. (1970), *The Prehistory of Africa*, New York: Thames & Hudson. #JAJG #FJK

CLARK, J.D. (1971), 'Problems of archaeological nomenclature and definition in the Congo Basin', *South African Archaeological Bulletin* 26: 67–8. #PM

CLARK, J.D. (1974), *Kalambo Falls prehistoric site. Vol. II: The late prehistoric remains*, Cambridge: Cambridge University Press. #JAJG #JD #MH

CLARK, J.D. (1974), 'Louis Seymour Bazett Leakey, 1903–1972', *Proceedings of the British Academy* 49; reprinted in Isaac, G.Ll. and McCown, E.R. (eds), *Human Origins: Louis Leakey and the East African Evidence*: 521–41. Menlo Park, California: Benjamin and Co. #JAJG

CLARK, J.D. (1976a), 'The domestication process in sub-Saharan Africa with special reference to Ethiopia', in *Origine de l'elevage et de la domestication*: 56–115. Nice: Union International des Sciences Préhistoriques et Protohistoriques. #SAB

CLARK, J.D. (1976b), 'Epi-Paleolithic aggregates from Greboun Wadi, Air, and Adrar Bous, Northwestern Tenere, Republic of Niger', in Abebe, B., Chavaillon, J. and Sutton, J.E.G. (eds), *Proceedings of the Panafrican Congress of Prehistory and Quaternary Studies, VIIth Session, Addis Ababa 1971*: 67–78. Addis Ababa: The Antiquities Administration. #PB

CLARK, J.D. (1980a), 'Thirty years of the Pan-African Congress, 1947–1977', in Leakey, R.E. and Ogot, B.A. (eds), *Proceedings of the 8th Pan-African Congress of Prehistory and Quaternary Studies, Nairobi, 1977*: 3–5. Nairobi: The International Louis Leakey Memorial Institute of African Prehistory. #JDC

CLARK, J.D. (1980b), 'Early human occupation of African savanna environments', in Harris, D.R. (ed.), *Human Ecology in Savanna Environments*: 41–72. London: Academic Press. #JDC

CLARK, J.D. (1980c), 'The origins of domestication in Ethiopia', in Leakey, R.E. and Ogot, B.A. (eds), *Proceedings of the 8th Panafrican Congress of Prehistory and Quaternary Studies*: 268–70. Nairobi: The Louis Leakey Memorial Institute for African Prehistory. #SAB

CLARK, J.D. (ed.) (1982), *The Cambridge History of Africa I: From the earliest times to c.500 B.C.*. Cambridge: Cambridge University Press. #DOC #WD

CLARK, J.D. (1986), 'Archaeological retrospect 10', *Antiquity* 60: 179–88. #JD #JDC #PR

CLARK, J.D., ASFAW, B., ASSEFA, G., HARRIS, J.W.K., KURASHINA, H., WALTER, R.C., WHITE, T.D. and WILLIAMS, M.A.J. (1984), 'Palaeoanthropological discoveries in the Middle Awash Valley, Ethiopia', *Nature* 307: 423–8. #JAJG

CLARK, J.D., COLE, G.H., ISAAC, G.Ll. and KLEINDIENST, M.R. (1966), 'Precision and definition in African archaeology', *South African Archaeological Bulletin* 21: 114–21. #JAJG #JD

CLARK, J.D. and KURASHINA, H. (1979), 'Hominid occupation of the east-central highlands of Ethiopia in the Plio-Pleistocene', *Nature* 282: 33–9. #JAJG

CLARK, J.D., OAKLEY, K.P., WELLS, L.H. and McCLELLAND, J.A.C. (1947), 'New studies on Rhodesian Man', *Journal of the Royal Anthropological Institute* 77: 7–32. #JAJG

CLARK, J.D. and WILLIAMS, M.A.J. (1978), 'Recent archaeological research in southeastern Ethiopia (1974–1975): some preliminary results', *Annales d'Ethiopie* 11: 19–44. #SAB

CLARK, J.D. and WILLIAMSON, K.D. (1984), 'A Middle Stone Age occupation site at Porc Epic cave, Dira Dawa (east-central Ethiopia): Part I', *African Archaeological Review* 2: 37–64.

CLARK, J.G.D. (1966), 'The invasion hypothesis in British archaeology', *Antiquity* 40: 172–89. #JD

CLARK, J.G.D. (1968), *Archaeology and Society*, London: Methuen. #AH

CLARK, J.G.D. (1969), *World Prehistory – A New Outline*, Cambridge: Cambridge University Press. #FJK

CLARK, J.G.D. (1971), *World Prehistory: A New Outline*, Cambridge: Cambridge University Press. #JD

CLARKE, D.L. (1968), *Analytical Archaeology*, London: Methuen, #JD

CLARKE, R.J., HOWELL, F.C. and BRAIN, C.K. (1970), 'More evidence of an advanced hominid at Swartkrans', *Nature* 225: 1217–20. #JAJG

CLARKE, SOMERS (1912), *Christian Antiquities in the Nile Valley*, Oxford: Clarendon Press. #PLS

CLEGG, JOHN (1982), 'Comment on Lewis-Williams 1982', *Current Anthropology* 23: 439–40. #WD

CLEUZIOU, S. and DEMOULE, J.-P. (1980), 'Situation de l'archéologie théorique', *Nouvelles de l'Archéologie* 3: 7–15. #PB

CLEUZIOU, S., DEMOULE, J.-P. and SCHNAPP, A. and A. (1973), 'Renouveau des méthodes et théorie de l'archéologie', *Annales Economie, Société, Civilisation* 1: 35–51. #PB

CLIST, B. (1981–2), 'Étude archéologique du matériel de la mission Maurits Bequaert de 1950–1952 au Zaïre', unpublished MA thesis: Université Libre de Bruxelles. #PM

CLOSE, A. (1977), 'The identification of style in lithic artifacts from North East Africa', *Mémoire de l'Institut d'Egypt*, No. 61. Cairo. #PJS

CNRS (Centre National de la Recherche Scientifique) (1978), 'Les recherches archéologiques dans les États d'Afrique au sud du Sahara et à Madagascar', Paris: CNRS Sophia Antipolis. Mimeographed, 193 pp. #PB

COCHETEUX, (1888–9), 'Communication préliminaire sur des instruments de pierre du Congo', *Bulletin de la Société d'Anthropologie de Bruxelles* 7: 325–6. #PM

COHEN, M. (1970), 'A reassessment of the Stone Bowl cultures of the Rift Valley, Kenya', *Azania* 5: 27–38. #PR

COHEN, M.N. (1977), *The Food Crisis in Prehistory*, New Haven: Yale University Press. #SAB

COLE, S. (1954) (rev. edn 1963), *The Prehistory of East Africa*, Harmondworth: Penguin. #JAJG #PR #JDC

COLE, S. (1975), *Leakey's Luck*, London: Collins. #JAJG

COLETTE, J. (1928), 'Trouvailles paléolithiques au Congo Belge', *Actes du Congrès International d'Anthropologie, IIIe Session, Amsterdam, 1927*, Paris: Nourry. #PM

COLETTE, J. (1929), 'Le préhistorique dans le Bas-Congo', *Bulletin de la Société Royale Belge d'Anthropologie et de Préhistoire* 44: 42–7. #PM

COLETTE, J. (1933a), 'Essai biométrique sur la station préhistorique de Kalina (Congo Belge)', *XVe Congrès International d'Anthropologie et d'Archéologie Préhistorique, Paris, 1931*: 278–85. Paris: Nourry. #PM

COLETTE, J. (1933b), 'Industries paléolithiques du Congo Belge', *XVe Congrès International d'Anthropologie et d'Archéologie Préhistorique, Paris, 1931*: 285–92. Paris: Nourry. #PM

COLETTE, J. (1933c), 'Comparaison entre les faciès Uélien et Léopoldien du Néolithique congolais', *Bulletin du cercle Zoologique Congolais* 10(4): 95–7. #PM

COLETTE, J. (1933d), 'Note sur la découverte d'une station anthropique dont la chronologie se rapporte à la transition du pléistocène à l'holocène', *Bulletin de la Société Royale d'Anthropologie et de Préhistoire* 48: 85–93. #PM

COLETTE, J. (1933e), 'Le Néolithique Uélien', *Bulletin de la Société Royale Belge d'Anthropologie et de Préhistoire* 48: 107–36. #PM

COLETTE, J. (1935), 'Complexes et convergences en préhistoire', *Bulletin de la Société Royale Belge d'Anthropologie et de Préhistoire* 50: 49–192. #PM #JDC

COLETTE, J. (1936a), 'Note sur la presence de fragments de nids fossiles d'insectes dans le Pléistocène supérieur du Stanley Pool (Congo Belge)', *Bulletin de la Société Belge de Géologie, de Paléontologie et d'Hydrologie* 45: 309–48. #PM

COLETTE, J. (1936b), 'Les rites de l'eau dans la néolithique congolais', *XVIe Congrès International d'Anthropologie et d'Archéologie Préhistorique, Bruxelles, 1935*: 1044–56. Brussels: Imprimerie médicale et scientifique. #PM

COLLETT, D. and ROBERTSHAW, P. (1983), 'Pottery traditions of early pastoral communities in Kenya', *Azania* 18: 107–25. #PR

COLLIE, G.L. (1928), 'The Aurignacians and their culture', *Beloit College Bulletin* 26(2). #PJS

COLLINGWOOD, R.G. (1939), *An Autobiography*, Oxford: Oxford University Press. #BGT

COLLINGWOOD, R.G. (1963), *The Idea of History*, Oxford: Oxford University Press. #DOC

COLLINS, E.R. and SMITH, R.A. (1915), 'Stone implements from South African gravels', *Journal of the Royal Anthropological Institute* 45: 79–91. #JAJG

CONGRÈS INTERNATIONAL D'ANTHROPOLOGIE ET D'ARCHÉOLOGIE PRÉHISTORIQUES, XIIE SESSION, PARIS (1900), *L'Anthropologie* 11: 569–604. #PB

CONNAH, G. (1975), *The Archaeology of Benin*, Oxford: Clarendon Press. #FJK #PRS

CONNAH, G. (1981), *Three Thousand Years in Africa*, Cambridge: Cambridge University Press. #FJK #AH

CONTI ROSSINI, C. (1928), *Storia d'Etiopia*, Bergamo: Istituto Italiano d'Arti Grafiche. #SAB

COOKE, C.K. (1955), 'The prehistoric artist of southern Matabeleland: his materials and technique as a basis for dating', in Clark, J.D. (ed.), *3rd Panafrican Congress on Prehistory, Livingstone, 1955*: 282–94. London: Chatto & Windus. #WD

COOKE, C.K. (1965), 'Evidence of human migrations from the rock art of southern Rhodesia', *Africa* 35: 263–85. #WD

COOKE, C.K. (1969), *Rock Art of Southern Africa*, Cape Town: Books of Africa. #WD

COOKE, C.K., SUMMERS, R.F. and ROBINSON, K.R. (1966), 'Rhodesian prehistory re-examined', *Arnoldia* (Rhod.) 2(12): 1–8. #JD

COOKE, H.B.S. (1952), 'Quaternary events in South Africa', in Leakey, L.S.B. and Cole, S. (eds), *Proceedings of the*

Pan-African Congress on Prehistory, Nairobi 1947: 26–35. Oxford: Basil Blackwell. #JAJG

COOKE, H.B.S. (1957), 'The problem of Quaternary glacio-pluvial correlation in east and southern Africa', in Clark, J.D. (ed.), *Third Pan-African Congress on Prehistory, Livingstone 1955*: 51–5. London: Chatto & Windus. #JD #PR

COOKE, H.B.S. (1958), 'Observations relating to Quaternary environments in East and southern Africa', *Transactions of the Geological Society of South Africa* 61(annex): 1–73 #PR #JDC

COOKE, H.B.S. (1976), 'Suidae from Plio-Pleistocene strata of the Rudolf Basin', in Coppens, Y., Howell, F.C. Isaac, G.Ll. and Leakey, R.E.F. (eds), *Earliest Man and Environments in the Lake Rudolf Basin: Stratigraphy, Paleoecology and Evolution*: 251–63. Chicago: University of Chicago Press. #JAJG

COON, C. (1968), *Yengema Cave Report*, Philadelphia: University Museum. #FJK

COOPER, W.G.G. (1927), 'Report on a rapid geological survey of the Gambia, B.W.A.', *Gold Coast Geological Review*, Bulletin no. 3. London. #FJK

COPPENS, Y. (1976), 'Introduction, to Part II, Paleontology and Paleoecology', in Coppens, Y., Howell, F.C. Isaac, G.Ll. and Leakey, R.E.F. (eds), *Earliest Man and Environments in the Lake Rudolf Basin: Stratigraphy, Paleoecology and Evolution*: 173–6. Chicago: University of Chicago Press. #JAJG

CORBEIL, R., MAUNY, R. and CHARBONNIER, J. (1948), 'Préhistoire et protohistoire de la presqu'île du Cap-Vert et de l'extrême Ouest sénégalais', *Bulletin de l'Institut Français d'Afrique Noire* 10: 378–460. #PB

CORNET, J. (1893), 'Aperçu géologique de la partie méridionale du bassin du Congo', *Bulletin de la Société Royale Belge de Géographie* 17: 153–9. #PM

CORNET, J. (1896), 'L'âge de la pierre dans le Congo Occidental', *Bulletin de la Société d'Anthropologie de Bruxelles* 15: 196–203. #PM

CORNEVIN, M. (1980), *Apartheid: Power and Historical Falsification*, Paris: UNESCO. #MH

CORVINUS, G. and ROCHE, H. (1976), 'La préhistoire dans la région de Hadar (bassin de l'Awash, Afar, Ethiopie): premiers résultats', *L'Anthropologie* 80: 315–24. #JAJG

CORVINUS, G. and ROCHE, H. (1980), 'Industries lithiques de la formation plio-pléistocène d'Hadar Ethiopie (campagne 1976)', in Leakey, R.E. and Ogot, B.A. (eds), *Proceedings of the 8th Panafrican congress of prehistory and Quaternary studies, Nairobi, September 1977*: 194–9. Nairobi: The International Louis Leakey Memorial Institute for African Prehistory. #JAJG

COTTEVIEILLE-GIRAUDET, REMY (1931), 'Les gravures protohistoriques de la montagne thébaine', *Bulletin de l'Institut français d'archéologie orientale* 30: 545–52. #WD

COULBEAUX, J.B. (1929), *Histoire politique et religieuse de l'Abyssinie*. Paris: Geuthner. #SAB

COURBIN, P. (ed.) (1963). *Études archéologiques: recueil de travaux*, Paris: SEVPEN. #PB

COUTIL, L. (1912), 'Tardenoisien, Capsien, Gétulien, Ibéro-Maurusien, Tellien, Loubirien, Généyenien, Intergétulo-Nolithique', *Congrès International d'Anthropologie et d'Archéologie Préhistoriques. Comptes rendu de la XIVème Session*: 1 : 310. Geneva. #PJS

COWGILL, G.L. (1979), Review of *The food crisis in prehistory* by M.N. Cohen, *American Anthropologist* 81: 658–60. #SAB

COX, A. (1972), 'Geomagnetic reversals – their frequency, their origin and some problems of correlation', in Bishop, W.W. and Miller, J.A. (eds), *Calibration of Hominoid Evolution*: 93–106. Edinburgh: Scottish Academic Press. #JDC

CRAWFORD, O.G.S. (1961), *Castles and Churches in the Middle Nile Region*, Sudan Antiquities Service Occasional Papers No. 2. Khartoum. #PLS

CROSSLAND, LEONARD, (in preparation), *Pottery from Begho, B2*. African Occasional Papers, No. 4. Calgary. #FJK

CROSSLAND, L.B. and POSNANSKY, M. (1978), 'Pottery, people and trade at Begho, Ghana', in Hodder, I. (ed.), *The Spatial Organization of Culture*: 77–89. London: Duckworth. #FJK #PB

CROVA, B. (1909), 'Notice sur les instruments néolithiques de la presqu'île du Cap Blanc (Mauritanie)', *Bulletin de la Société Préhistorique Française* 6: 369–75. #PB

CULWICK, A.T. (1931), 'Ritual use of rock paintings at Bahi, Tanganyika Territory', *Man* 31: 33–6. #WD

DAGET, J. and LIGERS, Z. (1962), 'Une ancienne industrie malienne: les pipes en terre', *Bulletin de l'Institut Français d'Afrique Noire* (B) 24: 12–53. #PB

DALE, L. (Delta) (1870), 'Stone implements in South Africa', *Cape Monthly Magazine* (NS) 1: 236–9. #JD

DALLONI, M. (1936), *Mission au Tibesti II*. Paris: Institut de France, Mémoires de l'Académie des sciences des l'Institut, 2e ser., 62. #WD

DALRYMPLE, G.B. (1972), 'Potassium-argon dating of geomagnetic reversals and North American glaciations', in Bishop, W.W. and Miller, J.A. (eds), *Calibration of Hominoid Evolution*: 107–34., Edinburgh: Scottish Academic Press. #JDC

DALTON, O.M. (1903), 'Note on an unusually fine bronze figure from Benin', *Man* 3: 185. #FJK

DANIEL, G.E. (1950), *A Hundred Years of Archaeology*, London: Duckworth. #PR

DANIEL, G.E. (1962), *The Idea of Prehistory*, Harmondsworth: Penguin. #PR #AH

DANIEL, G.E. (1967), *The Origins and Growth of Archaeology*, Harmondsworth: Penguin. #PR

DANIEL, G.E. (1968), 'One hundred years of Old World prehistory', in Brew, J.O. (ed.), *One Hundred Years of Anthropology*: 57–96. Cambridge, Mass: Harvard University Press. #PR

DANIEL G.E. (1975), *A Hundred and Fifty Years of Archaeology*, London: Duckworth. #JD #PB #PR

DANIEL, G.E. (ed.) (1981a), *Towards a History of Archaeology*, London: Thames & Hudson. #PR

DANIEL, G.E. (1981b), *A Short History of Archaeology*, London: Thames & Hudson. #PM #DOC

DANIEL, G.E. (1981c), 'Introduction: the necessity for an historical approach to archaeology', in Daniel, G. (ed.), *Towards a History of Archaeology*: 9–13. London: Thames & Hudson. #AH.

DANIELLI, G. and MARINELLI, O. (1912), *Risultati di un viaggio scientifico nella colonia Eritrea*, Firenze: Galletti e Cocci. #SAB

DARLING, P.J. (1984), *Archaeology and History in Southern Nigeria: The Ancient Linear Earthworks of Benin and Ishan*, Cambridge Monographs in African Archaeology 11. Oxford: BAR. #PRS

DART, R.A. (1925a), 'Australopithecus africanus: the man-ape of South Africa', *Nature* 115: 195–9. #JAJG

DART, R.A.(1925b), 'The historical succession of cultural impacts upon South Africa', *Nature* 115: 425–9. #WD

DART, R.A. (1953), 'Rhodesian engravers, painters and pigment miners of the fifth millennium B.C.', *South African Archaeological Bulletin* 8: 91–6. #WD

DART, R.A. (1957), 'The osteodontokeratic culture of Australopithecus prometheus', *Mem. Transv. Mus.* 10: 1–105. #JAJG

DARWIN, C. (1871), *The Descent of Man and Selection in Relation to Sex*, London: John Murray. #JAJG

DAVID, N. (1971), 'The Fulani compound and the archaeologist', *World Archaeology* 3: 111–31. #PM

DAVID, N. (1981a), ' "Unknown regions preserved": an essay on the state of archaeology in North Central Africa', in Ray I., Shinnie, P. and Williams, D. (eds), *Into the 80s*: 37–51. Proceedings of the 11th Annual Congress of the Canadian Association of African Studies. Vancouver: Tantalus Research Ltd. #PM

DAVID, N. (1981b), 'The archaeological background of Cameroonian history', in Tardits, Cl. (ed.), *Contribution de la recherche ethnologique à l'histoire des civilisations du Cameroun*: 79–99. Paris: CNRS. #AH

DAVID, N. (1982), 'Tazanu: Megalithic monuments of Central Africa', *Azania* 17: 43–77. #PM

DAVID, N. (1985), Editorial, *African Archaeological Review* 3: 1–2. #PB

DAVID, N. and HENNIG, H. (1972), *The Ethnography of Pottery: A Fulani Case Seen in Archaeological Perspective*, Reading, Mass: Addison-Wesley Modular Publication 21. #PM

DAVIES, OLIVER (1952), 'The raised beaches of the Gold Coast in relation to those of Natal and the Mediterranean', *Proceedings of the second Panafrican Congress of Prehistory and Quaternary Studies*: 259–61. #FJK

DAVIES, OLIVER (1956), 'The raised beaches of the Gold Coast and their associated archaeological material', *Quaternaria* 3: 91–3. #FJK

DAVIES, OLIVER (1957a), 'The Old Stone Age between the Volta and the Niger', *Bulletin d'I.F.A.N.* (Series B) 19: 592–616. #FJK

DAVIES, OLIVER (1957b), 'The distribution of Old Stone Age material in Guinea', *Bulletin d'I.F.A.N.* (Series B) 21: 1–2. #FJK

DAVIES, OLIVER, (1959a), 'The equipment of an Acheulean Man', *Archaeology* 12: 172–7. #FJK

DAVIES, OLIVER (1959b), 'The climatic and cultural sequence in the late pleistocene of the Gold Coast', in Clark, J.D. (ed.), *Proceedings of the 3rd Pan-African Congress on Prehistory, Livingstone*: 1–5. #FJK

DAVIES, OLIVER (1960), 'The neolithic revolution in Tropical Africa', *Transactions of the Historical Society of Ghana* 4: 14–20. #FJK

DAVIES, OLIVER (1961a), *Archaeology in Ghana*, Edinburgh: Edinburgh University Press. #FJK

DAVIES, OLIVER (1961b), 'The Invaders of Northern Ghana', *Universitas* 4: 134–6. #FJK

DAVIES, OLIVER (1962), 'Neolithic cultures of Ghana', in Mortelmans, G. and Nenquin, J. (eds), *Actes IVe Congrès Panafricaine Préhistorique et Étud. Quaternaire. Section III*: 291–302. Tervuren. #FJK #TS

DAVIES, OLIVER (1964a), *The Quaternary in the Coastlines of Guinea*, Glasgow. #FJK #TS

DAVIES, OLIVER (1964b), 'Gonja painted pottery', *Transactions of the Historical Society of Ghana* 7: 4–11. #FJK

DAVIES, OLIVER (1966a), 'The invasion of Ghana from the Sahara in the Early Iron Age', *Actas del V Congresso Panafricanco de Prehistoria (Tenerife)*: 27–42. #FJK

DAVIES, OLIVER (1966b), 'Comments on the Iron Age in sub-Saharan Africa', *Current Anthropology* 7: 470–1. #FJK

DAVIES, OLIVER (1967), *West Africa before the Europeans*, London: Methuen & Co. #FJK

DAVIES, OLIVER (1970), 'Northern Ghana', *Ghana Field Notes*, Part II. Legon. #FJK

DAVIES, OLIVER (1971), 'The archaeology of the flooded Volta Basin', *University of Ghana – Occasional Papers in Archaeology* No. 1. #FJK

DAVIES, OLIVER (1972), 'Ashanti', *Ghana Field Notes*. Part III. Legon. #FJK

DAVIES, OLIVER (1973), 'Excavation at Ntereso', Pietermaritzburg: mimeo. #FJK

DAVIES, OLIVER (1975), 'Excavations at Shongweni South Cave: the oldest evidence to date for cultigens in southern Africa', *Annals of the Natal Museum* 22: 627–62. #MH

DAVIES, OLIVER (1976), 'Southern Ghana', *Ghana Field Notes*. Part IV. Legon. #FJK

DAVIES, OLIVER (1980), 'The Ntereso culture in Ghana', in Swartz, B.K. and Dumett, R.A. (eds), *West African Culture Dynamics*: 205–25. The Hague: Mouton. #FJK

DAVIS, WHITNEY (1977), 'Toward a dating of Nile valley prehistoric rock-drawings', *Journal of the Society for the Study of Egyptian Antiquities* 8: 25–34. #WD

DAVIS, WHITNEY (1979), 'Sources for the study of rock art in the Nile valley', *Göttinger Miszellen: Beiträge zur ägyptologische Diskussion* 32: 59–74. #WD

DAVIS, WHITNEY (1984), 'Representation and knowledge in the prehistoric rock art of Africa', *African Archaeological Review* 2: 7–35. #WD

DAVIS, WHITNEY (1985a), 'The earliest art in the Nile valley', in Kryzaniak, L. and Kobusiewicz, M. (eds), *Origin and Early Development of Food-producing Cultures in North-eastern Africa*: 81–94. Poznan: Polish Academy of Sciences. #WD

DAVIS, WHITNEY (1985b), 'Present and future directions in the study of rock art', *South African Archaeological Bulletin* 50: 5–10. #WD

DAVIS, WHITNEY (1986), 'The origins of image making', *Current Anthropology* 27: 193–215. #WD

DAVIS, WHITNEY (1987), 'Style and history in art history', in Conkey, M.W. and Halstorf, C. (eds), *The Uses of Style in Archaeology*, Cambridge: Cambridge University Press. #WD

DAWSON, W.R. and UPHILL, E.P. (1972), *Who Was Who in Egyptology*, London: The Egypt Exploration Society. #DOC

DE MORGAN. J., CAPITAN, L. and BOUDY, P. (1910), 'Étude sur les stations préhistoriques du Sud-Tunisien', *Revue de l'École d'Anthropologie*. 20: 105–36, 206–21, 267–86, 336–47; 1911: 217–28. #PJS

DE PLOEY, J. and MOORSEL, H. van (1963), *Contributions à la connaissance chronologique et paléogéographique des gisements préhistoriques des environs de Léopoldville (Congo)*, Léopoldville: studia Universitatis 'Lovanium', 19. #PM

DE PRADENNE, A.V. (1940), *Prehistory*, London: Harrap. #JAJG

DEACON, H.J. (1969), 'Melkhoutboom Cave, Alexandria District, Cape Province: a report on the 1967 investigation', *Annals of the Cape Provincial Museums* 6: 141–69. #JD

DEACON, H.J. (1970), 'The Acheulian occupation at Amanzi Springs, Uitenhage District, Cape Province', *Annals of the Cape Provincial Museums (Natural History)* 8: 89–189. #JAJG

DEACON, H.J. (1972), 'A review of the post-Pleistocene in South Africa', *South African Archaeological Society Goodwin Series* 1: 26–45. #JD

DEACON, H.J. (1975), 'Demography, subsistence and culture during the Acheulian in southern Africa', in Butzer, K.W. and Isaac, G.Ll. (eds), *After the Australopithecines*: 543–70. The Hague: Mouton. #JAJG

DEACON, H.J. (1976), *Where Hunters Gathered: A Study of Holocene Stone Age People in the Eastern Cape*, Claremont: South African Archaeological Society Monograph 1. #JD

DEACON, H.J. (1979), 'Excavations at Boomplaas Cave: a sequence through the Upper Pleistocene and Holocene in South Africa', *World Archaeology* 10: 241–57. #JD

DEACON, H.J. (1983a), 'A comparative evolution of Mediterranean-type ecosystems: a southern perspective', in Kruger, F.J., Mitchell, D.F. and Jarvis, J.U.M. (eds), *Mediterranean-type Ecosystems. Ecological Studies* 43: 3–40. Berlin: Springer-Verlag. #JD

DEACON, H.J. (1983b), 'Another look at the Pleistocene climates of South Africa', *South African Journal of Science* 79: 325–8. #JD

DEACON, H.J. and DEACON, J. (1963), 'Scott's Cave: a late Stone Age site in the Gamtoos Valley', *Annals of the Cape Provincial Museums* 3: 96–121. #JD

DEACON, H.J., DEACON, J., BROOKER, M. and WILSON, M.L. (1978), 'The evidence for herding at Boomplaas Cave in the southern Cape, South Africa', *South African Archaeological Bulletin* 33: 39–65. #JD

DEACON, H.J., SCHOLTZ, A. and DAITZ, L.D. (1983), 'Fossil charcoals as a source of palaeoecological information in the fynbos region', in Deacon, H.J., Hendey, Q.B. and Lambrechts, J.J.N. (eds), 'Fynbos palaeoecology: a preliminary synthesis', *South African National Scientific Progress Report* 75: 174–82. Pretoria: CSIR. #JD

DEACON, H.J., DEACON, J., SCHOLTZ, A., THACKERAY, J.F., BRINK, J.S. and VOGEL, J.C. (1984), 'Correlation of palaeoenvironmental data from the Late Pleistocene and Holocene deposits at Boomplaas Cave, southern Cape', in Vogel, J.C. (ed.), *Late Cainozoic Palaeoclimates of the Southern Hemisphere*: 339–52. Rotterdam: Balkema. #JD

DEACON, H.J. and THACKERAY, J.F. (1984), 'Late Pleistocene environmental changes and implications for the archaeological record in southern Africa', in Vogel, J.C. (ed.), *Late Cainozoic Palaeoclimates of the Southern Hemisphere*: 375–90. Rotterdam: Balkema. #JD

DEACON, J. (1972), 'Wilton: an assessment after 50 years', *South African Archaeological Bulletin* 27: 10–45. #JD

DEACON, J. (1974), 'Patterning in the radiocarbon dates for the Wilton/Smithfield complex in southern Africa', *South African Archaeological Bulletin* 29: 3–18. #JD

DEACON, J. (1978), 'Changing patterns in the late Pleistocene/early Holocene prehistory of southern Africa as seen from the Nelson Bay Cave stone artefact sequence', *Quaternary Research* 10: 84–111. #JD

DEACON, J. (1984a), 'Later Stone Age people and their descendants in southern Africa', in Klein, R.G. (ed.), *Southern African Prehistory and Palaeoenvironments*: 221–328. Rotterdam: Balkema. #JD

DEACON, J. (1984b), *The Later Stone Age of Southernmost Africa*, Oxford: British Archaeological Reports International Series 213. #JD

DEBRUGE, A., (1923), 'Essai de chronologie sur "les escargotières"', *Recl. des Notes et Mémoires de la Société Archéologique de Constantine* 44: 61. #PJS

DEBRUGE, A. and MERCIER, G. (1912), 'La station préhistorique de Mechta Châteaudun', *Recl. des Notes et Mémoires de la Société Archéologique de Constantine* 36: 287–307. #PJS

DECORSE, C. (1980), 'An archaeological survey of protohistoric defensive sites in Sierra Leone', *Nyame Akuma* 17: 48–53. #FJK

DECORSE, C. (1981), 'Additional notes on archaeological fieldwork in northeastern Sierra Leone', *Nyame Akuma* 19: 14–16. #FJK

DELAFOSSE, L. (1976), *Maurice Delafosse, le Berrichon conquis par l'Afrique*. Paris: Société française d'Histoire d'Outre-Mer. #PB

DELAFOSSE, M. (1900), 'Sur des traces probables de civilisation égyptienne et d'hommes de race blanche à la Côte-d'Ivoire', *L'Anthropologie* 11: 677–83. #PB #AH

DELAFOSSE, M. (1912), *Haut-Sénégal-Niger*, Paris: Larose. #PB #AH

DELAFOSSE, M. (1916), 'La question de Ghana et la mission Bonnal de Mézières', *Annuaire et Mémoires du Comité d'études historiques et scientifiques de l'A.O.F.*, Gorée. #AH

DELAFOSSE, M. (1922), *Les Noirs de l'Afrique*, Paris: Payot. #PB

DELAFOSSE, M. (1924), 'Le Gâna et le Mali et l'emplacement de leurs capitales', *Bulletin du Comité d'Études historiques et scientifiques de l'A.O.F.* 9: 479–542. #PB

DELAFOSSE, M. (1925), *Les civilisations négro-africaines*, Paris: Stock. #PB

DELAFOSSE, M. (1931), *The Negroes of Africa, History and Culture*. Washington, D.C.: The Associated Publishers. [English translation of *Les Noirs de l'Afrique* (1922) and *Civilisations négro-africaines* (1925) by F. Fligelman]. #PB

DELCROIX, R. and VAUFREY, R. (1939), 'Le Toumbien de Guinée Française', *L'Anthropologie* 49: 265–312. #PM #PB

DELGADO, N. (1900–1), 'Quelques mots sur la collection de roches de la Province d'Angola récoltées par le Rev. Pe Antunes', *Communicações da Direcção des Serviços Geológicos de Portugal* 4: 201–5. #PM

DENBOW, J.R. (1984), 'Prehistoric herders and foragers of the Kalahari: the evidence for 1500 years of interaction', in Schrire, C. (ed.), *Past and Present in Hunter Gatherer Studies*: 175–93. Orlando: Academic Press. #PR

DENBOW, J.R. and WILMSEN, E.N. (1986), 'Advent and course of pastoralism in the Kalahari', *Science* 234: 1509–15. #PR

DEREFAKA, A. (1980), 'Cordage fabric and basketry of the Tichitt tradition', *West African Journal of Archaeology* 10: 117–54. #PB

DESCAMPS, C. (1981), 'Quelques réflexions sur le Néolithique du Sénégal', *Revue Ouest-Africaine d'Archéologie* 11: 145–52. #PB

DESPLAGNES, Lt. L. (1906), 'Notes sur les origines des populations nigériennes', *L'Anthropologie* 17: 525–9. #PB

DESPLAGNES, Lt. L. (1907), *Le Plateau Central Nigérien: une mission archéologique et ethnographique au Soudan français*, Paris: Emile Larose. #PB #AH

DESPLAGNES, Lt. L. (1915), 'Fouilles du tumulus d'El-Oualedji (Soudan)', *Bulletin de l'Institut Français d'Afrique Noire* 13: 1159–73. #PB

DEVISSE, J. (1981), 'La recherche archéologique et sa contribution à l'histoire de l'Afrique', *Recherche, Pédagogie et Culture* 55: 2–8. #PB

DEVISSE, J., BABACAR, A.O., BAH, T.M., BOUCHUD, J., COLIN, G.S., GHALI, N., LAUNOIS, A., LEBECQ, S., MEILLASSOUX, C., MOUSSIE, B., RICHIR, C., ROBERT–CHALEIX, D., VANACKER, C. and VAN–CAMPO, S. (1983), *Tegdaoust III, Recherches sur Aoudaghost: campagnes 1960–1965, enquêtes générales*. Paris: Eds Recherche sur les Civilisations, Mémoire 25. #PB #AH

DEWEY, H. and HOBLEY, C.W. (1925), 'Some obsidian implements from Kenya Colony', *Man* 25: 88–92. #PR

DIALLO, A.O. (1971), 'La céramique nianimba', INDRG Mémoire. Conakry. Mimeographed. #PB

DIETERLEN, G. (1966), 'Les fresques d'époque bovidienne du Tassili n'Ajjer et les traditions des Peul: hypothèses d'interprétation', *Journal de la société des Africanistes* 36: 141–57. #WD

DIOP, C.A. (1955), *Nations nègres et culture*, Paris: Collection Présence Africaine. #PB

DIOP, C.A. (1960a), 'Les intellectuels doivent étudier le passé non pour s'y complaire mais pour y puiser des leçons', Paris, *La Vie Africaine* 6: 10–11. #PB

DIOP, C.A. (1960b), *L'Afrique noire précoloniale*, Paris: Présence Africaine. #PB #AH

DIOP, C.A. (1962), 'Réponses à quelques critiques', *Bulletin de l'Institut Français d'Afrique Noire* (B) 24: 542–74. #PB

DIOP, C.A. (1967), *Antériorité des civilisations Nègres: mythe ou vérité historique?*, Paris: Présence Africaine. #PB #AH

DIOP, C.A. (1977), *Parenté génétique de l'égyptien pharaonique et des langues négro-africaines*, Dakar: Nouvelles Editions Africaines. #AH

DIOP, C.A. (1979), *Nations nègres et Culture*, Paris: Présence Africaine, 3ᵉ edn (first edition 1955). #AH

DIOP, C.A. (1981), 'Origin of the Ancient Egyptians', in Mokhtar, G. (ed.), *UNESCO General History of Africa II. Ancient Civilizations of Africa*: 27–57. California. #DOC

DIOP, L.M. (1968), 'Métallurgie traditionelle et âge du fer en Afrique', *Bulletin de l'Institut Fondamental d'Afrique Noire* (B) 30: 10–38. #PB #AH

DOLLIE, N. (1986), 'The National Forum', *South African Review* 3: 267–77. #MH

DOMBROWSKI, J.C. (1971), 'Excavations in Ethiopia: Lalibela and Natchabiet Caves, Begemeder Province', unpublished PhD thesis: Boston University. #SAB

DOMBROWSKI, J.C. (1976), 'Mumute and Bonoase – two sites of the Kintampo industry', *Sankofa* 2: 64–71. #FJK

DOMBROWSKI, J.C. (1980), 'Earliest settlements in Ghana: the Kintampo Industry', in Leakey, R.E. and Ogot, B.A. (eds), *Proceedings of the 8th Panafrican Congress of Prehistory and Quaternary Studies*: 261–2. Nairobi: The International Louis Leakey Memorial Institute for African Prehistory. #FJK

DONADONI, S. (ed.) (1963), *Le fonti indirette della storia Egiziana*, Rome: Università di Roma. Centro di Studi Semitici. 7. #DOC

DONADONI, S. (1964), 'Remarks about Egyptian connections of the Saharan rock shelter art', in Pericot Garcia, L. and Ripoll-Perello, E. (eds), *Prehistoric Rock Art of the Western Mediterranean and the Sahara*: 85–8. Chicago: Aldine. #WD

DONLEY–REID, L. (1984), 'The social uses of Swahili space and objects', unpublished PhD dissertation: University of Cambridge. #PRS

DOS SANTOS, J.R. (1934), 'Rui de Serpa Pinto e a arqueologia de Angola', *Actas di l Congresso Nacional de Antropologia Colonial* Porto: Edições da Exposição Colonial Portuguesa. #PM

DOUX, J. LEE (1914), 'Stone implements from South Africa', *Man* 14, no. 30. #JAJG

DREWES, A.J. (1962), *Inscriptions de l'Ethiopie Antique*, Leiden: E.G. Brill. #SAB

DROUX, G. (1937), 'Nouvelles stations préhistoriques au Congo Français (note préliminaire)', *Bulletin de la Société des Recherches Congolaises* 23: 171–80. #PM

DROUX, G. (1941), 'De la présence d'outils en pierre taillée dans la terrasse de 20m du Stanley-Pool', *Bulletin de la Société des Recherches Congolaises* 28: 137–42. #PM

DROUX, G. and BERGEAUD, G. (1937), 'Nouveaux ateliers préhistoriques à Brazzaville', *Bulletin de la Société des Recherches Congolaises* 24: 210–33. #PM

DROUX, G. and BERGEAUD, G. (1939), 'Le gisements préhistoriques de la Pointe hollandaise (Congo Brazaville)', *Bulletin de la Société des Recherches Congolaises* 28: 137–42. #PM

DROUX, G. and KELLEY, H. (1939), 'Recherches préhistoriques dans la région de Boko-Songho et à Pointe Noire (Moyen Congo)', *Journal de la Société des Africanistes* 9: 71–84.

DROWER, M.S. (1985), *Flinders Petrie. A Life in Archaeology*, London: Victor Gollancz. #DOC

DU TOIT, A.L. (1947), 'Palaeolithic environments in Kenya and the Union – a contrast', *South African Archaeological Bulletin* 2: 28–40. #JD

DUBOW, S. (in press), ' "Understanding the native mind": anthropology, cultural adaption, and the elaboration of a segregationist discourse in South Africa, c. 1920–36', in Hall, M. (ed.), *Collected Seminar Papers*, Cape Town: Centre for African Studies, University of Cape Town. #MH

DUCHEMIN, CAPTAIN (1905), 'Les mégalithes de la Gambie', *L'Anthropologie* 16: 633–8. #PB

DUCKWORTH, W.L.H. (1912), *Prehistoric Man*, Cambridge: Cambridge University Press. #JAJG

DUCKWORTH, W.L.H. (1925), 'The fossil anthropoid ape from Taungs', *Nature* 115: 236. #JAJG

DUNBAR, J.H. (1934), 'Some Nubian rock-pictures', *Sudan Notes and Records* 17: 139–66. #WD

DUNBAR, J.H. (1941), *The Rock-pictures of Lower Nubia*, Cairo: Department of Antiquities. #WD

DUNHAM, D. (1958), *The Egyptian Department and its Excavations*, Boston/Museum of Fine Arts. #DOC

DUNN, E.J. (1879–80), 'Stone implements of South Africa', *Transactions of the South African Philosophical Society* 2: 6–22. #PR

DUNN, E.J. (1931), *The Bushman*, London: Griffin. #JD

DUNNELL, R.C. (1982), 'Science, social science and common sense: the agonizing dilemma of modern archaeology', *Journal of Anthropological Research* 38: 1–25. #JD

DUPONT, E. (1887a), 'Découvertes faits par M. le Capitaine d'artillerie Zboïnski, d'instruments de l'âge de la pierre dans l'État du Congo', *Bulletin de l'Académie Royale de Belgique* 3ᵉ série, 13(4): 407–9. #PM

DUPONT, E. (1887b), 'Âge de la pierre au Congo', *Revue d'Ethnographie* 6: 509–10. #PM

DUPONT, E. (1889), *Lettres sur le Congo*, Paris: C. Reinwald éditeur. #PM

DUPRAT, C. (1894), 'L'âge de la pierre à Tébessa', *Recl. des Notes et Mémoires de la Société Archéologique de Constantine* 29: 543–51. #PJS

EBOUE, F. (1932), 'Les peuples de l'Oubangui–Chari. Essai d'ethnographie, de linguistique et d'économie sociale', *L'Ethnographie* 27: 3–79. #PM

ECHARD, N. (ed.) (1983), *Métallurgies africaines: nouvelles contributions*, Paris: Société des Africanistes, Mémoire 9. #PB

EDITORIAL (1970), *South African Archaeological Bulletin*, 25: 84. #JD

EDWARDS, I.E.S. (1985), *The Pyramids of Egypt*, Harmondsworth: Penguin Books. #DOC

EDWARDS, I.E.S., GADD, C.J. and HAMMOND, N.G.L. (eds) (1971), *The Cambridge Ancient History, 3rd edn, I.2 Early History of the Middle East*, Cambridge: Cambridge University Press. #DOC

EDWARDS, I.E.S., GADD, C.J., HAMMOND, N.G.L., and SOLLBERGER, E. (eds) (1973), *The Cambridge Ancient History, 3rd edn, II.1 History of the Middle East and the Aegean Region c. 1800–1380 B.C.*, Cambridge: Cambridge University Press. #DOC

EDWARDS, I.E.S., GADD, C.J., HAMMOND, N.G.L. and SOLLBERGER, E. (eds) (1975), *The Cambridge Ancient History, 3rd edn, II.2 History of the Middle East and the Aegean Region c. 1380–1000 B.C.*, Cambridge: Cambridge University Press. #DOC

EFFAH-GYAMFI, K. (1985), *Bono Manso: An Archaeological Investigation into Early Akan Urbanism*, African Occasional Papers No. 2, Calgary. #FJK

EGGERT, M. (1984), 'Imbonga und Lingonda: Zur frühesten Besiedlung des zentralafrikanischen Regenwaldes', *Beiträge zur Allgemeinen und Vergleicheden Archäologie* 6: 247–88. #PM

EGYPTOLOGY TITLES (1972–9) (No author), Brooklyn, Wilbour Library of Egyptology, The Brooklyn Museum and Faculty of Oriental Studies, University of Cambridge. #DOC

EHRET, C. (1976), 'Cushitic prehistory', in Bender, M.L. (ed.), *The non-Semitic Languages of Ethiopia*: 85–96. East Lansing: Michigan State University Press. #SAB

EHRET, C. (1979), 'On the antiquity of agriculture in Ethiopia', *Journal of African History* 20: 161–77. #SAB

ELLIOT SMITH, G. (1925), 'The fossil anthropoid ape from Taungs', *Nature* 115: 235. #JAJG

ELPHICK, R. (1977), *Kraal and Castle: Khoikhoi and the Founding of White South Africa*, New Haven: Yale University Press. #JD

ELUYEMI, O. (1977), 'Excavations in Isoya near Ile-Ife, Western Nigeria', *West African Journal of Archaeology* 7: 97–115. #PRS

EMPHOUX, J.P. (1965), 'Un site de protohistoire et de préhistoire au Congo: Mafanba', *Cahiers O.R.S.T.O.M., Sciences Humaines* 2(4): 89–95. #PM

EMPHOUX, J.P. (1970), 'La grotte de Bittori au Congà-Brazzaville', *Cahiers O.R.S.T.O.M., Sciences Humaines* 3(1): 2–20. #PM

ENGELMAYER, REINHOLD (1965), *Die Felsgravierung im Distrikt Sayala-Nubien, I, Die Schiffsdarstellungen*. Vienna: Österreichische Akad. d. Wissensch *Denkschriften (Phil.-Hist. Kl.)* 90. #WD

ESSOMBA, J.–M. (1986), *Bibliographie critique de l'archéologie camerounaise*, Yaoundé: Publications de l'Université de Yaoundé. #AH

EVANS, F.A. and BEALE, P.O. (1966), *The Anglo-Gambian Stone Circles Expedition, 1964/65*. Bathurst. #FJK

EVERNDEN, J.F. and CURTIS, G.H. (1965), 'The potassium-argon dating of late Cenozoic rocks in East Africa and Italy', *Current Anthropology* 6: 343–64. #JDC

EVERS, T.M. (1983), 'Mr Evers replies', *South African Journal of Science* 79: 261–4. #MH

EYO, EKPO (1965), 'Excavations at Rop Rock Shelter', *West African Archaeological Newsletter* 3: 5–13. #FJK

EYO, EKPO (1972), 'Excavations at Rop Rock Shelter', *West African Journal of Archaeology* 2: 13–16. #FJK

EYO, EKPO (1974), 'Recent excavations at Ife and Owo and their implications for Ife, Owo and Benin studies', unpublished PhD thesis: Ibadan. #FJK

EYO, EKPO and WILLETT, F. (1980), *Treasures of Ancient Nigeria*, New York: Knopf. #FJK

FAGAN, B.M. (1965a), *Southern Africa during the Iron Age*, London: Thames & Hudson. #MH

FAGAN, B.M. (1965b), 'Radiocarbon dates for sub-Saharan Africa III', *Journal of African History* 6: 107–16. #PB

FAGAN, B.M. (1970), 'The Greefswald sequence:- Bambandyanalo and Mapungubwe', in Fage, J.D. and Oliver, R.A. (eds), *Papers in African prehistory*: 173–99. Cambridge University Press. #MH

FAGAN, B.M. (1977), *The Rape of the Nile. Tomb Robbers, Tourists and Archaeologists in Egypt*, London: Macdonald & Jane. #DOC

FAGAN, B.M. (1981), 'Two hundred and four years of African archaeology', in Evans, J.D., Cunliffe, B. and Renfrew, C. (eds), *Antiquity and Man: Essays in Honour of Glyn Daniel*: 42–51. London: Thames & Hudson. #PR

FAGAN, B.M., PHILLIPSON, D.W. and DANIELS, S.G. (1969), *Iron Age Cultures in Zambia*, 2 vols, London: Chatto & Windus. #MH

FAGE, J.D. (1980), 'Evolution de l'historiographie de l'Afrique', in Ki-Zerbo, J. (ed.), *Histoire générale de l'Afrique I: méthodologie et préhistoire africaine*: 45–63. New York: Unesco. #PB

FAGG, B.E.B. (1945a), 'Preliminary report on a microlithic industry at Rop Rock Shelter, northern Nigeria', *Proceedings of 1st Inter. Conference of West Africanists*: 439–40. Dakar. #FJK

FAGG, B.E.B. (1945b), 'A preliminary report on a new series of pottery figures from northern Nigeria', *Proceedings of the 1st Inter. Conference of West Africanists*: 437–8. Dakar. #FJK

FAGG, B.E.B. (1962), 'The Nok terra-cottas in West African history', *Proceedings of the 4th Panafrican Congress on Prehistory (Léopoldville)*: 445–51. #FJK

FAGG, B.E.B. (1969), 'Recent work in West Africa: new light on the Nok culture', *World Archaeology* 1: 41–50. #FJK

FAGG, WILLIAM (1958), *The Sculpture of Africa*, London: Thames & Hudson. #FJK

FAGG, WILLIAM (1963), *Nigerian Images*. London: Lund Humphries. #FJK

FAGG, WILLIAM and UNDERWOOD, LEON (1949), 'An examination of the so-called "Olokun" head of Ife, Nigeria', *Man* 49: 1–7. #FJK

FAGG, WILLIAM and WILLETT, FRANK (1962), 'Ancient Ife: an ethnographical summary', *Proceedings of the 4th Panafrican Congress on Prehistory (Léopoldville)*: 357–73. #FJK

FAIRSERVIS, W. (1971–2), 'Preliminary report on the first two seasons at Hierakonpolis', *Journal of The American Research Center in Egypt* 9: 29–68. #DOC

FATTOVICH, R. (1977), 'Pre-Aksumite civilization of Ethiopia: a provisional review', *Proceedings of Seminar for Arabian Studies* 7: 73–8. #SAB

FATTOVICH, R. (1978), 'Traces of a possible African component in the Pre-Aksumite culture of Northern Ethiopia', *Abbay* 9: 25–30. #SAB

FATTOVICH, R. (1980), 'Materiali per lo studio della ceramica pre-aksumita etiopica', *Ann. ali Istituto Universitario Orientale di Napoli, supplemento* 25. #SAB

FATTOVICH, R. (1982), 'The problem of Sudanese-Ethiopian contacts in antiquity', in Plumley, J.M. (ed.), *Nubian Studies*: 76–86. Warminster: Arris and Phillips. #SAB

FATTOVICH, R. (1984), 'Remarks on the late prehistory and early history of Northern Ethiopia', Paper presented at the 8th International Conference of Ethiopian Studies, Addis Ababa, December 1984. #SAB

FATTOVICH, R. (in press), 'Some remarks on the origins of the Aksumite stelae', *Annales d'Ethiopie* 14. #SAB

FERRY, R. (1981), 'L'archéologie à Djibouti', *Archeologia* 60: 48–52. #SAB

FILIPOWIAK, W. (1979), *Études archéologiques sur la capitale médiévale du Mali*, Szczecin: Muzeum Narodowe. #PB

FISHER, R. (ed.) (1970), *Twilight Tales of the Black Baganda: The Traditional History of Bunyoro-Kitara, a former Uganda Kingdom*, London: Frank Cass. #PRS

FITCH, F.J. and MILLER, J.A. (1970), 'Radioisotopic age determinations of Lake Rudolf artefact site', *Nature* 226: 226–8. #JAJG

FITTING, J.E. (ed.) (1973), *The Development of North American Archaeology*, New York: Anchor Press-Doubleday. #PR

FLAMAND, G.–B.–M. (1921), *Les pierres écrites (Hadjrat-Mektoubat): gravures et inscriptions rupestres du nord-africain*, Paris: Masson. #WD

FLAMAND, G.–B.–M. and LAQUIÈRE, E. (1906), 'Nouvelles recherches sur la Préhistoire dans le Sahara et le Haut pays oranais', *Revue Africaine* 50: 204–43. #JAJG

FLANNERY, K.V. (1967), 'Culture history v. culture process: a debate in American archaeology', *Scientific American* 217: 119–22. #JD

FLETEMEYER, J.R. (1977), 'Age determination in the teeth of the Cape fur seal and its bearing on the seasonal mobility hypothesis proposed for the western Cape, South Africa', *South African Archaeological Bulletin* 32: 146–9. #JD

FLIGHT, C. (1976), 'Diffusionism and later African prehistory', in Abebe, B., Chavaillon, J. and Sutton, J.E.G. (eds), *Proceedings of the Panafrican Congress of Prehistory and Quaternary Studies, VIIth Session*: 317–23. Addis Ababa: The Antiquities Administration. #PB

FLINT, R.F. (1959a), 'On the basis of Pleistocene correlation in East Africa', *Geological Magazine* 96: 265–84. #JAJG #JD #PR

FLINT, R.F. (1959b), 'Pleistocene climates in eastern and southern Africa', *Bulletin of the Geological Society of America* 70: 343–74. #JD #JDC

FOCK, GERHARD J. (1979), *Felsbilder in Südafrika I, Die Gravierungen auf Klipfontein, Kapprovinz*. Cologne/Vienna: Böhlau/Institut für Ur- und Frühgeschichte der Universität zu Köln. #WD

FOCK, GERHARD J. and FOCK, DORA (1984), *Felsbilder in Südafrika, II, Kinderdam und Kalahari*. Cologne/Vienna: Böhlau/ Institut fur Ur- und Frühgeschichte der Universität zu Köln. #WD

FOCK, GERHARD J. *et al.* (1980), 'Rock engravings and the later stone age, Cape Province, South Africa: a multidisciplinary study', in Leakey, R.E. and Ogot, B.A. (eds), *Proceedings of the 8th Panafrican Congress on Prehistory and Quaternary Studies, Nairobi 1977*: 311–13. Nairobi: The International Louis Leakey Memorial Institute for African Prehistory. #WD

FONTAINE, A. (1967), 'Recherches statistiques et paramétriques sur l'industrie dite "Lupembien du Cap Manuel" (Sénégal)', *Bulletin de l'Institut Fondamental d'Afrique Noire* (B) 29: 28–39. #PB

FORDE, DARYLL (1951), 'The Yoruba-speaking peoples of south-western Nigeria', *Ethnographic Survey of Africa*, vol. 4. London. #FJK

FORTES, M. and EVANS–PRITCHARD, E.E. (1940), *African Political Systems*, London: International African Institute. #FJK

FOSSEY, D. (1983), *Gorillas in the Mist*, Boston: Houghton Mifflin. #JDC

FOUCHÉ, L. (ed.) (1937), *Mapungubwe: Ancient Bantu Civilization on the Limpopo*, Cambridge: Cambridge University Press. #MH #JDC

FOURNEAU, J. (1935), 'Le néolithique au Cameroun, les haches de pierre polie de Bafia et leur signifaction dans les sociétés indigènes actuelles', *Journal de la Société des Africanistes* 5: 67–84. #PM

FREDERIKSE, J. (1982), *None but ourselves. Masses vs. media in the making of Zimbabwe*, Johannesburg: Raven Press; London: James Currey. #MH

FRIEDE, H.M. and STEEL, R.H. (1977), 'An experimental study of iron-smelting techniques used in the South African Iron Age', *Journal of the South African Institute of Mining and Metallurgy* 77: 233–41. #MH

FROBENIUS, LEO (1911), *Auf dem wege Atlantis*, Berlin. #AH

FROBENIUS, LEO (1912), *Und Afrika spracht*, Berlin. #AH

FROBENIUS, LEO (1913), *The Voice of Africa*, London: Hutchinson & Co. #FJK #TS

FROBENIUS, LEO (1923), *Das Unbekannte Afrika*, München. #AH

FROBENIUS, LEO (1931), *Madsimu Dsangara*. 2 vols, Berlin/Zürich: Atlantis-Verlag (reprinted Graz: Akademische Druck- und Verlagsanstalt). #WD

FROBENIUS, LEO (1933), *Kulturgeschichte Afrikas*, Zürich: Phaidon Verlag. #AH

FROBENIUS, LEO (1937), *Ekade Ektab: die Felsbilder Fezzans*, Leipzig: Harrassowitz. #WD

FROBENIUS, LEO and OBERMAIER, HUGO (1925), *Hadschra Maktuba: Urzeitliche Felsbilder Kleinafrikas*, Münich: Wolff. #WD

FUCHS, PETER (1957), 'Felsmalereien und Felsgravuren in Tibesti', *Archiv für Völkerkunde* 12: 110–35. #WD

FURON, R. (1958), *Manuel de préhistoire générale*. Paris: Payot. #PM

GABEL, C. (1976), 'Microlithic occurrences in the Republic of Liberia', *West African Journal of Archaeology* 6: 21–35. #FJK

GABEL, C. (1985), 'Archaeology in sub-Saharan Africa', *International Journal of African Historical Studies* 18: 241–64. #PR

GABEL, C., BORDEN, R. and WHITE, S. (1975), 'Preliminary report on an archaeological survey of Liberia', *Liberian Studies Journal* 5: 87–105. #FJK

GADEN, H. and VERNEAU, R. (1920), 'Stations et sépultures néolithiques du territoire du Tchad', *L'Anthropologie* 30: 513–43. #PB

GADO, B. (1981), 'La recherche archéologique et historique au Niger: bilan, perspectives en archéologie et en histoire précoloniale', *Recherche, Pédagogie et Culture* 55: 33–40. #PB

GAILLARD, M. (1923), 'Niani, ancienne capitale de l'Empire mandingue', *Bulletin du Comité d'Études historiques et scientifiques de l'A.O.F.* 6: 620–36. #PB

GALLAY, A. (1966), 'Quelques gisements néolithiques du Sahara malien', *Journal de la Société des Africanistes* 36: 167–208. #PB

GALLAY, A. (1970), 'La poterie en pays sarakolé (Mali, Afrique Occidentale): étude de technologie traditionnelle', *Journal de la Société des Africanistes* 40: 7–84. #PB

GALLAY, A. (1984), 'Préface', in *Habitat lacustre du Bénin: une approche ethnoarchéologique* (A.-M. and P. Petrequin): 5–7. Paris: Eds Recherche sur les Civilisations, Mémoire 39. #PB

GALLAY, A., PIGNAT, G. and CURDY, P. (1981), 'Mission du Départment d'Anthropologie au Sénégal, Hiver 1980–81: contribution à la connaissance du mégalithisme sénégambien. Rapport préliminaire', Dakar: IFAN; Genève: Départment d'Anthropologie de l'Université de Genève. Mimeographed. 89 p. #PB

GALLOWAY, A. (1959), *The Skeletal Remains of Bambandyanalo*, Johannesburg: Witwatersrand University Press. #MH

De GANAY, S. (1940), 'Role protecteur de certaines peintures rupestres du Soudan français', *Journal de la Société des Africanistes*. 10: 87–98. #WD

GARDIN, J.-C. (1970), *Archéologie et calculateurs: problèmes mathématiques et semiologiques*, Paris: Eds du CNRS. #PB

GARDIN, J.-C. (1971), 'Archéologie et calculateurs: nouvelles perspectives', *Revue internationale des sciences sociales*: 204–18. #PB

GARDNER, G.A. (1963), *Mapungubwe Vol. 2*, Pretoria: Van Schaik. #MH

GARLAKE, P. (1973), *Great Zimbabwe*, London: Thames & Hudson. #MH

GARLAKE, P. (1976), 'An investigation of Manekweni, Mozambique', *Azania* 11: 25–47. #MH

GARLAKE, P. (1982), 'Prehistory and ideology in Zimbabwe', *Africa* 52: 1–19. #MH

GARLAKE, P. (1984), 'Ken Mufuka and Great Zimbabwe', *Antiquity* 58: 121–3. #MH

GASKIN, L.P.J. (1965), *A Bibliography of African Art*, London: International African Institute. #WD

GAUTIER, E.-E.-F. (1904), 'Gravures rupestres sud-oranaises et sahariennes', *L'Anthropologie* 15: 497–517. #WD

GAUTHIER, H. (1925–31), *Dictionnaire des noms géographiques contenus dans les textes hieroglyphiques*. Cairo: Société de Géographie d'Egypte. #DOC

GAVUA, KODZO (1985), 'Daboya and the Kintampo culture of Ghana', unpublished MA thesis: University of Calgary. #FJK

GERHART, G. (1978), *Black Power in South Africa. The Evolution of an Ideology*, Berkeley: University of California Press. #MH

GIFFORD, D.P., ISAAC, G.Ll. and NELSON, C.M. (1980), 'Prolonged Drift: evidence for predation and pastoralism at a Pastoral Neolithic site in Kenya', *Azania* 15: 57–108. #PR

GIFFORD-GONZALEZ, D.P. (1984), 'Implications of a faunal assemblage from a Pastoral Neolithic site in Kenya: findings and a perspective on research', in Clark, J.D. and Brandt, S.A. (eds), *From Hunters to Farmers: The Causes and Consequences of Food Production in Africa*: 240–51. Berkeley and Los Angeles: University of California Press. #PR

GIFFORD-GONZALEZ, D.P. and KIMENGICH, J. (1984), 'Faunal evidence for early stock-keeping in the central Rift of Kenya: preliminary findings', in Krzyzaniak, L. and Kobusiewicz, M. (eds), *Origin and Early Development of Food-producing Cultures in North-eastern Africa*: 457–71. Poznan: Polish Academy of Science. #PR

GILL, E.L. (1926), 'Can archaeological work in South Africa be regulated?', *South African Journal of Science* 23: 810–12. #JD

GLASER, E. (1895), *Die Abessinier in Arabien und Afrika*. Munich: Herman Lukaschik. #SAB

GLEADOW, A.J.W. (1980), 'Fission track age of the KBS tuff and associated hominid remains in northern Kenya', *Nature* 284: 225–30. #JAJG

GOBERT, E.G. (1910), 'Recherches sur le Capsien lre série', *Bulletin de la Société Préhistorique Française* 6: 595–604. #PJS

GOBERT, E.G. (1937), 'Les escargotières: le mot et la chose', *Revue Africaine* 81: 639–45. #PJS

GOBERT, E.G. (1950), 'Le gisement Paléolithique du Sidi Zin', *Karthago* 1: 1–51. #JDC

GOEDICKE, H. (1971), *Re-Used Blocks from the Pyramid of Amenemhet I at Lisht*, New York: Metropolitan Museum of Art. #DOC

GOOCH, W.D. (1881), 'The Stone Age of South Africa', *Journal of the Royal Anthropological Institute* 11: 124–82. #JD

GOODALL, ELIZABETH (1957), 'Styles in rock paintings', in Clark, J.D. (ed.), *Proceedings of the 3rd Panafrican Congress on Prehistory, Livingstone 1955*: 295–9. London: Chatto & Windus. #WD

GOODALL, ELIZABETH (1962), 'A distinctive mythical figure appearing in the rock paintings of Southern Rhodesia', in Mortelmans, G. and Nenquin, J. (eds), *Proceedings of the 4th Panafrican Congress on Prehistory*: 399–406. Tervuren: Musée royal de l'Afrique centrale. #WD

GOODALL, J. (1986), *The Chimpanzees of Gombe*, Cambridge: Harvard University Press. #JDC

GOODWIN, A.J.H. (1926), 'South African stone implement industries', *South African Journal of Science* 23: 784–8. #JAJG #JD

GOODWIN, A.J.H. (1935), 'A commentary on the history and present position of South African prehistory with full bibliography', *Bantu Studies* 9: 291–417. #JD #PR

GOODWIN, A.J.H. (1936), 'Vosburgh: its petroglyphs', *Annals of the South African Museum* 24: 163–210. #WD

GOODWIN, A.J.H. (1938), 'Archaeology of the Oakhurst Shelter, George, *Transactions of the Royal Society of South Africa* 25: 229–324. #JD #JDC

GOODWIN, A.J.H. (1946), *The Loom of Prehistory*, Cape Town: South African Archaeological Society Handbook No. 2. #JAJG #JD #PM

GOODWIN, A.J.H. (1947), 'The bored stones of South Africa', *Annals of the South African Museum* 37: 1–210. #JD

GOODWIN, A.J.H. (1950), 'Editorial notes and news', *South African Archaeological Bulletin* 5: 1–3. #JD

GOODWIN, A.J.H. (1952), 'The Van Riebeeck Festival Fair', *South African Archaeological Bulletin* 6: 53–4. #JD

GOODWIN, A.J.H. (1953), *Method in Prehistory*, Claremont: South African Archaeological Society Handbook. #JD

GOODWIN, A.J.H. (1954), 'Director and Survey', *South African Archaeological Bulletin* 9: 99–100. #JD

GOODWIN, A.J.H. (1958), 'Formative years of our prehistoric terminology', *South African Archaeological Bulletin*. 13: 25–33. #JD

GOODWIN, A.J.H. and VAN RIET LOWE, C. (1929), 'The Stone Age cultures of South Africa', *Annals of the South African Museum* 27: 1–289. #JAJG #JD #SAB #JDC

GOODY, J. (1954), *The Ethnography of the Northern Territories of the Gold Coast, West of the White Volta*, London: International African Institute. #FJK

GOODY, J. (1964), 'The Mande and the Akan hinterland', in Vansina, J. *et al.* (eds), *The Historian in Tropical Africa*: 190–218. London. #FJK

GORJU, J.L. (1920), *Entre le Victoria, l'Albert et l'Edouard: Ethnographie de la partie anglaise du Vicariat de l'Uganda*, Rennes: Oberthur. #PRS

GOUCHER, C. (1981), 'Iron is iron 'til it is rust: trade and ecology in the decline of West African iron-smelting', *Journal of African History* 22: 179–89. #PB

GOUCHER, C. (1983), 'Technological change in Bassar iron production', *Nyame Akuma* 23: 36. #PB

GOUCHER, C. (1984), 'The iron industry of Bassar, Togo: an interdisciplinary investigation of African technological history', unpublished PhD dissertation: University of California, Los Angeles. #PB #PRS

GOW, J. (1984), 'A survey of prehistoric beads from the Rift Valley and adjacent areas of Kenya', *MILA* 7: 17–35. #PR

GOWLETT, J.A.J., HARRIS, J.W.K., WALTON, D. and WOOD, B.A. (1981), 'Early archaeological sites, hominid remains and traces of fire from Chesowanja, Kenya', *Nature* 294: 125–9. #JAJG

GOYON, GEORGES (1957), *Nouvelles inscriptions rupestres du Wadi Hammamat*, Paris: Imprimerie Nationale. #WD

GRAMLY, R.M. and RIGHTMIRE, G.P. (1973), 'A fragmentary cranium and dated later Stone Age assemblage from Lukenya Hill, Kenya', *Man* (N.S.) 8: 571–9. #PR

GRAY, J.M. (1935), 'The riddle of Biggo', *Uganda Journal* 11: 226–33. #PRS

GRAY, J.M. (1940), *A History of the Gambia*, London: Cambridge University Press. #FJK

GRAZIOSI, P. (1933), 'Industrie preistoriche delle terrazze del Congo presso Leopoldville (Raccolta L. Cipriani)', *Archivio per l'Antropologia e l'Etnologia* 62: 115–31. #PM

GRAZIOSI, P. (1940), *L'Eta della Pietra in Somalia*, Firenze: Centro di Studi Coloniali: R. Universitas degli Studi di Firenze 18. #SAB

GRAZIOSI, P. (1942), *L'arte rupestre della Libia*, 2 vols. Naples: #WD

GRAZIOSI, P. (1954), 'Missione Preistorica Italiana in Somalia (Estate 1953)', *Revista di Science Preistoriche* IX: 121–3. #SAB

GRÉBÉNART, D. (1976), *Le Capsien des Régions de Tébessa et D'Ouled-Djellal, Algerie. Études Méditerranéens I*. Aix-en-Provence: Editions de l'Université de Provence. #PJS

GRÉBÉNART, D. (1985), 'La région d'In Gall – Tegidda N Tesemt. Programme Archéologique d'Urgence 1977–1981, Vol. 2: Le Néolithique final et les débuts de métallurgie', *Études Nigériennes* 49. Niamey: Institut de Recherches en Sciences Humaines. #PB

GREEN, F.W. (1903), 'Prehistoric drawings at El-Kab', *Proceedings of the Society for Biblical Archaeology* 25: 371–2. #WD

GREENBERG, J. (1949), 'Studies in African linguistic classification III. The position of the Bantu', *Southwestern Journal of Anthropology* 5: 309–17. #PM

GREENER, L. (1962), *High Dam over Nubia*, London: Cassell. #DOC

GREENER, L. (1966), *The Discovery of Egypt*, London: Cassell. #DOC

GREGORY, J.W. (1896), *The Great Rift Valley*, London: repr. Frank Cass (1968). #JAJG #PR

GREGORY, J.W. (1921), *The Rift Valleys and Geology of East Africa*, London: Seeley, Service. #JAJG

GRENADE, H. (1910), *Instruments en hématite polie recueillis dans le bassin de l'Uele*, Liège: Poncelet. #PM

GRIAULE, M. (1943), *Les Sao légendaires*, Paris: Gallimard. #PM

GRIAULE, M. and LEBEUF, J.P. (1948), 'Fouilles dans la région du Tchad, I', *Journal de la Société des Africanistes* 18: 1–128. #PM

GRIAULE, M. and LEBEUF, J.P. (1950), 'Fouilles dans la région du Tchad, II', *Journal de la Société des Africanistes* 20: 1–151. #PM

GRIMAL, N.C. (ed.) (1981), *Prospection et sauvegarde des antiquités de l'Egypte*, Le Caire: Institut français d'Archéologie orientale: Bibliotheque d'étude 88. #DOC

GROSLIER, B. (1981), 'Colloque de Valbonne, 25–26 mai 1978', *Recherche, Pédagogie et Culture* 55: 101. #PB

GUILLOT, R. and DESCAMPS, C. (1969), 'Nouvelles découvertes préhistoriques a Tiémassas (Sénégal)', *Bulletin de l'Institut Fondamental d'Afrique Noire* (B) 31: 602–37. #PB

GUITAT, R. (1972a), 'Projet de carte des sites néolithiques de l'Ouest Africain', in Hugot, H.J. (ed.), *Actes du VIe Congrès panafricain de préhistoire*, Dakar 1967: 70–1. Paris: Les Imprimeries Réunies de Chambéry. #PB

GUITAT, R. (1972b), 'Carte et répertoire des sites néolithiques de Mauritanie et du Sahara Espagnol', *Bulletin de l'Institut Fondamental d'Afrique Noire* 34: 192–227. #PB

HAALAND, R. (1980), 'Man's role in the changing habitat of Mema during the old kingdom of Ghana', *Norwegian Archaeological Review* 15: 31–46. #PB

HADDON, A.C. (1905), 'Presidential address, Section H', *Reports of the British Association for the Advancement of Science (South Africa)* 1905: 511–27. #JD

HALL, M. (1981), *Settlement Patterns in the Iron Age of Zululand*, Oxford: British Archaeological Reports. #MH

HALL, M. (1984a), 'The burden of tribalism: the social context of southern African Iron Age studies', *American Antiquity* 49: 455–67. #MH #SAB #FJK

HALL, M. (1984b), 'Pots and politics: ceramic interpretations in southern Africa', *World Archaeology* 15: 262–73. #AH

HALL, M. (1987), *The Changing Past: Farmers, Kings and Traders in Southern Africa. 200–1860*, Cape Town: David Philip; London: James Currey. #MH

HALL, M. and VOGEL, J.C. (1980), 'Some recent radiocarbon dates from southern Africa', *Journal of African History* 21: 431–56. #MH

HALL, R.N. (1905), *Great Zimbabwe*, London: Methuen. #MH #FJK

HALL, R.N. (1909), *Prehistoric Rhodesia*, London: Fisher Unwin. #MH

HAMILTON, C.A. (1982), 'The study of South African precolonial history: "Bantustan propaganda"?', *Reality* May: 6–9. #MH

HAMY, E.T. (1877), 'L'âge de la Pierre chez les Nègres', in *Materiaux pour l'histoire primitive et naturelle de l'Homme*, Vol. 12, 2eme séries, t. 8: 529–30. #AH

HAMY, E.T. (1897), 'L'âge de la pierre au Gabon', *Bulletin du Musée National d'Histoire Naturelle* 7: 154–6. #PM

HAMY, E.T. (1902), 'La Grotte de Kakimbon à Rotoma, près Konakry (Guinée Française)', in *Compte Rendu de la*

Bibliography

Douzième Session du Congrès international d'Anthropologie et d'Archéologie préhistoriques, Paris 1900: 232–47. Paris: Masson. #PB

HAMY, E.T. (1904), 'L'âge de pierre à la Côte d'Ivoire', *Bulletin du Musée d'histoire naturelle de Paris* 10: 534–6. #PB

HAMY, E.T. (1907), 'Anthropologie', in Desplagnes, L. (ed.), *Le Plateau Central Nigérien, une mission archéologique et ethnographique au Soudan français*: 87–94. Paris: Emile Larose. #PB

HARLAN, J.R. (1969), 'Ethiopia: a center of diversity', *Economic Botany* 23: 309–14. #SAB

HARRIS, J.W.K. (1983), 'Cultural beginnings: Plio-Pleistocene archaeological evidence from the Afar, Ethiopia', *African Archaeological Review* 1: 3–31. #JAJG

HARRIS, J.W.K. and GOWLETT, J.A.J. (1980), 'Evidence of early stone industries at Chesowanja, Kenya', in Leakey, R.E. and Ogot, B.A. (eds), *Proceedings of the Eighth Panafrican Congress of Prehistory and Quaternary Studies, Nairobi, 1977*: 208–12. Nairobi: TILLMIAP. #JAJG

HARRIS, J.W.K., GOWLETT, J.A.J., WALTON, D. and WOOD, B.A. (1981), 'Palaeoanthropological studies at Chesowanja', *Las Industrias mas antiquas*, Preprint, Union Internacional de ciencias prehistoricas y protohistoricas, X Congreso, Mexico D.F., 1981. #JAJG

HARRIS, J.W.K. and HERBICH, I. (1978), 'Aspects of early Pleistocene hominid behaviour east of Lake Turkana, Kenya', in Bishop, W.W. (ed.), *Geological Background to Fossil Man*: 529–48. Edinburgh: Scottish Academic Press. #JAJG

HARTLE, D.D. (1970), 'Preliminary report of the University of Ibadan's Kainji Rescue Archaeological Project', *West African Archaeological Newsletter* 12: 7–19. #FJK

HASSAN, F.A. (1981), *Demographic Archaeology*, New York: Academic Press. #SAB

HAUGHTON, S.H. (1918), 'Preliminary note on the ancient human skull remains from the Transvaal', *Transactions of the Royal Society of South Africa* 6: 1–8. #JAJG

HAWKES, C. (1931), 'Hill forts', *Antiquity* 5: 60–97. #MH

HAYES, W.C. (1953), *The Scepter of Egypt. I*, New York: Harper. #DOC

HAYES, W.C. (1959), *The Scepter of Egypt II*, New York: Harper. #DOC

HAZARD, P. (1964), *The European Mind 1680–1715*, Harmondsworth: Pelican Books. #DOC

HÉBRARD, L., HUGOT, H.J. and THILMANS, G. (1970), *Bulletin de l'Institut Fondamental d'Afrique Noire* (B) 32: 653–87. #PB

HEDGES, D. (1978), 'Trade and politics in southern Mozambique and Zululand in the eighteenth and early nineteenth centuries', unpublished PhD dissertation: University of London. #MH

HEINZELIN de BRAUCOURT, J. de (1948), 'Industrie lithique des graviers aurifères de la Lodjo (Ituri, Congo Belge), description de la collection Y. Piret', *Bulletin du Musée Royal d'Histoire Naturelle de Belgique* 25(8): 1–16. #PM

HEINZELIN de BRAUCOURT, J. de (1957), *Les fouilles d'Ishango. Exploration du Parc National Albert, mission J. de Heinzelin de Braucourt (1950)*, 2, Bruxelles: Institut des Parcs Nationaux du Congo Belge. #PM

HELCK, W. (1980), 'Ostrakon', Helck, W. und Westendorf, W. (herausgegeb.) *Lexikon der Ägyptologie IV*. Wiesbaden, 636–7. #DOC

HELLSTRÖM, PONTUS, with LANGBALLE, HANS (1970), *The Rock Drawings*, 2 vols, Odense: Scandinavian University Books. *Scandinavian Joint Expedition to Sudanese Nubia* 1. #WD

HENDEY, Q.B. and SINGER, R. (1965), 'The faunal assemblages from the Gamtoos Valley shelters', *South African Archaeological Bulletin* 20: 206–13. #JD

HERIN, A. (1973), 'Studie van een verzameling keramiek uit de Bushimaie vallei 'Kasai-Zaire' in het Koninklijk Museum voor Midden-Afrika te Tervuren', unpublished MA thesis: Rijksuniversiteit Gent. #PM

HERIN, A. (1977–8), 'Une collection de poteries protohistoriques de la vallée de la Bushimaie (Kasaï, Zaïre)', *Études d'Histoire Africaine* 9–10: 123–32. #PM

HEWITT, J. (1921), 'On several implements and ornaments from Strandloper sites in the eastern Province', *South African Journal of Science* 18: 454–67. #JD

HEWITT, J. (1955), 'Further light on the Bowker implements', *South African Archaeological Bulletin* 10: 94–5. #JD

HIERNAUX, J. (1962), 'Le début de l'âge des métaux dans la région des grands lacs africains', in Mortelmans, G. and Nenquin, J. (eds), *Actes du IVe Congrès Panafricain de Préhistoire et de l'Étude de Quaternaire, III Préhistoire et Protohistoire*: 381–9. Tervuren: Annales du Musée Royal de l'Afrique Centrale. #PM

HIERNAUX, J., LONGRÉE, E. de and DE BUYST, J. (1971), *Fouilles archéologiques dans la vallée du Haut-Lualaba. I. Sanga. 1958*, Tervuren: Annales du Musée Royal de l'Afrique Centrale. #PM

HIERNAUX, J. and MAQUET, E. (1956), 'Cultures préhistoriques de l'âge des métaux au Ruanda-Urundi et au Kivu (Congo Belge). Première partie', *Académie Royale des Sciences Coloniales. Bulletin des Séances* 2(6): 1126–49. #PM

HIERNAUX, J., MAQUET, E. and DE BUYST, J. (1972), 'Le cimetière protohistorique de Katoto', in Hugot, H. (ed.), *Sixième Congrès Panafricain de Préhistoire, Dakar 1967*. Chambéry: Les Imprimeries Réunies. #PM

HIGGS, E.S. (1972), *Papers in Economic Prehistory*, Cambridge: Cambridge University Press. #SAB

HILL, MATTHEW (1969), 'Archaeological fieldwork in Sierra Leone, 1967–68', *West African Archaeological Newsletter* 11: 11–18. #FJK

HILL, MATTHEW (1970), 'Ceramic seriation of archaeological sites in Sierra Leone, West Africa', unpublished PhD thesis: Southern Illinois University, Carbondale. #FJK

HILL, MATTHEW (1981), 'The Senegambian monument complex: current status and prospects for research', in M. Wilson *et al.* (eds), *Megaliths to Medicine Wheels*: 419–30. Calgary. #FJK

HILL, MATTHEW (n.d.), 'Magnetometer survey in the Gambia, 1977', mimeo. report on file with writer. #FJK

HINDSON, D. (1984), 'Union unity', *South African Review* 2: 90–107. #MH

HOBLEY, C.W. (1910), 'The Karianduss deposits of the Rift Valley', *Journal of the East African Natural History Society* 1: 52–6. #JAJG

HODDER, I. (1982), *Symbols in Action*, Cambridge: Cambridge University Press. #PR

HODDER, I. (1983), 'Archaeology, ideology and contemporary society', *Royal Anthropological Institute Newsletter* 56: 6–7. #MH

HODDER, I. (1986), *Reading the Past*, Cambridge: Cambridge University Press. #PR

HODDER, I. (ed.) (1987), *Material Culture and Symbolic Expression*, London: Allen & Unwin. #WD

HOFFMAN, MICHAEL (1979), *Egypt Before the Pharaohs*, New York: Knopf. #WD

HOLL, AUGUSTIN (1979), 'La politique sociale et économique française dans le Nyong et Sanaga de 1920 à 1940', unpublished Maîtrise thesis: Université de Yaoundé. #AH

HOLL, AUGUSTIN (1983a), 'Essai sur l'économie néolithique du Dhar Tichitt (Mauritanie)', Doctorate thesis: Université de Paris I, Panthéon-Sorbonne. #AH

HOLL, AUGUSTIN (1983b), 'La question de l'Age du Fer ancien de l'Afrique occidentale: essai de méthode', Paper read at the meeting 'Histoire et Archéologie de la métallurgie du fer', 21–27 March, Paris. #AH

HOLL, AUGUSTIN (1985a), 'Subsistence patterns of the Dhar Tichitt Neolithic, Mauritania', *African Archaeological Review* 3: 151–61. #PB #AH

HOLL, AUGUSTIN (1985b), 'Background to the Ghana Empire. Archaeological investigations on the transition to statehood in the Dhar Tichitt region, Mauritania', *Journal of Anthropological Archaeology* 4: 73–115. #PB #AH

HOLL, AUGUSTIN (1986a), 'The transition from Neolithic to Iron Age in the Sudano-Sahelian zone of West Africa: A case study in technological change', Paper presented at the 'World Archaeological Congress', 1–7 September, Southampton. #AH

HOLL, AUGUSTIN (1986b), *Économie et société néolithique du Dhar Tichitt, Mauritanie*, Paris: Editions Recherches sur les Civilisations, A.D.P.F. #AH

HOLM, S.E. (1966), *Bibliography of South African Pre- and Proto-historic Archaeology*, Pretoria: Van Schaik. #JD

HORE, E.C. (1882), 'Lake Tanganyika', *Proceedings of the Royal Geographical Society* 1: 1–28. #PM

HORNUNG, E. (1966), *Geschichte als Fest: Zwei Vortrage zum Geschichtsbild der frühen Menschzeit*, Darmstadt. #DOC

HORTON, M.C. (1984), 'The early settlement of the northern Swahili coast', unpublished PhD thesis: University of Cambridge. #PR

HOUDAS, O. (1900), *Tarikh es-Soudan*, by A. Es-Sa'di (translation into French), Paris: Leroux. #PB

HOUDAS, O. and DELAFOSSE, M. (1913), *Tarikh el-Fettâch*, by M. Kâti (translation into French), Paris: Leroux. #PB

HOWELL, F.C. (1967), 'Later Cenozoic studies in Africa and Palaeo-anthropology: a post-conference appraisal', in Bishop, W.W. and Clark, J.D. (eds), *Background to Evolution in Africa*: 903–22. Chicago: University of Chicago Press. #JDC

HOWELL, F.C. (1968), 'Omo Research Expedition', *Nature* 219: 567–72. #JAJG

HOWELL, F.C. (1978), 'Overview of the Pliocene and earlier Pleistocene of the lower Omo basin, southern Ethiopia', in Jolly, C. (ed.), *Early Hominids of Africa*: 85–130. London: Duckworth. #JAJG

HOWELL, F.C. (1982), 'Origins and evolution of African hominidae', in Clark, J.D. (ed.), *The Cambridge History of Africa, volume 1: From the Earliest Times to c. 500 BC.*: 70–156. Cambridge: Cambridge University Press. #JAJG

HOWELL, F.C., COLE, G.H. and KLEINDIENST, M.R. (1962), 'Isimila, an Acheulean occupation site in the Iringa Highlands, Southern Highlands Province, Tanganyika', in Mortelmans, G. and Nenquin, J. (eds), *Actes du IVe Congrès panafricain de Préhistoire*: 43–80. Tervuren. #JAJG

HOWELL, F.C. and COPPENS, Y. (1976), 'An overview of Hominidae from the Omo succession, Ethiopia', in Coppens, Y., Howell, F.C., Isaac, G.Ll. and Leakey, R.E.F. (eds), *Earliest Man and Environments in the Lake Rudolf Basin: Stratigraphy, Paleoecology and Evolution*: 522–32. Chicago: University of Chicago Press. #JAJG

HOWELLS, W.W. (1985), 'Taung: a mirror for American anthropology', in Tobias, P.V. (ed.), *Hominid Evolution: Past, Present and Future*: 19–24. New York: Alan Liss. #JD

HROMNIK, C. (1981), *Indo-Africa: Towards a New Understanding of the History of Sub-Saharan Africa*, Cape Town: Juta. #MH

HUARD, PAUL (1960), 'L'âge pastoral au Tibesti, I, II', *Notre Sahara* 10: 17–29; 14: 13–24. #WD

HUARD, PAUL (1961), 'Les figurations d'animaux à disques frontaux et attributs rituels au Sahara oriental', *Bulletin de l'Institut français de l'Afrique noire* 23: 476–517. #WD

HUARD, PAUL (1964), 'État des recherches sur les rapports entre cultures anciennes du Sahara tchadien, de Nubie et du Soudan', *Bibliotheca Orientalis* 21: 282–9. #WD

HUARD, PAUL (1965), 'Recherches sur les traits culturels des chasseurs anciens du Sahara centra-oriental et du Nil', *Revue d'Égyptologie* 17: 21–80. #WD

HUARD, PAUL and ALLARD-HUARD, L. (1978), 'Expansion sud-occidentale de la culture des Chasseurs du Sahara central', *Bulletin de l'Institut Fondamental d'Afrique Noire* 40: 15–27. #PB

HUARD, PAUL and LECLANT, JEAN (1980), *La culture des chasseurs du Nil et du Sahara*, 2 vols, Algiers: Centre de recherches anthropologiques, préhistoriques et ethnographiques. *Mémoires* 29. #WD

HUARD, PAUL and MASSIP, J.-M. (1964), 'Gravures rupestres de Ye Lulu Loga (confins nigéro-tchadiens)', *Bulletin de la Société préhistorique française, comptes rendues des séances mens.* 8: 192–7. #WD

HUARD, P., MASSIP, J.-M. and ROSSO, B. (1968), 'Grands outils de pierre polie du Sahara nigéro-tchadien', *Bulletin de la Société préhistorique française* 65: 631–41. #PB

HUBERT, H. (1920), 'Le dessèchement progressif en Afrique Occidentale', *Bulletin du Comité d'Études historiques et scientifiques de l'A.O.F.* 3: 401–67. #PB

HUBERT, H. (1922), 'Objets anciens de l'Afrique Occidentale', *Bulletin du Comité d'Études historiques et scientifiques de l'A.O.F.* 5: 382–99. #PB

HUBERT, H. (1925), 'Description d'objets néolithiques de l'Afrique Occidentale Française', *Bulletin du Comité d'Études historiques et scientifiques de l'A.O.F.* 8: 262–97. #PB

HUBERT, H., LAFORGUE, P. and VANELSCHE, G. (1921), 'Objets anciens de l'Aouker (Mauritanie)', *Bulletin du Comité d'Études historiques et scientifiques de l'A.O.F.* 4: 371–444. #PB

HUFFMAN, T. (1970), 'The Early Iron Age and the spread of the Bantu', *South African Archaeological Bulletin* 25: 3–21. #MH

HUFFMAN, T. (1974), 'The Leopard's Kopje Tradition', *National Museums and Monuments of Rhodesia. Museum Memoir* 6: 1–150. #MH

HUFFMAN, T. (1978), 'The origins of Leopard's Kopje: an 11th century difaquane', *Arnoldia* 7(7): 1–12. #MH

HUFFMAN, T. (1979), 'African origins', *South African Journal of Science* 75: 233–7. #MH

HUFFMAN, T. (1981), 'Snakes and birds: expressive space at Great Zimbabwe, *African Studies* 40: 131–50. #MH #PRS

HUFFMAN, T. (1982),'Archaeology and ethnohistory of the African Iron Age', *Annual Review of Anthropology* 11: 133–50. #MH

HUFFMAN, T. (1984a), 'Where you are the girls gather to play: the Great Enclosure at Great Zimbabwe', in Hall, M., Avery, G., Avery, D.M., Wilson, M. and Humphreys, A. (eds), *Frontiers: Southern African Archaeology Today*: 252–65. Oxford: British Archaeological Reports. #MH

HUFFMAN, T. (1984b), 'Expressive space in the Zimbabwe culture', *Man* (n.s.) 19: 593–612. #PRS

HUFFMAN, T.N. (1986a), 'Iron Age settlement patterns and the origins of class distinction in southern Africa', in Wendorf, F. and Close, A. (eds), *Advances in World Archaeology* 5, New York: Academic Press. #PRS

HUFFMAN, T.N. (1986b), 'Cognitive studies of the Iron Age in Southern Africa', *World Archaeology* 18: 84–95. #PRS

HUFFMAN, T. and VOGEL J.C. (n.d.), 'The chronology of Great Zimbabwe', unpublished typescript. #MH

HUGOT, H.G. (1955), 'Un gisement de "pebble-tools" à Aoulef', *Travails de l'Institut de Recherches sahariennes* 13: 131–49. #JAJG

HUGOT, H.J. (1966), 'Archaeology in Senegal, Mali, Mauretania and Guinea. Discussion', in Shaw, T. (ed.), 'Report on Conference of West African Archaeologists at Freetown, 28–30 June 1966', *West African Archaeological Newsletter* 5: 36–52. #PB

HUMPHREYS, A.J.B. (1972a), 'The Type R settlements in the context of the later prehistory and early history of the Riet River valley', unpublished MA thesis: University of Cape Town. #JD

HUMPHREYS, A.J.B. (1972b), 'Comments on aspects of raw material usage in the Later Stone Age of the Middle Orange River area', *South African Archaeological Society Goodwin Series* 1: 46–53. #JD

HUMPHREYS, A.J.B. and THACKERAY, A.I. (1983), *Ghaap and Gariep: Later Stone Age Studies in the Northern Cape*, Cape Town: South African Archaeological Society Monograph 2. #JD

HUMPHREYS, G.K. (1978), 'A preliminary report of some Late Stone Age occurrences in the Lake Ziway area of the central Ethiopian Rift Valley', *Annales d'Ethiopie* 11: 45. #SAB

HUNTINGFORD, G.W.B. (1933), 'The Azanian civilization of Kenya', *Antiquity* 7: 153–65. #PR

HUXLEY, T.H. (1863), *Evidence as to Man's Place in Nature*, London: John Murray. #JAJG

IMPEY, J. (1926), *Origin of the Bushmen and the Rock-paintings of South Africa*, Cape Town: Juta. #JD

INSKEEP, R. (1961a), 'The present state of archaeology in South Africa', *South African Museums Association Bulletin* 7: 225–9. #JD

INSKEEP, R. (1961b), Editorial, *South African Archaeological Bulletin* 16: 119–21. #MH

INSKEEP, R. (1962a), Editorial, *South African Archaeological Bulletin* 17: 85–6. #MH

INSKEEP, R. (1962b), 'The age of the Kondoa rock paintings in the light of recent excavations at Kisese II rock shelter', in Mortelmans, G. and Nenquin, J. (eds), *Proceedings of the 4th Panafrican Congress on Prehistory*: 249–56. Tervuren: Musée Royal de l'Afrique Central. #WD

INSKEEP, R. (1963), 'Cinderella III (or comments on archaeology in South African museums)', *South African Museums Association Bulletin* 8: 67–71. #JD

INSKEEP, R. (1964), Editorial, *South African Archaeological Bulletin* 19: 1–2. #MH

INSKEEP, R. (1967a), 'The Late Stone Age', in Bishop, W.W. and Clark, J.D. (eds), *Background to Evolution in Africa*: 557–82. Chicago: University of Chicago Press. #JD

INSKEEP, R. (1967b), Editorial, *South African Archaeological Bulletin* 21: 155–6. #MH

INSKEEP, R. (1967c), Editorial, *South African Archaeological Bulletin* 22: 127–8. #MH

INSKEEP, R. (1969a), 'The archaeological background', in Wilson, M. and Thompson, L. (eds), *The Oxford History of South Africa*, vol. 1: 1–39. Oxford: Clarendon Press. #MH

INSKEEP, R. (1969b), Editorial, *South African Archaeological Bulletin* 23: 117–19. #MH

INSKEEP, R. (1970), 'Archaeology and society in South Africa', *South African Journal of Science* 66: 301–11. #JD

INSKEEP, R. (1978), *The Peopling of Southern Africa*, Cape Town: David Philip. #JD

ISAAC, G.Ll. (1967), 'The stratigraphy of the Peninj Group – early Middle Pleistocene formations west of Lake Natron, Tanzania', in Bishop, W.W. and Clark, J.D. (eds), *Background to Evolution in Africa*: 229–58. Chicago: University of Chicago Press. #JAJG

ISAAC, G.Ll. (1972a), 'Early phases of human behaviour: models in Lower Palaeolithic archaeology', in Clarke, D.L. (ed.), *Models in Archaeology*: 167–99. London: Methuen. #JAJG

ISAAC, G.Ll. (1972b), 'Chronology and tempo of cultural change during the Pleistocene', in Bishop, W.W. and Miller, J.A. (eds), *Calibration of Hominoid Evolution*: 381–430. Edinburgh: Scottish Academic Press. #JAJG

ISAAC, G.Ll. (1976), 'Plio-Pleistocene artefact assemblages from East Rudolf, Kenya', in Coppens, Y., Howell, F.C., Isaac, G.Ll. and Leakey, R.E.F. (eds), *Earliest Man and Environments in the Lake Rudolf Basin: Stratigraphy, Paleoecology and Evolution*: 552–64. Chicago: University of Chicago Press. #JAJG

ISAAC, G.Ll. (1978), 'The food-sharing behavior of protohuman hominids', *Scientific American* 238(4): 90–108. #JAJG

ISAAC, G.Ll. (1980). 'Casting the net wide: a review of archaeological evidence for early hominid land-use and ecological relations', in Konigsson, L.-K. (ed.), *Current Argument on Early Man*, Royal Swedish Academy of Sciences; Oxford: Pergamon Press. #JDC

ISAAC, G.Ll. (1982), 'The earliest archaeological traces', in Clark, J.D. (ed.), *The Cambridge History of Africa, volume 1: From the Earliest Times to c. 500 BC.*: 157–247. Cambridge: Cambridge University Press. #JAJG

ISAAC, G.Ll. (1983), 'Bones in contention: competing explanations for the juxtaposition of Early Pleistocene artifacts and faunal remains', in Clutton-Brock, J. and Grigson, C. (eds), *Animals and Archaeology: I. Hunters and Their Prey*: 3–19. Oxford: BAR International Series 163. #PR

ISAAC, G.Ll. (1984), 'The archaeology of human origins: studies of the lower Pleistocene in East Africa, 1971–1981', *Advances in World Archaeology* 3: 1–87. #JAJG

ISAAC, G.Ll. (1985), 'Ancestors for us all: towards broadening international participation in palaeoanthropological research', in Delson, E. (ed.), *Ancestors: The Hard Evidence*: 346–51. New York: Alan R. Liss. #JAJG

ISAAC, G.Ll., and HARRIS, J.W.K. (1978), 'Archaeology', in Leakey, M.G. and Leakey, R.E. (eds), *Koobi Fora Research Project Volume I. The Fossil Hominids and an Introduction to Their Context*: 64–85. Oxford: Clarendon Press. #JAJG

ISAAC, G.Ll. HARRIS, J.W.K. and CRADER, D. (1976), 'Archaeological evidence from the Koobi Fora Formation', in Coppens, Y., Howell, F.C., Isaac, G. Ll. and Leakey, R.E.F. (eds), *Earliest Man and Environments in the Lake Rudolf Basin: Stratigraphy, Paleoecology and Evolution*: 533–51. Chicago: University of Chicago Press. #JAJG

JACQUES, V. (1901), 'Instruments de pierre du Congo, collection Haas', *Bulletin de la Société d'Anthropologie de Bruxelles* 19: 1–32. #PM

JACQUES, V. (1904), 'Étude comparée de l'âge de la pierre au Congo et dans l'Occident de l'Europe', *Congrès d'Archéologie et d'Histoire de Dinant, Compte rendu, 17e session*. 1: 493–510. #PM

JANMART, J. (1946a), 'Sur la position stratigraphique du Tumbien moyen et supérieur dans la Lunda (Angola du Nord-Est)', *Bulletin de la Société Royale Belge d'Anthropologie et de Préhistoire* 42: 174–80. #PM

JANMART, J. (1946b), *Stations préhistoriques de l'Angola du Nord-Est. Analyse géologique, climatologique et préhistorique d'un sondage fait en bordure de la rivière Luembe (Angola du Nord-Est)*, Diamang, Publicações Culturais, no. 1. Lisbon: Museu do Dundo. #PM

JANMART, J. (1953), *The Kalahari Sands of the Lunda (N.-E. Angola), their Earlier Redistributions and the Sangoan Culture*, Diamang, Publicações Culturais, no. 20. Lisbon: Museu do Dundo. #PM

JANSSEN, J. (1975), *Commodity Prices from the Ramessid Period*, Leiden:Brill. #DOC

JANSSEN, J. (1983), 'El-Amarna as a residential city', *Bibliotheca Orientalis* 40: 273–88. #DOC

JAUZE, J.B. (1944), 'Contribution à l'étude de l'archéologie du Cameroun', *Bulletin de la Société d'Études Camerounaises* 8: 105–23. #PM

JEFFREYS, D. (1985), *The Survey of Memphis I*, London: Egypt Exploration Society. #DOC

JEFFREYS, M.D.W. (1951), 'Neolithic stone implements (Bamenda, British Cameroons)', *Bulletin de l'IFAN* 13(4): 1203–17. #PM #AH

JOHANSON, D.C. and EDEY, M.A. (1981), *Lucy: The Beginnings of Humankind*, London: Granada. #JAJG

JOHANSON, D.C. and TAIEB, M. (1976), 'Plio-Pleistocene hominid discoveries in Hadar, Ethiopia', *Nature* 260: 293–7. #JAJG

JOHANSON, D.C. and WHITE, T.D. (1979), 'A systematic assessment of early African hominids', *Science* 203: 321–30. #JAJG

JOHNSON, G.A. (1982), 'Organizational structure and scalar stress', in Renfrew, C., Rowlands, M. and Seagraves, B.A. (eds), *Theory and Explanation in Archaeology: The Southampton Conference*: 389–421. New York: Academic Press. #SAB

JOHNSON, J.P. (1905), 'Discovery of a large number of stone implements of Palaeolithic type at Vereeniging, Transvaal', *South African Philosophical Society*, 16: 107–9. #JDC

JOHNSON, J.P. (1906), 'Contribution to our knowledge of the Stone Age of South Africa', *South African Journal of Science* 3: 293–308. #JD

JOHNSON, J.P. (1907a), 'The stone implements of South Africa', *Geological Magazine*, London. #JDC

JOHNSON, J.P. (1907b), 'The stone implements of South Africa', *Man* 7, no. 54. #JAJG

JOHNSON, J.P. (1910a), *The Pre-historic Period in South Africa*, London: Longman. #JD

JOHNSON, J.P. (1910b), *Geological and Archaeological Notes on Orangia*, London: Longman. #JD

JOHNSON, SAMUEL (1921), *History of the Yorubas*, London: G. Routledge & Sons. #FJK

JOHNSTONE, F.A. (1970), 'White prosperity and white supremacy in south Africa today', *African Affairs* 69: 124–40. #MH

JOIRE, J. (1952), 'La préhistoire de Guinée Française: Inventaire et mise au point de nos connaissances', in *Conferência internacional dos Africanistas ocidentais* II, Bissau 1947, Vol. 4: 295–365. #PB

JOLEAUD, LÉONCE (1933), 'Gravures rupestres et rites de l'eau en Afrique du nord', *Journal de la Société des Africanistes* 3: 197–282, 4: 285–302. #WD

JONES, N. (1920), 'On the implement-bearing deposits of Taungs and Tiger Kloof in the Cape Province of South Africa', *Journal of the Royal Anthropological Institute* 50: 412–24. #JAJG

JONES, N. (1924), 'On the Palaeolithic deposits of Sawmills, Rhodesia', *Journal of the Royal Anthropological Institute* 54: 276–86. #JAJG

JONES, N. (1926), *The Stone Age in Rhodesia*, Oxford: Oxford University Press. #JD

JONES, N. (1929), 'A hitherto undescribed Early Stone Age industry near Hope Fountain, Rhodesia', *South African Journal of Science* 26: 631–47. #JAJG

JONES, N. (1949), *The Prehistory of Southern Rhodesia*, Cambridge: Cambridge University Press. #JAJG #JDC

JOUENNE, P. (1918), 'Les monuments mégalithiques du Sénégal', *Bulletin du Comité d'Études historiques et scientifiques du l'A.O.F.* 1: 57–86. #PB

JOUENNE, P. (1920), 'Les roches gravées du Sénégal', *Bulletin du Comité d'Études historiques et scientifiques de l'A.O.F.* 3: 1–42. #PB

JOUENNE, P. (1930), 'Les monuments mégalithiques du Sénégal: les roches gravées et leur interprétation culturelle', *Bulletin du Comité d'Études historiques et scientifiques de l'A.O.F.* 13: 309–99. #PB

JOUSSEAUME, F. (1895), 'Réflexions anthropologiques à propos des tumulus et silex tailles des Comalis et des Danakils', *L'Anthropologie* VI. #SAB

JOYCE, T. (1909), 'Steatite figures from Sierra Leone', *Man* 9, no. 40. #FJK

JUNNER, N.R. (1939), 'River and beach terraces and peneplain residuals', *Gold Coast Geological Survey, Annual Report*, 1938–9. #FJK

JUNNER, N.R. (1940), 'Geology of the Gold Coast and Western Togo,' *Gold Coast Geological Survey Bulletin* no. 11. #FJK

KAISER, W. (1957), 'Zur inneren Chronologie der Naqadakultur', *Archaeologia Geographica* 6: 69–77. #DOC

KALB, J.E., JOLLY, C.J., MEBRATE, A., TEBEDGE, S., SMART, C., OSWALD, E.B., CRAMER, D., WHITEHEAD, P., WOOD, C.B., CONTROY, G.C., ADEFRIS, T., SPERLING, L. and KANA, B. (1982), 'Fossil mammals and artefacts from the Middle Awash Valley, Ethiopia', *Nature* 298: 25–9. #JAJG

KAMAL EL-DINE, LE PRINCE and BREUIL, HENRI (1928), 'Les gravures rupestres découvertes par le Prince Kamal el-Dine', *Revue scientifique* 4: 1–28. #WD

KAMMERER, A. (1926), *Essai sur l'histoire antique d'Abyssinie. Le royaume d'Aksoum et ses voisins d'Arabie et de Meroe*, Paris: Geuthner. #SAB

KANE–BERMAN, J. (1979), *South Africa. The Method in the Madness*. London: Pluto Press. #MH

KANNEMEYER, D.R. (1890), 'Stone implements: with a description of Bushman stone implements and relics: their names, uses, mode of manufacture and occurrence', *Cape Illustrated Magazine*. 1: 120–30. #JD

KARIG, J. (1984), *International Directory of Egyptology*, Berlin. #DOC

KATATE, A.G. and KAMUKUNGUNU, L. (1955), *Abagabe b'Ankole*, Kampala. #PRS

KATOKE, I. (1969), 'A History of Karagwe: Northwestern Tanzania from c. 1400–1915 AD', unpublished PhD dissertation: Boston University. #PRS

KATOKE, I. (1975), *The Karagwe Kingdom: a History of the Abanyambo of Northwestern Tanzania c. 1400–1915*, Nairobi: East African Publishing House. #PRS

KEENE, A.S. (1983), 'Biology, behavior and borrowing: a critical examination of optimal foraging theory in archaeology', in Moore, J.A. and Keene, A.S. (eds), *Archaeological Hammers and Theories*: 137–55. New York Academic Press. #SAB

KEES, H. (1961), *Ancient Egypt. A Cultural Topography*, London and Chicago: Faber & Faber. #DOC

KEITH, SIR ARTHUR (1925), 'The fossil anthropoid ape from Taungs', *Nature* 115: 234–5. #JAJG

KEITH, SIR ARTHUR (1931), *New Discoveries Relating to the Antiquity of Man*, London: Williams & Norgate. #JDC

KELLER, C.M. (1973), *Montagu Cave in Prehistory: a Descriptive Analysis*. Anthropological Records, 28, University of California. #JAJG

KEMP, B. (1976), 'Dating Pharaonic cemeteries. Part I: Non-mechanical approaches to seriation', *Mitteilungen des Deutschen Archaologischen Instituts Abteilung Kairo* 31: 259–91. #DOC

KEMP, B. (1977), 'The early development of towns in Egypt', *Antiquity* 51: 185–200. #DOC

KEMP, B. (1981), 'The character of the south suburb at Tell el-'Amarna', *Mitteilungen der deutschen Orient-Gesellschaft zu Berlin* 113: 81–97. #DOC

KEMP, B. (1983), 'Old Kingdom, Middle Kingdom and Second Intermediate Period c. 2686–1552 B.C.', in Trigger, B. et al., *Ancient Egypt. A Social History*: 71–182. Cambridge: Cambridge University Press. #DOC

KENDALL, D. (1971), 'Seriation from abundance matrixes', in Kendall, D. (ed.), *Mathematics in the Archaeological and Historical Sciences*: 215–52. Edinburgh: Edinburgh University Press. #DOC

KENSE, FRANÇOIS J. (1981), 'Daboya: a Gonja frontier', unpublished PhD thesis: University of Calgary. #FJK

KETEKU, E. (1978), 'Akwamu empire at Nyanawase: myth or reality?', *Nyame Akuma* no. 13: 11–13. #PRS

KETEKU, E. (1984), 'Radiocarbon dates from Nyanawase', *Nyame Akuma* no. 24/25: 4. #PRS

KIÉTHÉGA, J.-B. (1983), '*L'or de la Volta Noire: archéologie et histoire de l'exploitation traditionnelle*', Paris: Edition Karthala. #PB

KIRKMAN, J.S. (1954), *The Arab City of Gedi*, London: Oxford University Press. #PR

KITCHEN, K. (1986), *The Third Intermediate Period in Egypt*, Second edition with supplement, Warminster: Aris and Phillips. #DOC

KITSON, A. (1913), 'Southern Nigeria: some considerations of its structure, people and natural history', *Geographical Journal* 41: 16–38. #FJK

KITSON, A.E. (1916), 'The Gold Coast. Some considerations of its structure, people and natural history', *Geographical Journal* 48: 369–92. #FJK

KIWANUKA, M.S.M. (ed. and trans.) (1971), *The Kings of Buganda* by Sir Apolo Kaggwa, Nairobi: East African Publishing House. #PRS

KIYAGA-MULINDWA, DAVID (1976), 'The archaeology of the earthworks of Akim-Manso', unpublished MA thesis: Johns Hopkins University. #FJK

KLEBS, LUISE (1915), *Die Reliefs des alten Reiches*, Heidelberg: Winter. #WD

KLEIN, R.G. (1972a), 'Preliminary report on the July through September 1970 excavations at Nelson Bay Cave Plettenberg Bay (Cape Province, South Africa)', *Palaeoecology of Africa* 6: 177–208. #JD

KLEIN, R.G. (1972b), 'The late Quaternary mammalian fauna of Nelson Bay Cave (Cape Province, South Africa): its implications for megafaunal extinctions and environmental and cultural change', *Quaternary Research* 2: 135–42. #JD

KLEIN, R.G. (1974), 'Environment and subsistence of prehistoric man in the southern Cape Province, South Africa' *World Archaeology* 5: 249–84. #JD

KLEIN, R.G. (1978), 'Stone Age predation on large African bovids', *Journal of Archaeological Science* 5: 195–217. #JD

KLEIN, R.G. (1980), 'Environmental and ecological implications of large mammals from Upper Pleistocene and Holocene sites in southern Africa', *Annals of the South African Museum* 81: 223–83. #JD

KLEIN, R.G. (1981), 'Stone Age predation on small African bovids', *South African Archaeological Bulletin* 36: 55–65 #JD

KLEIN, R.G. (1984), 'The large mammals of southern Africa: Late Pliocene to Recent', in Klein, R.G. (ed.), *Southern African Prehistory and Paleoenvironments*: 107–47. Rotterdam: Balkema. #JD

KLEINDIENST, M.R. (1959), 'Composition and significance of a Late Acheulian assemblage based on an analysis of East African occupation sites', unpublished PhD dissertation, University of Chicago. #JAJG

KLEINDIENST, M.R. (1961), 'Variability within the late Acheulean assemblage in eastern Africa', *South African Archaeological Bulletin* 16: 35–52. #JAJG

KLEINDIENST, M.R. (1962), 'Components of the East African Acheulian assemblage: an analytic approach', in Mortelmans, G. and Nenquin, J. (eds), *Actes du IVe Congrès panafricain de Préhistoire*: 81–105. Tervuren. #JAJG

KLINDT-JENSEN, O. (1975), *A History of Scandinavian Archaeology*, London. #PR

KOBISHCHANOV, Y.M. (1966), *Aksum*, Moscow: Nauka. #SAB

KOBISHCHANOV, Y.M. (1979), *Aksum* (English translation), University Park: Pennsylvania State Press. #SAB

KOBISHCHANOV, Y.M. (1981), 'Aksum: political system, economics and culture, first to fourth century', in Mokhtar, G. (ed.), *General History of Africa II: Ancient Civilizations of Africa*: 381–400. Berkeley: University of California Press. #SAB

Bibliography

KOHL–LARSEN, L. (1943), *Auf den Spuren des Vormenschen*, 2 vols, Stuttgart: Stecker und Schröder Verlag. #PR

KRAUSS, R. (1985), *Sothis – und Monddaten, Studien zur astronomisch und technischen Chronologie Altägyptens*, Hildesheim. #DOC

KUEVI, D. (1985), 'Projet de recherche interdisciplinaire: étude des populations des zones montagneuses du Togo', Ministère de l'Education nationale et de la Recherche scientifique, mimeographed, 6 p. #PB

KUHN, HERBERT (1927), 'Alter und Bedeutung der nordafrikanischen Felszeichnungen', *IPEK* 1: 13–30. #WD

KUHN, T.S. (1970), *The Structure of Scientific Revolutions*, Chicago: University of Chicago Press. #PJS #AH

KUPER, A. (1980), 'Symbolic dimensions of the southern Bantu homestead', *Africa* 50: 8–23. #MH

KUPER, RUDOLPH (ed.) (1978), *Sahara, 10,000 Jahre zwischen Weide und Wüste*, Köln: Museen der Stadt. #AH

KURASHINA, H. (1978), 'An examination of prehistoric lithic technology in east-central Ethiopia', unpublished PhD thesis: University of California, Berkeley. #SAB

KUSSEL, U.S. (1974), 'Extractive metallurgy in Iron Age South Africa', *Journal of the South African Institute of Mining and Metallurgy* 74: 246–9. #MH

LABOURET, H. (1931), 'Préface', in *The Negroes of Africa, History and Culture*, Washington, D.C.: The Associated Publishers. [translation into English by F. Fligelman of *Les Noirs de l'Afrique* (1922) and *Civilisations négro-africaines* (1925), by M. Delafosse]. #PB

LABOURET, H. (1932), 'Plan de monographie régionale', *Bulletin du Comité d'Études historiques et scientifiques de l'A.O.F.* 15: 549–91. #PB

LACORRE, F. (1949), 'Le Gétulo-capsien: Abri 402 et Ain Metherchem', *Bulletin de la Société Préhistorique Française* 50: 258–73. #PJS

LAFORGUE, P. (1923), 'Essai sur l'influence de l'Industrie saharienne en Afrique Occidentale au cours de la période néolithique', *Bulletin du Comité d'Études historiques et scientifiques de l'A.O.F.* 6: 161–6. #PB

LAFORGUE, P. (1924), 'Quelques objets préhistoriques d'El Hoffrat Ouadane (Mauritanie)', *Bulletin du Comité d'Études historiques et scientifiques de l'A.O.F.* 7: 223–38. #PB

LAFORGUE, P. (1925), 'État actuel de nos connaissances sur la préhistoire en Afrique Occidentale Française', *Bulletin du Comité d'Études historiques et scientifiques de l'A.O.F.* 8: 105–71. #PB #AH

LAFORGUE, P. (1936), 'Note bibliographique sur la préhistoire de l'Ouest africain', *Bulletin du Comité d'études historiques et scientifiques de l'A.O.F.* 20: 113–30. #AH

LAFORGUE, P. and MAUNY, R. (1938), 'Contribution à la préhistoire du Cap-Vert', *Bulletin du Comité d'Études historiques et scientifiques de l 'A.O.F.* 21: 523–43. #PB

LAGOTALA, H. (1933), 'Industries lithiques de caractère paléolithique provenant du Congo Français', *Association Française pour l'Avancement des Sciences, 5ᵉ session, Chambéry 1933*: 342–4. #PM

LAMBERT, N. (1961), 'Le site néolithique de Medinet Sbat dans l'Ifozuiten (Mauritanie)', *Bulletin de l'Institut Français d'Afrique Noire* (B) 23: 423–55. #PB

LAMBERT, N. (1965), 'Note sur quelques céramiques de Mauritanie occidentale', *Bulletin de l'Institut Français d'Afrique Noire* 27: 413–44. #PB

LAMBERT, N. (1972), 'Objets en cuivre et Néolithique de Mauritanie Occidentale', in Hugot, H.J. (ed.), *Actes du VIe Congrès panafricain de préhistoire, Dakar 1967*: 159–74. Paris: Les Imprimeries Réunies de Chambery. #PB

LAME, M. (1978). 'Sénégal, Bilan archéologique', in *Les recherches archéologiques dans les états d'Afrique au Sud du Sahara et à Madagascar*: 53–6. Paris: CNRS Sophia Antipolis. #PB

LAMING–EMPERAIRE, A. (1964), *Origines de l'archéologie préhistorique en France*, Paris: Picard. #AH

LANFRANCHI, R. (1979), 'Recherches préhistoriques dans la moyenne vallée du Niari (République Populaire du Congo', 2 vols, unpublished thèse de doctorat de 3ᵉ cycle: Université de Paris. #PM

LANFRANCHI, R. (1986), 'Les industries préhistoriques congolaises dans le contexte du quaternaire récent', *INQUA Dakar Symposium. Changements globaux en Afrique*: 247–9. #PM

LANNING, E.C. (1970), 'Ntusi: an ancient capital site of Western Uganda, *Azania* 5: 39–54. #PR

LARICK, R.R. (1985), 'Spears, style and time among Maa-speaking pastoralists', *Journal of Anthropological Archaeology* 4: 206–20. #PR

LARICK, R.R. (1986), 'Iron smelting and inter-ethnic conflict among pre-colonial Maa-speaking pastoralists of north-central Kenya', *African Archaeological Review* 4: 165–76. #PR

LAWAL, BABATUNDE (1972), 'Archaeological excavations at Igbo-Ukwu – A reassessment', *Odu* (n.s.) 8: 72–97. #FJK

LAWAL, BABATUNDE (1973), 'Dating problems at Igbo-Ukwu', *Journal of African History* 14: 1–8. #FJK

LAWRENCE, A.W. (1963), *Trade Castles and Forts of West Africa*, London: Jonathan Cape. #FJK

LEACH, E. (1973), 'Concluding address', in Renfrew, C. (ed.), *The Explanation of Culture Change: Models in Prehistory*: 761–71. London: Duckworth. #MH

LEACH, E. (1984), 'Glimpses of the unmentionable in the history of British social anthropology', *Annual Review of Anthropology* 13: 1–23. #JD

LEAHY, A. (1985), 'The Libyan Period in Egypt: an essay in interpretation', *Libyan Studies* 16: 51–65. #DOC

LEAKEY, L.S.B. (1929), 'An outline of the Stone Age in Kenya', *South African Journal of Science* 26: 749–57. #JD #PR

LEAKEY, L.S.B. (1931), *The Stone Age Cultures of Kenya Colony*, London: Cambridge University Press. #JAJG #PR #SAB #JDC

LEAKEY, L.S.B. (1934a), *Adam's Ancestors*, London: Methuen. #JAJG.

LEAKEY, L.S.B. (1934b), 'The Oldoway Culture sequence', *Proceedings of the 1st Congress of Prehistoric and Protohistoric Sciences, London 1932*: 73–4. London: Oxford University Press. #JAJG

LEAKEY, L.S.B. (1935), *The Stone Age Races of Kenya Colony*, London: Oxford University Press. #JAJG #PR

LEAKEY, L.S.B. (1936a), *Stone Age Africa: An Outline of Prehistory in Africa*, London: Oxford University Press. #PR #JDC #WD

LEAKEY, L.S.B. (1936b), 'Fossil human remains from Kanam and Kanjera', *Nature* 138: 643. #JAJG

LEAKEY, L.S.B. (1937), *White African*, London: Hodder & Stoughton.

LEAKEY, L.S.B. (1945), 'Notes on the skulls and skeletal material from Hyrax Hill', in Leakey, M.D., 'Report on the excavations at Hyrax Hill, Nakuru, Kenya Colony, 1937–1938': 374–405. *Transactions of the Royal Society of South Africa* 30: 271–409. #PR

LEAKEY, L.S.B. (1949), *Tentative Study of the Pleistocene Climatic Changes and Stone Age Culture Sequences in North-Eastern Angola*, Diamang, Publicações Culturais, no. 4. Lisbon: Museu do Dundo. #PM

LEAKEY, L.S.B. (1950a), 'Part II: The crania', in Leakey, M.D. and L.S.B., *Excavations at the Njoro River Cave*: 41–73. Oxford: Clarendon Press. #PR

LEAKEY, L.S.B. (1950b), 'The archaeological aspect of the Tanganyika paintings with tentative notes on sequences', *Tanganyika Notes and Records* 29: 15–24. #WD

LEAKEY, L.S.B. (1951), *Olduvai Gorge*, Cambridge: Cambridge University Press, #JAJG

LEAKEY, L.S.B. (1952a), 'Capsian or Aurignacian? Which term should be used in Africa?', in Leakey, L.S.B. and Cole, S. (eds), *Proceedings of the Pan-African Congress on Prehistory, Nairobi 1947*: 205–6. Oxford: Basil Blackwell. #PR

LEAKEY, L.S.B. (1952b), 'The Tumbian culture in East Africa', in Leakey, L.S.B. and Cole, S. (eds), *Proceedings of the Pan-African Congress on Prehistory, Nairobi 1947*: 195–201. Oxford: Basil Blackwell. #PM

LEAKEY, L.S.B. (1952c), 'Olorgesailie', in Leakey, L.S.B. and Cole, S. (eds), *Proceedings of the Pan-African Congress on Prehistory, Nairobi 1947*: 209. Oxford: Basil Blackwell. #JAJG

LEAKEY, L.S.B. (1953). *Adam's Ancestors* (4th, revised edition), London: Methuen. #JAJG

LEAKEY, L.S.B. (1959), 'A new fossil skull from Olduvai', *Nature* 184: 491–3. #JAJG

LEAKEY, L.S.B. (1960a), 'Recent discoveries at Olduvai Gorge', *Nature* 188: 1050–2. #JAJG

LEAKEY, L.S.B. (1960b), 'The origin of the genus *Homo*', in Tax, S. (ed.), *The Evolution of Man*: 17–32. Volume 2 of *Evolution after Darwin: the University of Chicago Centennial*, Chicago: University of Chicago Press. #JAJG

LEAKEY, L.S.B. (1961a), 'New finds at Olduvai Gorge', *Nature* 189: 649–50. #JAJG

LEAKEY, L.S.B. (1961b), 'The juvenile mandible from Olduvai', *Nature* 191: 417–18. #JAJG

LEAKEY, L.S.B. (1965), 'The new Olduvai hominid discoveries and their geological setting', *Proceedings of the Geological Society of London* 1617: 104–9. #JAJG

LEAKEY, L.S.B. (1974), *By the Evidence. Memoirs 1932–1951*, New York: Harcourt Brace Jovanovich. #JAJG

LEAKEY, L.S.B. (1977), *The Southern Kikuyu before 1903*, 3 vols, London: Academic Press. #PR

LEAKEY, L.S.B. and COLE, S. (eds.) (1952), *Proceedings of the Pan-African Congress on Prehistory, Nairobi 1947*. Oxford: Basil Blackwell. #JAJG #PM

LEAKEY, L.S.B., EVERNDEN, J.F. and CURTIS, G.H. (1961), 'Age of Bed I, Olduvai Gorge, Tanganyika', *Nature* 191: 479. #JAJG #PR

LEAKEY, L.S.B. and OWEN, W.E. (1945), *A Contribution to the Study of the Tumbian Culture in East Africa*, Nairobi: Coryndon Memorial Museum, Occasional Papers, 1. #PM

LEAKEY, L.S.B., TOBIAS, P.V. and NAPIER, J.R. (1964), 'A new species of the genus *Homo* from Olduvai Gorge', *Nature* 202: 5–7. #JAJG

LEAKEY, M.D. (1945), 'Report on the excavations at Hyrax Hill, Nakuru, Kenya Colony, 1937–8', *Transactions of the Royal Society of South Africa* 30: 271–409. #PR

LEAKEY, M.D. (1967), 'Preliminary survey of the cultural material from Beds I and II, Olduvai Gorge, Tanzania' in Bishop, W.W. and Clark, J.D. (eds), *Background to Evolution in Africa*: 417–46. Chicago: University of Chicago Press. #JAJG

LEAKEY, M.D. (1970), 'Early artefacts from the Koobi Fora area', *Nature* 226: 228–30. #JAJG

LEAKEY, M.D. (1971), *Olduvai Gorge, Vol. III: Excavations in Beds I and II, 1960–1963*, Cambridge: Cambridge University Press. #JAJG

LEAKEY, M.D. (1975), 'Cultural patterns in the Olduvai sequence', in Butzer, K.W. and Isaac, G.Ll. (eds), *After the Australopithecines*: 477–94. The Hague: Mouton. #JAJG

LEAKEY, M.D. (1978), 'Olduvai Gorge 1911–1975: a history of the investigations', in Bishop, W.W. (ed.), *Geological Background to Fossil Man*: 151–6. Edinburgh: Scottish Academic Press. #JAJG

LEAKEY, M.D. (1983), *Africa's Vanishing Art: The Rock Paintings of Tanzania*, New York: Doubleday. #WD

LEAKEY, M.D. (1984), *Disclosing the Past*, London: Weidenfeld & Nicolson. #JD #PR

LEAKEY, M.D. and HAY, R.L. (1979), 'Pliocene footprints in the Laetoli Beds at Laetoli, northern Tanzania', *Nature* 278: 317–23. #JAJG

LEAKEY, M.D. and LEAKEY, L.S.B. (1950), *Excavations at the Njoro River Cave*, Oxford: Clarendon Press. #PR

LEAKEY, M.D., OWEN, W.E. and LEAKEY, L.S.B. (1948), *Dimple-based Pottery from Central Kavirondo, Kenya Colony*, Nairobi: Coryndon Memorial Museum Occasional Papers, 2. #PM

LEAKEY, M.G. and LEAKEY, R.E. (eds) (1978), *Koobi Fora Research Project volume 1. The Fossil Hominids and an Introduction to their Context*, Oxford: Clarendon Press. #JAJG

LEAKEY, R.E. (1970), 'New hominid remains and early artifacts from Northern Kenya', *Nature* 226: 223–34. #JAJG

LEAKEY, R.E. (1973), 'Evidence for an advanced Plio-Pleistocene hominid from East Rudolf, Kenya, *Nature* 242: 447–50. #JAJG

LEAKEY, R.E. (1980), *The Making of Mankind*, London: Michael Joseph. #PR

LEBEUF, J.-P. (1937), 'Rapport sur les travaux de la 4e mission Griaule, *Journal de la Société des Africanistes* 7: 213–9. #PM

LEBEUF, J.-P. (1962), *Archéologie tchadienne*, Paris: Hermann. #PM

LEBEUF, J.P. (1969), *Carte archéologique des abords du lac Tchad*, Paris: CNRS. #AH

LEBEUF, J.-P., LEBEUF, A.M.D., COURTIN, J. and TREINEN–CLAUSTRE, F.R. (1980), *Le gisement sao de Mdaga (Tchad)*, Paris: Société d'ethnographie. #AH

LEBEUF, J.-P. and MASSON DETOURBET, A. (1950), *La civilisation du Tchad*, Paris: Payot. #PM

LECLANT, J. (1950), 'Compte rendu des fouilles menés en Égypte durant les campagnes 1948–50', *Orientalia* 19: 360–73, 489–501. #DOC

LECLANT, J. (1951), 'Compte rendu des fouilles et travaux menés en Égypte durant les campagnes 1948–50 III', *Orientalia* 20: 340–51. #DOC

LECLANT, J. (1953), 'Fouilles et travaux en Égypte 1951–1952', *Orientalia* 22: 82–105. #DOC

LECLANT, J. (1955), 'Fouilles et travaux en Soudan, 1951–1954', *Orientalia* 24: 296–317. #DOC

LECLANT, J. (1962), 'Fouilles en Égypte et au Soudan 1960–1', *Orientalia* 31: 197–220, 322–38. #DOC

LECLANT, J. (1972), 'Afrika', Helck, W. und Otto, E. (herausgeb.), *Lexikon der Ägyptologie*, Band I, Wiesbaden, 86–94. #DOC

LECLANT, J. (1973), 'Une province nouvelle de l'art saharien: les gravures rupestres de Nubie', in *Maghreb et Sahara: études géographiques offertes à Jean Despois*: 239–46. Paris: #WD

LECLANT, J. (1983), 'Fouilles et travaux en Égypte et au Soudan, 1981–1982', *Orientalia* 52: 261–542. #DOC

LEE, H.N. and WOODHOUSE, B.C. (1970), *Art on the Rocks in Southern Africa*, Cape Town: MacDonald. #WD

LEE, R.B. (1965), 'Subsistence ecology of !Kung Bushmen', unpublished PhD thesis: University of California, Berkeley. #JD

LEE, R.B. (1968), 'What hunters do for a living or, how to make out on scarce resources', in Lee, R.B. and DeVore, I (eds), *Man the Hunter*: 30–48. Chicago: Aldine. #JD

LEE, R.B. and DEVORE, I. (eds) (1968), *Man the Hunter*, Chicago: Aldine. #JAJG #SAB #JDC

LEE DOUX, J. (1914), 'Stone implements from South Africa', *Man* 14: 49. #JAJG

LEFÈBVRE, G. (1967), 'Les styles de l'art rupestre pré- et protohistorique en Afrique du nord (essai de typologie)', in Hugot, H.-J. (ed.), *Proceedings of the 6th Panafrican Congress on Prehistory, Dakar 1967*: 266–30. Chambéry: Imprimeries réunies. #WD

LEFÈBVRE, G. and LEVÈBVRE, L. (1967), *Corpus des gravures et des peintures rupestres de la région de Constantine*, Paris: AMG. *Mémoires du CRAPE* 7. #WD

LEFÈBVRE, T. (1845–54), *Voyage en Abyssinie 1839–1843*, Paris. #SAB

LEGASSICK, M. (1975), 'South Africa: forced labour, industrialization and racial differentiation', in Harris, R. (ed.), *The Political Economy of Africa*: 227–70. Boston: Schenkman. #MH

LEGASSICK, M. (1980), 'The frontier tradition in South African historiography', in Marks, S. and Atmore, A. (eds), *Economy and Society in Pre-industrial South Africa*: 44–79. London: Longman. #MH

LE GROS CLARK, W.E. (1952), 'Anatomical studies of fossil hominoidea from Africa', in Leakey, L.S.B. and Cole, S. (eds), *Proceedings of the Pan-African Congress on Prehistory, Nairobi 1947*: 111–15. Oxford: Basil Blackwell. #JAJG

LE GROS CLARK, W.E. (1967), *Man-apes or ape-men? The story of discoveries in Africa*, New York: Holt, Rinehart & Winston. #JAJG

LEITE de VASCONCELOS, J. (1913), 'Instrumentos pre-históricos da Africa Portuguesa', *Argueólogo Português* 18: 174. #PM

LEONE, M. (1982), 'Some opinions about recovering mind', *American Antiquity* 47: 742–60. #MH

LEPSIUS, R. (1849–59), *Denkmaeler aus Aegypten und Aethiopien*, Berlin: #DOC

LEPSIUS, R. (1897–1913), 'Denkmaeler aus Aegypten und Aethiopien', Text hrsg. von L. Borchardt bearbeitet von K. Sethe. Leipzig.

LEROI-GOURHAN, A. (1950a), 'La caverne des Furtins', *Préhistoire* 11: 17–143. #PB

LEROI-GOURHAN, A. (1950b), *Les fouilles préhistoriques: technique et méthodes*, Paris: Picard. #JAJG #PB

LEROI-GOURHAN, A. (1964), *Les religions de la Préhistoire*, Paris: Presses Universitaires de France. #PB

LE ROY, P. (1950), 'Note documentaire sur la préhistoire de Brazzaville', *Encyclopédie Maritime et Coloniale* 6: 35–9. #PM

LÉVI–STRAUSS, CLAUDE (1962), *Totemism*, Boston: Beacon Press. #WD

LÉVI–STRAUSS, CLAUDE (1966), *The Savage Mind*, London: Weidenfeld & Nicolson. #WD

LEVY–LUXERAU, A. (1983), 'Métallurgie dans le Sahel nigérien: contraintes de l'écosysteme et effets de la technique. L'exemple de la région de Maradi (Niger)', in Echard, N. (ed.), *Métallurgies africaines: nouvelles contributions*: 225–36. Paris: Société des Africanistes, Mémoire 9. #PB

LEWIN, R. (1987), *Bones of Contention: Controversies in the Search for Human Origins*, New York: Simon & Schuster. #JAJG

LEWIS–WILLIAMS, J.D. (1981a), *Believing and Seeing: Symbolic Meanings in Southern San Rock Art*, London: Academic Press. #MH #WD

LEWIS–WILLIAMS, J.D. (1981b), 'The thin red line: southern San notions and rock paintings of supernatural potency', *South African Archaeological Bulletin* 36: 5–13. #WD

LEWIS–WILLIAMS, J.D. (1982), 'The economic and social context of Southern San rock art', *Current Anthropology* 23: 429–49. #JD #WD

LEWIS–WILLIAMS, J.D. (1983a), *The Rock Art of Southern Africa*, Cambridge: Cambridge University Press. #WD

LEWIS–WILLIAMS, J.D. (1983b), 'Science and rock art', *South African Archaeological Society Goodwin Series* 4: 3–13. #WD

LEWIS–WILLIAMS, J.D. (1983c), 'More on rock art: reply to Cooke and Willcox', *Current Anthropology* 24: 538–45. #WD

LEWIS–WILLIAMS, J.D. (1984), 'Ideological continuities in prehistoric southern Africa: the evidence of rock art', in Schrire, C. (ed.), *Past and Present in Hunter–Gatherer Studies*: 225–52. London: Academic Press: #JD #WD

LEWIS–WILLIAMS, J.D. (1986), 'Cognitive and optical illusions in San rock art research', *Current Anthropology* 27: 171–8. #WD

LEWIS–WILLIAMS, J.D. and BIESELE, MEGAN (1978), 'Eland hunting rituals among northern and southern San groups: striking similarities', *Africa* 48: 117–34. #WD

LEWIS–WILLIAMS, J.D. and LOUBSER, J.H.N. (1986), 'Deceptive appearances: a critique of southern African rock art studies', *Advances in World Archaeology* 5: 253–89. #WD

LHOTE, HENRI (1952a), 'Interprétations indigènes de quelques gravures, et peintures rupestres géometriques du Sahara occidental', *Notes africaines (Institut français de l'Afrique noire)* 53 (January, 1952): 5–6. #WD

LHOTE, HENRI (1952b), 'La connaissance du fer en Afrique occidentale', *Encyclopédie mensuelle d'Outre-Mer*: 269–72. #AH

LHOTE, HENRI (1953), 'Le cheval et le chameau dans les peintures et gravures rupestres du Sahara', *Bulletin de l'Institut français de l'Afrique noire* 15: 1138–228. #WD

LHOTE, HENRI (1959), *The Search for the Tassili Frescoes*, trans. Alan Broderick, London: Hutchinson. #WD

LHOTE, HENRI (1964), 'Faits nouveaux concernant la chronologie relative et absolute des gravures et peintures pariétales du Sud oranais et du Sahara', in Pericot Garcia, L. and Ripoll–Perello, E. (eds), *Prehistoric Art of the Western Mediterranean and the Sahara*: 191–214. Chicago: Aldine. #WD

LHOTE, HENRI (1970), 'Le peuplement du Sahara néolithique d'après l'interprétation des gravures et des peintures rupestres', *Journal de la Société des Africanistes* 40: 91–102. #PB

LHOTE, HENRI (1975), *Les gravures rupestres de l'Oued Djerat (Tassili-n-Ajjer)*, 2 vols, Paris: AMG. *Mémoires du CRAPE* 25. #ED

LHOTE, HENRI (1979), *Les gravures de l'Oued Mammanet (nord-ouest du massif de l'Air)*, Dakar: Nouvelles Éditions Africaines. #WD

LIDDELL, D. (1930–5), 'Hembury Fort Excavation Reports', *Proceedings of the Devon Archaeological Exploration Society* 1: 40–62, 90–119, 162–90; 2: 135–75. #TS

LINARES DE SAPIR, O. (1971), 'Shell middens of Lower Casamance and problems of Diola protohistory', *West African Journal of Archaeology* 1: 23–54. #PB

LINDGREN, H.E. and SCHOFFELEERS, J.M. (1978), *Rock Art and Nyau Symbolism in Malawi*, Limbe: Malawi Department of Antiquities, *Publications* 18. #WD

LIPTON, M. (1986). *Capitalism and Apartheid. South Africa, 1910–1986*, London: Wildwood House. #MH

LITTMAN, E., KRENCKER, S. and LUPKE, T. von (1913), *Deutsche-Aksum Expedition*, Vol. I–IV. Berlin: Reimer Verlag. #SAB

LLOYD, L.C. (1889), *A Short Account of Further Bushman Material Collected*, Third Report concerning Bushman Researches, presented to both Houses of Parliament of the Cape of Good Hope. London: David Nutt. #JD

LODGE, T. (1983), *Black Politics in South Africa since 1945*, Johannesburg: Ravan Press. #MH

LODGE, T. (1985), 'Introduction', in Gastrow, S., *Who's who in South African politics*: 1–26. Johannesburg: Ravan Press. #MH

LODGE, T. (1986), "Mayihlome! – let us go to war!": From Nkomati to Kabwe, the African National Congress, January 1984 – June 1985', *South African Review* 3: 226–47. #MH

LOMBARD, J. (1930), 'Présentation d'une série d'objets préhistoriques d'Afrique Equatoriale Française', *L'Anthropologie* 40: 285. #PM

LOMBARD, J. (1931), 'Matériaux préhistoriques du Congo Français', *Journal de la Société des Africanistes* 1: 49–59. #PM

LUBBOCK, JOHN (1865), *Prehistoric Times as Illustrated by Ancient Remains and the Manners and Customs of Modern Savages*, London: Williams & Norgate. #JAJG

LUBBOCK, JOHN (1869), 'On a collection of stone implements from the Cape of Good Hope', *Proceedings of the Anthropological & Ethnological Society of London* 1: 51. #JD

LUBBOCK, JOHN (1870a), 'Remarks on stone implements from Western Africa', *Atheneum* 2241: 467–8. #AH

LUBBOCK, JOHN (1870b), 'Notes on some stone implements from Africa and Syria', *Proceedings of the Ethnological Society of London* 1870: xcii–xcvii. #JD #AH

LUBBOCK, JOHN (1872), 'Note on stone implements from Africa and Syria', *Proceedings of the Royal Anthropological Institute* I: x cv–ii. #FJK

LUBELL, D., BALLAIS, J., GAUTIER, A. and HASSAN, F. (1975), 'The prehistoric cultural ecology of Capsian Escargotières: preliminary results of an inter-disciplinary investigation in the Chéria–Télidjène region (1972–1973)', *Libyca* 23: 43–121. #PJS

LUBELL, D., HASSAN, F., GAUTIER, A. and BALLAIS, J. (1976), 'The Capsian Escargotières', *Science* 191: 910–20. #PJS

LUBELL, D., SHEPPARD, P. and JACKES, M. (1984), 'Continuity in the epipalaeolithic of North Africa with special emphasis on the Maghreb', in Wendorf, F. and Close, A. (eds), *Advances in World Archaeology*, Vol. 3. New York: Academic Press. #PJS

LUCAS, A.J. (1931), 'Considération sur l'ethnique maure et en particulier sur une race ancienne: les Bafours. *Journal de la Société des africanistes* 1: 151–94. #AH

LUDOLF, J. (1691), *Historia Aethiopica*, Frankfurt. #SAB

LWANGA–LUNYIIGO, S. (1976), 'The Bantu problem reconsidered', *Current Anthropology* 17: 282–6. #PR

LYELL, C. (1863), *The Geological Evidences as to the Antiquity of Man*, London: John Murray. #JAJG

McBURNEY, C.B.M. (1960), *The Stone Age of Northern Africa*, Harmondsworth: Penguin Books. #JAJG #JDC

McBURNEY, C.B.M. (1967), *The Haua Fteah (Cyrenaica) and the Stone Age of the Southeast Mediterranean*, Cambridge: Cambridge University Press. #JAJG #JDC

McBURNEY, C.B.M. and HEY, R.W. (1955), *Prehistory and Pleistocene Geology in Cyrenaican Libya*, Cambridge: Cambridge University Press. #JAJG

McCULLOCH, M. (1950), 'Peoples of Sierra Leone', in Forde, D. (ed.), *Ethnographic Survey of Africa*, Part II, London: International African Institute. #FJK

MacCURDY, G.G. (1924), *Human Origins: A Manual of Prehistory*, New York: Appleton. #JAJG

McDOUGALL, I., MAIER, R., SUTHERLAND–HAWKES, P. and GLEADOW, A.J.W. (1980), 'K-Ar age estimate for the KBS Tuff, East Turkana, Kenya', *Nature* 284: 230–4. #JAJG

MacGAFFEY, W. (1966), 'Concepts of race in the historiography of northeast Africa', *Journal of African History* 7: 1–17. #PR #SAB

McHUGH, WILLIAM P. (1975), 'Some archaeological results of the Bagnold–Mold expedition to the Gilf Kebir and Gebel Uweinat, southern Libyan desert', *Journal of Near Eastern Studies* 34: 31–62. #WD

McINTOSH, R.J. and McINTOSH, S.K. (1981), 'The Inland Niger Delta before the Empire of Mali', *Journal of African History* 22: 1–22. #PB

McINTOSH, R.J. and McINTOSH, S.K. (1983), 'Forgotten tells of Mali: new evidence of urban beginnings in West Africa', *Expedition* 25: 35–46. #PB

McINTOSH, S.K. and McINTOSH, R.J. (1980a), *Prehistoric Investigations in the Region of Jenne, Mali*, Cambridge Monographs in African Archaeology 2. Oxford: BAR. #PB #PRS #AH

McINTOSH, S.K. and McINTOSH, R.J. (1980b), 'Jenne-jeno: An ancient African city', *Archaeology* 33: 8–14. #PRS

McINTOSH, S.K. and McINTOSH, R.J. (1981), 'West African Prehistory', *American Scientist* 69: 602–13. #FJK

McINTOSH, S.K. and McINTOSH, R.J. (1983), 'Current directions in West African prehistory', *Annual Review of Anthropology* 12: 215–58. #FJK #PB #WD #AH

McINTOSH, S.K. and McINTOSH, R.J. (1984), 'The early city in West Africa: Towards an understanding', *African Archaeological Review* 2: 73–98. #FJK #PB

McINTOSH, S.K. and McINTOSH, R.J. (1986), 'Recent archaeological research and dates from West Africa', *Journal of African History* 27: 413–42. #PB #PRS

MacIVER, D. RANDAL (1906), *Medieval Rhodesia*, London: MacMillan. #MH #JDC

MAES, J. (1924), 'Note sur les pierres taillées et gravées, sur les pierres alignées et sur une muraille de pierres en ruine situés près du village de Tundidara (Soudan)', *Bulletin du Comité d'études historiques et scientifiques de l'A.O.F.* 8: 31–8. #AH

MAGGS, T.M.O'C (1967a), 'Microdistribution of some typologically linked rock paintings from the western Cape', in Hugot, H.-J. (ed.), *Proceedings of the 6th Panafrican Congress on Prehistory*: 218–20. Chambéry: Imprimeries réunies. #WD

MAGGS, T.M.O'C. (1967b), 'A quantitative analysis of the rock art from a sample area in the western Cape', *South African Journal of Science* 63: 100–4. #WD

MAGGS, T.M.O'C. (1973). 'The NC3 Iron Age tradition', *South African Journal of Science* 69: 326. #MH

MAGGS, T.M.O'C. (1976a), *Iron Age Communities of the Southern Highveld*, Pietermaritzburg: Natal Museum. #MH

MAGGS, T.M.O'C. (1976b), 'Some recent radiocarbon dates from eastern and southern Africa', *Journal of African History* 17: 71–96. #MH

MAGGS, T.M.O'C. (1976c), 'Iron Age patterns and Sotho history on the southern Highveld', *World Archaeology* 7: 318–32. #MH #PRS

MAGGS, T.M.O'C. (1980a), 'Mzonjani and the beginnings of the Iron Age in Natal', *Annals of the Natal Museum* 24(1): 71–96. #MH

MAGGS, T.M.O'C. (1980b), 'Msuluzi Confluence: a seventh century Early Iron Age site on the Tugela River', *Annals of the Natal Museum* 24(1): 111–45. #MH

MAGGS, T.M.O'C. (1980c), 'The Iron Age sequence south of the Vaal and Pongola Rivers: some historical implications', *Journal of African History* 21: 1–15. #MH

MAGGS, T.M.O'C. (1982a), 'Mgoduyanuka: terminal Iron Age settlement in the Natal grasslands', *Annals of the Natal Museum* 25(1): 83–114. #MH

MAGGS, T.M.O'C. (1982b), 'Mabhija: pre-colonial industrial development in the Tugela Basin', *Annals of the Natal Museum* 25(1): 123–41. #MH

MAGGS, T.M.O'C. (1984a), 'The Iron Age south of the Zambezi', in Klein, R.G. (ed.), *Southern African Prehistory and Palaeoenvironments*: 329–60. Rotterdam: Balkema. #MH

MAGGS, T.M.O'C. (1984b), 'Ndondondwane: a preliminary report on an Early Iron Age site on the lower Tugela River', *Annals of the Natal Museum* 26(1): 71–94. #MH

MAGGS, T.M.O'C. and MICHAEL, M. (1976), 'Ntshekane, an Early Iron Age site in the Tugela Basin, Natal', *Annals of the Natal Museum* 22(3): 705–39. #MH

MAITRE, J.-P. (1979), 'Schémas d'évolution culturelle, I. Note sur la répartition régionale des décors céramiques néolithiques sahariens', *L'Anthropologie* 83: 584–601. #PB

MALAN, B.D. (1959), 'Obituary: Astley John Hilary Goodwin 1900–1959', *South African Archaeological Bulletin* 141: 123–5. #JD

MALAN, B.D. (1962), 'Biographical sketch', *South African Archaeological Bulletin* 17 (Suppl): 38–42. #JD

MALLOWS, W. (1984), *The Mystery of the Great Zimbabwe*, New York: Norton. #MH

MANHIRE, A.H., PARKINGTON, J. and VAN RIJSSEN, W. (1983), 'A distributional approach to the interpretation of rock art in the south-western Cape', *South African Archaeological Society Goodwin Series* 4: 29–33. #JD #WD

MARCHAL, J.-Y. (1981), 'Une enquête de géographie fondamentalement utile pour les archéologues', *Recherche, Pédagogie et Culture* 55: 87–94. #PB

MARET, P. de (1978), 'Chronologie de l'âge du fer dans la dépression de l'Upemba en République du Zaïre', 3 vols, unpublished PhD thesis: Université Libre de Bruxelles. #PM

MARET, P. de (1980), 'Preliminary report on 1980 fieldwork in the Grassfield and Yaoundé, Cameroon', *Nyame Akuma* no. 17: 10–12. #AH

MARET, P. de (1982), 'New survey of archaeological research and dates for West-Central and North-Central Africa', *Journal of African History* 23: 1–15. #AH

MARET, P. de (1985a), *Fouilles archéologiques dans la vallée du Haut-Lualaba. Zaïre. II.Sanga et Katongo, 1974.* Tervuren: Annales du Musée Royal de l'Afrique Centrale. #PM

MARET, P. de (1985b), 'Recent archaeological research and dates from Central Africa', *Journal of African History* 26: 129–48. #PM

MARET, P. de (1986), 'The Ngovo Group: an industry with polished stone tools and pottery in Lower Zaïre', *African Archaeological Review* 4: 103–33. #PM

MARET, P. de, VAN NOTEN, F. and CAHEN, D. (1977). 'Radiocarbon dates from West Central Africa: a synthesis', *Journal of African History* 18: 481–505. #PM #PRS

MARKS, S. (1986a), 'The historiography of South Africa. Recent developments', in Jewsiewicki, B. and Newbury, D. (eds), *African Historiographies. What History for Which Africa?*: 165–76. Beverly Hills: Sage. #MH

MARKS, S. (1986b), 'Patriotism, patriarchy and purity: Natal and the politics of Zulu ethnic consciousness', Africa Seminar paper, Centre for African Studies, University of Cape Town. #MH

MARLIAC, A. (1975), *Contribution à l'étude de la préhistoire au Cameroun septentrional*, Paris: ORSTOM, Travaux et Documents no. 43. #PM

MARSHALL, F.M. (1986), 'Aspects of the advent of pastoral economies in East Africa', unpublished PhD thesis: University of California, Berkeley. #PR

MARTIN, A. (1960), *Tipología de la cerámica de Fernando Poo*, Santa Isabel: Estudios del Instituto Claretiano de Africanistas. #PM

MARTIN, A. (1965), *Secuencia cultural en el neolítico de Fernando Poo*, Madrid: Trabajos de Prehistoria, Seminario de Historia Primitiva del Hombre de la Universidad de Madrid. #PM

MARTIN, V. and BECKER, C. (1974), 'Répertoire des sites protohistoriques du Sénégal et de la Gambie', *Kaolack*, mimeographed, 92 p. #PB

MARTINEZ SANTA OLALLA, J. (1947), *Africa en las actividades del Seminario de Historia Primitiva del Hombre*, Madrid: Trabajos de Prehistoria, Seminario de Historia Primitiva del Hombre de la Universidad de Madrid. #PM

MASAO, F. (1976), 'Some common aspects of the rock paintings of Kondoa and Singida', *Tanzania Notes and Records* 77–8: 51–64. #WD

MASAO, F. (1979), *The Later Stone Age and the Rock Paintings of Central Tanzania*, Wiesbaden: Steiner. #WD

MASON. R.J. (1951), 'The excavation of four caves near Johannesburg', *South African Archaeological Bulletin* 6: 71–9. #MH

MASON, R.J. (1957), 'The Transvaal Middle Stone Age and statistical analysis', *South African Archaeological Bulletin* 12: 119–43. #JD

MASON, R.J. (1962), *The Prehistory of the Transvaal*, Johannesburg: Witwatersrand University Press. #JAJG #JD #MH

MASON, R.J. (1966), 'The excavation of Doornlaagte Earlier Stone Age camp, Kimberley district', *Actas del V Congreso Panafricano de Prehistoria y del estudio del Cuaternario, Tenerife 1963* 2: 187–8. #JAJG

MASON, R.J. (1967a), 'Prehistory as a science of change – new research in the South African interior', *Occasional Papers of the Archaeological Research Unit (University of the Witwatersrand)* 1: 1–19. #MH

MASON, R.J. (1967b), 'The archaeology of the earliest superficial deposits in the Lower Vaal Basin near Holpan, Windsorten District', *South African Geographical Journal* 49: 39–56. #JDC

MASON, R.J. (1968), 'Transvaal and Natal Iron Age settlement revealed by aerial photographs and excavation', *African Studies* 27: 167–80. #MH

MASON, R.J. (1986), 'Origins of black people of Johannesburg and the southern western central Transvaal AD 350–1880', *Occasional Papers of the Archaeological Research Unit (University of the Witwatersrand)* 16: 1–937. #MH

MASSOULARD, EMILE (1949), *Préhistoire et protohistoire de l'Égypte*, Paris: Institut d'Ethnologie. *Travaux et mémoires* 53. #WD

MAUNY, R. (1947), 'Une route préhistorique à travers le Sahara occidental', *Bulletin de l'Institut Français d'Afrique Noire* 9: 341–57. #PB

MAUNY, R. (1949), 'État actuel de nos connaissances sur la préhistoire de la Colonie du Niger', *Bulletin de l'Institut Français d'Afrique Noire* 11: 141–58. #PB

MAUNY, R. (1950a), 'État actuel de nos connaissances sur la préhistoire du Dahomey et du Togo', *Études dahoméennes* 4: 5–11. #PB

MAUNY, R. (1950b), 'Les ruines de Tegdaoust et la question d'Aoudaghost', *Notes Africaines* 48: 107–9. #PB

MAUNY, R. (1951a), 'Un âge du cuivre au Sahara occidental?', *Bulletin de l'Institut Français d'Afrique Noire* 13: 168–80. #PB

MAUNY, R. (1951b), 'Poteries néolithiques du Cap-Vert (Sénégal)', *Bulletin de l'Institut Français d'Afrique Noire* 13: 153–67. #PB

MAUNY, R. (1951c), 'État actuel de la question de Ghana', *Bulletin de l'Institut Français d'Afrique Noire* 13: 463–75. #PB

MAUNY, R. (1951d), 'Notes d'archéologie au sujet de Gao', *Bulletin de l'Institut Français d'Afrique Noire* 13: 837–52. #PB

MAUNY, R. (1952), 'Essai sur l'histoire des métaux en Afrique occidentale', *Bulletin de l'Institut Français d'Afrique Noire* 14: 545–95. #PB #AH

MAUNY, R. (1953a), 'Les recherches archéologiques en A.O.F., particulierement de 1938 à 1952', *Bulletin de l'Institut Français d'Afrique Noire* 15: 684–730. #PB

MAUNY, R. (1953b), 'Notes historiques autour des principales plantes cultivées d'Afrique occidentale', *Bulletin de l'Institut Français d'Afrique Noire* 15: 684–730. #PB

MAUNY, R. (1953c), 'Autour de l'historique de l'introduction du fer en Afrique occidental', *Encyclopédie mensuelle d'Outre-Mer*: 109–10. #AH

MAUNY, R. (1954), 'Gravures, peintures et inscriptions rupestres de l'Ouest africain', *Bulletin de l'Institut Français d'Afrique Noire, Initiations Africaines* 11. #PB

MAUNY, R. (1955a), 'Les gisements néolithiques de Karkarichinkat (Tilemsi, Soudan Français)', in Balout, L. (ed.), *Actes du IIe Congrès panafricain de préhistoire, Alger 1952*: 616–29. Paris: Arts et Métiers Graphiques. #PB

MAUNY, R. (1955b), 'Autour de la repartition des chars rupestres sahariens', in *Proceedings of the 2nd Panafrican Congress on Prehistory. Algiers 1952*: 741–6. Paris: Arts et métiers graphiques. #WD

MAUNY, R. (1957), 'État actuel de nos connaissances sur la préhistoire et l'archéologie de la Haute Volta', *Notes Africaines* 73: 16–25. #PB

MAUNY, R. (1960), 'Notes bibliographiques', *Bulletin de l'Institut Français d'Afrique Noire* (B) 22: 544–55. #PB

MAUNY, R. (1961a), *Tableau géographique de l'Ouest Africain au Moyen Age, d'après les sources écrites, la tradition, et l'archéologie*, Mémoire de l'Institut Français d'Afrique Noire 61, Dakar. #PB #FJK

MAUNY, R. (1961b), 'Catalogue des restes osseux humains prehistoriques trouvés dans l'Ouest africain', *Bulletin de l'Institut Français d'Afrique Noire* (B) 23: 388–410. #PB

MAUNY, R. (1962), 'Séminaire d'Ethno-Histoire (Dakar, 11–20 décembre 1961)', *Bulletin de l'Institut Français d'Afrique Noire* (B) 24: 614–19. #PB

MAUNY, R. (1964a), 'Les fossiles directeurs en archéologie ouest africaine', in *The Historian in Tropical Africa. Studies presented and discussed at the 4th international African Seminar at the University of Dakar, Senegal, 1961*, London: International African Institute. #PB

MAUNY, R. (1964b), 'Le Centre de recherches africaines de la Sorbonne', *Bulletin de l'Institut Français d'Afrique Noire* (B) 26: 271–3. #PB

MAUNY, R. (1968), 'Bibliographie de la préhistoire et de la protohistoire de l'Ouest africain', *Bulletin de l'IFAN* 29 (série B): 879–917. #AH

MAUNY, R. (1970), *Les siècles obscurs de l'Afrique noire. Histoire et archéologie*, Paris: Fayard. #PB

MAUNY, R. (1972), 'Contribution à la connaissance de l'archéologie préhistorique et protohistorique ivoiriennes', *Annales de l'Université d'Abidjan*, Série I (Histoire), Vol. 1: 11–32. #PB

MAUNY, R. and HALLEMANS, J. (1957), 'Préhistoire et protohistoire de la région d'Akjoujt (Mauritanie)', in Clark, J.D. (ed.), *Compte rendu du IIIe Congrès panafricain de préhistoire, Livingstone 1955*, 248–61. London: Chatto & Windus. #PB

MAUNY, R. and MONOD, T. (1957), 'Découverte de nouveaux instruments en os dans l'Ouest africain', in Clark, J.D. (ed.), *Compte rendu du IIIe Congrès Panafricain de préhistoire, Livingstone 1955*: 242–7. London: Chatto & Windus. #PB

MAXWELL, J.W. (1898), 'Stones circles in Gambia', *Geographic Journal* 12: 522–7. #AH

MAYR, ERNST (1982), *The Growth of Biological Thought*. Cambridge: Harvard University Press. #AH

MAZEL, A.D. (1983), 'Eland, rhebuck and cranes: identifying seasonality in the paintings of the Drakensberg', *South African Archaeological Society Goodwin Series* 4: 34–7. #JD

MAZEL, A. and PARKINGTON, J. (1978), 'Sandy Bay revisited: variability among Late Stone Age tools', *South African Journal of Science* 74: 381–2. #JD

MAZEL, A. and PARKINGTON, J. (1981), 'Stone tools and resources: a case study from southern Africa', *World Archaeology* 13: 16–30. #JD

MBAE, B.N. (1986), 'Aspects of Maasai ethno-archaeology: implications for archaeological interpretation', unpublished MA thesis: University of Nairobi. #PR

MEHLMAN, M.J. (1979), 'Mumba-Höhle revisited: the relevance of a forgotten excavation to some current issues in East African prehistory', *World Archaeology* 11: 80–94. #PR

MENGHIN, O. (1925), 'Die Tumbakultur am unteren Kongo und der westafrikanische Kulturkreis', *Anthropos* 20: 516–57. #PM

MENGHIN, O. (1926), 'Neue Steinzeitfunde aus dem Kongostaate und ihre Beziehungen zum europäischen Campignien', *Anthropos* 21: 833–50. #PM

MENGHIN, O. (1931), *Weltgeschichte der Steinzeit*, Vienna: Anton Schroll. #PM

MENGHIN, O. (1949), 'El Tumbiense africano y sus correlaciones intercontinentales', *R.U.N.A. Archivo para las ciencias del Hombre* 2(1–2): 89–125. #PM

MERCIER, G. (1915), 'L'Homme de Mechta–Châteaudun (Algérie)', *Bulletin de la Société Préhistorique Française*. 12: 160–6. #PJS

MERCIER, G. and DEBRUGE, A. (1912), 'La station préhistorique de Mechta Châteaudun', *Recl. des Notes et Mémoires de la Société Archéologique de Constantine* 46: 287–307. #PJS

MERRICK, H.V. (1976), 'Recent archaeological research in the Plio-Pleistocene deposits of the lower Omo valley, southwestern Ethiopia', in Isaac, G.Ll. and McCown, E.R. (eds), *Human Origins: Louis Leakey and the East African Evidence*: 461–81. Menlo Park, California: Benjamin. #JAJG

MERRICK, H.V. (1983), 'An annotated bibliography of Kenyan prehistoric archaeology, 1896–1981', *African Archaeological Review* 1: 143–77. #PR

MERRICK, H.V., DE HEINZELIN, J., HAESARTS, P. and HOWELL, F.C. (1973), 'Archaeological occurrences of early Pleistocene age from the Shungura Formation, lower Omo valley, Ethiopia', *Nature* 242: 572–5. #JAJG

MÊTINHOUÉ, G. and ADANDE, A. (1984), 'Recherches sur les productions céramiques artisanales d'hier à aujourd'hui en République populaire du Bénin', Abomey–Calavi: Equipe de Recherche Archéologique Béninoise, mimeographed, 13 p. #PB

MEYEROWITZ, EVA L.R. (1941a), 'Ancient Nigerian Bronzes – 1', *Burlington Magazine* 79: 89–93. #FJK

MEYEROWITZ, EVA L.R. (1941b), 'Ancient Nigerian Bronzes – II', *Burlington Magazine* 79: 121–6. #FJK

MEYEROWITZ, EVA L.R. (1943), 'Ancient bronzes in the royal palaces at Benin', *Burlington Magazine* 8: 248–53. #FJK

MEYEROWITZ, EVA L.R. (1951), *The Sacred State of the Akan*, London: #FJK

MEYEROWITZ, EVA L.R. (1952), *Akan Traditions of Origin*, London: Faber & Faber. #FJK

MEYEROWITZ, H. and MEYEROWITZ, V. (1939), 'Bronzes and terra-cottas from Ile-Ife', *Burlington Magazine* 75: 150–5. #FJK

MICHELS, J. (1979), 'Axumite archaeology: an introductory essay', in Kobishchanov, Y.M., *Aksum*: 1–34. University Park: Pennsylvania State Press. #SAB

MICHELS, J.W. (1986), 'The Aksumite kingdom: a settlement pattern perspective', Paper presented at the 9th International Conference of Ethiopian Studies, Moscow, August 1986. #SAB

MIGEOD, F.W.H. (1926), *A New History of Sierra Leone*, London: Kegan Paul. #FJK

MODAT, LT. COL. (1919), 'Les populations primitives de l'Adrar mauritanien', *Bulletin du Comité d'Études historiques et scientifiques de l'A.O.F.* 2: 372–92. #PB

MOKHTAR, G. (ed.) (1981), *UNESCO General History of Africa II. Ancient Civilization of Africa*, London: Heinemann; Berkeley: University of California Press; Paris: Unesco. #DOC

MOLTENO, F. (1983), 'The schooling of black South Africans and the 1980 Cape Town students' boycott: a sociological interpretation', unpublished M Soc. Sci. thesis: University of Cape Town. #MH

MONNERET De VILLARD, UGO (1935 1957), *La Nubia Medioevale*, 4 vols, Cairo: Service des Antiquités de L'Egypte. #PLS

MONOD, T. (1937), 'Gravures et inscriptions rupestres du Sahara occidental: renseignements pratiques et inventaire', *Bulletin du Comité d'Études historiques et scientifiques de l'A.O.F.* 20: 155–78. #PB

MONOD, T. (1938), *Contributions à l'étude du Sahara occidental*, I, *Gravures, peintures et inscriptions rupestres*, Paris: Larose. Publication du Comité d'études historiques et scientifiques de l'Afrique occidentale française ser. A, no. 7. #PB #WD

MONOD, T. (1963), 'The late tertiary and pleistocene in the Sahara and adjacent southerly regions', in Clark Howell, F. and Bourlière, François (eds), *African Ecology and Human Evolution*: 117–229. Chicago: Aldine. #WD

MONTEIL, C. (1929), 'Les Empires du Mali (étude d'histoire et de sociologie soudanaise)', *Bulletin du Comité d'Études historiques et scientifiques de l'A.O.F.* 12: 291–447. #PB

MOORE, H.L. (1986), *Space, Text and Gender*, Cambridge: Cambridge University Press. #PR

MOORSEL, H. van (1944), 'Les ateliers préhistoriques de Léopoldville', *Belgique d'Outre-Mer* 1: 32–7. #PM

MOORSEL, H. van (1947), 'Recherches préhistoriques de 1936 à 1946 dans la plaine de Lemba', *Bulletin du Service géologique du Congo Belge et du Ruanda-Urundi* 3: 49–67. #PM

MOORSEL, H. van (1948), 'Une industrie céramique ancienne dans la plaine de Léopoldville', *Brousse* 3/4: 17–39. #PM

MOORSEL, H. van (1968), *Atlas de préhistoire de la plaine de Kinshasa*, Kinshasa: Lovanium, Publications Universitaires. #PM

MORAIS, J. (1984), 'Mozambican archaeology: past and present', *African Archaeological Review* 2: 113–28. #MH

MORAIS, J. and SINCLAIR, P. (1980), 'Manyikeni, a Zimbabwe in southern Mozambique', in Leakey, R. and Ogot, B. (eds), *Proceedings of the 8th Panafrican Congress of Prehistory and Quaternary Studies*: 351–4. Nairobi: International Louis Leakey Memorial Institute for African Prehistory. #MH

De MORGAN, JACQUES (1896), *Recherches sur les origines de l'Égypte I*. Paris: Leroux. #WD

MORI, FABRIZIO (1965), 'Contributions to the study of the pre-historic pastoral peoples of the Sahara: chronological data from the excavations in the Acacus', in Ripoll–Perello, E. (ed.), *Miscelanea en homenaje al Abate Henri Breuil* II: 172–9. Barcelona. #WD

MORI, FABRIZIO (1974), 'The earliest Saharan rock-engravings', *Antiquity* 48: 87–92. #WD

MORRIS, CHARLES W. (1938), *Foundations of the Theory of Signs*, Chicago: University of Chicago Press. #WD

MORTELMANS, G. (1947), 'Préhistoire et Quaternaire du Sud du bassin du Congo', *La géologie des terrains récents dans l'Ouest de l'Europe. Session extraordinaire des Sociétés belges de géologie, 1946*: 215–44. Brussels: Hayez. #PM

MORTELMANS, G. (1952a), *Les dessins rupestres gravés, ponctués et peints du Katanga: essai de synthèse*: 35–55. Tervuren: Annales du Musée Royal du Congo Belge. #PM #WD

MORTELMANS, G. (1952b), 'La préhistoire du Congo belge et de l'Afrique sud-saharienne', *Problèmes d'Afrique Centrale* 18: 233–63. #PM

MORTELMANS, G. (1953), 'Vue d'ensemble sur le Quaternaire du bassin du Congo', *Congrès International des Sciences Préhistoriques et Protohistoriques. Actes de la IIIe Session, Zurich 1950*: 114–20. Zurich. #PM

MORTELMANS, G. (1956), 'Le Congrès Panafricain de Préhistoire visité le Katanga. Compte rendu de l'excursion (7–14 août 1955)', *Bulletin de la Société Belge de Géologie, de Paléontologie et d'Hydrologie* 65: 73–115. #JAJG

MORTELMANS, G. (1957a), 'Le Cénozoïque du Congo Belge', in Clark, J.D. (ed.), *Proceedings of the Third Pan-African Congress on Prehistory, Livingstone 1955*: 23–50. London: Chatto & Windus. #PM

MORTELMANS, G. (1957b), 'La préhistoire du Congo Belge', *Revue de l'Université de Bruxelles* 9e année, 2–3: 119–71. #JAJG #PM

MORTELMANS, G. (1962), 'Vue d'ensemble sur la préhistoire du Congo occidental', in Mortelmans, G. and Nenquin, J. (eds), *Actes du IVe Congrès Panafricain de Préhistoire et de l'Étude du Quaternaire. Section III. Pré- et protohistoire*: 129–64. Tervuren: Annales du Musée Royal de l'Afrique Central. #PM

MORTELMANS, G. and MONTEYNE, R. (1962), 'La grotte peinte de Mbafu, témoignage iconographique de la première évangélisation du Bas-Congo', in Mortelmans, G. and Nenquin, J. (eds), *Actes du IVe Congrès Panafricain de Préhistoire et de l'Étude du Quaternaire. Section III. Pré- et Protohistoire*: 457–86. Tervuren: Annales du Musée Royal de l'Afrique Centrale. #PM

MORTILLET, G. de (1882), *La Préhistorique: Antiquité de l'Homme*, Paris: Reinwald. #PJS

MORTILLET, G. de and MORTILLET, A. de (1881), *Musée Préhistorique*, Paris: Reinwald. #JAJG

MOURA, J. de (1957), 'Una história entre lendas', *Boletim do Instituto de Angola* 10. #PM

MOUTA, F. (1934), 'Contribuїção para o estudo da prehistória angolense (Distrito de Malange)', *Communicações dos Serviços Geologicos de Portugal* 19: 12 p. #PM

MOUTH, L. (1899), 'Rapport sur une fouille exécutée dans la grotte de Rotoma près Konakry', *Revue coloniale*, Septembre: 497–501. #PB #AH

MOYSEY, C.F. (1930), 'Some notes on surface hunting', *Proceedings of the Devon Archaeological Exploration Society* 1: 29–34. #TS

MOYSEY, F. (1943), 'Excavation of a rock shelter at Gorgora, Lake Tana, Ethiopia', *Journal of the East Africa and Uganda Natural History Society* 17: 196–8. #SAB

MUFUKA, K. (1983), *Dzimbahwe: Life and Politics in the Golden Age 1100–1500 AD*, Harare. #MH

MÜLLER–BECK, H. (ed.) (1978–86), *Die Archäologischen und Anthropologischen Ergebnisse der Kohl–Larsen-Expeditionen in Nord-Tanzania 1933–1939*, Band 4, 1–4. Tübingen: Institut für Urgeschichte. #PR

MUNRO–HAY, S. (1981), 'A tyranny of sources: the history of Aksum from its coinage', *Northeast African Studies* 3: 1–16. #SAB

MUNRO–HAY, S. (1982), 'The foreign trade of the Aksumite port of Adulis', *Azania* 17: 107–25. #SAB

MUNSON, P. (1971), 'The Tichitt Tradition: a late prehistoric occupation of the northwestern Sahara', PhD thesis: University of Illinois at Urbana. Ann Arbor: University Microfilms. #PB

MURDOCK, G.P. (1959), *Africa: Its Peoples and their Culture History*, New York: McGraw-Hill. #PR #SAB #TS

MURRAY, K.C. (1939), 'The provision of a Nigerian Museum', *Nigeria Field* 8: 169–75. #FJK

MURRAY, K.C. (1941), 'Nigerian Bronzes: works from Ife', *Antiquity* 15:71–80. #FJK

MURRAY, T. and WHITE, J.P. (1981), 'Cambridge in the bush? Archaeology in Australia and New Guinea', *World Archaeology* 13: 255–63. #PR

MUSONDA, F.B. (1976), 'The Late Stone Age in Ghana in the light of excavations along the Voltaian scarp', unpublished MA thesis: University of Ghana, Legon. #FJK #TS

MUSSI, M. (1974–5), 'États des connaissances sur le Quaternaire de la Somalie'. #SAB

MUSSI, M. (1984), 'Excavations in southern Somalia', *Nyame Akuma* no. 24/25: 18. #SAB

MUSSI, M. (1987), 'Preliminary report on Buur Medow 1, a LSA site in the Middle Juba Valley (Southern Somalia)', *Nyame Akuma* no. 28: 33–7. #SAB

MUZZOLINI, A. and KOLMER, H. (1982), 'Les peintures des "têtes rondes" et les peintures de l'ère "pastorale" dans l'Acacus (Libye): chronologie relative et chronologie absolue', *Ars Praehistorica* 1: 99–122. #WD

MUZZOLINI, A. and KOLMER, H. (1983), 'Les gravures et peintures rupestres de l'Acacus (Libye): une révision de la classification et de la chronologie relative traditionelles', *Bulletin de la Société préhistorique de l'Ariège* 38: 165–86. #WD

MYERS, OLIVER (1958), 'Abka re-excavated', *Kush* 6: 131–41. #WD

MYERS, OLIVER (1967), 'Excavations at Ife, Nigeria', *West African Archaeological Newsletter* 6: 6–11. #FJK

NADEL, S.F. (1942), *A Black Byzantium*, London: International African Institute. #FJK

NATIONAL COMMISSION FOR MUSEUMS (1983), *Source Book on Nigerian Archaeology*, Lagos. #FJK

NEEL, H. (1913), 'Statuettes en pierre et en argile de l'Afrique Occidentale', *L'Anthropologie* 24: 433–43. #PB

NELSON, C.M. (1973), 'A comparative analysis of twenty-nine late Stone Age occurrences from East Africa', unpublished PhD thesis: University of California, Berkeley. #PR

NELSON, C.M. (1976), 'Flaked stone tool variations in the Later Stone Age of eastern and southern Africa', in Abebe, B., Chevaillon, J. and Sutton, J.E.G. (eds), *Proceedings of the Panafrican Congress of Prehistory and Quaternary Studies, VIIth session – 1971*: 131–52. Addis Ababa. #PR

NISBET, J., MACHIN, I., MAGGS, T. and KINGWILL, R. (1984), *History Alive. Standard 5*, Pietermaritzburg: Shuter & Shooter. #JD

NENQUIN, J. (1959), 'Dimple based pots from Kasai, Belgian Congo', *Man* 59(242): 153–5. #PM

NENQUIN, J. (1963), *Excavations at Sanga, 1957. The Protohistoric Necropolis*, Tervuren: Annales du Musée Royal de l'Afrique Centrale. #PM

NENQUIN, J. (1967), *Contribution to the Study of the Prehistoric Cultures of Rwanda and Burundi*, Tervuren: Annales du Musée Royal de l'Afrique Centrale. #PM

NENQUIN, J. (1969), 'Symposium on the nomenclature of the Stone Age Industries of the Lower Congo, with special reference to the Colette excavations at Kalina Point (Tervuren, Belgium, 20th–23rd September 1968)', *Commission of Nomenclature and Terminology, Berkeley Office, Bulletin* 2: 2–35. #PM

NEUVILLE, R. and RUHLMANN, A. (1941), 'La place du Paléolithique ancien dans le Quaternaire marocain', *Publications de l'Institut des Hautes Études marocaines, coll. Hesperis* 8. #JAJG

NEWBOLD, DOUGLAS (1928), 'Rock-pictures and archaeology in the Libyan desert', *Antiquity* 2: 261–91. #WD

NEWMAN, T. (1966), 'Archaeological survey of Sierra Leone', *West African Archaeological Newsletter* 4: 19–22. #FJK

NICOLAS, J.P. (1951), 'Préhistoire-Protohistoire', in Guernier, E.L. (ed.), *Encyclopédie de l'Afrique Française, Cameroun, Togo*: 47–50. Paris: Editions de l'Union Française. #PM

NILSSON, E. (1940), *Ancient Changes of Climate in British East Africa and Abyssinia*, Meddalanden fran Stockholms Hogskoles Geologiska Institut, #56, Stockholm. #JDC

NIVEN, C.R. (1937), *A Short History of the Yoruba Peoples*, London: Longman Green & Co. #FJK

NUNOO, R.B. (1948), 'A report on excavations at Nsuta Hill, Gold Coast', *Man* 90: 73–6. #FJK

NUNOO, R.B. (1959), 'Archaeological survey at the College of Technology', *Journal of Kumasi College of Technology* 1: 17–19. #FJK

NURSE, D. and SPEAR, T. (1985), *The Swahili: Reconstructing the History and Language of an African Society, 800–1500*. Philadelphia: University of Pennsylvania Press. #PR

NYAKATURA, J.W. (1973), *Anatomy of an African Kingdom: A History of Bunyoro-Kitara*, ed. by G.N. Uzoigwe. New York: NOK Publishers. #PRS

NZEWUNWA, N. (1980), *The Niger Delta: Prehistoric Economy and Culture*. Oxford: BAR. #AH

OAKLEY, K.P. (1957), 'Tools makyth Man', *Antiquity* 31: 199–209. #JAJG

OAKLEY, K.P. (1969), *Frameworks for Dating Fossil Man*, 3rd edition, London: Weidenfeld & Nicolson. #JAJG

OAKLEY, K.P. (1974), 'Revised dating of the Kanjera hominids', *Journal of Human Evolution* 3: 257–8. #JAJG

OAKLEY, K.P. (1975), 'A reconsideration of the date of the Kanam jaw', *Journal of Archaeological Science* 2: 151–2. #JAJG

OAKLEY, K.P. (1976), 'Obituary, Sir Wilfrid Le Gros Clark', in *Proceedings of the Panafrican Congress of Prehistory and Quaternary Studies, VII Session, Addis Ababa, 1971*: 22–3. #JAJG

OBAYEMI, HUDSON (1969), 'History of archaeology in West Africa', incomplete draft of Masters thesis: University of Legon, Ghana. #PB

OBENGA, T. (1973), *L'Afrique dans l'Antiquité: Égypte pharaonique-Afrique noire*. Paris: Présence africaine. #AH

OBERMAIER, HUGO (1931), 'L'âge de l'art rupestre nord-africain', *L'Anthropologie* 51: 65–74. #WD

O'BRIEN, T.P. (1939), *The Prehistory of Uganda Protectorate*, Cambridge: Cambridge University Press. #JAJG #PR #PM

O'CONNOR, D. (1974), 'Political systems and archaeological data in Egypt: 2600–1780 B.C.', *World Archaeology* 6: 15–38. #DOC

O'CONNOR, D. (1983), 'New Kingdom and Third Intermediate Period', in Trigger, B. *et al.*, *Ancient Egypt: A Social History*: 183–278. Cambridge: Cambridge University Press. #DOC

O'CONNOR, D. (1987a), 'The locations of Yam and Kush and their historical significance', *Journal of the American Research Centre in Egypt* XXIII. #DOC

O'CONNOR, D. (1987b), 'The location of Irem', *Journal of Egyptian Archaeology* 73: 99–136. #DOC

O'CONNOR, D. (1987c), 'The nature of Tjemhu (Libyan) society in the New Kingdom', in Leahy, A. (ed.), *Libyans in Egypt in the First Millennium B.C.* London: Croom Helm. #DOC

O'CONNOR, D. and SILVERMAN, D. (1979), 'The University Museum in Egypt', *Expedition* 21: 4–43. #DOC

ODAK, O. (1980), 'Comments on "Archaeology and development" by D. Miller', *Current Anthropology* 21: 721. #PR

ODNER, K. (1971), 'An archaeological survey of Iramba, Tanzania', *Azania* 6: 151–98. #WD

OLIVER, R. (1953), 'A question about the Bachwezi', *Uganda Journal* 17: 135–7. #PRS

OLIVER, R. (1959), 'Ancient capital sites of Ankole', *Uganda Journal* 23: 51–64. #PRS

OLIVER, R. (1963), 'Discernible developments in the interior, c. 1500–1840', in Oliver, R. and Mathew, F. (eds), *Oxford History of East Africa*: 169–211. Oxford: Clarendon Press. #PRS

OLIVER, R. (1966), 'The problem of the Bantu expansion', *Journal of African History* 7: 361–76. #PR

OLIVER, R. (1977), 'The East African interior', in Oliver, R. (ed.), *The Cambridge History of Africa, Volume 3, from c. 1050 to 1600*: 621–69. Cambridge: Cambridge University Press. #PR

OLIVER, R. (1979), 'Cameroun – The Bantu cradleland?' *SUGIA* 1: 7–20. #PR

OLIVER, R. and FAGAN, B.M. (1975), *Africa in the Iron Age c. 500 BC to AD 1400*, Cambridge: Cambridge University Press. #MH #FJK

ONYANGO–ABUJE, J.C. (1976), 'Reflections on culture change and distribution during the Neolithic period in East Africa', *Hadith* 6: 14–30. #PR

ONYANGO–ABUJE, J.C. (1980), 'Temporal and spatial distribution of Neolithic cultures in East Africa', in Leakey, R.E. and Ogot, B.A. (eds), *Proceedings of the 8th Panafrican Congress of Prehistory and Quaternary Studies, Nairobi, September 1977*: 288–92. Nairobi: The International Louis Leakey Memorial Institute for African Prehistory. #PR

ONYANGO–ABUJE, J.C. and WANDIBBA, S. (1979), 'The palaeoenvironment and its influence on man's activities in East Africa during the latter part of Upper Pleistocene and Holocene', *Hadith* 7: 24–40. #PR

OPOKU–GYAMFI, Y. (1975), 'Operation Feed Yourself in the 2nd Millennium B.C. in Ghana', *Sankofa* 1: 79–82. #AH

OPPENHEIM, A.L. (1964), *Ancient Mesopotamia. Portrait of a Dead Civilization*, Chicago: University of Chicago Press. #DOC

OPPERMAN, H. (1978), 'Excavations in the Buffelskloof rock shelter near Calitzdorp, southern Cape', *South African Archaeological Bulletin* 33: 18–28. #JD

ORPEN, J.M. (1874), 'A glimpse into the mythology of the Maluti Bushmen', *Cape Monthly Magazine* (NS) 9(49): 1–13. #JD

ÖSING, J. (1980), 'Libyen, Libyer', Helck, W. und Westendorf, W. (herausgegeb.), *Lexikon der Agyptologie* III, Wiesbaden, 1015–33. #DOC

OTTO, B. and OBERMAIER, H. (1909), 'Ein "in situ" gefundener Faustkeil aus Natal', *Anthropos* 4: 972–5. #JAJG

OZANNE, PAUL (1962), 'Notes on the early historic archaeology of Accra', *Transactions of the Ghana Historical Society* 6: 51–70. #FJK

OZANNE, PAUL (1965), 'Adwuku: a fortified hill-top in Shai', *Ghana Notes and Queries* 7: 4–5. #FJK

OZANNE, PAUL (1966a), *Tobacco Pipes of Accra and Shai*, Legon: Institute of African Studies, University College of Ghana. #FJK

OZANNE, PAUL (1966b), 'A preliminary archaeological survey of Sierra Leone', *West African Archaeological Newsletter* 5: 31–5. #FJK

OZANNE, PAUL (1969), 'The diffusion of smoking in West Africa', *Odu* (n.s.) 2: 29–42. #FJK

OZANNE, PAUL (1971), 'Ghana', in Shinnie, P.L. (ed.), *The African Iron Age*, Oxford: Clarendon Press. #PRS

PAGER, HARALD (1971), *Ndedema*, Graz: Akadeische Druck- und Verlagsanstalt. #WD

PALLARY, P. (1907a), 'Le préhistorique saharien', *L'Anthropologie* 18: 140–5. #JAJG

PALLARY, P. (1907b), 'Revue de préhistoire nord-africaine, 1904–1906', *Revue Africaine* 51: 57–99. #JDC

PALLARY, P. (1909), 'Instructions pour les recherches préhistoriques dans le Nord-Ouest de l'Afrique', *Mémoires de la Société Historique Algérienne*, Vol. III. #PJS

PALLARY, P. (1911), 'Les collections préhistoriques du Musée des Antiquités algériennes', *Revue Africaine* 55: 306–26. #JAJG

PALLARY, P. (1918–19), 'Revue de Préhistoire maghrebine', *L'Anthropologie* 29: 92. #JAJG

PALMER, H.R. (1931), *The Carthaginian Voyage to West Africa in 500 B.C.*: 50–1. Bathurst: J.M. Lawani. #AH

PALMER, H.R. (1936), *The Bornu Sahara and Sudan*, London: John Murray. #FJK

PANOFSKY, ERWIN (1939), *Studies in Iconology*, Oxford: Oxford University Press. #WD

PARIBENI, R. (1907), 'Ricerche sul luogo dell'antica Adulis', *Monumenti Antichi* 1907: 437–572. #SAB

PARIS, F. (1984). 'La région d'In Gall-Tegidda N Tesemt. Programme Archéologique d'Urgence 1977–1981, Vol. 3: Les sépultures du Néolithique final à l'Islam', *Etudes Nigériennes* 50. Niamey: Institut de Recherches en Sciences Humaines. #PB #AH

PARKER, H. (1923), 'Stone circles in Gambia', *Journal of the Royal Anthropological Institute* 53: 173–228. #FJK

PARKINGTON, J.E. (1970), Review of *Background to Evolution in Africa*, *South African Archaeological Bulletin* 25: 48–50. #PR

PARKINGTON, J.E. (1972a), 'Seasonal mobility in the Late Stone Age', *African Studies* 31: 223–43. #JD

PARKINGTON, J.E. (1972b), 'Stone implements as information', *South African Archaeological Society Goodwin Series* 1: 10–20. #JD

PARKINGTON, J.E. (1976), 'Coastal settlement between the mouths of the Berg and Olifants rivers, Cape Province', *South African Archaeological Bulletin* 31: 127–40. #JD

PARKINGTON, J.E. (1977), 'Soaqua: hunter-fisher-gatherers of the Olifants River, western Cape', *South African Archaeological Bulletin* 32: 150–7. #JD

PARKINGTON, J.E. (1980), 'Time and place: some observations on spatial and temporal patterning in the Later Stone Age sequence in southern Africa', *South African Archaeological Bulletin*', 35: 73–83. #JD

PARKINGTON, J.E. (1984), 'Changing views of the Later Stone Age of South Africa', in Wendorf, F. and Close, A. (eds), *Advances in World Archaeology* 3: 90–142. New York: Academic Press. #JD

PARKINGTON, J.E. and POGGENPOEL, C. (1971), 'Excavations at De Hangen 1968', *South African Archaeological Bulletin* 26: 3–36. #JD

PARKINGTON, J. and HALL, M. (1987), 'Patterning in recent radiocarbon dates from southern Africa as a reflection of prehistoric settlement and interaction', *Journal of African History* 28: 1–25. #MH

PARKINGTON, J. and SMITH, A.B. (1986), Guest editorial, *South African Archaeological Bulletin* 41. #JD

PARTRIDGE, T.C. (1973), 'Geomorphological dating of cave opening at Makapansgat, Sterkfontein, and Taung', *Nature* 246: 75–9. #JAJG

PEDRALS, D.P. de (1948), *Manuel scientifique de l'Afrique noire*, Paris: Payot. #AH

PEDRALS, D.P. de (1950), *Archéologie de l'Afrique noire*, Paris: Payot. #AH

PENNING, W.H. (1886), 'Notes on a few stone implements found in South Africa', *Journal of the Royal Anthropological Institute* 16: 68–70. #JD

PENNING, W.H. (1898), 'Exhibition of stone implements from South Africa', *Journal of the Royal Anthropological Institute* 28: 54. #JD

PERINGUEY, L. (1907–9), 'On rock engravings of animals and the human figure, found in South Africa', *Transactions of the South African Philosophical Society* 18: 401–19. #WD

PERINGUEY, L. (1911), 'The Stone Ages of South Africa', *Annals of the South African Museum* 8: 1–218. #JAJG #JD

PERINGUEY, L. and CORSTOPHINE, G.S. (1900), 'Stone implements from Bosman's Crossing, Stellenbosch', *Minutes of the Proceedings of the South African Philosophical Society* 11: xxiv. #JD

PERRAMON, R. (1968), *Contribución a la prehistoria y protohistoria de Rio Muni*, Santa Isabel: Instituto Clarentiano de Africanistas. #PM

PERSON, Y. (1961), 'Les Kissi et leurs statuettes de pierre dans le cadre de l'histoire ouest-africaine', *Bulletin de l'Institut Français d'Afrique Noire* (B) 23: 1–59. #PB

PETIT-MAIRE, N. (1979a), 'Cadre écologique et peuplement humain: le littoral ouest-saharien depuis 10000 ans', *L'Anthropologie* 83: 69–82. #PB

PETIT-MAIRE, N. (1979b), *Le Sahara atlantique à l'Holocene: peuplement et écologie*, Alger: Mémoires du CRAPE. #AH

PETIT-MAIRE, N., CELLES, J.C., COMMELIN, D., DELIBRIAS, G. and RAIMBAULT, M. (1983), 'The Sahara in northern Mali: man and his environment between 10,000 and 3500 years bp. (Preliminary results)', *African Archaeological Review* 1: 105–25. #PB

PETIT-MAIRE, N. and RISER, J. (eds) (1984), *Sahara ou Sahel: le Quaternaire récent du bassin de Taoudenni (Mali)*. Marseille. #AH

PETREQUIN, A.-M. and PETREQUIN, P. (1984), *Habitat lacustre du Bénin: une approche ethnoarchéologiqu*, Paris: Eds. Recherche sur les Civilisations, Mémoire 39. #PB

PEYRONY, D. (1933), 'Les industries aurignaciennes dans le bassin de la Vézère. Aurignacien et Périgordien', *Bulletin de la Société Prehistorique Française* 30: 543–59. #PB

PHILLIPSON, D.W. (1968), 'The Early Iron Age site at Kapwirimbwe, Lusaka', *Azania* 3: 87–105. #MH

PHILLIPSON, D.W. (1970), 'Excavations at Twickenham Road, Lusaka', *Azania* 5: 77–118. #MH

PHILLIPSON, D.W. (1972), 'Zambian rock paintings', *World Archaeology* 2: 313–27. #WD

PHILLIPSON, D.W. (1976a), 'The Early Iron Age in Eastern and Southern Africa: a critical re-appraisal', *Azania* 11: 1–23. #PR

PHILLIPSON, D.W. (1976b), *The Prehistory of Eastern Zambia*, Nairobi: British Institute in Eastern Africa. #WD

PHILLIPSON, D.W. (1977a), *The Later Prehistory of Eastern and Southern Africa*, London: Heinemann. #MH #PR #WD

PHILLIPSON, D.W. (1977b), 'The excavation of Gobedra rock-shelter, Axum: an early occurrence of cultivated finger millet in northern Ethiopia', *Azania* 12: 53–82. #SAB

PHILLIPSON, D.W. (1985), *African Archaeology*. Cambridge: Cambridge University Press. #MH #FJK

PIGGOTT, S. (1934), Cartoon, *Antiquity* 60: 3 (March 1986). #TS

PIGGOTT, S. (1981), 'Summary and conclusions', in Daniel, G. (ed.), *Towards a History of Archaeology*: 186–9. London: Thames & Hudson. #AH

PIPERNO, M. (1980), 'Les sols d'occupation oldowayens évolués de Garba IV, Melka–Konturé, Ethiopie (fouilles 1972–1976), in Leakey, R.E. and Ogot, B.A. (eds), *Proceedings of the 8th Panafrican Congress of Prehistory and Quaternary Studies, Nairobi, September 1977*: 202–4. Nairobi: The Louis Leakey Memorial Institute for African Prehistory. #JAJG

PITT-RIVERS, A.H. LANE–FOX (1900), *Antique Works of Art from Benin*, London: Harrison & Sons. #FJK

POLE, L.M. (1975), 'Iron-working apparatus and techniques: Upper Region of Ghana', *West African Journal of Archaeology* 5: 11–39. #FJK

POLET, J. (1981), 'Archéologie d'une région lagunaire. Le Pays Eothilé', *Recherche, Pédagogie et Culture* 55: 47–51. #PB

POLLARD, SHEILA H.M. and RUSSELL, P.M.G. (1969), 'Excavations of Round Barrow 248b, Upton Pyne, Exeter', *Proceedings of the Devon Archaeological Society* 27: 49–78. #TS

PONCET, Y., BERNUS, E., BERNUS, S., CRESSIER, P., ECHARD, N., GOULETQUER, P., GREBENART, D. and PARIS, F. (1983), 'La région d'In Gall-Tegidda N Tesemt (Niger). Programme Archéologique d'Urgence 1977–1981. Atlas', *Études Nigeriennes* 47. Niamey: Institut de Recherches en Sciences Humaines. #PB #AH

POND, A., ROMER, A. and COLE, F. (1928), 'A contribution to the study of prehistoric man in Algeria, North Africa', *Logan Museum Bulletin* (II), Beloit. #PJS

POND, A., CHAPIUS, L., ROMER, A. and BAKER, F. (1938), 'Prehistoric habitation sites in the Sahara and North Africa', *Logan Museum Bulletin* No. 5, Beloit. #PJS

POPE, M. (1975), *The Story of Archaeological Decipherment*, New York: Thames & Hudson. #DOC

POSNANSKY, M. (1959), 'A Hope Fountain site at Olorgesailie, Kenya Colony', *South African Archaeological Bulletin* 14: 83–9. #JAJG

POSNANSKY, M. (1961), 'Bantu genesis', *Uganda Journal* 25: 86–93. #PM

POSNANSKY, M. (1966), 'Kingship, archaeology and historical myth', *Uganda Journal* 30: 1–12. #PRS

POSNANSKY, M. (1967a), 'Wayland as an archaeologist', *Uganda Journal* 31: 9–12. #PR

POSNANSKY, M. (1967b), 'The Iron Age in East Africa', in Bishop, W.W. and Clark, J.D. (eds), *Background to Evolution in Africa*: 629–49. Chicago: University of Chicago Press. #PR

POSNANSKY, M. (1968), 'The excavation of an Ankole capital site at Bweyorere', *Uganda Journal* 32: 165–82. #PR #PRS

POSNANSKY, M. (1969), 'Bigo bya Mugenyi', *Uganda Journal* 33: 125–50. #PR #PLS #PRS

POSNANSKY, M. (1971), 'Ghana and the origins of West African trade', *African Quarterly* 11: 110–26. #FJK

POSNANSKY, M. (1972), 'The early development of trade in West Africa – some archaeological considerations', *Ghana Social Science Journal* 2: 87–101. #FJK

POSNANSKY, M. (1973), 'Aspects of early West African trade', *World Archaeology* 2: 149–63. #FJK

POSNANSKY, M. (1975), 'Archaeology, technology and Akan civilization', *Journal of African Studies* 2: 24–39. #FJK

POSNANSKY, M. (1976), 'Archaeology and the origins of Akan society in Ghana', in Sieveking, G. de G. *et al.* (eds), *Problems in Economic and Social Archaeology*: 49–60. London: Duckworth. #FJK

POSNANSKY, M. (1979), 'Excavations at Begho, Ghana, 1979', *Nyame Akuma* no. 15: 23–7. #FJK

POSNANSKY, M. (1981), 'Archaeology in West Africa', in Ray, D.I., Shinnie, P. and Williams, D. (eds), *Proceedings of the Eleventh Annual Conference of the Canadian Association of African Studies, Vol 1: 'Into the 80s'*: 73–85. Vancouver: Tantalus Research. #FJK #PB

POSNANSKY, M. (1982), 'African archaeology comes of age', *World Archaeology* 13: 345–58. #PR #PB

POSNANSKY, M. and DE BARROS, P.L.F. (1980), *An Archaeological Reconnaissance of Togo, August 1979*. Report prepared for H.E. the Minister of National Education and Scientific Research of the Republic of Togo. #PB

PRATT, I. (1925), *Ancient Egypt. Sources of Information in the New York Public Library*, The New York Public Library. #DOC

PRIDDY, A.J. (1970a), 'RS63/32: An Iron Age site near Yelwa, Sokoto Province: Preliminary Report', *West African Archaeological Newsletter* 12: 20–32. #FJK

PRIDDY, A.J. (1970b), 'Kagoge: a settlement site near Bussa, Ilorin Province: preliminary report', *West African Archaeological Newsletter* 12: 33–42. #FJK

PUCCIONI, N. (1936), *Antropologici e Etnografici delle gente della Somalia*, Vol. III. Bologna. #SAB

QUECHON, G. and ROSET, J. (1974), 'Prospection archéologique du Massif de Termit (Niger)', *Cahiers de l'ORSTOM* (Série Sciences Humaines) 11: 85–104. #PB

RAHTZ, P. and FLIGHT, COLIN (1974), 'A quern factory near Kintampo, Ghana', *West African Journal of Archaeology*, 4: 1–31. #FJK

RAIMBAULT, M. (1980), 'La poterie traditionelle au service de l'archéologie: les ateliers de Kalabougou (cercle de Ségou, Mali)', *Bulletin de l'Institut Fondamental d'Afrique Noire* 42: 441–74. #PB

RAIMBAULT, M. (1981), 'Les recherches archéologiques au Mali: histoire, bilan, problèmes et perspectives', *Recherche, Pédagogie et Culture* 55: 16–25. #PB

RANGER, T. (1979), 'The mobilization of labour and the production of knowledge: the antiquarian tradition in Rhodesia', *Journal of African History* 20: 507–24. #MH

RATTRAY, R.S. (1923), *Ashanti*, Oxford: Clarendon Press. #FJK

RAVISE, A. (1975), 'Recensement de sites paléolithiques et néolithiques du Senegal', *Bulletin de l'Institut Fondamental d'Afrique Noire* 37: 234–45. #PB

READER, J. (1988), *Missing Links*, 2nd edition, Harmondsworth: Penguin Books. #JAJG

RECK, H. (1914), 'Erste Vorläufige Mitteilung über den Fund eines fossilen Menschenskelets aus Zentral-afrika', in *Sitzungsberichte der Gesellschaft naturforschender Freunde* 3: 81–95. #JAJG #PR

RECK, H. (1926), 'Prähistorische Grab- und Menschenfunde und ihre Bezeihungen zur Pluvialzeit in Ostafrika', *Mitteilungen aus den deutschen Schutzgebieten* Band 34, Heft 1, Berlin. #JAJG #PR

REDFORD, D. (1984), *Akhenaten. The Heretic Pharaoh*, Princeton: Princeton University Press. #DOC

REEVE, HENRY (1912), *The Gambia*, London: Smith, Elder & Co. #FJK

REGNAULT, P. (1894), 'L'âge de la pierre grossièrement taillée au Congo Français', *Bulletin de la Société d'Anthropologie de Paris* 5: 477–80. #PM

REID, D. (1985), 'Indigenous Egyptology: The decolonization of a profession', *Journal of the American Oriental Society* 105: 233–46. #DOC

REINDORF, C.C. (1895), *History of the Gold Coast*, Basel; reprinted 1966, London: Oxford University Press. #FJK

REISNER, G. (1923), *Excavations at Kerma I-III, IV-V*. Cambridge, Mass.: Harvard African Studies. #DOC

REISNER, G. (1932), *A Provincial Cemetery of the Pyramid Age Nag-ed Der III*, London: Oxford University Press. #DOC

REISNER, G. (1942), *A History of the Giza Necropolis I*, Cambridge, Mass.: Harvard University Press. #DOC

RENOUX, A. (1937), 'Vestiges humains dans la région d'Aouchiche (Mauritanie)', *Bulletin du Comité d'Études historiques et scientifiques de l'A.O.F.*, 20: 147–52. #PB

RESCH, W.F.E. (1963), 'Neue Felsbilderfunde in der ägyptischen Ostwüste', *Zeitschrift für Ethnologie* 8: 86–97. #WD

RESCH, W.F.E. (1967), *Die Felsbilder Nubiens*, Graz: Akademische Druck- und Verlagsanstalt. #WD

RESCH, W.F.E. (1969), 'Das alter der ostägyptischen und nubischen Felsbilder', *IPEK* 22: 114–22. #WD

REVOIL, G. (1882), *La Vallée du Daroor*, Paris: Challamel. #SAB

REYGASSE, M. (1920), 'Études de paléthnologie maghrébine (nouvelle serie)', *Recl. des Notes et Mémoires de la Société Archéologique de Constantine* 52: 513–70. #PJS

REYGASSE, M. (1922), 'Etudes de paléthnologie maghrébine – deuxième série)', *Recl. des Notes et Mémoires de la Société Archéologique de Constantine* 53: 159–204. #PJS

REYGASSE, M. (1931), 'Les Âges de la pierre dans l'Afrique du Nord (Algerie)', *Histoire et Historiens d'Algérie*: 37–70. Algiers. #JDC

REYGASSE, M. (1935), 'Gravures et peintures rupestres du Tassili des Ajjers', *L'Anthropologie* 45: 533–71. #WD

RHOTERT, HANS (1952), *Libysche Felsbilder*, Darmstadt: Wittich. #WD

RHOTERT, HANS and KUPER, RUDOLPH (1981), *Felsbilder aus Wadi Ertan und Wadi Tarhoscht (Südwest-Fezzan, Libyen)*. Graz: Akademische Druck- und Verlagsandstalt. #WD

RICCI, L. (1984), 'L'expansion de l'Arabie Meridionale', in Chelhod, S. (ed.), *L'Arabie du Sud, histoire et civilisation I: le peuple Yemenite et ses racines*: 249–57. Paris: Maisonneure et Larose. #SAB

RICKARD, J.C. (1881a), 'Notes on four series of palaeolithic implements from South Africa', *Cambridgeshire Antiquaries Society* 5: 57–66. #JD

RICKARD, J.C. (1881b), 'Notes on some Neolithic implements from South Africa', *Cambridgeshire Antiquaries Society* 5: 67–74. #JD

RIGHTMIRE, G.P. (1975), 'New studies of post-Pleistocene human skeletal remains from the Rift Valley, Kenya', *American Journal of Physical Anthropology* 41: 351–69. #PR

RIGHTMIRE, G.P. (1984), 'Human skeletal remains from Eastern Africa', in Clark, J.D. and Brandt, S.A. (eds), *From Hunters to Farmers: The Causes and Consequences of Food Production in Africa*: 191–9. Berkeley and Los Angeles: University of California Press. #PR

RIVALLAIN, J. (1981), 'Un artisanat ancien: la poterie dans le sud du Bénin', in *2000 ans d'histoire africaine: le sol, la parole et l'écrit. Mélanges en hommage à Raymond Mauny*, 1: 247–63. Paris: Société Française d'Histoire d'Outre-Mer. #PB

RIVALLAIN, J. (1983), 'Sites littoraux du pays alladian (Côte d'Ivoire): premières enquêtes et premiers sondages', *Annales de l'Université d'Abidjan* (Série 1, Histoire) 11: 27–60. #PB

RIVIÈRE, J. (1896), 'L'industrie préhistorique du silex en Tunisie', *25e Congrès Association française pour l'Avancement des Sciences, Carthage-Tunis, 1st part*: 199–200. #JAJG

ROBBINS, L.H. (1973), 'Turkana material culture viewed from an archaeological perspective', *World Archaeology* 5: 209–14. #PB

ROBERT, D., ROBERT, S. and DEVISSE, J. (eds) (1970), *Tegdaoust I: recherches sur Aoudaghost*. Paris: Arts et Métiers Graphiques. #PB

ROBERT, S. and ROBERT, D. (1972), 'Douze années de recherches archéologiques en République Islamique de Mauritanie', *Annales de la Faculté des Lettres de l'Université de Dakar* 1: 195–233. #PB

ROBERT–CHALEIX, D. (1983), 'Fusaïoles décorées du site de Tegdaoust', in Devisse, J.*et. al.*, *Tegdaoust III, Recherches sur Aoudaghost: campagnes 1960–1965, enquêtes générales*: 447–514. Paris: Eds Recherche sur les Civilisations, Mémoire 25. #PB

ROBERTS, A.F. (1984), '"Fishers of men": religion and political economy among colonized Tabwa', *Africa* 54: 49–70. #PM

ROBERTSHAW, P.T. (1977), 'Excavations at Paternoster, south-western Cape', *South African Archaeological Bulletin* 32: 63–73. #JD

ROBERTSHAW, P.T. (1978), 'The origin of pastoralism in the Cape', *South African Historical Journal* 10: 117–33. #JD

ROBERTSHAW, P.T. (1979), 'The first archaeological excavation in Southern Africa?' *South African Archaeological Bulletin* 34: 52–3. #PR

ROBERTSHAW, P.T. (1986), 'Engaruka revisited: the excavations of 1982', *Azania* 21: 1–26. #PR

ROBERTSHAW, P.T. and COLLETT, D. (1983), 'A new framework for the study of early pastoral communities in East Africa', *Journal of African History* 24: 289–301. #PR

ROBERTSHAW, PETER (in press), *Early Pastoralists of South-Western Kenya*, Nairobi: British Institute in Eastern Africa. #PR

ROBIN, M. (1939), 'Notes sur les premières populations de la région de Dosso', *Bulletin du Comité d'études historiques et scientifiques de l'A.O.F.* 23. #AH

ROBINSON, K.R. (1959), *Khami Ruins*, Cambridge: Cambridge University Press. #MH

ROBINSON, K.R. (1961), 'Excavations on the Acropolis Hill', *Occasional Papers of the National Museums of Southern Rhodesia* 23a: 159–92. #MH

ROBINSON, J.T. and MASON, R.J. (1957), 'Occurrence of stone artifacts with Australopithecus at Sterkfontein', *Nature* 180: 521–4. #JAJG

ROCHE, H. (1980), *Premiers outils taillés de l'Afrique*, Paris: Société d'Ethnographie. #JAJG

RODNEY, W. (1976), *How Europe underdeveloped Africa*, Dar es Salaam: Tanzania Publishing House. #SAB

ROE, D.A. (1981), *The Lower and Middle Palaeolithic Periods in Britain*, London: Routledge & Kegan Paul. #JAJG

ROFFO, P. (1934), 'Les civilisations du Mzab, Alger, Heintz. Compte rendu par R. Vaufrey', *L'Anthropologie* 45: 417. #JAJG

ROSET, J.P. (1983), 'Nouvelles données sur le problème de la néolithisation du Sahara méridional: Aïr et Ténéré, au Niger', *Cahiers de l'ORSTOM* (Série Géologie) 13: 119–42. #PB

ROUBET, C. (1979), *Economie pastorale préagricole en Algerie Orientale. Le Néolithique de tradition capsienne, exemple: l'Aurès*, Paris: C.N.R.S. Études Antiquités Africaines. #PJS

ROUBET, C., HUGOT, H.J. and SOUVILLE, G. (eds) (1981), *Préhistoire africaine. Mélanges offerts au doyen L. Balout*, Paris: A.D.P.F. #PJS #AH

ROWLANDS, M. (1986), 'Colonialism, archaeology and constituting the African peasantry', in *Comparative Studies in the Development of Complex Societies* vol. 3, precirculated papers of the 'World Archaeological Congress', Southampton. #AH

RUDNER, J. (1979), 'The use of stone artefacts and pottery among the Khoisan peoples in historic and protohistoric times', *South African Archaeological Bulletin* 34: 3–17. #JD

RUDNER, J. and RUDNER, I. (1970), *The Hunter and His Art*, Cape Town: Struik. #WD

RUDNER, J. and RUDNER, I. (1973), 'End of an era? A discussion', *South African Archaeological Bulletin* 28: 13–26. #JD

RUST, A. (1937), *Das altsteinzeitliche Rentierjagerlager Meiendorf*, Neumunster. #JAJG

RUSTAD, JOHN (1980), 'The emergence of iron technology in West Africa, with special emphasis on the Nok Culture of Nigeria', in Swartz, B.K. and Dummett, R.A. (eds), *West African Culture Dynamics*: 227–46. The Hague: Mouton. #AH

SACKETT, J.R. (1966), 'Quantitative analysis of Upper Paleolithic stone tools', *American Anthropologist* 68: 356–94. #JD

SACKETT, J.R. (1981), 'From de Mortillet to Bordes: a century of French Palaeolithic research', in Daniel, G. (ed.), *Towards a History of Archaeology*: 85–99. London: Thames & Hudson. #PR #PB #PJS

SAGGS, H. (1962), *The Greatness that was Babylon*, London: Sidgwick & Jackson. #DOC

SALÉE, A. (1924–5), 'Une hache en quartz de type acheuléen du Ruanda (Est Africain Belge)', *Annales de la Société Scientifique de Bruxelles* 44: 360–2. #PM

SALÉE, A. (1926), 'Coup de poing de l'Afrique Centrale', *L'homme préhistorique* 13: 139. #PM

SALÉE, A. (1927), 'Un atelier de style paléolithique dans l'Urundi (Est Africain Belge)', *Annales de la Société Scientifique de Bruxelles* 47: 76–7. #PM

SALIÈGE, J.-F., PERSON, A., BARRY, I. and FONTES, P. (1980), 'Premières datations de tumulus préislamiques au Mali: site mégalithique de Tondidarou', *Compte Rendu de l'Académie des Sciences de Paris, Série D* 291: 981–4. #PB

SALT, H. (1814), *A Voyage to Abyssinia and Travels into the Interior of that Country*, London: F.C. and J. Risvington. #SAB

SAMPSON, C.G. (1970), 'The Smithfield Industrial Complex: further field results', *Memoirs of the National Museum, Bloemfontein* 5: 1–172. #JD

SAMPSON, C.G. (1972), 'The Stone Age industries of the Orange River Scheme and South Africa', *Memoirs of the National Museum, Bloemfontein* 6: 1–283. #JD

SAMPSON, C.G. (1974), *The Stone Age Archaeology of Southern Africa*, New York: Academic Press. #JD #WD

SAMPSON, C.G. (1984), 'Site clusters in the Smithfield settlement pattern', *South African Archaeological Bulletin* 39: 5–23. #JD

SAMPSON, C.G. (1986), 'Model of a prehistoric herder-hunter contact zone: a first approximation', *South African Archaeological Society Goodwin Series* 5: 50–6. #JD

SANDFORD, K.S. (1934a), 'Recent work on Palaeolithic man in the Nile valley', *Proceedings of the 1st Congress of Prehistoric and Protohistoric Sciences, London 1932*: 69. London: Oxford University Press. #JAJG

SANDFORD, K.S. (1934b), *Palaeolithic Man and the Nile Valley in Upper and Middle Egypt*. Chicago: Oriental Institute Publications 18. #JAJG

SANDFORD, K.S. and ARKELL, A.J. (1929). *Palaeolithic Man and the Nile–Faiyum Divide*, Chicago: Oriental Institute Publications 10. #JAJG

SANDFORD, K.S. and ARKELL, A.J. (1933), *Palaeolithic Man and the Nile Valley in Nubia and Upper Egypt*, Chicago: Oriental Institute Publications 17. #JAJG #WD

SANDFORD, K.S. and ARKELL, A.J. (1939), *Palaeolithic Man and the Nile Valley in Lower Egypt*, Chicago: Oriental Institute Publications 46. #JAJG

SANTOS Jr, J.R. and ERVEDOSA, C. (1970), 'A estação arqueologica de Benfica Luanda, Angola', *Ciências Biologicas* 1: 31–51. #PM

SAUER, C.O. (1952), *Agricultural Origins and Dispersals*, New York: American Geographic Society. #SAB

SAUL, J.S. and GELB, S. (1981), *The Crisis in South Africa. Class Defense, Class Revolution*, New York: Monthly Review Press. #MH

SBACCHI, A. (1985), *Ethiopia under Mussolini: Fascism and the Colonial Experience*, London: Zed Books. #SAB

SCHAPERA, I. (1925), 'Some stylistic affinities of Bushman art', *South African Journal of Science* 22: 504–15. #WD

SCHAPERA, I. (1930), *The Khoisan Peoples of South Africa*, London: Kegan Paul. #JDC

SCHAPIRO, MEYER (1953), 'Style', in Kroeber, Alfred L. (ed.), *Anthropology Today*: 287–312. Chicago: University of Chicago Press. #WD

SCHARFF, ALEXANDER (1942), 'Die frühen Felsbilderfunde in den ägyptischen Wüste und ihr Verhältnis zu den vorgeschichtlichen Kulturen des Niltals', *Paideuma* 2: 161–77. #WD

SCHERZ, E.-R. (1970–86), *Felsbilder in Südwest-Afrika*, 3 vols, Cologne/Vienna: Böhlau/Institut für Ur- und Frühgeschichte der Universität zu Köln. *Fundamenta*, ser. A, 7. #WD

SCHILD, R. and WENDORF, F. (1977), *The Prehistory of Dakhla Oasis and Adjacent Desert*, Wroclaw: Polska Akademia Nauk Instytut Historii Kultury Materialnej. #JAJG

SCHMIDT, P.R. (1975), 'A new look at interpretations of the Early Iron Age in East Africa', *History in Africa* 2: 127–36. #PR

SCHMIDT, P.R. (1978), *Historical Archaeology: A Structural Approach in an African Culture*, Westport: Greenwood Press. #PR #PRS

SCHMIDT, P.R. (1983a), 'An alternative to a strictly materialist perspective: a review of historical archaeology, ethnoarchaeology, and symbolic approaches in African archaeology', *American Antiquity* 48: 62–79. #SAB #PRS

SCHMIDT, P.R. (1983b), 'Cultural meaning and history in African myth', *International Journal of Oral History* 4: 167–83. #PRS

SCHMIDT, P.R. and CHILDS, S.T. (forthcoming), 'Advanced technology in ancient Tanzania'. #PRS

SCHNEIDER, R. (1976), 'Les débuts de l'histoire ethiopienne', *Documents, Histoire Civilisation Ethiopienne* 7: 47–54. #SAB

SCHOFIELD, J.F. (1926), 'Zimbabwe: a critical examination of the building methods employed', *South African Journal of Science* 23: 971–86. #MH

SCHOFIELD, J.F. (1937), 'The pottery of the Mapungubwe district', in Fouché, L. (ed.), *Mapungubwe: Ancient Bantu Civilization on the Limpopo*: 32–60. Cambridge: Cambridge University Press. #MH

SCHOFIELD, J.F. (1948), *Primitive Pottery. An Introduction to South African Ceramics, Prehistoric and Protohistoric*, Cape Town: South African Archaeological Society. #MH

SCHOONRAD, MURRAY (ed.) (1971), *Rock Paintings of Southern Africa. South African Journal of Science*, spec. publ. 2. #WD

SCHRIRE, C. (1980), 'An enquiry into the evolutionary status and apparent identity of San hunter-gatherers', *Human ecology* 8: 9–32. #PR

SCHRIRE, C., DEACON, J., HALL, M. and LEWIS–WILLIAMS, J.D. (1986), 'Burkitt's milestone', *Antiquity* 60: 123–31. #JD #WD

SCHWEINFURTH, G. (1884), 'Note sur des objets en minerai de fer provenant du pays des Monbouttous', *Bulletin de l'Institut Égyptien* 2e serie, 4: 211–14. #PM

SCHWEINFURTH, G. (1912), 'Über alte Tierbilder und Felsinchriften bei Assuan', *Zeitschrift für Ethnologie* 44: 627–58. #WD

SCHWEITZER, F.R. (1970), 'A preliminary report on excavations of a cave at Die Kelders', *South African Archaeological Bulletin* 25: 136–8. #JD

SCOTT, L. (1984), 'Palynological evidence for Quaternary palaeoenvironments in southern African', in Klein, R.G. (ed.), *Southern African Prehistory and Paleoenvironments*: 65–80. Rotterdam: Balkema. #JD

SCULLY, R.T.K. (1969), 'Fort sites of East Bukusu, Kenya', *Azania* 4: 105–14. #PRS

SCULLY, R.T.K. (1979), 'Nineteenth-century settlement sites and related oral traditions from the Bungoma areas, western Kenya', *Azania* 14: 81–96. #PRS

SEALY, J.C. and VAN DER MERWE, N.J. (1986), 'Isotope assessment and the seasonal-mobility hypothesis in the southwestern Cape of South Africa', *Current Anthropology* 27: 135–50. #JD

SELIGMAN, C.G. (1921), 'The older Palaeolithic age in Egypt', *Journal of the Royal Anthropological Institute* 51: 115–44. #JAJG

SELIGMAN, C.G. (1930), *Races of Africa*, Oxford: Clarendon Press. #PB #TS

SERPA PINTO, R. de (1930), 'Pre-história angolense', *Trabalhos da Sociedade Portuguesa de Antropologia e Etnologia* 4: 302. #PM

SERPA PINTO, R. de (1933), 'La préhistoire de l'Afrique portugaise', *Comptes-rendus du XVe Congrès International d'Anthropologie et Archéologie Préhistorique, Paris 1931*: 325–8. Paris: Nourry. #PM

SEVERO, R. (1890), 'Primeiros vestigios de periódo neolítico na província de Angola', *Revista de Sciencias Naturais e Sociais* 1: 152–61. #PM

SHAW, THURSTAN (1944), 'Report on excavations carried out in the cave known as "Bosumpra" at Abetifi, Kwahu, Gold Coast Colony', *Proceedings of the Prehistoric Society* 10: 1–67. #FJK #TS

SHAW, THURSTAN (1945), 'Prehistory and archaeology in the Gold Coast', *Proceedings of the 1st International Conference of West Africanists*: 467–99. Dakar. #FJK

SHAW, THURSTAN (1946), *The Study of Africa's Past*, International African Institute Memorandum XXI. Oxford. #TS

SHAW, THURSTAN (1960), 'Early smoking pipes in Africa, Europe and America', *Journal of the Royal Anthropological Institute* 90: 272–305. #FJK

SHAW, THURSTAN (1961), *Excavation at Dawu*, Edinburgh: Thomas Nelson & Sons. #FJK #TS

SHAW, THURSTAN (1962), 'Chronology of excavation at Dawu, Ghana', *Man* 62: 36–7. #TS

SHAW, THURSTAN (1963a), 'Field research in Nigerian archaeology', *Journal of the Historical Society of Nigeria* 2: 449–64. #FJK

SHAW, THURSTAN (1963b), *Archaeology and Nigeria*, Ibadan: Ibadan University Press. #TS

SHAW, THURSTAN (1969a), 'Archaeology in Nigeria', *Antiquity* 43: 187–99. #FJK

SHAW, THURSTAN (1969b), 'Further spectographic analyses of Nigerian bronzes', *Archaeometry* 11: 85–98. #FJK

SHAW, THURSTAN (1970a), *Igbo-Ukwu*, 2 vols, Evanston: Northwestern University Press. #FJK

SHAW, THURSTAN (1970b), 'The analysis of West African bronzes: a summary of the evidence', *Ibadan* 28: 80–9. #FJK

SHAW, THURSTAN (1972a), 'The prehistory of West Africa', in Ade Ajayi, J.F. and Crowder, M. (eds), *History of West Africa* 1: 33–77. London: Longman. #FJK

SHAW, THURSTAN (1972b), 'Early agriculture in Africa', *Journal of the Historical Society of Nigeria* 6: 143–91. #PB

SHAW, THURSTAN (1975), 'Those Igbo-Ukwu radiocarbon dates: facts, fictions and probabilities', *Journal of African History* 16: 503–17. #FJK

SHAW, THURSTAN (1976), 'Changes in African archaeology in the last forty years', in Fyfe, C. (ed.), *African Studies Since 1945: A Tribute to Basil Davidson*: 156–68. London: Longman. #PR #TS

SHAW, THURSTAN (1978), *Nigeria: Its Archaeology and Early History*. London: Thames & Hudson. #FJK #AH

SHAW, THURSTAN (1981a), 'The Late Stone Age in West Africa and the beginnings of African food production', in *Préhistoire Africaine: Melanges offerts au Doyen L. Balout*: 213–35. Paris: Rech. civilisations, Synthèse 6. #FJK

SHAW, THURSTAN (1981b), 'Synthesis and reflections', in Ray, D.I., Shinnie, P. and Williams, D. (eds), *Proceedings of the Eleventh Annual Conference of the Canadian Association of African Studies, Vol. 1, 'Into the 80s'*: 99–120. Vancouver: Tantalus Research Limited. #PB #TS

SHAW, THURSTAN (1984), *Filling Gaps in African Maps: Fifty Years of Archaeology in Africa*, Bloomington: Indiana University Press. #TS

SHEPPARD, P.J. (1987), *The Capsian of North Africa: Stylistic Variation in Stone Tool Assemblages*, Oxford: British Archaeological Reports. International series. #PJS

SHINNIE, MARGARET (ed.) (1958), *Linant de Bellefonds – Journal d'un voyage à Meroe dans les années 1821 et 1822*, Khartoum: Sudan Antiquities Service Occasional Papers No. 4. #PLS

SHINNIE, P.L. (1954), 'Excavations at Tanqasi', *KUSH* 2: 66–85. #PLS

SHINNIE, P.L. (1955), *Excavations at Soba*, Khartoum: Sudan Antiquities Service Occasional Papers No. 3. #PLS

SHINNIE, P.L. (1960a), 'Socotra', *Antiquity* 34: 100–10. #PLS

SHINNIE, P.L. (1960b), 'Excavations at Bigo, 1957', *Uganda Journal* 24: 16–28. #PLS #PRS

SHINNIE, P.L. (1967), *Meroe – A Civilization of the Sudan*, London: Thames & Hudson. #PLS

SHINNIE, P.L. (1981), 'Archaeology in Gonja, Ghana', *Le Sol, la Parole et l'Ecrit* 2: 65–70. #FJK

SHINNIE, P.L. and CHITTICK, H.N. (1961), *Ghazali – A Monastery in the Northern Sudan*, Khartoum: Sudan Antiquities Service Occasional Papers No. 5. #PLS

SHINNIE, P.L. and HAALAND, R. (eds) (1985), *African Iron Working: Ancient and Traditional*, Oslo: Norwegian University Press. #PRS

SHINNIE, P.L. and KENSE, FRANÇOIS J. (n.d.), 'Excavations at Daboya, Northern Ghana: 1978–83'. #FJK

SHINNIE, P.L. and OZANNE, PAUL (1962), 'Excavations at Yendi Dabari', *Transactions of the Historical Society of Ghana* 6: 87–118. #FJK #PLS

SHINNIE, P.L. and SHINNIE, MARGARET (1978), *A Medieval Nubian Town – Debeira West*, Warminster: Aris and Phillips. #PLS

SHINNIE, P.L. *et. al.* (eds) (1972 *et seq.*), *Nyame Akuma: a newsletter of African archaeology*, Calgary and Edmonton: mimeo. #DOC

SIDIBE, S. (1981), 'Review of La Protohistoire du Sénégal 1, by Thilmans, G., Descamps, C. and Khayat B. Mémoire de l'Institut Fondamental d'Afrique Noire 91', *Recherche, Pédagogie et Culture* 55: 118–19. #PB

SILBERBAUER, G. (1965), *Bushman Survey Report*, Gaborone: Bechuanaland Government. #JD

SINGER, R. and WYMER, J. (1982), *The Middle Stone Age at Klasies River Mouth in South Africa*, Chicago: Chicago University Press. #JD

SIRET, H. and L. (1887), *Les premiers Ages du Métal dans le sud-est de l'Espagne*, Louvain: Anvers. #PJS

SIRET, L. (1924), 'La taille de trapèzes tardenoisien', *Revue Anthropologique* 34: 115–34. #PJS

SLATER, H. (1976), 'Transitions in the political economy of south-east Africa before 1840', unpublished PhD thesis: University of Sussex. #MH

SMITH, A.B. (1974), 'Preliminary report of excavations at Karkarichinkat Nord and Karkarichinkat Sud, Tilemsi Valley, Republic of Mali, Spring 1972', *West African Journal of Archaeology* 4: 33–55. #PB

SMITH, A.B. (1975), 'Radiocarbon dates from Bosumpra Cave, Abetifi, Ghana', *Proceedings of the Prehistoric Society*, 41: 179–82. #TS

SMITH, A.B. (1976), 'A microlithic industry from Adrar Bous, Tenere Desert, Niger', in Hugot, H.J. (ed.), *Actes du VIᵉ Congrès panafricain de préhistoire, Dakar 1967*: 181–94. Paris: Les Imprimeries Réunies de Chambéry. #PB

SMITH, A.B. (1983), 'The Hotnot syndrome: myth-making in South African school textbooks', *Social Dynamics* 9: 37–49. #JD #MH

SMITH, A.B. (1986), 'Competition, conflict and clientship: Khoi and San relationships in the western Cape', *South African Archaeological Society Goodwin Series* 5: 36–41. #JD

SMITH, H.S. (1985), 'Settlements in the Nile Valley', *Mélanges Gamal eddin Mokhtar* II: 288–94. Institut français d'Archéologie orientale du Caire. Bibliothèque d'étude. #DOC

SMITH, I.F. (1965), *Windmill Hill and Avebury*, Oxford: Clarendon Press. #TS

SMITH, P.E.L. (1968), 'Problems and possibilities of the prehistoric rock art of northern Africa', *Africa Historical Studies* 1: 1–39. #WD

SMITH, P.E.L. (1982), 'The late palaeolithic and epipalaeolithic of northern Africa', in Clark, J.D. (ed.), *The Cambridge History of Africa Vol. 1: From the earliest times to c. 500 BC*: 342–409. Cambridge: Cambridge University Press. #WD

SMITH, W. (1972), *Sunbird*, London: Heinemann. #MH

SMITH WOODWARD, A. (1925), 'The fossil anthropoid ape from Taungs', *Nature* 115: 235–6. #JAJG

SMITH, W.S. (1958), Revised by Simpson, W.K. (1981), *The Art and Architecture of Ancient Egypt*, Harmondsworth: Pelican History of Art, Penguin Books. #DOC

SMITS, L.G.A. (1971), 'The rock paintings of Lesotho, their contents and characteristics', in Schoonrad, M. (ed.), *Rock Paintings of Southern Africa*: 14–19. *South African Journal of Science* spec. publ. 2. #WD

SMITS, L.G.A. (1983), 'Rock paintings in Lesotho: site characteristics', *South African Archaeological Bulletin* 38: 62–76. #WD

SMUTS, J.C. (1932), 'Climate and man in Africa', *South African Journal of Science* 29: 98–131. #JD

SOHNGE, P.G., VISSER, D.J.L. and VAN RIET LOWE, C. (1937), 'The geology and archaeology of the Vaal River basin', *Geological Survey Memoir* 35. Pretoria: Government Printer. #JD #JDC

SOLIGNAC, MARCEL (1928), *Les pierres écrites de la Berberie orientale*, Tunis: J. Barlier. #WD

SOLOMON, J.D. (1939), 'The Pleistocene succession in Uganda', in O'Brien, T.P., *The Prehistory of Uganda Protectorate*: 15–50. Cambridge: Cambridge University Press. #PR

SOPER, R.C. (1965), 'The Stone Age in northern Nigeria', *Journal of the Historical Society of Nigeria* 3: 175–94. #FJK

SOPER, R.C. (ed.) (1971), 'The Iron Age in eastern Africa, *Azania* 6: 1–244. #PR

SOPER, R.C. (1979), 'Iron Age archaeology and traditional history in Embu, Mbeere and Chuka areas of central Kenya', *Azania* 14: 31–59. #PRS

SOPER, R.C. and GOLDEN, B. (1969), 'An archaeological survey of Mwanza region, Tanzania', *Azania* 4: 15–79. #PRS

SOUSTELLE, J. (1975), *Rapport sur la recherche française en archéologie et anthropologie*, Paris: La Documentation Française. #PB

SOUTHORN, B.S. (1952), *The Gambia: The Story of the Groundnut Colony*, London: Allen & Unwin. #FJK

SOWUNI, M.A. (1985), 'The beginnings of agriculture in West Africa: botanical evidence', *Current Anthropology* 26: 127–9. #FJK

SPENCER, A. (1979), *Brick Architecture in Ancient Egypt*, Warminster: Aris and Phillips. #DOC

SPENCER, A. (1982), *Death in Ancient Egypt*, Harmondsworth: Penguin Books. #DOC

SPIEGELBERG, WILHELM (1921), *Ägyptische und andere Graffiti (Zeichnungen) aus der Thebanischen Nekropolis*, Heidelberg: Winter. #WD

SPRATT, D.A. (1982), 'The analysis of innovation processes', *Journal of Archaeological Science* 9: 79–94. #JD

SPRIGGS, M. (ed.) (1984), *Marxist Perspectives in Archaeology*, Cambridge: Cambridge University Press. #MH

STAHL, A.B. (1984), 'A history and critique of investigations into early African agriculture', in Clark, J.D. and Brandt, S.A. (eds), *From Hunters to Farmers: The Causes and Consequences of Food Production in Africa*: 9–21. Berkeley: University of California Press. #SAB

STAHL, A.B. (1985a), 'Reinvestigation of Kintampo 6 Rock Shelter, Ghana: implications for the nature of culture change', *African Archaeological Review* 3: 117–50. #FJK #AH

STAHL, A.B. (1985b), 'The Kintampo Culture: Subsistence and Settlement in Ghana during the Mid-second Millennium B.C., unpublished PhD thesis: University of California, Berkeley. #AH

STAHL, A.B. (1986), 'Early food production in West Africa: Rethinking the role of the Kintampo Culture', *Current Anthropology* 27: 532–6. #AH

STAINIER, X. (1897a), 'Découverte d'une hache polie préhistorique au Congo', *La Belgique Coloniale* 1: 7–8. #PM

STAINIER, X. (1897b), 'Archéologie préhistorique', in Masui, T. (ed.), *Guide de la section de l'État Independent du Congo à l'Exposition de Bruxelles-Tervuren en 1897*: 279–80. Brussels: Monnom. #PM

STAINIER, X. (1899), *L'âge de la pierre au Congo*, Brussels: Annales du Musée du Congo, Série III, Ethnographie et Anthropologie I–1, Impr. Vande Weghe. #PM #PR

STEWART, P. and MAZEL, A. (1986), 'Perpetual poisoning of the mind: a consideration of the treatment of the San and the origins of South Africa's black population in South African school history textbooks since 1972 for Standards 8, 9, 10 and 1974 for Standards 5, 6, 7', Workshop paper, Centre for African Studies, University of Cape Town. #MH

STILES, D. (1979a), 'Recent archaeological findings at the Sterkfontein site', *Nature* 277: 381–2. #JAJG

STILES, D. (1979b), 'Early Acheulian and Developed Oldowan', *Current Anthropology* 20: 126–9. #JAJG

STORY, R. (1958), 'Some plants used by the Bushmen in obtaining food and water', *Memoirs of the Botanical Survey of South Africa* 30: 1–115. #JD

STORY, R. (1964), 'Plant lore of the Bushmen', in Davis, D.H.S. (ed.), *Ecological Studies in Southern Africa*, The Hague: W. Junk. #JD

STOW, G.W. (1905), *The Native Races of South Africa*, London: Swan Sonnenschein. #MH

STRIEDTER, K.H. (1976), 'Zeichentheoretische Aspekte der Felsbilder Nordafrikas', *Paideuma* 22: 11–52. #WD

STRIEDTER, K.H. (1983), *Felsbilder Nordafrikas und der Sahara*, Wiesbaden: Steiner. *Studien zur Kulturkunde* 64. #WD

STRIEDTER, K.H. (1984), *Felsbilder der Sahara*, Munich: Prestel. #WD

SUMMERS, R. (1950), 'Iron Age cultures in Southern Rhodesia', *South African Journal of Science* 47: 95–107. #MH

SUMMERS, R. (1958), *Inyanga. Prehistoric Settlements in Southern Rhodesia*, Cambridge: Cambridge University Press. #MH

SUMMERS, R. (ed.) (1959), *Prehistoric Rock Art of the Federation of Rhodesia and Nyasaland*, Salisbury: National Publications Trust. #WD

SUMMERS, R. (1961), 'Excavations in the Great Enclosure', *Occasional Papers of the National Museums, Southern Rhodesia* 23a: 236–88. #MH

SUMMERS, R. (1967a), 'Archaeological distributions and a tentative history of tsetse infestation in Rhodesia and the northern Transvaal', *Arnoldia* 3(3): 1–18. #MH

SUMMERS, R. (1967b), 'Iron Age industries of southern Africa, with notes on their chronology, terminology and economic status', in Bishop, W.W. and Clark, J.D. (eds), *Background to Evolution in Africa*: 687–700. Chicago: University of Chicago Press. #MH

SUMMERS, R. (1970), 'Forty years' progress in Iron Age studies in Rhodesia, 1929–1969', *South African Archaeological Bulletin* 25: 95–103. #MH

SUMMERS, R. (1971a), 'Archaeology in southern Africa 1869–1970: bibliographical notes', *South African Museums Association Bulletin* 10: 20–8. #JD

SUMMERS, R. (1971b), *Ancient Ruins and Vanished Civilizations of Southern Africa*, Cape Town: Bulpin. #MH

SUMMERS, R. (1972), 'Editorial', *South African Archaeological Bulletin* 27: 1–2. #MH

SUTTON, J.E.G. (1966), 'The archaeology and early peoples of the highlands of Kenya and northern Tanzania', *Azania* 1: 37–57. #PR

SUTTON, J.E.G. (1968), 'The settlement of East Africa', in Ogot, B.A. and Kieran, J.A. (eds), *Zamani: A Survey of East African History*: 69–99. Nairobi: East African Publishing House. #PR

SUTTON, J.E.G. (1973), *The Archaeology of the Western Highlands of Kenya*, Nairobi: British Institute in Eastern Africa Memoir no. 3. #PR #PRS

SUTTON, J.E.G. (1984), 'Irrigation and soil-conservation in African agricultural history', *Journal of African History* 25: 25–41. #PR

SUTTON, J.E.G. (1986), 'The irrigation and manuring of the Engaruka field system', *Azania* 21: 27–52. #PR

SUTTON, J.E.G. and ROBERTS, A.D. (1968), 'Uvinza and its salt industry', *Azania* 3: 45–86. #PR #PRS

SZUMOWSKI, G. (1956), 'Fouilles à l'abri sous roche de Kourounkorokale (Soudan)', *Bulletin de l'Institut Français d'Afrique Noire* (B) 18: 462–509. #PB

SZUMOWSKI, G. (1957), 'Fouilles au Nord du Macina et dans la région de Segou', *Bulletin du Comité d'Études historiques et scientifiques de l'A.O.F.* (B) 19: 224–58. #PB

TAIEB, M., JOHANSON, D.C., COPPENS, Y. and ARONSON, J.L. (1976), 'Geological and palaeontological background of Hadar hominid site, Afar, Ethiopia', *Nature* 260: 289–93. #JAJG

TALBOT, M.R. and DELIBRIAS, D. (1977), 'Holocene variations in the level of Lake Bosumtwi', *Nature* 268: 722–4. #FJK

TALBOT, P.A. (1926), *The Peoples of Southern Nigeria*, London: Humphrey Milford. #FJK

TARAMELLI, A. (1902), 'Quelques stations de l'âge de la pierre découvertes par l'ingenieur Pietro Gariazzo dans l'État Indépendant du Congo', *Congrès International d'Anthropologie et d'Archéologie préhistoriques. Compte-rendu de la douzième session, Paris 1900*: 248–64. Paris: Masson #PM

TAYLOR, T. (1988), 'Mainz 1987: the state of world archaeology', *Current Anthropology* 29: 671–9. #BGT

TEILHARD DE CHARDIN, P. (1930), 'Le Paléolithique en Somalie française et en Abyssinie', *L'Anthropologie* 40: 331–4. #JAJG #SAB

TEN RAA, E. (1969), 'Sandawe prehistory and the vernacular tradition', *Azania* 4: 91–103. #PRS

THACKERAY, A.I. (1983), 'Dating the rock art of southern Africa', *South African Archaeological Society Goodwin Series* 4: 21–6. #WD

THACKERAY, A.I. et. al. (1981), 'Dated rock engravings from Wonderwerk Cave, South Africa', *Science* 214: 64–7. #WD

THEAL, G. McC. (1907), *History and Ethnography of Africa South of the Zambezi. Vol. 1 1505–1795*, London: Swan Sonnenschein. #MH

THILMANS, G., DESCAMPS, C. and KHAYAT, B. (1980), *Protohistoire du Sénégal 1: les sites mégalithiques*, Mémoire de l'Institut Fondamental d'Afrique Noire 91*. Dakar: IFAN. #FJK #PB #AH

THILMANS, G. and RAVISE, A. (1980), *Protohistoire du Sénégal 2: Sintiou–Bara et les sites du fleuve*, Mémoire de l'Institut Fondamental d'Afrique Noire 91**. Dakar: IFAN. #PB #AH

THOMASSEY, P. and MAUNY, R. (1951), 'Campagne de fouilles à Koumbi Saleh', *Bulletin de l'Institut Français d'Afrique Noire* 13: 438–62. #PB

THOMASSEY, P. and MAUNY, R. (1956), 'Campagne de fouilles de 1950 à Koumbi–Saleh (Ghana?)', *Bulletin de l'Institut Français d'Afrique Noire* (B) 18: 117–40. #PB

TIETZE, C. (1985), 'Amarna. Analyse der Wohnhäuser und Soziale Struktur der Stadtbewohner', *Zeitschrift für ägyptischen Sprache und altertumskunde* 111: 48–84. #DOC

TIETZE, C. (1986), 'Amarna (Teil II). Analyse der ökonomischen Beziehungen der Stadtbewohner', *Zeitschrift für ägyptischen Sprache und altertumskunde* 113: 55–78. #DOC

TILLET, THIERRY (1983), *Le Paléolithique du bassin tchadien septentrional (Niger, Tchad)*. Paris: CNRS. #AH

TIXIER, J. (1957), 'Le hachereau dans l'Acheuléen nord-africain', *Congrès préhistorique de France, compte rendu de la XVᵉ session (1956)*: 914–23. #JAJG

TIXIER, J. (1963), 'Typologie de l'epipaléolithique du Maghreb', *Mémoire de Centre de Recherches Anthropologiques, Préhistoriques et Ethnographiques*, No. 2. Paris: Arts et Métiers Graphiques. #PB #PJS

TIXIER, J. (1967), 'Procédés d'analyse et questions de terminologie concernant l'étude des ensembles industriels du Paléolithique et de l'Epipaléolithique dans l'Afrique du Nord-Ouest', in Bishop, W.W. and Clark, J.D. (eds), *Background to Evolution in Africa*: 771–819. Chicago: University of Chicago Press. #PB

TIXIER, J., INIZAN, M.-L. and ROCHE, H. (1980), *'Préhistoire de la pierre taillée*, Valbonne: Cercle de recherches et d'études préhistoriques. #PB

TOBIAS, P.V. (1976), 'White African: an appreciation and some personal memories of Louis Leakey', in Isaac, G.Ll. and McCown, E.R. (eds), *Human Origins: Louis Leakey and the East African Evidence*: 55–74. Menlo Park, California: Benjamin. #JAJG

TOBIAS, P.V. (1978), 'The South African australopithecines in time and hominid phylogeny, with special reference to the dating and affinities of the Taung skull', in Jolly, C. (ed.), *Early Hominids of Africa*: 45–84. London: Duckworth. #JAJG

TOBIAS, P.V. (1985a), 'Prehistory and political discrimination', *South African Journal of Science* 81: 667–71. #JD

TOBIAS, P.V. (1985b), 'History of physical anthropology in southern Africa', *American Journal of Physical Anthropology* 28: 1–52. #FJK

TODD, J.L. (1903), 'Notes on stone circles in Gambia', *Man* 3: 164–5. #FJK

TODD, J.L. and WOLBACH, G.B. (1911), 'Stone circles in the Gambia', *Man* 11: 161–4. #FJK

TONGUE, HELEN (1909), *Bushman Paintings*, Oxford: Clarendon Press. #WD

TREINEN–CLAUSTRE, Fr. (1982), *Sahara et Sahel à l'Age du Fer: Borkou, Tchad*, Paris: Musée de l'Homme. #AH

TRIGGER, B.G. (1965), *History and Settlement in Lower Nubia*, New Haven: Yale University Press. *Yale University Publications in Anthropology* 69. #WD

TRIGGER, B.G. (1969), *Beyond History: The Methods of Prehistory*, New York: Holt, Rinehart & Winston. #SAB #WD

TRIGGER, B.G. (1976), *Nubia under the Pharaohs*, London: Thames & Hudson. #DOC

TRIGGER, B.G. (1979), 'Egypt and the comparative study of early civilizations', in Weeks, K. (ed.), *Egyptology and the Social Sciences*: 23–56. American University in Cairo Press. #DOC

TRIGGER, B.G. (1980), 'Archaeology and the image of the American Indian', *American Antiquity* 45: 662–76. #SAB

TRIGGER, B.G. (1983), 'The rise of Egyptian civilization', in Trigger B.G. *et al.*, *Ancient Egypt. A Social History*: 1–70. Cambridge: Cambridge University Press. #DOC

TRIGGER, B.G. (1984), 'Alternative archaeologies: nationalist, colonialist, imperialist', *Man* (NS) 19: 355–70. #JD #MH #FJK #BGT

TRIGGER, B.G. (1985), 'The past as power: anthropology and the North American Indian', in McBryde, Isabel (ed.), *Who owns the Past?*: 11–40. Melbourne: Oxford University Press. #BGT

TRIGGER, B.G. (1986), 'Prospects for a world archaeology', *World Archaeology* 18: 1–20. #BGT

TRIGGER, B.G. and GLOVER, I.C. (1981), Editorial, *World Archaeology* 13: 133–6. #PB

TRIGGER, B.G. and GLOVER, I.C. (eds) (1981-2), 'Regional traditions of archaeological research', *World Archaeology* 13 (2 & 3). #PR

TRIGGER, B., KEMP, B., O'CONNOR, D. and LLOYD, A. (1983), *Ancient Egypt. A Social History*, Cambridge: Cambridge University Press. #DOC

TRINGHAM, R. (1983), 'V. Gordon Childe 25 years after: his relevance for the archaeology of the eighties', *Journal of Field Archaeology* 10: 85–100. #JD

TSCHUDI, J. (1955), *Les peintures rupestres du Tassili-n-Ajjer*, Neuchâtel: La Baconnière. #WD

TUCKEY, J.K. (1818), *Narrative of an Expedition to explore the River Zaire usually called the Congo in South Africa, in 1816 under the Direction of Captain J.K. Tuckey*, London: John Murray. #PM

UCKO, PETER J. and ROSENFELD, ANDRÉE (1967), *Palaeolithic Cave Art*, New York: McGraw-Hill. #WD

URVOY, Y. (1936), *Histoire des populations du Soudan central (Colonie du Niger)*, Paris: Emile Larose. #PB

VANACKER, C. (1979), *Tegdaoust II, Recherches sur Aoudaghost. Fouilles d'un quartier artisanal*, Mémoire de l'Institut Mauritanien de la Recherche Scientifique 2. Paris. #PB

VANDENHOUTE, J. (1972–3), 'De Begraafplaats van Ngongo Mbata (Neder–Zaire). Opgravingsverslag en historische situering', unpublished MA thesis: Rijksuniversiteit Gent. #PM

VAN DER MERWE, N. (1980), 'Production of high carbon steel in the African Iron Age: the direct steel process', in Leakey, R.E. and Ogot, B.A. (eds), *Proceedings of the 8th Panafrican Congress of Prehistory and Quaternary Studies*: 331–4. Nairobi: International Louis Leakey Memorial Institute for African Prehistory. #MH

VAN DER MERWE, N. and KILLICK, D. (1979), 'Square: an iron smelting site near Phalaborwa', *South African Archaeological Society Goodwin Series* 3: 86–93. #MH

VAN DER MERWE, N. and SCULLY, R. (1971), 'The Phalaborwa story: archaeological and ethnographic investigation of a South African Iron Age group', *World Archaeology* 3: 178–96. #MH

VAN GRUNDERBEEK, M.–C., ROCHE, E. and DOUTRELEPONT, H. (1983), *Le premier âge du fer au Rwanda et au Burundi. Archéologie et environnement*, Butare: Institut National de Recherche Scientifique. #PM

VAN HAMM, R. and ANQUANDAH, J. (1986), *Civilization of Komaland, North Ghana*, Rotterdam. #FJK

VAN NEER, W. (1981), 'Archeozoölogische studie van Matupi (Ijzertijd en Late Steentijd) en Kiantapo (Ijzertijd) in Zaire, 2 vols, ScD thesis: Katholieke Universiteit Leuven. #PM

VAN NOTEN, F. (1972), *Les tombes du Roi Cyirima Rujugira et de la Reine-Mère Nyirahuyhi Kanjogera. Description archéologique*, Tervuren: Annales du Musée Royal de l'Afrique Centrale. #PM #PRS

VAN NOTEN, F. (1977), 'Excavations at Matupi cave', *Antiquity* 51: 35–40 #PM

VAN NOTEN, F. (1977–8), 'Une prospection au Nord et Nord–Est du Zaïre', *Études d'Histoire africaine* 9–10: 75–7. #PM

VAN NOTEN, F. (1978), *Rock Art of the Jebel Uweinat (Libyan Sahara)*, Graz: Akademische Druck- und Verlagsanstalt. #WD

VAN NOTEN, F. (ed.) (1982), *The Archaeology of Central Africa*, Graz: Akademische Druck u. Verlagsanstalt. #PM

VAN NOTEN, F. (1983), *Histoire archéologique du Rwanda*, Tervuren: Annales du Musée Royal de l'Afrique Centrale. #PM

VAN RIET LOWE, C. (1929), 'Further notes on the archaeology of Sheppard Island', *South African Journal of Science* 26: 665–83. #JD

VAN RIET LOWE, C. (1937), 'Prehistoric rock engravings in the Vaal River basin', *Transactions of the Royal Society of South Africa* 24, Pt 3. #WD

VAN RIET LOWE, C. (1944), 'Notes on Dr Francis Cabu's collection of stone implements from the Belgian Congo', *Transactions of the Royal Society of South Africa* 30: 169–74. #JAJG #PM

VAN RIET LOWE, C. (1952a), *The Pleistocene Geology and Prehistory of Uganda. Part II: Prehistory*. Colchester: Geological Survey of Uganda Memoir no. 6. #PR #JDC

VAN RIET LOWE, C. (1952b), *The Distribution of Prehistoric Rock Engravings and Paintings in South Africa*, Cape Town: Archaeological Survey. *Archaeological Series* 7. #WD

VAN RIET LOWE, C. (1952c), 'The development of the hand-axe culture in South Africa', in Leakey, L.S.B. and Cole, S. (eds), *Proceedings of the Pan–African Congress on Prehistory, Nairobi 1947*: 167–77. Oxford: Basil Blackwell. #JAJG

VAN RIET LOWE, C. (1953), 'The Kafuan culture of South Africa', *South African Archaeological Bulletin* 8: 27–31. #JDC

VANSINA, J. (1965), *Oral Tradition: A Study in Historical Methodology*, Chicago: Aldine. #PRS

VANSINA, J. (1967), 'The use of oral tradition in African culture history', in Gabel, C. and Bennett, N.R. (eds), *Reconstructing African Culture History*, Boston: Boston University Press. #PRS

VANSINA, J. (1979), 'Bantu in the crystal ball I', *History in Africa* 6: 287–333. #PM

VANSINA, J. (1980), 'Bantu in the crystal ball II', *History in Africa* 7: 293–325. #PM

VANSINA, J. (1985), *Oral Tradition as History*, London: James Currey; Madison: The University of Wisconsin Press. #PM

VAN ZINDEREN BAKKER, E.M. (1967), 'Upper Pleistocene and Holocene stratigraphy and ecology on the basis of vegetation changes in sub-Saharan Africa', in Bishop, W.W. and Clark, J.D. (eds), *Background to Evolution in Africa*: 125–47. Chicago: University of Chicago Press. #JD

VAUFREY, R. (1928), 'La Paléolithique Italien', *Archéologique Institut de Paléontologie Humaine*. Mémoire 3. Paris. #PJS

VAUFREY, R. (1933a), 'Notes sur le Capsien', *L'Anthropologie* 43: 457–83. #PJS

VAUFREY, R. (1933b), 'Stratigraphie et répartition des faciès capsiens, *L'Anthropologie* 43: 648–9. #PJS

VAUFREY, R. (1934), 'Les plissements acheuléo-mousteriens des alluvions de Qafsa', *Proceedings of the 1st Congress of Prehistoric and Protohistoric Sciences, London, 1932*: 66–8. London: Oxford University Press. #JAJG

VAUFREY, R. (1936), 'L'âge des spirales de l'art rupestre nord-africain', *Bulletin de la Société Préhistorique Française* 33: 624–34. #WD

VAUFREY, R. (1938), 'L'âge de l'art rupestre nord-africain', *IPEK* 12: 10–29. #WD

VAUFREY, R. (1939), *L'art rupestre nord-africain*, Paris: Institut de paléontologie humaine. *Archives/Mémoire* 20. #WD

VAUFREY, R. (1953), 'L'Age de la Pierre en Afrique', *Journal de la Société des Africanistes* 23: 103–38. #PB

VAUFREY, R. (1955), *Préhistoire de l'Afrique: Afrique du Nord et Maghreb*, Tunis: Publication de l'Institut des hautes études de Tunis. #PJS #AH

VAUFREY, R. (1969), *Préhistoire de l'Afrique: au nord et à l'est de la grande forêt*, Tunis: Publication de l'Institut des hautes études de Tunis. #AH

VAVILOV, N.I. (1926), *Studies on the Origin of Cultivated Plants*, Leningrad: Institute of Applied Botanical Plant Breeding. #SAB

VAYSON de PRADENNE, A. (1938), *La préhistoire*, Paris: A. Colin. #PM

VERMEERSCH, P.M., PAULISSEN, E., OTTE, M., GIJSELINGS, G. and DRAPPIER, D. (1980), 'Acheulean in Middle Egypt', in Leakey, R.E. & Ogot, B.A. (eds), *Proceedings of the 8th Panafrican Congress of Prehistory and Quaternary Studies, Nairobi, September 1977*: 218–21. Nairobi: The Louis Leakey Memorial Institute for African Prehistory. #JAJG

VERNEAU, R. (1905), 'Note sur quelques crânes du 2ᵉ territoire militaire de l'A.O.F.', *L'Anthropologie* 16: 41–56. #PB

VERNEAU, R. (1920), 'Nouveaux documents sur l'ethnographie ancienne de la Mauritanie', *L'Anthropologie* 30: 323–68. #PB

VERNET, R. (1984), 'La préhistoire de la Mauritanie: état de la question', Doctoral thesis: Université de Paris I, Pantheon-Sorbonne. #AH

VIDAL, J. (1923a), 'Au sujet de l'emplacement de Mali (ou Melli), capitale de l'ancien empire mandingue', *Bulletin du Comité d'Études historiques et scientifiques de l'A.O.F.* 5: 251–68. #PB

VIDAL, J. (1923b), 'Le veritable emplacement de Mali', *Bulletin du Comité d' Études historiques et scientifiques de l'A.O.F.* 6: 606–19. #PB

VIDAL, P. (1969), *La civilisation mégalithique de Bouar: prospections et fouilles 1962–1966*, Recherches oubanguiennes 1. Paris: Firman–Didot. #PM

VIGNARD, E. (1934), 'Présentation d'une belle série de triangles et trapèzes du Capsien en connexion avec leur microburins', *Bulletin de la Société Préhistorique Française* 33: 217–32. #PJS

VINNICOMBE, PATRICIA (1967), 'Rock painting analysis', *South African Archaeological Bulletin* 22: 129–41. #WD

VINNICOMBE, PATRICIA (1972a), 'Motivation in African rock art', *Antiquity* 46: 124–33. #WD

VINNICOMBE, PATRICIA (1972b), 'Myth, motive and selection in southern African rock art', *Africa* 42: 192–204. #WD

VINNICOMBE, PATRICIA (1975), 'The ritual significance of the eland (*Taurotragus oryx*) in the rock art of southern Africa', in Anati, E. (ed.), *Les religions de la préhistoire*: 379–400. Capo di Ponte (Brescia): Centro Camuno di Studi Preistorici. #WD

VINNICOMBE, PATRICIA (1976), *People of the Eland*, Pietermaritzburg: Natal University Press. #WD

VOGEL, J.C. (1978), 'Isotopic assessment of the dietary habits of ungulates', *South African Journal of Science* 74: 298–301. #JD

VOGEL, J.C. (1983), 'Isotopic evidence for past climate and vegetation of South Africa', *Bothalia* 14: 391–4. #JD

VOGEL, J.C. (ed.) (1984), *Late Cainozoic palaeoclimates of the southern hemisphere*, Rotterdam: Balkema. #JD

VOGEL, J.C. and BEAUMONT, P.B. (1972), 'Revised radiocarbon chronology for the Stone Age in South Africa', *Nature* 237: 50–1. #JDC

VOIGT, E. (1980), 'Reconstructing Iron Age economies of the northern Transvaal: a preliminary report', *South African Archaeological Bulletin* 35: 39–45. #MH

VOIGT, E. (1983), *Mabungubwe: An Archeozoological Interpretation of an Iron Age Community*, Pretoria: Transvaal Museum. #MH

VOIGT, E. (1984), 'The faunal remains from Magogo and Mhlopeni: small stock herding in the Early Iron Age of Natal', *Annals of the Natal Museum* 26(1): 141–63. #MH

VOIGT, E. and PLUG, I. (1981), 'Early Iron Age herders of the Limpopo valley', unpublished report, Transvaal Museum, Pretoria. #MH

VOIGT, E. and VON DEN DRIESCH, A. (1984), 'Preliminary report on the faunal assemblage from Ndondondwane, Natal', *Annals of the Natal Museum* 26(1): 95–104. #MH

VON BECKERATH, J. (1975), 'Chronologie', Helck, W. und Otto, E. (herausgeb.), *Lexikon der ägyptologie*: Band I, 967–72. Wiesbaden: Otto Harrowswitz. #DOC

VON KOENIGSWALD, G.H.R. (1956), *Meeting Prehistoric Man*, London: Thames & Hudson. #JAJG

VON LUSCHAN, FELIX (1897), *Beiträge zur Völkerkunde der deutschen Schutzgebiete*, Berlin: Reimer. #WD

VON LUSCHAN, FELIX (1922), 'Uber Petroglyphen bei Assuan und bei Demir–Kapu', *Zeitschrift für Ethnologie* 54: 177–92. #WD

WADE, W.D. (1971), 'The skeletal biology of human remains from sites in the Lake Kainji area of Nigeria', *West African Journal of Archaeology* 1: 61–85. #FJK

WADLEY, L. (1979), 'Big Elephant Shelter and its role in the Holocene prehistory of central South West Africa', *Cimbebasia* (B) 4: 51–60. #JD

WADLEY, L. (1984), 'Subsistence strategies in the Transvaal Stone Age: a preliminary model', in Hall, M., Avery, G., Avery, D.M., Wilson, M.L. and Humphreys, A.J.B. (eds), *Frontiers: Southern African Archaeology Today*: 207–14. Oxford: British Archaeological Reports International Series 207. #JD

WADLEY, L. (1986), 'Segments of time: a mid-Holocene Wilton site in the Transvaal', *South African Archaeological Bulletin* 41: 54–62. #JD

WADLEY, L. (1987), 'A social and ecological interpretation of the Later Stone Age in the southern Transvaal', unpublished PhD thesis: University of the Witwatersrand. #JD

WANDIBBA, S. (1980), 'The application of an attribute analysis to the study of the Later Stone Age/Neolithic pottery ceramics in Kenya (summary)', in Leakey, R.E. and Ogot, B.A. (eds), *Proceedings of the 8th Panafrican Congress of Prehistory and Quaternary studies, Nairobi, September 1977*: 283–5. Nairobi: The International Louis Leakey Memorial Institute for African Prehistory. #PR

WARD, W.E.F. (1948), *A History of Ghana*, London: George Allen & Unwin. #FJK

WARNIER, J.P. (1984), 'Histoire du peuplement et genèse des paysages dans l'Ouest camerounais', *Journal of African History* 25: 395–410. #AH

WARNIER, J.P. (1985), *Échanges, développement et hiérarchies dans le Bamenda précolonial (Cameroun)*, Stuttgart: Franz Steiner Verlag. #AH

WARNIER, J.P. and FOWLER, I. (1979), 'A nineteenth century Ruhr in Central Africa', *Africa* 49: 329–51. #AH

WASHBURN, S.L. (ed.) (1961), *Social Life of Early Man*, Viking Fund Publications in Anthropology 31. Chicago: University of Chicago Press. #JAJG

WASHBURN, S.L. (1963), *Classification and Human Evolution*, Viking Fund Publications in Anthropology 37. Chicago: University of Chicago Press. #JAJG

WATERLOT, G. (1909), *Rapport addressé à M. le Gouverneur général de l'A.O.F. sur les recherches faites sur la préhistoire dans la presqu'île du Cap-Vert (Sénégal)*, Dakar: Documents IFAN. #AH

WAYLAND, E.J. (1923), 'Palaeolithic types of implements in relation to the Pleistocene deposits of Uganda', *Proceedings of the Prehistoric Society of East Anglia* 4: 96–112. #JAJG

WAYLAND, E.J. (1924), 'The Stone Age in Uganda', *Man* 24: no. 124. #JAJG #PR

WAYLAND, E.J. (1927), 'A possible age correlation of the Kafu Gravels', *Uganda Protectorate, Annual Report of the Geological Department for the year ended 31st December, 1926, Appendix A*: 40–1. #JAJG

WAYLAND, E.J. (1929), 'African pluvial periods', *Nature* 123: 31–3. #JDC

WAYLAND, E.J. (1934a), 'Rifts, rivers, rains and early man in Uganda', *Journal of the Royal Anthropological Institute* 64: 333–52. #JAJG #PR #JDC

WAYLAND, E.J. (1934b), 'Some notes of the Bigo bya Mugenyi', *Uganda Journal* 2: 24–7. #PRS

WEBLEY, L. (1986), 'Pastoralist ethnoarchaeology in Namaqualand', *South African Archaeological Society Goodwin Series* 5: 57–61. #JD

WELLS, M.J. (1965), 'An analysis of plant remains from Scott's Cave in the Gamtoos Valley', *South African Archaeological Bulletin* 20: 79–84. #JD

WENDORF, F. (ed.) (1968), *The Prehistory of Nubia*, 2 vols, Dallas: Southern Methodist University Press. #JAJG

WENDORF, F. and SCHILD, R. (1974), *A Middle Stone Age Sequence from the Central Rift Valley, Ethiopia*, Warsaw: Ossolineum. #SAB

WENDT, W.E. (1972), 'Preliminary report on an archaeological research programme in South West Africa', *Cimbebasia* (B) 2(1): 1–61. #JD

WENDT, W.E. (1976), '"Art mobilier" from Apollo XI Cave, South West Africa: Africa's oldest dated works of art', *South Africa Archaeological Bulletin* 31: 5–11. #WD

WHEELER, M. (1970), *The British Academy 1949–1968*, London: Oxford University Press. #PR

WIESSNER, P. (1983), 'Style and social information in Kalahari San projectile points', *American Antiquity* 48: 253–76. #JD

WILD, R.P. (1927a), 'Stone artefacts of the Gold Coast and Ashanti', *Gold Coast Review* 3(1). #FJK

WILD, R.P. (1927b), 'Stone artefacts of the Gold Coast and Ashanti', *Gold Coast Review* 3(2). #FJK

WILD, R.P. (1931), 'A stone implement of paleolithic type from Gold Coast Colony', *Gold Coast Review* 5(2). #FJK

WILD, R.P. (1934), 'Ashanti: baked clay heads from graves', *Man* 34: 1–4. #FJK

WILD, R.P. (1935a), 'An ancient pot from Tarkwa, Gold Coast', *Man* 35: 136–7. #FJK

WILD, R.P. (1935b), 'Bone dagger and sheath from Obuasi, Ashanti', *Man* 35: 10–11. #FJK

WILD, R.P. (1935c), 'The inhabitants of the Gold Coast and Ashanti before the Akan invasion', *Gold Coast Teachers' Journal* 6–7. #FJK

WILD, R.P. (1937), 'A method of bead making practised in the Gold Coast', *Man* 38: 115. #FJK

WILK, RICHARD (1985), 'The ancient Maya and the political present', *Journal of Anthropological Research* 41: 307–26. #AH

WILKS, IVOR (1961), *The Northern Factor in Ashanti History*, Legon: Institute of African Studies, University College of Ghanna. #FJK

WILKS, IVOR (1962), 'A medieval trade-route from the Niger to the Gulf of Guinea', *Journal of African History* 3: 337–41. #FJK

WILKS, IVOR (1968), 'The transmission of Islamic learning in the western Sudan', in Goody, J. (ed.), *Literacy in Traditional Societies*: 161–97. Cambridge: Cambridge University Press. #FJK

WILLCOX, A.R. (1956), *Rock Paintings of the Drakensberg*, London: Max Parrish. #WD

WILLCOX, A.R. (1963), *The Rock Art of South Africa*, London: Nelson. #WD

WILLCOX, A.R. (1968), 'A survey of our present knowledge of rock paintings in South Africa', *South African Archaeological Bulletin* 23: 20–3. #WD

WILLCOX, A.R. (1984), *The Rock Art of Africa*, New York: Holmes & Meier. #WD

WILLETT, FRANK (1960a), 'Investigations at Old Oyo, 1956–57', *Journal of the Historical Society of Nigeria* 2: 59–77. #FJK

WILLETT, FRANK (1960b), 'Ife and its archaeology', *Journal of African History* 1: 231–48. #FJK #PRS

WILLETT, FRANK (1962), 'The microlithic industry from Old Oyo, Western Nigeria', in *Proceedings of the 4th Panafrican Congress on Prehistory (Léopoldville, 1959)*: 261–71. Tervuren. #FJK

WILLETT, FRANK (1967), *Ife in the History of West African Sculpture*, London: Thames & Hudson.

WILLETT, FRANK and FLEMING, S.F. (1976), 'A catalogue of important Nigerian copper-alloy castings dated by thermoluminescence', *Archaeometry* 18: 135–46. #FJK

WILLEY, G.R. and SABLOFF, J.A. (1974), *A History of American Archaeology*, London: Thames & Hudson. #PR #PJS #PB

WILLEY, G.R. and SABLOFF, J.A. (1980), *A History of American Archaeology*, 2nd edition, San Francisco: W.H. Freeman. #SAB

WILMAN, MARIA (1933), *The Rock-engravings of Griqualand West and Bechuanaland, South Africa*, Cambridge: Deighton Bell. #WD

WILSON, C. (1952), *Before the Dawn in Kenya*, Nairobi: The English Press. #PR

WILSON, C. (1954), *Kenya's Warning*, Nairobi. #PR

WILSON, GODFREY and HUNTER, MONICA (1942), *The Study of African Society*, Rhodes-Livingstone Paper No. 2. Livingstone. #TS

WILSON, J. (1964), *Signs and Wonders upon Pharaoh. A History of American Egyptology*, Chicago: University of Chicago Press. #DOC

WINKLER, HANS A. (1934), *Bauern zwischen Wasser und Wüste*, Stuttgart: Kohlhammer. #WD

WINKLER, HANS A. (1937), *Völker und Völkerbewegungen im vorgeschichtlichen oberägypten im Lichte neuer Felsbilderfunde*, Stuttgart: Kohlhammer. #WD

WINKLER, HANS A. (1938), *The Rock-drawings of Southern Upper Egypt I*, London: Egypt Exploration Society. #WD

WINKLER, HANS A. (1939), '*The Rock-drawings of Southern Upper Egypt II*', London: Egypt Exploration Society. #WD

WRIGLEY, C.C. (1958), 'Some thoughts on the Bacwezi', *Uganda Journal* 22: 11–17. #PRS

Y . . . . (G. LE RUMEUR) (1933), 'Les témoins d'une civilisation ancienne dans le cercle de Tahoua', *Bulletin du Comité d'Études historiques et scientifiques de l'A.O.F.* 16: 299–318. #PB

YATES, R., GOLSON, J. and HALL, M. (1985), 'Trance performance: the rock art of Boontjesskloof and Sevilla', *South African Archaeological Bulletin* 40: 70–80. #JD

YELLEN, J.E. (1977), *Archaeological Approaches to the Present: Models for Reconstructing the Past*, New York: Academic Press. #JD #JDC

YORK, RICHARD (1973), 'Excavations at New Buipe', *West African Journal of Archaeology* 3: 1–189. #FJK

YORK, RICHARD, MATHEWSON, DUNCAN, CALVOCORESSI, DAVID and FLIGHT, COLIN (1967), *Archaeology in the Volta Basin*, Legon. #TS

ZELTNER, F. de (1913a), 'Les schistes taillés de Nioro', *L'Anthropologie* 24: 17–23. #PB

ZELTNER, F. de (1913b), 'Des dessins sur des roches à Aïr qui appartient au territoire des Touaregs', *L'Anthropologie* 23: 101–4, 24: 171–84. #WD

ZONHOVEN, L.M.J. (1983), *Annual Egyptological Bibliography 1979*, Warminster: Aris & Phillips. #DOC

ZONHOVEN, L.M.J. (1985), *Annual Egyptological Bibliography 1981*, Warminster: Aris & Phillips. #DOC

ZWERNEMANN, J. (1982), *Culture History and African Anthropology*, Stockholm: Uppsala Studies in Cultural Anthropology 6. #AH

General Index

Index of People